# Money, Banking, and the Economy

# MONEY, BANKING, and the ECONOMY

**FIFTH EDITION**

# John A. Cochran

ARIZONA STATE UNIVERSITY

**MACMILLAN PUBLISHING CO., INC.**
NEW YORK

**COLLIER MACMILLAN PUBLISHERS**
LONDON

Copyright © 1983, John A. Cochran.

Printed in the United States of America.

Earlier editions copyright © 1967, 1971, 1975, and 1979 by John A. Cochran.

Macmillan Publishing Co., Inc.
866 Third Avenue, New York, New York 10022

Collier Macmillan Canada, Inc.

Library of Congress Cataloging in Publication Data

Cochran, John A.
    Money, banking, and the economy.

    Includes bibliographies and index.
    1.   Money—United States.    2.   Banks and banking—
United States.    3.   Monetary policy—United States.
I. Title.
HG540.C63     1983          332′.0973          82-7227
ISBN 0-02-323050-9                             AACR2

    Printing:  1 2 3 4 5 6 7 8          Year:  3 4 5 6 7 8 9 0

ISBN   0-02-323050-9

To my wife, Mary, and my three daughters,
Jackie Sue, Cindy, and Cathy

# PREFACE

In the decade of the 1980s public policy questions relating to money and banking seem even more crucial than in earlier decades. In 1980 an important law governing the rules affecting banks and other financial institutions was passed by Congress. This law is nearly as important as the 1913 law establishing the Federal Reserve System. The 1980 law gives power to the Federal Reserve to control the expansion of transaction accounts by all financial institutions and changes some of the rules governing competition between financial institutions. Control of inflationary pressures through tighter control of the various monetary aggregates by our central bank has also received greater emphasis in the early 1980s. In addition, the effect of greater monetary discipline has impacted on interest rates and the financial markets in which they are determined.

Because of the greater emphasis on the importance of money supply expansion in a period of inflationary pressures, the material on creating money appears earlier than in the previous edition. The money market chapters are also presented earlier so as to emphasize the importance of interest rates in the 1980s. There is even an early discussion of interest rates and inflation in Chapter 1. The chapters on banks and their competitors now follow the chapters on financial markets. Subsequently, there are chapters on central banking followed by the monetary theory chapters and, in conclusion, the public policy chapters.

As well as reorganizing the order of presentation of chapters in order to highlight the subject matter that is of critical importance in the 1980s, there is, of course, substantial revision and updating of all chapters throughout. Inflation continues to be of great concern, not only in the United States, but in every country in the world. This concern comes up not only in the separate chapter on inflation but in numerous other chapters throughout the book. This is particularly true in the chapters on interest rates, monetary policy, and the American balance of payments and the international monetary system.

The United States in the 1980s is even more of an "open economy" in which both exports and imports are of greater importance to the economy than they were in earlier decades. Furthermore, American interest rates have an impact on the value of the U.S. dollar in foreign exchange markets and thus on the value of other foreign currencies. Changes in the values of various currencies in turn affect the balance of payments of various countries and their domestic economies as well.

For the beginning student of money and banking, a number of terms likely to be unfamiliar are set in bold type and defined in the Glossary at the end of the book. This is a new feature of this edition.

As in earlier editions, both students and colleagues at Arizona State University have been helpful with their critical and encouraging comments. Professors Tim Hogan, Dennis Hoffman, and Don Schlagenhauf all reviewed chapters in their particular areas of interest. Naturally, any errors that remain are my responsibility.

Once again, my wife, Mary, has been most helpful with her labor of love. This has included editorial suggestions and many hours of typing both the book and the accompanying expanded Instructors' Manual. With all of the innovations in money and banking this remains a most stimulating and rewarding field of study. We hope that this proves true for new students as well as for more senior scholars.

**J. A. C.**

# CONTENTS

ix

# PART **7**   PUBLIC POLICY

# LIST OF
# TABLES AND FIGURES

## TABLES

xiii

# FIGURES

# PART 1

# MONEY

No complaint, however, is more common than that of a scarcity of money. Money, like wine, must always be scarce with those who have neither wherewithal to buy it, nor credit to borrow it.*

THE WEALTH OF NATIONS

1

# CHAPTER

# Introduction to Money and Interest Rates

In the more than two hundred years since Adam Smith published his classic work in which the foundations of modern economics were established, most people have continued to be fascinated with the subject of money. Monetary policy is debated in political campaigns and receives a great deal of attention on the financial pages of daily newspapers. The American economy is not only a market economy but also a monetary economy and, as John Maynard Keynes, noted British economist, pointed out in 1936, a monetary economy is different from a pure market economy without money. Interest rates, or the cost of borrowed money, are also quite important to a market economy. By the decade of the 1980s, such interest rates to would-be borrowers, whether charged by financial institutions, such as banks, or those prevailing in the impersonal financial markets, had become quite volatile. We are concerned with understanding the reasons for changes in interest rates, as well as the nature and functioning of money.

*All the quotations at the beginning of each chapter come from the classic work, first published in 1776, by Adam Smith, *An Inquiry Into the Nature and Causes of the Wealth of Nations*.

## THE IMPORTANCE OF MONEY

The American market economy is intimately affected by the stock and flow of money. People use **money**, or credit substitutes for money, whenever they buy goods and services. If they save part of their income, they may hold part of these savings in the form of money balances. The prices of goods are quoted in money terms. When credit is extended to finance expenditures, it too is expressed in terms of money as a measure of the amount of credit involved. Money is almost everywhere in the economic system where the production and exchange of goods and services are involved.

But money, which is such a useful and desired servant, at times misbehaves. Sometimes a country has so much money that the money price of everything keeps increasing in an inflationary spiral. Then the value of money tomorrow in terms of its purchasing power will be less than its value today. On the other hand, sometimes a country seems to have so little money that hardly anyone has enough to spend. When money is in too short a supply, as in the Great Depression of the 1930s, the wheels of factories do not turn as rapidly as they can and breadlines of unemployed workers form. Money can be either a great blessing or a great curse.

## PRIVATE FINANCIAL INSTITUTIONS AND CENTRAL BANKING

The functioning of major financial institutions in our financial system is a matter of importance for the entire economy. Many **financial institutions**, including commercial banks, are financial intermediaries in that they transfer surplus funds from those who save to those who want to spend more than their current income would permit. In transferring these financial funds, financial intermediaries are also aiding efficient resource allocation. They tend to lower the real rate of interest and thus increase real investment, which in turn increases economic growth.

A number of these financial intermediaries, such as commercial banks and savings and loan associations, also create transaction accounts to facilitate expenditures. Demand deposits of banks, however, are still the largest part of transaction accounts. Beginning in 1980, Congress permitted the Federal Reserve System (the central bank of the United States) to impose uniform reserve requirements on all financial institutions offering transaction accounts. (These reserve requirements are discussed in Chapter 15.) Transaction accounts, such as demand deposits of commercial banks, are created when financial institutions make loans or acquire investments.

**Central banks** regulate a country's supply of money, affect the level of interest rates, and issue regulations applying to all financial institutions creating transactions accounts. Because a central bank has so much power over financial institutions, it in turn has power over the entire economy. In the United States the federal government, too, in its taxing, spending, and borrowing operations affects the entire economy in various important ways. For example, the government has a significant impact on the supply of money and interest rates, depending on the deficit or surplus in the budget and the methods of debt management used. If the government continues to run a chronic budget deficit, it is difficult, if not impossible, for the central bank not to increase the money supply—with possible inflationary consequences.

Thus far we have used the term *money* as if its meaning were obvious to the student. We now consider more carefully the nature and meaning of money.

## THE GENERAL NATURE AND DEFINITION OF MONEY

What money is, where it comes from, and how it is used are important questions. In ancient times money was a kind of useful commodity. Certain metals, including gold and silver, were most often used for the medium of exchange, but many other useful commodities were used at various times by various people. In the United States, we have used gold, silver, paper currency, and even demand deposits of commercial banks.

As the American industrial system became more dominant and the scope and extent of the market for all types of goods and services grew after the Civil War, the use of bank deposits became more widespread. Increasingly, business firms discovered that it was simpler to pay their creditors by check than by currency. In the twentieth century the custom of paying bills by check has also spread to many persons.

Other cultures have had kinds of money other than those used in the United States today. For example, cigarettes have been used as money in times of war or of great social disruption even in highly advanced countries, and primitive societies today still use great stones, spears, cattle, and the like as their forms of most liquid wealth (i.e., money). What is needed, therefore, is a definition of money that fits all the seemingly bizarre forms of money as well as the more conventional forms. Money may therefore be defined as *anything generally acceptable in payment for goods, services, and debts*. The words *generally acceptable* are quite important in this definition, because they focus attention on the fact that any commodity or symbolic article, whether issued by a legal government or not, may serve as money.

Society itself, through its use and acceptability of an item as money, gives the item the generalized purchasing power of money. The attitude and behavior of people determine what is money and what is not. Sometimes the legal money issued by the government of a country may not even be accepted as money by most of the inhabitants. Thus during the civil war in China, the population substituted cigarettes as the preferred form of money, because runaway inflation was destroying the value of the official paper currency almost hourly. Money, to be money, must be generally acceptable.

Money is also the most liquid asset by which the market value of all goods and services may be determined. Money is mainly, however, a medium of exchange by which goods or services can be sold; it in turn can be used to buy whatever is desired in the market. If what is desired costs more than an individual or institution is able to pay for out of current income, then money can be used to measure the extension of credit needed to secure the desired item. Money is thus used as a measure of debt contracts. Money has many uses in a complex market economy, such as that of the United States today, but above all by serving as a medium of exchange, it eliminates the inconveniences of a barter economy.

## The Barter System

**Barter** is the direct exchange of one good or service for another, without the intermediate step of an exchange for money. Barter is used in a few sectors of the American economy even today, but most of the experience with barter in the United States was during earlier periods. In the early colonial period and on the western frontier, settlers helped each other with barn and house raisings, cooperated with clearing land and planting crops on occasion, and in other ways exchanged services with one another. If a man secured help from his neighbors in a project involving a substantial amount of shared labor in a given period, say, at harvest time, it was expected that he would also help his neighbors when they needed his services. This exchange of labor services was a form of implicit barter with the reciprocity clearly understood, even if not literally expressed in the form of a contract.

Much barter of goods was a simple matter of one good being directly exchanged for some quantity of another good in a single market transaction. In still other cases, goods might be exchanged for services.

The frontier doctor and teacher often had to accept goods in kind as part payment for their services. In such a primitive economy, money was in quite short supply and the advantages of society's specializing in either the production of goods or services were often secured through direct barter.

The barter system, nevertheless, has a number of serious disadvantages. First, the functioning of this system necessitates a double coincidence of wants on the part of those involved in the barter of goods or services. One party must want exactly what the other party offers for trade and vice versa. If this double coincidence of wants is not matched exactly, then either no trade takes place, or more likely, one party to the barter is seriously disadvantaged in terms of trade.

The history of the American Indian trade is replete with examples of the Indians receiving an unfair price for the commodities they offered for the white man's goods. The sale of Manhattan island by an Indian tribe for $24 of trade goods offered by the white man is only one incident in a long series of such barters in which the Indians suffered from the lack of an exact double coincidence of wants. Similar incidents could also be offered of trade among the settlers themselves in which advantage was taken of one party to the trade. Although disadvantageous terms of trade can be imposed on one party to an exchange even with the use of money, such unfair trade is particularly likely under a barter system.

The second disadvantage of the barter system is that it limits the scope of the market. It is difficult if not impossible to make barter transactions over long distances, particularly when the communications system is primitive. A barter system usually goes hand in hand with a local market.

A third disadvantage is the difficulty of trading goods over time. Debt contracts are not impossible in a barter system, but equity in such transactions is more difficult without money. If I borrow one bushel of wheat from you in the spring and return a bushel of wheat in the fall, we could easily have a dispute about the respective qualities of the grain. Money is a more exact measure of value, particularly if the price level remains stable.

Finally, the barter system is usually associated with a production system, as on the frontier, where each person is a jack-of-all-trades. A high degree of specialization is difficult to secure under a barter system. Specialization and interdependence of productive units come only with an expanded market system. The market can expand and take on such specialized functions only with the widespread use of money. Furthermore, lower transaction costs are associated with money than with barter. Let us discuss the functions of money.

## The Four Functions of Money

The four major functions of money are (1) medium of exchange, (2) standard unit of account or standard of value, (3) standard of deferred payments, and (4) store of value. The most important function of money, as already stated, is that of serving as a medium of exchange. This function of money is more efficient than the barter system.

*Medium of Exchange*   With money serving as a medium of exchange, we can work for money, knowing that the money we secure from selling our labor services can be used to acquire useful goods and services, which is the real economic justification for our work in the first place. We do not want money for its own sake, but we have learned from experience that the possession of money gives us a good deal of economic independence. With money in our pockets, we are free to sample the wares of the marketplace. Without money we have limited access to the production of others. Money makes it possible for us to extend our economic capacities, so that we can enjoy an assorted bundle of goods and services, which it would be impossible for us to produce singlehandedly.

*Standard Unit of Account*   The second function of money is that it serves as a generally accepted standard of value, or standard unit of account. Goods and services can be priced in terms of money, and this price is understandable to the would-be buyer as well as to the seller. The use of money as a measure of value eliminates the necessity to quote the price of apples in terms of nuts, the price of nuts in terms of oranges, and so on. Furthermore, we can add the market value of goods, once they are expressed in monetary terms.

Money is used as a standard unit of account in arriving at the **gross national product (GNP),** the market value of all final goods and services produced in a country in a year. The money value of GNP tells a great deal about the economic activity of a country, without the necessity of itemizing each amount of physical production of each type of good and service. The money value of goods becomes the common denominator in which they can all be expressed.

*Standard of Deferred Payments*   The third function of money is that it is a measure of value over time when used as a standard of deferred payments. Just as money is used to measure the market value of goods or services at a given time, so it serves to indicate the sum of purchasing power being lent and borrowed. Although a specific, useful commodity can be lent with the same commodity or one similar to it due in repayment, different interpretations about the quality of the two commodities being exchanged over time may occur, as mentioned. With money being lent there is no difficulty about the amount due in return.

Nevertheless, a qualitative problem may also develop with money debt contracts, for the value of money sometimes changes over time. The value of money is determined by how much actual goods and services it will buy. If the price of these goods and services is changing, then the amount of real goods and services that can be acquired with a given amount of money will be different at times. If I borrow $100 now and repay the same $100 in ten years, I may or may not be repaying the same amount of purchasing power. If the price level has doubled in this ten-year period, I must repay only half the real amount of purchasing power that I borrowed. Whenever the price level is rising, debtors usually benefit and creditors usually lose. If creditors have previously lost real purchasing power because of inflation, they may insist on indexation of interest rates or increase interest rates sufficiently to take account of the rate of anticipated inflation.

Money as a measure of value over time thus sometimes behaves like the remarkable mushroom in *Alice's Adventures in Wonderland*. When Alice ate from one side of the magic mushroom, she shot up to an amazing height, whereas when she ate from the other side, she dwindled to a tiny size. Although such properties may be useful in a magic mushroom, they are somewhat disconcerting when associated with a measure of the amount of purchasing power owed by a debtor to a creditor. Money as a standard of deferred payments does perform a useful function, but the efficiency of this function is somewhat at the mercy of the forces that determine the price level.

*Store of Value*     The store of value function of money also suffers the same inconvenience, in that a change in the price level interferes with this intended function of money. Money has the ability to satisfy a desire to save purchasing power when it is used as a store of value. Sometimes individuals and institutions do not wish to spend all current income today. Acquiring an amount of money today makes available purchasing power tomorrow, or at any future time. The amount of purchasing power available tomorrow is the same as the purchasing power saved today, however, only if tomorrow's prices of commodities and services are the same as they are today. Considerable hazard is thus introduced in using money or any asset, such as a bond, with a given nominal dollar value as a store of value if there is considerable uncertainty about the future course of prices. If prices are expected to rise in the future, it is better to spend money now on acquiring some useful asset, rather than holding money in a sterile form, which moreover is depreciating in value.

Efforts are sometimes made to improve the way in which money performs these four major functions, particularly because of the major disadvantage incurred when price-level changes interfere with the desired use of money as a standard of deferred payments or as a store of value. The most basic approach, of course, is to try to stabilize the price level itself and thereby stabilize the value of money in terms of its purchasing power.

A second approach used in some countries at various times is to fix debt or labor union contracts in terms of a price index that measures changes in the value of money. Such a contract over time, therefore, would guarantee that the future payment of a debt or supply of labor services would in fact be compensated for by the same amount of purchasing power as when the contracts were entered into. Even when these efforts at ensuring a stable value of money are not completely successful, money has still been necessary as a measure of debt and as a store of value.

## MONEY IN THE UNITED STATES TODAY

The use of checks to buy most goods and services, or to repay debt, has meant a great stress on *all transaction accounts* in the common definitions of money in the United States. Although various definitions of "money" are somewhat arbitrary, the ones most generally used are those employed by the Federal Reserve in establishing growth targets for the **monetary aggregates**. Prior to the passage of the Monetary Control Act of 1980, only the currency component and demand deposits of commercial banks were included in the narrowest Federal Reserve definition of the monetary aggregates but in the two years after that act this definition of money was considerably broadened. Nonbank travelers' checks were added to the currency component and demand deposits of commercial banks, while other checkable deposits were added too. These include NOW accounts, checking accounts on which interest is paid; ATS balances, savings accounts that may be transferred automatically to a checking account when you write a check; credit union share draft balances; and demand deposits at thrift institutions.

By 1982, this definition of money was called M1. All checkable deposits, or transaction accounts, made up nearly three fourths of the total money supply. The currency component of the money supply, which consists of all currency outside the U.S. Treasury, the Federal Reserve Banks, and vaults of commercial banks, is largely composed of Federal Reserve notes, because some 90 percent of such currency is issued by the Federal Reserve. In early 1982, M1 totaled some $450 billion, of which some $124 billion was in the currency component.

M2, which is a broader definition of money, consists of overnight repurchase agreements (federal funds), Eurodollars, money market mutual funds, and savings and small time deposits. This definition of money is not only larger than M1, because it totaled some $1,841 billion at the end of 1981, but it also typically grows at a faster rate than M1. Money market mutual funds, for example, which totaled only $75.8 billion at the end of 1980, had more than doubled at the end of 1981 to $185 billion.

Most of the other components of M2 also showed growth in 1981, but not at the high rate of the money market mutual funds. The funds grew so rapidly because they paid very high rates of interest in 1981. M3 is defined as M2 plus large time deposits and term repurchase agreements. It totaled some $2,187 billion at the end of 1981.

The **Federal Reserve** looks at all three major definitions of money, and bank credit as well, in establishing its targets for monetary policy. For 1982, for example, the Federal Reserve set target ranges of growth for M1 of 2½ to 5½ percent, for M2 of 6 to 9 percent, for M3 of 6½ to 9½ percent, and for commercial bank credit of 6 to 9 percent. Most economists, however, usually stress the M1 definition of money. Let us now consider the value of money.

## The Value of Money

We have already mentioned that the **value of money** is determined by its purchasing power, that is, by the bundle of goods and services that it will buy at any one given time. Therefore, when the price level goes up, the value of the dollar goes down; when the price level falls, the value of the dollar rises. It does not matter how much or how little gold and silver a country may have, because the mere possession of gold and silver does not determine the value of a particular currency at home or abroad.

The value of the currency is determined by the real goods and services for which it can be exchanged. The only way that the store of gold and silver held by a country can affect the value of its monetary unit is if these gold or silver stocks somehow affect the price level of that country by affecting its supply of money. As we discover in the next two chapters, the supply of money in a country is determined by its holdings of gold or silver only if the country is on a gold standard, a silver standard, or a bimetallic monetary standard based on both gold and silver.

Inasmuch as the United States had not been on a traditional gold coin standard since 1933, the value of the dollar today is not directly affected by a gold flow out of the country, or a gold flow into it, even though such gold flows result in changes in our total stock of gold. The value of the dollar was in fact declining during most of the depressed

1930s, even though the country was receiving large quantities of gold from abroad beginning in 1934, because the price level was rising after 1933. In some years in the 1960s, there was virtually no change in the value of the dollar, even when the country experienced large outflows of gold, because of the relative overall price stability of goods and services. After August 15, 1971, the United States did not permit convertibility of dollars held by foreign countries into gold. There were still, however, some gold flows in and out of the United States because of sales and purchases of gold between the United States and the International Monetary Fund.

It should also be noted that the value of the dollar and the amount of real income available to the average family are not the same thing. The value of the dollar may increase because of a decline in the price level, but if the number of workers without jobs greatly increases, the average real income available to the typical family has not risen but actually declined. Similarly, in a period of inflation, with the price level rising, if more workers have jobs than earlier and if the average level of money wages is rising as fast as or faster than prices are increasing on most goods and services, then real gains in real income are being enjoyed by the average family, even though the value of the dollar is declining.

***Differential Impacts of Inflation***   We must also note, however, that either a rising or a declining price level, with concomitant changes in the value of the dollar, affects different economic groups in quite different ways. Debtors need not fear the ravages of **inflation** if the inflation does not become too serious, because they find that they are repaying less in real purchasing power than they have borrowed. Creditors, on the other hand, invariably lose in a period of inflation with its decline in the value of the dollar. Even high interest rates in an inflationary period may not be high enough to compensate creditors for the loss in real value they will experience during the period of the loan. If this is true, it means that creditors have not correctly predicted the future course of inflation so as to charge a high enough interest rate now.

An understanding of the differential impacts of inflation on debtors and creditors can be used as a key to unlock the meaning of a good deal of political history in the United States both in the nineteenth and twentieth centuries. The populist, greenback, and free silver movements in the nineteenth century were all consciously determined to bring about inflation of the price level. These movements were representative of the farmer and worker, both of whom were nearly always heavily in debt. The merchant and creditor groups, who would suffer from inflation, obviously opposed such efforts to depreciate the value of the dollar by pushing up the price level. Each group was acting in its own special interest and neither was necessarily any more enlightened as to the public interest than the other. In the twentieth century, debtors and creditors have also sometimes been arrayed in different political group-ings, which have assumed different, and sometimes quite emotional, positions relative to the value of the dollar.

*Inflation as a Tax*   Inflation has sometimes been called "the most unfair of all taxes." Whether it is unfair or not depends upon one's set of social values, but that it is a tax transferring real income from one group to another cannot be denied. A rise in the price level, like a fall in the price level, not only changes the value of the dollar but also redistributes real income from certain groups to other groups. Retired persons, those in white-collar positions, and anyone else with a relatively fixed income face a loss of real income when the value of the dollar declines. Those with sharply increasing money incomes, such as profit recipients and wage earners in strong unions, may benefit in terms of real income in a period of inflation, even while others are losing.

**Changes in the Value of Money**   Thus although money is a very useful servant, it sometimes misbehaves, as when its purchasing power de-clines in a period of inflation. Such a possible change in the value of money detracts from its smooth functioning in a complex economy in which the granting and discharge of debts, for example, amounts to many billions of dollars each year. Why, then, may the value of money change in such a quixotic manner from time to time?

As every principles of economics course emphasizes, the value of anything is determined by the demand for it compared with its supply. If it is initially assumed that the demand for money is given, it must follow that the value of money is determined by its supply. Although this simple formulation has many qualifications, as is indicated later in a number of chapters, it has a certain usefulness as a first approximation. The neo-classical economists of the late nineteenth and early twentieth centuries often called attention to the relationship between the quantity of money and the value of each unit of money. This so-called **quantity theory of money** argued, *ceteris paribus*, that the value of money was simply de-termined by its quantity. As the amount of money increased, each unit of it would be worth less, because the price level would be expected to rise *pari passu* with the rise in the quantity of money.

**Interest Rates and Inflation**   The price of borrowed money, or the **interest rate**, is also importantly affected by changes in the value of money. When the price level rises and is expected to continue to rise (inflationary expectations), lenders may add an inflation premium to the interest rate that they would otherwise charge. If there is no change in the price level, lenders may still be expected to charge an interest rate for their savings, or foregoing of present consumption, for the period of the loan.

Lenders are not only giving up present consumption, but they are also foregoing liquidity (i.e., money), which would allow them to buy goods and services "tomorrow" if not "today." Borrowers are willing to pay an interest rate, especially if they are in business planning to add to their stock of capital goods, because additional capital has a marginal productivity. This is often called the "real rate of interest" (i.e., the real rate of return charged on borrowed funds, ignoring the effects of any inflation). Individuals are also willing to pay such a rate of interest if they want to buy capital goods, such as a car or a house, and sometimes even if they want to buy services, such as airline tickets.

In the 1970s and early 1980s, there was often accelerating and even double-digit inflation, so that market or nominal rates of interest (real rates of interest plus an inflation premium) tended to be very volatile. This was true whether we look at short-term rates of interest for one year or less, intermediate-rates of interest from one to five years, or even long-term rates of interest on bonds with maturities of ten years or more.

Irving Fisher of Yale in the 1920s estimated the real rate of interest for long-term loans at about 3 percent, and this still seems to be a fairly good approximation for the 1980s. Market rates of interest, however, for all maturities of debt in the early 1980s have often been double-digit because a high premium for future expected inflation was added to the real rate of interest. Otherwise, lenders would be paid back much less real purchasing power in the future than they were lending now. High present rates of inflation, or large budget deficits by the federal government, along with large credit demands by personal and business borrowers, have all tended to push up interest rates. Since judgments in the financial markets about the prospects of future inflation tend to change, sometimes sharply from time to time, interest rates in the markets have also tended to move up and down considerably.

This volatility of interest rates in and of itself tended to increase the level of interest rates, because investors in debt had to add an additional risk premium into the yield they expected to receive because of market risk involved. Risk of default, as well as the productivity of capital, could account for differences in interest rates between one bond, say, and another bond. But if there were substantial fluctuations in the rate of inflation, which in turn led to fluctuations in interest rates on new debt and in yields on outstanding bonds, bond prices would also change in the opposite direction.

That is to say, if interest rates and bond yields rose, then market bond prices on outstanding bonds would fall. If bond holders wished to sell their bonds before maturity, they would suffer a capital loss. Because of the risk of such variations in the price of bonds in periods when interest rates were volatile, higher yields would be demanded by the bond investor than would be necessitated solely by the real rate of interest and the premium for expected inflation.

Nevertheless, changes in the rate of inflation alone seemed to offer a very good first approximation explaining changes in interest rates in the two decades from 1960 to 1980. This can be seen in Figure 1–1, where percentage changes in the Consumer Price Index from the year earlier are graphed along with the interest rate on three-month Treasury bills. For most of this period the relationship is reasonably close, although, in general, in 1980 and even in 1981 this was not true. In that period, changes in market risk must be added to changes in the inflation premium to explain the observed market variability in interest rates.

Other major factors affecting interest rates besides the inflation rate are Federal Reserve policy and the demand for borrowed funds. The demand for borrowed funds tends to rise when aggregate economic activity (output and employment) is rising and to fall when real economic activity is falling. The Federal Reserve tends to restrict the growth of the money supply when inflationary pressures are increasing, which is an additional reason for interest rates to increase in such a period. Loan demand is also usually rising in an inflationary period, which likewise tends to push up interest rates. Part 2 discusses in some detail the money

**Figure 1–1     Interest Rates and Inflation**

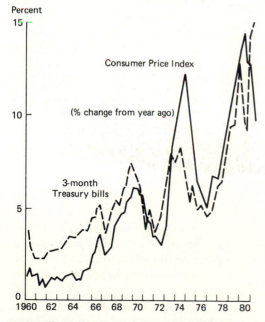

SOURCE: *The Morgan Guaranty Survey*, Sept. 1981, p. 7.

and capital markets, where interest rates are determined. Part 3 deals with commercial banks and their competitors. Part 4, Commercial Banking Practices, notes the interactions between bank lending and investing activities and interest rates. The effects of interest rates on bank portfolio policies are also considered. Impacts of Federal Reserve policy on interest rates are discussed in Part 5, Central Banking. Interest rate theory is discussed in Chapters 23 and 24 in Part 6, Monetary and Income Theory. Finally, public policy is discussed in Part 7.

Because interest rates and the price level are significantly affected, if not determined, by the change in the quantity of the money stock as compared with the growth in real output, we should introduce some of the factors determining the stock of money. We have already noted earlier that most money in the United States consists of demand deposits of commercial banks and other transaction accounts of banks and other financial institutions. Let us now summarize the process of money creation.

## The Creation of Money

The creation of money in the form of added demand deposits of commercial banks takes place whenever these banks increase their total loans and investments. The same is true for other financial institutions when their transactions accounts outstanding rise as a result of an increase in their portfolio of loans or investments. Because banks and other financial institutions are involved in profit-making, they usually make more loans or add to their investment portfolio whenever their cash reserves increase. (Legal reserves are either deposits in a Federal Reserve Bank or vault cash.)

Although an individual bank or other financial institution receives more cash reserves whenever its customers increase their demand or time deposits, such an increase in deposits by one institution usually means a loss in deposits by another institution. The total cash reserves of the financial system increase only when the Federal Reserve is supplying more reserves. Let us briefly note the use of added reserves by commercial banks in particular.

*The Use of Added Reserves by Banks*    If there is no substantial quantity of unused, excess bank reserves, it can be expected that, whenever the Federal Reserve makes more reserves available to the banking system, these added cash reserves will be employed by the banks receiving them. The mechanism whereby the banks expand their deposits by a multiple of any new cash reserves is discussed in Chapter 4, and Part 5 is devoted to the rationale and *modus operandi* of the Federal Reserve in supplying reserves to the financial system. It is sufficient for this introductory discussion to note that final control over changes in the money supply is in the hands of the Federal Reserve. This is true even though a given change in the money supply depends upon the behavior of the commercial banking system and other institutions in changing their total amount of earning assets, as well as on Federal Reserve policy. Initially, it is usually assumed that demands of banks and other financial institutions for excess reserves and the public's demand for money are unchanged.

## Broad Federal Reserve Policy Objectives

Insofar as the broad objectives of Federal Reserve policy are concerned, these goals of policy relate to the best performance of the economy as a whole. In particular, the Federal Reserve wishes to encourage and assist noninflationary economic growth. Because disturbances in the path of an equilibrium rate of growth may originate either in the financial markets or in the real product markets, the Federal Reserve is usually trying to offset these disturbances to stable economic growth by varying the tools of policy under its control. Hence if the flow of money expenditures is rising either because of a deficit in the federal budget, a sharp rise in consumer outlays, or a higher rate of private investment expenditures, then the price level is likely to start rising, as already indicated. Under these circumstances, the Federal Reserve usually moves gradually toward a policy of less credit ease or greater credit restraint—depending on the prior monetary policy stance.

*Slowdown in Inflationary Pressures*    This means that the rate of growth of the monetary aggregates, such as the money supply (e.g., M1 and M2) will tend to slacken off, while interest rates on borrowed money are likely to start rising. Eventually, if the Federal Reserve has moved quickly and strongly enough, a slowdown in the pace of inflationary price increases should take place. However, if the rise in money expenditures has been very sharp in a short period of time and the Federal Reserve is at all laggard in changing its prior policy to one of less credit ease or more credit restraint, the time lag before the inflationary pressures are capped may be considerable. The lessons of the 1970s are instructive in this regard. In fact, if the needed credit restraint comes too late, the inevitable result may be an economic recession, such as that of 1973–1975 or 1981–1982.

*Economic Recession Will Lead to Monetary Easing*    Whenever an economic **recession** does occur, whether brought on by Federal Reserve credit restraint, a sharp cutback in government expenditures, or a major decline in one of the important categories of private spending, such as a sharp reduction in the rate of inventory accumulation by business firms, then a decline in aggregate demand will take place. This decline in aggregate demand results in falling sales, reduction in production schedules, and rising worker layoffs. Despite the rise in unemployment, prices may still continue rising for some months. In fact, prices will rarely decline, although they did in March 1982 in a recession period. Usually, the rate of inflation only slackens for a time.

However, if the rise in unemployment in the judgment of the monetary authorities is serious enough, an easing in monetary policy will undoubtedly occur. This will mean an increase in the **monetary base** in the form of more bank reserves, while the money supply will tend to increase and interest rates will fall.

## A LOOK AHEAD IN THE TEXT

Some monetary history is introduced in the next several chapters. Although the traditional gold standard is now primarily of historical interest, it is a subject of seemingly perennial interest to students. In 1981, the possibility of a return to the traditional gold standard was raised seriously for the first time in nearly fifty years with the appointment of a seventeen-member Gold Policy Commission by the Reagan administration and Congress. Most of the members of this gold commission, however, appeared to be against such a change in our monetary system.

Yet gold still plays some part in international monetary relationships, even though its role is clearly declining. Some understanding of the past role of silver is also of interest. Even in the midst of the 1980s when great stress is placed on "relevance," one may argue that a historical perspective sometimes helps to reduce the apparent uniqueness of every present problem. Inflation, which continues to be a serious problem in the 1980s, has also been a problem many times in the past. Surely history may have something of value to teach us here. The apparently mystical process of money creation is considered before examining the financial markets. Considerable emphasis is then placed on commercial banks, because they continue to be the largest financial intermediary.

Finally, we are ready for the exciting questions of monetary theory and monetary policy. The daily newspaper and the weekly magazines almost invariably have some discussion of current monetary and banking questions. After studying money and banking the student should be able to follow these current developments with greater understanding. Furthermore, students should be able to come to their own conclusions on matters of public policy.

## Questions for Discussion

1. Discuss the importance of money and various money substitutes, such as credit cards, in the American economy of the 1980s.
2. Even with the growth of the use of credit cards, why is money still important? If one is to study money, why does one need to study banking as well?
3. Why must value judgments be carefully weighed in discussing controversial public policy issues in this field? Cite some conflicting judgments about monetary policy that you have recently read.
4. Discuss some common objects that have been used as money in some countries in recent years. What is money in the United States today?
5. Define money and discuss its four functions. Which function is the most important in your judgment?
6. Discuss what determines the value of money. Why does the value of money vary over time? How can the value of money be stabilized?
7. Discuss the advantages and disadvantages of inflation at different periods of time. What groups support inflationary policies and which groups oppose inflation? Why?
8. How do changing rates of inflation affect interest rates? Why did interest rates become so volatile in the early 1980s?
9. Discuss the causes and impacts of inflation in the United States in the 1970s and 1980s. What public policies were tried (with what effect?) to curb growing inflation in these decades?

## Selected Bibliography for Further Reading

In order to enrich the study of money and banking students should be aware of numerous current articles on various money and banking topics. Not only the hometown newspaper but *The New York Times* and *The Wall Street Journal* carry frequent articles on topics relevant to this course. Every Friday—about 4:10 P.M. after the stock market has closed—the money supply statistics and other current financial data are released by the Federal Reserve. These are published on Saturday in *The New York Times* and local newspapers and on Monday in *The Wall Street Journal*. Each of the twelve Federal Reserve Banks publishes either a monthly or quarterly *Review* with statistics and articles of current interest. The Board of Governors of the Federal Reserve System also publishes the *Federal Reserve Bulletin* each month and releases various studies to the general public, including its *Annual Reports*.

# 2
# CHAPTER

# Gold and Other Commodity Money Standards

The earliest forms of money were various useful commodities— particularly metals of all kinds. Today we tend to think of precious metals such as gold and silver as well suited to serve a monetary purpose. In earliest civilized life, any metal—whether it be iron, tin, copper, gold, or silver—was precious. The known ore of metals was so scarce and the refining methods so difficult and expensive that any metal was valuable. The military state of Sparta in ancient Greece appropriately used iron, whereas the Romans used both tin and copper as money. The fabled Midas, a king of ancient Lydia in Asia Minor, was one of the first to put a stamp on gold and thus provide the first legal tender gold coins for circulation.

## PRIMITIVE MONEY

Even before metals were available in sufficient quantity to provide a crude monetary system, primitive peoples found it necessary and desirable to have money of sorts. Each primitive group's distinctive money often depended upon the nature of its livelihood. Useful commodities common to a particular culture were often used, so that a hunting society would use the skins of wild animals for money. A pastoral culture often used livestock, whereas agricultural communities often used grain and foodstuffs. Almost every useful commodity was probably used by some group somewhere as money. These early moneys are not completely forgotten, as evidenced by the fact that a number of modern money terms derive from some of the ancient forms of money. For example, the modern word *pecuniary* comes from the Latin *pecus* for cattle. Similarly, *salary* derives from the Latin word for salt, *salarium*. Both salt and cattle were used as money at different times in ancient Rome.

On the North American continent, certain Indian tribes used wampum, a beaded belt of seashells, as money. Some Indian tribes even used woodpecker scalps as money, and among the plains Indians, buffalo hides were common currency. Horses were also used as a measure of wealth and for trading purposes among many Indian tribes.

In Africa cattle were most commonly regarded as a store of wealth and were available to buy other useful commodities, such as wives. In the Pacific islands of Melanesia, pigs were the desired form of wealth. Snouts and ears of animals were used as currency in early Russia, whereas even in the twentieth century, squirrel skins have continued to be used as a medium of exchange in Mongolia. Shells and beads of all sorts and colors have been used in various regions of the world, although certain tribes have had a marked preference for particular shapes and colors. Another tribe, even close by, might have a different monetary preference. Feather money was used in the South Banks Islands of the Pacific. Cubes of salt and animal skins were often used by different cultures for exchange purposes. Spears, fishhooks, bits of wire, and many other useful articles have also served in various parts of the world in place of direct barter of goods.

Whatever useful commodity serves as money in a given primitive society, some form of money is needed to fulfill commercial or trade needs and noncommercial needs, such as those required to make payments for marriage purposes. In either case, the emphasis is on money as a medium of exchange, because primitive moneys did not always fulfill the other functions of money discussed in Chapter 1. The noncommercial uses of money, which some anthropologists say first developed in early primitive societies, included not only marriage payments but payments for taxes or tribute, in sacrifices, in other religious ceremonies, in festive gifts, in blood money, in fines, in peace offerings, in funerals, in payments for skilled or ritual labor, and in ornaments and prestige tokens. As trade developed, particularly "foreign trade," the benefits of using money rather than barter greatly increased, particularly among the early Mediterranean peoples, some of whom settled rather early into trading cities.

## Money As an Instrument of Trade

In the cradle of Western civilization, around the Mediterranean Sea, many early civilized peoples used cattle as a measure of wealth. When seaborne commerce became increasingly important with the rise of merchant nations on the Mediterranean shore, something more portable than cattle was needed to carry on the thriving commerce. Furthermore, in such an expanded market system not every commodity used as money in a local self-sufficient tribal economy would be acceptable to merchants of different nations.

Although many of these Mediterranean civilizations displayed warlike tendencies, others were interested in expanding their wealth and influence through trading. The first of these merchant, or shopkeeper, nations was averred by the ancient historian Herodotus to be Lydia. Inasmuch as merchants needed a medium of exchange to carry on commerce, it is not surprising that King Midas of Lydia was the first soverign to put his imprint on ingots of gold, thus giving civilization its first coins. These early gold coins possessed all the characteristics of desirable money and become widely accepted in trade.

It has been said that gold is the "natural standard of merchants." Certainly, gold was used very early in trade among merchants; but among the common people, silver or baser metals were more likely to serve in hand-to-hand circulation. Alfred Marshall, the great English economist of the nineteenth century, suggested that silver and money were almost synonymous throughout most of history and that silver was the dominant basis of currency in most of the world prior to the discoveries of gold in Australia and California in the nineteenth century. Some nations alternated between a monetary system based on one or the other of these two precious metals, or a system combining them in some manner.

Nations often resorted to gold or silver, or both, as their monetary base because these precious metals possessed in great measure certain monetary characteristics needed by a commodity used as money in an expanded market. These desirable characteristics of money are (1) portability, (2) durability, (3) divisibility, and (4) general acceptability.

The earliest forms of money did not always possess all these characteristics. Soft commodities obviously were not as durable as gold, silver, or stones. Larger stones, however, were not very portable. Only through much trial and error did crude forms of money evolve into more sophisticated monetary systems suitable for widespread production and trading activities. The evolution of different forms of money in England illustrates some of the stages through which money has changed its form, as economic organization itself has developed into a more elaborate market system.

## EARLY COINAGE IN BRITAIN

The early Britons were a primitive agricultural people living in isolated self-contained settlements. Livestock and goods were bartered with neighbors. Some currency was in use, however, in the form of gold, silver, or iron rings worn on the arms of their chiefs. This "ring money" was similar to that used in some of the early Mediterranean civilizations. Also some Apollo gold coins were struck in crude mints in imitation of the coins used in Gaul in the fourth century B.C.

The first gold coin of England to be continuously struck was produced in the reign of Henry III (1216–1272); it was pure gold of 24 carats. This gold coin, the first to be struck in Britain after the Norman invasion, appeared in 1257, only five years after a gold coin was struck in Florence, which came to be known as a florin. The great popularity of florins undoubtedly aided public acceptance of the new English gold coins.

Coin clipping was such a serious problem of currency debasement for every new coinage that various measures were taken in an attempt to halt the practice. Severe punishments were inflicted. When these failed in their purpose, scriptural texts were engraved around the edges of the coins to appeal to the religious instincts of the populace. Even this, however, did not eliminate the problem.

Observing that such debased coins continued to circulate, whereas full-bodied coins were hoarded or even melted down for their specie content, the chancellor of the exchequer under Elizabeth I enunciated a now famous principle. Sir Thomas Gresham made the discovery in 1558, which we now call **Gresham's law**. Simply stated, it is that bad money drives good money out of circulation. As the nineteenth-century English economist Alfred Marshall phrased it: "whenever the specie value of a certain class of coins exceeds their currency value, the coins will begin to go into the melting pot, or be exported."

## THE EARLY ENGLISH GOLD STANDARD

In the Middle Ages in western Europe the principal standard of value was silver, even though the Byzantine Empire in the eastern Mediterranean was on a gold standard. Gold was used by merchants, particularly in international trade, in such currencies as the florin of Florence and the ducat of Venice, but such gold coin had to be given a value by each country in its money of account, which was silver. Because different countries adopted slightly different ratios between gold and silver, gold tended to flow toward those countries where it was valued highest in terms of silver, whereas silver flowed away from such a country to pay for the gold. Although silver was the indispensable medium for everyday transactions, it was too bulky and heavy for larger commercial transactions. Nevertheless, as far as western Europe is concerned, the gold standard virtually originated in England, and there attained the greatest refinement of both theory and practice.

In 1663 Charles II of England issued a gold coin called the guinea, which was officially valued at £1. A troy pound of gold 11/12 fine was coined into 44½ guineas. A given weight of fine gold was valued at 14.485 times an equal weight of fine silver. This ratio of the value of gold to silver undervalued gold in terms of its value in the European market. Rather than dispense with gold coins entirely, gold coins were traded at a premium over their official value. The price of such gold coins, as the price of any commodity like wheat or iron, varied from time to time, but the coins were still used as a medium of exchange.

In 1717 Sir Isaac Newton, then master of the mint, studied the shortage of gold coins in the country. He correctly attributed the shortage to the disparity of the official value of gold in Britain from the market value of gold in Europe. By raising the value of the gold guinea to 21 silver shillings, the ratio of gold to silver became 15:1, which was even higher than the market ratio in Europe. Because silver was then undervalued, little of it remained in circulation and England in effect went on the gold standard. This gold standard, therefore, was really founded on nothing but the overvaluation of gold in the coinage system. The deliberate adoption of gold as the basis of the English monetary standard did not take place until one hundred years later. Before that event, however, England tried a paper money standard.

Both England and France abandoned the use of gold and silver during the French Revolution in favor of **fiat,** or paper, money standards for some years thereafter. England went off the gold standard in 1798 when it made the notes of the Bank of England inconvertible into gold. England also suspended the coinage of silver at the same time. England did not return to gold until the Act of 1816, which prescribed gold coins as the sole standard of value with unlimited legal tender rights. Silver coins were declared to be representative, or tokens for, money. However, by this time the public had become so adjusted to the idea of using paper currency that the new coins did not readily pass into general circulation.

The continued use of paper currency alongside gold coins seemed to call for some regulation of the amount of bank notes that could be issued. This regulation was achieved by the Act of 1844, which placed great stress on the limitation of the quantity of representative money (bank notes) so as to ensure the maintenance of the monetary standard on principles somewhat similar to those of purely gold commodity standard.

## Spread of the Gold Standard

The gold discoveries in Australia and California in the middle of the nineteenth century assisted the process whereby many other countries, in addition to England, adopted the **gold standard** as their monetary standard. Traditionally, the countries of Europe had been on a silver standard, although some of them in the nineteenth century adopted the **bimetallic standard**. In the first half of the nineteenth century France was the leading European country on this bimetallic standard in which both silver and gold are standard money. (In the same period the United States was also on a bimetallic standard.) Holland, which like France had been on the bimetallic standard, returned to silver in 1847. Belgium and Switzerland adopted bimetallism and, along with Italy, joined France in the Latin Monetary Union of 1865.

     The **silver standard** remained effective only in Germany, Holland, and Scandinavia. By 1871 Russia, Austria-Hungary, Italy, and the United States were using irredeemable paper currency. In that year, however, Germany took a significant step that led it, and many other nations as well, to the gold standard. After the conclusion of the Franco-Prussian War, Germany received a substantial indemnity from France and in 1871 adopted a new currency unit, the mark, that was based on gold. Using the funds acquired from France, Germany was able to buy large quantities of gold while selling silver on a large scale.

     By 1900 most of the countries of Latin America, which earlier had been on silver or bimetallic standards, had resorted to **paper money standards**. Only Peru, Argentina, Uruguay, and Mexico had adopted gold. Chile and Brazil were moving toward a gold standard. The United States had officially adopted the gold standard by 1900, though it had been on it in effect since 1879, when the greenbacks of the Civil War period were made redeemable in specie. Coinage of silver dollars had ceased in the United States in 1873.

## Characteristics of the Nineteenth-Century Gold Standard

The greatest period of the gold standard began after the Napoleonic wars, when England officially adopted the gold standard in 1816, though the other major countries of the world did not adopt gold until the 1870s. This period ended in 1914 when, at the beginning of World War I, England departed the gold standard. The period of the ascendancy of the gold standard throughout the world also corresponded with the apogee of the British Empire. Britain was the most powerful nation on earth, and the world's money market center was London. Britain was also on the gold standard. Not surprisingly, therefore, many other nations were attracted to the gold standard. When the gold strikes of the midnineteenth century made available a sufficient abundance of gold, it became possible for many other countries, in addition to wealthy Britain, to play by the rules of the fashionable gold game. Furthermore, English economists had persuasively argued that the gold standard had many advantages, not only for an individual country but also for the encouragement of world trade with great benefits to all trading nations.

***Advantages of the Gold Standard***    The main advantages of the gold standard were thought to be (1) the stability of international exchange rates brought about by most of the world's important trading countries valuing their respective currencies in terms of gold, and being willing to see gold flow in or out of their individual countries in order to maintain exchange rate stability, and (2) the internal discipline imposed on the supply of money by the scarcity of the country's gold reserves. Because gold was so limited in supply, it was held to be virtually impossible for a country on the gold standard to have widespread inflation or general increases in the prices of goods and services. With no important changes in the overall price level likely, the value of a country's money was thus preserved.

Stable exchange rates, by increasing the confidence of businesspeople engaged in international trade, would tend to increase trade between countries. Beginning with Adam Smith, all economists were in agreement that the internal division of labor made possible by international trade would increase the standard of living of all trading countries. Moreover, the internal stability in value of a country's currency brought about by the limitation in the supply of money, which was a characteristic of the gold standard, would assist a country in maintaining a given level of exports by reason of stable prices of export goods. With the major trading countries on such a stable internal monetary standard in terms of gold, the value of each currency in terms of one another—international exchange rates—would also be stable.

To secure these presumed great advantages relating to international trade, and internal price stability as well, countries that followed England's lead and adopted the gold coin standard in the nineteenth century were supposed to follow certain basic rules. In order to define the monetary unit in terms of gold, each country needed to (1) determine a given price of gold, or what is the same thing, decide how much gold was stated as backing for each unit of money, (2) indicate that gold coin was to be legal tender (i.e., acceptable in payment of debt), (3) provide for unlimited coinage of all gold presented to the mint with only a very small charge for the cost of minting the metal, (4) permit the public to secure virtually unlimited quantities of gold coin, which could be used in circulation, hoarded, or even melted down for industrial or ornamental purposes, (5) permit the import or export of gold without hindrance, and (6) provide that paper currency in use could be converted into a specific amount of gold coin or bullion at the option of the holder of the paper currency. Some version of this gold standard, following the lead of Great Britain as the most powerful nation of the period, became the imitated kind of monetary standard from 1875 to 1914.

***Disadvantages of the Gold Standard***   The great disadvantage of the gold standard for an individual country was that it subjected the domestic economy to all the vagaries of foreign trade, movements of capital, including "hot money" or speculative capital movements, and so on. If a country really played according to the rules of the gold standard game, a loss of gold abroad, for example, resulted in a decrease in the money supply of the country losing gold, restrictive credit measures by the central bank (e.g., the Bank of England) in raising interest rates and attracting capital from abroad, and, finally, deflation, which often proved to be most painful.

Costs of production, such as wages, are often quite "sticky," so that substantial unemployment of labor and other resources may be necessary to achieve much success in the reduction of labor and product market prices. Hence external stability was achieved at the price of internal instability.

## Gold and World Trade

In addition to the internal difficulties to which a country on the gold standard was often exposed, there was difficulty in increasing the world supply of gold rapidly enough in the nineteenth century to support a rapidly growing volume of world trade. As has been suggested earlier, many countries probably would not have followed the lead of Britain, and Germany later, in adopting the full gold standard as their monetary system, if substantial gold discoveries had not occurred in the midnineteenth century. These additions to the world stock of gold were soon absorbed in the reserve holdings of the world's central banks, such as the Bank of England, and shortages of monetary reserves again developed.

The quantity of gold and foreign exchange holdings of other countries on the gold standard available to a given country was important, because ultimately the aggregate money supply and its growth for a given country were limited by these monetary reserves. A limited stock of gold thus acted as a drag on the growth of the money supply of the major industrial countries during a period when their productive capacities were greatly increasing. This slow growth in world gold production and the concomitant slow growth in the money supply of most countries have sometimes been given as major factors responsible for downward pressure on world price levels during the period 1873–1896.

After 1890 new gold mines were discovered both in South Africa and the United States and new processes were developed for increasing the output of existing gold mines. International liquidity, in the form of an increased supply of gold, was thereby greatly eased. Various methods in economizing the use of gold by gold standard countries were also employed.

**Economizing Scarce Gold Reserves**    Although a country on the gold standard needed at all times to be able to redeem claims on its gold stock (i.e., representative paper money backed by gold), it did not need to have 100 percent in gold behind its money supply. Indeed, every country on this standard used a fractional reserve system, though the proportion of gold reserves to ultimate monetary claims on this gold varied substantially from one country to the next. In that bastion of the gold standard, England, the ratio of aggregate demand liabilities of the banking system to gold reserves appeared to have been less than 5 percent in the later period of the gold standard, from 1880 to 1914. In other gold standard countries, the gold ratio was somewhat higher than this, but in no country was it 100 percent, In England, in fact, the availability of gold was so limited, in view of possible internal and external drains on the gold reserves of the Bank of England, that some public concern was expressed as to the adequacy of such reserves. Similar concern was expressed in such countries as Germany and Belgium.

In addition to having only a fractional ratio of gold behind ultimate monetary claims, other economizing techniques were used by various countries. For one thing, only a limited number of countries, such as England, Germany, and the United States, were on a full gold standard in the late nineteenth century. Other countries, such as France, Belgium, and Switzerland, were on a "limping" gold standard. In these latter countries legal convertibility of notes into gold or full-legal-tender silver coins was at the option of the authorities. Still other nations, such as Russia, Japan, Austria-Hungary, the Netherlands, most of the Scandinavian countries, Canada, South Africa, Australia, New Zealand, and some of the Asian and South American countries, were on a gold exchange standard. Countries on the gold exchange standard held a substantial part or the bulk of their monetary reserves in foreign exchange of such countries as England, which were on a full gold standard. Both internally and externally, therefore, there was a pyramid of money on a fractional reserve gold base.

## Gold As the International Monetary Standard

The fortunes of all countries on the gold standard were interrelated, because the gold standard in the late nineteenth century was truly an international monetary standard. A **favorable balance of trade** for a country meant that a country with an excess of exports over imports of goods would be receiving gold from abroad. A country with an unfavorable balance of trade would suffer a loss of gold. This movement of gold affected not only the country with the gold outflow but the country with the gold inflow as well. A loss of gold from a country importing more merchandise than it exported put pressure on the monetary reserves of that country.

Loss of monetary reserves restricted the growth in the internal money supply of a country or perhaps even contracted the money supply. Such deflationary pressure on the price level tended to reduce the prices of exports as well as those of all other goods and services, and ultimately led to an increase in exports of merchandise. An internal decline in prices also made domestically produced goods in comparison with foreign goods relatively cheaper than before, so imports of merchandise would decline. Finally, therefore, the country with a deficit in its balance of payments caused by an unfavorable balance of trade would reach a new equilibrium in its balance of payments. Gold flows were thus self-correcting.

This self-correcting process was reinforced by the opposite conditions occurring in the country receiving gold. A country with augmented monetary reserves of gold would tend to have an increase in its supply of money. Increased quantities of money were expected to be reflected in increased expenditures on goods and services. Higher levels of money expenditures would lead to higher prices of most goods and services.

Higher internal prices meant that foreign goods would now appear more attractive than previously in terms of their prices. Imports, therefore, would increase. On the other hand, higher prices of goods in the country receiving gold would make it more difficult for the exporters of that country to compete in world markets. Exports of that country would then decline.

For the country with a surplus in its balance of payments caused by a favorable balance of trade, an inflow of gold was therefore as self-correcting as an outflow of gold for the country with an unfavorable balance of trade. The economies of various countries on a gold standard became more sensitive to economic developments in other countries on a gold standard. Many such economic developments would be reflected in international trade and finally in an actual or possible flow of gold.

## Central Banks and the "Automatic" Gold Standard

A number of writers on the traditional gold standard seem to suggest that some invisible hand aided the international flows of gold in some "automatic" way to achieve the necessary equilibrium of trade and money for the various countries involved. It is true that certain flows of capital and gold across national frontiers helped attain a new equilibrium in the balance of trade. On the other hand, powerful central banks, like the Bank of England, operated virtually as a financial arm of the government in each country helping the process to work the way the writers said it should work. (A central bank is a bank to the government and a bankers' bank, as well as having responsibility for regulating the supply of money in a country. From 1836, after the demise of the Second Bank of the United States, until 1913 the United States did not have a central bank. Since 1913, the Federal Reserve System has been the central bank of the United States.)

The monetary authorities in each gold standard country were vitally concerned that the national currency should always be convertible directly or indirectly into gold at the legal parity. Therefore the currency of a given country had to be worth at all times approximately the same amount in the currencies of other countries. Because each gold standard country's currency was defined as being worth so much in gold, each currency had to have a certain ratio to other currencies. The ratio or price of one currency in terms of another currency is called the *exchange rate*. As long as countries did not change the price of their currency in terms of gold, each currency would remain at a fixed, stable mint exchange rate in terms of other currencies, even though the market exchange rates could fluctuate somewhat until gold moved in or out of the country.

Protection of the value of a given currency in terms of gold was the basic objective of central bank policy for gold standard countries. The resultant stable exchange rates aided the flow of trade and capital and were regarded as one of the important advantages of the gold standard. So the central bank had to assist with whatever policies were needed to preserve this established exchange rate. In practice, this meant that a central bank always became concerned when a country lost gold, because this reduction of monetary reserves could pose a threat to the value of that country's currency.

***Reversing the Outflow of Gold***    Raising interest rates at home was the usual method of the central bank to protect the currency of the country losing gold. In England, a higher Bank rate established by the Bank of England by tradition meant that all commercial bank rates and money market rates would also be raised immediately. (It was not until 1971 that this tradition was discontinued, whereas in 1972 the Bank rate was automatically tied to money market rates rather than the reverse relationship.) Higher interest rates might attract foreign capital seeking investment and would certainly make it more attractive for indigenous capitalists to invest their funds internally. Keeping funds at home reduced the gold outflow, whereas attracting funds from abroad resulted in an inflow of gold. In either case the vital gold monetary reserves of the country would be protected.

If the country losing gold had no central bank, interest rates would have risen eventually anyway. A reduction in the money supply caused by the loss of gold would have made it necessary for banks, and other lenders, to increase the cost of borrowed funds. The central bank was able to do quickly what the forces of the marketplace would have done more slowly and more painfully. A small loss of gold could sometimes, therefore, be stopped from developing into a larger loss of gold. The central bank was thus working with rather than against the forces of the market.

It should be noted, however, that central banks normally did not take corrective action in the face of a gold inflow. Any such increase in monetary reserves was usually welcomed rather than offset. It was really up to the country losing gold to undertake needed corrective steps.

***Loss of Gold and Deflation***    Whenever a country lost gold, and thereby experienced higher interest rates and perhaps a decline in its money supply, deflation of its economy often occurred. If the loss of gold came after a substantial upswing in economic activity with considerable price increases, or inflation, the subsequent corrective deflationary period might be quite unpleasant. Wages and prices often tend to be somewhat rigid, or "sticky," in a downward direction. A substantial rise in unemployed workers was thus the usual price of the deflationary process imposed by the loss of gold. The greater the inflationary excesses of the expansionary period, the more severe the subsequent contraction was likely to be.

If a loss of gold was quite substantial in a short period of time, the deflationary pressures resulting therefrom assisted by the central bank increasing interest rates might very well bring on a financial panic. Whenever a financial panic occurred in a country, the resulting loss of confidence and the failure, perhaps, of a number of commercial banks and other financial institutions combined to make the ensuing deflation and depression more severe than it would have been without such drastic financial pressures. In such cases the cure might seem even worse than the disease.

Once the deflationary process had wrung out many of the inflationary price increases of the previous expansionary period, the country that had earlier lost gold was then in a position to compete more aggressively in world markets. Lower prices of export goods usually meant higher exports. Lower incomes and lower prices at home undoubtedly meant lower imports of goods from abroad, so a more favorable trade balance almost inevitably resulted.

## A New Equilibrium in Trade

The effects of central bank policy in gold standard countries in the nineteenth century reinforced the "automatic" pressures of a loss or gain of gold on a country's money supply. In the short run, the increase in interest rates brought about by central bank action for a country losing gold reduced the export of funds and even attracted some short-term funds from abroad. In the long run, such deflationary policies lowered the country's price level, even if a depression resulted thereby, and thus enabled the country to compete better in world markets. The ultimate adjustment of a flow of gold between countries was to be on the flow of goods and services between countries.

With such an international mechanism contributing to the establishment of new equilibria as a result of an increase or decrease in the gold stock of a country, the value of the country's currency both in terms of gold and foreign currencies could be preserved. In the long run, preserving the value of a country's currency depended upon an equilibrium growth in the gold stock of that country relative to the growth of its foreign trade. Preserving the value of the currency was a cardinal part of the gold standard. Even with some representative paper currency backed by gold outstanding, hard money was supposed to be sound money. If a country's money was as good as gold, it was thought to be very good indeed.

## THE DECLINE AND FALL OF THE GOLD STANDARD

How could most of the countries of the world ever discard such a sound, hard, commodity money standard as the gold standard? We have already suggested that the major disadvantage of the gold standard was that it exposed the health and prosperity of a country's economy to all the economic winds that might buffet the markets of the world. Any major change in demand and supply conditions anywhere in the world's leading commodity markets would have repercussions on the terms and volume of international trade. A depression in one country, for example, would represent a decline in demand for the products another country produced for export. If the latter country were prosperous and continued to import as many products from abroad as before, a decline in its exports would soon eliminate any surplus in its current account and could lead to a loss of gold. The gold outflow would then result in this country's experiencing a depression similar to that in some other major country. Both depressions and inflations could be exported among the members of the gold club. It used to be said that "whenever America sneezed, the rest of the world caught pneumonia." Although this is not true today, even if it were partly true in an earlier period, the international gold standard always made the economies of various countries more sensitive to one another through the effects of gold flows on international trade.

The gold standard was always a fair-weather standard in that a country could not afford to continue to play by the rules of the gold game if serious financial or political difficulties were being experienced by other major trading nations. Any serious financial crisis anywhere was bound to affect all nations to some degree. A war, of course, was the kind of crisis that would lead all participants, and sometimes nonparticipants as well, to suspend the gold standard. In retrospect, the nineteenth century had fewer serious wars than the twentieth. Furthermore, the peace of the world and much of its financial stability as well was perhaps partly the result of the great world power status of the British Empire after 1815. With the end of World War I the status of Great Britain was greatly diminished and its mantle of world leadership largely fell on the United States.

The political world of the twentieth century has been quite different from that of the nineteenth century. It was not merely a question of a new leader taking the place of a former one. The legacy of World War I has been a series of revolutions and new states around the world. Communism as a serious political force did not exist before World War I, but after that war communism came to power in Russia, and after World War II it came to power in China. Each of these nations has accumulated satellites and none of these countries has been willing even to consider operating by the rules of the gold game.

Even the great powers on the gold standard before World War I have largely abandoned gold as the centerpiece of their monetary systems. Many of these powers did return to gold in the 1920s, but the remarriage of gold and money was brief. Britian returned to gold in 1925 but abandoned it in 1931. The United States left the traditional gold standard in 1933, and France in 1936.

The Great Depression of the 1930s, which began in October 1929, finished the work of World War I in demolishing the political and financial world of the nineteenth century. Gold no longer seemed to have quite the same glitter for countries that it once had. For one thing, many countries were experiencing serious political upheavals in the 1930s. Spokesmen for the masses were assuming control and to them mass unemployment seemed too high a price to pay for stable exchange rates. The old doctrines of limited central government and admiration of the automatic workings of the marketplace were not quite so hallowed as they had once been. The gold standard was, therefore, an early casualty of this political upheaval. Gold still remained part of the monetary reserves of all countries, but it was not the touchstone of the monetary systems of great powers that it had been in the nineteenth century.

## *After Gold?*

No other commodity has replaced gold as the foundation of monetary systems around the world. War spawns its own forms of commodity money, as was discussed earlier, but none survives the reestablishment of a new social and political order. Gold itself retains a great deal of popular interest and still serves the cause of international trade by its flow between countries. For a number of years the United States was able to run a deficit in its balance of payments by exporting gold.

After 1970, although gold still remained part of the monetary reserves of countries, the new "paper gold," or special drawing rights (SDRs) of the International Monetary Fund, contributed more to the growth of world monetary reserves than did gold. Gold and convertible currencies, such as the dollar, continued to be part of the monetary reserves of most countries in addition to SDRs, but for international monetary transactions gold had lost a great deal of its usefulness. In fact, after August 15, 1971, the United States refused to allow the free convertibility of dollars held by foreign central banks into gold held by the U.S. Treasury. For private speculators and some individual countries, however, gold continued to exercise an almost hypnotic attraction, so that the free market price of gold fluctuated, as did that of other commodities, even though the official price of gold among central banks was only $42.22 per ounce after February 1973. The peak price of gold was $875 in early 1980. Thereafter it fell to about $400 by late-1982. Higher rates of inflation and expectations of still more inflation drove up the price of gold. When the inflation rate fell, the price of gold fell too.

Silver and other commodity metals still serve in fractional currency as token money for most countries. But paper currency and notations on bank balance sheets in the form of demand deposit liabilities make up the bulk of the money supplies of such highly industrialized countries as the United States, Britain, and France. The backing for this paper money and bank money is mostly credit, particularly the credit of the central government. Money in the modern era has thus become much less concrete and much more abstract. This evolutionary historical process of movement from concrete commodity money to abstract bank money can be traced well in the monetary experience of such a country as the United States. This is the subject of the next chapter.

## Questions for Discussion

1. List and discuss some of the various useful commodities used by primitive peoples as money.

2. Discuss the monetary use of gold and silver as instruments of trade by early civilizations.
3. Why did Britain mint gold coins as early as the thirteenth century? What problems sometimes developed in the use of these early gold coins?
4. What led Britain to adopt the gold standard in the late eighteenth and early nineteenth centuries? What role did silver play?
5. Discuss the major characteristics of the nineteenth-century gold standard.
6. Why did most of the major industrial countries follow the lead of Great Britain and adopt the gold standard by the end of the nineteenth century?
7. What were the major advantages and disadvantages of this traditional gold coin standard?
8. Discuss the "self-adjusting" process of gold flows among countries and the effects of these gold flows on international trade and the balance of payments of the countries involved.
9. Why did the major industrial countries abandon the traditional gold standard in the 1930s?
10. What has taken the place of gold within most countries? What is the role of gold now in international monetary relations among central banks?
11. Why did the free market price of gold rise sharply by 1980 to over $800 an ounce, even though the official price was only $42.22? Do you think this means that gold will be more significant in international monetary affairs in the 1980s than in the 1970s?

# Selected Bibilography for Further Reading

*Books*

BERNSTEIN, PETER L., *Primer on Money, Banking and Gold* (New York: Random House, 1968).

BLOOMFIELD, ARTHUR, *Monetary Policy Under the International Gold Standard* (New York: Federal Reserve Bank of New York, 1959).

CASSELL, FRANCIS, *Gold or Credit: The Economics and Politics of International Money* (New York: Praeger, 1965).

CRAIG, SIR JOHN, *The Mint* (Cambridge, England: Cambridge University Press, 1953).

CROWTHER, GEOFFREY, *An Outline of Money*, rev. ed. (London: Thomas Nelson and Sons Ltd., 1950).

EINZIG, PAUL, *Primitive Money* (London: Eyre & Spottiswoode, 1948).

GILBERT, MILTON, *The Gold Dollar System, Conditions of Equilibrium and the Price of Gold* (Princeton, N.J.: International Financial Section, 1968).

GREEN TIMOTHY, *The World of Gold Today* (New York: Walker, 1973).

HAWTREY, R. C, *The Gold Standard in Theory and Practice*, 5th ed. (London: Longmans, Green and Co., 1947).

JOSSET, C. R., *Money in Britain* (London: Frederick Warne and Co., Ltd., 1962).

LINDERT, PETER H., *Key Currencies and Gold, 1900–1913* (Princeton, N.J.: International Financial Section, 1969).

MARSHALL, ALFRED, *Money Credit & Commerce* (London: Macmillan and Co., Ltd., 1924).

QUIGGIN, A. HINGSTON, *A Survey of Primitive Money* (London: Methuen & Co., Ltd., 1949).

## *Articles*

BARRO, R. J., "Money and the Price Level Under the Gold Standard," *Economic Journal*, **89** (March 1979), 13–33.

NEWBURGER, H. M. and H. H. STOKES, "Relationship Between Interest Rates and Gold Flows Under the Gold Standard: A New Empirical Result," *Economica*, **46** (August 1979), 261–279.

PRYOR, FREDERIC L., "The Origins of Money," *Journal of Money, Credit and Banking*, **9**, No. 3 (Aug. 1977), 391–409.

WHITAKER, J.K., "Essay in the Pure Theory of Commodity Money," *Economic Papers*, **31**, No. 3 (Nov. 1979), 339–357.

The Americans, it has been said, indeed have no gold or silver money; the interior commerce of the country being carried on by a paper currency and the gold and silver which occasionally come among them being all sent to Great Britain in return for the commodities which they receive from us.

THE WEALTH OF NATIONS

# CHAPTER

# The American Monetary Standard

America from its founding as a collection of English colonies has always experienced monetary difficulties. The basic problem was that there was never enough money—hard **specie**, that is. The situation was aggravated by England's refusal to allow the colonists to coin their own money. Barter of goods directly for other goods, therefore, had to be done. But some money was always available. It was mostly foreign coins, not only English but French, Spanish, and Portuguese coins as well. Even local Indian wampum was used, at first in trade with the Indians but later among the colonists as well. Any money was better than none at all.

   After independence, and most especially after the Constitution was ratified, the new country embarked upon its own efforts to establish a national currency. The new currency most certainly had to be based on one or more of the precious metals after a bad experience with paper currency during the Revolutionary War. As it turned out, the new currency was founded on both gold and silver. Difficulties in keeping the price of gold and silver at the mint at the same value as their market value meant, however, that the country alternated from silver to gold. The country tried paper again, in the Civil War, and then returned to gold. After World War I and the Great Crash of 1929 demolished the gold

37

standard around the world, the United States went on a new credit standard at home but remained on a gold bullion standard settling for international obligations.

After August 15, 1971, the United States refused to allow foreign central banks freely to convert their dollars into gold. It still remained on the **gold bullion standard,** however, in that it sold and purchased certain other currencies with gold from the International Monetary Fund. Gold thus remained as part of the international monetary reserves of the United States. Less gold was nevertheless behind each dollar after February 1973, when the official price of gold was raised to $42.22 an ounce. In November 1973, the 1968 agreement formally recognizing the two-tier gold system was terminated. This meant that central banks could now sell gold for more than the official price, if they wished to.

Regardless of which monetary standard prevailed in America at a particular moment in its history, the sound and fury of controversy has invariably swirled around the subject of money. Someone has always been certain that a monetary standard other than the official one in force would be better for the United States. And, naturally, there have always been defenders of the status quo. America's monetary history, therefore, has been almost as exciting as its political history, particularly because the two have been intertwined. But let us start at the beginning with the colonial experience in money matters.

## COLONIAL CURRENCY

The basic fact of colonial life was that everything except land was scarce. Scarcity applied to hard specie as it did to goods. The early colonists had brought little specie with them from England, and whatever currency they later acquired through trade went back to England to purchase badly needed tools and occasionally luxuries. An unfavorable balance of trade persisted with England, for each year the colonies purchased more goods than they sold to the mother country. The flight of specie to England left the colonists with little to serve the needs of growing trade within and among the colonies.

The barter system quickly developed and always persisted to some degree on the western frontier. But the inconveniences of barter discussed in the first chapter made themselves felt, so "country pay" in the form of various useful commodities developed in the different colonies. In New England the wampum money (seashells) of the Indians was used for country pay. From 1643 to 1649 wampum was even considered legal tender by the Massachusetts Bay Colony. In the Middle Atlantic colonies wampum was also used, along with fur skins, powder, and shot. In the Southern colonies country pay consisted of tobacco and rice. Tobacco was the most popular type of money and was even given an exchange rate in terms of English money. In 1619 in Virginia the best grade of tobacco had an exchange value per pound of three shillings, and the second grade of tobacco was worth 18 pence.

Foreign currency, however, especially from Spain and England, was always the most popular and uniformly accepted currency throughout the colonies. The Spanish milled dollars were the favorite silver coins in circulation. These coins were originally termed *pesos*, but they became known as pieces of eight or dollars in English-speaking countries. The Spanish dollars not only circulated in the colonies but even made their appearance in England and on the Continent. The heavy output of silver from Spanish colonial mines made it possible for Spain to issue these coins in great quantity and also meant that they continued to be issued as full-valued coins. Though the favorite coin of the colonists was always the Spanish silver dollar, the shortage of hard money of all kinds made almost any coin acceptable.

## CURRENCY DURING THE REVOLUTIONARY WAR

After the Revolutionary War began in 1775, the problem of financing the war was one of great urgency. The central authority embodied in the Continental Congress had little real power, because the ultimate power to make decisions remained in the hands of each former colony. Unable to raise funds through obligatory taxes, the Continental Congress issued bills of credit. These continental bills, or *continentals*, were based on the pledge of the confederated colonies to provide for eventual redemption in Spanish milled dollars, which thereupon assumed the role of the unit of common account and standard of value. One such four-dollar paper currency note issued in 1776 indicated, "This bill entitles the bearer to receive four Spanish milled dollars, or the value thereof in gold or silver according to a Resolution of Congress passed at Philadelphia, July 22, 1776." Continental paper currency was originally issued in denominations from one to eight dollars, but later fractional parts, such as one half, one third, and even two thirds of a dollar, were added.

These bills, which were declared to be legal tender to be accepted in payment of all private and public debts by the various states, were issued in fairly small amounts by Congress at first. In mid-1775, the first issue of $2 million was authorized and was followed by another issue of $4 million later in the year. Each subsequent year, however, the difficulties of financing the war, and rising prices, necessitated an ever larger issue of paper currency. Under Gresham's law the bad paper money soon drove all the good gold and silver specie money out of circulation.

By 1779 there were more than $241 million in continentals outstanding. By that time the currency was nearly worthless because of the sharp rise in prices caused by its overissue. "Not worth a continental" became a popular expression. The various states in 1780 and 1781 completed the destruction of this paper currency as money by canceling its legal-tender status.

The different states had also issued paper currency at the beginning of the Revolutionary War, though the Continental Congress forbade this practice in 1777. After the collapse of the continental currency, the states resumed their issuance of paper currency until such issuance was forbidden once again—this time in 1789 by the new Constitution. The various state issues, which finally totaled about the same amount as the continental currency, suffered, for the most part, the same fate of excessive depreciation in value that had befallen the continentals. The early American experience with fiat money, or paper currency backed only by a vague promise of some eventual redemption in specie, was thus not very promising.

## THE BIMETALLIC STANDARD

Not surprisingly, therefore, the Founding Fathers of the new government established by the Constitution were determined that a currency standard better and stronger than the paper standard should be quickly established. Both gold and silver had forceful proponents among leaders in the government. Robert Morris, superintendent of finance in 1782, urged that the dollar be based on silver. Alexander Hamilton, the first secretary of the treasury, was inclined to believe that if a single metal were adopted, then it should be gold. Nevertheless, he proposed a compromise monetary standard based on both gold and silver.

The greatest difficulty in establishing a bimetallic standard was determining the mint ratio between gold and silver. After studying the commodity prices of these metals, Hamilton proposed that the mint ratio be 15:1 (i.e., 15 ounces of silver would be regarded by the mint as equal in value to 1 ounce of gold). Prior to the passage of the Coinage Act of 1792, which established bimetallism in the United States, the relative value of these two metals both here and in Europe had been fairly steady for some years at 15:1. The official mint ratio between silver and gold was therefore set at 15:1. Unfortunately, however, for the smooth operation of this dual monetary standard, the market ratio of these metals began to change very shortly after 1792, so that gold was valued at a higher price in terms of silver in the free bullion market than it was at the mint.

## The Silver Standard, 1792–1834

The divergence of the relative price of gold in terms of silver in the bullion market was the result of a great increase in the output of the silver mines, which caused the price of silver to decline steadily after 1792. Because silver was now overvalued at the mint, whereas gold was undervalued, Gresham's law came into play. The overvalued specie, silver, drove the undervalued specie, gold, out of circulation. Instead of being on a bimetallic monetary standard after 1792, we were on a *de facto* silver standard practically from the very beginning.

With the decline in the market value of silver, 15½ or even 16 ounces of silver in the bullion markets were required to buy 1 ounce of gold. At the American mint, however, a moneybroker could secure legal money for 15 ounces of silver, which then could be exchanged for 1 ounce of gold coins in circulation. Because 1 ounce of gold coins really had a market value of 16 ounces of silver, rather than 15, the search for profit on the part of the moneybroker soon led to the disappearance of all gold coins from circulation. The gold coins were then melted down and exported as gold bullion to Britain or some other gold standard country.

Silver dollars also tended to disappear from circulation because they were accepted at their face value in Spanish possessions, even though they were minted lighter than their Spanish counterparts. The steady export of silver dollars was checked only when President Jefferson ordered a halt to the coinage of silver dollars in 1806, thereby making such dollars virtually unobtainable. Gresham's law had thus resulted in the disappearance not only of gold coins but silver dollars as well. With each succeeding decade of our early history, the shortage of hard specie grew more acute.

***The Money Mess of the 1820s and 1830s***    The flight of hard specie from circulation, even though the mint continued to coin gold coins and fractional silver currency, resulted in a greater shortage of hand-to-hand circulating money. Foreign coins, therefore, continued to circulate in the United States, even as they had in the colonial period. But the great bulk of money in circulation was paper money.

The best paper money, because it could still be redeemed in specie, was issued at the First Bank of the United States, which operated as a central bank on a charter from Congress from 1791 to 1811. Its successor, the Second Bank of the United States, also on a charter from Congress, was in existence from 1816 to 1836. This bank also issued redeemable paper currency and even regulated somewhat the issue of bank notes by private state banks.

When Andrew Jackson was reelected president in 1832 after a campaign in which he pledged destruction of the Second Bank of the

United States, a mounting money mess had to be resolved somehow. Many state banks issued paper bank notes that were virtually worthless because the public could rarely redeem them in specie. Furthermore, many of these unsound banks went into periodic bankruptcies that reduced the amount of circulating money still further. Something had to be done particularly to restore some hard money to the circulatory stream.

## The Early Gold Standard, 1834–1862

By 1834, the money problem had become so serious that a legislative remedy had to be applied by Congress. Congress acted in the statute of June 28, 1834, by changing the ratio of silver to gold at the mint from 15:1 to 16:1. Previously, the fine gold weight of the dollar had been 24.75 grains, whereas it was now reduced to 23.2 grains. The silver dollar was left unchanged at 371.25 grains fine. Because the ratio of silver to gold in the market was 15.625:1, gold was now being overvalued at the mint. The effect of this legislation was to replace the notes of the newly defunct Second Bank of the United States with gold coins. In January 1837, Congress further amended the basic monetary standard act of 1792. Both gold and silver coins were to be 9/10 fine. The full weight of the silver dollar was declared to be 412.5 grains, whereas the weight of the gold dollar was increased slightly from 23.2 to 23.22 grains.

These legislative changes by Congress resulted in a substantial gold inflow into the United States, because of the new attractive mint prices of gold. Gold coins were now used in actual circulation and the United States was on a *de facto* gold standard. With the continuance of the coinage of fractional silver coins, the availability of hard specie to the public was greatly improved. This new hard money policy of the government was further emphasized by the Specie Circular issued by the Treasury in 1836, which provided that all public lands had to be paid for in gold or silver notes recognized by the treasurer of the United States as convertible into specie.

The coinage of gold coins at the mint took a decisively sharp spurt upward after the gold strikes in this country, beginning with the one at Sutter's Mill, California, in 1848. The mining of gold in the United States, which had been valued at $889,000 in 1847, rose to $10 million in 1848, $40 million in 1849, and $50 million in 1850. For decades thereafter, the annual output of gold remained in a range of $40 million to $50 million.

In March 1849, Congress authorized the minting of $10 gold pieces to supplement the existing $5 gold pieces and also approved a tiny $1 gold piece, because silver dollars continued to be scarce. The coinage of silver dollars had been resumed in 1840, but only a negligible amount was coined each year. In 1851 and 1853, Congress reduced the silver content of fractional silver coins, so that they became subsidiary, or token, coins. Finally, in 1857, Congress canceled the legal-tender status of all foreign coins. Henceforth, the monetary standard of the United States was to be purely American.

## THE GREENBACK STANDARD

The outbreak of the Civil War in April 1861 revived the war financing problems faced during the Revolutionary War. Unfortunately for the stability of the dollar's value, the same expedient of issuing irredeemable paper currency was followed. From the outset the Union government was unwilling to impose the high levels of taxation necessary to avoid the depreciated paper dollar. Secretary of the Treasury Salmon P. Chase recommended to Congress in a special session in July 1861 a budget for the following twelve months that would provide only one fourth of the needed revenue through taxes. The other three fourths of the financing needed to raise and equip an army would come from borrowing.

Monetary problems facing the country were also troublesome. A shortage of currency developed at the end of 1861, when the New York City banks announced that they were suspending specie payments. When the Legal Tender Act of 1862 was introduced in early January, it appeared that if Congress refused to grant the request of the Treasury to issue irredeemable paper currency, the government would have no means to pay its bills. Congress therefore promptly passed the requested legislation on February 25 and the greenbacks came into existence. The formal name of this currency was United States notes. Some of it is still in circulation today as $2 bills, which are regarded by some people as unlucky.

Originally, the notes were issued in round numbers of $5, $10, $20, $50, $100, and above. The issue of $150 million of these notes was authorized with $50 million of the new notes to take the place of demand notes issued by the Treasury the previous year. The greenbacks were declared to be "lawful money and a **legal tender** in payment of all debts, public and private, within the United States, except duties on imports and interest on the public debt," which were to be payable in coin. In subsequent congressional action the amount of authorized greenbacks was raised to $450 million. Bills in denominations of $1 and $2 were also issued later.

Throughout the Civil War the price of gold in the bullion market steadily rose, as did the cost of living. This increase in the price level of goods and services meant that the value of the greenbacks in real purchasing power was steadily depreciating. The greenbacks and similar paper currency issued during the Civil War did not decline in value as greatly as the continentals had during the Revolutionary War, which may be partly because the Civil War did not last as long as the Revolutionary War.

***Other Paper Currencies***    After March 3, 1863, no further issues of greenbacks were authorized, for a new way of borrowing money had been discovered. The new technique was to sell special types of government bonds to private banks, against which they could issue bank notes. The only banks with this privilege of note issue against part of the government debt were newly authorized national banks.

The National Bank Act was passed by Congress on February 25, 1863. Banks taking out a national bank charter could issue bank notes at 90 percent of the face value or market value, whichever was the lower, of the government bonds purchased by the bank. In addition, banks had to maintain cash reserves of 15 to 25 percent of the total of their notes and deposits, though a considerable amount of these reserves were permitted to be in the form of deposits with other banks in reserve cities, such as New York City. When the war ended on April 9, 1865, nearly $100 million of these national bank notes were in circulation.

State bank notes were finally taxed out of existence by a 10 percent tax imposed by Congress in a statute passed on March 3, 1865. Many state banks then took out national charters, so that the number of national banks, which had totaled only 638 at the end of 1864, rose to 1,582 a year later. State bank notes gradually disappeared from circulation.

The legal-tender status of greenbacks was upheld by the Supreme Court in May 1871. Four years later, in January 1875, Congress passed the Specie Resumption Act to make it possible to redeem the greenbacks in specie. This resumption of specie payment was to take place on January 1, 1879.

## THE DE FACTO GOLD STANDARD, 1879–1900

The effect of the Specie Resumption Act of 1875 was to return the country to a **de facto** gold standard on January 1, 1879. The reason for this was that the Coinage Act of 1873 had not even mentioned the silver dollar. This omission of reference to silver was later called by certain political groups "the crime of 1873," because the price of silver began to decline sharply after 1873. Though this decline in the price of silver was probably the result of a great increase in the output of silver mines, the fact remains that greenbacks were redeemed only in gold specie after 1879. Silver had lost its legal-tender status.

On July 12, 1881, Congress added still another kind of paper money in the form of gold certificates. Such certificates had been provided for earlier under the act of March 3, 1863, but until 1882 gold certificates had been issued only in large denominations for the use of banks and clearinghouses. Now gold certificates were to be available for public use.

## Silver Versus Gold

The worldwide shift to the gold standard in the 1870s following the leadership of Great Britain and Germany, as discussed in the previous chapter, led to a worldwide decline in commodity prices. For the United States, the ensuing period of deflation and depression in the 1870s was quite severe and led to political demands that the money supply be increased. Rather than urging the expansion of the amount of greenbacks, the battle cry became bimetallism. This would have meant the unlimited coinage of silver and probably would have led through Gresham's law to a shift from the gold standard to the silver standard, as in the period before 1834.

In the 1880s and 1890s, the free-silver forces representing the farmer debtors of the Midwest and the silver mining interests of the Far West continued their political agitation. William Jennings Bryan of Nebraska, an ardent defender of silver, secured the nomination of the Democratic party by making his inflammatory "Cross of Gold" speech to the 1896 party convention. In the November election, however, the Republican William McKinley won. His election virtually finished the political power of the free-silver movement and set the course of the country firmly on the route to a full gold standard.

## THE FULL GOLD STANDARD, 1900–1933

The gold standard was officially adopted by the United States with the Gold Standard Act of March 14, 1900. The country had been, as was indicated, on the *de facto* gold standard since 1879, when the resumption of gold specie payments was permitted for the greenbacks of the Civil War era. In 1900, the country was officially and completely on the **de jure** gold standard. The gold dollar consisting of 25.8 grains 9/10 fine was declared to be "the standard unit of value."

The amount of gold certificates outstanding subsequently grew tremendously, rising from $201 million in 1900 to $803 million in 1910, and finally even to $1 billion in 1913. Bank notes were also increasing in this period from $300 million in 1900 to $716 million in 1913. After the passage of the Federal Reserve Act in 1913, only the twelve Federal Reserve Banks or the Treasury could issue any new paper currency.

The new paper currency of the Federal Reserve was tied firmly to gold, because the Federal Reserve Act required that these notes be backed by not less than 40 percent in gold. Therefore most of the currency in circulation after 1913 consisted either of gold coins or of paper money backed either 100 percent by gold (gold certificates) or 40 percent by gold (**Federal Reserve notes**). Admittedly, some other currency was still outstanding in the form of some remaining greenbacks, the newer silver certificates, national bank notes, and, of course, fractional silver coins. Nevertheless, the bulk of our hand-to-hand money was ultimately based on gold.

Even before actually entering World War I, the United States became a major provider of military supplies and food to the belligerent powers. This profitable trade changed America from a debtor to a substantial creditor nation. By the end of the war in 1918, foreign countries owed the United States more than $3 billion. In addition to buying goods on credit, other nations had shipped substantial quantities of their gold holdings to the United States to pay for needed materials. By the end of the war, the United States owned some 40 percent of the world's known gold reserves. The American gold standard was clearly on a firm base.

The large stock of gold that the United States had accumulated during the early years of the hostilities in Europe made it unnecessary for the United States to suspend all operations of the gold standard, as had been true for the combatants in Europe. Therefore the United States did not have to return to the gold standard after the war, because it had really never left it. (England returned to the gold standard in early 1925, followed by most of the other major industrial countries. A few countries had restored the gold standard before England's return.)

## The Gold Standard in the 1920s

The United States throughout the 1920s was on a full gold coin standard, although many other countries adopted a modified version of the gold standard in the form of a gold bullion standard or a gold exchange standard. Great Britain was on a kind of gold bullion standard prior to 1931 in that the Bank of England had to sell bars of gold to anyone presenting to it a certain minimum amount of bank notes. France, on the other hand, used foreign exchange of gold standard countries to supplement its gold stock, so it was on a partial gold exchange standard.

## *The End of the Gold Standard*

The 1920s was, however, the twilight of the traditional gold standard. At the end of this decade of postwar prosperity, storm clouds were gathering for a serious crisis of capitalism. Significantly enough, some of the major causes of this crisis were financial in their origin. The threatened collapse of the free market system had begun with overspeculation on the stock exchanges, leading finally to a panic on the New York Stock Exchange in the autumn of 1929. Thereafter the financial shock wave initiated in New York City spread the panic throughout the world. In Europe, particularly, new shock waves developed, which reverberated across the Atlantic to hit the United States with additional financial pressures.

The ever increasing financial panic in the United States virtually stopped overseas investment by Americans. Thus many European countries, such as Austria, Germany, England, and France, were no longer able to secure needed American dollars to repay their substantial debt and interest payments on their foreign debts. Many of these debts had been incurred in the United States during World War I and the early years of the postwar reconstruction period. Faced with their inability to meet scheduled debt payments and the ever present danger of gold outflows, European governments applied exchange controls on the exportation of gold and payments in general to other countries. The application of these direct controls meant the eventual abandonment of the gold standard by these European countries.

England was the first country to leave the gold standard in 1931, after having been on it for only six years after World War I. France did not leave gold completely until 1936 but had imposed certain exchange controls before then. Most other countries, including the United States, abandoned the traditional gold standard even before France.

## THE AMERICAN INTERNATIONAL GOLD BULLION STANDARD, 1933 TO DATE

In the face of severe financial pressures both at home and abroad, the United States found it necessary to leave the gold standard in the depths of the Great Depression. Five days after the inauguration of President Franklin D. Roosevelt on March 4, 1933, Congress passed the Emergency Banking Act. On March 10, the president issued an executive order prohibiting the export of gold and gold certificates except under license by the secretary of the treasury. The first steps toward a complete nationalization of gold were also taken in that executive order, though a number of years were required to achieve virtually complete compliance. Gold held both by Americans and by foreigners, with a few minor exceptions, had to be surrendered to the government. Gold certificates too were withdrawn from public circulation and gold clauses in contracts were canceled. All domestic circulation of gold coin or domestic hoarding of gold was thus forbidden. However, as of January 1, 1975, Americans could again legally own gold as a result of a law passed by Congress in August 1974.

In the Thomas Amendment to the Agricultural Adjustment Act, passed in May 1933, all U. S. coins and currencies were declared legal tender. This amendment also gave the president a number of discretionary powers with respect to the monetary standard, some of which were never used. Perhaps the most important provision of the Thomas Amendment was the one permitting the president to reduce the gold content of the dollar by 50 percent or less. As a result of this provision the Treasury increased the price of gold toward the end of 1933, that is, reduced the amount of gold behind each dollar. It thus became perfectly clear that the United States had definitely abandoned the traditional gold standard.

After 1933, therefore, gold would be used by the United States only in settlement of international financial claims and in part as backing by the Federal Reserve of its outstanding liabilities of Federal Reserve notes and member bank reserve deposits. Even then, the Federal Reserve Banks were required to have only a fraction of the total amount of gold certificates that had been deposited with them by the Treasury behind these liabilities. Until 1945 this legal reserve ratio of gold certificates for the Federal Reserve was 40 percent; in that year it was reduced to 25 percent. In 1965 the requirement on the Federal Reserve of holding fractional gold certificate reserves behind member bank reserves was removed completely by Congress. The 25 percent gold requirements behind outstanding Federal Reserve notes was removed by Congress in 1968.

All the gold stock was henceforth to be held only behind the international dollar liabilities of the United States. But as has been previously noted, the gold window of the United States Treasury was closed to foreign redemption of dollars in gold on August 15, 1971. The United States, however, continued to pay out (or acquire) gold in dealings with the International Monetary Fund. In December 1971, the dollar was devalued 8.5 percent by raising the official price of gold in the United States from $35 to $38 an ounce. Fourteen months later in February 1973, the dollar was devalued by an additional 10 percent by raising the official United States price of gold to $42.22; in November 1973 the agreement to separate the official gold market from the free market, as set up in a two-tier market in March 1968, was terminated. By 1982 the free market price of gold was more than $400 an ounce.

## THE MODERN AMERICAN CREDIT-DEBT MONEY STANDARD

With the demise of the American gold coin standard in 1933 and the American gold bullion standard (for the most part) in 1971, the domestic American monetary standard became entirely a credit-debt money standard. The small amounts of Treasury currency outstanding, either fractional coins or paper currency still outstanding from the greenbacks of the Civil War period, are, of course, debt of the federal government and are backed by the credit of the federal government. The great bulk of currency outstanding (more than four fifths by value) consists of Federal Reserve notes, which are debt of the twelve Federal Reserve Banks. These notes are backed by the credit extended by the Federal Reserve Banks, which consists mostly of U. S. government securities held by the Federal Reserve System and some loans to depository institutions.

Most of the money supply in the United States, however, consists of demand deposits of commercial banks, other transaction accounts, and other monetary liabilities of various financial institutions. These kinds of "money" are shown in Table 3–1, where data for the six years from 1976 to 1981 are shown. Four definitions of money—M1, M2, M3, and L—are shown in this table. But no matter how money is defined, it still consists of debt of financial institutions.

Prior to 1980, M1-A was the definition of money to which the Federal Reserve gave most of its attention in formulating monetary policy. In 1980 and 1981, M1-B received most of the attention of policymakers. In 1982, M1-B was redefined as M1. M1 includes demand deposits of commercial banks, which are debts of commercial banks, other checkable deposits, traveler's checks and currency. By the end of 1981, such demand deposits of commercial banks and other checkable deposits were 71 percent of the total of M1.

M2 is a much broader definition of money than M1. M2 includes M1 plus savings and small denomination time deposits at all depository institutions, overnight repurchase agreements at commercial banks, overnight Eurodollars held by U. S. residents other than banks at Caribbean branches, and balances of money market mutual funds. The Federal Reserve has growth targets each year for both M1 and M2. Still broader definitions of money are M3 and L, which are defined in the footnotes to Table 3–1.

Returning to Table 3–1, we can note the growth rates of the

**Table 3–1   Money Stock Measures and Liquid Assets (In billions of dollars, seasonally adjusted. December data.)**

| | *M1* | *M2* | *M3* | *L* |
|---|---|---|---|---|
| *Date* | *Currency plus demand deposits*[a] *plus other checkable deposits at banks and thrift institutions*[b] | *M1 plus overnight RPs and Eurodollars MMMF shares and savings and small time deposits at commercial banks and thrift institutions*[c] | *M2 plus large time deposits and term RPs at commercial banks and thrift institutions* | *M3 plus other liquid assets*[e] |
| 1976 | 307.7 | 1,166.7 | 1,299.7 | 1,523.5 |
| 1977 | 332.5 | 1,249.1 | 1,460.3 | 1,715.5 |
| 1978 | 363.2 | 1,403.9 | 1,629.0 | 1,938.9 |
| 1979 | 389.0 | 1,518.9 | 1,779.3 | 2,153.9 |
| 1980 | 414.5 | 1,656.1 | 1,963.1 | 2,370.4 |
| 1981 | 440.9 | 1,822.4 | 2,187.8 | 2,685.0 |

[a]Includes (1) demand deposits at all commercial banks other than those due to domestic banks, the U.S. government, and foreign banks and official institutions less cash items in the process of collection and F.R. float, and (2) currency outside the Treasury, F.R. banks, and the vaults of commercial banks.

[b]NOW and ATS accounts at banks and thrift institutions, credit union share draft accounts, and demand deposits at mutual savings banks.

[c]Overnight (and continuing contracts) RPs are those issued by commercial banks to the nonbank public, and overnight Eurodollars are those issued by Caribbean branches of member banks to U.S. nonbank customers. Small denominations time deposits are those issued in amounts of less than $100,000. M2 will differ from the sum of components presented in subsequent tables by a consolidation adjustment made to avoid double counting of the public's monetary assets. The difference represents the amount of demand deposits held by thrift institutions at commercial banks.

[d]Large denomination time deposits are those issued in amounts of $100,000 or more and are net of the holdings of domestic banks, thrift institutions, the U.S. government, money market mutual funds, and foreign banks and official institutions. Term RPs are net of RPs held by money market mutual funds.

[e]Other liquid assets include the nonbank public's holdings of U.S. savings bonds, short-term Treasury securities, commercial paper, and bankers' acceptances net of money market mutual fund holdings of these assets.

SOURCE: Federal Reserve data.

various types of money from the end of 1976 to the end of 1981. M1 increased by more than 43 percent from $307.7 billion to $440.9 billion. The broader definitions of money in this six-year period grew even faster, with M2 growing by 56 percent, M3 by 68 percent, and L by 76 percent. Because money in the United States is debt based on credit, as existing financial institutions innovate in the types of liabilities that they offer to savers, and new financial institutions appear (e.g., money market mutual funds in the late 1970s), the broader definitions of money grow even faster than the narrower definitions. The Federal Reserve, however, in its money policy determination focuses mostly on the medium of exchange function of money and for that reason puts most of its attention, as will we, on M1 and M2.

# Questions for Discussion

1. Discuss the major characteristics of American colonial currency. What was "country pay"? Illustrate this type of money. What role did foreign coins play in the Americans colonies?
2. Discuss the financing used during the Revolutionary War and the effect of financing needs of the colonies on their currency outstanding.
3. Why did the new United States adopt a bimetallic standard using both gold and silver rather than one metal or the other?
4. What problems developed under the *de jure* bimetallic standard, so that the United States was *de facto* either on a silver standard or a gold standard prior to the Civil War?
5. Why was the greenback standard adopted during the Civil War? What was the experience with this type of fiat money?
6. When, and why, did the United States return to the *de facto* gold standard? What economic impact did this change in monetary standard have on the United States? What political groups particularly objected to the gold standard? Why?
7. When did the United States adopt the full gold standard? What happened to the American money supply after this full gold standard was adopted?
8. Discuss the experiences of some of the major industrial countries with the gold standard in the 1920s. How was a possible shortage of gold for monetary purposes averted in that decade?
9. What kind of a mixed monetary system did the United States adopt in 1933 after it went off the traditional gold standard? How was that system further modified by the 1980s?
10. What was the effect on the international monetary system of the closing by the United States of its "gold window" to foreign holders of dollars on August 15, 1971? Why did the United States subsequently devalue the dollar in two steps by raising the price of gold in December 1971 and again in February 1973? Briefly, discuss the floating of the dollar since then.
11. In what sense is the United States now on a credit-debt standard? What are the major forms of money now in use in the United States?

# Selected Bibliography for Further Reading

BLOOMFIELD, ARTHUR, *Monetary Policy Under the International Gold Standard* (New York: Federal Reserve Bank of New York, 1959).

GILBART, JAMES WILLIAM, *The History of Banking in America*, Reprints of Economic Classics (New York: A. M. Kelley, 1967).

KROOSS, HERMAN EDWARD, *Documentary History of Banking and Currency in the United States* (New York: Chelsea House Publishers, 1969).

LAUGHLIN, J. LAURENCE, *The History of Bimetallism in the United States* (New York: D. Appleton and Co., 1886).

LINDERT, PETER H., *Key Currencies and Gold, 1900–1913* (Princeton, N. J.: Princeton University International Finance Section, 1969).

MITCHELL, WESLEY CLAIR, *A History of the Greenbacks (Chicago:* University of Chicago Press, 1903, New Impression, 1960).

NUSSBAUM, ARTHUR, *A History of the Dollar* (New York: Columbia University Press, 1957.).

STUDENSKI, PAUL, and HERMAN KROOS, *Financial History of the United States*, 2d ed. (New York: McGraw-Hill, 1963).

# CHAPTER 4

# Creating Money

In the previous chapter, we noted that the American monetary standard is now a credit-debt standard. We also noted that most money (M1) in the United States today is either demand deposits of commercial banks or other transactions accounts of these same commercial banks and other financial institutions. In this chapter we focus on the creation of new money (demand deposits and other transactions accounts) that occurs when commercial banks and other financial institutions increase their loans and investments. The process of creation of new money is essentially the same for all financial intermediaries. Because commercial banks are the largest financial intermediary, we center our discussion here on the creation of new demand deposits at commercial banks.

It should first be noted that there is a multiplier relationship between the amount of bank deposits a given bank can have in terms of cash reserves. The **simple monetary multiplier**, which we will shortly discuss, is simply the reciprocal of the average reserve ratio requirement on transactions accounts of depository institutions. (The **reserve requirement on transactions accounts** in 1981 was 3 percent for institutions having less than $25 million of such accounts and 12 percent on such transactions accounts of more than $25 million). It is this fractional reserve requirement for commercial banks that makes it possible for them to create money, even though each individual bank only lends out its excess reserves. Because each bank can lend only funds that it has, how can the entire banking system create new money? Money creation by the banking system sometimes strikes the student as being almost as

53

mysterious as the processes of the medieval alchemist, who was trying to create gold out of baser metals.

## THE PROCESS OF MONEY CREATION

The creation of money may seem much less mysterious after the process is examined step by step. It may then be realized that this process of money creation depends upon (1) a fractional legal reserve requirement, so that banks do not have to maintain 100 percent reserves against their demand deposits, (2) a fractional legal reserve ratio against time deposits, (3) the provision of added reserves by the central bank (i.e., the Federal Reserve System), (4) the demand for currency on the part of the public, which may be viewed as a ratio of demand deposits held by the public, (5) the demand for time deposits by the public, which again may be viewed as a ratio of demand deposits, and (6) the demand for excess reserves by commercial banks.

### Factors Determined by the Central Bank

Three of these six factors affecting the money supply are determined by the central bank—total bank reserves, the legal reserve ratio behind demand deposits, and the legal reserve ratio behind time deposits. Two other factors, the demand for currency and the desired ratio of time deposits to demand deposits, are under the control of the public, whereas the demand for excess reserves is a function of commercial bank behavior. Only if we regard the public's and bank's portfolio policies as being constant (i.e., not affected by interest rate and income demand changes) can we regard the money supply as being exogenously, or externally, determined by the central bank.

After the Monetary Control Act of 1980, the control over the money supply by the Federal Reserve was increased in that there was no further incentive for member banks to leave the system in search of lower reserve requirements. In fact, reserve requirements imposed by the Federal Reserve were extended to the transactions deposits of all financial institutions, which certainly increased the power of the Federal Reserve to control ultimately the creation of added money by such financial institutions. On the other hand, the early years of the decade of the 1980s, as had been true of the 1970s, saw the continued growth in nonreservable highly liquid assets, such as nonbank repurchase agreements (RPs) and money market mutual funds. Time deposits of commercial banks also continued to grow in amount and importance.

Nevertheless, in considering the determination of the supply of money we should consider the demand for money and the cost of creating more money. When reserve requirements are imposed on an asset called money (i.e., transactions balances), there is a cost to the financial institution creating such added transactions balances. If there is no legal reserve requirement, as on money market mutual funds, there may still be customary cash reserves held by the institution plus the interest paid on additional amounts of such funds. The same point can be made about the NOW accounts (demand deposits on which interest is paid) available throughout the country after December 31, 1980. In this case there are two costs of added NOW accounts to the financial institutions: the added required reserves and the interest rate (usually 5¼ percent) that has to be paid.

## Ratio of Time Deposits Desired by the Public

Insofar as the demand for monetary assets, including money, is concerned, both changes in national income and interest rates affect the portfolio holdings of monetary assets of the public. As national income rises, we expect that the ratio of currency to income will fall, because larger transactions in dollar terms tend to be paid for by check. The ratio of **time deposits**, on the other hand, can be expected to increase as national income increases, because time deposits, unlike demand deposits, may be regarded as "luxury goods," of which more are demanded at higher levels of income. In fact, by the 1980s time deposits of commercial banks greatly exceeded the dollar amount of demand deposits. By 1982, time and savings deposits at all commercial banks totaled more than $900 billion, more than 2½ times the amount of the $335 billion in demand deposits at these banks.

Time deposits seem to bear an inverse relationship to market rates of interest, so that the public shifts out of holdings of time deposits into other money market assets, such as Treasury bills and money market mutual funds, when market yields rise, and vice versa. Research studies have shown that the excess reserve ratio of banks varies inversely with interest rates on loans and securities. That is, as interest rates on such earning assets increase, banks are willing to reduce their excess holdings of cash, even though the risk factor increases somewhat.

Disregarding the risk factor and uncertainty and assuming profit-maximizing behavior on the part of commercial banks, excess reserves held by banks would be zero. Such excess reserves have fallen in recent years as a result of (1) higher interest rates, (2) lower valuation of risk, and (3) greater emphasis on profit-maximizing behavior.

## MONETIZATION OF DEBT

Whenever commercial banks exchange their debt (demand deposits) for a private or governmental debt, they are creating money. It does not matter whether an individual or business firm is securing a new loan from a bank, or whether the bank is buying an outstanding U.S. government security; the result is the same—**debt** has been **monetized**. The banks secure an earning asset, whereas the increase in their liabilities (demand deposits) means that someone else now has money who did not have it before.

Commercial banks once had the privilege of printing bank notes, which were used as money in hand-to-hand circulation, but the bank note privilege is now restricted to the Treasury and the Federal Reserve System. Nevertheless, the great growth in recent years in the use of checks for payment of goods, services, financial assets, and so on has meant that the banking system has kept its importance as the immediate source of most new money. The banks can still create money, but they do it by making changes in their balance sheets rather than by resorting to a printing press. Before we examine the mechanics of bank deposit creation, however, let us first consider the major kinds of bank assets and liabilities, inasmuch as we use the balance sheet, or **T-accounts**, approach in our explanation of bank deposit creation.

### *The Commercial Bank Balance Sheet*

Like all business firms, commercial banks use balance sheets on which the total value of assets must equal the total value of liabilities plus net worth. The major kinds of bank assets and liabilities are shown on the sample balance sheet of the First National Bank of Yourtown. The classification of assets and liabilities in Table 4–1 is actually taken from the annual report of a major commercial bank. Other banks have a somewhat different method of presenting balance sheet items; for example, demand deposits and time deposits may simply be presented as one item, deposits.

The major items of concern are the first four on the asset side and the first three on the liability side. Before we examine the nature of these items, the student should be reminded that no particular item on the asset side is matched by a corresponding item on the liability side. It is necessary, however, in using a balance sheet to change the total amount of assets, say, if the total amount of liabilities plus net worth changes, and vice versa. The balance sheet must always balance, because total assets always equal total liabilities plus net worth.

**Table 4-1   First National Bank of Yourtown, Statement of Condition, December 31, 1984**

| Assets | Liabilities and Net Worth |
|---|---|
| Cash and due from banks | Demand deposits |
| U.S. government securities | Time deposits |
| Other bonds and securities | Deposits of public funds |
| Loans and discounts | Capital stock |
| Bank premises and equipment | Surplus |
| Federal Reserve Bank stock | Undivided profits |
| Interest earned, not collected | Discount collected, but not earned |
| Other assets | Dividends declared, but unpaid |
|  | Reserve for taxes, etc. |
|  | Other liabilities |

***Cash Held by Banks***    A bank's "cash" includes (1) vault cash, or coins and paper currency actually held in the vaults of the bank, (2) deposits in the regional Federal Reserve Bank, if the bank is a member of the system, and (3) deposits in other commercial banks. Only the first two categories may be considered as legal reserves by member banks in the Federal Reserve System, although all three "cash" categories are considered as primary reserves available to each bank in meeting any requirements for ready money.

***Securities Held by Banks***    The second item on the asset side, "U.S. government securities," includes all debt obligations of the federal government held by banks. This term is not restricted to bonds, but includes Treasury bills and Treasury notes as well. Banks consider short-term government securities to be secondary reserves, because they can be readily turned into cash.

    "Other bonds and securities" refers primarily to municipal bonds, or tax-exempts, which are the debt obligations issued by states, toll-road authorities, counties, school districts, water districts, and the like, as well as those debt securities sold by cities and towns. "Loans and discounts" is an item of great concern to banks, because making loans is a prime function of a bank. Although banks obtain some of their income from interest received on U.S. government securities, municipal securities, and service charges, the bulk of their earnings comes from the loans they make. Loans, however, do involve some risk, so that they are sometimes referred to collectively as risk assets.

***Bank Deposits***    On the liability side, total bank deposits are separated into (1) demand deposits, (2) time deposits, and (3) deposits of public funds. (These "public funds" are demand deposits if held by the federal government, but the deposits of state and local governments may be either demand or time deposits.) Demand deposits of individuals and businesses are included in our definition of money, whereas time deposits are referred to as near-money. State and local government deposits of public funds on demand in commercial banks are also included in the Federal Reserve System's definition of money, though federal government deposits in commercial banks are not.

From the point of view of the individual bank, an increase in its deposits provides added funds with which it can increase its earning assets, such as loans and investments. This appearance of causality from deposits to earning assets, however, is somewhat misleading, because for the banking system as a whole the direction of change is the reverse. Whenever cash reserves of the banking system are increased, usually as a result of more reserves supplied by the monetary policy of the Federal Reserve System, the banks are thereby enabled to acquire more earning assets. When the banks are adding to their total portfolio of loans and investments, their liabilities (demand deposits and time deposits) are also increasing. Hence, the supply of money and near-money increases as a direct result of the extension of bank credit by the banking system.

## The Monetary Base

Before the individual bank can increase its earning assets, it must first have added cash reserves. If a given bank has not simply increased its cash position at the expense of another bank, total bank reserves or the monetary base must have grown. *The monetary base consists of all bank reserves and all currency held by the public.* The public decides how much currency it desires in relation to demand deposits by withdrawing or depositing currency into checking accounts, and banks can determine their demand for excess reserves. Nevertheless, the monetary authorities (the central bank and the Treasury) decide what the total monetary base shall be.

Whenever the Federal Reserve System increases Federal Reserve credit or whenever the Treasury mints more coins or prints more currency, the monetary base increases. If the public's demand for currency is constant, when the monetary base increases, so too do total bank reserves (i.e., member bank deposits in the Federal Reserve Banks and vault cash held by commercial banks). If the banks have more reserves, they can increase the money supply by adding to their portfolio of earning assets. The money supply, however, is increased by a multiple of the increase in bank reserves as determined by the size of the monetary multiplier.

## The Simple Monetary Multiplier

The simple monetary multiplier is determined by finding the reciprocal of the average legal ratio reserve requirement behind demand deposits. This, of course, assumes no change in currency holdings by the public, no change in time deposits, and no change in excess reserves of the banks. In that event, $D = R/r_d$. Likewise, the change in demand deposits is found by multiplying the change in bank reserves by the reciprocal of the average legal ratio behind demand deposits, or $\Delta D = (1/r_d)\Delta R$.

In either case, the reciprocal of the legal ratio behind demand deposits, $1/r_d$, is the simple monetary multiplier. If the legal reserve ratio is 10 percent, the monetary multiplier is 10. If the ratio is raised to 12 percent, the multiplier falls to 8. If the ratio is lowered to 8 percent, the multiplier increases to 12.5. The simple monetary multiplier, then, is under the control of the central bank, because it is the Board of Governors of the Federal Reserve System that establishes the legal reserve ratios required behind different amounts of transactions accounts of financial institutions.

## The More Complex Monetary Multiplier

A more **complex monetary multiplier** can be calculated by considering the legal ratio behind time deposits ($r_t$) and the public's desire for time deposits relative to demand deposits ($t$), as well as the public's desire for currency relative to demand deposits ($c$). Likewise, bank demand for excess reserves as a ratio to demand deposits ($e$) must be included. The Federal Reserve System is still assumed to control any change in bank reserves ($\Delta R$), and it still sets the legal reserve ratio behind demand deposits ($r_d$) and the legal ratio behind time deposits ($r_t$). Recognizing that currency is a leakage from bank reserves, when more currency is demanded by the public, the equation for expanding demand deposits becomes

$$\Delta D = [1/(r_d + r_t t + c + e)]\ \Delta R.$$

This new coefficient makes clear that the expansion of demand deposits depends not only on the legal reserve ratios for demand and time deposits and the provision of added bank reserves by the monetary authorities but also on the portfolio preferences of commercial banks and the portfolio preferences of the public as well. If the portfolio preferences of banks and the public are stable (the relevant ratios are constant), it is still essentially true that the money creation process is ultimately under the control of the Federal Reserve. In reality, these ratios do shift cyclically and secularly, which presents certain problems for the prediction and control of monetary aggregates for the monetary authorities. Some of these difficulties are discussed later in connection with monetary policy. (In fact, at the end of 1981, the money supply M1 was about $440 billion, whereas total reserves of depository institutions were slightly under $45 billion. This would yield a complex multiplier of about 9.)

## Multiple Expansion of Demand Deposits by the Banking System

The commercial banking system today expands the money supply when bank credit is increased as a result of added bank reserves. The freedom of the commercial banking system to monetize private or public debt, and thus increase the money supply, is much greater under our present fractional reserve system of banking than it would be under a 100 percent reserve system. The process of the multiple expansion of demand deposits is illustrated in Table 4–2, which contains as examples three commercial banks in three different cities, the First National Banks of Albany, Boston, and Chicago, Banks A, B, and C.

*Pyramiding of the Money Supply*   Several major assets and liabilities of commercial banks are given here on skeleton balance sheets, or T-accounts, for these three banks. The problem is to see how an increase in cash reserves can be pyramided by a number of commercial banks into a money supply that is considerably greater than the original increase in cash reserves. This pyramiding of the money supply by the banks, on the basis of a given amount of cash reserves, is possible because in our banking system commercial banks are required only to have legal reserves that are a fraction of their outstanding demand and time deposits. In this exercise we assume that all banks must maintain legal reserves equal to 10 percent of their demand deposits. Because we are omitting any reference to time deposits in this example, we do not need to take account of the fact that legal reserve ratios against time deposits are always lower than those required against demand deposits.

*Public Deposit of Paper Currency*   Let us assume that a distant relative, Aunt Matilda, died, leaving you $1,000. Because your aunt had no confidence in banks, the inheritance came to you in the form of paper currency, which might be either Treasury currency or Federal Reserve

**Table 4–2  Bank Lending and Expansion of Bank Deposits at Three Banks for Seven "Days"[a] (10 percent reserve ratio)**

### First National Bank of Albany (Bank A)

| | Assets | | | | Liabilities | | |
|---|---|---|---|---|---|---|---|
| | Day 1 | Day 2 | Day 3 | | Day 1 | Day 2 | Day 3 |
| Cash | | | | Demand | | | |
| reserves | $1,000 | $1,000 | $1,000 | deposits | $1,000 | $1,000 | $1,900 |
| | | | −900 | | | +900 | −900 |
| | | | $ 100 | | | $1,900 | $1,000 |
| Required | | | | | | | |
| reserves | 100 | 190 | 100 | | | | |
| Excess | | | | | | | |
| reserves | 900 | 810 | 0 | | | | |
| Loans | 0 | 900 | 00 | | | | |

### First National Bank of Boston (Bank B)

| | Assets | | | | Liabilities | | |
|---|---|---|---|---|---|---|---|
| | Day 3 | Day 4 | Day 5 | | Day 3 | Day 4 | Day 5 |
| Cash | | | | Demand | | | |
| reserves | $900 | $900 | $ 900 | deposits | $900 | $ 900 | $1,710 |
| | | | −810 | | | +810 | −810 |
| | | | $ 90 | | | $1,710 | $ 900 |
| Required | | | | | | | |
| reserves | 90 | 171 | 90 | | | | |
| Excess | | | | | | | |
| reserves | 810 | 729 | 0 | | | | |
| Loans | 0 | 810 | 810 | | | | |

### First National Bank of Chicago (Bank C)

| | Assets | | | | Liabilities | | |
|---|---|---|---|---|---|---|---|
| | Day 5 | Day 6 | Day 7 | | Day 5 | Day 6 | Day 7 |
| Cash | | | | Demand | | | |
| reserves | $810 | $810 | $810 | deposits | $810 | $ 810 | $1,539 |
| | | | −729 | | | +729 | −729 |
| | | | $ 81 | | | $1,539 | $ 810 |
| Required | | | | | | | |
| reserves | 81 | 154 | 81 | | | | |
| Excess | | | | | | | |
| reserves | 729 | 81 | 0 | | | | |
| Loans | 0 | 729 | 729 | | | | |

[a]The "days" used here are arbitrary time periods to measure changes in the balance sheets of these three banks. On Day 3 when Bank A loses cash reserves of $900, Bank B acquires cash reserves of the same amount as a result of a check deposited in Bank B written on Bank A. The same is true on Day 5 when Bank B loses $810 in cash received by Bank C. There are no "leakages" of cash from the banking system through a rise in currency in circulation in these seven "Days." Each bank is assumed to have a legal reserve ratio requirement of 10 percent against demand deposits. These legal reserves may be either deposits in the regional Federal Reserve Bank or currency held in these banks' vaults.

notes. However, inasmuch as you have confidence in the safety of your deposits, especially because the Federal Deposit Insurance Corporation has insured your bank up to $100,000 for each depositor, you place the $1,000 in your checking account, or demand deposit, in the First National Bank of Albany (Bank A) on Day 1. In order to see what effect your deposit of currency can have on the entire banking system, we have ignored other prior deposits of the bank, and we have also assumed that the bank has no excess legal reserves, either as deposits in its Federal Reserve Bank or as vault cash.

*Required Reserves*     Bank A now has a $1,000 demand deposit liability, but it also has $1,000 on the asset side of its balance sheet in the form of cash reserves on Day 1. Subsequent changes for Bank A, and the two other banks after each receives a new initial deposit, are shown each "day" for a total of seven days. Because we have assumed a 10 percent average reserve requirement for all these member banks of the Federal Reserve System, Bank A is required to earmark $100 of its vault cash as legal reserves or deposit this amount with the Federal Reserve Bank of New York.

*Excess Reserves*     Bank A now has $900 in excess cash reserves on Day 1, which it can invest in some desirable earning asset. As far as the logic of the process of the multiple expansion of demand deposits is concerned, it does not matter whether the bank buys U.S. government securities of whatever maturity, makes a short-term business loan, or acquires some other earning asset. Because the special function of commercial banks is often considered to be that of extending short-term self-liquidating credit to businesses, we assume that Bank A makes a short-term business loan.

*A New Bank Loan*     Let us assume that Bank A makes a loan on Day 2 to a local shoe store in Albany so that it can order a fresh inventory of ladies' shoes prior to the Easter selling season. The loan is for the amount of $900 and has a maturity of ninety days. The bank credits the shoe store's checking account with the amount of the loan, and also adds the amount of the loan to its business loan assets. Because Bank A now temporarily has $1,900 in demand deposits on Day 2, it is required to have $190 in reserves. The Albany shoe store, which has already placed a substantial order for ladies' shoes with its supplier in Boston, now sends the Boston shoe manufacturer a check for $900 to secure a cash discount. As soon as the shoe manufacturer receives the check from the Albany store, it deposits the check in its Boston bank, Bank B, on Day 3. After the check clears, either through a bank correspondent or the Federal Reserve System, which we assume here occurs on Day 3 when the check is deposited, Bank B will have a demand deposit liability of $900 and an asset of $900 in cash.

***Summary of the Deposit Expansion Process***   Summarizing what has happened thus far to three banks on seven "days," we may note that already a substantial expansion of the money supply has occurred. (It should never be forgotten that the most important part of the money supply in the United States today is that of demand deposits of commercial banks.) We started out with $1,000 in paper currency, which was deposited in Bank A in Albany on Day 1. On Day 5, we already have a total of $2,710 in demand deposits of Banks A, B, and C added together. On Day 7, we also have the same total of bank deposits in the three banks. What accounts for this substantial expansion in the stock of money?

The total of bank deposits in Banks A, B, and C of $2,710 on Day 7 is accounted for by (1) the initial cash deposit of $1,000 in Bank A on Day 1, plus (2) the $900 loan made by Bank A on Day 2, which became an initial deposit for Bank B on Day 3, plus (3) the $810 loan of Bank B on Day 4, which became an initial deposit of Bank C on Day 5. We would actually have total bank deposits of $3,439 on Day 7 if we added in the $729 loan made by Bank C on Day 6, which resulted in a secondary deposit for Bank C on Day 6, but which was withdrawn on Day 7.

Several factors made possible this lending activity, which resulted in this substantial expansion in bank demand deposits. First, the commercial banks were not required to have 100 percent reserves behind their outstanding demand deposits, so that they could lend out the amount in excess of their required reserves. (Although the same result would have been accomplished if each bank had purchased government securities of the same amount rather than increased its business loans.) Second, there were businesspeople who were good credit risks and wished to borrow from a bank, and we have assumed that in its search for profits no bank wants unnecessary excess reserves. Third, we have assumed that each bank loses the entire amount of the deposit it creates by its new loan, though this need not be true for very large banks. In the latter event, the expansion of demand deposits can proceed even more rapidly, as some lending banks receive redeposits and thus do not suffer losses in reserves of the full amount of their new loans.

***Additional Steps in Bank Deposit Expansion***   Thus far we have proceeded through only three steps. If additional alphabetical banks up to the mathematical limit of $n$ are added to this sequence, the combined balance sheet for all commercial banks would be as shown in Table 4–3. In this T-account we can see what has happened after all banks have had an opportunity to lend out their added excess reserves. The result is that

**Table 4–3    Bank Deposit Expansion for All Banks**[a]

| Assets | | Liabilities | |
|---|---|---|---|
| Cash reserves | $1,000 | Demand deposits | $10,000 |
|    Required reserves | $1,000 | | |
|    Excess reserves | 0 | | |
| Loans | $9,000 | | |

[a]Legal reserve cash ratio assumed to be 10 percent for all banks against their demand deposits, adjusted.

demand deposits total $10,000 against which there is $1,000 in cash reserves, all of which is now required reserves. The reason why bank deposits expanded from the original $1,000 deposit to the present $10,000 is shown by the fact that bank loans expanded from 0 to the present $9,000.

The money supply thus becomes ten times the amount of the original increase in cash reserves as a result of bank monetization of private debt. Ten is the reciprocal (1/10) of the average reserve requirement of 10 percent assumed here. If the average reserve requirement were 9 percent, the coefficient of bank demand deposit expansion would be approximately 11; if the average reserve requirement were 8 percent, the coefficient would be approximately 12, and so on. It should therefore be clear that whenever the Federal Reserve System lowered the legal ratio reserve requirement for its member banks, as it did on several occasions prior to the sharp reduction in 1980, there was a larger coefficient of possible bank deposit expansion. The actual coefficient of bank deposit expansion based on the ratio of legal reserves required for member banks is probably about 9 in the 1980s, as already noted.

*Factors Limiting Bank Expansion of Deposits*    Regardless of what the legal reserve requirement may be, or how much it may be reduced, it is still necessary for the banks to be willing to lend money or acquire investments. At the same time credit-worthy, would-be borrowers or bank-eligible investments must also be available. These factors were quite important in limiting bank deposit expansion during the Depression of the 1930s. However, in the post-World War II period, city banks in particular have generally been willing to utilize any added excess reserves provided them by the Federal Reserve System, because these banks tend to reduce their excess reserves to zero in order to try to maximize their possible profits. The great expansion of federal debt in World War II also meant that a large amount of short- and intermediate-term bank-eligible securities has been available in the postwar period for the banks to acquire, even if private loan demand is weak in a period of economic recession. In such a period of economic decline when the Federal Reserve wishes the money supply to expand, it provides the banks with added reserves. The banks then use these new reserves to acquire government securities, which increases demand deposits of banks just as making more business loans does.

Additional factors limiting the amount of expansion of demand deposits by the banking system, as already noted in the earlier discussion of the monetary multiplier, include any loss of currency from the banks caused by an increase in currency in circulation, any increase in desired holdings of cash or excess reserves by the banks, or an increase in the legal reserve ratio imposed by the Federal Reserve Board. If these three factors are held constant, added reserves will be utilized in creating added demand deposits until no excess reserves remain. The coefficient of such multiple demand deposit creation is the reciprocal of the legal cash reserve ratio behind demand deposits, plus the legal reserve ratio for time deposits, times the ratio of time to demand deposits, plus the ratio of currency to demand deposits, plus the ratio of excess bank reserves to demand deposits.

For students to be certain that they understand this process of creation and destruction of bank demand deposits, they should see how the total demand deposits of the banking system tend to contract if a withdrawal of currency of $1,000 occurs from one of these three commercial banks. If students work through such a contractionary process using the T-accounts, they will discover that demand deposits tend to contract by the same coefficient that they tend to expand. The process of multiple expansion and contraction of demand deposits by the commercial banking system is thus a symmetrical process. Also, the same expansion or contraction of transactions accounts occurs for nonbank financial institutions when they gain or lose cash reserves.

Once this money, in the form of new transactions accounts or demand deposits, has been created, it can be spent or loaned over and over again. As long as the financial institution has the same dollar amount of assets in the form of loans and investments, it will have the same liabilities (e.g., transactions accounts). As the new money moves into the economy, some of it flows through the financial markets. This is the subject of the next chapter.

# Questions for Discussion

1. To what extent did the passage of the Monetary Control Act of 1980 affect the creation of "money"? Although financial institutions other than banks can now have transactions accounts, how important do banks remain in the

process of the creation of money? Was the Federal Reserve's control over the ultimate creation of money increased or decreased by the 1980 act?

2. List and discuss the various factors affecting the major part of money creation (i.e., the multiple expansion of demand deposits in the United States).

3. What is meant by monetization of debt by commercial banks? Are there any possible dangers in this process? What are the advantages to the entire economy of the banks and other depository institutions being able to monetize private or public debt?

4. List the major assets and the major liabilities appearing on commercial banks' balance sheets. Be sure to define each asset or liability (e.g., cash). What are the possible directions of change on a bank's balance sheet (i.e., does an increase in liabilities result in an increase in assets, or vice versa)?

5. Define and discuss the "monetary base" and the "monetary multiplier." What is the difference between the simple and the more complex monetary multiplier? To what extent do the monetary authorities control the monetary base and the monetary multiplier, and to what extent does the public control or affect them?

6. Explain the multiple expansion of bank deposits by using T-accounts for three or more banks. Is it true, as has sometimes been stated, that no single bank or depository institution can increase the money supply? What legal requirements affecting banks make possible this multiple expansion of bank credit and hence bank deposits? How do these requirements affect other depository institutions?

7. Is there discretionary behavior on the part of the banks and other depository institutions in this deposit expansion process? Is it necessary for business people, or other possible would-be borrowers, to want to borrow from commercial banks or other depository institutions? What is the role of the Federal Reserve in affecting the expansion of transactions accounts by depository institutions?

8. How is the coefficient of multiple expansion of bank deposits computed? Is it possible for a single bank to expand its deposits by a multiple of its added cash reserves? If this is not possible, how can the banking system do what no single bank can do?

9. In the exercise, what is assumed to happen to the deposits and reserves of an individual bank after it makes a bank loan? What effect on the time lags in this expansionary process would there be if all banks receive an increase in their cash reserves at the same time?

10. How far can the entire banking system and other depository institutions go in this multiple expansion of transactions accounts? List and discuss all the factors that affect this expansionary process.

# Selected Bibliography for Further Reading

BALBACH, ANATOL B., "How Controllable is Money Growth?" *Review*, Federal Reserve Bank of St. Louis, **63**, No. 4 (April 1981), 3–12.

BOORMAN, JOHN T., and THOMAS M. HARILESKY, *Money Supply, Money Demand, and Macroeconomic Models* (Boston: Allyn and Bacon, 1972).

ENTINE, ALAN, *Monetary Economics: Readings* (Belmont, Calif.: Wadsworth, 1968).

HART, ALBERT GAILORD, and PETER B. KENEN, *Money, Debt and Economic Activity*, 5th ed. (Englewood Cliffs, N.J.: Prentice-Hall, 1969).

NICHOLS, DOROTHY, *Modern Money Mechanics* (Chicago: Federal Reserve Bank of Chicago, 1968).

RITTER, LAWRENCE, *Money and Economic Activity*, 3rd ed. (Boston: Houghton Mifflin, 1967).

WRIGHTSMAN, DWAYNE, *An Introduction to Monetary Theory and Policy* (New York: Free Press, 1971).

# PART 2

# THE MONEY AND CAPITAL MARKETS

The great wheel of circulation is altogether different from the goods which are circulated by means of it.

**THE WEALTH OF NATIONS**

## 5

# CHAPTER

# Flow of Funds and Income-Product Accounts

The borrowing and lending of money for various periods of time takes place not only in individually negotiated transactions, as when a would-be borrower approaches a bank lending officer, but also in vast impersonal financial markets. Commercial banks and other financial institutions enter these markets primarily as lenders, though occasionally as borrowers. Although banks are restricted by legal regulations as to the type of investment they acquire, they do enter both the short-term money market and the long-term capital market. The restrictions on banks are not on the maturity of the investment they acquire, except for maturity restrictions on mortgages, but pertain rather to the quality of the debt instruments in which they invest their depositors' funds. Both federal and state authorities permit banks to acquire any of the marketable securities of the federal government and its instrumentalities, and the various high-grade obligations of state and local governments. Banks ordinarily cannot buy either corporate bonds or common stocks, unless these securities are being acquired for personal trusts under bank management.

It is not enough, however, to look only at commercial bank participation in these financial markets, though we focus on this exclusively in Chapter 7. Before narrowing our consideration to commercial banks alone, it is necessary to examine the nature and functioning of these financial markets. In examining the functioning of these markets, we find that the flow of funds analysis and the alternative income-product accounts are both helpful. Let us first look at the nature of money and capital markets.

## THE MONEY AND CAPITAL MARKETS

In either the **money market**, narrowly defined, or the **capital market**, money is being bought and sold for varying periods of time. Money is here for hire. But in the narrowly defined money market, the period of hire is one year or less. In the capital markets, on the other hand, the period of time is anything over one year. Another significant difference between these two markets is that the money market is restricted to highly marketable liquid debt instruments, whereas the capital market includes both equity instruments (common stocks) and long-term debt instruments (**bonds**). Because the capital market has so many different kinds of securities offered for sale by so many different kinds of private and public borrowers, it is sometimes referred to in the plural as the *capital markets.*

Both the money market and the capital markets may be jointly referred to as the *financial markets.* Consideration of the short and long ends of the financial markets together, as well as separately, is warranted by a number of factors. First, all of the financial markets of a country influence the nature, scope, and rate of its economic development. A full range of borrowing and lending markets is needed to realize the most complete economic potential of a country. For certain purposes, borrowers want very short-term funds, whereas for other purposes they need long-term borrowed funds or equity funds invested as ownership shares in the business. Lenders, likewise, need a variety of securities, diversified as to maturity as well as to risk, in their investment portfolio.

Second, a number of borrowers participate in all maturities of the money and capital markets. The federal government, for example, borrows money for ninety-one days by issuing Treasury bills, which are sold in the money markets. On the other hand, it may issue bonds with maturities of ten to forty years in the capital markets. Large corporations also borrow funds in all sectors of these financial markets. A corporation may issue commercial paper maturing in four to six months, or it may issue bonds with a maturity of thirty years, or issue new common stock with no maturity at all, because such stock is evidence of ownership in the corporation. Funds may thus be raised in either the debt or equity market, and in various maturities.

Third, various **financial institutions** operate as ultimate lenders in diverse sectors of the financial markets, or perhaps as intermediaries in the channeling of funds from the ultimate lender to the borrower. Commercial banks, life insurance companies, and savings and loan institutions operate in many sectors of these markets. Various types of underwriters, including investment bankers and government security dealers, operate in a number of different parts of these financial markets.

Fourth, because of the participation of a number of important borrowers and lenders in different segments of the financial markets, influences originating in one maturity sector will be transmitted, though sometimes with a lag, to other sectors. In the upswing of the business cycle, for example, when borrowing demands of business firms in particular are becoming stronger and more urgent, interest rates in all sectors of money and capital markets tend to rise, though short-term interest rates usually increase the greatest amount. In the downswing of the business cycle, all maturities of market yields tend to fall, though here, too, short-term interest rates usually decline the most. Influences at work in any part of the financial markets thus tend to spread to other sectors, although the influence becomes somewhat weaker the farther away in maturity from the original impulse.

## Analyzing Factors at Work in the Money and Capital Markets

Anything that influences the stream of money and credit in the economy ultimately affects some part of the financial markets, and vice versa; whatever affects the money and capital markets, by influencing the terms on which borrowing is done and the liquidity of both borrowers and lenders, also has an impact on total spending on goods and services. Viewing the total money-credit circuit of funds is one simple way of looking at the interrelationship of financial factors with spending affecting the level of output of real goods and services. When the flow of total money spending on new goods and services expands, we normally expect the total output of such goods and services to increase also, at least until bottlenecks and ceilings are reached in the production process. When ceilings are reached, prices are likely to rise. A simple aggregative approach to the flow of funds is thus useful for certain purposes.

For many other purposes, however, additional information is needed concerning the direction of the flows of money and credit. Furthermore, it is often useful not only to know where money is being spent but also where it came from. So the sources and uses approach to financing is often indicated. Large commercial banks (e.g., Bankers

Trust in New York City), typically use this analytical approach in fore-casting the behavior of the financial markets for the forthcoming year. To provide this additional analytical detail, it is necessary to divide the economy into different sectors of activity (e.g., households and different types of financial institutions). Once the sectoring has been completed, it is then necessary to construct summary balance sheets for each sector to examine the flow of money and credit by sectors in a given time period.

These flows, and the changes in them, are useful not only for understanding productive forces at work in the aggregate but also for understanding the demand and supply financial factors that affect in-terest rates in different maturity sectors of the money and capital mar-kets. Certain large commercial banks, as well as various agencies of the federal government, have found it quite useful to study carefully changes in these flows of money and credit.

## The Income-Product Accounts

Before looking at the framework of the **flow of funds accounts,** which measure changes in the flows of money and credit in the money and capital markets and the economy generally, we will examine the major concepts in an older social accounting system. The older income-product accounts were originally pioneered by Nobel prize winner Simon Kuznets at the National Bureau of Economic Research in the 1930s but were subsequently taken over and published on a regular basis by the U. S. Department of Commerce beginning in 1942.

This national income accounting system, which has been revised a number of times in the postwar period, now provides historical data back to 1929 and current data on a quarterly basis. The flow of funds system was first developed in the postwar period by Morris Copeland and others for the Federal Reserve System and does not permit the historical perspective of the income-product accounts. Since the 1980s, however, the data in the newer accounting system are available on a half-year basis, though the income-product accounts data are available quarterly.

## Gross National Product

The most comprehensive measure of the nation's output in a given quarter or year is the gross national product (GNP), which is the market value of all final goods and services produced in that time period. The other national income aggregates may be derived by deducting certain items from this overall number. Net national product (NNP) is thus obtained by subtracting depreciation charges and other allowances for the consumption of durable capital goods from the gross national product. Further subtraction of indirect business tax and nontax liability, business transfer payments, a statistical discrepancy, and addition of subsidies less current surplus of government enterprises gives us national income.

**National income** may also be regarded as the aggregate earnings of labor and property in the current production of goods and services. National income thus measures the total factor cost of the goods and services produced in a quarter or year. Personal income is the current income received by persons from all sources, inclusive of transfers from government and business but exclusive of transfers among persons. Disposable personal income is the income remaining to persons after deduction of personal tax and nontax payments to general government. This is the income available to persons for spending or saving. All these concepts are shown, along with data for certain selected years, in Table 5–1.

Each national income concept shown in this table is useful for particular purposes. A bank economist making a forecast of economic activity for the coming year would probably forecast GNP for quarters and for the entire year. An economist working in a company making appliances might be more interested in disposable personal income, because that is the amount of income actually available to persons for spending or saving. Even here, the economist would probably forecast GNP first before arriving at the derivative disposable personal income figure. These various national income concepts can also be put in constant dollars to erase the effect of inflation, as shown for disposable personal income in Table 5–1 on the bottom line in constant 1972 dollars.

## Major Components of the Gross National Product

*Consumer Spending*    In addition to being broken down into various categories as in Table 5–1, the four major expenditure components can be given as shown in Table 5–2. The most important component by dollar volume is clearly that of personal consumption expenditures. As a percentage of GNP, consumption expenditures typically approach two thirds of the total spending in the economy on currently produced goods and services in that time period.

In 1980, for example, consumption expenditures totaling $1,670.1 billion represented 63.5 percent of the $2,627.4 billion GNP in that year. The largest category of consumption spending in that year was devoted

**Table 5-1   Relation of Gross National Product, National Income, and Personal Income and Saving, 1929–1980 (In billions of dollars)**

| Item | 1929 | 1933 | 1941 | 1950 | 1970 | 1975 | 1978 | 1979 | 1980 |
|---|---|---|---|---|---|---|---|---|---|
| **Gross national product** | **103.4** | **55.8** | **125.0** | **286.5** | **992.7** | **1,549.2** | **2,151.1** | **2,413.9** | **2,627.4** |
| *Less:* Capital consumption allowances | 9.7 | 7.4 | 10.0 | 23.5 | 88.1 | 159.3 | 221.2 | 253.6 | 287.8 |
| Indirect business tax and nontax liability | 7.1 | 7.1 | 11.3 | 23.4 | 94.3 | 140.1 | 178.1 | 188.4 | 211.7 |
| Business transfer payments | .6 | .7 | .5 | .8 | 4.1 | 7.4 | 8.7 | 9.4 | 10.5 |
| Statistical discrepancy | 1.1 | .7 | .6 | -1.3 | -1.5 | 5.5 | 6.4 | 2.2 | 1.7 |
| *Plus:* Subsidies less current surplus of government enterprises | 0.2 | .0 | .1 | .1 | 2.9 | 2.4 | 3.6 | 3.1 | 4.7 |
| **Equals: National income** | **84.8** | **39.9** | **102.7** | **237.6** | **810.7** | **1,239.4** | **1,745.4** | **1,963.3** | **2,120.5** |
| *Less:* Corporate profits and inventory valuation adjustment | 9.0 | -1.7 | 14.1 | 33.9 | 71.4 | 110.5 | 185.5 | 196.8 | 181.7 |
| Contributions for social insurance | .2 | .3 | 2.8 | 7.1 | 58.6 | 110.9 | 161.8 | 187.1 | 203.7 |
| Excess of wage accruals over disbursements | ··· | ··· | ··· | ··· | ··· | ··· | ··· | ··· | ··· |
| *Plus:* Government transfer payments to persons | .9 | 1.5 | 2.6 | 14.4 | 76.1 | 170.9 | 214.6 | 239.6 | 284.0 |
| Personal interest income | 6.9 | 5.5 | 5.3 | 9.7 | 69.4 | 123.2 | 173.2 | 209.6 | 256.3 |
| Dividends | 5.8 | 2.0 | 4.4 | 8.8 | 22.2 | 29.9 | 43.1 | 48.6 | 54.4 |
| Business transfer payments | .6 | .7 | .5 | .8 | 4.1 | 7.4 | 8.7 | 9.4 | 10.5 |
| **Equals: Personal income** | **85.0** | **47.0** | **95.4** | **227.2** | **811.1** | **1,265.0** | **1,721.8** | **1,943.8** | **2,160.5** |
| *Less:* Personal tax and nontax payments | 2.6 | 1.4 | 3.3 | 20.6 | 115.8 | 168.9 | 258.8 | 302.0 | 338.7 |
| **Equals: Disposable personal income** | **82.4** | **45.6** | **92.2** | **206.0** | **695.3** | **1,096.1** | **1,462.9** | **1,641.7** | **1,821.7** |
| *Less:* Personal outlays | 79.1 | 46.5 | 81.8 | 194.7 | 639.5 | 1,001.8 | 1,386.6 | 1,555.5 | 1,717.6 |
| Personal consumption expenditures | 77.3 | 45.8 | 80.8 | 192.0 | 621.7 | 976.4 | 1,348.7 | 1,510.9 | 1,670.1 |
| Consumer interest payments | 1.5 | .5 | .9 | 2.3 | 16.7 | 24.4 | 37.1 | 43.7 | 46.4 |
| Personal transfer payments to foreigners | .3 | .2 | .2 | .4 | 1.1 | .9 | .8 | 1.0 | 1.1 |
| **Equals: Personal saving** | **3.3** | **-.9** | **10.3** | **11.9** | **55.8** | **94.3** | **76.3** | **86.2** | **104.2** |
| **Disposable personal income in constant (1972) dollars** | **229.5** | **169.6** | **277.9** | **362.9** | **751.6** | **875.8** | **981.5** | **1,011.5** | **1,017.7** |

SOURCE: *Economic Report of the President*, January 1981, pp. 252–253, 258–259.

to services, which was $785.5 billion, or 47 percent of total consumption spending. This was far larger than consumer spending on durables or nondurables. The consumer in the 1980s was thus continuing long-term trends toward increased spending on services. In earlier years, service spending rose faster than spending on nondurables, for example, but it was not until 1971 that the dollar volume of such service spending exceeded spending on nondurables. Consumer durable goods spending, though showing a rising trend in total dollars, often fluctuates more from year to year than either nondurable or service spending.

***Gross Private Domestic Investment***    The volatility of consumer durable spending is shared by producers' durable equipment spending, and indeed by all parts of gross private domestic investment expenditures. Hence such investment spending, which rose by $36.3 billion from 1971 to 1972, and by $1.7 billion in 1973, fell by $5 billion in 1974, by $9 billion in 1975, and by $20.7 billion in 1980. Change in business inventories shows even more volatility than does total investment spending. This was particularly the case for the recession years of 1974–1975, when inventories swung by $17.6 billion from a $10.7 billion accumulation rate in 1974 to a liquidation of $6.9 billion in 1975.

***Government Expenditures***    Government expenditures have loomed ever larger in the gross national product, not only absolutely but also relatively. In 1929 such government spending accounted for only 8.2 percent of GNP, but by 1980 the proportion had risen sharply to 20.4 percent. Of this larger allocation of resources to the government, nearly two thirds (62 percent) in 1980 was spent on purchases of goods and services by state and local governments. To be sure, an important part of this spending by state and local governments was financed by various grants-in-aid by the federal government, but the allocation of resources within the economy was directly affected by decision making at the state and local government level.

***Net Exports of Goods and Services***    Net exports of goods and services accounts for a small part of GNP. Both exports and imports of goods and services grew strongly in the postwar period. The difference between them, however, which is the amount that enters into GNP, is very small, only $0.7 billion in 1971 and $3.3 billion in 1972. The small surplus of $7.1 billion and $7.5 billion in 1973 and 1974, respectively, grew to a large $20.5 billion in 1975, as a serious recession led to a decline in the imports of goods. A weaker dollar abroad in the last part of the 1970s, which had the effect of cutting the price of American exports, produced another larger export surplus of $27.5 billion in 1980, as shown in Table 5–2.

**Table 5–2   Gross National Product, 1929–1980 (In billions of dollars)**

| Item | 1929 | 1933 | 1941 | 1950 | 1960 | 1970 | 1975 | 1980 |
|---|---|---|---|---|---|---|---|---|
| **Gross national product** | **103.4** | **55.8** | **125.0** | **286.5** | **506.5** | **982.4** | **1,549.2** | **2,627.4** |
| **Personal consumption expenditures** | **77.3** | **45.8** | **80.8** | **192.0** | **324.9** | **618.8** | **976.4** | **1,670.1** |
| Durable goods | 9.2 | 3.5 | 9.7 | 30.0 | 43.1 | 84.9 | 132.2 | 210.2 |
| Nondurable goods | 37.7 | 22.3 | 42.9 | 98.2 | 151.1 | 264.7 | 407.3 | 674.4 |
| Services | 30.3 | 20.1 | 28.2 | 63.0 | 130.7 | 269.1 | 437.0 | 785.5 |
| **Gross private domestic investment** | **16.2** | **1.4** | **17.9** | **53.8** | **75.9** | **140.8** | **206.1** | **395.1** |
| *Fixed investment* | *14.5* | *3.0* | *13.4* | *47.0* | *72.9* | *137.0* | *213.0* | *399.0* |
| *Nonresidential* | *10.6* | *2.4* | *9.4* | *27.3* | *48.5* | *100.5* | *157.7* | *295.0* |
| Structures | 5.1 | 1.0 | 3.0 | 9.5 | 18.8 | 37.7 | 55.4 | 108.1 |
| Producer's durable equipment | 5.5 | 1.4 | 6.4 | 17.8 | 29.7 | 62.8 | 102.3 | 186.9 |
| Residential structures | 3.9 | .6 | 4.0 | 19.8 | 24.5 | 36.6 | 55.3 | 104.0 |
| Nonfarm | 3.6 | .5 | 3.6 | 18.6 | 23.3 | 35.1 | 52.4 | 99.1 |
| Change in business inventories | 1.7 | –1.6 | 4.5 | 6.8 | 3.0 | 3.8 | –6.9 | –3.9 |
| Nonfarm | 1.8 | –1.4 | 4.0 | 6.0 | 2.7 | 3.7 | –10.5 | –2.6 |
| **Net exports of goods and services** | **1.1** | **.4** | **1.5** | **2.2** | **5.5** | **3.9** | **26.8** | **27.5** |
| Exports | 7.0 | 2.4 | 6.1 | 14.4 | 28.9 | 62.5 | 154.9 | 341.2 |
| Imports | 5.9 | 2.0 | 4.7 | 12.2 | 23.4 | 58.5 | 128.1 | 313.6 |
| **Government purchases of goods and services** | **8.8** | **8.2** | **24.9** | **38.5** | **100.3** | **218.9** | **339.9** | **534.8** |
| *Federal* | *1.4* | *2.1* | *16.9* | *18.7* | *53.7* | *95.6* | *122.7* | *198.9* |
| National defense | ... | ... | 13.7 | 14.0 | 44.5 | 73.5 | 83.0 | 132.0 |
| Other | ... | ... | 3.2 | 4.7 | 9.3 | 22.1 | 39.7 | 66.9 |
| State and local | 7.4 | 6.1 | 8.0 | 19.8 | 46.5 | 123.2 | 217.2 | 335.9 |
| *Gross national product in constant (1972) dollars* | *315.7* | *222.1* | *400.4* | *534.8* | *737.2* | *1,085.6* | *1,233.9* | *1,483.0* |

SOURCE: *Economic Report of the President 1981*, pp. 233, 234, 248–249.

## Goods and Services Included in Gross National Product

The aggregate dollar value of national output may be arrived at either by summing product values or by summing income flows. (For a technical discussion of the GNP accounts, see *National Income*, 1954 Edition, cited at the end of the chapter.) If product flows are summed, we arrive at the GNP, whereas if income flows are summed we have national income. Considering the GNP, certain goods and services are included, whereas others are excluded. The value of housewives' services, do-it-yourself projects, and illegal transactions are all excluded. So too is the value of goods produced in previous years and sold this year, such as secondhand automobiles or older houses. (The value of services contributed by brokers or salespeople would be included in current GNP, even when they are selling previously produced products.)

For those goods and services that are included, "double counting" is avoided. Only the "value added" by each firm and each industry in the process of production of the final good or service is included in GNP, rather than adding the total market value of the good at each stage of production.

Certain goods and services are included in GNP even though they are not sold in the marketplace. These "imputed" goods and services include food grown and consumed by the farmer and "payment in kind," such as the provision of board and room for a live-in maid. The rental value of owner-occupied homes is also included in GNP. By the 1980s, nearly one fourth of the $785.5 billion spent by consumers on services was accounted for by the rental value of owner-occupied homes. All these imputed goods and services are, of course, valued at what is presumed to be their current market value.

## Reliability of Data in Gross National Product Accounts

All data in the GNP accounts do not have the same degree of reliability. The reliability of particular data depends upon (1) whether the economic units, such as businesses, governmental agencies, or individuals, are reporting on an item represented by straightforward transactions of simple definition or on an item that requires complex calculations on their part or is somewhat vaguely defined; (2) the quality of the records kept by the economic units whose transactions are being measured; (3) the nature of the data produced by the reporting system, such as the distinction between complete census-type coverage and sampling; and (4) the extent that items that enter the income and product accounts are different from those actually reported. In general, a long and involved estimating process is a sign of statistical weakness. Imputed data should be regarded as having less reliability, because they are estimated, than data directly collected from reporting units involving actual market transactions.

Applying the factors affecting reliability to the components of national income, it is generally agreed that wages and salaries rank highest in reliability because of the relative simplicity of the concept, the comprehensiveness, and the high quality of the record keeping, and the reporting system. Much of these data are derived as by-products of the Social Security system. On the low end of the reliability scale must be placed rental income of persons. A profit-type of income is involved, which may involve a vague definition of the reporting unit. Furthermore, record keeping and reporting systems are fragmentary and poor, and complex calculations are necessary to convert the reported data into those incorporated in the national income entries.

Estimates of the other income shares rank between these two extremes in reliability. Thus supplements to wages and salaries follow wages and salaries closely, whereas at the lower end of the scale, the income of unincorporated enterprises and inventory valuation adjustment are only somewhat superior in reliability to rental income of persons. Corporate profits before taxes, on the other hand, rank next to the two items involving employee compensation.

Government purchases of goods and services are highest on the scale of reliability among the components of GNP, whereas estimates of changes in business inventories are lowest on the product scale. Producers' purchases of durable equipment and personal consumption expenditures for durable and nondurable goods—both of which are based largely on producers' records—come next after government purchases in reliability on the product side. Although personal consumption expenditures for services are also based largely on producers' sales records, such sources yielding census-type data are available only infrequently, which reduces the reliability of the estimates that must be made in the interim of such comprehensive reporting.

The reliability of personal income is higher than that of national income, because the two major items entering into personal income, but not national income, are highly reliable: government transfer payments and government interest. The deduction of corporate inventory valuation adjustment and other components of corporate profits, except dividends, from national income before arriving at personal income also makes for greater reliability in personal income.

Finally, there is a statistical discrepancy in these accounts that arises from the excess of GNP over national income. The summing of the component product flows yields a larger total than the components of the national income and all other charges against the total value of gross national product. This arises from errors in the component estimates and is also relevant to the problem of data reliability.

## The Flow of Funds Accounts

The flow of funds accounts, compiled and published by the Board of Governors of the Federal Reserve System, take an entirely different approach to the economy than the income-product accounts of the Department of Commerce. The GNP deliberately avoids double counting and focuses only on the market value of currently produced goods and services. The flow of funds accounts, on the other hand, are concerned with all transactions in the economy accomplished by a transfer of credit or money. Not only transactions in current output but also sales of land, existing homes, used automobiles, and so on are included. Even flows of funds that arise from transactions in mortgages, securities, trade credit, and other financial instruments are specifically traced in these accounts.

Because of the different focuses of these two data sytems and also because they were developed quite separately from each other, there are inconsistencies between the two systems. It is therefore necessary to reconcile the data from one system with the other, if, for example, one wishes to trace the flow of funds going into real investment in the United States in a given period of time.

## The Difficulties of Data Reconciliation

The difficulties in reconciling these two national data systems are not only that each system has certain peculiar advantages and disadvantages, but also that the data in various categories are defined and used in different ways. Furthermore, flow of funds data are now published only on a half year and annual basis rather than the quarterly basis of the income-product accounts. Four important differences between flow of funds and national income accounts may be summarized as follows: (1) national income accounts confine themselves exclusively to nonfinancial transactions and contain no data on borrowing, lending, or hoarding; (2) income accounts, contrary to flow of funds accounts, in order to avoid double counting, report only transactions in the current output of final goods and services and do not show transactions in intermediate goods or in already existing assets; (3) income accounts restrict the use of the term **real investment** to producers' durable goods and changes in business inventories, except that residential construction is included along with commercial and industrial construction under investment, whereas in the flow of funds accounts consumer purchases of durable goods are considered as investment and are shown both gross and net; and (4) the sectoring of the data is much more detailed in the flow of funds accounts than in the older system of national income accounting, so that the analyst desiring to move from one type of accounts to the other finds the burden of integration and reconciliation a rather complicated matter.

Because it is difficult for the ordinary user of these data to make all the adjustments necessary, the usual tendency for most analysts is to use the national income accounts, or perhaps sources and uses of funds statements, rather than to make use of the potential information that can be derived from careful study and analysis of flow of funds accounts. The solution to this problem seems to lie, for most observers, in changing the definitions and form of presentations of the data at the source of the two parts of the government so that they are compatible and complementary to one another. The National Accounts Review Committee, made up of a number of users of these data, suggested that a national income accounting system should be designed compatible either with a flow of funds or an input-output accounting system. If this recommendation were adopted, most but not all of the compromise would have to be made by the constructors of the flow of funds data.

*Need for Integrated National Accounting*     If such an integrated system is developed, the resulting integrated transactions accounts will probably be harmonized with essentially the present national and expenditure accounts. Financial transactions then would be added to the data showing transactions in goods, services, and transfers. If this were done, however, the existing national income accounts would also have to be modified somewhat. Residential construction presently under gross private domestic investment would probably be placed back in the consumer sector under a consumer capital transactions account. Consequently, it might be reasonable to add consumer purchases of durable goods—now classified as investment in the flow of funds accounts but not in the national income accounts—to that same consumer capital sector.

Some other modifications in the present income-product accounts would doubtless be necessary to achieve the final desired result of an integrated transactions and financial data system for the entire economy, but the present income-product accounts could provide the basic framework for such an integrated macrodata system. Even though such an integrated national data system may be some years away, the serious student of financial markets should not overlook the rich possibilities of achieving new insights into relationships between financial transactions and real transactions that may be achieved by a careful study of the flow of funds data published regularly by the Board of Governors of the Federal Reserve System. In essence, the flow of funds accounts consist of a statement of the capital account for the economy as a whole.

*The Capital Account Matrix*   This capital account is presented as a matrix with columns of different sectors and rows of different types of transactions. The major groups of transactors, such as households, businesses, and governments, are organized into various sectors. Although the Federal Reserve maintains data on a continuing basis for about twenty such sectors, only eleven aggregate sectors are given in the published data. Transactions data, which are given for each of the published sectors, are arranged in three major transactions groups: (1) current nonfinancial, (2) capital nonfinancial, and (3) financial.

## SECTORS IN THE FLOW OF FUNDS ACCOUNTS

Each sector is composed of economic units that are similar in function and institutional structure. These eleven flow of funds sectors are (1) consumers and nonprofit organizations, (2) farm business, (3) nonfarm business, (4) corporate business, (5) the federal government, (6) state and local governments, (7) commercial banking and monetary authorities, (8) savings institutions (mutual savings banks, savings banks, savings and loan associations, and credit unions), (9) insurance companies and private pension plans, (10) finance not classified elsewhere (security brokers and dealers, open-end investment companies, and sales finance companies), and (11) a sector for the rest of the world, which includes all foreign transactions with the United States.

  This flow of funds accounting system is designed to provide a statistical framework for the analysis of problems involving interrelationships between financial and nonfinancial flows arranged in a single consistent structure. The sector accounts can be visualized as a set of interlocking balance-of-payments similar to those that record the flow of international payments. Each transaction recorded is reflected in at least four entries in the accounts of the sectors. For a transaction consisting of a purchase of goods for cash, there are four entries: (1) purchase of goods by buyer, (2) sale of goods by seller, (3) reduction in cash for buyer, and (4) increase in cash for seller. There are thus two nonfinancial entries and two financial entries. If such a transaction were partly for cash and partly for credit, there would have been more than four entries. Some transactions, such as a purchase of securities for cash or repayments of debt in cash, are, of course, entirely financial in character.

*Financial Flows for Each Sector*    Financial flows for each sector are generally recorded on a net basis for each category of financial transaction. The asset entry for each category represents funds used to acquire assets of that type in the accounting period less funds realized from the disposition of assets of that type in the accounting period. The liability entry, on the other hand, represents funds raised by borrowing less funds used in repayment in the accounting period. In addition to estimates of financial flows, estimates of amounts of financial assets and liabilities outstanding are provided in partial balance sheets for the various sectors. These balance sheets are partial because they do not include estimates for net worth or for net equity of owners in the sector's assets.

*Borrowing and Saving*    Borrowing and saving together are the two sources of funds used to acquire physical and financial assets. A distinction is drawn, however, between nonfinancial transactions, such as the purchase and sales of goods and services, transfer payments and receipts, and taxes, and financial transactions, such as net changes in the capital amounts of claims owed as liabilities or held as assets for each sector. All the financial transactions of a sector are combined together in net financial investment, which is the excess of the financial uses of a sector over its financial sources. In other words, if the sector has positive saving, it will be supplying through lending (the acquisition of some financial asset) the deficit spending of some other sector. If a sector, such as the government, is basically a deficit sector but is also lending to some other sector, this sector is performing an intermediation function of borrowing and then relending.

    This intermediation function is largely isolated in the flow of funds accounts by grouping together varous types of financial institutions that perform most of this intermediation. However, the source of most credit in the flow of funds is ultimately from the nonfinancial sector, whether the credit is provided directly or passes through a financial intermediary. That is, the total flow in the credit markets is almost completely matched by financial investment in one form or another by the nonfinancial sectors. The uses of credit, likewise, are almost entirely by the nonfinancial sectors.

## SAVINGS AND INVESTMENT IN THE FLOW OF FUNDS ACCOUNTS

For each sector, **saving** equals that sector's physical capital formation plus net financial investment, which measures the sector's excess of lending to other sectors over its borrowing from other sectors. At the national level total savings equals capital formation plus net foreign investment. Saving may be regarded as a diversion from the current payments stream, whereas physical investment outlays, government deficits, and foreign deficits inject spending back into the current income stream.

The totals of current saving and current investment for each sector as well as for the overall economy, however, are regarded as identical. If the dollar total of current saving is not shown as being equal to the dollar total of current investment, a statistical discrepancy exists. To balance the total flow of funds matrix, a discrepancy column and a discrepancy row are utilized to absorb such discrepancies.

## Components of Investment and Saving

For the consumer and nonprofit sector, tangible **investment** consists of net purchases of consumer durable goods, purchases of residential construction for owner occupancy, and plant and equipment expenditures by nonprofit organizations. Net financial investment for this sector includes saving through life insurance, saving through private and government pension plans, and proprietors' net investment in unincorporated businesses, net of depreciation. Because net investment of unincorporated firms is thus included in this sector, gross saving in the "farm and noncorporate business" sectors is shown equal to capital consumption charges. Net saving is thus shown as being equal to zero in these sectors.

Net saving for the corporate business sector is equal to retained earnings after tax payments. These data are shown after inventory valuation adjustment. Saving of government sectors is the excess of all nonfinancial receipts over all nonfinancial expenditures including net purchases of tangible assets. Saving of the insurance sector consists of change in the surplus and other reserves of life insurance companies, except legal reserves on life insurance and pension plan contracts, plus the total change in surplus and other reserves for nonlife insurance companies.

*Larger Flow of Savings Than in National Income Accounts*    In the Department of Commerce national income accounts, all financial claims within the United States are offset against one another. Hence there is no recording of financial flows within the economy or of financial investment by individual sectors. In the flow of funds accounts, there is a deconsolidation of these national totals of saving and tangible investment among the domestic sectors. Furthermore, there is explicit recording of financial flows among sectors, detailed by the type of instrument. Using these accounts, we can follow the routes, whether direct or through intermediaries, whereby saving is allocated. Some sectors, such as households, have excesses of saving over physical investment, which they lend to sectors, such as businesses and governments, that may have an excess of spending over current income.

***Consumer Durables Are in Saving and Investment*** As previously indicated, another important difference between the flow of funds accounts and the national income accounts is that in the former system of social accounting total gross national saving and gross investment expenditures include purchases of consumer durable goods. This reduces the amount of current outlays and increases the total amount of saving in the flow of funds accounts. The reasons why the Board of Governors chose to include consumer durables along with producer durables in gross investment are several: (1) a household purchase of durables usually represents an investment in a product that will be useful over a period of several years or more, (2) such consumer durable goods are significant substitutes for business capital equipment, and (3) purchases of consumer durables are debt-financed to a large extent.

The inclusion of consumer durables in gross national investment or capital outlays increases the total of such investment spending considerably. The contribution of households to gross national saving is also correspondingly increased, because the total for household saving is taken before deduction for the purchases of durables. In the national income accounts, however, one type of household expenditure, that on residential construction, is already considered part of gross investment and gross saving.

## Sector Uses and Sources

As already indicated, the economy is divided into eleven major groups of transactors in the flow of funds accounts. For each column for a sector there are two subcolumns with one headed *U* for uses of funds and the other headed *S* for sources of funds. Every receipt of funds by a sector is reflected in one or more uses of funds, if only to increase cash balances. Hence, a balance must exist between total sources of funds and total uses of funds. Any differences between these totals for the various sectors are finally accounted for in the last row of the accounts, which is labeled sector discrepancies.

*Financial Transactions in Claims* Every transaction in financial claims appears both as a source of funds and a use of funds, because all borrowing is someone else's lending. These claims include the money supply, which consists of demand deposit liabilities of commercial banks, and currency, which is a liability of the monetary authorities. Each row of the flow of funds matrix summarizes purchase and sales in markets for individual transaction categories (e.g., the various credit market instruments).

The tables for the individual columns, however, are sector statements of sources and uses of funds. Summation of all uses of funds along a given row by all the sectors of the matrix gives the total of outlays made to acquire a particular kind of asset (e.g., bank loans, not elsewhere classified). Summation of sources along the same row results in the total of funds raised in that particular manner. Each row or set of rows for financial claims, therefore, is a summary of all funds coming into and going out of a particular financial market or group of markets.

*Interrelationship of all Items in the Matrix*    Because of the interrelationship of all items in matrices like the flow of funds accounts, a change in one item results in changes in other items. No one cell of the matrix can be changed without altering at least three others. These would include one in the same sector column, one in the same row, and at least one other for the corresponding column and second row. This means that this system of accounts is a severely constrained accounting system, which undertakes to place every transaction of the economy into direct juxtaposition to its counterparts, both vertically in sector accounts and horizontally in transaction or market summary accounts.


## FUNDS RAISED IN UNITED STATES CREDIT MARKETS IN 1975–1980

Table 5–3 presents in summary form the flow of funds data for funds raised and advanced for the six years 1975–1980. The various concepts that have already been discussed can be illustrated by the data shown here. For example, the household sector, like the corporate sector, in the six years shown in Table 5–3 borrowed large amounts of funds from the credit markets and both sectors peaked in this period in their borrowing needs in 1979.

In that year, the household sector borrowed a total of $164.9 billion, which included $109.1 billion for mortgages on houses alone. Corporate borrowing in the same year was $114.3 billion, which was substantially less than household borrowing. In 1980, however, household borrowing fell sharply, particularly as a result of a severe economic recession in the second quarter, so that annual corporate borrowing of $101.1 billion was slightly larger than annual household borrowing of $100.8 billion.

## Business Sector

The nonfinancial corporate business sector thus made great demands for credit on the various financial institutions in the late 1970s and early 1980s and also resorted to direct flotation of debt and equity issues in the money and capital markets. These pressures for outside business financing rose much faster throughout this period than did capital outlays themselves. From 1975 to 1980 inclusive, business fixed investment outlays (on structures and producers' durable equipment) rose by 26 percent, from $161.5 billion to $205.2 billion, but corporate borrowing nearly tripled as shown earlier in Table 5–3, from $37.9 billion in 1975 to $101.1 billion in 1980.

## Government Sectors

In addition to the heavy borrowing needs of the private household and business sectors, state and local governments and the federal government were also heavy borrowers in the late 1970s and the early 1980s. The federal government borrowed substantially more than state and local governments, as, for example, they borrowed $79.8 billion in 1980 and state and local governments borrowed only $20.7 billion. Both levels of government exhibited strong variability in their borrowing year by year (e.g., the federal government borrowed $55.1 billion in 1978, then declined sharply in borrowings to $38.8 billion in 1979, and rose sharply to $79.2 billion in 1980).

State and local governments showed similar variability with a drop in borrowing in 1979 and a sharp upswing in 1980. Furthermore, such sharp variability in government borrowing, at all levels, has considerable impact on interest rates in various sectors of the financial markets.

## Sources of Funds to Credit Markets, 1975–1980

Variations in interest rates, particularly changes in interest rate differentials, in turn help to explain changes in the relative importance of different sources of credit. In periods of tight credit and rising yields in the financial markets, for example, funds are pulled out of financial intermediaries and loaned directly by savers in the markets. This disintermediation, or nonintermediation if savings are loaned directly in the credit markets without having been placed on deposit in a financial intermediary, varies substantially from year to year. Financial intermediation in general, as shown in Table 5–4, increased in the six years

**Table 5–3    Funds Raised in U.S. Credit Markets, 1975–1980 (In billions of dollars)**

| | Transaction Category, Sector | 1975 | 1976 | 1977 | 1978 | 1979 | 1980 |
|---|---|---|---|---|---|---|---|
| | Nonfinancial Sectors | | | | | | |
| 1 | **Total funds raised** ................. | **210.8** | **271.9** | **338.5** | **400.4** | **394.9** | **363.3** |
| 2 | Excluding equities .................. | 200.7 | 261.0 | 335.3 | 398.3 | 390.6 | 349.8 |
| | *By sector and instrument* | | | | | | |
| 3 | U.S. government ................... | 85.4 | 69.0 | 56.8 | 53.7 | 37.4 | 79.2 |
| 4 | Treasury securities ............... | 85.8 | 69.1 | 57.6 | 55.1 | 38.8 | 79.8 |
| 5 | Agency issues and mortgages ...... | −.4 | −.1 | −.9 | −1.4 | −1.4 | −.6 |
| 6 | All other nonfinancial sectors ....... | 125.4 | 202.8 | 281.7 | 346.7 | 357.6 | 284.1 |
| 7 | Corporate equities ................ | 10.1 | 10.8 | 3.1 | 2.1 | 4.3 | 13.6 |
| 8 | Debt instruments ................. | 115.3 | 192.0 | 278.6 | 344.6 | 353.2 | 270.6 |
| 9 | Private domestic nonfinancial | | | | | | |
| | sectors......................... | 112.1 | 182.0 | 267.8 | 314.4 | 336.4 | 254.2 |
| 10 | Corporate equities .............. | 9.9 | 10.5 | 2.7 | 2.6 | 3.5 | 11.4 |
| 11 | Debt instruments ................ | 102.2 | 171.5 | 265.1 | 311.8 | 333.0 | 242.8 |
| 12 | Debt capital instruments......... | 98.4 | 123.5 | 175.6 | 196.6 | 199.9 | 175.6 |
| 13 | State and local obligations ...... | 16.1 | 15.7 | 23.7 | 28.3 | 18.9 | 22.2 |
| 14 | Corporate bonds.............. | 27.2 | 22.8 | 21.0 | 20.1 | 21.2 | 27.6 |
| | Mortgages | | | | | | |
| 15 | Home ...................... | 39.5 | 63.6 | 96.3 | 104.6 | 109.1 | 81.5 |
| 16 | Multifamily residential ........ | | 1.8 | 7.4 | 10.2 | 8.9 | 8.7 |
| 17 | Commercial .................. | 11.0 | 13.4 | 18.4 | 23.3 | 25.7 | 21.6 |
| 18 | Farm ....................... | 4.6 | 6.1 | 8.8 | 10.2 | 16.2 | 14.0 |
| 19 | Other debt instruments .......... | 3.8 | 48.0 | 89.5 | 115.2 | 133.0 | 67.2 |
| 20 | Consumer credit .............. | 9.7 | 25.6 | 40.6 | 50.6 | 44.2 | 3.1 |
| 21 | Bank loans n.e.c. .............. | −12.3 | 4.0 | 27.0 | 37.3 | 50.6 | 37.9 |
| 22 | Open market paper ............ | −2.6 | 4.0 | 2.9 | 5.2 | 10.9 | 5.8 |
| 23 | Other....................... | 9.0 | 14.4 | 19.0 | 22.2 | 27.3 | 20.4 |
| 24 | By borrowing sector.............. | 112.1 | 182.0 | 267.8 | 314.4 | 336.4 | 254.2 |
| 25 | State and local governments ..... | 13.7 | 15.2 | 20.4 | 23.6 | 15.5 | 20.7 |
| 26 | Households .................... | 49.7 | 90.5 | 139.9 | 162.6 | 164.9 | 100.8 |
| 27 | Farm ........................ | 8.8 | 10.9 | 14.7 | 18.1 | 25.8 | 19.0 |
| 28 | Nonfarm noncorporate.......... | 2.0 | 4.7 | 12.9 | 15.4 | 15.9 | 12.5 |
| 29 | Corporate..................... | 37.9 | 60.7 | 79.9 | 94.8 | 114.3 | 101.1 |
| 30 | Foreign......................... | 13.3 | 20.8 | 13.9 | 32.3 | 21.2 | 29.9 |
| 31 | Corporate equities .............. | .2 | .3 | .4 | −.5 | .9 | 2.2 |
| 32 | Debt instruments ............... | 13.2 | 20.5 | 13.5 | 32.8 | 20.3 | 27.7 |
| 33 | Bonds ...................... | 6.2 | 8.6 | 5.1 | 4.0 | 3.9 | .8 |
| 34 | Bank loans n.e.c. .............. | 3.9 | 6.8 | 3.1 | 18.3 | 2.3 | 11.8 |
| 35 | Open market paper ............ | .3 | 1.9 | 2.4 | 6.6 | 11.2 | 10.1 |
| 36 | U.S. government loans .......... | 2.8 | 3.3 | 3.0 | 3.9 | 3.0 | 5.0 |
| | Financial Sectors | | | | | | |
| 37 | **Total funds raised** ................. | **12.7** | **24.1** | **54.0** | **81.4** | **88.5** | **70.8** |

SOURCE: Board of Governors of the Federal Reserve System, *Federal Reserve Bulletin*, May 1981, p. A42.

from 1975 to 1980 inclusive, as commercial banks expanded their advance of funds to the credit markets from $29.4 billion in 1975 to $103.5 billion in 1980. Also, insurance and pension funds expanded their contribution to the credit markets from $40.6 billion in 1975 to $76.4 billion in 1980.

However, savings institutions such as savings and loan associations and mutual savings banks exhibited considerable variability in their furnishing of funds to the credit markets. Such funds furnished rose from $53.5 billion in 1975 to $82.0 billion in 1977 and declined to $57.6 billion in 1980. Even commercial banks, in addition to their strong growth over this period, had substantial variability in furnishing funds to credit markets. Their funds furnished rose from $87.6 billion in 1977 to $128.7 billion in 1978 but fell in 1979 and 1980 to $121.1 billion and $103.5 billion, respectively. Insurance and pension funds had far less variability and much steadier growth, as an inspection of Table 5–4 reveals.

## DISCREPANCIES IN THE DATA IN THE FLOW OF FUNDS SYSTEM

Although the flow of funds national accounting system is an interlocking and balancing set of sector and transaction accounts with total sources of funds equal to total uses of funds for each sector account and total re-

---

Table 5–4   **Direct and Indirect Sources of Funds to Credit Markets, 1975–1980 (In billions of dollars)**

|  | *Transaction Category, or Sector* | *1975* | *1976* | *1977* | *1978* | *1979* | *1980* |
|---|---|---|---|---|---|---|---|
| 1 | **Total funds advanced in credit markets to nonfinancial sectors** . . . . . . . | **200.7** | **261.0** | **335.3** | **398.3** | **390.6** | **349.8** |
|  | *By public agencies and foreign* | | | | | | |
| 2 | Total net advances . . . . . . . . . . . . . . . . | 44.6 | 54.3 | 85.1 | 109.7 | 80.1 | 95.8 |
| 3 | U.S. government securities . . . . . . . . . | 22.5 | 26.8 | 40.2 | 43.9 | 2.0 | 22.3 |
| 4 | Residential mortgages . . . . . . . . . . . . . | 16.2 | 12.8 | 20.4 | 26.5 | 36.1 | 32.0 |
| 5 | FHLB advances to savings and loans . . . . . . . . . . . . . . . . . . . . . | −4.0 | −2.0 | 4.3 | 12.5 | 9.2 | 7.1 |
| 6 | Other loans and securities . . . . . . . . . | 9.8 | 16.6 | 20.2 | 26.9 | 32.8 | 34.5 |
|  | *Total advanced, by sector* | | | | | | |
| 7 | U.S. government . . . . . . . . . . . . . . . . . . . | 15.1 | 8.9 | 11.8 | 20.4 | 22.5 | 26.0 |
| 8 | Sponsored credit agencies . . . . . . . . . . | 14.8 | 20.3 | 26.8 | 44.6 | 57.5 | 48.6 |
| 9 | Monetary authorities . . . . . . . . . . . . . . . | 8.5 | 9.3 | 7.1 | 7.0 | 7.7 | 4.5 |
| 10 | Foreign . . . . . . . . . . . . . . . . . . . . . . . . . . | 6.1 | 15.2 | 39.4 | 37.7 | −7.7 | 16.7 |
| 11 | Agency borrowing not included in line 1 . . . . . . . . . . . . . . . . . . . . . . . . | 13.5 | 18.6 | 26.3 | 41.4 | 52.4 | 47.5 |

**Table 5–4** *(Continued)*

| | Transaction Category, or Sector | 1975 | 1976 | 1977 | 1978 | 1979 | 1980 |
|---|---|---|---|---|---|---|---|
| | *Private domestic funds advanced* | | | | | | |
| 12 | Total net advances .................. | 169.7 | 225.4 | 276.5 | 330.0 | 362.9 | 301.5 |
| 13 | U.S. government securities......... | 75.7 | 61.3 | 44.1 | 51.3 | 87.9 | 104.6 |
| 14 | State and local obligations ......... | 16.1 | 15.7 | 23.7 | 28.3 | 18.9 | 22.2 |
| 15 | Corporate and foreign bonds....... | 32.8 | 30.5 | 22.5 | 22.5 | 25.6 | 25.5 |
| 16 | Residential mortgages............. | 23.2 | 52.6 | 83.3 | 88.2 | 81.8 | 58.1 |
| 17 | Other mortgages and loans......... | 17.9 | 63.3 | 107.3 | 152.2 | 157.9 | 98.2 |
| 18 | LESS: Federal Home Loan Bank | | | | | | |
| | advances...................... | −4.0 | −2.0 | 4.3 | 12.5 | 9.2 | 7.1 |
| | *Private financial intermediation* | | | | | | |
| 19 | Credit market funds advanced by | | | | | | |
| | private financial institutions ...... | 122.5 | 190.1 | 257.0 | 296.9 | 292.5 | 265.6 |
| 20 | Commercial banking.............. | 29.4 | 59.6 | 87.6 | 128.7 | 121.1 | 103.5 |
| 21 | Savings institutions .............. | 53.5 | 70.8 | 82.0 | 75.9 | 56.3 | 57.6 |
| 22 | Insurance and pension funds....... | 40.6 | 49.9 | 67.9 | 73.5 | 70.4 | 76.4 |
| 23 | Other finance.................... | −1.0 | 9.8 | 19.6 | 18.7 | 44.7 | 28.1 |
| 24 | Sources of funds.................... | 122.5 | 190.1 | 257.0 | 296.9 | 292.5 | 265.6 |
| 25 | Private domestic deposits.......... | 92.0 | 124.6 | 141.2 | 142.5 | 136.7 | 163.9 |
| 26 | Credit market borrowing .......... | −1.4 | 4.4 | 26.9 | 38.3 | 33.8 | 19.8 |
| 27 | Other sources ................... | 32.0 | 61.0 | 89.0 | 116.0 | 122.0 | 81.9 |
| 28 | Foreign funds .................. | −8.7 | −4.6 | 1.2 | 6.3 | 26.3 | −20.0 |
| 29 | Treasury balances .............. | −1.7 | −.1 | 4.3 | 6.8 | .4 | −2.0 |
| 30 | Insurance and pension reserves ... | 29.7 | 34.5 | 49.4 | 62.7 | 49.0 | 58.5 |
| 31 | Other, net...................... | 12.7 | 31.2 | 34.1 | 40.3 | 46.3 | 45.4 |
| | *Private domestic nonfinancial investors* | | | | | | |
| 32 | Direct lending in credit markets ..... | 45.8 | 39.7 | 46.3 | 71.5 | 104.2 | 55.7 |
| 33 | U.S. government securities......... | 24.1 | 16.1 | 23.0 | 33.2 | 57.8 | 30.7 |
| 34 | State and local obligations ......... | 8.4 | 3.8 | 2.6 | 4.5 | −2.5 | −1.8 |
| 35 | Corporate and foreign bonds....... | 8.4 | 5.8 | −3.3 | −1.4 | 11.1 | 5.4 |
| 36 | Commercial paper ................ | −1.3 | 1.9 | 9.5 | 16.3 | 10.7 | −2.4 |
| 37 | Other........................... | 6.2 | 12.0 | 14.5 | 18.8 | 27.1 | 23.9 |
| 38 | Deposits and currency.............. | 98.1 | 131.9 | 149.5 | 151.8 | 144.7 | 173.5 |
| 39 | Security RPs ..................... | .2 | 2.3 | 2.2 | 7.5 | 6.6 | 4.7 |
| 40 | Money market fund shares......... | 1.3 | | .2 | 6.9 | 34.4 | 29.2 |
| 41 | Time and savings accounts......... | 84.0 | 113.5 | 121.0 | 115.2 | 84.7 | 131.8 |
| 42 | Large at commercial banks ....... | −15.8 | −13.2 | 23.0 | 45.9 | .4 | 12.7 |
| 43 | Other at commercial banks ....... | 40.3 | 57.6 | 29.0 | 8.2 | 39.3 | 62.9 |
| 44 | At savings institutions ........... | 59.4 | 69.1 | 69.0 | 61.1 | 45.1 | 56.2 |
| 45 | Money........................... | 12.6 | 16.1 | 26.1 | 22.2 | 18.9 | 7.8 |
| 46 | Demand deposits ................ | 6.4 | 8.8 | 17.8 | 12.9 | 11.0 | −1.8 |
| 47 | Currency........................ | 6.2 | 7.3 | 8.3 | 9.3 | 7.9 | 9.6 |
| 48 | **Total of credit market instruments,** | | | | | | |
| | **deposits and currency**............ | **143.9** | **171.6** | **195.8** | **223.3** | **248.9** | **229.1** |

SOURCE: Board of Governors of the Federal Reserve System, *Federal Reserve Bulletin*, May 1981, p. A43.

ceipts equal to total payments for each transaction account, discrepancies in the actual data presented within this framework do occur. Usually these sector discrepancies are between $1 billion and $2 billion, except for a typically large discrepancy in the household sector, even though saving and investment are regarded as being conceptually equal. Discrepancies may arise from a variety of factors, such as inconsistencies in timing, valuation, coverage, and classification, or from such statistical inadequacies as errors in the basic data or omissions of pertinent transactions or transactors. The mere appearance of discrepancies, however, should not be interpreted by itself as indicating errors in the basic data.

Whenever an entry in a sector or transaction account is estimated as a residual, there can be no discrepancy shown for that item. The consumer sector account usually shows one of the largest of the sector discrepancies inasmuch as so many of the individual transaction items in the consumer account are themselves computed as residuals in other accounts. The consumer accounts thus serve as a resting place for discrepancies actually originating in other accounts but not shown there. The corporate sector account and the U.S. government sector contain the other major sector discrepancies. Curiously enough, some of the sector accounts show marked seasonal variations in their discrepancies because of timing problems and inconsistencies in the available measures on seasonally adjusted flow of funds.

Insofar as financial transactions are concerned, a substantial number of these accounts show no discrepancy because they are residuals. These residual calculations include savings shares, U.S. savings bonds, saving through life insurance, saving through pension funds, state and local obligations, corporate bonds, corporate stock, mortgages, consumer credit, security credit, and proprietors' net investment in noncorporate business. The flow accounts for some other financial transactions, such as gold and Treasury currency, time deposits, federal obligations, bank loans not otherwise classified, other loans, and miscellaneous financial transactions, have relatively small discrepancies. Where substantial discrepancies take place in financial transactions, they occur in the demand deposit and currency account and in the trade credit account. The discrepancy in the former account is largely a timing discrepancy arising from mail float, which occurs when checks are in the mail between the drawer and the drawee, whereas the discrepancy in the trade credit account comes partly from timing or float but also is caused by deficiencies in the basic statistics for this account.

The discrepancies in each sector account are the sum of all the discrepancies in each sector. The discrepancy, however, may be shown in several different ways depending upon the method of grouping and summarizing entries in the various accounts. In the Federal Reserve flow of funds accounts, the sector discrepancies appear as the difference between gross saving and gross investment.

# Questions for Discussion

1. Define gross national product (GNP). List and discuss the four major components of GNP. Which is the most important? What does this suggest about the orientation of the American economy? Which component is the most volatile? What is the significance of this volatility?
2. Discuss the two major ways of arriving at the aggregate dollar value of national output. Which goods and services are included in GNP and which are excluded? Why? Briefly discuss the reliability of the major components of data included in GNP.
3. Discuss the use of the Federal Reserve flow of funds accounts as a set of concepts for analyzing changes in the financial markets, which might, for example, be reflected in changes in interest rates. How useful do you think these accounts are for the student of these financial markets?
4. Discuss the differences in concepts (e.g., saving and investment) in the flow of funds system and the national income accounts. Indicate some of the difficulties in data reconciliation between these two systems.
5. Name the economic sectors in the flow of funds accounts and indicate how they are interrelated in a single consistent structure. For what time periods are data for these different sectors available?
6. Discuss the intermediation function of financial flows as shown in the flow of funds accounts. Include in your discussion stocks and flows of financial assets and liabilities.
7. Why is there a larger flow of saving and investment in the flow of funds accounts than in the national income accounts? Discuss the major sources of savings and the major uses of savings as shown in the flow of funds accounts.
8. Discuss the summary of the flow of funds accounts for a recent year in the 1980s. Look in the back of a recent *Federal Reserve Bulletin* for the latest data.
9. Discuss the principal financial flows and direct lending in the credit markets as shown in recent flow of funds annual data for a period of five years or more.
10. Discuss the variation from year to year in commercial bank credit as part of total financial flows in recent years. Why does the proportion of such bank credit show so much volatility from year to year? How does this variability compare with that of other financial intermediaries? Why?
11. Discuss some of the major discrepancies in the data in the flow of funds system. If an entry is estimated as a residual, can there be a discrepancy for that item? Can all discrepancies for these data be eliminated?

# Selected Bibliography for Further Reading

BANKERS TRUST COMPANY, *Credit and Capital Markets 1981*, New York, 1981.
BOARD OF GOVERNORS OF THE FEDERAL RESERVE SYSTEM, *Flow of Funds in the United States, 1939–1953* (Washington, D.C.: 1955).

——, *Flow of Funds Accounts 1945–1967* Washington, D.C.: 1969).

COPELAND, M. A., *A Study of Moneyflows in the United States* (New York: National Bureau of Economic Research, 1952).

HEARINGS BEFORE THE SUBCOMMITTEE ON ECONOMIC STATISTICS OF THE JOINT ECONOMIC COMMITTEE, Congress of the United States, October 29 and 30, 1959, *The National Economic Accounts of the United States* (Washington, D.C.: U.S. Government Printing Office, 1957).

U.S. Department of Commerce Office of Business Economics, *National Income*, 1954 edition (Washington, D.C.: 1954).

——, *U.S. Income and Output* (Washington, D.C.: 1958).

——, *The National Income and Product Accounts of the U.S., 1929–1965* (Washington, D.C.: 1966).

——, *The Economic Accounts of the U.S.: Retrospect and Prospect* (Washington, D.C.: 1971).

In addition, see the latest *Federal Reserve Bulletin* for the most recent flow of funds data.

# 6

## CHAPTER

# The Money Market

The *money market*, as the term was defined in the last chapter, for both the United States and other market economies, is now centered in New York City and in London. There are regional money centers in this country, whose operations are connected with the market in New York City, however, just as the money market centers of Europe and the rest of the world have ties with the market in London and in New York City. The money market is a market that trades in short-term highly liquid, negotiable debt instruments of one year or less in maturity.

## MAJOR FUNCTIONS OF THE MONEY MARKET

The two major functions of the money market are (1) to provide short-term financing for the public and private institutions needing such financing, and (2) to provide an impersonal market where institutions with a temporary supply of surplus funds may find profitable employment for such funds. These institutions include not only commercial banks and other financial institutions but also large nonfinancial corporations and even state and local governments. When nonfinancial institutions, or individuals, put their surplus funds directly into the money market, they are avoiding the intermediation function provided by the financial institutions.

If funds are withdrawn from financial institutions in order to receive higher rates in the money market, this is called *disintermediation*, whereas using the funds directly in the money market is called *nonintermediation*. Such disintermediation or nonintermediation becomes particularly prevalent in periods of credit restraint, such as in 1966, 1969, 1973–1974, and 1981–1982. In these years, the yields on Treasury bills, for example, became higher than the interest rates paid to depositors by banks and other financial institutions and hence attracted funds into the money market out of such financial institutions.

*Money Market Instruments*    The major debt instrument in the money market is the **Treasury bill,** which is issued for three months, six months, and one year, and for varying periods of less than one month in the form of cash management bills. The call loan to brokers and their customers is also part of this money market, but it no longer has the central place in this market that it had in the 1920s. Other short-term, highly liquid debt securities (**money market instruments**) traded in this market include bankers' acceptances, usually of ninety days maturity, commercial paper, which often comes in four-to-six-month maturities, and certificates of deposit issued by commercial banks in maturities from thirty days to one year. In addition to these kinds of money market paper, there is a highly specialized part of the money market that deals in federal funds, or deposits in Federal Reserve Banks, for as short a period as twenty-four hours. Most of these federal funds transactions, like other money market transactions, either occur in New York City or involve interdistrict transfers of funds, most of which involve New York City banks or other financial institutions in the center of the money market. A recent money market instrument available in the late 1970s and early 1980s is the money market mutual fund, which offered high money market rates of return to small investors.

## The New York Money Market

Surplus funds desiring temporary employment flow to New York City from the rest of the country and from other countries as well. Any stringency in the money market is felt first in New York, where funds flow out of the city to meet seasonal and other demands for funds in the rest of the country, or flow to foreign money market centers in search of a better rate of return. Flows into the central money market in New York City may be generated by higher yields in the money market caused, perhaps, by increased credit restraint imposed by the Federal Reserve.

One of the basic points about the money market is that this impersonal market typically involves directly only very large institutions. Direct involvement in the money market is limited to large institutions, because the standard unit of account in this market is $1 million. In addition to large borrowers and lenders, however, smaller lenders can now invest in money market funds and may be indirectly involved insofar as commercial banks, insurance companies, and similar financial institutions may pool the loanable funds of large numbers of individual savers.

These funds may pour into New York City through the correspondent banking facilities of the banking system, through repurchase agreements directly between corporations and government security dealers, or through foreign investment accounts or similar investment channels.[1] The surplus funds are absorbed both by federal government and corporate short-term borrowing. In the latter category are included not only nonfinancial corporations but financial institutions as well that are acting as intermediaries in using the borrowed funds thus secured for someone else's ultimate utilization.

The money market is an over-the-counter market that employs a complex network of telephonic communications in order to clear the market. There is no single physical location where one can go to observe the money market at work, as in the case of the New York Stock Exchange, where high-grade corporate common stock is traded. There are about thirty-six trading rooms in New York City, which are in telephonic communication not only with each other but with important customers and borrowers in New York City and throughout the country. Contracts for the purchase and sale of these money market instruments thus concluded over the telephone are scrupulously honored and are regarded as being just as binding as contracts executed on legal paper in a lawyer's office.

## THE GOVERNMENT SECURITIES MARKET

The fact that Treasury bills, and other short-term government securities, within one year to maturity are so important to the money market indicates that a brief look at the **government securities market** should be taken. There appears to be a tendency on the part of some persons to use the term *government bonds* as a synonym for *government securities*, but this usage is incorrect. The total interest-bearing federal debt at the end of 1980 was $928.9 billion, of which $623.2 billion was marketable.

Of the marketable debt on that date, $216.1 billion was in the form of Treasury bills, $321.6 billion was in the form of Treasury notes, and

---

[1]Some funds in the form of Eurodollars, which are discussed later, pour into the home office of New York banks from their London branches.

only $85.4 billion was in the form of Treasury bonds. It can thus be seen that over four fifths of the marketable federal debt was in the form of some security other than bonds. Furthermore, the bond or long end of the market is much less actively traded than the short end of the market. Prices in the long end, therefore, are much more sensitive to any substantial change in supply or demand conditions.

## A Dealer Market

It is also important to emphasize that the direct participants in the government securities markets are dealers rather than brokers, as is the case in the stock exchange. Of the thirty-six primary dealer firms in the 1980s, twelve are large dealer banks, whereas there are about twenty-four nonbank dealers. (Primary dealers are those who report data on their transactions and holdings of government securities to the Federal Reserve Bank of New York.)

There were a total of only about twenty such primary dealers in the 1960s, but high profits in this industry in 1975 and 1976 brought in fifteen new firms from the beginning of 1974 to the end of 1977. The great expansion in the number of firms reduced the market concentration in this industry, so that the top five firms in the industry in 1976 accounted for only a third of trading activity, whereas earlier they had accounted for half of all trading activity.

Dealers buy for their own position, or inventory, and sell from their holdings. As a result each dealer runs a greater risk from market fluctuations than do brokers, who buy only to fill orders of others. Only three of the nonbank dealers deal in government securities as their principal activity; the others are departments of firms that underwrite corporate and municipal bonds and even corporate stocks.

***Functions of the Government Securities Dealers***    Most **government security dealers** have their main offices in New York City and branches in the other major cities. Some of the dealers also deal in other debt instruments, such as bonds of state and local governments; others specialize exclusively in federal government securities. In carrying out their market function, the dealers develop contacts with commercial banks, the Trading Desk of the Federal Reserve System, insurance companies, pension funds, large nonfinancial corporations, and foreign central banks. In catering to the specialized needs of each of their customers, government security dealers are able, for example, to sell large nonfinancial corporations Treasury bills with exactly the right maturity for the individual corporation and geared to its future dividend dates, tax dates, interest payments, and similar large cash commitments. Both corporations and state and local governments that have raised substantial amounts of cash from the capital markets through the sale of bonds will temporarily invest some of these proceeds in Treasury bills until the time for necessary disbursement on new construction projects.

The government securities dealers play a key role in the new cash and refunding operations of the Treasury. They subscribe for a significant share of new marketable securities sold by the Treasury and they subsequently distribute the new securities to investors. The dealers also maintain a secondary market for Treasury securities, which guarantees the marketability of such securities.

*Dealer Operations in the Bill Market*  Because government security dealers do most of their trading in Treasury bills, it is important to summarize their usual methods of operations in the bill market. First, dealers carry a portfolio or inventory of securities and stand ready to buy or sell at quoted prices. Second, dealers make their profit in the spread between the bid (buying) and asking (selling) price. Third, quotations are given in basis points. Fourth, the usual spread on short-term Treasury bills is around four basis points, though market uncertainty concerning future money market trends will induce the dealers to widen this spread so as to protect themselves against unexpected factors leading to sharp price and yield changes. Fifth, outside financing is necessary to enable the dealers to carry their inventory, because equity capital is not sufficient for this purpose.

**Difficulties in Forming New Government Security Dealer Firms**
Although it is theoretically possible for anyone to become a dealer in government securities, in fact certain practical factors have a restrictive effect on entry into this line of business. These factors may be summarized as (1) financial, (2) the difficulty of doing regular business with the Trading Desk of the Federal Reserve, and (3) the uncertain profitability of the government securities market. The financial restrictions are that not only must prospective dealers be willing to invest a relatively large sum in their business, but, more important, they must have established arrangements for financing their position. This usually means that new entrants to this market have established prior contracts by reason of having been a trader for one of the established government securities dealers, or by reason of being a dealer in other debt instruments.

It is likewise quite important that the prospective new firm can do business with the Trading Desk of the Federal Reserve. Only those dealers who can make a market will be able to enter into this valuable business, along with the ability to borrow, on occasion, from the Federal Reserve by executing repurchase agreements with the Federal Reserve

Bank of New York. Dealers must have borrowing arrangements so that they can carry a large enough position to make a market.

*Five New Dealers in the 1960s*    Despite difficulties in new firms entering the government securities market, five new dealers entered this market in the 1960s and three nonbank dealers withdrew. The 1960s thus contrasted with the 1950s, because no new dealers entered the market in the earlier period. Of the new dealers in the 1960s, two were nonbank dealers and three were bank dealer departments. These five new dealers accounted for over one fifth of total activity in U.S. government and federal agencies securities in the mid-1960s, whereas the trading volume of old dealers remained at about the 1961 level. There was a relative increase in the importance of bank dealers in the 1960s and 1970s, though nonbank dealers still account for somewhat more than half the trading volume.

*Fifteen New Dealers in the 1970s*    As already noted, fifteen new dealers entered this industry in the 1970s as a result of high profits in 1975, 1976, and 1977. The great growth of Treasury debt and large declines in interest rates resulted in such profits. Many of the new entrants were investment banking firms who sought to expand the range of their operations as activity in the intermediate and long-term Treasury market grew.

Some of the smaller dealers, however, are little more than brokers in the long-term sector of the market, because they are often unwilling in practice to undertake substantial transactions at quoted prices. The present over-the-counter organization of the government securities market is such that this market is particularly geared to servicing of large orders from banks, savings institutions, nonfinancial corporations, and the like. Odd-lot orders from individuals are typically processed through a commercial bank. The total volume of orders from individuals for marketable government securities still appears to be quite small because of the greater individual preference for savings bonds or money market mutual funds for those of modest income, or for common stock and tax-exempt state and local government securities for those in higher income tax brackets.

*The Underwriting Function of Dealers*    Dealers, along with commercial banks and the Federal Reserve System, help to underwrite the issuance of new government securities not only by bidding regularly on new cash and refunding issues for their own inventory but also by regularly inserting throwaway bids in each auction so that oversubscription for many regular Treasury issues is common. This oversubscription by dealers at low throwaway bids (i.e., the dealers bid for more bills than they really desire to purchase) means that the Treasury can always be certain of selling its bill tender. The Federal Reserve aids the dealers in these underwriting efforts by often easing pressures in the money market before a large Treasury financing and by extending financial assistance (through the execution of repurchase agreements) to those dealers who may find themselves unable to secure adequate financing from their normal sources.

## Transactions in the Government Securities Market

Although the total dollar volume of government securities traded in the 1970s and 1980s showed an impressive increase (e.g., total dollar volume rose from $3.5 billion in 1974 to $10.4 billion in 1976, to $13.1 billion in 1979, and averaged $27.4 billion in December 1981), dealers have continued to emphasize the short end of the market. About two thirds of daily trading is concentrated in securities maturing in less than one year, whereas the bulk of this trading is in Treasury bills.

The Treasury bill market is thus broader than for other government securities, because a greater amount of trading takes place. *Making a market* means that dealers stand ready to buy from, or sell outright to, customers reasonable amounts of government securities on the basis of quotations given on the telephone. To carry out this function of making a market, dealers must carry a substantial inventory, particularly of Treasury bills. The amount of market trading is many times larger in such bills than in bonds.

Although Treasury bills make up about one third of the outstanding marketable federal debt, they account for well over half the daily trading in government securities. Probably because of this very active trading in bills, they are quoted in terms of yield, and changes in yield are given in basis points. (It takes 100 basis points to make 1 percent.) Treasury bonds, on the other hand, are quoted in price terms, and changes in such prices are given in $1/32$ of one point.

*Greater Risk in the Bond Market*    The foregoing suggests some increase in market risk in the long end of the market. After October 6, 1979, when the Federal Reserve abruptly tightened credit policy and shifted its emphasis in open market operations from controlling the federal funds rate to controlling bank reserves, bond yields became increasingly volatile. In late 1979, 1980, and 1981 this caused substantial swings in bond dealers' profits and losses. Yields on short-term debt instruments, however, continued to be even more volatile than bond yields. Furthermore, the level of all interest rates was substantially higher in the early 1980s than it had been a decade earlier. There were higher interest rates because of the intractability of inflation and the necessity of including in all yields a factor to offset the risk of still further inflation. Also when

**Figure 6-1    Dealer Positions in United States Government and Federal Agency Securities**

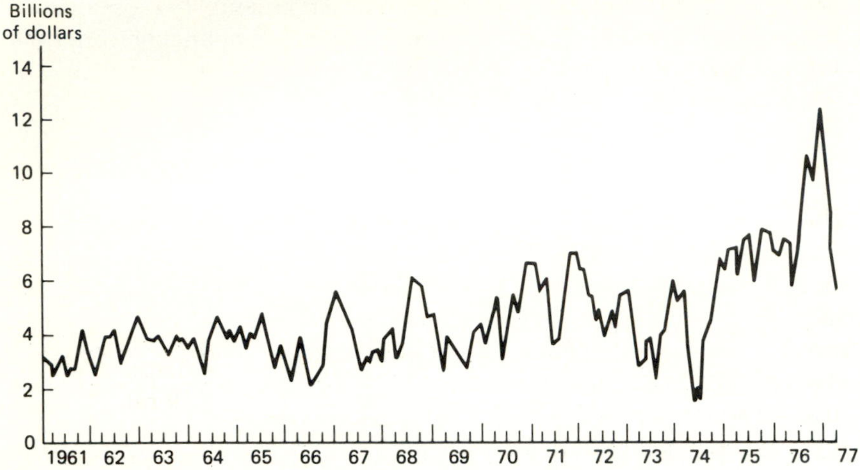

SOURCE: Federal Reserve Bank of New York, *Quarterly Review*, Summer 1977, Vol. 2, p. 43.

yields were rising, bond prices were falling (as in the "October Massacre" of 1979), which imposed a further market risk and often losses on dealers.

The **dealer positions,** or inventory, of U.S. government and federal agency securities are shown in Figure 6-1, which contains data for the sixteen years from 1961 through early 1977. In addition to the substantial intrayear fluctuations in the holdings of such securities, the average inventory holdings of the dealers were greater in the mid-1970s than in the 1960s. This meant that dealers' financing needs in the 1970s were greater, because these positions are highly leveraged. That is, dealers borrow a very high percentage of the cost of purchasing securities. About 95 percent of the dealers' position is financed by borrowed funds.

In the late 1970s and early 1980s, sharp fluctuations in dealer positions still occurred, as shown in Figure 6-1 for the 1960s and the earlier part of the 1970s. However, the sharp price fluctuations of marketable debt and the higher cost of borrowing to finance dealer positions led to lower average positions of government security dealers. For all of 1977, for example, the average daily position of dealers was $5.1 billion. It fell to $2.6 billion in 1978 and was $3.2 billion in 1979 and $4.3 billion in 1980. In December 1981, it was $4.1 billion. Dealers held such low average inventories even though the Treasury sold more new securities in the late 1970s and early 1980s than it had a decade earlier.

The income of the dealer is earned either as carry income or trading profits. Carry income (or loss) is the difference between the interest cost of a dealer's portfolio and the cost of the borrowed funds needed to support that portfolio. Trading profits are the gain (or loss) of the dealer from selling securities for more (or less) than was paid for them. Let us now consider the means by which government securities dealers secure their needed financing.

## FINANCING OF GOVERNMENT SECURITY DEALERS

Since the mid-1950s, three of the five major New York City banks making dealer loans have regularly extended to dealers both federal fund loans (immediately available funds) and Clearing House loans (funds available in twenty-four hours after clearing a check through the Clearing House). These loans are made at a preferential rate below the call rate on other security loans but at a rate that is often higher than the average yield on securities held by the dealers. This loss on the carry has driven dealers to search for other sources of borrowed funds. Borrowings from out-of-town lenders are invariably federal fund loans with the funds transferred the same day over the Federal Reserve wire facilities.

### The Repurchase Agreement

The **repurchase agreement,** which was developed in the bankers' acceptance market in the 1920s, was successfully applied on a large scale in the government securities market of the 1970s and 1980s as a technique for financing part of the position of the dealers. In this way, a dealer secures "immediately available funds" as does a commercial bank when it buys federal funds. In a typical repurchase agreement the dealer sells government securities to a bank, nonfinancial corporation, or similar customer and at the same time makes a commitment to repurchase an equivalent amount of these securities at a later date. A spread in prices between the selling and repurchase price is established so that the buyer, or lender, of funds is provided a return. The maturity of these repurchase agreements ranges from one or two days to several months, in a few isolated cases. In general, the maturity is quite short.

The dealer uses the repurchase agreement not only to finance a trading or investment position but also to tailor investment in debt maturities to lenders' requirements. Also, the dealers sometimes act as money brokers through the use of offsetting repurchase and resale agreements. The great growth of the repurchase agreement in the government securities markets in the 1970s and 1980s gave a new role of financial lender to many of our large nonfinancial corporations. The greater importance of still another money substitute, such as that represented by the repurchase agreement, is that it provides still another possibility for the velocity of money to increase, even while the stock of money remains much more stable. A rise in the velocity of money means that the prices of goods and services can increase (i.e., inflation takes place) even when the Federal Reserve is restricting the growth of the stock of money.

The seasonal utilization of the repurchase agreement also has become quite significant. It is common for government security dealers to enter into agreements to repurchase large amounts of government securities on important tax and dividend dates during each year. The clustering of repurchase agreements around certain dates adds to the normal seasonal strains and stresses placed on the money market by business borrowing demands. This often forces the Federal Reserve to come to the aid of the dealers at such times by providing them with needed financing help through the vehicle of the repurchase agreement.

## *Position and Sources of Dealer Financing*

Position and sources of dealer financing for the last three years of the 1970s are shown in Table 6–1. Although the average daily position of the dealers was markedly lower in 1979 than in 1977, nevertheless their financing requirements had soared from $9.8 billion to $16 billion in the same two years. Commercial banks, particularly outside New York City, corporations, and "all others," which includes pension funds and the Federal Reserve Trading Desk, all continued to be major suppliers. Repurchase agreements continued to be the favorite vehicle for supplying such financing to the dealers, because about two thirds of borrowed funds are channeled through this device.

Most of these repurchase agreements are quite short, with the typical maturity running from one to fifteen days. Less than one third of dealer financing involves the use of repurchase agreements longer than fifteen days. For example, if the dealer secures a repurchase agreement from the Federal Reserve, the initial maturity is always fewer than fifteen days, though sometimes, around Christmas particularly, such repurchase agreements may be renewed at the option of the Federal Reserve.

The rate on funds obtained from private lenders through repurchase agreements is a matter of negotiation between dealer and lender. There is, however, a money market framework within which such negotiations take place. Other money market yields that influence the negotiated repurchase agreement yield include (1) the federal funds rate, (2) the dealer loan rates at New York City banks, and (3) yields on Treasury

**Table 6–1  U.S. Government Securities Dealers' Positions and Sources of Financing (par value; average of daily figures in millions of dollars)**

| | Item | 1977 | 1978 | 1979 |
|---|---|---|---|---|
| | | | Positions[a] | |
| 1 | **U.S. government securities** ... | **5,172** | **2,656** | **3,223** |
| 2 | Bills ....................... | 4,772 | 2,452 | 3,813 |
| 3 | Other within 1 year.......... | 99 | 260 | −325 |
| 4 | 1–5 years.................... | 60 | −92 | −455 |
| 5 | 5–10 years.................. | 92 | 40 | 160 |
| 6 | Over 10 years............... | 149 | −4 | 30 |
| 7 | **Federal agency securities**..... | **693** | **606** | **1,471** |
| | | | Financing[b] | |
| 8 | **All sources**................. | **9,877** | **10,204** | **16,003** |
| | Commercial banks | | | |
| 9 | New York City.............. | 1,313 | 599 | 1,396 |
| 10 | Outside New York City ...... | 1,987 | 2,174 | 2,868 |
| 11 | Corporations[c] .............. | 2,358 | 2,379 | 3,373 |
| 12 | All others .................. | 4,158 | 5,052 | 4,104 |

[a]Net amounts (in terms of par values) of securities owned by nonbank dealer firms and dealer departments of commercial banks on a commitment, that is, trade-date basis, including any such securities that have been sold under agreements to repurchase. The maturities of some repurchase agreements are sufficiently long, however, to suggest that the securities involved are not available for trading purposes. Securities owned, and hence dealer positions, do not include securities purchased under agreement to resell.

[b]Total amounts outstanding of funds borrowed by nonbank dealer firms and dealer departments of commercial banks against U.S. government and federal agency securities (through both collateral loans and sales under agreements to repurchase), plus internal funds used by bank dealer departments to finance positions in such securities. Borrowings against securities held under agreement to resell are excluded when the borrowing contract and the agreement to resell are equal in amount and maturity, that is, a matched agreement.

[c]All business corporations except commercial banks and insurance companies.

*Note:* Averages for positions are based on number of trading days in the period; those for financing, on the number of calendar days in the period.

SOURCE: Board of Governors of the Federal Reserve System, *Federal Reserve Bulletin*, Feb. 1981, p. A32.

bills. Because dealers can usually satisfy their credit needs at the posted rates of New York City banks if they have to, the maximum rate that dealers would pay for one-day repurchase agreements secured outside the city would be equal to the posted rate at New York City banks minus the additional costs in obtaining the funds elsewhere.

The minimum rate that the dealer would be able to obtain is determined by the yield that the lender could obtain on alternative investments. This alternative yield for commercial banks is the federal funds rate, inasmuch as banks can always sell excess reserves in this one-day market at the going federal funds rate. For business corporations the alternative yield would be that on short Treasury bills, finance company paper, or similar short-dated money market assets.

## Characteristics of Dealer Financing Arrangements

In the 1970s, there were no major shifts among the sources of nonbank dealer financing, though there was some increase in the availability of funds. Nonfinancial corporations continue to finance about one sixth to one fifth of the dealer positions, whereas banks inside and outside of New York City finance about two fifths of the total. Nonbank dealers also receive financing from time to time from the Federal Reserve Trading Desk and other sources such as pension funds through repurchase agreements. Bank dealers, on the other hand, finance their positions with bank funds, though their funds are generally costed at some approximation of the federal funds rate.

*Day-to-Day Dealer Financing*    Most of the dealer financing continues to be on a day-to-day basis. This means that such borrowing influences, and is influenced by, the terms on which banks and other lenders and borrowers adjust their liquidity positions. The total financing requirements of the dealers are very large, growing out of the large volume of transactions in the market and the substantial size of the position, or inventory, of government securities that the dealers must carry in order to make a market.

## THE TREASURY BILL MARKET

After an overview of the entire government securities market, one should focus on that part of the market that is directly part of the money market. This is, of course, the Treasury bill market.

## Three Kinds of Treasury Bills

As already indicated, there are three kinds of regular Treasury bills, as well as special bills such as cash management bills. The 91-day or 3-month Treasury bill and the 182-day or 6-month Treasury bill are both auctioned on Monday and dated for issue on the following Thursday. Usually the Treasury offers about $5 billion of 91-day bills and about $5 billion of 182-day bills for a total of $10 billion in the regular Monday auction. Around $5 billion of 1-year bills are offered in the regular monthly auction.

In the mid-1970s the Treasury added very short or "cash management" bills, dated to mature in fewer than 30 days. On June 3, 1981, the Treasury sold $3 billion in 15-day cash management bills to yield a record 18.480 percent. The previous day a comparable issue of $6 billion in 20-day bills yielded 17.946 percent. In March 1981, the Treasury sold 22-day bills at a much lower yield of 13.762 percent. A year later, in March 1982, the Treasury sold $8 billion of 20-day bills at an average yield of 14.87 percent. In December 1981, and in August 1981, the Treasury had sold 16-day bills. Cash management bills thus have varying maturities, though they are all very short (i.e., less than one month).

*The Weekly Bill Tender*     Tenders in the **Monday auction** are accepted at any Federal Reserve Bank until 1:30 P.M. Eastern time. Bills are issued in denominations of $10,000, $15,000, $50,000, $100,000, $500,000, and $1,000,000. Small investors are likely to submit noncompetitive bids, so that they can be sure that they will receive the exact amount of bills desired. Noncompetitive tenders from any one bidder of less than $200,000 for bills are filled in full at the average price (in three decimals) of accepted competitive bids. Large bidders, such as money market banks, government security dealers, the Federal Reserve System, and foreign central banks regularly enter competitive bids in the Monday auction. The lowest price (highest yield) at which bills are awarded is called the *stop out* price. Usually only a fraction of the bids at the low price are accepted.

Because these Treasury bills have no coupon rate and are sold at auction below their par or face value, the yield is determined on a discount basis. The Treasury computes this discount on the basis of a 360-day year so that the average yield stated is somewhat below the actual interest rate computed on the basis of a calendar year. For example, the average price of the 91-day bill in the regular weekly auction on May 18, 1981 was $9,594.70 for a $10,000 face value bill, which had an equivalent annual yield of 16.034 percent for a 360-day year. In the same auction the average price for a $10,000 face value 182-day bill was $9,240.40, which was an annual yield for a 360-day year of 15.025 percent. These yields were almost double what they had been only a year earlier, when the auction yield averaged 8.953 percent for 3-month bills and 8.923 percent for 6-month bills. Because monetary policy often changes year by year, such changes in Treasury bill yields are common.

*The Monthly Bill Tender*     By the 1980s the Treasury had regularized its 52-week Treasury bills by offering them on a once-a-month basis. By offering approximately $5 billion in such bills each month, the Treasury was able to avoid possible competition with its weekly bill issues or possible unsettlement of the money market that might be caused by irregularity and uncertainty as to the timing of future Treasury bill borrowings.

## Ownership of Treasury Bills

The ownership of Treasury bills is shown in Table 6–2, as given in the Treasury survey of ownership for December 31, 1981. On this date 71 percent of the bills were owned by "all other investors," and the Federal Reserve Banks owned 20 percent of total Treasury bills. Commercial banks, state and local governments, and nonfinancial corporations followed in the size of their Treasury bill holdings. In most periods, ignoring "all other investors," commercial banks are the largest private holder of Treasury bills.

The Treasury has always been able to sell the desired amount of bills in the weekly or monthly auction. Treasury bills outstanding in the 1970s more than doubled from $80.6 billion at the end of 1969 to $172.6 billion at the end of 1979. In the next two years ending in December 1981, Treasury bills outstanding grew by $72.4 billion to a total of $245 billion.

## MONEY MARKET MUTUAL FUNDS

Although individual investors with $10,000 or more can, and often do, buy Treasury bills, a newer money market instrument for the small depositor with $1,000 or more appeared in the mid-1970s. This was the money market fund offering competitive money market yields on small deposits and even check-writing in amounts of $500 or more.

Prior to 1974, the assets of money market funds were virtually zero, and by the end of 1974 there were only fifteen such funds. Beginning in 1977 and 1978 the assets and number of these funds began to soar. At the end of 1978, there were sixty-one funds, up from fifty in 1977, and assets totaled more than $10 billion. Each year thereafter until the early 1980s, they doubled at least. In 1981, they had more than doubled their size, growing to about $3 billion a week. By the end of July 1982, there were 234 such funds and their assets totaled $212.5 billion. The reason for this phenomenal growth was not only the small amount of savings that they accepted but also the very high levels of interest rates as compared with alternative forms of liquid assets. In May 1982, for example, the average yield for the money funds was about 13.5 percent.

**Table 6–2   Ownership of Treasury Bills, December 31, 1981 (par value, $ millions)**

| | |
|---|---:|
| Total all holders | 245,015 |
| U.S. government agencies and trust funds | n.a. |
| Federal Reserve Banks | 49,679 |
| Held by private investors | 195,335 |
| Commercial banks | 9,667 |
| Mutual savings banks | 423 |
| Insurance companies | 760 |
| Nonfinancial corporations | 1,173 |
| Savings and loan associations | 363 |
| State and local governments | 5,126 |
| All other investors[a] | 177,824 |

[a]Included with all other investors are those banks, insurance companies, savings and loan associations, and corporations not reporting in the Treasury survey. Details may not add to totals owing to rounding.

SOURCE: Board of Governors of the Federal Reserve System, *Federal Reserve Bulletin*, March 1982, p. A33.

In general, there are two types of money market funds. One invests in short-term debt of large banks and corporations, as well as U.S. Treasury issues. These funds have a somewhat higher rate of return. Other funds emphasizing maximum safety, but yielding lower income, invest only in securities issued or guaranteed by the U.S. Treasury. Both types of funds are discussed in Chapter 11, Financial Intermediaries.

## THE FEDERAL FUNDS MARKET

Another important part of the money market is the **federal funds** market. Federal funds are deposits in Federal Reserve Banks, such as member bank deposits. The federal funds market primarily involves borrowing and lending between commercial banks of excess commercial bank reserves on deposit in the Federal Reserve Banks, typically for periods of only twenty-four hours. The yield on these overnight (one-day) federal funds transactions measures the return on the most liquid of all financial assets and for this reason is critical to investment decisions. This yield is compared by financial managers with yields on all other investments before investment decisions are made as to the combinations of maturities of financial assets that will be purchased, or the term over which the institution will borrow.

Furthermore, the federal funds market is important because the yield in this market is closely related to the conduct of Federal Reserve monetary policy. The interest rate on federal funds is highly sensitive to

Federal Reserve actions in supplying or withdrawing bank reserves. Also, other money market yields tend to move up and down in parallel action with yield changes in the federal funds market.

## Market Dominance of Commercial Banks

Although government securities dealers, foreign agency banks, and large nonfinancial corporations all trade in the federal funds market at times, this section of the money market is dominated by the commercial banks. By February 1982, average daily volume in the one-day and continuing contract federal funds market was nearly $100 billion. Large commercial banks ($1 billion or more assets as of December 31, 1977) accounted for more than half of these average daily transactions. In dollar amount these banks traded each week from $53 billion to $57 billion, or more than twice as much federal funds as they had four years earlier.

Although the federal funds market is a national market centered in New York City, as is the government securities market, it is a much more loosely organized market. For example, no dealers maintain a position in federal funds and stand ready to buy or sell at quoted prices. Some large banks, however, do stand ready to make limited purchases or sales of federal funds on any given day, depending sometimes on the needs of their correspondent banks.

## Dominance of Large Banks

About 90 percent of the federal funds transactions of banks are made by 134 large banks. Furthermore, fewer than ten large banks account for more than half of all reported purchases of federal funds. The percentage of commercial banks that participate at times in the federal funds market has nevertheless risen in recent years. In 1969, only 55 percent of all member banks either bought or sold federal funds.

By 1976, that percentage had risen to 88 percent, with most of the new entrants to the market being small banks. The market, however, is still dominated by a relatively small number of large banks. In particular, a growing portion of the federal funds market has consisted of large bank borrowings of correspondent balances from small banks.

*The 134 Reporting Banks*    Because of this substantial concentration among a few large banks in this part of the money market, the Federal Reserve is able to restrict its reported data on federal funds purchases and sales to a group of 134 large reporting banks. In a three-year survey period, these banks accounted for four fifths of the purchases, whereas their sales were equal to three fifths of the total purchases. Of this number, 46 very large commercial banks account for the bulk of federal funds transactions. (Until recently, the Federal Reserve secured data only from these 46 very large banks.)

Figure 6–2 shows the tremendous growth in federal funds and repurchase agreements (which are also part of the market for immediately available funds) held by these 46 very large commercial banks in the ten years from 1967 to 1977. Although there are intrayear variations in such holdings, the strong trend of growth is clear from average holdings of about $2.5 billion in 1967 to holdings in excess of $35 billion by 1977. Spurts of rapid growth in this market have taken place during periods when short-term interest rates were either rising rapidly or were at high levels. Also, in some periods of credit restraint, the discount window has not been freely available to banks short of required reserves.

The rise of liability management in the past twenty years has led to banks borrowing federal funds more frequently and in larger amounts. Some individual banks continually borrow as much as four times their required reserves in the federal funds market. Some bank transactions have recently been for longer than a single business day, though that is still the typical maturity for federal funds transactions. If immediately available funds, such as federal funds, are desired for longer than a day, a repurchase agreement is often used rather than an unsecured federal funds transaction.

**Figure 6–2    Federal Funds and RPs Held by Large Domestic Commercial Banks**

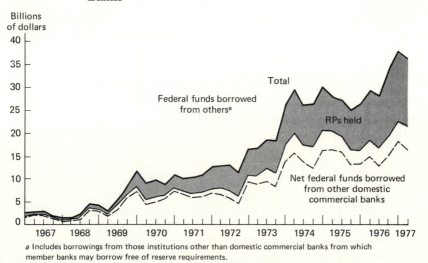

a Includes borrowings from those institutions other than domestic commercial banks from which member banks may borrow free of reserve requirements.

SOURCE: Federal Reserve Bank of New York, *Quarterly Review*, Summer 1977, Vol. 2, p. 40.

*The Importance of Daily Data on Federal Funds*    The daily data on federal funds transactions are valuable to the monetary authorities, particularly to those officials who are responsible for conducting system open market operations. These data combined with other data, such as information on member banks' excess reserves and member bank borrowing, make it possible to assist in forming judgments on such matters as (1) the likelihood of changes in short-term money rates, (2) the possible need for funds by government securities dealers, (3) the potential pressure on the reserve positions of the major money market banks, and (4) probable changes in a number of other factors, such as contemplated borrowings in the financial markets.

Many of these financial developments occur because of changes in the real sectors of the economy, and such financial indicators are thus helpful in formulating a monetary policy designed ultimately to affect the real sectors of the economy. These federal funds data available throughout a trading day help to form a "feel of the market," which is important in the conduct of Federal Reserve open market operations.

## Transactions in the Federal Funds Markets

As already indicated, most of the buying and selling of federal funds takes place among a relatively small number of large commercial banks. Among these money market banks, the New York City banks play a particularly important role, because they account for about one third of average daily transactions. Most of these federal funds transactions of the New York City banks, however, involve buying and selling federal funds with banks outside of New York City. Less than 20 percent of the volume of trading of the New York City banks is with one another, whereas about 80 percent is with other commercial banks.

*Three Forms of Federal Funds Contracts*    Regardless of the location of the transacting bank, there are three major forms of contracts for federal funds transactions: (1) the transaction may be unsecured, (2) it may be secured by the pledge of short-term U.S. government securities, or (3) it may take the form of a sale of U.S. government, federal agency, or municipal issues under a repurchase agreement. By securing a transaction in federal funds with short-term government securities, a state-chartered bank selling federal funds is exempt from many state statutes, which provide that in general loans made to a single borrower may not exceed 10 percent of the bank's capital and surplus. (In June 1963, the Comptroller of the Currency ruled that federal funds transactions by national banks were no longer subject to such borrowing and lending limits.) Regardless of legal considerations, interbank transactions are more likely to be secured when large banks purchase funds from small banks, rather than vice versa.

Because the typical bank entering the federal funds market is a rather large bank, some three fourths of these transactions are in the form of overnight unsecured loans, whereas the remainder involve the use of repurchase agreements or buybacks, with the bank listing either of these transactions on its books as an outright purchase or sale. When a repurchase agreement is involved, the lender of federal funds buys short-term government securities, whereas the seller agrees to repurchase them within a stated time at an agreed price.

If Treasury bills are involved, the original purchase and the later repurchase are expressed in terms of rates of discount instead of price. When the buyback is used, lenders enter into two contracts at the same time. They agree to buy securities, usually Treasury bills, for delivery and payment the same day. They also agree to sell the same issue of securities for delivery and payment in federal funds the next day.

Transactions in federal funds, like government security transactions, are usually negotiated by telephone and confirmed subsequently by wire or letter. When banks in different cities are involved in a given federal funds agreement, the funds move over the leased wire of the Federal Reserve System. The interest payment is made through a correspondent bank. In New York City, transactions among banks are settled by an exchange of checks, with the lender giving a check on its reserve balance with the Federal Reserve Bank of New York, whereas the borrower gives its own check payable through the local clearinghouse the next day.

*The Role of Correspondent Banks and Brokers*    Federal funds transactions among banks are often accomplished between correspondent banks. Therefore some of the large New York City banks with many correspondent banks play an important role in this particular market. Two stock brokers (Garvin Guy Butler, and Mabon Nugent and Company) are important brokers in bringing together buyers and sellers of federal funds. These firms furnish the Federal Reserve Bank of New York data on federal funds rates for a given day.

## Interest Rate on Federal Funds

Variations in the interest rate on federal funds are shown in Figure 6–3 for the sixteen-year period from 1961 to 1977. Marked peaks in the federal funds rate, which are particularly notable in 1966, 1969, 1973, and 1974, are clearly observable in this graph. In each case, the peaks correspond with periods of increasing credit restraint by the Federal Reserve.

**Figure 6–3**     **Interest Rate on Federal Funds**

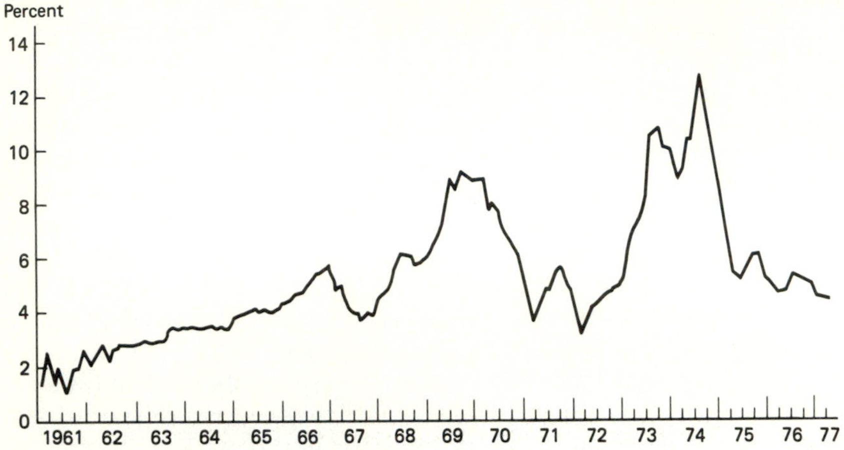

Percent

SOURCE: Federal Reserve Bank of New York, *Quarterly Review*, Summer 1977, Vol. 2, p. 41.

In the even more severe period of credit restraint in 1981–1982, the **federal funds rate** in some weeks averaged close to 20 percent, which was markedly higher than the earlier peak of 1974. The degree of pressure placed on bank reserve positions is more clearly noted in these data on federal funds rate, because in each of these peak periods the federal funds rate exceeds the discount rate established by the Federal Reserve Banks.

      The discount rate was held at 4½ percent through 1966, whereas the federal funds rate exceeded 5 percent in late 1966. In 1969, the federal funds rate was nearly 9 percent, when the discount rate was only 6 percent. In 1973 and 1974 the difference was even more marked, because the peak discount rate in 1973 was 7½ percent and the peak discount rate in 1974 was 8 percent. But by the spring of 1981, the basic discount rate was 14 percent with a 4 percent surcharge for large banks borrowing continuously from the Federal Reserve. Later in 1981, the surcharge was reduced until it was eliminated in November. The basic discount rate was also cut to 13 percent in November and to 12 percent in December. By mid-1982, it was down to 10 percent. In this credit restraint period, the spread between the federal funds rate and the discount rate was often much smaller than in several earlier credit restraint periods.

*The Range of Federal Fund Rates*     The range of federal fund rates is also sometimes very wide. For example, on Wednesday, May 20, 1981, the day's high for federal funds in the open market was 27 percent, whereas the low was 19 percent. The very next day, the range of federal funds was only from 19¾ percent to 21 percent. Wednesday is the last day of the reserve week, and such extreme variations in the price of excess member bank reserves, which occur in the federal funds market at times, are particularly likely to occur on the last day of the week.

The federal funds rate may be either below or above the discount rate, which is the interest rate member banks pay when they borrow reserves (which are also federal funds) from their regional Federal Reserve Bank. Up until the credit restraint period of 1966, the federal funds rate was always below the discount rate, but in periods of credit restraint since then the federal funds rate has often been above the discount rate, as already noted. Under these circumstances, the discount window of the Federal Reserve Bank must impose nonprice-rationing procedures on depository institutions wishing to borrow reserves continuously from them. These procedures are discussed in Chapter 18.

*Accommodating Banks in Federal Funds*    Some banks in the federal funds market may be considered accommodating banks in that they will sell federal funds to country correspondent banks, even when the transactions run against their own reserve positions. Most banks in the market, however, should be considered adjusting banks. The adjusting banks may be divided into three groups: (1) banks that shift between lending and borrowing from day to day so as to try to balance out the reserve week without either an excess or deficiency of reserves, (2) some of the smaller banks in the federal funds market that usually keep a cushion of excess reserves and thus are typically sellers, and (3) a small group of generally buying banks that appears to use the federal funds market primarily to meet persistent reserve deficiencies.

In addition to differences among types of banks in this market, several regional differences exist. Although New York City is very important both in buying and selling federal funds, it is on net balance a buyer of these funds. Other large cities, such as San Francisco, Cleveland, and Boston, are primarily sellers of federal funds. Chicago, like New York City, on net balance is a buyer of these funds. The federal funds market and the Treasury bill market together now occupy the strategic place in the money market that was occupied by the call loan in the money market of the 1920s.

## THE EURODOLLAR MARKET

An important appendage to the New York money market is the Eurodollar market, which is centered in London. This international money market, which first developed in the late 1950s after the removal of currency restrictions by European countries, had become quite important by the 1980s. Eurodollars consist largely of dollar-denominated deposits in European banks, which include branches of American banks in London. These Eurodollars are freely convertible into dollars in New York City and, indeed, are partly backed by dollars held in New York banks. Eurodollars are loaned typically for three or four months— though often for one month or less—at interest rates higher than those in the New York money market. The New York banks, however, usually provide the clearinghouse function for the Eurodollar market, so that transfers of balances can be quickly accomplished.

## The Origin and Growth of Eurodollars

Eurodollars originate when foreigners gain ownership over U.S. dollars and decide to transfer their dollars from New York to other money market centers such as London, Paris, or Zurich. The chronic deficit in the American balance of payments has given increasing amounts of such American dollars into the hands of private and public foreign institutions. The growth of the Eurodollar market, however, has presented another alternative to foreigners gaining dollars to the earlier alternatives of holding dollars in New York City, perhaps in Treasury bills or in time deposits in commercial banks.

    The Eurodollar market also represents an alternative to selling these dollars to foreign central banks, which prior to August 15, 1971, might have demanded payment in gold from the U.S. Treasury. Furthermore, the growth of this new money market has increased international liquidity, because Eurodollars are backed only by a fractional reserve of dollars on deposit in New York banks. Finally, the existence and growth of this money market has made it possible for American banks to escape some of the pressures of credit restraint periods, such as 1966, 1969, 1973, and 1982, by securing added loanable funds, even though the interest rates on these Eurodollar deposits are often quite high.

## Eurodollars by the 1980s

In the decade of the 1970s, the Eurodollar market flourished, with time deposits in this market growing at an annual rate above 25 percent, as compared with annual growth rates of about 10 percent, for broad measures of the money supply both in the United States and West Germany. Liabilities denominated in other hard currencies, such as German marks, Swiss francs, and even Japanese yen, are also traded in this market, but nearly 75 percent of all Eurocurrency deposits are denominated in dollars (i.e., Eurodollars). Data on the Eurocurrency market are collected by the Bank for International Settlements (BIS) in Basle, Switzerland. For 1979, the BIS estimated that gross Eurocurrency deposits (inclusive of interbank deposits) totaled about $900 billion. Considering only Eurocurrency liabilities to nonbanks, a still substantial total of less than $200 billion is reported. Both these numbers were considerably greater than they had been a decade earlier.

Eurodollars are not considered part of the narrow definition of the money supply (M1) of the United States, because they are not available as a medium of exchange to buy goods and services in the United States. Nevertheless, they may be regarded, as are U.S. Treasury bills and other money market assets, as a close substitute for money in that they can serve the store of value function of money. Hence, overnight Eurodollar holdings of U.S. residents are included in M2. Because this is true, in periods when Eurodollars are increasing substantially, as in the decade of the 1970s, domestic inflation may be promoted because the velocity of domestic money (M1) can rise, even though the Federal Reserve is controlling the rate of growth in the money supply. If the velocity of money changes unpredictably, severe problems are posed for the monetary policy authorities.

## BANKERS' ACCEPTANCES

Another one of the money market instruments of growing importance in recent years has been the bankers' acceptance. This instrument, though used in the 1920s, assumed an even greater role by the 1980s. A simple definition of a **bankers' acceptance** is that it is a negotiable draft, which is drawn against an accepting bank and is usually payable in ninety days.

### Use in Foreign Trade

The bankers' acceptance is particularly used in connection with imports, exports, or storage of goods. For example, an importer of coffee in New York City may need short-term credit to finance a purchase of coffee from a Brazilian exporter. The exporter may be unable or unwilling to extend the credit needed, so the importer goes to a New York City bank. Rather than giving the importer a direct loan, the bank may agree to accept a bank bill, which indicates the amount owed by the importer to the exporter and is due, say, ninety days later.

The accepting bank thus guarantees that the importer will pay the debt at maturity. By guaranteeing payment of the trade bill (after having investigated the credit standing of the importer), the bank substitutes its credit for that of the importer. The Brazilian exporter is then willing to receive the bankers' acceptance in lieu of cash payment. If the exporter wishes to have cash now, he may sell the bankers' acceptance on the open market (probably to another New York City bank).

The most typical use of bankers' acceptances has been in financing imports and exports. Only about 3 percent of acceptances are for domestic shipment and storage. Because world trade and that of the United States expanded rapidly in the 1970s and early 1980s, it is not surprising that the amount of bankers' acceptances also expanded sharply. In December 1981, for example, bankers' acceptances outstanding totaled more than $69 billion, which was nearly triple the $25.4 billion outstanding at the end of 1977. At the end of 1969, acceptances totaled only $5.4 billion.

***Growth in Tight Money Periods***    The use of bankers' acceptances as a way of securing short-term credit to finance imports or exports is not only tied to the volume of foreign trade but is also related to the degree of tightness or ease in the money market generally. When credit restraint policies of the Federal Reserve and an upswing in private demand for borrowed funds force up money market rates, a noticeable increase in the volume of bankers' acceptances outstanding occurs. The reasons for this are not hard to find. First, importers, for example, can sometimes secure credit in this way at a cheaper rate than if they negotiated a direct bank loan. At the end of March 1981, for example, the prime bank interest rate for the best business borrowers was 18 percent, whereas the market rate on prime bankers' acceptances, ninety days, was 13.38 percent. Even if we add on to the market discount rate at the customary bank charge of 1.5 percent for accepting the bankers' acceptance originally, the total cost of funds thus obtained is less than 16 percent, which was still lower than the effective interest rate for business borrowers, who must maintain a 20 percent compensating balance when borrowing from banks, as well as paying a higher prime rate.

The accepting commercial bank is especially happy to make this kind of commitment in periods of tight money, because no bank funds are directly involved. In recent years there have been practically no losses involved in bankers' acceptances, so the bank is making what it regards as a safe commitment without any use of its scarce loanable funds. The accepting bank receives 1.5 percent discount merely for lending the use of its name.

## Dealers in Bankers' Acceptances

The market for bankers' acceptances is an over-the-counter market with about ten to fifteen dealer firms. Some of these are large firms with nationwide branches. Most of these firms deal in a variety of marketable obligations with acceptance trading only a modest part, in some cases, of their overall activities.

Movements in acceptance rates are closely aligned with other short-term money market instruments but are also influenced by the size of dealers' portfolios. The normal dealer spread between buying and selling rates is ⅛ to ¼ percent, but it can be 1 percent or higher in a sharply fluctuating market. Some of the dealers' financing needs can be satisfied by securing repurchase agreements from the Trading Desk of the Federal Reserve Bank of New York, and this is also an outlet for outright sales of acceptances or for the extension of repurchase agreements.

In recent years, the Trading Desk has not usually purchased bankers' acceptances outright, but it has bought them under repurchase agreements. At the end of 1981, the Desk held $195 million of bankers' acceptances under such repurchase agreements. When the Federal Reserve extends repurchase agreements in acceptances, it is for the purpose of supplying bank reserves for a short time, usually one to seven days.

## COMMERCIAL PAPER

Another important part of the money market is the buying and selling of **commercial paper.** Commercial paper consists of marketable short-term unsecured promissory notes of businesses, usually in denominations of $100,000 or more with maturities typically of sixty days or less, but sometimes up to six months. In the 1970s an increasing number of large corporations met part of their short-term credit needs through the issuance of such commercial paper. These notes are either placed directly with large investors, such as insurance companies, nonfinancial corporations, and bank trust departments, or are sold to other investors through the ten dealers in this market. In the eleven years prior to the end of 1976, such commercial paper outstanding increased fivefold from $10.1 billion in January 1966 to $52.6 billion at the end of December 1976. At the end of 1981, commercial paper outstanding totaled $165.5 billion.

### Limited Number of Issuing Firms

The commercial paper market is a highly select one in which only the very largest firms with the highest credit rating are able to participate. Although commercial paper is unsecured in the sense of not being a claim on specific collateral, it is supported by unused lines of credit at commercial banks. Only about 90 finance companies and 345 of the nation's leading nonfinancial corporations can tap this market for short-term capital.

About 60 percent of commercial paper is placed directly by about seventy-five companies, and the remaining 40 percent is sold through dealers. In either case, the financial or nonfinancial company issuing the commercial paper is able to obtain short-term funds at a rate that is typically less than is being charged for bank credit. The seventy-five firms that place their commercial paper directly account for about 60 percent of the amount of commercial paper outstanding. These firms are likely to be large finance and bank holding companies. Bank holding companies did not enter this market until 1969 but have been quite active since then.

For investors commercial paper, because of its relatively low risk and short maturity, is a close substitute for other money market instruments such as Treasury bills and large-denomination **certificates of deposit (CDs)**. As a result, yields on commercial paper move closely with yields on these other money market instruments. Dealers holding inventories of commercial paper finance them either by overnight repurchase agreements (RPs) or by secured call loans from banks. In either case the financing costs are closely tied to the federal funds rate.

The average amounts of commercial paper placed by major dealers with a given investor varies from $1.5 million to $2.5 million, with the minimum amount usually $100,000. In bearer form, the notes are sold in even amounts of $5,000 or more, usually at a discount. Yields are usually quoted in eighths of 1 percent, but quotes increase in multiples of five basis points.

## Funds to Finance Consumer Hard Goods

Although the origins of this part of the money market date from the midnineteenth century, it was only in the 1920s and again in the 1970s and 1980s that the commercial paper market attained its present importance. The reason for the growth of this kind of financing is that most of the funds acquired in this manner ultimately provide the basis for the extension of credit to consumers. It is, therefore, the increased purchase of hard goods on credit by consumers that has resulted in the increased volume of this kind of short-term business credit. Sales finance companies, for instance, often buy consumer installment sales contracts from retail dealers who have sold cars, refrigerators, ranges, furniture, or similar hard goods to a consumer on time. About four fifths of all commercial paper is issued by such finance companies, including sales finance companies that specialize in financing purchases of such durable goods as automobiles, commercial finance companies that lend to small business firms for working capital, and consumer finance companies.

***Commercial Paper Dealers***　If the commercial paper is not placed directly, it will be marketed through a small number of commercial paper houses, which typically are associated with, or even constitute departments of, investment brokers. These commercial paper houses act as dealers by purchasing the paper outright from the issuer at the going market rate of discount, which was 15.49 percent for 3-month commercial paper in February 1981, and charging in addition a commission of ⅛ to ¼ percent of the face value of the paper. (The prime bank lending rate at that time averaged 19.43 percent.) The dealers then sell the paper not only to commercial banks but to nonfinancial corporations having a short-term surplus of funds generated from tax accruals, depreciation allowances, retained earnings, or even from funds borrowed in the capital markets for a new plant or equipment but not yet expended. The major nonfinancial industry investing in this market is the oil industry, which often holds from one third to two thirds of the corporate total.

*Commercial Paper Placed Directly*　By the 1980s, a number of the largest borrowers in the commercial paper market, consisting particularly of nine of the largest sales finance companies, had discovered that they could sell their notes directly to investors rather than using the services of the dealers. The amount of commercial and finance company paper placed through dealers rose sharply from $8.8 billion at the end of 1977 to $19.8 billion at the end of 1980. Directly placed commercial paper, however, totaled even more than dealer-placed paper and rose from the end of 1977 to the end of 1980 from $40.6 billion to $68 billion. Finance company borrowings are usually continuous throughout the year, whereas manufacturers in such industries as textiles, grain, flour, fertilizer, and seed have a pronounced seasonal swing in their borrowings, which continue to be handled through the dealer intermediaries.

***Advantages of Commercial Paper Financing***　The advantages of borrowing money through the issuance of commercial paper instead of through direct bank borrowing include (1) the lower discount rate attached to commercial paper, (2) the lack of a need to maintain a compensatory balance as is usually the case with a bank loan, which therefore raises the cost of the effective bank rate, (3) the ability to tap nonbank sources that have idle funds for short-term investment, and (4) the flexibility afforded to the borrower by being able to move in and out of the impersonal open market so that a sales finance company, for example, can retrench rather quickly in its borrowings in this manner if the demand for its services drops as a result of a sharp fall in consumer installment credit. One possible disadvantage of this type of borrowing is that because of its impersonal character there might be an inability to renew the debt contract if this seemed advisable. Also, the funds going into the commercial paper market are marginal funds, which could suddenly disappear if economic adversity hit the lenders.

*Investors Gain by Buying Commercial Paper*      The major advantage to investors of buying commercial paper is that the yield is typically somewhat higher than on other money market instruments. In mid-1981, for example, the yield on prime commercial paper was more than 1 percentage point above that on 91-day Treasury bills. This yield differential was higher than the typical ½ of 1 percentage point differential of the mid-1970s, because corporations rather than selling bond issues in early 1981 were often floating commercial paper issues in the market.

*One-Bank Holding Companies Now Issue Commercial Paper*      The advantage of one-bank holding companies issuing commercial paper, as they did importantly in the late 1970s and early 1980s, is that this is an attractive source of funds in a period of credit restraint. Credit restraint, not only in 1973–1974 but also in 1981–1982, led to substantial flotations of commercial paper by bank holding companies. The amount of such paper outstanding rose some two and a half times in four years, from $7 billion at the end of 1977 to $26.9 billion at the end of 1981. Access to such a source of borrowed funds was one of the important motives in establishing new one-bank holding companies in the 1970s and early 1980s.

## BANK CERTIFICATES OF DEPOSIT

In early 1961, the large New York City banks had become quite active in the money market through their issuance of a new marketable liability. This new money market asset was interest-bearing, negotiable certificates of deposit (**bank CDs**), which were issued to domestic business corporations. This was a change in banking practice, which represented a break in tradition of some thirty years standing.

Prior to the new time certificates, the New York City banks accepted time deposits, which paid interest to the holder, from foreign depositors, governmental authorities, as well as domestic religious, educational, and similar institutions, but not from domestic business firms. To the extent that corporations chose to sell another money market instrument, such as Treasury bills, and then build up their holdings of CDs, New York City banks could suffer a decline in corporate demand deposits but still enjoy an increase in corporate time deposits. The loss of reserves implied by the drop in demand deposits would be partially offset by the fact that time deposits require a lower percentage of legal reserves than do demand deposits.

## Competition with Other Money Market Assets

The New York City banks acted to pay interest on such marketable time certificates issued to domestic corporations originally in denominations of $1 million or more (later CDs were sold in $100,000 units or less) as a defensive measure designed to attract some of the short-term funds of those corporations away from direct investment in the money market. With increasingly higher yields in the money market over the postwar period, particularly in periods of Federal Reserve credit restraint, corporate treasurers had become increasingly desirous of keeping their cash balances at an absolute minimum and investing any funds above that amount in the money market. As a result of this search for some return on their temporarily idle funds, nonfinancial corporations have become important sources of financing of government securities dealers, a financing function that earlier had been the exclusive prerogative of commercial banks.

***Great Popularity of CDs*** The new negotiable time certificates of deposit proved to be popular almost immediately. In the first year of their issue, some $2 billion of them were bought by large business corporations. Throughout the 1960s (except for a decline in 1969) and the 1970s and well into the 1980s, these large CDs continued to grow in popularity. By the end of 1981, they totaled some $305.41 billion, which was up from $147.7 billion at the end of 1977. Small CDs (less than $100,000) also grew strongly in this period. From the end of 1977 to the end of 1981, they rose from $451.3 billion to $851.7 billion.

# Questions for Discussion

1. Define the term *money market* in both a broad and a narrow sense. Why is one definition used at some times and another at other times?
2. How would you differentiate between the money and capital markets? How are they interrelated?
3. What is the most important debt instrument in the money market today and why is it so important? What was the most important money market instrument in the 1920s and why has it declined in importance? What are repurchase agreements and how are they used in the money market?

4. How is the government securities market organized? Are the participants in this market dealers or brokers? How many direct market participants are there and what is their typical trading unit?

5. What are the regular Treasury bill issues and how often are they offered? Are they sold on a discount basis or with a coupon? Who buys these Treasury bills and why? Why has the total amount of Treasury bills outstanding increased in recent years?

6. Compare the profile of market performance of the Treasury bill market with that of the government bond market. How do you explain the differences?

7. Discuss the sources and techniques of financing the position of the government securities dealers. What factors must the dealers consider in deciding which alternative source of financing to use?

8. Discuss the development of the federal funds market by the 1980s. What is the economic function performed by this market and who are the major participants? Discuss the role of the large money market banks in this market.

9. Discuss the nature and characteristics of the Eurodollar market and its relationship with the New York money market. To what extent can credit restraint policies of the Federal Reserve in a period of inflation (e.g., 1981–1982) influence this international money market? What role might such a money market play in the remainder of the 1980s?

10. What are bankers' acceptances and how are they used? Under what conditions does the volume of bankers' acceptances outstanding tend to rise and why? What are the advantages of using this type of short-term credit instrument?

11. What is commercial paper and what kind of borrowers use this type of paper? What changes had occurred in the commercial paper market by the 1980s and why? What economic factors affect the volume of commercial paper outstanding?

12. Why do you believe New York City banks issued marketable certificates of deposit (CDs) for the first time in February 1961? Why have these large and small CDs been so popular? What effect has this growth in bank time deposits had on bank lending, if any? What may cause variations in the total amount of large CDs outstanding?

# Selected Bibliography for Further Reading

## *Books and Monographs*

BECKHART, BENJAMIN (ed.), *The New York Money Market*, four volumes (New York: Columbia University Press, 1932).

BOARD OF GOVERNORS OF THE FEDERAL RESERVE SYSTEM, *The Federal Funds Market* (Washington, D.C.: 1959).

CHASE MANHATTAN BANK, *Euro-Dollar Financing*, 2nd ed. (New York: Chase Manhattan Bank, Sept. 1968).

DOUGALL, HERBERT EDWARD, and JACK E. GAUMNITZ, *Capital Markets and Institutions*, 4th ed. (Englewood Cliffs, N.J.: Prentice-Hall, 1980).

FEDERAL RESERVE BANK OF NEW YORK, *Essays in Domestic and International Finance* (New York: 1969).

GREEF, ALBERT O., *The Commercial Paper House in the United States* (Cambridge, Mass.: Harvard University Press, 1938).

JOINT ECONOMIC COMMITTEE, Congress of the United States, *A Study of the Dealer Market for Federal Government Securities* (Washington, D.C.: U.S. Government Printing Office, 1960).

MADDEN, CARL, *The Money Side of "The Street"* (New York: Federal Reserve Bank of New York, Sept. 1959).

NADLER, MARCUS, SIPA HELLER, and SAMUEL SHIPMAN, *The Money Market and Its Institutions* (New York: Ronald Press, 1955).

NICHOLS, DOROTHY M., *Trading in Federal Funds: Finding of a Three-Year Survey* (Washington, D.C.: Board of Governors of the Federal Reserve System, 1965).

ROOSA, ROBERT V., *Federal Reserve Operations in the Money and Government Securities Markets* (New York: Federal Reserve Bank of New York, July 1956).

TREASURY DEPARTMENT AND THE FEDERAL RESERVE SYSTEM, *Treasury–Federal Reserve Study of the Government Securities Market*, three parts (Washington, D.C.: 1960).

———, *Report of the Joint Treasury–Federal Reserve Study of the U.S. Government Securities Market* (Washington, D.C.: U.S. Government Printing Office, 1969).

# *Articles*

BOARD OF GOVERNORS OF THE FEDERAL RESERVE SYSTEM, "Interest Rates, Credit Flows, and Monetary Aggregates Since 1964," *Federal Reserve Bulletin*, June 1971, pp. 425–440.

———, "Developments in International Financial Markets," *Federal Reserve Bulletin*, Oct. 1975, pp. 605–617.

FRYDL, EDWARD J., "The Debate over Regulating the Eurocurrency Markets," *Quarterly Review*, Federal Reserve Bank of New York, Vol. 4, No. 4, Winter 1979–1980, pp. 11–20.

HELFRICH, RALPH T., "Trading in Bankers' Acceptances: A View from the Acceptance Desk of the Federal Reserve Bank of New York," *Monthly Review*, Federal Reserve Bank of New York, Vol. 58, No. 2, Feb. 1976, pp. 51–57.

HERVEY, JACK L., "Bankers' Acceptances," *Business Conditions*, Federal Reserve Bank of Chicago, May 1976, pp. 3–11.

HURLEY, EVELYN M., "The Commercial Paper Market," *Federal Reserve Bulletin*, June 1977, pp. 525–536.

LUCAS, CHARLES M., MARCOS T. JONES, and THOM B. THURSTON, "Federal Funds and Repurchase Agreements," *Quarterly Review*, Vol. 2, Summer 1977 (New York: Federal Reserve Bank of New York), pp. 33–48.

Melton, William C., and Jean M. Mahr, "Bankers' Acceptances," *Quarterly Review*, Vol. 6, No. 2, Summer 1981 (New York: Federal Reserve Bank of New York), pp. 39–55.

## Government Periodical Publications

Annual Reports of the Board of Governors of the Federal Reserve System.
Annual Reports of the Federal Reserve Bank of New York.
Board of Governors of the Federal Reserve System, *Federal Reserve Bulletin* (monthly).
Monthly and Quarterly Reviews of the Twelve Federal Reserve Banks. (The articles in each *Quarterly Review* of the Federal Reserve Bank of New York are particularly valuable.)
United States Treasury Department, *Treasury Bulletin* (monthly).

## Newspapers

*The Wall Street Journal*
*The New York Times*
Each Monday these newspapers, and some others as well, carry an article and statistical tables relating to factors affecting the money market in the previous reserve week (Thursday to Wednesday).

Yet, partly, by discounting real bills of exchange, and partly by lending upon cash accounts, banks and bankers might still be able to relieve the greater part of those dealers from the necessity of keeping any considerable part of their stock by them, unemployed and in ready money, for answering occasional demands.

THE WEALTH OF NATIONS

# CHAPTER

# Commercial Banks and the Money Market

Although the money market has a number of important participants, **commercial banks** play a particularly significant role, which should be carefully examined. Furthermore, it is largely through its varying impact upon commercial bank reserve positions that the Federal Reserve is able to affect the cost and availability of funds in the money and capital markets and thus to influence aggregate economic activity. The relationships of commercial banks to this short-term debt market are therefore of special significance.

Because banks are now concerned with both asset and liability management, they may approach the impersonal money market for either of these purposes, particularly if they are large banks. Liability management for large commercial banks requires interaction with the money market, because an important tool of such liability management is, as has been noted, the issuance of large certificates of deposit in denominations of $100,000 or more. These CDs, in turn, are an important money market asset.

If these commercial banks wish more funds, say, to expand their business lending, then they can "buy" such funds by offering a higher interest rate on such marketable deposits. Smaller commercial banks may also wish to be more aggressive in attracting additional deposits in periods of rising loan demand. However, the smaller banks are usually restricted to offering "consumer-type" certificates of deposit in much smaller dollar amounts than are traded in the money market.

Nearly all commercial banks, however, no matter what their size, interact with the money market either directly or indirectly in their asset management. Because we will deal with the principles of liability management in Chapter 12, our main emphasis in this chapter will be on asset management of banks in relationship to the money market. In this context, banks may approach the money market when their reserve positions require some adjustment. A commercial bank with temporary excess reserves may wish to find temporary employment for them in the money market, whereas a bank with a temporary deficiency of reserves may wish to sell some of its Treasury bills in the money market, or perhaps buy federal funds. Furthermore, because the center of the money market is New York City, it is the large commercial banks, either located in New York City or having correspondent relationships with New York City banks, that are likely to place initial pressure or ease on the money market through their reserve adjusting operations. The eight New York City money market banks and the other reporting banks (134 in all) are the banks that resort most to the money market. These large banks are defined as those having had assets of $1 billion or more as of December 31, 1977.

These banks are also likely to find their reserve positions affected first by any change in money market conditions arising from nonbank sources. Because of the critical importance of the participation of these large commercial banks in the money market, we pay particular attention to the character of their operations. These 134 reporting banks account for about 90 percent of the gross purchases and sales of federal funds. Even nonmoney market banks, though, have some connection with the money market through their correspondent relationships. In short, the whole commercial banking system, by putting in or taking out excess funds from the money market, affects the market level of short-term interest rates and availability of short-term credit. In turn, the entire banking system is affected by pressures or ease in the money market by reason of the impact of such changes on the liquidity of the banking system.

## DIRECT PARTICIPATION BY BANKS IN THE MARKET

Banks participate directly in the money market not only because of **liability management**, but also because in addition to having primary reserves in the form of cash in the till, deposits in the Federal Reserve

Banks, and deposits in other commercial banks, they also must have secondary reserves. Secondary reserves are highly liquid assets that can be quickly turned into cash with very little risk of loss. In short, secondary bank reserves consist of those debt instruments that are the stock in trade of the money market, such as Treasury bills, bankers' acceptances, and commercial paper. The existence of an active money market gives such marketability, and hence liquidity, to these assets. If it were not for the money market, these assets would be much more difficult to turn into cash quickly. The large money market banks also contribute to the money market by their creation of bank CDs, which in large denominations are traded in the money market, as noted in the previous chapter.

## The Money Market As a Source of Bank Funds

Any of the money market assets held by commercial banks may be liquidated whenever additional funds are needed by banks to offset deposit declines or a rise in loan demand. The sale of such secondary reserve assets by the banks means that the money market is being tapped as a source of needed bank funds. There are other ways, however, in which banks can tap the money market.

*Interbank Borrowing of Reserves*   Interbank borrowing of reserves in the federal funds market has soared in the last two decades as the practice of bank liability management has spread. This is indicated by the ratio of gross purchases of federal funds to required reserves, which rose sharply from less than 20 percent in 1962 for large banks to well over 200 percent by 1982. Even small banks increased substantially their participation rate in the **federal funds market** by the 1980s, although they were still more likely to be sellers than buyers. The availability of this market for borrowing and lending excess reserves has made for greater efficiency in the use of reserves and higher bank profits for both borrowing and lending banks. This has also made possible lower interest rates for bank borrowers than would otherwise have been the case.

*Bank CDs*   The changed attitude on the part of banks in the early 1960s, which led to the sharp increase in lending and borrowing of excess bank reserves, had been expressed in the issuance of the large-denomination ($100,000 or more) CDs in early 1961. Instead of passively waiting for the public to put deposits in banks, large banks in particular decided to "buy" deposits (and subsequently reserves) in order to secure the bank funds needed to support lending and investing activities. By early 1982, large-denomination time deposits of banks had soared to $308 billion from $145.2 billion at the end of 1977. Small-denomination time deposits in the same period also rose sharply, from $454.9 billion to $851.6 billion.

Although such time deposits have become increasingly important to commercial banks, they are costlier than the more traditional passbook accounts or interest-free checking accounts (until December 31, 1980), and they are also more volatile. Depositors in recent decades have become more and more sensitive to interest rate differentials. When money market rates are higher than rates paid by commercial banks on small time deposits still regulated by the interest-rate ceilings of Regulation Q of the Federal Reserve Board, then deposits are often withdrawn from banks and reinvested in the money market.

*Bank Commercial Paper*   Because of the loss of deposits occurring with the fall in the level of CDs in periods of credit restraint, such as 1966, 1969, 1973–1974, and 1981–1982, commercial banks developed other methods of raising funds in the money market by the late 1960s. One new device of some importance by the 1980s was the issuance of commercial paper through a corporation affiliated with the bank. Banks used their newly created one-bank holding companies commonly as the issuing agent for this commercial paper, though direct subsidiaries of the bank or other affiiliates of the bank were also used. The bank guaranteed the commercial paper in order to assure its ready marketability through a commercial paper dealer. This source of bank funds was not subject to interest rate ceilings, as applied by Regulation Q, or reserve requirements, as applied by Regulation D. By 1982, $35 billion of such bank commercial paper was outstanding, which was up sharply from the $7.1 billion outstanding at the end of 1977.

**Sale of Participations**   Banks have also raised funds in the financial markets by selling participations in individual loans or pools of loans. When this is done, the bank usually agrees to repurchase the participation at a specified date or on demand. The loans thus sold continue to be serviced by the bank, so that the borrower may not be aware of the transaction. Although loan participations have long been a feature of correspondent relationships, by the 1980s some such loan participations were being sold to nonbank customers. This permitted banks to bid for funds with competitive interest rates and maturities, which would not otherwise have been possible for them.

**Borrowing As a Source of Bank Funds**   By the 1980s commercial banks have come to rely on borrowing as a major source of bank funds. In early 1981, for example, bank borrowings (federal funds purchased and securities sold under agreements to repurchase) were nearly $53 billion, which was about one-third of the total of $166 billion in cash held by banks, including items in the process of collection. Such borrowings were also nearly equal to the $54.6 billion held in interbank demand deposits and were nearly half of the total holdings of U. S. government securities of $113.7 billion.

The large city banks relied even more on borrowings as a source of funds than did the smaller banks. New York City banks in early 1981 had borrowed $40.8 billion, as compared with their cash assets holdings of $41.5 billion and $11.3 billion held in the form of U. S. government securities. At the same time, other large member banks borrowed $50 billion, as compared with their cash asset holdings of $49.7 billion and $16.2 billion in U. S. government securities.

Such bank borrowing had increased dramatically since the mid-1970s. In early 1976, all bank borrowings totaled $66.8 billion, which more than doubled five years later to $163 billion. The same phenomenal growth was recorded for each size and location of commercial banks.

## Employment of Excess Reserves

Commercial banks, wherever they are located in the United States, can put temporary surplus funds, such as excess reserves, to work in the money market. The interest return will not be as great as that on business loans, for instance, but the funds are more secure and can be readily recalled when needed. Furthermore, to earn even a small interest return is better than none at all. Of course, in periods of rising interest rates, such as often happens in periods of great economic prosperity, the opportunity cost of holding idle funds becomes even greater, so that the money market tends to activate idle pools of cash all over the country. Country banks, which often hold some excess reserves, now find it more profitable to lend these excess reserves through the mechanism of the federal funds market to large city banks.

When city banks have a deficiency of legal reserves as a result of substantial borrowing pressures on them, these large city banks will often even telephone their country correspondent banks to tap their excess funds. If interest rates were not high, it might not be worth the trouble to activate the numerous small pools of excess reserves in the country banks; but when loan demand and interest rates are rising, it becomes profitable to do so. If loan demand subsequently increases at the country bank, then, of course, the amount of idle excess reserves available for borrowing by the city banks declines.

***Financing of Other Money Market Participants***    Commercial banks also affect the money market through their financing of other participants in the money market. Banks will make direct loans to dealers, brokers, and their customers to help finance money market transactions. Of the $8 billion of loans for purchasing or carrying securities to brokers and dealers by large weekly reporting banks at the end of February 1982, 33 percent, or $2.7 billion, was made by New York City banks alone. Of the $50.2 billion of loans to financial institutions on that date, $15.6 billion, or 31 percent, was made by New York City banks.

Not only the size of the New York City banks but the centering of so much of the national money and capital markets in the city helps account for the importance of this type of financial lending for New York City banks. In interbank demand deposits, also, New York City banks loom large as they hold one fifth of the total held by the entire commercial banking system. With the funds generated by these interbank deposits, New York City banks are able to increase their participation in the money market. Of course, seasonal withdrawal of some of these deposits puts particular pressure on the New York City banks and causes them at such times to liquidate some of their money market holdings.

## LIQUIDITY OF COMMERCIAL BANKS

Bank reserves, either owned or available through borrowing from a particular bank, affect other aspects of its participation in the money market and also make up part of the needed liquidity of a bank. **Liquidity** of an asset can be defined as the ease with which the asset can be converted into cash. The various forms of cash, including bank reserves, are, of course, the most liquid of all assets. Some liquidity needs of a bank are prescribed by law, whereas others are determined by custom or management decisions of the particular bank. The amount of required reserves for an individual bank depends on both the legal reserve ratio imposed by various regulatory authorities, such as the Federal Reserve Board, and the amount of bank deposits in the bank.

### *Bank Needs for Liquidity*

In addition to these legally established liquidity ratios, banks need to have liquidity reserves for their own business purposes. **Bank liquidity** needs relate to (1) possible deposit fluctuations, and (2) possible loan demands. The higher the amount of liquid assets held by a commercial bank, the greater its feeling of safety in being able to meet either an unexpected deposit withdrawal or an unexpected loan demand. On the other hand, the greater the amount of safety purchased by the bank by having larger amounts of cash or other highly liquid reserves, the lower will be the level of possible bank profits.

Each bank is always faced with this choice between maximum safety through a high level of liquidity or maximum profits with a low level of liquidity. Because the state of confidence varies from one stage of the business cycle to another, one would expect to find different ratios of bank liquidity at different times. Furthermore, city banks in recent years seem to have placed more emphasis on maximizing profits than earlier, so that most of them now seem to strive toward zero excess legal reserves. This does not mean that they give no consideration to liquidity, because liquidity can be met in different ways.

By the 1980s, most commercial banks seemed to have developed considerable confidence in the stability of the American monetary and economic system. This greater confidence meant that most banks were willing to reduce their liquidity position in their liability management operations (i.e., borrowing of deposits or reserves) to enhance the profitability of their operations. As in earlier years, however, the larger city banks were the most aggressive in this regard. Some of these banks increased their loans and reduced their portfolio of government securities so far that they pushed their loan-deposit ratios to 80 percent or even more. Such a high ratio would have been unthinkable for most bankers even a decade earlier.

***Sources of Bank Liquidity***    Banks are able to meet their liquidity needs through their holdings of vault cash and deposits in other banks, including Federal Reserve Banks, and also through their holdings of money market instruments such as Treasury bills, the maturity composition of their loan and investment portfolio, and repayment, amortization, or serial repayments on loans and investments. In addition to the amount and character of cash and near-cash assets, the ability of commercial banks to borrow deposits in the money market by issuing CDs or by borrowing reserves from other commercial banks or from the regional Federal Reserve Banks greatly increases the potential liquidity of those banks having access to such borrowed cash reserves. The sources of bank liquidity, as well as the needs for bank liquidity, are summarized in Table 7–1.

If a bank knows that it can easily borrow reserves if a reserve deficiency develops, it is more likely to be willing to aim for zero excess reserves as a profit-maximizing goal, even though it knows that at times reserves may drop below the anticipated level owing to unexpected loan demands or unexpected cash drains. Because of this reserve borrowing potential, many large city banks seem to have been content in recent years to see their loan-deposit ratios rise to very high levels. Furthermore, these same banks have been willing to extend the average maturity of their loan portfolio as indicated by their increased eagerness to extend increasing amounts of term loans to large business firms desiring this kind of credit accommodation.

**Table 7-1    Sources and Needs for Bank Liquidity**

| *Sources of Liquidity* | *Needs for Liquidity* |
|---|---|
| Primary Reserves<br>  1.  Cash in bank vaults<br>  2.  Deposits in Federal Reserve Bank<br>  3.  Deposits in correspondent banks<br>Secondary reserves<br>  4.  Holdings of Treasury bills and other<br>      money market assets<br>Loan portfolio<br>  5.  Repayment of loans<br>Borrowings<br>  6.  Issuance of certificates of deposit<br>  7.  Purchase of federal funds<br>  8.  Borrowing from Federal Reserve<br>      Bank<br>  9.  Borrowing from correspondent bank | 1.  Legal reserve ratios required behind<br>     deposits<br>2.  Possible fluctuations in deposits<br>3.  Future loan demands<br>4.  Cash needs of customers |

*The Loan Portfolio and Liquidity*    The greatest source of liquidity, however, to meet new loan requests at banks comes from the loan portfolio itself. As loans mature and are repaid, cash is made available to the loan officers for the purpose of extending new credit. The entire loan need not be repaid at one time, because many large-term loans provide for serial repayment over a period of time. The cash flow thus provides much liquidity, as well as the stock of money and near-money held by the bank. One might also argue that the quality of the loan portfolio also provides liquidity for the bank, as well as the composition of the varying maturities of loans outstanding.

A rise in the loan deposit ratio, even when it is accompanied by an increase in the proportion of the loan portfolio occupied by term loans, does not necessarily indicate a serious weakening in the liquidity position of the bank or group of banks in this situation. The low credit risk of the borrowers receiving such loans may compensate at least in part for any reduction in the liquidity ratio to be attributed to a higher percentage of risk assets in the total assets of the bank. As long as loan defaults are low and outstanding credit is repaid on time, a particular bank may well conclude that the desired level of its liquidity is being adequately maintained.

## Deposit Variability and Bank Liquidity

The desired level of bank liquidity is also affected, as has been suggested by the deposit variation of an individual bank. This deposit variation is one of the main causes, outside of legal reserve requirements, that forces the bank to maintain certain liquid cash and near-cash asset reserves. These deposit variations arise from (1) variations in loan demands related to cyclical changes in business activity, (2) seasonal variations in the demand for bank credit, (3) seasonal variations in currency in circulation (i.e., whenever currency in circulation rises, bank deposits and bank reserves tend to fall and vice versa), (4) different rates of population and economic activity growth in different parts of the country, (5) competitive shifts in which some banks grow faster than other banks in the area, and (6) changes caused by shifts in the relative prosperity of different groups of depositors.

Commercial banks, as both a legal and practical matter, need more liquidity behind demand deposits than behind time deposits. The relative rate of growth of demand versus time deposits thus affects the liquidity needs of banks. The volatility of bank demand deposits is generally greater than that of time deposits, which means that banks must be prepared for a more rapid turnover of their demand deposits than they reasonably expect from their time deposits.

Foreign depositors, large corporations, or governmental units holding time deposits, however, may suddenly withdraw substantial amounts of these deposits, particularly if money market rates begin to move upward sharply. When these kinds of depositors are importantly represented among the time deposits of a particular commercial bank, the bank is only prudent to have a somewhat higher protection of liquidity than might otherwise appear to be necessary. Even when time deposits have specific maturities, as is the case for large CDs, a bunching of large amounts of these CDs around particular dates may cause concern to bank managements if the holders of these deposits demand cash instead of renewing them on the maturity date.

## Variability in Loan Demands and Bank Liquidity

Variability in potential loan demand is also an important basic determinant affecting the amount of liquidity that any bank feels it needs. In part, as already indicated, variations in loan demands may move with variations in bank deposits. If both loan demands and deposits are increasing or declining at the same rate, provision for a change in the level of anticipated deposits also, in effect, takes care of some of the likely change in loan demand. If, however, these two variables do not move in the same direction at the same rate, certain special liquidity problems relating to loan demand alone arise. Seasonal variations in anticipated loan demand are particularly important in connection with the provision of anticipated liquid assets, which can be liquidated at the times when the bank will need increased loanable funds.

*Sources of Loanable Funds*   Although alternative methods of securing loanable funds, such as buying federal funds or borrowing from the regional Reserve Bank, may be feasible on occasion, they may not be considered desirable to meet most anticipated seasonal loan demands. For example, prior to April 1973 the Federal Reserve System frowned on regular seasonal borrowing by member banks for the purpose of meeting customer loan demands when these loans might reasonably be anticipated by banks from their past experience. Even after the initiation of the seasonal borrowing privilege in April 1973, the amount of such borrowing averaged less than $200 million in each subsequent month of 1973 and was less than $150 million in early 1982. This was largely true because this new privilege was specifically designed for small member banks who do not usually borrow as much and as often as some of the larger member banks. Therefore a small commercial bank ordinarily can still be expected to acquire money market assets and cash in anticipation of higher loan demand.

*Added Bank Reserves Needed for Economic Growth*   The cyclical or secular problem of bank liquidity is not so easily solved, however, as the seasonal problem for the individual commercial bank. For the longer period of time that is involved in either cyclical or secular time periods, it must be the responsibility of the Federal Reserve System, and to some extent the Treasury, to provide an adequate amount of liquidity for the entire commercial banking system. As the level of economic activity arises, so too can the level of business and individual demand for bank credit be expected to increase.

In satisfying this increased demand for bank credit, however, growing numbers of commercial banks, and eventually the entire commercial banking system, find that liquidity is being progressively impaired as loan-deposit ratios continue to rise. This may be accepted by many banks if they believe that their prospective profits outweigh the greater risk of a reduction in bank liquidity. Asset management by banks may also lead to a relative decline in liquidity, if it is believed that the quality of the assets being acquired justifies some apparent decline in liquidity.

*Liability Management by Banks*   In addition to asset management, which has been a traditional concern for commercial bankers, the credit restraint periods of 1966, 1969, 1973–1974, and 1981–1982 brought a greater emphasis on liability management. This means that the sources and availability of bank funds become of vital concern to commercial banks. We have already noted the great expansion of bank borrowing since the mid-1960s. In a later chapter it is also pointed out that one of the prime motives for establishing a one-bank holding company is to be able to raise more funds for the bank through selling commercial paper. The resort to the Eurodollar market, particularly in 1966 and 1969, was widespread by many of the larger banks, even though interest rates there were considerably higher than those in the New York money market.

In 1981–1982, although the Federal Reserve permitted and encouraged interest rates to rise, it did not force the disintermediation on the banks that it had in 1969. The banks were still able to get time deposit funds by issuing large CDs, providing they were willing to pay the high competitive interest rates. The alternative cost and availability of borrowed funds thus made liability management of central importance to banks, expecially in credit restraint periods. Should the bank borrow federal funds, borrow at the discount window, issue more CDs, or what? The cost and availability of funds from each of these sources thus had to be carefully evaluated.

*Added Reserves Can Also Increase Secondary Reserves of Banks*
Commercial banks in meeting their liquidity requirements also place a heavy dependence on the accumulation of secondary reserves, by which we mean mainly money market assets such as Treasury bills. The profit-oriented bank will seek to have only the minimum required amounts of cash on hand, due from banks, and deposits in its reserve account.

In fact, when cash reserves are increased as a result of credit easing activities of the Federal Reserve, the ordinary response of such a bank is to try to employ the added cash immediately in some earning asset. Even a small interest return, such as is received on most money market instruments, is better than no return at all. In short, idle cash is costly in that it could conceivably be earning an interest return. Furthermore, certain liquidity requirements of the bank may be served just as well by an adequate amount of short-term, highly liquid assets as by having the same amount in idle cash.

## MANAGING THE MONEY POSITION OF A BANK

The entry of a commercial bank into the money market comes in connection with the management of its money position, which means management of the liquid assets of the bank to avoid either excesses or deficiencies of required reserves on an average daily basis for the reserve period. In 1982, the Federal Reserve proposed lengthening this reserve period to two weeks. This took effect on February 2, 1984.

The money desk managers, who manage the cash reserve position in large commercial banks, must thus keep close track of the factors that determine reserve requirements, mainly a change in both demand and time deposits. Often for large city banks at least, future required reserves are projected for several weeks ahead with daily or even hourly revisions of the projections. The money desk must also make certain that the bank has an adequate amount of highly liquid assets, such as Treasury bills, that can be liquidated if needed to add to the supply of loanable funds, or to restore the legal reserve position of the bank.

## Reserve Adjustments and the Bill Market

Banks are likely to be most eager to invest in Treasury bills during a period of credit easing by the Federal Reserve System in an economic recession, when the system is supplying bank reserves in greater abundance. The problem for commercial banks then becomes what to do with these added reserves. To let them lie idle in large amounts (as was true in the 1930s) seems the height of folly in the 1980s. When interest rates even on short-term investments reach the high levels of the early 1980s, the opportunity cost of idle cash reserves becomes considerable. Because these added reserves may not be available indefinitely, and because the number of eligible would-be borrowers invariably drops sharply during such a recession period, the problem becomes one of considering alternative forms of short-term investment.

## Federal Funds Versus Treasury Bills

Projection of future cash flows and expected levels of demand and time deposits help determine the type of investment alternative for employing available excess reserves. The most serious short-term investment alternatives appear to be to sell federal funds or to buy various types of short- and intermediate-term government securities or tax anticipation notes of local governments.

Simplifying the choices, we might narrow the alternatives to selling federal funds versus buying Treasury bills. Which of the two alternatives seems the more tempting at the moment depends importantly on the differential between the market yield on bills and the effective rate on federal funds transactions. The federal funds rate is the interest rate charged by banks with excess reserves when they lend these reserves to banks with a deficiency of reserves.

The rate on these transactions, which are regularly sold for one day except for holidays or weekends, is determined by the supply of excess reserves in the banking system and the demand for such funds. When the differential of the Treasury bill rate over this federal funds rate widens, bank demand for Treasury bills ordinarily increases. When this differential narrows, bank demand for Treasury bills ordinarily falls.

***Temporary Excess Bank Reserves*** In some instances, when there is an increase in the loanable funds of a bank caused by a deposit that is not expected to remain very long with the bank, the manager of the money desk of the bank will almost automatically invest the temporary funds in the federal funds market. Such might be the case with a large corporate deposit made by the corporation in preparation for the payment of dividends in a few days. However, if the new deposit is expected to remain for more than a few days, we would expect a careful considera-tion of the respective advantages of Treasury bills versus federal funds. In every case, we would expect the bank to consider its present and expected primary reserve position before deciding what if anything should be done toward adding or reducing secondary reserves (e.g., Treasury bills).

*Temporary Reserve Deficiency* A present or prospective reserve deficiency faces the money desk manager with the same set of alterna-tives as does the presence of excess reserves. If the bank faces a reserve deficit, should it purchase federal funds or sell Treasury bills? If the deficit is expected to be of only short duration, it appears probable that the decision will be made to buy federal funds, whereas a more per-manent reserve deficit will more likely involve a present or future reduction in the bank's holdings of Treasury bills, either through sale in the open market or runoff at maturity. The short-term decision to buy federal funds or sell Treasury bills in the face of a reserve deficiency is also presumably affected by the interest rate differential between these two short-term investments, as was the opposite decision to sell federal funds or buy Treasury bills when excess reserves increased. The bank may also carry a reserve deficiency or reserve surplus of 2 percent into the next reserve period or borrow reserves from its regional Reserve Bank.

## ADJUSTING THE BANK'S RESERVE POSITION

A rather careful adjustment in reserve position is called for when, as is usually the case for large city banks, the money desk manager seeks to keep a fully invested asset position without involving reserve deficits. If a deposit inflow supplies funds expected to be retained by the bank for a considerable period of time, such as several months, then it is to be expected that such short-term funds would enter a longer part of the money market than the federal funds market. Such funds would probably be invested in Treasury bills or possibly commercial paper or bankers' acceptances. Likewise, a persistent deposit drain is ordinarily met by selling such securities from the investment portfolio of the bank. But when it seems likely that the increase or decrease in funds arising from changed levels of bank deposits is temporary, one might then expect the large bank to buy or sell federal funds.

## 134 Large Banks Regularly Buy and Sell Federal Funds

As has already been noted, the federal funds market is dominated by a small number of large **money market banks**. Out of the 14,700 commercial banks in the United States, only about 134 large weekly reporting banks carry on about 90 percent of federal funds purchases and sales, whereas fewer than 50 banks account for about three fourths of all transactions. Fewer than 10 banks account for more than half of all purchases. Only about 40 banks have total daily average transactions of $10 million or more.

In periods of credit restraint, however, such as 1966, 1969, 1973–1974, and 1981–1982, both the number of banks participating in the market (including smaller banks) and the total volume of transactions greatly increase. By the 1980s, the size and scope of commercial bank participation in this part of the money market had increased considerably. For example, during the last week of April 1981, about $50 billion of net federal funds transactions involving large commercial banks occurred. This was nearly triple the amount of such transactions in late August 1974, which was also a severe credit restraint year. The monetary authorities are greatly interested in such developments in the federal funds market, because transactions and interest rates in this very short end of the money market reflect the degree of pressure or ease of the prevailing monetary policy on the commercial banking system.

*Bank Selling of Federal Funds*    When a bank that ordinarily participates in the federal funds market has a temporary reserve surplus of, say, $10 million, it can be expected to sell these surplus reserves immediately. The average reserve requirements for member banks are calculated on the basis of the five-day reserve week, and normally the money market banks wish to employ profitably all their cash reserves. These large banks still aim for zero excess reserves, even though the Federal Reserve now permits them to carry both excess and deficient reserves into the next reserve week.

*The Mechanics of Dealing in Federal Funds*    When a selling (lending) transaction is desired, the mechanics of the market normally require only several phone calls plus confirming letters. Usually the decision to sell surplus reserves is made by the money desk manager by 11 A.M. based on the data of actual reserve requirements at the previous day's close, plus the effect of the morning's clearing on reserves, plus adjustments needed in correspondent bank balances. Estimates are also made of expected deposit movements for the day, which would involve direct transfer of funds to or from other banks. Past records showing usual seasonal patterns plus possible advance notice of large deposits or withdrawals from customers help in making these daily projections each morning.

Once the final decision to sell federal funds is made, the usual procedure is to call nearby banks that often buy such funds, as well as to take account of requests for such borrowed funds from correspondent banks. Any residual amount not already sold in these ways can be readily disposed of through the federal funds brokerage facilities provided by several brokers, such as Garvin Guy Butler, and Mabon Nugent and Company in New York City. Once an agreement to sell federal funds with a bank wishing to buy federal funds has been reached over the telephone, another phone call is made to the regional Reserve Bank so that it can immediately transfer funds from the selling to the buying bank. A confirming letter then is mailed to provide a written record of the transaction. If the two banks buying and selling federal funds are in the same city, it is customary for the buying bank to give the selling bank a check on itself, which is cleared through the clearinghouse so that repayment of the federal funds transaction is automatically made the next day. Of course, if the two banks are in different Federal Reserve districts, the wire transfer facilities of the Federal Reserve are used, so that the reserve account of the borrowing bank is immediately credited the same day, whereas a reverse flow of funds occurs the following day.

*Making a Market in Federal Funds*    Some commercial banks make regular markets in federal funds (i.e., they stand ready to buy or sell reasonable amounts of federal funds at any time). At times, in order to accommodate federal funds needs of correspondent banks, for example, such a bank may have to sell federal funds, even though the bank has no excess funds of its own. In this case the trading bank has to secure federal funds from another participant in the market or else run a temporary reserve deficiency in its own reserve account. Other banks over a period of several months may be either predominantly buyers or predominantly sellers of federal funds. If for some reason a bank wishing to buy federal funds is unable to secure all the borrowed reserves needed, it may, if it is a member bank, borrow from its regional Reserve Bank. In a few cases, banks needing added reserves typically borrow from their Reserve Bank and enter the federal funds market only if they have surplus reserves.

*Bank Buying of Federal Funds*    In still other cases banks strongly prefer to buy federal funds rather than borrow from their Reserve Bank because (1) these funds may sometimes be secured at a rate lower than the discount rate, although in periods of credit restraint, such as 1966, 1969, 1973–1974, and 1981–1982, the federal funds rate is often appreciably above the discount rate, (2) it may appear to banks with reserve deficiencies that buying federal funds is simpler than borrowing from the Federal Reserve, particularly because the Reserve Banks discourage continuous borrowing by banks, and (3) fairly frequent buying and selling of federal funds may give the trading bank a better feel of the money market, as well as improve its relationship with other banks including correspondents.

*Federal Funds Market Increases Use of Bank Reserves*    Although for the individual bank the buying of federal funds is an alternative manner of securing needed reserves as compared with the possibility of borrowing from its Reserve Bank, that activity in the federal funds market, unlike borrowing from the system, does not increase total member bank reserves. Thus, federal funds transactions, which may reach an average daily level around $50 billion or more over a considerable period of time, simply permit a more intensive use of existing reserves. With higher interest rates prevailing, idle bank reserves become more costly to the holding bank in respect to foregone interest return than was true at a lower level of interest rates.

Because reserve requirements for city banks are based on deposits at the opening of business but are met by reserves held at the end of the day, it is possible for considerable activity to take place in the federal funds market in the afternoon as banks seek to adjust their reserve position. And at the end of the reserve period on a Wednesday, the federal funds rate can also be quite volatile as bank activity in this market tends to increase.

## TRADING IN THE TREASURY BILL MARKET

In addition to adjusting their reserve position by buying or selling federal funds, commercial banks also buy and sell Treasury bills for this purpose. As already indicated, banks normally hold some Treasury bills in their secondary reserves to offset unexpected cash drains and to be able to meet substantial increases in the demand for bank credit from business firms particularly. In addition to these more or less normal holdings of Treasury bills, a bank might find it expedient to buy more Treasury bills if it has a cash inflow expected to be retained for some weeks or even months.

## High Liquidity of Treasury Bills

Regular Treasury bills, because they are issued with original maturities of less than one month, three months, six months, or one year, are subject to very little market risk. They are nearly cash inasmuch as they do become cash at the expiration of their short maturity period. Moreover, they are better in one sense than cash because they earn an interest return, though there is always some possibility of market loss. Furthermore, because a broad and active market in Treasury bills exists, the bank is always certain that it can sell any part of its Treasury bill holdings at any time with very little possible capital loss arising from market fluctuations in the price of Treasury bills.

***Treasury Bills and Bank Reserve Positions*** The extent to which commercial banks use the treasury bill market to adjust their reserve positions depends importantly on the relationship of the Treasury bill rate to the federal funds rate and to the discount rate of the Federal Reserve System, as has been suggested. As one would expect, the banks tend to use the least-cost or highest-return alternative. For example, if the Treasury bill rate is above the discount rate, many banks will prefer to borrow from their regional Reserve Bank when they have a reserve deficiency, rather than sell Treasury bills. Contrariwise, if the Treasury bill rate and the federal funds rate are below the discount rate, most banks will prefer to buy federal funds or sell Treasury bills rather than borrow from their regional Reserve Bank.

## SPECIAL RESERVE REQUIREMENTS

Although banks tend to try to keep the amount of their idle cash at a minimum, some banks simply need to have more cash on hand than other banks. The distance of a bank from the source of its cash—its regional Reserve Bank or a city correspondent bank—is a main determinant of the average level of cash needed by the bank. Not surprisingly, smaller banks as a group typically carry a higher percentage of their assets in the form of vault cash than do larger banks.

Seasonal requirements for cash holdings of banks are also a factor in determining the amount of cash held by a bank at a specific time. When the public is demanding more cash, as before holidays, the bank must build up its inventory of cash to satisfy this customer need. After the holiday period is over, a heavy return flow of cash into banks takes place until the abundancy of cash received by the commercial banking system is deposited ultimately in the regional Reserve Banks. No bank is entirely happy with having superfluous cash in its vault, even though such cash is counted as legal reserves, because of the problem of guarding against possible bank robbers.

## Correspondent Balances

**Correspondent balances** also are a form of primary reserves, or cash, of commercial banks. A city correspondent requires its country correspondent to maintain a balance sufficient to cover the cost of services furnished to the country correspondent. Despite these services, however, it is always in the interest of the country bank to keep its city correspondent balances as low as possible. These correspondent balances sometimes get so low in relation to the cost of the services being performed that the city bank finds it necessary to encourage the country bank to maintain a balance somewhat larger than it has been running. If the account continues to be unprofitable, the city correspondent may even terminate the relationship, though such extreme action is unlikely. Correspondent accounts normally yield a comfortable profit for the city bank. Indeed, the likelihood of profit from such accounts leads most large city banks to seek out actively correspondent deposit business.

## Deposits in a Federal Reserve Bank

Deposits in the regional Reserve Bank are the third kind of cash, or **primary reserves**, for member banks, although they are now nearly perfect substitutes for vault cash, because vault cash or deposits in Reserve Banks are each considered legal reserves for member banks in the Reserve System. The bulk of legal reserves of member banks continues to be held in the Reserve Banks, however, because of the greater protection of keeping surplus cash in such a safe place, as well as legal requirements that make it necessary for the member banks to keep part of their legal reserves in their regional Reserve Bank. The process of check clearance through the Federal Reserve normally adds to member bank reserves, as well as the depositing of excess cash by the member bank after the postholiday return cash flow to the banking system.

## OTHER MONEY MARKET ADJUSTMENTS BY COMMERCIAL BANKS

Banks also may adjust their reserve position through other money market assets. Commercial paper, repurchase agreements, and loan participations with correspondents may all be used in a variable fashion not only for income purposes but for liquidity purposes as well.

## Purchase of Commercial Paper

Prime finance companies, which originate a substantial amount of commercial paper, will write such paper for any maturity from 30 to 270 days with a scaled interest rate pattern in the maturity desired by the banker. Although such paper is an unsecured IOU of the company issuing it, it is regarded favorably by commercial banks because losses prior to the 1970s were almost nonexistent. (In May 1970, however, the bankruptcy of the Penn Central Railroad did result in some losses to holders of commercial paper of that company.) Rates on such commercial paper are generally ¼ to 1 percent above the Treasury bill rate and are continually adjusted to reflect changes in Treasury bill rates.

One disadvantage to the bank in having such commercial paper is that it has no marketability if it has been secured by the bank directly from the finance company. It receives its liquidity therefore simply from its safety and its short maturity. Prime industrial paper, on the other hand, along with the paper of lesser known finance companies, is marketed through dealers and may be resold in the open market if necessary. The disadvantage of this particular kind of commercial paper is that its fixed predetermined maturity may not fit the particular portfolio needs of the commercial bank. On the other hand, prime industrial paper usually provides yields that range from ⅛ to ⅜ of 1 percent above comparable yields on paper of prime finance companies.

## Repurchase Agreements

Another money market instrument of increasing importance is the use of repurchase agreements (RPs) by a bank with a temporary surplus of funds. Rather than sell these funds for only twenty-four hours in the federal funds market, the surplus bank may buy Treasury obligations for a fixed number of days from a government security dealer or another commercial bank in need of funds for the same number of days. In entering into a repurchase agreement, the seller agrees to repurchase the given amount of government obligations at a fixed price, or rate, at the end of the contract period. The yield on RPs to the buying bank usually falls between the federal funds rate and the Treasury bill rate for a comparable maturity.

In some ways, the use of repurchase agreements is similar to buying and selling federal funds, except that the market unit trade is sometimes smaller than the $1 million unit that is standard in the federal funds market. Furthermore, national banks are not restricted by the legal loan limit of 10 percent of capital and surplus, which formerly applied to them in federal funds sales to any one purchaser. The freedom from this legal lending limit for national banks applies, however, only to repurchase agreements in government securities with less than eighteen months to maturity. State banks must still conform to their respective state requirements on lending limits.

## Call Loan Participation

**Call loan participations** extended by city banks to their country correspondents is another avenue of entrance into the money market available for banks outside the money market centers. Although loan participations with city correspondents have long been standard practice, only in recent years have city banks been willing to extend this participation to call loans. This major innovation was generally introduced in the mid-1950s and is now usually available to country correspondents. When available, such call loan participations represent an attractive employment of short-term funds, because the call feature makes the loan available within one day of call. Moreover, the interest return on such loans is considerably above the lower yields at the short end of the money market. Country banks sharing in these call loan participations, however, are usually expected to leave their funds in such employment at least a week or two. In some cases country banks have continuously employed funds in call loan participations for a number of months at a time.

# SECONDARY RESERVE REQUIREMENTS OF BANKS

The main reason for holding secondary reserves is the probable future need for cash by the commercial bank. If future cash requirements of the bank can be forecast with a high degree of probability, the portfolio manager can arrange the maturities of highly liquid assets to meet these future cash needs.

## Recapitulation of Bank Liquidity Needs

We should recall that the liquidity needs of a bank are determined by (1) seasonal variations in both deposits and loan demands, (2) random factors affecting bank deposits, (3) unstable deposit accounts, and (4) cyclical factors affecting bank liquidity needs. Even though large banks in large cities may be somewhat more fortunate in seasonal movements than smaller banks in smaller cities in that the seasonal peak requirements of some customers will be offset by the seasonal low points of others, there are still fluctuations in the loan portfolio of city banks. One of the large New York City banks found in a study of one postwar year that commercial, industrial, and agricultural loans reached a seasonal peak in December, 12 percent above the annual average, and fell to a seasonal low of 11 percent below the annual average in June. Food processors, tobacco firms, finance companies, and department stores particularly seem important in helping explain such a large degree of seasonal fluctuations in loan demand at banks.

*Seasonal Variations in Bank Deposits*     In addition to noting that loan demands vary importantly over the year, it is also necessary to take account of seasonal variations in deposits. Unfortunately, these two kinds of seasonal movements for some banks are likely to have the worst kind of conjuncture. It often seems that bank deposits will fall at the very time that demands for loan accommodations are increasing. The reason for this adverse coincidence is that bank customers, unless restricted by minimum compensating balance requirements, often tend to draw down their deposit accounts before seeking loan accommodation. Conversely, once loans are repaid, deposit balances tend to accumulate. For banks that have a high concentration of customers in a particular industry, such adverse coincidence may produce very difficult results. A solution to this problem might be greater diversification of the loan portfolio, or provision of adequate secondary reserves to meet such seasonal cash requirements, or both.

*Unstable Bank Deposits and Cyclical Factors*     Although causes of random deposit fluctuations cannot usually be identified, such fluctuations do occur and secondary reserves should be adequate to take care of them. In addition, certain deposit accounts are widely recognized as unstable, such as (1) accounts due to banks or correspondent bank demand balances, (2) public funds—this includes the tax and loan accounts of the Treasury and the deposits of state and local governmental authorities, (3) large accounts in small banks—this may be particularly critical for single-industry towns.

In each case in which such unstable accounts loom importantly in the total deposit balances held by a bank, prudent management demands that the bank be readily able to meet the loss of such an unstable account by disposing of some of the secondary reserves, which should be available against such a contingency. Finally, cyclical needs of banks for cash may be partially anticipated through their secondary reserves. In periods of recession when the Federal Reserve is generously supplying added amounts of bank reserves and business demand for added loans from banks has declined, it is possible for banks to add to their secondary reserves by the acquisition of short-term government securities, which subsequently can be disposed of in the following upswing to accommodate increased business demand for bank loans then.

## Secondary Reserve Assets Are Shiftable

More than liquidity as such is required of the **secondary reserve assets.** The loan portfolio, including even the mortgage portfolio, through amortization and repayment of loans provides a cash flow, which thus gives some liquidity to these assets. But the characteristic that is specially needed for the secondary reserve is shiftability. Thus an asset to qualify for a commercial bank's secondary reserve must have (1) high quality, (2) short maturity, and (3) a high degree of marketability with minimum risk of market fluctuations in price. Treasury bills, as already indicated, qualify particularly well on these grounds as secondary reserves.

***Treasury Bills in Bank Secondary Reserves***    Bills have a ready marketability and, because of their narrow bid-asked trading spreads, can usually be sold without any loss even if held only a short time. As a rule, the higher the yield of a bill at purchase, or the shorter the maturity of the bill at purchase, the wider can be the subsequent market fluctuation over a given period without the bank that sells the bill incurring a loss on the transaction. The greater safety from possible adverse market fluctuations in price that Treasury bills give the bank holding them helps account for the popularity of Treasury bills as a major component of bank secondary reserves. The greater trading activity in the short end of the government securities market, as compared with the long end of this market, also means that bills can readily be marketed at any time.

*Other Secondary Reserve Assets*    In addition to Treasury bills and other short-term Treasury obligations, it is possible for the commercial bank to use Federal Agency issues, Public Housing Authority notes, bankers' acceptances, and commercial paper in its secondary reserves. These other money market assets do not have quite as much shiftability as Treasury bills, though they usually have higher yields than Treasury bills. The reduced shiftability of these assets, however, makes them attractive only if seasonal or other liquidity requirements can be forecast with some degree of accuracy. There may be more reluctance to sell such other secondary reserve assets freely because the spreads between the bid and asked prices on marketable agency issues and the Housing Authority notes, to take two examples, are both wider than is true for Treasury bills. There is thus somewhat more market risk for these other money market assets.

# Questions for Discussion

1. Discuss the ways in which commercial banks use the money market to adjust their reserve positions. Why would a bank buy federal funds, for example, rather than sell Treasury bills?
2. How many banks not in the larger money market centers still enter the money market? How widespread is such commercial bank participation in the money market in the 1980s?
3. How has the use of Regulation Q by the Federal Reserve Board affected member bank participation in the money market? Do you approve of its scheduled termination in 1986? Why or why not?
4. What is the relationship between bank liquidity and a bank's participation in the money market? Why do banks need liquidity? In what ways can banks satisfy their liquidity requirements? How does deposit variability affect bank need for liquidity? What impact on bank liquidity is felt by variability in demand for bank loans?
5. How many commercial banks typically use the federal funds part of the money market? Why? How would you define the federal funds market? How important is this part of the money market in the 1980s?
6. What is meant by saying that a bank makes a market in federal funds? What is the range of possible rates in the federal funds market during any given reserve week? Why? What sometimes happens in the federal funds market on a Wednesday, the last day of the reserve period? Why?
7. How can federal funds transactions be moved from one region to another? What part does the correspondent banking system play in the federal funds market?
8. Why do banks trade in the Treasury bill market? What is the market risk on Treasury bills as compared with long-term government securities? Why? How active is trading in the short end of the government securities market as compared with trading activity in the long end of the market?
9. What considerations might induce a bank to sell Treasury bills, say, when it has a reserve deficiency rather than to buy federal funds or borrow from its regional Reserve Bank? If a bank has a temporary surplus of reserves, what options are open to its money manager?
10. Define and discuss the basic reserve position of banks. Why has the percentage of required reserves in the form of borrowed reserves been rising in the 1980s as compared with the 1960s and 1970s?
11. How does the growing use of liability management by banks affect their liquidity? How does such liability management affect the banks' use of the resources of the money market?

# Selected Bibliography for Further Reading

FEDERAL RESERVE BANK OF NEW YORK, *Essays in Money and Credit* (New York: 1964).

——, *Essays in Domestic and International Finance (New York:* 1969).

GAMBS, CARL M., AND DONALD V. KIMBALL, "Small Banks and the Federal Funds Market," *Economic Review*, Federal Reserve Bank of Kansas City, Nov. 1979, Vol. 64, No. 9, pp. 3–12.

LAURENT, ROBERT D., "Interbank Lending—An Essential Function," *Business Conditions*, Federal Reserve Bank of Chicago, Nov. 1974, pp. 3–7.

LYON, ROGER A., *Commercial Bank Investment Portfolio Management* (Princeton, N. J.: Princeton University Press, 1961).

MADDEN, CARL, *The Money Side of "The Street"* (New York: Federal Reserve Bank of New York, 1959).

RITTER, LAWRENCE, ed., *Money and Economic Activity Readings in Money and Banking*, 3rd ed. (Boston: Houghton Mifflin, 1967).

ROBINSON, ROLAND, *The Management of Bank Funds*, 2nd ed. (New York: McGraw-Hill, 1962).

ROOSA, ROBERT V., *Federal Reserve Operations in the Money and Government Securities Markets* (New York: Federal Reserve Bank of New York, 1956).

SMITH, WAYNE, "Repurchase Agreements and Federal Funds," *Federal Reserve Bulletin*, May 1978, pp. 353–360.

SPINDT, PAUL A., AND VEFA TARHAN, "Liquidity Structure Adjustment Behavior of Large Money Center Banks," *Journal of Money, Credit and Banking*, Vol. XII, No. 2, Part 1, May 1980, pp. 198–208.

# PART 3

# COMMERCIAL BANKS AND THEIR COMPETITORS

> The banks, when their customers apply to them for money, generally
> advance it to them in their own promissory notes.
>
> **THE WEALTH OF NATIONS**

# 8

## CHAPTER

# The Development of American Banking

To a large degree, the development of American commercial banking has been marked by the experimental attitude that characterized the country's experience with different monetary standards, as discussed earlier in Chapter 3. The exigencies of financing a new and growing country necessitated different approaches to banking from time to time. In the colonial period Great Britain severely limited the number of banks allowed to operate in the colonies. After independence the number of banks grew somewhat larger, but a new bank could be started only by securing a charter from a state legislature, or perhaps Congress.

Not until 1838 did the state of New York inaugurate the **free banking** era, when it became relatively easy for bank promoters to start a new bank. Other states quickly imitated the example of New York, and the period of underbanking was succeeded by a period of overbanking. Various abuses such as **wildcat banking** occurred, which inevitably resulted in greater regulation of banking by the states and the federal government.

It took the Civil War to get Congress to pass the National Banking Act, and it took the panic of 1907 to get Congress to pass the Federal Reserve Act in 1913. When the charter of the Second Bank of the United States expired in 1836, there had been no central bank to regulate the money supply created by commercial banks either through note issue or by the creation of demand deposits.

Furthermore, throughout its financial history the United States has had massive liquidation of banks during periods of serious financial panic. The Great Depression of the 1930s alone eliminated more than 5,000 independent banks. The Depression did, however, lead to banking reform that, through the Federal Deposit Insurance Corporation and a stronger Federal Reserve System, assisted the banking system to meet the trials of World War II and the early postwar period without a recurrence of widespread bankruptcies among banks.

In the period following World War II, commercial banks grew and prospered despite increased competition from nonbanking financial institutions. New forms of bank credit were developed and larger banks were managed with increased efficiency through improved management techniques and a growing use of electronic devices such as computers. Banks managed to convey to the public an image of responsibility and strength and a progressive attitude toward meeting legitimate credit needs. This favorable acceptance of banks by the public has not always characterized American banking history.

## COMMERCIAL BANKING BEFORE THE CIVIL WAR

Early American experience with commercial banks did not inspire much public confidence in banks and bankers. The earliest banks were often state monopolies run in the interests of the merchants who organized and managed them. These banks concentrated on making short-term commercial loans rather than making available the long-term agricultural credit desired so strongly by the bulk of the population living outside the few cities. Furthermore, many of these early banks were so poorly managed that they went bankrupt in the numerous financial panics that swept the country from time to time.

### Many Early Banks Were Local Monopolies

In the entire colonial period England issued charters to only four banks in the colonies. After independence the number of American banks proliferated greatly, although certain states permitted only a single monopoly bank. In 1781 the Bank of North America began operations in Philadelphia as a result of a statute passed by Congress. Most of the new banks, however, secured state charters. By 1794 a total of eighteen banks had been chartered in the United States, but in Pennsylvania, New York, Massachusetts, and Maryland a single monopoly bank was located in the principal city of the state.

## The First Bank of the United States

During the period when a number of **state banks** were being chartered, a national bank—the First Bank of the United States—was established by Congress in 1791. This was the brainchild of Alexander Hamilton, then secretary of the treasury, who argued that the bank would make three major contributions to the new American economy: (1) increase the country's active or productive capital, since $2 or $3 in paper money could be issued for every specie dollar held by the bank, (2) help the government in borrowing, and (3) facilitate the payment and collection of taxes. The charter passed by Congress for the bank provided that (1) the charter was to be in effect for twenty years, (2) capital was to be $10 million, of which the federal government was to subscribe one fifth, (3) private subscriptions were to be made, one fourth in specie and three fourths in 6 percent government bonds, (4) the bank was not permitted to buy or sell goods or real estate except when acquired as forfeited collateral, and (5) interest on loans and discounts was not to exceed 6 percent.

The bank cooperated closely with the Treasury in attempting to stabilize the money market and protect the banking system. Several other banks were prevented from going into bankruptcy because of timely deposits of funds by the bank. Nevertheless, considerable popular opposition developed to the bank. Opponents argued that it was controlled by foreigners, because a considerable amount of bank stock was held in England, and that it was an unconstitutional monopoly, which was far less efficient than the state banks. An effort to recharter the bank failed in 1811, when the Senate was divided on the issue and Vice-President George Clinton voted against the bank.

Without the restraining influence of a national bank to regulate the issuance of bank notes by requiring redemption in specie reserves, the war years of 1812–1815 saw a tremendous growth in state banks and their bank note issues. The number of state banks increased from 88 in 1811 to 208 in 1815; circulation of bank notes in the same period rose from $22.7 million to $99 million. In 1814 the excessive note issue even forced the banks to suspend specie redemption. Furthermore, the Treasury had no fiscal agent to act as a central depository, but rather had deposits in ninety-four different banks.

## The Second Bank of the United States

To create some order in the mounting monetary and banking chaos, Congress finally chartered the Second Bank of the United States in 1816. Like the First Bank of the United States, the charter was for twenty years. Capital, however, was enlarged to $35 million. Notes of the bank were to be acceptable in payment of all public dues, but these notes had to be redeemable in specie on demand, or the bank would be liable to the noteholder for 1 percent per month on the value of the unredeemed note. Congress also provided that after February 20, 1817, all payments to the government were to be made in coin, Treasury notes, notes of the Bank of the United States, or bank notes payable on demand in specie. State banks therefore had only ten months to reorganize their note issues in order to have them accepted by the Treasury. Such resumption of specie payment was accomplished on the date set.

Despite considerable success in limiting the excesses of state banking, popular opposition again developed to this national bank on the grounds of monopoly, which had also been charged against the First Bank of the United States. The supporters of Andrew Jackson in the South and the West were particularly opposed to this bank. Although Congress passed a bill in 1832 to recharter the bank, President Jackson vetoed the bill and Congress could not muster enough votes to override the veto.

## Early State Banking

Even under the watchful eye of the Second Bank of the United States, the number of state banks grew substantially. In the fifteen years from 1811 to 1829, the number of state banks rose from 90 to 329. By 1834, the number had grown to 506. Likewise, state bank note issues rose sharply, more than doubling from 1830 to 1837. The growth in state bank note issues paralleled the growth in bank lending. Despite a growth in assets, many of these early commercial banks seemed to be in almost chronic difficulties.

Banking difficulties centered around an inadequate and poorly distributed supply of hard specie of gold and silver, as well as poor management practices. When a bank made a short-term commercial loan, it gave the borrower its bank notes as money. When these notes were later presented to the bank for redemption in specie, the loans on which the notes were based were often still outstanding. The inadequate specie reserves of the bank then quickly evaporated and the bank became insolvent. In order to avoid public demands for redemption in hard specie, some banks were located for note issue purposes as far west in the wilderness as Ohio, "with the wildcats." In time these banks became known as wildcat banks; in fact, they were little better than counterfeiters.

Despite the constant bank failures and the poorly backed bank notes, the great shortage of money of all kinds led to the establishment of more and more "printing press" banks. These numerous weak banks were, of course, quite vulnerable to any widespread economic and financial difficulties. In the panic of 1837, banks failed in large numbers throughout the country. In the state of New York alone, some eleven banks became insolvent, with nine becoming completely bankrupt.

*The Free Banking Act of 1838*    These widespread bank failures, along with public revulsion against the monopolistic privileges available to only a few banks under the special legislative acts then required to establish banks, led to the Free Banking Act of 1838 in the state of New York. Under this act any group of people could incorporate a bank by depositing with the state comptroller United States bonds, state bonds, real estate bonds, or mortgages. This act was widely adopted by other states and led to a great boom in the formation of new banks.

*Growth in State Banks*    By 1844 the number of state banks had increased to 696, but a decade later the total had nearly doubled to 1,208. Despite the great growth in state banks, many states still suffered from inadequate banking facilities. In fact, some states had no incorporated banks at all. In 1852 there were no incorporated banks in Arkansas, California, Florida, Illinois, Iowa, Michigan, and Wisconsin, in the territories of Oregon and Minnesota, and in the District of Columbia. In Indiana and Missouri, banking was a state monopoly.

In other states, however, the number of banks continued to rise. In 1860, on the eve of the Civil War, the number of state banks had grown to 1,562. The monetary value of state bank notes in circulation was $207 million in 1860, as compared with $131 million in 1850. The decade of the 1850s then saw pronounced growth both in state banks and in their note issues. Many of these notes had depreciated in value, whereas other bank notes were purely fraudulent.

## The National Banking System

The chaotic state banking system, as well as the urgent need for financing the military conflict, led to the enactment of an important banking reform measure in the middle of the Civil War. The National Bank Act, passed by Congress in February 1863, required each new national bank to deposit with the comptroller of currency United States bonds equal to one third of its capital. In return the national bank received national bank notes equal to 90 percent of the par or market value of the deposited bonds, whichever was lower. By October 1863, some 66 banks had taken national charters; a year later the number had grown to 508.

*Tax on State Bank Notes*    To encourage state banks to take out national charters, in June 1864 Congress imposed a 2 percent tax on state bank notes. Legislation passed by Congress in March 1865 increased the tax to 10 percent beginning on July 1, 1866, which led a great number of state banks to convert to **national banks**. In October 1865 there were 1,513 national banks, whereas there had been only 508 banks a year earlier. By late 1866 the number had further increased to 1,644. By this time the national banking system had become well established, although a few state banks remained in operation.

*Strength of The National Banking System*    In certain respects the new national banking system was a vast improvement on the former state banking system. Most of the national banks were stronger than the state banks, and the note issues of the national banks held their value better than the state bank note issues prior to the Civil War. Reserve requirements imposed by Congress limited the creation of deposits, whereas the required deposit of government bonds with the Comptroller of the Currency by the national bank limited the national bank note issue.

National banks in reserve cities were required to keep in their vaults a 25 percent reserve in lawful money against deposits. Those in other cities, although also subject to the 25 percent reserve requirement, could keep one half of these legal reserves on deposit in New York City banks. Country banks had to meet only 15 percent legal reserve requirement, and three fifths of it could be deposited in a city bank.

*Defects of The National Banking System*    The national banking system suffered from certain major defects. The supply of bank notes was inelastic, as it had been under the old state banking system. An **inelastic money supply** means that the supply of money cannot expand and contract with the needs of trade and the economy. In periods of prosperity, merchants and other businessmen needed more loanable funds and a greater supply of money to transact business. In such periods, the national bank note currency actually displayed a perverse elasticity. Banks tended to sell government securities in order to secure more loanable funds to make more profitable business loans. But when the banks sold such government securities the supply of money in circulation was forced to contract, because the backing for such paper currency was government securities owned by the national banks.

*Inadequate Distribution of National Bank Notes*    The supply of national bank notes was both limited and poorly distributed among the states, which gave rise to great shortages of hand-to-hand money in many localities. The total value of such bank notes was originally fixed at $300 million. Half of this total was to be distributed to the states on the basis of population; the other half was to be assigned by the secretary of the treasury on the basis of the existing banking capital resources and business of the states and territories. The older states, with the slowest rate of economic growth, thus received the bulk of this paper currency, whereas the newer and rapidly growing frontier states and territories were hampered in their growth by a chronically inadequate stock of money. The state of Connecticut, for example, had a greater circulation of the new paper money than Michigan, Iowa, Minnesota, Kansas, Missouri, Kentucky, and Tennessee combined.

*Reserve Requirements*    The system of required reserves also placed the Western states in great financial dependency on the East, for the bulk of bank reserves came to be held in New York City. This was not an unalloyed blessing for the New York City banks, however, because they were regularly subject to heavy seasonal withdrawals of cash reserves by their country bank correspondents. Credit pressures converged from the New York City banks twice each year, in the spring and in the fall, when country banks needed more funds to make loans for planting and harvesting.

Furthermore, these pressures on the banking system were accentuated by the fact that the system of required reserves, by permitting a bank to hold part of its legal reserves in New York City banks, resulted in a pyramiding of bank reserves. The reserves were pyramided because they were counted twice as cash, both by the country bank and the New York City bank. Usually these pressures created only a mild financial crisis, but in 1873, 1893, and 1907 full-blown financial panics resulted.

**The Revival of State Banking**    The defect of the inelasticity of the supply of national bank notes was partially offset by the increased use of bank deposits. Checkbook money came into greater use in the 1870s and 1880s, particularly in the cities. In country areas, farmers continued to transact most of their business in currency, so that the growing use of bank deposits did not satisfy their needs for money. For much of industry and commerce, however, checks proved to be a more satisfactory form of payment than paper currency for large transactions. The growing use of checks actually revived the state banking system.

With the prohibitive tax on the state bank notes in 1865, most of the existing state banks were forced to take out national charters in order to continue to pay out their own bank notes when loans were made. In the early years after the Civil War there were so few state banks that statistics are unavailable. By 1876 a renascence in state banking was underway with 633 state banks reported for that year. Twelve years later, in 1888, the number of state banks had more than doubled to 1,523. It appeared by this time that the country was going to have a dual banking system of both national and state banks, rather than national banks alone.

## BANKING IN THE EARLY YEARS OF THE TWENTIETH CENTURY

By 1892 the number of state banks had actually surpassed the number of national banks. The slower growth of national banks, together with political demands for an expanded currency, helped provide some of the impetus required for Congress to pass the Currency Act of 1900, otherwise known as the Gold Standard Act. Certainly the greatest significance of this act was that it firmly established our monetary system on the *de jure* gold standard, after having been on the *de facto* gold standard for some years. Several provisions of the act also were significant for commercial banking: the capital requirement for a national bank was reduced; national bank notes could be issued up to the full par value of the deposited government bonds rather than 90 percent as formerly; and the federal tax on such bank notes was reduced.

***Growth in New Banks*** The provision of the Currency Act of 1900 resulted in a significant increase in the number of new national banks; 3,046 new national banks were formed between 1900 and 1908, practically doubling the total of 1900. The amount of national bank notes in circulation also more than doubled in the same period, rising from $265 million in 1900 to $614 million in 1908. By 1914 the number of national banks had risen to 7,525. It was now more profitable to start a national bank in order to take advantage of the liberalized provisions of the law regarding the issue of bank notes.

State banks, however, also continued to grow in number and importance. From 1900 to 1908 the number of state banks more than doubled from 6,650 to 14,522. By 1914 there were 19,240 state banks in the United States. State banking was far from dead, as had seemed the case in the early years after the Civil War. Instead, state banking was expanding at a more rapid rate than national banking.

***The Panic of 1907*** The growth of substantial numbers of both new national and new state banks did not give the banking system, or the monetary system, enough strength to withstand the panic of 1907. In fact, increased numbers of small, relatively weak banks, with bank reserve holdings concentrated in New York City, probably made the panic more likely. When the panic had run its course, from mid-October to mid-December, the country finally seemed determined to take the necessary steps to strengthen the banking system. What was needed most of all was a central bank. Since 1836 and the demise of the Second Bank of the United States, commercial banks had had no dependable "lender of last resort." Furthermore, there was little effective regulation of the issuance of bank notes. In particular, there was no offset to the inelastic currency of the state banks before the Civil War and of the national banks after the Civil War.

***The Federal Reserve Act of 1913***    One purpose of the Federal Reserve Act of 1913 was "to furnish an elastic currency." The inelastic currency of the national banks was to be withdrawn from circulation, though the last of this currency was not eliminated until 1935. The new paper currency was Federal Reserve notes. These would be paid out by Federal Reserve Banks whenever they bought government securities, or whenever the member commercial banks borrowed reserves from their district Federal Reserve Bank.

The average reserve requirement on member commercial banks (all national banks were required to join the new system, although state banks had the option of not joining) was only about 14 percent as compared with the average reserve requirement in excess of 20 percent under the National Bank Act. Commercial banks, therefore, were able to expand credit substantially, because available reserves had been increased as a result of the reduction in the reserve requirement. A more elastic and expanded money supply was thus provided by increased demand deposits of commercial banks, as well as by an increased supply of paper currency. (There is further discussion of the Federal Reserve System in Chapter 15.)

## COMMERCIAL BANKING IN THE 1920s

The passage of the Federal Reserve Act just before World War I had helped the commercial banking system weather that crisis and also strengthened the banking system when the war was over. Both the commercial banking system and the American monetary system were thus in a much stronger position at the end of World War I than in the immediate postwar periods of earlier wars. The dollar had not depreciated in World War I as rapidly as in earlier wars, thanks to the imposition of heavier taxes, direct and indirect controls over production and prices, and the development of a more productive economic system. Internationally, the dollar was in a stronger position than previously because of the significant change from America's position as a debtor nation at the beginning of the war to that of creditor nation at the end. The financial stage was set for the prosperous 1920s.

***Bank Failures***    Despite the apparent strength of the financial system, the number of bank failures in this new era of prosperity was appallingly high. In less than a decade, from 1921 to 1929 inclusive, some 5,712 banks suspended operations. Although one might have expected some bank failures to occur in the postwar recession of 1920–1921, a large number of failures occurred in the last years of the decade.

Most of the banks that failed were small state banks that had been formed in large numbers before World War I. Some 88.4 percent of the failures occurred among banks with a capital of less than $100,000. These failures were largely among nonmembers of the Federal Reserve System concentrated in agricultural areas of the South and West. At least one of the reasons why bank failures were so high in these areas is that the agricultural sector did not share in the prosperity of the 1920s, which was largely confined to the industrial sectors of the economy. Agricultural prices reached their peak in World War I and drifted downward steadily after that time.

***Expansion of Branch Banking***   **Branch banking** expanded throughout the 1920s. In 1920 there were 547 banks operating 1,455 branches; by 1929 there were 763 banks with 3,349 branches. Mergers among banks were also common, particularly after 1926. The banks that were eliminated were generally the small, weak banks.

## THE BANKING CRISIS OF 1929–1933

Strong banks as well as weak ones failed in the years after the collapse of the stock market in October 1929, a financial panic of the greatest dimensions. The failure of the Credit Anstalt, a large commercial bank in Austria, in 1931 brought a new wave of financial panic to Wall Street. In that year the number of commercial bank failures in the United States was double the previous year's figure. In all, some 5,000 banks failed in the Great Depression, and an additional 1,200 were absorbed by other, stronger banks. There was thus a great wringing out of liquidity and banks before the panic ran its course.

So many banks were failing in late 1932 and early 1933 that many governors declared banking holidays in their respective states. The first banking holiday, which was declared on October 31, 1932, in Nevada lasted 12 days. By the time President Roosevelt was inaugurated on March 4, 1933, most of the banks in the country were already closed. One of the first acts of the new president was to declare a national banking holiday. Only the stronger banks were permitted to open their doors after the holiday.

But the worst of the storm was over by then; what remained of the commercial banking system could breathe more easily. In 1934, which was still a year of depression, new banks were being formed. By 1939 there were a total of 14,531 commercial banks in the United States, as compared with slightly fewer than 14,000 in the dark days of 1933. In the fourteen years from 1920 to 1933, however, nearly half the commercial banks in this country had been eliminated through bankruptcy or merger.

## STRENGTHENING THE BANKING SYSTEM IN 1933 AND 1935

Once the country's worst fears had been alleviated in the spring of 1933, the task of trying to prevent the recurrence of such a panic remained to be accomplished. Because the Depression had been triggered and subsequently aggravated by financial factors, including a near collapse of the commercial banking system, some shoring-up of banks seemed urgently needed.

*The Federal Deposit Insurance Corporation*   Congress therefore passed the Banking Act of June 16, 1933, which established the **Federal Deposit Insurance Corporation** to insure bank deposits. This bank insurance was designed to discourage the public from ever again engaging in the panicky bank runs that were such a damaging feature of late 1932 and early 1933. All commercial banks were eligible to join the FDIC, although all member banks of the Federal Reserve System were required to have such insurance. Individual accounts were originally insured up to $2,500, but through various amendments to the law Congress progressively increased the limit, until it was raised to $100,000 as of March 31, 1980. By the 1980s nearly 99 percent of all commercial bank deposits were in banks so insured.

*Strengthening the Federal Reserve in 1935*   The commercial banking system was also aided by the Banking Act of 1935, which modernized the Federal Reserve System. This act removed the Secretary of the Treasury from the **Federal Reserve Board of Governors** and established the **Federal Open Market Committee** to control open market operations, or the buying and selling of government securities by the system. The board was also given greater flexibility in setting reserve requirements for member commercial banks. This act did not, however, as some proponents had wished, make membership in the Federal Reserve System compulsory for all banks.

Even in 1980, when important banking reforms were inaugurated, membership was not compulsory. Nevertheless, transactions accounts of all financial institutions were subjected to uniform reserve requirements imposed by the Federal Reserve Board. Moreover, access to the Federal Reserve **discount window** was made available to more financial institutions.

## WORLD WAR II AND COMMERCIAL BANKS

As a result of new techniques of war finance, bank deposits doubled from 1941 to 1945, and holdings of government securities by banks nearly quadrupled. In both the Revolutionary War and the Civil War the government had resorted to issuing fiat paper currency to secure the funds that could not be raised by taxation. Beginning in World War I, however, the government discovered that selling bonds and other government securities directly to commercial banks accomplished the same result as issuing paper money. This technique was brought to a high development in World War II.

The banks, of course, also benefited from this financing of the government, because they received some earning assets at a time when the opportunities to make private loans were being subordinated to the needs of the war. The Federal Reserve also provided added reserves to the banking system throughout the war, so that the banks could acquire whatever debt the Treasury chose to sell to them.

At the end of World War II, the banking system had some $90 billion in government securities, more than $34 billion in cash and $150 billion in total deposits. The great liquidity of the banking system was increased in the immediate postwar period by the continuation of support of the government securities market by the Federal Reserve System—a policy undertaken in World War II to assist the Treasury in the sale of its debt securities. Because the prices of government securities were still being supported, the banks could sell off substantial quantities of government securities to make more profitable business and personal loans. Bank loans, therefore, showed a strong upswing after the war. This strong bank lending, along with the great holdings of liquid assets such as savings bonds well dispersed throughout the economy, probably helped maintain buying power and so served to help stave off a feared depression, which never happened.

## POSTWAR BANKING TRENDS

A number of postwar recessions in economic activity did affect the banking system, as well as other parts of the economy, but there were no waves of bank failures to match those of the early 1930s. The decline in the number of commercial banks, which occurred in the postwar period, was mainly among small noninsured state banks. These banks dropped from 714 at the end of 1945 to 310 at the end of 1978. In the same period, the number of insured commercial banks actually rose from 13,297 to

14,381. The total number of commercial banks grew in the late 1960s and 1970s and was more than 14,700 by the 1980s.

*Growth in Banking Assets*     Total **bank assets** grew considerably in the postwar period. Total loans of all commercial banks, for example, rose sharply from $25.7 billion at the end of 1945 to $912.7 billion at the end of 1980. U. S. government securities held by these same banks rose from $88.9 billion to $110.7 in this period. Other securities held by these banks, which were mainly state and local government securities, rose by thirty-fold in this period, from $7.1 billion in 1945 to $230 billion in 1982.

  For the most part, banks just kept getting larger and larger in size, even in the face of severe competition from nonbanking financial institutions. In the states in which branching was permitted on a statewide basis, such as California, the number of branching offices increased substantially with the population growth. Elsewhere, new banks were formed or branches were established in urban areas if permitted by law. Despite an earlier decline in the total number of commercial banks, by the 1980s, as noted, the number of banks exceeded 14,700. The growth in bank branches meant that there were 40,000 bank offices in the United States in the early 1980s.

*The Depository Institutions Deregulation and Monetary Control Act of 1980*     On March 31, 1980, a new law passed by Congress seemed destined to have a very significant impact on commercial banking and the financial system generally. This act had two parts. The Depository Institutions Deregulation part of the act broadened the area of competition between financial institutions by easing regulatory barriers to competition. This involved granting thrift institutions greater freedom in making consumer and even business loans, which had heretofore been reserved to commercial banks. On the other hand, there was also a provision for the gradual removal of interest rate ceilings on deposits, which gave a competitive edge to banking institutions. The Monetary Control part of the act required all institutions with transaction accounts to meet reserve ratios set by the Federal Reserve Board. Both parts of the 1980 act will be discussed in more detail in later chapters.

# Questions for Discussion

1. Discuss the First and Second Banks of the United States. What impact did they have on the banking and monetary system during the years they were in existence? Why were their charters not renewed by Congress?
2. Discuss the nature of commercial banking in the United States before the

Civil War. What state legislation in this period resulted in a substantial growth in the number of banks?

3. Discuss the major provisions of the National Bank Act of 1863. Discuss the impact on American commercial banking of this act and the two subsequent acts of Congress in 1864 and 1865, which imposed a tax on state bank notes.

4. Discuss the strengths and weaknesses of the national banking system as compared with the state banking system. Why did both banking systems have an inelastic currency?

5. What happened to state banking immediately after the Civil War? What developments occurred in state banking in the later years of the nineteenth century? Explain your answers.

6. Discuss the Currency Act of 1900 with regard to its impacts on the banking system. What were some of the major characteristics of commercial banking in the United States just prior to World War I?

7. Discuss the major characteristics of commercial banking in the 1920s. What was the effect on commercial banking of the passage of the Federal Reserve Act of 1913?

8. Why was the Great Depression, beginning with the stock market crash of 1929, so severe in its impact on commercial banking? Could any of its effects have been mitigated by different private or public policies?

9. Discuss the banking reform legislation of the 1930s with its implications for commercial banking today.

10. Discuss some of the major changes in the American banking system after World War II. In particular, indicate changes in the number and size of commercial banks.

11. Discuss some of the major provisions of the Depository Institutions Deregulation and Monetary Control Act of 1980. What impact on commercial banks in particular, and financial institutions in general, do you expect to develop in the 1980s as a result of this act?

# Selected Bibliography for Further Reading

AMERICAN BANKERS ASSOCIATION, *The Commercial Banking Industry* (Englewood Cliffs, N. J.: Prentice-Hall, 1962).

BURNS, HELEN M., *The American Banking Community and New Deal Banking Reforms, 1933–35* (Westport, Conn.: Greenwood Press, 1974).

DWYER, GERALD P., JR., "The Effects of the Banking Acts of 1933 and 1935 on Capital Investment in Commercial Banking," *Journal of Money, Credit and Banking*, Vol. XIII, No. 2, May 1981, pp. 192–204.

FRIEDMAN, MILTON, and ANN JACOBSON SCHWARTZ, *A Monetary History of the United States, 1867–1960* (Princeton, N. J.: Princeton University Press, 1963).

GAMBS, CARL M., "State Reserve Requirements and Bank Case Assets," *Journal of Money, Credit and Banking*, Vol. XII, No. 3, Aug. 1980, pp. 462–470.

GOLDBERG, LAWRENCE G. and ANTHONY SAUNDERS, "The Causes of U.S. Bank

Expansion Overseas: The Case of Great Britain," *Journal of Money, Credit and Banking*, Vol. XII, No. 4, Part 1, Nov. 1980, pp. 630–643.

HILDERMAN, LEONARD C., *National and State Banks: A Study of Their Origins* (Boston: Houghton Mifflin, 1931).

STAUFFER, ROBERT F., "The Bank Failures of 1930–31," *Journal of Money, Credit and Banking*, Vol. XIII, No. 1, Feb. 1981, pp. 109–113.

STUDENSKI, PAUL, and HERMAN KROOSS, *Financial History of the United States*, 2d ed. (New York: McGraw-Hill, 1963).

The judicious operations of banking by providing, if I may be allowed so violent a metaphor, a sort of waggon-way through the air; enable a country to convert, as it were, a great part of its highways into good pastures and cornfields, and thereby to increase very considerably the annual produce of its land and labour.

THE WEALTH OF NATIONS

# 9
# CHAPTER

# The Commercial Banking System

There are a large number of commercial banks in the United States, as we noted in the previous chapter. The growth and development of these national and state banks were also discussed in this prior chapter. Although the late nineteenth and early twentieth centuries were periods of growth in the number of these banks, the half century after 1920 was marked by a substantial attrition in their numbers. The 30,000 separate banks in operation after World War I were more than cut in half in the ensuing decades. By the 1980s, there were about 14,700 commercial banks. The number of banking offices today, however, is more than the number of separate banks in 1920. Other financial institutions, such as savings and loan associations, which are competing increasingly with commercial banks, particularly since they were able to offer what amounts to checking accounts after December 31, 1980, will be discussed elsewhere. Commercial banks, however, are still "the department stores of finance."

## THE BANKING SYSTEM

Large banks with substantial numbers of branches are becoming common in a number of states, though branch banking is still prohibited in other states. Branch banking across state boundaries is still impossible in the United States, although permissive legislation to allow such branching was being discussed in the early 1980s. Nevertheless, banks do establish links with one another through the **correspondent banking system** and sometimes through holding companies. Furthermore, banks are unified into a banking system by the various common regulations applied to the large banks, which are members of the Federal Reserve System, and to the great bulk of all banks, who are insured members of the Federal Deposit Insurance Corporation. Before considering the links between banks, let us first consider the formation of a new bank.

## The Dual Banking System

In forming a new bank, promoters have the option of applying either to the comptroller of the currency for a national bank charter, or if a state charter is desired, to their state banking office. Many of the new banks in the postwar period have been state banks, because the various state banking regulations are usually less strict than those imposed by the federal government. New national banks nevertheless have been established, and some banks may feel that greater prestige is thereby achieved.

One of the differences between a state and a national bank is that all national banks must have the word *national* in their title. Second, all national banks must belong to the Federal Reserve System (since 1913), and all members of the Federal Reserve System must be insured members of the Federal Deposit Insurance Corporation (since 1933). However, qualified state banks may also join the Federal Reserve System. Furthermore, even if a state bank does not join the Federal Reserve System, it may have its individual deposits insured by the Federal Deposit Insurance Corporation up to $100,000 for each account. Most new state banks in the 1980s immediately apply for deposit insurance in order to secure greater public acceptance. Before applying for insured status, however, the organizers of a new state bank must first secure a charter from a state.

***The Needs Test in New York State***    The fifty states have a great deal of variability in their banking laws relating to the formation of new commercial banks. A number of states have a needs test that bank incorporators must meet before they receive their charter. In deciding whether a new bank will meet community needs for a new bank, a substantial amount of information must be collected. In New York State, the information submitted to the banking authorities must include (1) census data on population and population forecasts, (2) sales and market data on the number of commercial and industrial establishments in the area,

(3) payroll information and average family income, and even (4) information about the average value of local homes. In most states, however, the information required is not so extensive or so detailed. Some supervisory authorities appear to follow a rule of thumb that the application for a new bank will be approved only if it can be shown that total deposits for the bank will rise to a level of at least $3,000,000 within a three-year period.

***The Illinois Requirements***    In Illinois, the main requirements in the state law governing bank incorporation appear to be proof of the good character of the organizers and minimum capital and surplus requirements varying according to the size of the town. If no bank already exists in a city, village, or incorporated town of less than 2,500 population, only $25,000 is required to meet the minimum capital stock requirement. In a town of more than 2,500 and less than 10,000 population, the minimum capital requirement is $50,000; from 10,000 to 50,000 population, the minimum capital requirement is $100,000; in all cities over 50,000 population, the minimum capital required is $200,000. In addition, the Illinois law requires the establishment of a surplus of at least 10 percent of the capital and a reserve for operating expenses of at least 5 percent to be provided at the time of the organization.

## Securing a National Bank Charter

Although many new banks formed are state banks, the organizer of a new bank may prefer to apply for a national bank charter. In making an application to the comptroller of the currency for a national bank charter, information must be submitted on the following factors: (1) management—character, experience, and financial responsibility of the proposed management, as well as the personal history of each organizer: (2) ownership—concentrated or well distributed; (3) capital—adequacy of capital structure in relation to estimated deposits and assets, as well as adequacy in relation to competitive banks; (4) earnings—availability of banking business to support the proposed bank, as well as a three-year projection of earnings and expenses; and (5) convenience and needs—economy and banking history of community, population and size of the area to be served, future growth prospects of area, location of proposed bank in relation to existing banking or other financial facilities, and major type of loan demands the proposed bank expects to serve.

A rather thorough justification must be prepared to secure a national banking charter. In addition, before approving or disapproving the application, the comptroller of the currency receives the recommendations of his bank examiners, as well as recommendations from the

Board of Governors of the Federal Reserve System and from the Federal Deposit Insurance Corporation. Local opinion is also sampled regarding the proposed bank with opportunity available for any protests against the proposed bank. Under these stringent conditions it may seem surprising that any new national banks are ever organized. Nevertheless, some new national banks continue to be organized, though the net number of national banks declined by 221 in the 1970s to stand at 4,448 at the end of 1979.

## Some Increase in State Banks

The number of state banks increased somewhat in the 1970s, even though the number of national banks fell slightly. There were 9,169 state banks at the end of 1979, an increase of 373 state banks in that decade. Lower reserve requirements for nonmember banks of the Federal Reserve System before 1980 was largely responsible for the increase in such state banks. Furthermore, the total number of state banks grew in that decade even though some banks were absorbed through bank mergers. Although banks are still not permitted to merge across state lines and thus have branches in other states, they are still able to achieve some of the advantages of interstate banking through the correspondent bank relationship.

## CORRESPONDENT BANKING

Correspondent relationships that banks maintain with one another are very important in making the large number of independent commercial banks in the United States into a banking system. When a bank has a deposit in another bank, these banks have a correspondent relationship with each other. Country banks generally have deposits in city banks, and city banks have deposits in banks in the same and other cities.

## Advantages for the Country Bank

*Rapid Check Clearance*     There are many reasons for having interbank deposits. First, the depositing bank still has primary reserves, or cash, when it has a deposit in another bank. Second, the depositing bank receives valuable services from the correspondent bank holding the deposit. Checks can be cleared and funds moved rapidly through the facilities of the correspondent banking system. Checks can often be cleared faster through the city correspondent bank than through use of the regional Reserve Bank. For this reason country banks clear more than 90 percent of their out-of-town checks through their city correspondent.

*Buying and Selling Securities*    Second in importance only to **check clearance** as a service secured by country banks through their correspondent city bank is the buying and selling of securities. All commercial banks have an investment portfolio, and country banks usually have a higher percentage of their earning assets in this form than do city banks. Consequently, the dealer or broker service provided by the city bank in buying or selling investments for the country banks is quite important. Furthermore, the investment specialists of the city correspondent bank will ordinarily analyze the bond portfolio of the country bank, if desired, and advice on future additions to the investment portfolio is available. Safekeeping of the purchased securities in the vaults of the city bank, along with crediting the account of the country bank at the maturity of the security, is also usually provided without charge.

*Loan Participations with City Banks*    The next most important function of the correspondent bank relationship consists of loan participations by banks. Large city banks often associate themselves into syndicates for the purpose of making large loans to giant business firms. City and country correspondents likewise can participate in loans, to the great benefit of the country bank especially. At certain seasons of the year the country bank is likely to have peak loan demands that it alone is unable to handle. By turning to its city correspondent for help, the country bank may be able to persuade the city bank to enter into loan participations in some instances. Loan participations, direct correspondent-to-customer loans, sale of assets, and interbank loans are all ways in which a country bank can secure external funds from the city correspondent bank.

*Technical Advice*    Technical advice and counsel from the city bank is of great aid to the country bank. The regular visit of the representative of the city bank to its country bank customer may help in the dissemination of information of value to the country banker, as does the correspondent bank conference usually held annually by the larger city banks. New operating procedures can be employed and new machines can be installed with the welcome technical advice of the city correspondent. The impetus to modernization of the country bank may have come from a visit from the country banker to the city bank. Information on current economic and general credit conditions is likewise regularly provided to the country bank by its city correspondent. Credit inquiries about large would-be borrowers can also usually be answered.

## Advantages for the City Bank

The city bank, in turn, gains valuable deposits and new business from its country correspondent banks. Correspondent bank business is quite important to a few large city banks. For example, the Chase Manhattan Bank of New York City has nearly 4,000 correspondents. With the cost of servicing a correspondent balance at 1 percent or less and short-term money market rates in recent years at double-digit levels, it is clear that these correspondent balances received from country banks, or other city banks, are worthwhile for the city correspondent banks.

## Economic Advantages of Correspondent Banking

The entire economy gains from having a complex interrelated correspondent banking system. With the large number of independent banks in the commercial banking industry in the United States, it is necessary to have links between banks to enable bank customers to transfer funds from one part of the country to another. Small-town customers of local banks can receive travelers' checks of large city banks, foreign currency can be easily purchased from local banks, business and other customers of local banks have ready access to investment in the money market through their local bank's ties with large city banks, and so on.

New and improved ways of conducting business are also more readily transmitted to the smaller country banks from the large city banks, which are most likely to be innovators in such matters. This in turn results in greater efficiency and convenience of operations for local bank customers. The spread of drive-in bank facilities from cities to small towns is a case in point. Greater automation of clerical functions is another example of a gain in speed and accuracy, which is of benefit to customers as well as to the management of the local bank.

***Interbank Deposits***    The monetary nexus of the correspondent banking system, which plays such an important role in linking more than 14,700 independent banks, is the interbank deposit. Interbank deposits (both demand and time) in recent years have aggregated about $60 billion, which is some sixfold what they were in the prewar period. Banks making the deposits obviously felt a greater need to increase their deposits in another bank—often in a large city bank. For such banks, correspondent balances provide a liquid asset out of which vault cash can be drawn or deposits can be made in Federal Reserve Banks. The depositing bank can use interbank deposits as a ready source of funds when customers' demands for cash are heavy. These deposits may also be utilized as an outlet for temporary surpluses. Also, by having these deposits in the city bank, the country bank enjoys a number of services that are important to its successful operations.

## Growth in Check Clearance

As already indicated, one fundamental advantage for the country bank having a city correspondent bank is rapid check clearance and the immediate credit provided by the city bank for the cash letters it receives from its country correspondents. Hence, the check clearance burden on the city correspondents has been increasing steadily.

A survey made in 1954 showed that over 90 percent of the dollar amount of money payments in the United States was made by check, and that the average check passed through 2.3 banks in the collection process. Almost three decades later, the average check passes through 2.6 banks and the total number of checks has increased enormously, because check volume has been rising about 7 to 8 percent per year in the last three decades. Only banks with deposits in excess of $100 million normally clear checks directly through the Federal Reserve System. But large correspondents clear about one fourth of their checks through other correspondents.

Less than half of all checks written each year (44 percent) clear through the facilities of the Federal Reserve System. Nevertheless, such check clearance is a major task for the Federal Reserve. To expedite clearings, some forty-eight check-processing centers serve as regional and national clearinghouses for checks deposited at the Federal Reserve Banks by commercial banks. In 1977, for example, more than 13 billion check items with a total dollar value in excess of $6.4 trillion were processed.

## Electronic Funds Transfer Arrangements

In light of this heavy volume of paper checks processed each year because of continued public preference for writing checks, it is not surprising that the Federal Reserve has tried to encourage the growing use of **electronic transfer of funds.** Wire transfers of funds between commercial banks and clearance of check-like deposit items electronically did in fact become more common by the late 1970s and early 1980s. More than 24 million wire transfers of funds with a dollar value of $48 trillion were processed by the Federal Reserve System in 1977. In the same year, automated clearinghouse associations (ACH) had clearings that totaled around $40 billion, represented by 106 million items.

Because of lagging consumer acceptance of the electronic

transfer of funds, however, the available technology has not been fully used. Still, point of sale (POS) machines have been installed in some grocery stores and department stores whereby funds can be immediately transferred from the customer's account to that of the merchant's. Automated teller machines have also been used by increasing numbers of banks. In the early 1980s some 22,000 such machines were in use.

There has also been an impressive growth in the use of automated clearings by the Federal Reserve. Government direct deposit programs have been especially successful and by the end of the 1970s accounted for more than four fifths of such electronic transfers. Undoubtedly, further growth in the use of electronic transfer will occur throughout the 1980s.

## BANKING IN THE DIFFERENT STATES

Because each of the fifty states may have different regulations on banking within its jurisdiction, there is considerable variation in the size and type of banking carried on in the states. The ability of banks to have branches varies from state to state depending upon the appropriate state legislation. Hence, Massachusetts, which permits limited branch banking, has fewer but larger banks than does Minnesota, which is predominantly a unit banking state. In 1979, both of these states had about the same total of bank deposits, with $24 billion being held in Massachusetts and nearly $23 billion of bank deposits in Minnesota.

Massachusetts, however, had only 149 commercial banks in that year with 939 branches, whereas Minnesota had 762 banks and only 227 branches. Banking, nevertheless, was more concentrated in Minnesota than might appear from these data, since two large bank holding companies in Minnesota control the bulk of banking deposits in that state. Where branch banking is prohibited or little developed in a state, strong bank holding companies often tend to develop as substitutes.

To cite another state, Illinois had 1,288 banks and 452 branches, with total bank deposits of $103 billion in 1979. (After August 16, 1976, Illinois banks were permitted to establish at most two limited service facilities, the most distant of which must be within 3,500 yards of the main office.) This was some 21 percent greater than the total bank deposits of $85 billion in Texas, which had 1,427 banks and 234 branches. The state of New York, with 302 banks, or only one fourth the number of banks in Illinois or Texas, still had $326 billion of bank deposits, or more than triple the total in Illinois and nearly quadruple that of Texas. California, similarly, had only 257 banks in 1979 but had total bank deposits of nearly $178 billion.

It is clear from these data that the average size of commercial banks varies considerably from state to state. The availability of commercial bank services also changes substantially in the different states, though this cannot be determined from these data, which are restricted to separately incorporated banks rather than including all bank offices. For a state permitting limited branch banking, such as Massachusetts, or one permitting statewide branching, such as California, this makes a great deal of difference.

## THREE FORMS OF BANK ORGANIZATION

The three different legal forms of bank organization in the banking industry are (1) the unit bank, which limits its business to a single bank location, (2) the branch bank, which has a number of branches for its banking operations as well as the main office, and (3) the holding company, which holds controlling stock interests in a group of banks. Holding company banking is also sometimes called group banking, because a number of banks are associated together in a network of banks.

### Unit Banking

Some **unit banks** have grown to large size, even though they may be operating under state restrictions severely limiting or completely prohibiting the establishment of branches. Through correspondent relationships with other banks, unit banks have been able to provide their customers with services that would be unavailable if they had to rely entirely on their own resources. But the inability to establish branches restricts the ability of a unit bank to provide at least some of the services that its customers might desire. For example, some customers living in the suburbs might prefer a branch of their city bank in the local shopping center, just as they expect large department stores to have nearby branches.

### Branch Banking

When **branch banking** is permitted, large city banks have branches not only within the legal limits of the city but in the metropolitan area as well, and perhaps through the entire state. California, which has been permissive toward branch banking, has the largest bank in the United States. The Bank of America National Trust and Savings Association had about $121 billion in assets at the end of 1981 and nearly 1,100 branches throughout the entire state. Wherever a substantial number of potential customers are congregated, an aggressive branch banking system can be expected to establish yet another branch.

Table 9–1 presents data relating to the number of banks and the number of branches in the different states. All states permitted branch banking in at least some form in 1980, although some states in the Midwest, Texas, and Wyoming were still predominantly unit banking states. In the country as a whole, as Table 9–1 indicates, the number of new branches in 1980 was nearly 2,000 and there was an increase of 132 banks in that year. Some of the states that were considered unit banking states in the 1960s had moved into the category of limited branching by 1980 (e.g., Iowa and Illinois), whereas New York, a limited branching state in the 1960s, permitted statewide branching on January 1, 1976.

**Table 9–1  Commercial Banks and Branches in the United States (States and Other Areas) During 1980, by State**

| State | In Operation Dec. 31, 1980 | | Net Change During 1980 | |
|---|---|---|---|---|
| | *Banks* | *Branches* | *Banks* | *Branches* |
| Total United States | 14,870 | 38,779 | +132 | +1,929 |
| Alabama | 318 | 624 | +1 | +46 |
| Alaska | 12 | 113 | N.A. | +4 |
| Arizona | 35 | 537 | +8 | +32 |
| Arkansas | 262 | 415 | +1 | +22 |
| California | 297 | 4,288 | +40 | +198 |
| Colorado | 442 | 111 | +32 | +14 |
| Connecticut | 64 | 603 | −1 | +10 |
| Delaware | 20 | 148 | N.A. | +1 |
| District of Columbia | 18 | 151 | +1 | +11 |
| Florida | 565 | 1,184 | −20 | +239 |
| Georgia | 435 | 839 | −4 | +47 |
| Hawaii | 12 | 165 | N.A. | +2 |
| Idaho | 26 | 247 | −1 | +11 |
| Illinois | 1,292 | 534 | +4 | +82 |
| Indiana | 407 | 1,129 | 0 | +34 |
| Iowa | 657 | 572 | 0 | +4 |
| Kansas | 620 | 272 | +3 | +18 |
| Kentucky | 345 | 761 | +2 | +64 |
| Louisiana | 269 | 805 | +7 | +41 |
| Maine | 41 | 308 | N.A. | +9 |
| Maryland | 102 | 942 | 0 | +37 |
| Massachusetts | 144 | 953 | −5 | +17 |
| Michigan | 376 | 2,159 | +4 | +159 |

**Table 9–1    (Continued)**

| State | In Operation Dec. 31, 1980 | | Net Change During 1980 | |
|-------|-------|----------|-------|----------|
|       | Banks | Branches | Banks | Branches |
| Minnesota | 764 | 273 | +2 | +46 |
| Mississippi | 178 | 697 | −5 | +31 |
| Missouri | 731 | 438 | +4 | +23 |
| Montana | 166 | 36 | +1 | +8 |
| Nebraska | 464 | 283 | +3 | +47 |
| Nevada | B | 143 | +2 | +8 |
| New Hampshire | 76 | 160 | −3 | +12 |
| New Jersey | 169 | 1,588 | −7 | +34 |
| New Mexico | 90 | 244 | +3 | +6 |
| New York | 317 | 3,418 | +15 | +29 |
| North Carolina | 80 | 1,742 | −3 | +19 |
| North Dakota | 178 | 128 | +3 | +5 |
| Ohio | 385 | 2,237 | −23 | +131 |
| Oklahoma | 502 | 255 | +16 | +7 |
| Oregon | 90 | 582 | +10 | +31 |
| Pennsylvania | 367 | 2,559 | −11 | +80 |
| Rhode Island | 17 | 233 | N.A. | +2 |
| South Carolina | 85 | 729 | 0 | +42 |
| South Dakota | 153 | 166 | −2 | +8 |
| Tennessee | 353 | 1,032 | +1 | +40 |
| Texas | 1,472 | 260 | +45 | +26 |
| Utah | 78 | 286 | +2 | +13 |
| Vermont | 29 | 167 | −1 | +8 |
| Virginia | 230 | 1,410 | −4 | +38 |
| Washington | 111 | 942 | +1 | ·8 |
| West Virginia | 237 | 64 | +2 | +5 |
| Wisconsin | 641 | 525 | +5 | +25 |
| Wyoming | 103 | 3 | +9 | N.A. |

N.A.—No activity.

SOURCE: Federal Deposit Insurance Corporation, *Annual Report 1980*, Washington, D.C., 1981, pp. 224–225.

## Growth in Both Banks and Branches

The data in Table 9–1 indicate clearly that the growth in the banking industry in 1980 was in the area of branching, because 1,929 new branches were established that year. Nevertheless, although there are now nearly 39,000 bank branches in the United States, there were still 14,870 separate banks in 1980. Most banks, by number, have no branches at all, because most branches are part of large statewide systems, such as in California and New York, or in still sizable branching systems in limited branching states, such as in Massachusetts and Michigan. Unit banking is thus far from dead, even though dramatic expansions in the number of new bank offices take place each year.

***California Branch Banking***    Statewide branch banking is clearly most important in California. Some 4,288 branches had been established by the 297 banks in that state by the end of 1980, and five of the fifteen largest U.S. banks call California their home. The five most important intercity branch systems in California are Bank of America National Trust and Savings Association, Security-First National Bank, Wells Fargo Bank, America Trust Company, and the Crocker-Citizens National Bank. Only the Bank of America, with about one fourth of the total of bank branches, covers the entire state; most of the other banks tend to cluster most of their branches in contiguous counties.

Some of these localized large California banks, however, are starting to expand elsewhere in the state. For example, the third largest California bank, Wells Fargo, used to restrict its branching largely to the San Francisco area, but by 1981, 117 of its 384 branches were in southern California. Other Western states, such as Arizona and Oregon, also have growing statewide branching systems.

In 1980 eleven Western states established 109 new banks out of the 132 set up that year. This was 80 percent of the total of new banks. Oddly enough, because these Western states often have statewide branching, they did not dominate the number of new bank branches set up that year. Only 18 percent of the substantial total of 1,929 new branches were established in those same eleven Western states. Most of the new bank branches opened in 1980 were in the East, the Midwest, or the South. Branching by banks was truly becoming a national phenomenon.

***Limited Branch Banking***    Among the states permitting limited branch banking, New York before 1976 had the largest number of branches, with some 3,204 by the end of 1975. By the end of 1980 after statewide branching had gone into effect, there were 3,418 branches in New York. Most of the branches, by number, are located in New York City, although in recent years the larger banks in the city have been establishing more branches in suburban communities.

States that have very limited branch banking, such as Illinois and Texas, tend in consequence to have a larger number of unit banks. Each of these states has more than triple the number of banks in New York, even though total banking resources in each of these states is less than 40 percent of those in New York. Where branch banking is not normally permitted, therefore, it appears that the tendency is for a large number of relatively smaller banks to operate. This impression is further confirmed by referring to data for California. In this state, commercial banks, which in 1980 were only 20 percent of the number of banks in Illinois, had nearly 60 percent greater total resources than Illinois banks. Clearly, the typical California bank with its branches is larger than the typical unit bank in Illinois.

***Increase in Branch Banking***    The total number of new bank branches established in the United States in recent years is on the upswing. In 1980, as Table 9–1 shows, 1,929 bank branches were established, which is down only slightly from the 1,991 branches set up in 1978. The number of bank branches, which totaled 11,358 in 1981, had increased by more than threefold by 1980 to a total of 38,779.

## Branch Banking and Competition

There was a lively controversy as to the merits of branch banking in various states in the early 1980s. The Federal Reserve Bank of Philadelphia, a decade earlier in 1972, did a simulation study of limited branching, statewide branching, and multibank holding companies in a projection for Pennsylvania for 1982. This study showed that statewide branching would improve the competitive performance of banking in local markets in Pennsylvania, as compared with the extant branching law, which permitted branching only in contiguous counties. Regardless of whether branching laws were changed, the study predicted a decline in Pennsylvania banks from the 1972 total of 450 to only 330–340 in 1982.

Moreover, in 1981 for the first time the Pennsylvania Bankers Association's governing council voted to support the concept of statewide banking. Historically, banks in Pennsylvania could open branches only in counties bordering their headquarters. Under the new proposal, banks would be permitted to expand into counties immediately beyond the contiguous ones. As a result of this support, such a proposal was introduced into the state legislature and was passed in 1982, permitting such expanded banking.

In general, statewide branch banking predominates in the West and on the East Coast, whereas unit banking prevails from the Mississippi to the Rockies. However, some Midwestern states are now permitting limited branching; for example, in 1976 Illinois banks were permitted to establish branches within two miles of the home office. Regardless of the legal form of banking permitted, most states had a decline in the percentage of deposits held by the five largest banks or bank groups in the 1960s and 1970s. In California, for example, the percentage of deposits held by the five largest banks declined from 82 to 78 percent in the 1960s. Similarly, in a unit banking state such as Illinois the percentage of deposits dropped from 42 to 38 percent. Growth in the size of individual banks or increase in bank branches, where permitted, does not therefore necessarily mean that there will be increased concentration of deposits in given states. Furthermore, the increase in the number of banks in the 1970s, especially in Western states experiencing population growth, resulted in a somewhat smaller concentration in particular banking markets.

## American Bank Branches Abroad

In addition to vigorous branching at home in states that permitted it, many American banks after 1965 began actively to branch abroad. In 1965, only eleven American banks had branches abroad, but by the 1980s the number of banks with foreign branches had increased to 140. The number of bank branches abroad increased correspondingly from only 180 in 1965 to 532 in 1970 and to 789 by the end of 1979. The real explosion in bank branching abroad was in the second half of the 1960s, although growth continued in the 1970s at a slower pace.

The largest number of American branches was in the United Kingdom, where there were sixty-four branches at the end of 1979. The top twenty U.S. banks have over 82 percent of all foreign branches and nearly 92 percent of total branch assets. At the end of 1979, the combined assets of the overseas branches of U.S. banks totaled $312.9 billion, an increase of $55.3 billion, or 21.5 percent, during the year. There were also twenty-eight new foreign branches established in 1979.

Prior to the explosion of bank branching abroad in the mid-1960s, only a few coastal city large banks had foreign branches for their customers. But the credit restraint periods of 1966 and 1969, the earlier imposition of controls on the outflow of funds from the United States in 1964 and 1965, and the great growth of the Eurodollar market discussed in Chapter 6 all led to a wider participation of American banks in foreign branching. By this technique, U.S. banks could better serve their corporate customers, who were expanding their foreign investments. With new foreign branches, American banks could tap foreign sources of funds and assist in loan placement as well as provide more service facilities for their corporate customers.

Branch banking is obviously a growth industry. Another kind of bank organization, the holding company, has also expanded its area of operations in recent years.

## *Bank Holding Companies*

Not only have states formerly forbidding, or strictly limiting branching, liberalized these restrictions, but state limitations on **bank holding companies** have also recently been eased, (e.g., Pennsylvania and Illinois). Where bank holding companies are established, their operations may be restricted to a single state (e.g., bank holding companies in New York State); or they may operate over a number of states, as is true of holding companies in the Far West states. Some holding companies may hold limited but nevertheless controlling stock interests in a few banks in a limited area, although other holding companies may hold substantially all the stock of a considerable number of banks perhaps over a wide area.

The chief characteristics of a bank holding company system are (1) each commercial bank belonging to the group is a separately chartered bank with its own board of directors and officers and subject to the same laws and supervision as other banks under the same legal jurisdiction, (2) the holding company owns part or substantially all the stock of each member bank of the group and exercises control through its stockholder relationship, (3) the holding company is separately incorporated and subject to separate regulation over its own board of directors and officers, and (4) bank holding companies must register with the Federal Reserve Board, as required by the Bank Holding Company Act of 1956 and the 1970 amendments to this act. This legislation is discussed in the next chapter.

# Questions for Discussion

1. Why is it still important to focus on commercial banks in the 1980s, even though such banks have many other competitors among financial institutions?
2. How meaningful is the term "dual banking system" today? Why has that term been used? Why were new banks prior to 1980 more likely to be "state" than "national" banks?
3. How are banks in different parts of a state, or in different states, connected? (Hint: consider bank holding companies, branch banking, and correspondent banking.)
4. How important is correspondent banking today? What are the advantages that both small and large banks receive from this relationship?
5. Discuss the different possibilities of moving funds, either by using paper (checks) or electronically. Why has the electronic funds transfer system not grown faster than it has?
6. Why is banking different in the different states? Why are banks in some

states on average larger than banks in other states? What are the advantages and disadvantages of size in banking?

7. Why did branch banking grow so rapidly in the 1970s and early 1980s? Do you think this trend will continue?

8. Discuss the advantages and disadvantages of branch banking. Which form of banking exists in your state? Why? Why has interstate branching not yet been permitted? Do you think it will come about? Defend your answer.

9. Why have American banks established branches abroad? Where do these branches tend to be concentrated? Why?

# Selected Bibliography for Further Reading

## Books and Monographs

AMERICAN BANKERS ASSOCIATION, *The Commercial Banking Industry*, a monograph prepared for the Commission on Money and Credit (Englewood Cliffs, N.J.: Prentice-Hall, 1962).

ANNUAL REPORTS of the Federal Deposit Insurance Corporation.

ASSOCIATION OF RESERVE CITY BANKERS, *Correspondent Banking* (Chicago: 1945).

BEATY, JOHN Y., *Correspondent Banking* (Cambridge, Mass.: Bankers Publishing Company, 1951).

CHAPMAN, JOHN, and RAY WESTERFIELD, *Branch Banking* (New York: Harper and Brothers Publishers, 1942).

FINNEY, KATHERINE, *Interbank Deposits* (New York: Columbia University Press, 1958).

FIRST NATIONAL CITY BANK OF NEW YORK, *Correspondent Bank Services* (New York: 1956).

HOGENSON, PALMER T., *The Economics of Group Banking* (Washington, D.C.: Public Affairs Press, 1955).

LENT, GEORGE E., *The Changing Structure of Commercial Banking* (The Amos Tuck School of Business Administration, Tuck Bulletin 24, July 1960).

NADLER, MARCUS, and JULES I. BOGEN, *The Bank Holding Company* (New York: Graduate School of Business Administration, New York University, 1959).

RHOADES, STEPHEN A., *Banking Structure and Performance at the State Level During the 1970s*, Staff Studies of Board of Governors of the Federal Reserve System (Washington, D. C.: March 1981).

## Articles

BOARD OF GOVERNORS OF THE FEDERAL RESERVE SYSTEM, "Recent Changes in the Structure of the Commercial Banking Industry," *Federal Reserve Bulletin*, March 1970, pp. 195–210.

FEDERAL RESERVE BANK OF CHICAGO, "Rival Bank Needs for External Funds," *Business Conditions*, May 1972, pp. 12–19.

FEDERAL RESERVE BANK OF NEW YORK, "Bank Expansion in New York State: The 1971 Statewide Branching Law," *Monthly Review*, Vol. 53, No. 11, Nov. 1971, pp. 266–274.

FEDERAL RESERVE BANK OF PHILADELPHIA, "Changing Pennsylvania's Branching Law: An Economic Analysis," *Business Review*, Dec. 1972, pp. 3–24.

JUNCKER, GEORGE R. "A New Supervisory System for Rating Banks," *Quarterly Review*, Federal Reserve Bank of New York, Vol. 3, No. 2, Summer 1978, pp. 47–55.

KNIGHT, ROBERT E., "The Impact of Changing Check Clearing Arrangements in the Correspondent Banking System," *Monthly Review*, Federal Reserve Bank of Kansas City, Dec. 1972, pp. 14–42.

——, "The Changing Payments Mechanism: Electronic Funds Transfer Arrangements," *Monthly Review*, Federal Reserve Bank of Kansas City, July–Aug. 1974, pp. 10–20.

KOROBOW, LEON, DAVID P. STUHR, and DANIEL MARTIN, "A Nationwide Test of Early Warning Research in Banking," *Quarterly Review*, Federal Reserve Bank of New York, Vol. 2, Autumn 1977, pp. 37–52.

SANTAMERO, ANTHONY M., and JEREMY J. SIEGEL, "Bank Regulation and Macro-Economic Stability," *American Economic Review*, Vol. 71, No. 1, March 1981, pp. 39–53.

SHORT, GENIE DUDDING, and BETSY BUTTRILL WHITE, "International Bank Lending: A Guided Tour Through the Data," *Quarterly Review*, Federal Reserve Bank of New York, Vol. 3, No. 2, Autumn 1978, pp. 39–46.

# 10
# CHAPTER

# The Market Structure of the Commercial Banking Industry

Although the banking system in the United States consists of more than 14,700 separate commercial banks, such large numbers are not, in and of themselves, enough to guarantee aggressive competition in the industry. The market in which most borrowers find themselves is a local lending market, particularly if the would-be borrower is an individual or a small business firm. The number of alternative sources of funds in a particular lending market rather than the total number of banks in the country is the important factor.

Furthermore, banks compete not only with one another; they also compete with other financial institutions as well. The competition among different types of financial institutions takes the form of efforts to attract depositors, who lend funds to the bank or other financial institution, as well as attracting would-be borrowers. In this interinstitutional competition, commercial banks are somewhat hampered by various regulations unlike those applying to their competitors. Different rules of the game are partly responsible for the slower rate of growth of commercial banks in the postwar period as compared with other financial institutions such as savings and loan associations and life insurance companies.

After the **Depository Institutions Deregulation Act of 1980** was passed, thrift institutions were given a greater opportunity to compete with commercial banks. They were permitted to offer transactions accounts on which they could pay interest (NOW accounts) and were also permitted more freedom to make consumer installment loans. In addition, they were required to have reserves behind their transactions accounts. Commercial banks also were given greater regulatory freedom to compete with one another and with thrift institutions, but they were not permitted to branch across interstate lines.

Individual banks have also been slowed in their efforts to grow by antitrust suits beginning in February 1961. Before then many banks had believed that they were not restricted in their desire to merge with other banks by the Sherman Act of 1890 and the Clayton Act of 1914. The office of the attorney general believed otherwise, however, and the Supreme Court upheld the government's contention in two important leading cases, one decided in April 1963 and the other in June 1964. Since then banks, particularly large banks, have been forced to curb their urge to merge. After the 1970 Phillipsburg case, even smaller banks were forced to reconsider any merger plans. Banks of all sizes can still expand through securing more business. In states that permit branching, large branch banks have continued to establish new offices in rapidly growing areas to attract more business.

## RESTRICTED BANK ENTRY

Throughout American banking history several different points of view have been enacted into legislation regarding the question of freedom of entry into the banking industry. Prior to 1838, as indicated earlier, a special act of Congress, or more usually of one of the state legislatures, was needed to secure a bank charter. After the legislature of New York enacted the free banking law of 1838, the other states quickly followed suit and it became relatively easy to secure a bank charter. Critics of this legal approach to banking usually ascribe the early evils of wildcat banking and later excesses of overbanking to this permissive approach to entry into banking.

The widespread bank failures of the 1920s and early 1930s led to a sharp change in attitude toward easy entry into banking and also resulted in restraints on bank competition. Congress apparently concluded that one of the principal underlying reasons for the financial collapse of 1929–1933 was excessive competition in banking. The Banking Acts of 1933 and 1935 therefore severely limited the degree of competition permitted banks. Consequently, entry into banking was made more difficult.

In addition to the limitations imposed by Congress on bank entry and other forms of bank competition, the various federal and state regulatory agencies adopted a sterner approach toward the granting of new bank charters. In some cases this attitude was justified on grounds of protecting the profits of existing banks. Wherever banking authorities took this approach, very few new charters were granted to would-be bankers. It is almost always possible to demonstrate that a new bank will take away some business and deposits from existing banks in a given territory and thereby adversely affect their profits. Public hearings are usually held before new bank charters are granted, either by state or federal authorities, and certainly before admission to the Federal Deposit Insurance Corporation. Existing banks are thus given ample opportunity to protest that a new bank may reduce their profits, perhaps even to the point of bankruptcy. This is certainly a factor restricting the number of new banks organized in some areas.

## COMPETITION BY THE NUMBERS

Most of the 14,700 commercial banks in the country are independent unit banks, largely because various important states such as Minnesota and Texas prohibit branching, and a number of other states permit branching only on a limited basis. Although the number of independent banks seems sufficient to ensure a great deal of competition, the total number of banks in the postwar period was slowly eroded until 1962. In the decade of the 1950s alone, some 5 percent of the number of banks was reduced, mostly as a result of merger activity by large banks. Antitrust suits by the government in the 1960s slowed the merger movement, but the number of new banks organized still increased considerably over the decade. In the 1970s more than 1,000 commercial banks were added to the total. Furthermore, these banks had nearly 40,000 branches with more than 2,000 branches added in 1979 alone.

### Bank Mergers and Bank Size

This increase in the total number of banks and branches occurred despite a number of mergers involving large banks in the 1950s and smaller banks in the 1960s and 1970s. Even with the importance and significance of this **bank merger** movement, there still remained a large number of small banks throughout the country. By 1979, there were still some 3,251 banks with less than $10 million in total assets and an additional 9,895 banks with assets ranging from $10 million to $100 million.

Nevertheless, there is a great deal of concentration of assets in the banking industry. The 186 largest banks with assets of $1 billion or more control some 60 percent of all bank assets. The medium-sized banks under them with $100 million to $1 billion in assets total only 1,406 banks and have about 20 percent of all bank assets.

## Bank Concentration Varies from State to State

As noted in the previous chapter, some states permit statewide branching, some permit branching within a limited geographic area, and still others prohibit branching. These varied laws result in different **bank concentration** ratios in various banking markets. States between the east coast and the Mississippi River generally permit limited branching, those between the Mississippi and the Far West states generally prohibit branching, and those in the Far West permit statewide branching. As might be expected, there is more concentration in states with statewide branching than in the other states.

For example, in 1975 the three largest banks in Hawaii had 77 percent of total bank deposits, the three largest in Nevada had 83 percent, the three largest in Arizona had 86 percent, and the three largest in California had 62 percent. By way of contrast (even including bank holding companies as well as banks) in states with limited branching in 1975, the three largest banks in Michigan had 34 percent of total bank deposits, in Wisconsin 28 percent, and in Massachusetts 46 percent. Where branch banking was prohibited in 1975 and multibank holding companies were not active, the three largest banks in Nebraska had only 20 percent of bank deposits in the state, in Oklahoma only 21 percent, and in Illinois 37 percent.

Of course in states prohibiting branching but where multibank holding companies are active, the concentration percentages are higher. In 1975, the three largest bank groups had 52 percent of bank deposits in Minnesota, 46 percent in Montana, and 41 percent in Colorado. Clearly, differing state legislation does make a difference in the degree of bank concentration in the various states.

Other factors are at work, however, as well as differing state legislation. High or low growth in state population, for instance, can result in changed banking concentration. In general, over a fifteen-year period from 1960 through 1975, states with a high deposit concentration in 1960 had a lower degree of concentration fifteen years later and vice versa. Furthermore, states with slower population growth experienced an increase in deposit concentration, while states like Arizona and California with rapid population growth experienced a decrease in deposit concentration.

Finally, since 1965 a number of states have liberalized their laws with respect to bank branching. This, in turn, might be expected to result in some increase in bank concentration in such states. For example, Arkansas, Florida, Iowa, and Virginia, which formerly prohibited any branching, now permit limited branching.

Maine, New Jersey, New York, and South Dakota now permit statewide branching. Ohio, formerly a limited branching state, passed a law in the late 1970s that would provide for statewide branching ten years after the law was passed. Illinois, formerly a unit branching state, now permits banks to establish two walk-up, drive-up facilities within 3,500 yards of the main office. Pennsylvania has liberalized its banking law. Other states are reviewing their branching laws with a view to making them less restrictive.

***Bank Concentration in Various Cities***   In some cities there is a large disparity among the bank deposits of different banks. In the 1980s the two largest Chicago banks held about 42 percent of deposits in that urban area. The two largest banks in Dallas, however, accounted for about 64 percent of the city's total bank deposits. The two big banks in Philadelphia had 36 percent of total deposits, whereas in Boston the two largest banks held approximately 52 percent of total deposits. In New York City the two largest banks also held about 52 percent of that city's bank deposits.

The two largest banks in San Francisco had 65 percent of total deposits, whereas in Seattle the two largest banks held nearly 60 percent of deposits. At the same time, a number of small banks exist side by side with the few large banks in each of the cities cited. The banking industry apparently tolerates a good deal of diversity in operating size. Nevertheless, the dominant position of a few large banks in many of the nation's largest cities is mute testimony to the importance of past bank mergers, as well as the growth of large banks. There was, however, no greater concentration in the banking industry in the 1960s and 1970s, in contrast to the increased concentration during the 1950s. The continuance of the merger movement among small banks was offset by the greater numbers of newly organized banks.

## Economies of Scale

The lure of greater earnings through greater size had been an important expectation leading to a number of bank mergers. The **economies of scale** (i.e., lower unit costs as a result of expanding production) are a familiar characteristic of most manufacturing industries in the United States. The banking industry also appears to have economies of scale. Several important studies of bank costs and bank earnings in recent years clearly show economies of scale for increase in the size of banks.

George Bentson studied variation in costs by size of eighty to eighty-three member banks in the Federal Reserve Bank of Boston district for three years, 1959–1961. Costs ranged from $3.4 million to $55 million. F. W. Bell and N. B. Murphy extended the study to larger banks ($2.8 to $801 million), to other Federal Reserve districts (New York and Philadelphia as well as Boston), and to the later years of 1963–1965. Both studies find consistent and significant economies of scale (elasticities of cost under 1.0) for all size of banks studied. In general, there was an elasticity of cost of 0.93 for the average operating costs of these banks. That means that an increase in output of 10 percent, say, in number of loans serviced, would mean an increase in costs of 9.3 percent. These studies, unlike some other studies that measure output in dollar amounts of deposits or dollar amounts of numbers, measured output in terms of number of deposit and loan accounts.

A study of profitability of all insured commercial banks in the United States in the twenty-one-year period from 1954 to 1974 inclusive was one by Edward Gallick of the Federal Reserve Bank of Kansas City. Gallick, like Bentson, found a positive association between bank size and bank profitability. The smallest banks, those with deposits of less than $5 million, had an average rate of return on capital of only 11.43 percent, which was the lowest ratio of any bank size group. As the size of the bank increased, so too did profitability, so that banks with deposits of more than $100 million had the highest average pretax rate of return of 15.71 percent.

Another study focusing only on economies of scale associated with a rise in the number of demand deposit accounts involved a cross section of 967 banks, which participated in the Federal Reserve's functional cost analysis in 1968. This study by D. Daniel, W. Longbrake, and N. Murphy attributed most of the economies of scale to the use of computers by larger banks. Small banks that used computers had higher costs than similar-sized banks that did not use computers. Banks that had computers for less than one year had higher costs than banks that had had computers for longer than one year. Finally, the authors noted that once a bank had attracted more than 10,000 demand deposit accounts the use of computers led to a substantial decrease in average per unit costs.

**Automation and Lower Bank Costs**    Reasons for increased efficiency as bank size increases are thus not too difficult to find. A 1964 study of the Federal Reserve Bank of Chicago emphasized the impact of automation over a period of time in reducing wage and salary cost. By 1962 the percentage of total expenses for Chicago district banks attributable to wages and salaries had declined to 34 percent from the 1952 figure of 49 percent. The introduction of expensive machinery for accounting duties is particularly attractive for larger banks. The Bell and Murphy study likewise found that economies of scale arise from the use of lower skilled labor, fewer processing and administrative officers, and shifts of technology available from larger-scale operations. In addition, administrative costs per dollar of a loan decline sharply with increasing size of the loan. Larger banks as a group tend to make larger loans than do smaller banks. The larger size of loan possible was advanced publicly as an important factor in a number of bank mergers in the 1960s and 1970s.

## The Bank Merger Act of 1960

The possibility of excessive concentration within the banking industry as a result of a wave of bank mergers in the 1950s, designed perhaps at least in part to achieve economies of scale, led Congress to pass the Bank Merger Act of 1960. This law gave regulatory power to approve the merger, consolidation, acquisition of assets, or assumption of liabilities of one insured bank with or by another such bank to the Comptroller of the Currency, the Board of Governors of the Federal Reserve System, or the Federal Deposit Insurance Corporation. The appropriate agency depended on whether the resulting, acquiring, or assuming bank was to be a national bank, a state member bank, or a nonmember insured bank. The law required that the specific action agency involved should also request from the two other agencies and from the Attorney General advisory reports on the competitive factors in the case. As it turned out, this particular provision of the law unleashed a veritable Pandora's box of troubles involving differing interpretations of competitive factors by these different parts of the federal government.

After 1960 there was a number of highly significant bank merger cases where the relevant action agency gave approval to the proposed merger, even though one or more of the other agencies did not approve of the merger. This clash of different policy interpretations might have come to naught, except that the Attorney General had recourse to the courts in a number of bank merger cases where he believed that bank competition would be significantly reduced. The Antitrust Division under the Attorney General met with considerable success in the courts. The government argued in 1961 in different cases that both the Sherman and Clayton Acts applied to possible bank mergers. In leading cases in 1963 and 1964, the Supreme Court upheld these contentions of the government.

# THE BANKING INDUSTRY AND BANKING MARKETS

At issue in these suits involving two Philadelphia banks (1963) and two banks in Lexington, Kentucky (1964) were a number of important legal and economic principles. For many years a number of lawyers and bankers had believed that banks were immune to prosecution under the Sherman and Clayton Acts. The Supreme Court in its 1963 and 1964 decisions completely laid this belief to rest and ruled that unless Congress granted a specific exemption, banks were covered by the acts. Also, in the first of these cases, the Supreme Court accepted the government's definition of the relevant banking market. The District Court had earlier indicated that banking was a "line of commerce."

## *The 1963 Philadelphia Bank Case*

The government had gone to court in February 1961 to try to prevent the proposed merger of two Philadelphia banks. On June 17, 1963, the Supreme Court ruled in favor of the government. In its decision the Supreme Court enjoined the proposed merger of the Philadelphia National Bank (the second largest commercial bank in Philadelphia) and the Girard Trust Corn Exchange Bank (the third largest bank in Philadelphia) under Section 7 of the Clayton Act on the grounds that this merger would "result in a significant increase in the concentration of firms in that market" and thereby lessen competition.

When the Justice Department initiated the suit against the Philadelphia banks, it alleged that the proposed merger would violate both the Sherman and the Clayton acts by unduly restraining competition and tending toward monopoly. Even though the Comptroller of the Currency had approved the proposed merger under the 1960 Bank Merger Amendment to the Federal Deposit Insurance Act, the government filed a civil suit in February 1961 to prevent the proposed merger.

The government contended that the proposed combine would hold 35 percent of the commercial banking assets and 42 percent of the commercial and industrial loan assets in the Philadelphia area. The Philadelphia National and Girard Trust would jointly be 50 percent larger than the previous leader, the First Pennsylvania Banking and Trust Company. With total resources of $1.8 billion, the consolidated bank would have been the sixteenth largest in the country.

It was believed that both the Board of Governors of the Federal Reserve System and the Federal Deposit Insurance Corporation had recommended against approving the merger. Because one of the two banks proposing to merge was a national bank, the final decision was up to the Comptroller of the Currency. The Bank Merger Act of 1960, however, also required a study of the competitive factors involved by the office of the Attorney General. This latter government agency in this case had decided to invoke provisions of the Sherman and Clayton Antitrust Acts.

***Banking as a Line of Commerce***    When the case was first tried before a District Court in Philadelphia in 1962, the government argued that commercial banking constituted a major line of commerce, so that mergers in this industry should be treated in the same way that industrial and commercial mergers had been considered under Section 7 of the Clayton Act. Furthermore, the government argued that the relevant market in which the effect of banking concentration should be considered, if the proposed merger took place, should be a four-county Philadelphia metropolitan area.

Both of these concepts advanced by the government were challenged by the merging banks, who argued (and the district judge agreed) that the market should be defined as an eight-county metropolitan area, including three New Jersey counties. The Philadelphia banks also argued, contrary to the government's position, that commercial banking should not be treated as a relevant line of commerce. The defendant banks believed that banking was more complex than a single industry with a single definable market. They believed instead that there were a number of separate financial markets, each with different degrees of competition, in which all commercial banks are involved.

The defendant banks held that commercial banking had two main subdivisions, the securing of deposits and the granting of loans, and that each of these subdivisions could be further divided into various types of deposits and loans. For each type of loan or deposit, the banks argued that there were different customers, different types of competitors, different geographic areas, and therefore different degrees of competition. With this line of argument, specific inclusion could be made of nonbank competitors, such as life insurance companies and savings and loan associations. The District Court did not accept this line of argument but ruled instead that commercial banking was the relevant line of commerce. Inasmuch as the District Court upheld the banks' contention that their merger did not violate the provisions of the Clayton Act, the banks did not continue this line of reasoning when their case was argued before the Supreme Court.

***The Four-County Banking Market***    The Supreme Court followed the District Court in holding that commercial banking was the relevant line of commerce, but it rejected the District Court's opinion that an eight-county market was the relevant one. Instead the Supreme Court accepted the government's position that the four-county market was the proper one to consider in this case, because under Pennsylvania law banks can establish branches only in counties contiguous to the county in which the bank's home office is established. Thus for the two merging banks a four-county market was the only one in which they could establish branches. It was the four-county market, therefore, to which statistical measures of concentration were applied.

*The 30 Percent Rule*    The Supreme Court in its decision set 30 percent as the critical figure for undue concentration in a given banking market. It said in the Philadelphia case: "Without attempting to specify the smallest market share which would still be considered to threaten undue concentration, we are clear that 30 per cent presents that threat." The merging Philadelphia banks would have had 36 percent of the deposits in the four-county metropolitan area.

No questions of public interest in a broad sense were admissible but only the narrow issue of the probable effect of the merger on a lessening of competition in the defined banking market. (This meant, for example, that possible economies of scale resulting from the merger would not be considered by the Court.) When the Supreme Court in 1963 enjoined this proposed merger, it firmly laid to rest the contentions of some that commercial banks were not even subject to the provisions of the Clayton Act. However, this decision in 1963 and the similar Supreme Court decision in 1964 led directly to Congress passing the Bank Merger Act of 1966.

## The Lexington Bank Case

In an important 1964 antitrust decision involving commercial banks, the Supreme Court invoked the Sherman Act, rather than the Clayton Act as it had in the case of the two Philadelphia banks. This was another suit instituted originally by the Attorney General in February 1961. On April 6, 1964, the Supreme Court voided the merger of two Lexington, Kentucky, banks under Article I of the Sherman Act. The merger involved the First National Bank and Trust Company, Lexington, Kentucky, with the Security Trust Company, the first and fourth largest banks in Lexington.

The Supreme Court decided that significant competition would be eliminated by the merger and that this would constitute an unreasonable restraint of trade forbidden by the Sherman Act. To make it crystal-clear that commercial banks would be treated in the same manner as other business firms, the Supreme Court offered as authority for its decision four railroad cases decided earlier by the Court in which mergers were involved. In these cases the substantial competition previously existing between the railroads came to an end when the merger occurred. Therefore the Court asserted that when merging companies are major competitive factors in a relevant market, the elimination of such competition by merger in itself constitutes a violation of Article I of the Sherman Act.

## THE BANK MERGER ACT OF 1966

An important bank merger case in 1965 had led to the passage of the Bank Merger Act of 1966. In September 1961, the Federal Reserve Board had approved the merger of Manufacturers Trust Company and the Hanover Bank, both of New York City. The Attorney General's office, however, subsequently challenged the legality of this merger after it had won the Philadelphia and Lexington Bank cases. On March 10, 1965, the Federal District Court of New York ruled in the government's favor, even though the assets and managements of the two banks had already been commingled for some time.

This favorable decision for the government was appealed to Congress. Legislation was introduced in Congress that would force the government to drop further prosecution not only of Manufacturers-Hanover but of two other bank merger cases as well. This legislation was enacted into law in February 1966 as the Bank Merger Act of 1966. It was hoped that all regulatory government agencies would henceforth examine similar competitive factors, though there was considerable vague language in the act.

Several things were clear, however, in the 1966 act. First, Manufacturers-Hanover and two other bank merger cases were to have no further prosecution. Second, the Justice Department was to have only thirty days to challenge in the courts any favorable rulings on proposed mergers handed down by the Comptroller of the Currency, the Federal Reserve Board, or the Federal Deposit Insurance Corporation. Third, all the regulatory agencies and the courts were supposed to apply common standards whereby any proposed merger that would "substantially lessen competition" would be prevented unless outweighed by other considerations. The vagueness of the law is apparent in this phraseology.

Although the Bank Merger Act of 1966 was supposed to end conflicting standards in bank merger cases, it still remained for the Supreme Court to clarify the ruling legal principles. The high court had clarified the application of the law to large banks in its 1963 and 1964 decisions, and it would now have to establish the legal ground rules for mergers of small banks.

### The 1970 Phillipsburg Bank Case

The Supreme Court finally turned its attention on June 29, 1970, to the problem of mergers of small banks in a ruling barring the proposed merger of two small banks in Phillipsburg, New Jersey. Although the Comptroller of the Currency had approved the proposed merger in 1967, the Justice Department brought suit under the Bank Merger Act of 1966 by charging that the proposed bank merger would violate the Clayton Act. When a Federal District Court in New Jersey dismissed the case, the government appealed to the Supreme Court.

As in the Philadelphia bank case, the proper size of the banking market was an important issue. The Justice Department argued that the proper market for measuring concentration was the Phillipsburg, New Jersey–Easton, Pennsylvania area, because Easton is just across the Delaware River from Phillipsburg. These two communities have a total of seven commercial banks. The merged bank would have been the second largest bank in the combined area with assets of $41 million, or 19 percent of total commercial bank deposits in the combined area. The Comptroller of the Currency took the whole Lehigh Valley area as the proper market area. In this area there are more than thirty commercial banks, plus thirteen savings and loan associations and thirty-four finance companies. Hence the comptroller argued that the merger would not substantially lessen competition. The Federal District Court picked still a different market area, which covered Phillipsburg, Easton, and Bethlehem, Pennsylvania, and contained eighteen banks.

In its 1970 ruling in favor of the government, the Supreme Court noted that the merged bank would have 19 percent of the total assets of all banks in the two-city area. This percentage was termed unduly high, because the merged bank would control "an undue percentage share of the market." This was essentially the same standard applied earlier to big bank mergers, though the earlier 30 percent share of the market standard had now been abandoned. The Phillipsburg case is important for possible commercial bank mergers, because some 85 percent of the nation's banks have deposits of less than $25 million. Prior to this 1970 decision, it seemed possible that the Clayton and Sherman acts might not be invoked against bank mergers between small banks. As a result of this key decision, it became clear that all commercial banks were covered by the antitrust laws. Still greater difficulties were thus interposed in cases of contemplated merger between two commercial banks.

## The 1974 Connecticut National Bank Case and the Monetary Control Act of 1980

In a 1974 ruling on a proposed merger involving the Connecticut National Bank, the Supreme Court noted that savings banks were "fierce competitors" of commercial banks in certain markets. Nevertheless, the "line of commerce" definition of commercial banking first enunciated in the 1963 Philadelphia bank case was retained. However, in this case the Court emphasized bank competition for commercial business.

On these grounds, even after the passage of the Monetary Control Act of 1980, thrifts would be excluded from the Federal Reserve's competitive analysis of mergers and acquisitions. Although all depository institutions may offer NOW accounts, they are not available to commercial and business enterprises. Of course, if thrift institutions were considered direct competitors of commercial banks, concentration ratios applied to a possible merger or acquisition would be diluted. This would make possible more mergers, even under current standards. On the other hand, concentration analysis could be applied only to banks except in cases where thrifts are seen as "significant competitors." This still seems to be the attitude of bank regulatory authorities, despite the passage of the Monetary Control Act of 1980.

## Bank Mergers in the Late 1970s

Despite legal impediments to unrestrained bank mergers in the 1960s and 1970s, such mergers, especially those involving smaller banks, did continue each year. By the late 1970s, considerable activity was occurring in bank mergers. In 1975, sixty-seven operating banks were absorbed in mergers approved by federal bank supervisory agencies. In 1976 there were eighty-one such approved mergers. Some seventy-two merger proposals were approved by the FDIC in 1977 and seventy in 1978. The number of bank mergers approved by the FDIC, however, dropped to fifty-three in 1979.

In general, the number of bank mergers in the late 1970s was somewhat greater than the number in the early 1970s. They were also higher than the typical number of mergers in the 1960s, although 1965 had fifty mergers and 1968 had fifty-four mergers. Despite the strong bank merger movement in the 1970s, the number of operating banks actually rose by more than 1,000 as new national and state banks were being chartered in each year of that decade.

Over the two decades from 1960 to 1979 inclusive, there were some 3,840 mergers and acquisitions in the banking industry. Almost half of these mergers occurred in only seven states: Florida, New Jersey, New York, Ohio, Pennsylvania, Texas, and Virginia.

## Concentration of Banking Assets by the 1980s

By the end of the 1970s and in the early years of the 1980s there was considerable evidence that a substantial amount of concentration of bank assets had occurred through rapid growth of large banking organizations despite the difficulties of bank mergers. In 1976, eighteen banks with assets of $5 billion or more had total assets of $264.4 billion, or 25 percent of total bank assets. Such very large banks had nearly doubled in numbers in only three years from 1976 to 1979. The thirty-three such large banks in 1979 had $724 billion in bank assets, or 41 percent of total bank assets.

Expanding the number of banks considered to include all commercial banks with assets of $50 million or more gives us a total of 3,364 such banks in 1979. This was only 22 percent of total banks in that year, but these banks held about 87 percent of total bank assets. There must be considerable advantages in the banking industry for such larger-size banks or they would not account for such a sizable amount of bank assets. Furthermore, if there were not such size advantages, such large banks would not still be growing in number and size.

It is thus not surprising that banks attempt to grow still larger through mergers and by consolidations into regional bank holding companies as well as by expanding their amount of bank business. By the 1980s, more than two thirds of all deposits and 70 percent of all banking assets were accounted for by banks belonging to holding companies. The largest bank holding company, which is the ninth largest banking company in the United States, continued to be First Interstate Corporation, formerly Western Bancorporation, which in 1981 changed the name of all its member banks to First Interstate Bank of Arizona, or whatever state in which they are located. First Interstate had twenty-two banks in eleven Western states with more than $30 billion in assets in the early 1980s.

Like the six smaller multistate bank holding companies, First Interstate had a "grandfather" status when the 1956 Bank Holding Company Act, discussed later, blocked further interstate bank holding companies. In order to take advantage of its large size (i.e., to secure various economies of scale), First Interstate in the early 1980s achieved tighter control over the individual banks in its "family." In 1982, First Interstate pioneered in granting First Interstate franchises to certain independent banks.

A systemwide data network via satellite, a common bank card, and an interstate network of teller machines made the more than 870 banking offices of First Interstate more integrated parts of one giant bank. Individual banks were assigned given companies and even given industries, such as the Oregon bank dealing with forest products and the California bank with energy companies. Loan sharing arrangements were developed between the component banks through a clearing house at First Interstate's headquarters. Foreign corporate lending was also handled by one banking group.

All of this coordination of lending and investing efforts, as well as more sophisticated management to deal with a large banking system, resulted in profit rates, whether measured on assets or equity, among the top five banking organizations in the United States. Economies of scale thus clearly resulted in greater profits.

An even greater degree of bank consolidation could still take place because of the great cost advantages of greater size. More expensive and complicated electronic technology applied to banking has made such greater concentration more likely, whereas bank regulators increasingly have looked to the test of public benefit in deciding on proposed bank mergers or acquisition of banks by bank holding companies. If federal legislation were enacted approving branching across state lines, a further impetus to the growth of large banks would be provided.

The size of many existing bank holding companies continued to increase in the 1970s and new bank holding companies were also being formed. After 1970, the newer one-bank holding companies, as well as the older multiple-bank holding companies, were being regulated by the Federal Reserve Board. Altogether 3,644 bank holding companies were registered with the Federal Reserve Board at the end of 1981.

## Advantages of Regional Holding Companies

Group or holding company banking seemed to offer not only most of the advantages of branch banking but also several unique features. In general, group banking thrived in states in which branch banking was forbidden by state law or restricted geographically. Even in states in which branch banking was permitted, the holding company could expand across state lines, which was not permitted to the branch bank. Bank holding companies can thus obtain geographic diversification both within states and across state lines. Such holding companies can also enter closely related areas such as factoring, consumer finance, mortgage banking, and investment banking. Although these activities are permitted for banks, they may often be conducted more easily as subsidiaries of a holding company. Unlike commercial banks, holding companies can issue commercial paper. This can be an important source of added bank funds, especially in credit restraint periods such as 1969, 1973, 1981 and 1982.

Furthermore, group banking gives all the appearance of home rule in ownership for local banks, even when the facts of ownership and control are quite different. In group banking the affiliated banks retain their individual corporate existence while reaping many of the benefits of multiple-location banking. From the viewpoint of the local community, the head of the local banking office remains a bank president rather than becoming a branch manager, as is true under branch banking. The familiar name of the local bank is also retained and is not replaced by the name of a city bank in a metropolis some miles distant.

Other advantages of group banking, under the legal form of a holding company, are many of the same ones attributed to branch banking. The common ownership under a unified direction makes possible the mobilization of lending resources and technical management talents that would not otherwise be available. Loans and investments for the entire group of banks can be better diversified, thus retaining safety. In addition, funds can be more fully employed in the most profitable manner (meaning largely loans rather than investments), so that the total group can attain a higher rate of profits than would be possible by each bank acting separately. Part of this greater focus on more profitable loans may be achieved through the employment of management specialists in particular economic areas of activity. For example, the large holding company groups in the Far West have been able to staff their constituent banks with officers and specialists equipped to serve local agricultural needs, which are undergoing rapid technological change and require outside capital to help secure the needed new capital goods.

## BANK HOLDING COMPANIES MAY PROMOTE COMPETITION

Increased competition with the large money center banks in New York City and Chicago has also come about as a result of the sharp growth of a number of regional banks, often as a result of the use of the holding company device. For example, the Commerce Trust Company of Kansas City, Missouri, formed a holding company (Commerce Bancshares, Inc.) in 1967, which in five years acquired twenty-one banks and a mortgage company. As a result, the legal lending limit (calculated as 10 percent of capital surplus, undivided profits, and valuation reserves) climbed from $6 million to more than $11 million. United Jersey Banks, incorporated in October 1970, likewise grew rapidly in its first two years as it acquired fifteen banks and raised its loan limit from $4.5 million to $11.4 million. Even older bank holding companies, such as BancOhio Corporation founded in 1929, have sharply stepped up their acquisition rate of banks in recent years and thereby increased their assets and legal lending limit. In 1970, BancOhio Corporation acquired four banks, added two more in 1971, and four more in 1972. From the end of 1966 to the end of 1972, assets doubled, from $1.11 billion to $2.36 billion.

The rapid growth of these and other regional banks by the aggressive use of the holding company device, along with the credit restraint periods of 1966, 1969, 1973, and 1981 and 1982, which forced large industrial companies to search for more loanable funds outside their normal sources at New York and Chicago banks, means that many regional banks are now making larger business loans than they once did. Hence from the end of 1966 to the end of 1972, loans of member banks of the Federal Reserve System outside New York City and Chicago grew by 76 percent, as compared with a growth of 59 percent at New York and Chicago banks. Deposits likewise grew by 56 percent at these regional banks in this period, as compared with a deposit growth of only 43 percent in New York and Chicago. The rapid growth of bank holding companies earlier in the 1950s, however, had led Congress to pass the Holding Company Act of 1956.

## The Holding Company Act of 1956

The Banking Act of 1933 had separated member banks of the Federal Reserve System from securities companies and provided for limited regulation by the Board of Governors of holding company affiliates of member banks. This regulation, however, proved to be inadequate, because the expansion of bank holding companies in the banking field and their interests in nonbanking businesses were not adequately regulated. The expanding activities of bank holding companies in the 1950s finally led Congress to give control over the expansion of holding company banking to the Board of Governors of the Federal Reserve System. This new regulatory power was contained in the Holding Company Act of 1956.

***Registered Bank Holding Companies***    The act required bank holding companies to register with the board and defined a holding company as a corporation that "directly or indirectly owns 25 per cent or more of the voting shares of each of two or more banks," so that one-bank holding companies were specifically excluded from the coverage of the act. Approximately 1,450 one-banking holding companies later filed registration with the Federal Reserve System in compliance with the Bank

Holding Company Amendments of 1970. At the end of 1981, there were a total of some 3,644 bank holding companies.

*Acquisition of Added Banks*    The 1956 act had provided that holding companies had to secure board approval before acquiring 25 percent or more of the stock of additional banks. The formation of new holding companies likewise necessitated board approval. The act also specifically forbade bank holding companies from engaging in nonbanking businesses. Likewise, additional multistate bank holding companies could not be formed, though the seven then in existence were given "grandfather" status.

Section 3(c) of the 1956 Holding Company Act required the board to take into consideration five factors in ruling on the expansion of operations of holding companies through the acquisition of additional banks: (1) the financial history and condition of the holding company and bank concerned, (2) their prospects, (3) the character of their management, (4) the convenience, needs, and welfare of the communities and area concerned, and (5) whether or not the effect of the acquisition would expand the size or extent of the bank holding company system beyond limits consistent with adequate and sound banking, the public interest, and the preservation of competition in the field of banking. In applying these provisions of the act, the Federal Reserve Board approved a number of proposed acquisitions, while denying others.

**Greater Bank Regulation**    The significance of this act is that it placed another major form of corporate banking under specific regulatory control. The other major type of corporate banking, branch banking, had been under regulatory control of the various states from the beginning of its important growth after World War I. As indicated in the previous chapter, some states do not even permit branch banking, whereas other states permit branch banking only within certain limited geographical areas. Even where branch banking is permitted, specific approval of the supervisory authorities must be obtained before a new branch is established. Furthermore, no bank may establish a branch outside the state of its home office.

The prime objective of the 1956 law was to slow the unregulated growth of group banking through the holding company device. There were fears in some quarters that a continued lack of regulation of this form of banking might lead to a serious decrease in competition in the banking industry.

That this objective was not achieved can be seen by referring to Figure 10–1, which shows that the number of multibank holding companies more than doubled in the decade of the 1960s, with the rate of growth particularly rapid after 1965. In this same decade, the number of banks acquired by multibank holding companies increased by more than 400, which also represented a doubling of such banks acquired. Furthermore, the deposits of commercial banks affiliated with multibank holding companies grew three times faster than the deposits of all commercial banks in the 1960s. At the end of 1970, 121 multibank holding companies controlled 895 banks with one sixth of all bank deposits. As earlier noted, by the end of 1981 there were some 3,644 bank holding companies registered with the Federal Reserve Board. These bank holding companies had about three-fourths of the assets held by all commercial banks.

## Market Entry of Multibank Holding Companies

An expanding multibank holding company enters a new market in three ways: *de novo* entry, foothold entry through acquisition of a small bank, and acquisition of a relatively large bank, or a leading bank, in the market. Because of the possible anticompetitive effects involved in the acquisition of a leading bank, this method of entry into new markets has been greatly restricted by the regulatory authorities. Although favorable competitive effects may obtain if the bank holding company sets up a brand new bank (**de novo** entry), this type of entry is expensive, entails

**Figure 10–1    Growth of Multibank Holding Companies**

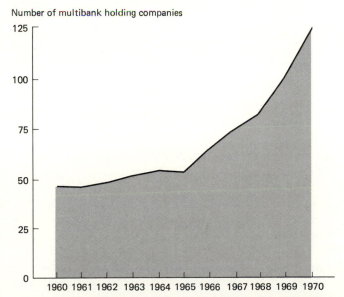

Number of multibank holding companies

SOURCE: Federal Reserve Bank of Philadelphia, *Business Review*, May 1972, p. 8.

considerable risk, and requires considerable time for the establishment of new customer relationships. Hence the predominant form of entry by bank holding companies is the foothold entry, wherein a small existing bank is acquired in the market.

When the bank holding company then uses its considerable management resources to strengthen the newly acquired bank, the result should be that the new affiliate becomes a stronger competitor and thus experiences a faster rate of growth of deposits and possibly an increase in its market share. However, no significant adverse competitive effects on independent banks have been uncovered in most research studies on this matter. In general, *no* significant positive relationship has been found between multiple-bank holding company affiliation and increases in local market concentration. At the same time, bank affiliates of bank holding companies offer a slightly wider range of services and increased consumer and business credit.

## One-Bank Holding Companies

After the mid-1960s, another serious threat to competition developed from the rapid growth of one-bank holding companies. By the end of 1964, forty-three of the nation's largest banks had formed one-bank holding companies. In the four years from January 1, 1965, to January 1, 1969, 239 one-bank holding companies operating 575 nonbank subsidiaries were formed. These new one-bank holding companies operated in thirty-one states and had over $15 billion in bank deposits. Furthermore, the one-bank holding company had moved into 119 different non-banking activities, including transportation, real estate, manufacturing, wholesale and retail sales, mining, petroleum, agriculture, and insurance.

By 1970, twenty-three of the fifty-one largest banks in the country were owned by one-bank holding companies. These banks included the six largest banks in the country, which hold more than one fifth of total bank deposits. There were then 1,116 one-bank holding companies, which controlled 32.6 percent of the deposits of all commercial banks in the United States. At the end of 1970, 162 one-bank holding companies controlled banks with deposits in excess of $100 million each. About 70 percent of these same one-bank holding companies were also engaged in activities not closely related to banking. By the end of 1977, 40 percent of banks owned by holding companies were owned by one-bank holding companies.

As a result of the rapid expansion of one-bank holding companies, the president, the Federal Reserve Board, and various congressional leaders proposed in 1969 and 1970 that such holding companies should be brought under the 1956 Bank Holding Company Act. Such an act was passed by Congress on December 31, 1970. The unregulated growth of such bank holding companies could lead, it was feared, to a greater concentration of economic power by a selective use of the extension of bank credit.

## The 1970 Amendments to the Bank Holding Company Act

As a result of the 1970 amendments to the Bank Holding Company Act of 1956, one-bank holding companies were to be treated in the same manner as multibank holding companies. A bank holding company was now defined as "any company which has control over any bank or over any company that is or becomes a bank holding company." That is, one-bank holding companies now had to register with the Federal Reserve System and submit their current or proposed nonbanking activities to the scrutiny of the Federal Reserve regulators. On September 1, 1971, the Federal Reserve Board delegated to the twelve Federal Reserve Banks certain authority to approve applications to form one-bank holding companies.

Permissible activities of bank holding companies must not only be closely related to banking, but these activities must also be in the public interest. This latter phrase sugggests that the board may see fit to restrict expansionary activities of bank holding companies if adverse effects on competition are expected, even though the activities may otherwise be permitted. Geographical restrictions on bank holding companies will probably be avoided, however, since expansion of bank holding companies into new geographical areas may tend to foster competition.

## Bank Holding Companies and Interstate Banking

The McFadden Act of 1927 expressly prohibits interstate banking and thereby created major barriers to entry in local banking markets by banks in other states. Loan production offices that do not accept deposits, however, do not violate the law. And what banks cannot do, bank holding companies often can. Furthermore, foreign banks can have offices in more than one state. About half of the 150 foreign banks in the United States do have offices in two or more states. The largest interstate presence of large banking organizations, however, is felt in the non-banking activities of bank holding companies.

Bank holding companies have acquired many of the largest mortgage banking firms in the country and a considerable number of consumer finance companies. Local market, consumer-oriented companies have been particular acquisition targets for a number of such bank holding companies. In the 1970s, more than 100 mortgage banks and over 500 consumer and commercial finance companies were acquired by bank holding companies.

These acquisitions and the establishment of loan production offices has given extensive national coverage to some of the large American banks. By the 1980s, the Bank of America had 350 offices in forty-one states; Citicorp had about 400 offices in thirty-eight states; and Manufacturers Hanover Trust Company had 190 offices in eighteen states. Many other bank holding companies had interstate offices, too, though fewer offices in a smaller number of states.

The International Banking Act of 1978 limited interstate expansion by foreign banks but directed the administration to study the McFadden Act, which prohibits such interstate expansion by American banks. Some observers believed that widespread interstate activities by bank holding companies and the directive to study possible interstate bank branching might lead to further legal liberalization. In fact, in January 1981, the outgoing Carter administration recommended gradual legislative moves permitting direct interstate branching by banks. In the event that Congress eventually accepts some of these recommendations, new competitors could enter a number of local banking markets now closed to interstate branching. At the same time, the large number of 14,700 commercial banks might be reduced through increased mergers across state lines.

## Small Banks and Interstate Banking

If interstate branch banking is permitted, it might be expected that some of the first impacts of such liberalized bank regulation would be felt by small banks (i.e., large banks might tend to acquire small banks across state lines). In 1980, profits grew faster at small banks than at large banks because rural loan demand was depressed by high rates of interest rates, so that small banks could lend substantial amounts of funds to large banks at high rates of interest. Their high profitability and the large number of small banks seems to make them likely targets for takeover efforts. Some 300 small banks were acquired or merged in 1980, a rise of 50 percent over 1979.

There are about 13,000 small banks, or banks with about $100 million in assets or less. Although they make up about 88 percent of all commercial banks in the United States, they hold just 21 percent, or $315.8 billion, of total bank deposits. In order to fend off possible acquisition efforts, many small banks are making increased efforts to become more efficient (e.g., dropping unprofitable accounts and imposing additional service fees) to remain profitably independent.

## Questions for Discussion

1. Why are there entry restrictions for the banking industry? Why have these been different for different periods of American history?
2. How many commercial banks are there now in the banking industry? How competitive are they with each other? Discuss the advantages and disadvantages of different size banks?
3. Discuss the Holding Company Act of 1956 and indicate its significance for commercial banking. Why did Congress amend this act to cover one-bank holding companies in 1970? What bank regulatory authority was given certain discretionary powers over holding companies in 1956? What are some of the factors taken into account by this authority before approving or disapproving proposed new bank acquisitions by holding companies?
4. Discuss the Bank Merger Act of 1960. Do you think that the division of authority among regulatory authorities for the approval or disapproval of a proposed bank merger is good or bad? Is any coordination needed among such authorities?
5. What were the reasons given by the government in the antimerger suits against commercial banks instituted beginning in February 1961? What were some of the arguments used by the merging banks in defense of their proposed mergers?
6. Discuss the important Supreme Court decisions of June 1963, April 1964, June 1970, and June 1974 as they relate to commercial banking. Why were these highly significant decisions? What may be the effect on the commercial banking industry of these decisions?
7. Discuss the difficult problem of defining a banking market. Do you think that nonbanking financial institutions as well as banks should be included in a banking market? What line of reasoning did the courts use in deciding that banking was a relevant line of commerce under the antitrust laws?
8. Discuss the bank merger movement in the 1960s, which resulted in the Bank Merger Act of 1966. What was the effect of this act in the 1970s on mergers in banking?
9. Discuss some of the major economic factors affecting the bank merger movement. Which of these factors do you think are the most important?
10. Discuss bank consolidations through multibank holding companies. To what extent may some of the advantages of bank mergers be achieved by bank holding companies?
11. Discuss the growth of one-bank holding companies after the mid-1960s and their subsequent regulation under the 1970 amendments to the 1956 Bank Holding Company Act.
12. What are the implications of the Monetary Control Act of 1980 for bank mergers and acquisitions?

13. Why is interstate bank branching still prohibited across state lines? If such prohibitions are relaxed, what do you believe will be some of the implications for the commercial banking industry?

# Selected Bibliography for Further Reading

## Monographs

ADVISORY COMMITTEE ON BANKING TO THE COMPTROLLER OF THE CURRENCY, *National Banks and the Future* (Washington, D.C.: U.S. Treasury Department, Comptroller of the Currency, 1962).

AMERICAN BANKERS ASSOCIATION, *The Commercial Banking Industry* (Englewood Cliffs, N.J.: Prentice-Hall, 1962).

BOARD OF GOVERNORS OF THE FEDERAL RESERVE SYSTEM, *Forty-Ninth Annual Report Covering Operations for the Year 1962* (Washington, D.C.: 1963).

FEDERAL DEPOSIT INSURANCE CORPORATION, *1979 Annual Report*, (Washington, D.C.: 1980).

FEDERAL RESERVE BANK OF CHICAGO, *Annual Proceedings of a Conference on Bank Structure and Competition* (Chicago: 1971, 1979, 1980).

ROSENBLUM, HARVEY, "Bank Holding Companies: An Overview," *Business Conditions*, Federal Reserve Bank of Chicago, Aug. 1973, pp. 3–13.

SELECTED AUTHORS, *Studies in Banking Competition and the Banking Structure* (Washington, D.C.: Articles reprinted from *The National Banking Review*, The Administrator of National Banks, United States Treasury, 1966).

## Articles

BENTSON, GEORGE J., "Economies of Scale of Financial Institutions," *Journal of Money, Credit and Banking*, Vol. IV, No. 2, May 1972, pp. 312–341.

BERKELEY, NORBORNE, Jr., "The Coming Consolidation of Banking," *Banking the Changing Order*, a special issue of *Executive* published by the Graduate School of Business, Cornell University, Winter 1977, pp. 33–34.

BOARD OF GOVERNORS OF THE FEDERAL RESERVE SYSTEM, "Recent Changes in the Structure of Commercial Banking," *Federal Reserve Bulletin*, March 1970, pp. 195–209.

DRUM, DALE S., "MBHCs: Evidence After Two Decades of Regulation," *Business Conditions*, Federal Reserve Bank of Chicago, Dec. 1976, pp. 3–15.

ERDEVIG, ELEANOR, "District Trends in Banking Concentration," *Economic Perspectives*, Federal Reserve Bank of Chicago, March–April 1981, Vol. V, Issue 2, pp. 6–12.

GALLICK, EDWARD C., "Bank Profitability and Bank Size," *Monthly Review*, Federal Reserve Bank of Kansas City, Jan. 1976, pp. 11–16.

GRUNEWALD, ALAN E., "The Economic Necessity for Interstate Banking," *Proceedings of a Conference on Bank Structure and Competition, May 3–4, 1979*, Federal Reserve Bank of Chicago, 1979, pp. 232–262.

KAUFMAN, GEORGE G., "Banking as a Line of Commerce: The Changing Competitive Environment," a series of occasional papers in draft form prepared by members of the Research Department, Federal Reserve Bank of Chicago, June 1981.

MULLER, RONALD, and ROBERT COHEN, "U.S. Banking and Economic Instability: A Systemic Dilemma," *Banking the Changing Order*, a special issue of *Executive* published by the Graduate School of Business, Cornell University, Winter 1977, pp. 37–44.

RHOADES, STEPHEN A., "The Competitive Effects of Interstate Banking," *Federal Reserve Bulletin* (Washington, D.C.: Board of Governors of the Federal Reserve System, Jan. 1980), pp. 1–8.

———, Federal Reserve Decisions on Bank Mergers and Acquisitions During the 1970s, Staff Studies of the Board of Governors of the Federal Reserve System (Washington, D.C.: Aug. 1981).

TREBING, MICHAEL E., "The New Bank-Thrift Competition: Will It Affect Bank Acquisition and Merger Analysis?" *Review*, Federal Reserve Bank of St. Louis, Feb. 1981, Vol. 63, No. 2, pp. 3–11.

> What is annually saved is as regularly consumed as what is annually
> spent, and nearly in the same time too; but it is consumed by a
> different set of people.
>
> THE WEALTH OF NATIONS

# 11
# CHAPTER

# Financial Intermediaries

The stage has been set for the decade of the 1980s to be a period of increased competition not only among banks, with the possibility of some increase in concentration, but also for increased competition between banks and thrift institutions. In short, there is likely to be increased competition among all kinds of **financial intermediaries.** Such increased competition is to be encouraged as a result of the passage of the Depository Institutions and Monetary Control Act of 1980, which has already been alluded to.

Under this act, after December 31, 1980, commercial banks and other financial institutions could pay interest on checking accounts **(NOW accounts).** Financial institutions other than commercial banks were also given greater freedom to acquire earning assets. What was not clear was whether commercial banks could acquire **thrift institutions** and whether commercial banks could have interstate branches. The outcome of this new competitive struggle was thus in doubt.

What was not in doubt was that all financial intermediaries would continue to grow in the 1980s, as they have in recent decades. Increasingly, savers turn to various institutional arrangements to channel their savings into productive investments. Which institutional arrangement will be favored depends importantly on interest rate differentials among the institutions, which had in earlier years often favored the growth of thrift institutions at the expense of commercial banks.

An intense interest of more and more individuals in their personal security and that of their dependents had also led to a rapid growth in pension funds and life insurance companies. Different rates of growth in the demand for credit, which in part tend to be supplied by financial institutions with different kinds of specialization, also affect the differential rates of growth of different financial intermediaries. If, for example, the demand for business credit, which impinges importantly on commercial banks, is high, such banks will "buy" deposits and reserves through the techniques of liability management and thus grow faster than they otherwise would.

All financial intermediaries perform an important middleman function as intermediaries between surplus and deficit spending units. They borrow from savers and lend to those who make real investments. As the financial intermediaries perform this function, they create money (transactions accounts or checking accounts) and other liquid assets called near-money. In short, they monetize credit by substituting their nonetary liabilities for monmonetary liabilities.

The six major types of financial intermediaries are (1) commercial banks, (2) savings and loan associations, (3) mutual savings banks, (4) credit unions, (5) life insurance companies, and (6) pension funds. Various of these intermediaries have been forced to specialize both by statute and by regulation, even though some of these regulations were eased after 1980. Commercial banks, as the department stores of finance, have the broadest range of latitude in employing the funds that they attract.

# THE DEPOSITORY INSTITUTIONS DEREGULATION ACT OF 1980

On March 31, 1980, Congress changed some of the fundamental ground rules under which financial intermediaries compete with one another. This was the first act providing for permanent nationwide authorization for depository institutions to offer interest-bearing transactions accounts (checking accounts) effective December 31, 1980. Other deposit offerings and service capabilities were also made possible. In addition to being able to offer NOW accounts (negotiable orders of withdrawal, or checking accounts with interest—originally set at 5¼ percent), banks were able to continue offering **automatic transfer services (ATS)** for shifting funds from savings to checking accounts. All federally chartered credit unions were now enabled to issue share drafts (in effect, checking accounts.) Savings and loan associations were authorized to establish remote service units (RSUs) to facilitate debits and credits to savings accounts, loan payments, and related transactions. **Deposit insurance** at federally insured banks, **savings and loan associations,** and **credit unions** was increased from $40,000 to $100,000.

Important new powers conferred on federally chartered savings and loan associations were (1) investment of up to 20 percent of their assets in consumer loans, commercial paper, and corporate debt securities, (2) investment in shares or certificates of open-end investment companies registered with the SEC and that restrict their portfolios to the same investment instruments that savings and loan associations are allowed to hold directly, (3) investment of up to 5 percent of their assets in loans for education and community development and unsecured construction loans, (4) issuance of credit cards and extension of credit in connection with credit cards, (5) provision of trust and fiduciary powers under restrictions and protections similar to those applicable to national banks, (6) inclusion of shares of open-end management investment companies among the assets eligible to satisfy liquidity requirements, (7) issuance of mutual capital certificates to be included as part of general reserves and net worth.

It is apparent that this broadening of lending functions for savings and loan institutions should reduce somewhat their former great specialization in mortgage lending and make them more nearly full-service financial institutions. This, in turn, should mean that they can compete even more effectively with commercial banks for both deposits and earning assets.

**Mutual savings banks,** likewise, were given greater latitude with respect to their loans and their acceptance of deposits. Savings banks with federal charters could now invest up to 5 percent of their total assets in commercial, corporate, and business loans within the home state of the bank or within seventy-five miles of the bank's home office. They were also allowed to accept **demand deposits** in connection with commercial, corporate, and business loan relationships.

## THE GROWTH OF BANKING AND NONBANKING FINANCIAL INTERMEDIARIES

In the years since World War II, nonbanking financial institutions have grown at a rapid rate—in some decades even faster than commercial banks. However, banks have sought out and received increasing amounts of savings and other time deposits in direct competition with these nonbanking financial institutions. The interest rates paid by commercial banks on time deposits as compared with the interest rates paid by savings and loan associations on their shares, or the yields on commercial paper issued by finance companies, have been important factors affecting the flows of funds to these various financial institutions.

In many respects, therefore, the liabilities of other financial institutions have come to be recognized as close substitutes for the liabilities of commercial banks, especially because financial institutions in all fifty states were able to have NOWs (interest-yielding checking accounts) after December 31, 1980. Furthermore, by the 1980s the time deposits of commercial banks were considerably greater in dollar amount than the demand deposits of these same commercial banks. Some forty years earlier, demand deposits of commercial banks were three times greater than their time deposits.

## Growing Intermediary Role of Commercial Banks

The growing intermediary role of commercial banks has made them appear to be more similar to other financial institutions than was earlier believed, whereas other financial institutions seem to be becoming somewhat more like commercial banks. Commercial banks, however, still furnish the bulk of increases in the money supply through the creation of added demand deposits. In 1981 these bank demand deposits were about 60 percent of the money supply M1, whereas transactions accounts of other financial institutions were less than 3 percent of the money supply. Some of these added demand deposits can be exchanged with the bank for added time deposits if the public's preference for various monetary assets and the interest rate structure encourage this exchange. The lending and investing activities of commercial banks might then result in the creation of more money (NOW accounts) and more near-money in the form of time deposits. Likewise, the lending and investing activities of other financial institutions can result in the creation of more near-money in the form of their liquid liabilities, such as shares in savings and loan associations.

## Liabilities of Financial Intermediaries

Banks, therefore, appear to be only one type of financial intermediary that borrows short and lends long. All financial intermediaries intervene between the final saver and the final investor by offering short-term liabilities and acquiring long-term assets. Those spending units that have a surplus of income over expenditures will desire to acquire various assets of value, including financial assets. Financial assets, unless they are the direct debt of deficit spending units, are largely the short-term **financial intermediaries.**

These liabilities of financial intermediaries are created to satisfy the portfolio preferences of the surplus spending units while the same financial intermediaries are acquiring earning assets in the form of debt of the deficit spending units. This changing of debt into credit is the major function of financial intermediaries. Even though total debt and total credit must be equal, the financial intermediaries are able to change the composition of each to conform with borrowing and lending preferences of the ultimate savers and the ultimate investors.

## The Function of Financial Intermediaries

In changing the composition of **debt-credit**, the financial intermediaries are able to reduce the risk accruing to the ultimate lender. The financial institution can do this through a diversification of assets and through expertise acquired by long experience in the financial markets. The assumption of some of the risk in lending on the part of the financial institution makes it possible for interest rates to be lower than they otherwise would be and for economic growth to be higher than it otherwise would be.

    The instruments issued by financial intermediaries can satisfy one or more of the qualities sought most by savers, such as safety of principal, liquidity, convenience, and accessibility in readily divisible denominations. The rise and diffusion of income in the period after World War II has created a large class of small savers. This type of saver has traditionally emphasized liquidity and safety of principal over immediate return or growth potential. Furthermore, the development of government insurance (both for commercial banks and savings and loan associations) and increased government supervision of financial intermediaries have made the liabilities of such institutions even more liquid and safe. Such liabilities intended for the small saver are almost all of a fixed face value. That is, they do not fluctuate with changes in the price level.

### Financial Intermediaries Specialize in Their Assets and Liabilities
These financial intermediaries, however, differ among themselves in the type of liabilities they offer to the public and the type of earning asset that they specialize in acquiring. Commercial banks, for example, are especially important in being able to create demand liabilities, which are the largest part of the means of payment, or money supply, though mutual savings banks now furnish a small amount of demand deposits, and other financial institutions (e.g., savings and loan associations) have a certain amount of transactions or NOW accounts.

    Life insurance companies, on the other hand, supply a different financial service to the public. This involves assuming certain risks of mortality, while still permitting the public the accumulation of certain assets of value in the form of cash reserves. Savings and loan associations create savings and loan deposits, which are still a different type of financial asset preferred in certain individual portfolios. Financial intermediaries thus appear to differ from one another in degree rather than kind.

# GROWTH OF FINANCIAL INTERMEDIARIES

Financial intermediaries have grown rapidly in the postwar period at the same time that debt of all kinds has been increasing considerably. In fact, much of the increase in debt by deficit spending units has been made possible by the growth of these intermediary financial institutions. Growth in total assets of the major types of financial intermediaries in the three decades from 1950 to the end of 1979 can be seen in Table 11–1.

All financial intermediaries grew at a rapid rate in these three decades with the assets of all intermediaries rising each decade from 100 to 150 percent. Some intermediaries, such as credit unions, private pension funds, state and local pension funds, and finance companies had extremely high rates of growth throughout these three decades. It should be noted, however, that each of these intermediaries cited started from a very low base of total assets, so that it was relatively easy for them to have high rates of growth.

But savings and loan associations, which started from a low base of assets in 1950, had a high rate of growth not only in the 1950s but in the 1970s as well, when the base of assets (in 1970) was quite substantial. Only in the decade of the 1960s, which was marked by severe **credit restraint** in 1966 and 1969 and considerable disintermediation of funds from savings and loan associations in these same periods of credit restraint, was there a relatively low rate of growth (47 percent) for savings and loan associations.

## *Commercial Banks Still the Largest Intermediary*

Although commercial banks during these three decades were surpassed in their rate of growth by credit unions and savings and loan associations, this category of financial intermediary is still the largest by a considerable margin and had quite respectable rates of growth in each decade (e.g., 156 percent in the 1970s). Some 44 percent of all assets held by financial intermediaries in 1979 was in fact held by commercial banks, though this percentage was down somewhat from the 56 percent of all assets held by commercial banks three decades earlier in 1950.

**Table 11-1 Total Assets and Percentage Rate of Growth by Decade for Financial Intermediaries, 1950–1979 (In billions of dollars. Percentages were computed.)**

| Financial Intermediary | 1950 | 1960 | Percentage Increase in 1950s | 1970 | Percentage Increase in 1960s | 1979 | Percentage Increase in 1970s |
|---|---|---|---|---|---|---|---|
| Commercial banks | $168.9 | $257.6 | 52 | $576.2 | 124 | $1,480.3 | 156 |
| Savings and loan associations | 16.9 | 71.5 | 322 | 176.2 | 47 | 579.3 | 234 |
| Life insurance companies | 64.0 | 119.6 | 86 | 207.3 | 81 | 431.0 | 107 |
| Mutual savings banks | 22.4 | 40.6 | 81 | 79.0 | 94 | 163.4 | 107 |
| Finance companies | 9.3 | 27.6 | 186 | 64.0 | 132 | 168.9 | 164 |
| Investment companies | 3.3 | 17.0 | 415 | 47.6 | 180 | 49.5 | 4 |
| Credit unions | 1.0 | 5.7 | 470 | 18.0 | 215 | 65.9 | 266 |
| Private pension funds | 7.1 | 38.1 | 436 | 110.4 | 190 | 236.8 | 114 |
| State and local pension funds | 4.9 | 19.7 | 302 | 60.3 | 206 | 178.9 | 196 |
| Total | $297.8 | $597.4 | 100 | $1,339.0 | 124 | $3,354.0 | 150 |

SOURCE: U.S. League of Savings Associations, *Savings and Loan Fact Book '80*, Chicago, Ill., 1980, p. 46.

Looking at particular financial competitors of commercial banks, we might note that the total assets of commercial banks in 1979 were more than two and a half times the total assets of savings and loan associations that year. The growth in assets over the three decades of commercial banks was nearly equal to the total assets in 1979 of savings and loan associations, life insurance companies, mutual savings banks, and finance companies. It should be quite apparent that commercial banks have been very vigorous in their growth efforts and are very effective competitors of other financial intermediaries. One rapidly growing financial intermediary—the **money market mutual fund**—will now be discussed.

## Money Market Mutual Funds

In the 1970s and 1980s, high and fluctuating interest rates in the money market attracted a growing amount of attention from small savers. Large financial institutions, discussed in the money market chapter, have always invested surplus funds in this short-term market for borrowed funds. In order to discourage small savers from taking deposits out of thrift institutions and putting them in Treasury bills, the minimum amount of Treasury bills had already been raised to $10,000. To make it easier, however, for the small saver to enter the money market, a new form of investment, and a new financial intermediary, developed after the mid-1970s. This was the money market mutual fund, in which small savers could invest $1,000 or more, depending on the fund, and on which they could even write checks for $500 or more.

Even after June 1, 1978, when commercial banks and savings and loan associations were able to offer **money market certificates** for six months tied to the latest auction yield on six-month Treasury bills, money market funds continued to grow rapidly. For one thing, the new money market certificates were available only in minimum amounts of $10,000. For another thing, even though the yields were significantly above those paid on passbook savings accounts, they were still below the yield available from funds invested in money market mutual funds. For example, in early March 1981 (during the 1981–1982 credit restraint period), the return on six-month money market certificates was about 14 percent, whereas the yield of the money market mutual funds averaged about 15.7 percent.

The average maturity of investments, such as large bank CDs or Treasury bills, held by these money funds was typically about thirty-one days, which meant that yields could, and would, change considerably even from one week to the next, but the return invariably was higher than that on money market certificates. Hence it is not difficult to understand that savers in a period of inflation would find money market mutual funds an attractive place in which to hold some of their savings and would often invest maturing money market certificates in money market funds in order to get a higher yield.

## COMPETITION BETWEEN BANK AND NONBANK FINANCIAL INSTITUTIONS

One effect of this intense competition between banks and nonbank financial institutions was to lower the share of total consumer savings deposits held by commercial banks. By the early 1980s, only 30 percent of such consumer savings deposits were held by commercial banks, as compared with about 42 percent a decade earlier. In their search for more funds, the banks were forced to bid more aggressively for large time deposits. The suspension of **Regulation Q** interest rate ceilings on large bank CDs in the early 1970s accelerated such growth in bank time deposits, as well as the six-month money market certificates offered by banks and savings and loan associations after June 1, 1978. Another money market certificate was for only three months and required only $7,500 in savings. This was available beginning May 1, 1982. The yield offered on it was tied to the latest yield on 91-day Treasury bills, as the earlier six-month certificate yield had been tied to that on six-month Treasury bills.

An improved regulatory climate, such as the liberalization of Regulation Q and its eventual phaseout by March 31, 1986, and the permission for mutual savings banks, credit unions, and savings and loan associations throughout the country to offer NOW accounts had also led to increased competition among financial intermediaries. Technological changes, such as the electronics funds transfer system (EFTS) and the growing use of magnetic bank cards, have made it possible for funds to be transferred instantaneously from interest-bearing accounts to demand accounts and thereby blurred the distinction between the two, despite some difficulties in gaining full public acceptance of electronic transfer systems.

Economic growth and a greater concentration of capital in bank holding companies and branch institutions—both commercial banks and savings and loan associations—have made for increased competition. Also, financial institutions other than financial banks, which are full-line financial institutions, finally received more freedom. In the March 31, 1980, Depository Institutions Deregulation Act they received the right to extend loans, such as installment loans, which had previously been denied them by law or regulation. All of these factors have certainly increased the amount of competition in the 1980s.

Such intense competition among financial intermediaries has resulted in certain benefits both for savers and borrowers. The competition has increased the efficiency of intermediation by reducing its cost, that is, by narrowing the spread between the cost of funds to ultimate borrowers and the returns to savers. Furthermore, such competition, as well as the ravages of chronic inflation, has also resulted in a proliferation of savings instruments, which can thus increase the supply of assets desired by the saver. Insurance companies, for example, by the 1980s had greatly reduced their acquisition of fixed-income investments, such as corporate bonds and mortgages, and were moving increasing amounts of new cash directly into stocks and real estate ownership.

## Savings and Loan Associations

Savings and loan associations, as already noted, are second only in size to commercial banks and moreover have had at least three decades of rapid growth in assets. The principal business of savings and loan associations is to make loans secured by residential real estate and share account loans, although they have been permitted to diversify their lending activities somewhat after the passage of the 1980 act. At the end of 1979, there were 4,709 savings and loan associations in the United States, a decline of 1,611 from the peak number of 6,320 in 1960. In the early 1980s, they continued to decline in number as a result of mergers and bankruptcies. Although every one of the fifty states has savings and loan offices, nearly half of them are in the eight states of Ohio (399 associations), Pennsylvania (387), Illinois (381), Texas, New Jersey, Maryland, North Carolina, and California.

Nearly 2,000 savings and loan associations are federally chartered and supervised by the Federal Home Loan Bank Board. In addition to these federally chartered associations, some 2,050 state-chartered associations are also insured by the Federal Savings and Loan Insurance Corporation (FSLIC) up to $100,000 on each account, as are most commercial banks. Only 670 associations are noninsured. The majority of insured associations hold 98 percent of the total assets of the savings and loan business.

Most savings and loan associations are of moderate size, with 2,678 associations at the end of 1979 having assets of at least $10 million but less than $100 million. Nevertheless, the larger associations with assets over $100 million held 79.4 percent of total assets of such thrift institutions at the end of 1979. Mergers of associations have played some role in the growth of larger associations, particularly after the mid-1960s. From 1960 to 1965 inclusive there were a total of 164 such mergers. But thereafter the number of mergers each year increased considerably until the peak year of 1974, when 132 mergers occurred. The number of mergers declined somewhat each year after that, but there were still thirty-seven mergers in 1979.

In 1981 and 1982, there were a number of significant mergers of savings and loan associations. The two most important ones occurred in September 1981. First, there was the merger of Franklin Society Federal Savings and Loan of New York City, with assets totaling $1 billion, which was merged into the First Federal Savings and Loan of Rochester, New York, with assets of $1.2 billion. The combined savings and loan association had fifty-five offices across New York state.

Several days later, an even more important merger took place involving three different associations in three different states. West Side Federal Savings and Loan Association of New York City, with assets of $2.6 billion, and Washington Savings and Loan Association of Miami, with assets of $1.3 billion, were both merged into Citizens Savings and Loan Association of San Francisco, with assets of $3 billion before the merger. It is also interesting to note that Citizens Savings is owned by the United Financial Corporation, which is a subsidiary of National Steel Company of Pittsburgh. After the merger, the new association was the fourth largest savings and loan association in the country, with $6.8 billion of assets and 136 offices in California, New York, and Florida.

In the first two months of 1982 alone, there were six government-assisted mergers of failing S and Ls. In March and April 1982, there were more mergers of thrift institutions. Not only savings and loan assoications but savings banks also needed mergers in order to prevent bankruptcy of the merging institutions. In late March, the New York Bank for Savings merged into the Buffalo Savings Bank for combined deposits of $8.1 billion. In early April, two Philadelphia savings banks merged with FDIC assistance. Failing Western Savings Bank with more than $2 billion in deposits was merged into the Philadelphia Savings Fund Society, which already had $6.3 billion of deposits.

In addition to mergers of local thrift institutions in the East and Midwest, four major California Savings and Loan Associations had also acquired some failing thrift institutions. By mid-1982, one California S and L (Home Savings of America, Los Angeles, the largest in the U.S. with $14.5 billion in assets) had acquired nine S and Ls in Illinois, Texas, Missouri, and Florida. California Federal, Los Angeles, with $8.4 billion in assets had acquired four S and Ls in Florida, and Georgia. Two other S and Ls in Florida and one in New York, were acquired by two other

California S and Ls. Still other troubled savings and loan associations might still be absorbed by mergers in the 1980s, even across state lines.


## The Thrift Problem

Many of the difficulties of the savings and loan associations that led to this wave of mergers in the early 1980s had arisen from the **thrift problem.** This involved maturity imbalance between the assets and liabilities of thrift institutions. Until the mid-1960s, lenders were able to profit from a fairly stable spread between returns on their mortgage loan portfolios and interest costs on predominantly savings account liabilities.

Since then, however, high and often accelerating rates of inflation have been accompanied by rapidly rising and highly volatile interest rates. The prior advantage of a steady stream of interest and principal payments from fixed-rate mortgages was thus converted into a very serious disadvantage. In fact, several times in the late 1970s and early 1980s the yield curve showing the relationship between yields and maturities on the same quality security was downward sloping (i.e., short-term rates were higher than long-term rates).

Given a negative slope on the yield curve, thrift institutions have had to pay more for some of their short-term funds than most of their mortgage loans were yielding. Furthermore, recurrent bouts of disintermediation were suffered by thrift institutions beginning in 1966 as depositors withdrew funds from savings institutions to receive a higher yield in the money market. This disintermediation occurred during various periods of credit restraint by the Federal Reserve.

In such a period not only did the thrift institutions suffer, but likewise did the housing industry. A shortage of loanable funds by lenders of mortgage funds sharply reduced housing starts and resulted in idle resources in the construction industry from time to time. Even after the inauguration of money market certificates, as of June 1, 1978, as already noted, some disintermediation was reduced, but the thrift problem continued.

In 1981–1982, as the Federal Reserve pushed up market interest rates in a continuing policy of credit restraint, the cost of new deposits, especially in the form of money market certificates, began to soar. At the same time, the existing portfolio of mortgage assets consisted largely of long-term, fixed-rate mortgages made in earlier years, when interest rates were much lower. Furthermore, thrift institutions suffered disintermediation in this period, as money market yields rose faster and higher than the interest rates offered on deposits in the thrift institutions.

The problem really became intense for savings and loan associations and other thrift institutions in 1981 and 1982. The 3,786 federally insured S and Ls had a small profit of $800 million in 1980, but posted large losses in 1981 and 1982. In 1981, alone, there was recorded a loss of $4.6 billion for those institutions and losses in 1982 were expected to be even larger. Such thrift institutions were not only suffering profit losses, but they were also losing deposits as savers often sought the higher yields available on money market funds.

Associations, therefore, had to reduce their mortgage commitments and lending activity, borrow heavily, and reduce liquid asset holdings to extend any mortgages at all. As a result of this serious reduction in institutional liquidity, the Federal Home Loan Bank Board added at least 100 more savings and loan institutions to the list of most troubled thrift institutions, which brought the total to 363 at the end of 1981. At the end of 1980, only 121 such institutions were on the troubled list.

## Adjustable-rate Versus Fixed-rate Mortgages

Because of this serious thrift problem, a number of thrift and other financial institutions lending significant amounts of mortgage money began in the late 1970s and early 1980s to offer **adjustable-rate mortgages (ARMs)** in addition to their traditional fixed-rate mortgages (FRMs). Previously, mortgage lending institutions had assumed the risk of predicting future interest rates on their deposits when they offered fixed interest rates to mortgage borrowers. Now they wanted to shift some of these risks of future interest rate variability (resulting from changing rates of inflation) to the mortgage borrower.

The Federal Home Loan Bank Board (FHLBB) in 1979, 1980, and again in 1981 permitted federally chartered savings and loan associations to offer various forms of these adjustable-rate mortgages to borrowers. In 1981, the Comptroller of the Currency likewise authorized national banks, within specified guidelines, to offer adjustable-rate mortgages. In neither case did the regulatory authorities specify how many of these newer mortgages could be offered compared with the traditional fixed-rate mortgages. Presumably, the market was to make that decision.

Adjustable-rate mortgages are usually limited in the various ways that interest rates and monthly payments may be changed over the life of the mortgage. When they were first proposed by the FHLBB in January 1979, federally chartered savings and loan associations making ARMs, which were then called variable-rate mortgages or VRMs, could change The mortgage cost to borrowers by no more than ½ percentage point once a year and by no more than 2¼ percentage points over the life of the mortgage. Monthly payments would change accordingly. The following year (1980), however, the FHLBB permitted greater discretion to the lending institution.

Now the lending institution was able to change the interest rate by a maximum of 5 percentage points over the life of the mortgage, though still by no more than ½ percentage point each year. Monthly payments were to be changed only once every three to five years. Any changes in the mortgage rate were to be based on the FHLBB contract mortgage rate index for conventional mortgages for the purchase of existing homes, rather than to the cost of funds to the lenders. On April 30, 1981, the FHLBB granted still greater flexibility to its member institutions. Interest rate adjustments could now be tied to any reference rate, provided that it could be verified by the borrower and was not controlled by the lender. Furthermore, the interest rate could be adjusted by changes in the monthly payment and/or in the loan term, subject to the conditions that the loan term from the date of closing be limited to forty years. Also, the payment amount had to be adjusted at least every five years to a level sufficient at the existing interest rate to amortize the loan fully over its remaining life.

The Comptroller of the Currency had already, on March 23, 1981, authorized national banks to offer within specified guidelines, adjustable-rate mortgages for the purchase of one-to-four-family owner-occupied homes. Any such adjustments in mortgage rates were to be tied to one of three possible reference rates: (1) the six-month Treasury bill auction rate, (2) the three-year constant maturity Treasury note rate, (3) the FHLBB national average contract mortgage rate on conventional mortgages for the purchase of existing homes. Using one of these reference rates, the national bank making a mortgage could change its mortgage interest rate by a maximum of 1 percentage point every six months with no limit on the cumulative change over the life of the mortgage.

At the option of the bank, monthly payments could be maintained at a fixed dollar amount for a specified time up to five years, regardless of changes in the interest rate. If this option were used, there might even be negative amortization on the principal amount of the mortgage (i.e., the borrower might owe a larger total amount on the mortgage at the end of five years than the amount originally borrowed). The bank was required periodically (say, every five years) to adjust the monthly payments so that they would fully amortize the loan over the remaining term.

It should be evident that these more liberal regulations on mortgage lending place the burden of developing marketable mortgage products on lenders. It should also be evident that many different products can be, and probably will be, developed. Some possible terms of a mortgage contract may be more desirable to the borrower than other terms, while the same can be said for the lender. Competition between lenders—and between borrowers—will have to determine the final mix of mortgage products offered throughout the 1980s. Let us now consider other nonbank financial intermediaries.

## Mutual Savings Banks

At the beginning of the 1980s, there was another major type of financial intermediary, the mutual savings bank. There are about 463 mutual savings banks with a total of 3,338 offices chartered in seventeen states (largely in the Northeast) with assets (at the end of 1979) of nearly $158 billion. About 85 percent of these mutual savings banks are insured by the Federal Deposit Insurance Corporation. Mutual savings banks are owned by their depositors, who receive all earnings after provision for adequate reserves. Like savings and loan associations, nearly four fifths of assets of mutual savings banks are typically in mortgages. Both of these institutions are considered thrift institutions.

Historically, thrift institutions such as savings and loan associations and mutual savings banks and even commercial banks have relied on their ability to attract a significant amount of household savings. Gains in household savings from 1961 to 1979, with bar graphs showing the average from 1954 to 1960, are graphed in Figure 11-1 for savings and loan associations, mutual savings banks, and commercial banks.

Several things can be clearly seen in this figure. Savings and loan associations traditionally have done better at attracting gains in household savings than mutual savings banks and commercial banks. The average figure for 1954–1960 was over 50 percent for savings and loan associations, less than 20 percent for mutual savings banks, and less than 30 percent for commercial banks. In 1981 and 1982, as earlier noted, there were a number of mergers of savings banks, as well as mergers of savings and loan associations.

On the other hand, all of these financial intermediaries have had great fluctuations in their ability to attract household savings from 1961 to 1979, with commercial banks having even greater fluctuations than savings and loan associations. Finally, both savings and loan associations and mutual savings banks had smaller gains in household savings in 1979 than they had had in 1961. Commercial banks, however, showed an uptrend in attracting such savings at the end of the period.

## Disintermediation and the New Money Market Certificates

Partly as a result of a desire to compete more effectively with commercial banks and to maximize profits, various thrift institutions such as

**Figure 11–1    Gains in Household Savings at Major Financial Institutions (percentage distribution), 1961–1979**

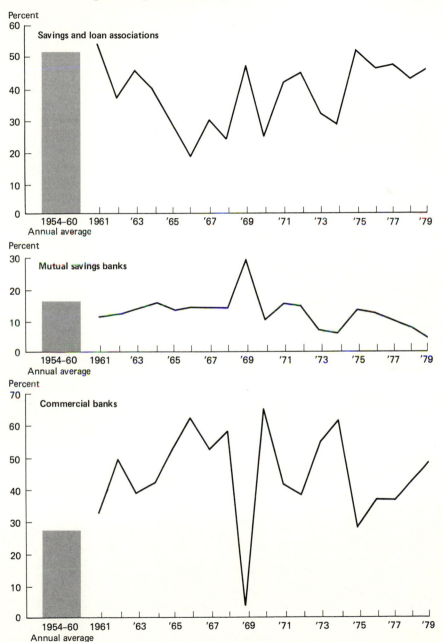

SOURCE: U.S. League of Savings Associations, *Savings and Loan Fact Book '80*, Chicago, Ill., 1980, p. 13.

savings and loan associations found themselves in a very difficult situation in the early 1980s. In order to prevent or reduce recurrent disintermediation of funds from financial intermediaries in periods of credit restraint, federal regulators as of June 1, 1978, had permitted the issuance of money market certificates of $10,000 or more, which would carry a yield that would be on the latest six-month Treasury bills sold at auction each Monday. Because of this competitive money market yield, it was believed there would be no incentive for savers to withdraw funds from thrift institutions, at least in amounts of $10,000 or more, in periods when money market yields were soaring.

The immediate popularity of these money market certificates substantially reduced subsequent disintermediation, until money market yields, including that on money market funds, soared in 1981-1982. But solving one problem, even temporarily, brought other problems in its wake. Increasingly, savers reduced their percentage of savings held in low-yielding passbook accounts and put an ever higher percentage into deposits paying money market rates. By January 1981, a record high of 56.2 percent of deposits was in savings and loan associations in such market-sensitive certificates. This percentage rose even higher, later in 1981 and 1982.

At the same time that the cost of deposits used as the major source of loanable funds for thrift institutions was becoming higher and more

**Figure 11–2    Money Market Certificates (MMC), Interest Rates and Balances at Savings Associations**

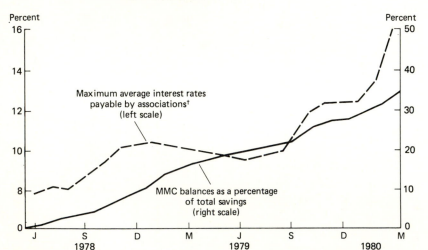

† Continuous 365/360 compounding until March 15, 1979; annual yield on a 182/360 day basis since then.

SOURCE: U.S. League of Savings Associations, *Savings and Loan Fact Book '80*, Chicago, Ill., 1980, p. 13.

volatile, depending on developments in the money market, the rates of return on assets, which were typically fixed-interest rate mortgages for savings and loan associations, were averaging under double-digit rates for about half of their portfolio. The cost of interest-sensitive deposits, on the other hand, was often 14 or 15 percent or more.

Hence the thrift problem, discussed already, put a severe squeeze on both profitability and the equity position of many thrift institutions in the early 1980s. Commercial banks were usually in a somewhat better position because they had a higher percentage of their earning assets in short-term, higher-yielding loans, such as business loans.

The steady relative increase in significance in such interest-sensitive deposits after June 1, 1978, when they were first authorized, in the form of money market certificates for savings and loan associations is shown in Figure 11–2. On the left side of the figure, the fluctuating, and often rising, interest rates are shown. This is a graphic demonstration of the thrift problem.

## Possible Mergers Between Banks and Thrift Institutions

After two decades of increasing difficulty in arranging bank mergers after the antitrust suits beginning in February 1961, and because of the thrift problem facing many nonbank financial intermediaries, some banks and other financial intermediaries contemplated mergers in the early 1980s. This was in addition to the wave of mergers between savings and loan associations and between savings banks. The first such merger apparently was between a small state bank and a savings and loan association in Arizona, first proposed in November 1980. The merger joined Surety Savings and Loan Association (Phoenix) with City Bank (Sun City) into the fifth largest state-chartered bank in Arizona. The new bank's assets originally were $131 million. The merger was approved by the FDIC, the Comptroller of the Currency, the Federal Reserve Board, and the U. S. Justice Department.

At the same time that this innovative merger was taking place, a number of similar mergers were reported as being seriously considered. In late 1980, the National Bank of Detroit asked the Federal Reserve Board for permission to acquire Landmark Savings and Loan Association of Saginaw, Michigan. It was also reported that Citicorp (New York City) was considering the acquisition of a large California savings and loan association in the same period. Although the Federal Reserve Board had previously prevented banks from acquiring savings institutions except where the thrift was insolvent, there was sufficient widespread concern about the necessity of such possible mergers that legislation was proposed in Congress to permit them.

## Life Insurance Companies

In addition to the depository institutions that have been discussed, other important financial intermediaries are growing in importance over time. Life insurance companies, for example, increased their total assets from the end of 1960 to the end of 1977 by $224 billion—from $126.5 billion to $350.5 billion. By the end of 1980, life insurance companies' assets totaled about $472 billion. In the 1970s, as in the 1960s, about one third of such life insurance assets were accounted for by mortgages. Most of the rise of such assets was accounted for by the continued rise in life insurance policies in force. From the point of view of the insured, some of the premiums paid to the life insurance companies represented "savings," as measured by the cash value of life insurance policies.

In the late 1970s, however, the privilege of borrowing at low interest rates against their "savings" in the cash value of life insurance policies resulted in some serious problems for the life insurance industry. High and often accelerating rates of inflation also forced the industry to reexamine its traditional investment policies of placing funds largely into private corporate bonds and mortgages, both of which traditionally involve long maturities and fixed interest rates. As late as the end of 1980, some 27 percent of total life insurance company assets were in mortgages and more than 40 percent of all assets were held in corporate bonds. Historically, in fact, about 90 percent of privately placed corporate debt has been acquired by life insurance companies, as well as significant amounts of corporate bonds sold publicly.

Largely because of the strong participation of life insurance companies, the private placement market for corporate bonds grew rapidly between 1971 and 1977, as annual volume climbed from $8.7 billion to a record $23.7 billion. Thereafter it began to decline as life insurance companies became less and less interested in buying corporate bonds. In 1980, for example, the private placement market accounted for only 26 percent of corporate bond financing, which was down sharply from the 48 percent only two years earlier.

By the early 1980s, for those corporate bonds purchased by life insurance companies the maturity had shrunk to fifteen years or less. Moreover, as already noted, the shift in emphasis in the portfolio of life insurance companies was to acquire stocks, real estate ownership, and even oil and gas ventures and **leverage buyouts** of companies in which a significant equity interest could be acquired. (Leveraged buyouts are purchases of companies using large amounts of borrowing.)

# Real Estate Purchases by Life Insurance Companies and Pension Funds

As shown earlier in Table 11-1, both life insurance companies and pension funds grew strongly in the 1970s and early 1980s. Assets of life insurance companies rose by 107 percent in the 1970s and that of pension funds by 114 percent. The pressure of a large flow of new savings each year along with volatile and uncertain interest rates, and the ravages of continuing inflation, led inevitably to greater interest by these financial institutions in the real estate market.

In 1980, for example, the Metropolitan Life Insurance Company purchased the fifty-nine-story Pan Am Building in New York City for $400 million, the largest one-building real estate deal on record. In 1981, despite the competition of the British National Coal Board's $8 billion pension plan, the Prudential Insurance Company with its $60 billion in assets was the successful bidder in another large financial transaction. Metropolitan paid $340 million for Connecticut General Mortgage, headquartered in Springfield, Massachusetts, a real estate investment trust with a collection of commercial real properties. Prudential was bidding on behalf of some 350 United States pension fund clients.

Although European pension funds have been buying real estate for years, this is a relatively new investment strategy for United States financial institutions. In the early 1980s, pension funds in the United States had less than 3 percent of their $286 billion assets in real estate. A number of pension managers, however, have talked about raising that figure to 10 percent. Life insurance companies, likewise, have tended to be large holders of mortgages but relatively small holders of real estate. At the end of 1980, for example, life insurance companies held mortgages totaling some $131.1 billion but had only $15 billion in real estate.

In 1981, however, some major new building projects involving life insurance funds provided life insurance companies with a major equity interest as well as an interest-earning mortgage asset. On July 20, 1981, Metropolitan Life invested $250 million in a joint venture with a Chicago developer, which gave the insurance company a 50 percent interest in new building projects. Likewise, Aetna Life and Casualty Company in the same year agreed to invest as much as $200 million in a realty development plan with Twentieth-Century Fox Film Corporation, which would also be a 50 percent partner.

Prudential Life Insurance Company has in many ways led the way in the United States for both life insurance companies and pension fund investments in real estate. In 1970, Prudential set up its Prudential's Property Investment Separate Account (PRISA), the oldest and largest real estate account set up by insurers to buy property with pension fund cash. Although it got off to a slow start in the early 1970s, its activities were greatly enhanced by a 1974 law that required pension funds to diversify their investments.

Sharp drops in stock prices in the mid-1970s and the subsequent fall of the bond market also increased the appeal of real estate. From 1978 to 1981, PRISA's holdings tripled to $2.75 billion, while it served some 350 pension clients. The holdings of PRISA include 200 office buildings, more than 500 industrial structures, 75 hotels and motels, 50 shopping centers, 55 apartment buildings, and more than three dozen farms. Similar separate real estate accounts are offered by other insurance companies and banks, although some big pension funds are buying real estate without a middleman.

## Credit Unions

Another fast-growing financial intermediary has been credit unions. In only three years from the end of 1972 to the end of 1975, time and savings accounts rose from $1.2 billion to $33 billion. By the end of 1980, credit union assets had more than doubled again, to a total of $71.5 billion.

## New, and More Diversified, Financial Institutions

In the early 1980s, there was a ferment of new approaches (**financial innovations**) by existing financial institutions and the entry of non-financial firms into the financial industry. For example, Merrill-Lynch, the largest stock brokerage firm, set up a wholly-owned subsidiary to go into brokerage and investment in real estate. Commercial banks expanded their activities in making consumer installment loans, often through subsidiaries, as well as establishing business service companies. Perhaps the most dramatic new entry into the financial industry, however, was that of Sears and Roebuck, which had long been essentially a major retailer. Sears, however, had long had its Allstate Insurance Group.

In 1982, Sears began new operations in real estate, stock brokerage, and other financial services. These activities were facilitated by the acquisition of the Dean Witter Financial Services Group and the Coldwell Banker Real Estate Group. Further financial expansion was most likely, particularly if interstate banking was approved by Congress.

## Nonbank Intermediaries

Nonbank intermediaries include not only private intermediaries such as mutual savings banks, savings and loan associations, life insurance companies, and credit unions, but also governmental intermediaries, such as Federal Land Banks and various trust funds, such as government insurance and pension funds. Many of these financial institutions, like commercial banks, borrow short at a given interest rate and lend long at a higher interest rate. This interest rate differential is their compensation for the particular financial service that they provide.

In their lending operations, all these kinds of financial institutions create debt that can serve as a liquid asset for the holders. Each financial institution, it is true, creates its own unique form of debt, of which money is one kind and various near-moneys are others.

*Government-Sponsored Credit Agencies*   Although agencies of the federal government make direct loans, insure, and guarantee loans made by private lenders directly to private borrowers, an increasing amount of credit activities involves direct lending by agencies that are legally privately owned but are federally sponsored and operate to serve a public interest. Of the five major **government sponsored credit agencies**, three serve the agricultural sector of the economy and two provide financial support for the housing sector. The agricultural agencies, all of which are under the general supervison of the Farm Credit Administration, are (1) the Federal Land Banks, (2) the Federal Intermediate Credit Banks, and (3) the Banks for Cooperatives.

All credit agencies are highly specialized lenders. The land banks supply long-term real estate loans to farmers and ranchers through 643 local Land Bank Associations. The twelve Intermediate Credit Banks, on the other hand, supply working capital by acting as banks of discount for agriculture. The thirteen Banks for Cooperatives specialize entirely in financing the operations of farmers' cooperatives with short-term loans.

*Borrowing by Government-Sponsored Agencies*   The housing-related agencies are the Federal Home Loan Bank System (FHLB) and the Federal National Mortgage Association (FNMA). Although the Land Banks and the FHLB became fully privately owned a few years after World War II, it was not until late in 1968 that the remaining three credit agencies, which had previously been under mixed federal and private ownership, shifted to full private ownership. Some of the functions of the FNMA were then transferred to the new federally owned agency, the Government National Mortgage Association (GNMA).

*FNMA and the Secondary Mortgage Market*   Insofar as the housing agencies are concerned, FNMA, since becoming privately owned, has operated almost entirely in the secondary market for home mortgages, mostly with those mortgages insured by the Federal Housing Administration, guaranteed by the Veterans Administration, or insured by the

Farmers Home Administration. In the early 1970s, however, FNMA began some secondary market operations (buying and then subsequently selling mortgages made by primary mortgage lenders) that involved conventional mortgages; their participation in this area has subsequently increased substantially. The twelve Federal Home Loan Banks assist the mortgage markets in a less direct fashion, because their function is to supply credit directly to their member savings and loan associations. This makes possible a larger portfolio of mortgages at savings and loan associations than would otherwise be possible.

In the 1970s and 1980s, the federally sponsored lending agencies continued the strong growth that they had experienced in the 1960s. In just four years—from 1973 to 1976 inclusive—the outstanding debt of these agencies grew by one third, from $60 billion to more than $80 billion. In the next four years outstanding debt doubled to more than $164 billion at the end of 1980. The Federal National Mortgage Association, the Federal Land Banks, and the Federal Intermediate Credit Banks all showed particularly strong growth.

Another way of showing the strong growth of such government-sponsored credit agencies is to note that annual borrowing of these agencies, which was less than $1 billion as recently as fiscal year 1972, had risen to $22.8 billion in fiscal 1981. In fiscal 1982, it was estimated to be $31.2 billion. Because these enterprises are privately owned, there is little that any presidential administration can do to control their continued expansion, but it should be noted that this off-budget borrowing can be added to the direct borrowing of the federal government in order to get some idea of the impact of federal and federally assisted borrowing on the credit markets. By the early 1980s, this total borrowing was more than one third of all funds raised in the credit markets.

## THE FEDERAL FINANCING BANK

To coordinate and consolidate the borrowing activities of about twenty federal agencies, Congress passed an act in December 1973 establishing the **Federal Financing Bank (FFB)** under the secretary of the treasury. The large government-sponsored agencies already discussed are excluded from using the facilities of this new agency, but the numerous government-owned financial agencies now have access to the credit facilities and expertise of this Treasury-directed borrowing agency. The Federal Financing Bank (FFB) can buy obligations that the federal agencies have issued, sold, or guaranteed in the credit markets. The FFB finances these purchases by selling its own obligations directly in the credit markets. Initially, the FFB was given authority to issue up to $15 billion of its own obligations so as to borrow from the public. There is no limit on the amount of borrowing that is possible from the Treasury.

As an arm of the Treasury Department, the Federal Financing Bank can reduce the borrowing costs of the various government agencies that previously had raised funds in the credit markets at a higher cost than the Treasury paid on its general obligations. In 1973, prior to the FFB, some seventy-three separate offerings were made in securities marketed by agencies now eligible to use the bank's facilities. At the end of 1976, the FFB had purchased some $28.7 billion in agency debt. Four years later—at the end of 1980—this debt of the Federal Financing Bank had more than tripled, to $87.4 billion.

The FFB also purchases federal government "loan assets" that otherwise would have been sold to private investors with agency guarantee of payment of principal and interest. The bank also makes direct loans to guaranteed borrowers. With the exception of one public borrowing in 1974, all needed funds to acquire such assets have been secured in borrowings from the Treasury. When the FFB makes a loan, it charges the borrower a rate that is one eighth of 1 percent over comparably dated issues. To illustrate the bank's operations we might note that in fiscal 1976, the bank received income of more than $60 million, whereas its expenses were only $250,000. The bank's low costs may be attributed to the fact that the Treasury's debt managers run the bank's operations as a sideline to their regular responsibilities. Nevertheless, more than 15 percent of the estimated $200 billion in Treasury borrowings during fiscal years 1975–1977 can be traced to satisfying the credit needs of the FFB.

*Similarity of Function of Financial Intermediaries*    The basic similarity of function uniting all these financial institutions, whether private or government-sponsored, is that by creating financial claims these institutions act as intermediaries in transferring unspent incomes from those with a surplus to those spending units who wish to have a deficit. In helping to bring about such transfers of savings these financial institutions actually raise the level of saving and investment above what it would otherwise be. In addition, they help to allocate more efficiently these scarce savings among alternative investment opportunities. If these financial intermediaries did not exist, each income-spending unit would either have to run a balanced budget position or borrow directly from surplus income units. Units not wishing to consume all of present income would have to lend directly to deficit units or else invest any such surplus in new tangible assets. The lack of financial intermediaries, therefore, by making it more difficult for certain units to run a deficit would impose more severe budget restraints upon them. Such budget restraints would inevitably restrict savings and investments to a relatively low level and hence lead to a relatively low rate of growth in final output.

Private financial intermediaries—most particularly commercial banks, mutual savings banks, and savings and loan associations—which have demand deposits, or transactions accounts in the form of NOW accounts, also provide an important economic function of adding to the stock of money when they provide more credit to borrowers. This is particularly the case for commercial banks when they acquire more earning assets in their loan and investment portfolio. When bank assets rise, their liabilities, which include demand deposits, must also rise. In the next chapter, we consider bank portfolio management and its regulation.

# Questions for Discussion

1. List the six major types of financial intermediaries and indicate in what respects each of them has specialized functions. To what extent is this specialization market-determined and to what extent is it made necessary by governmental regulations?
2. List and discuss the major provisions of the Depository Institutions Deregulation Act of 1980. What effects of this act would you expect to see on the growth and competitive behavior of the various financial intermediaries?
3. Discuss the relative rate of growth of the various intermediaries in the postwar period before 1980. Distinguish in your discussion between contractual savings institutions and depository institutions. To what extent, and why, have commercial banks become more of a financial intermediary in recent years?
4. Discuss the characteristics and behavior of thrift institutions (e.g., savings and loan associations and mutual savings banks). How do changing yields on their earning assets affect their lending and investing activities?
5. Discuss the functions of various financial intermediaries and indicate why some have grown at a more rapid rate than others. Why are commercial banks still the largest financial intermediary?
6. Discuss the growth and development of money market mutual funds in the late 1970s and early 1980s. How did the creation of money market certificates in 1978 enable banks and savings and loan associations in part to meet the growing competition of money market funds? What difference does it make whether there is disintermediation from the thrift institutions into the money market?
7. Discuss the nature and functioning of savings and loan associations. How did "the thrift problem" develop in the early 1980s? What were some of the

consequences of this thrift problem? Do you believe that the 1980 act will help or hurt the savings and loan industry?

8. Discuss adjustable-rate mortgages as contrasted with traditional fixed-rate mortgages. Why did savings and loan associations eagerly embrace this new type of mortgage in the early 1980s? What impact do you think this new mortgage will have on the housing industry?

9. Why have life insurance companies and pension funds in the 1980s tended to reduce their purchase of corporate bonds, particularly of long maturities, and increase their investment in real estate? Do you believe this is wise or unwise?

10. Describe and discuss mutual savings banks. How well have they competed with commercial banks? How will they be affected by the 1980 act?

11. Discuss the competitive behavior among different types of financial intermediaries in trying to attract a larger flow of savings. To what extent do you believe this competition should be regulated by some part of the government, such as the Board of Governors of the Federal Reserve System? Why? Will such competition be increased or diminished by the 1980 act?

12. Discuss the similarities and differences in investment behavior among the various types of financial intermediaries. Do you believe that the various financial institutions should be encouraged to remain somewhat specialized, or should they be permitted to become more like one another? What are likely to be the effects of the 1980 act on such investment behavior?

13. How likely will be mergers between different kinds of financial intermediaries? What developments were in this direction in the early 1980s? Why?

14. Discuss the characteristics and functions of government-sponsored credit agencies (e.g., the FHLB and FNMA). Will these agencies increase or decrease in importance in the rest of the 1980s? Why do you think so?

15. Discuss the importance of the newest government financial intermediary—the Federal Financing Bank (FFB) established in 1974. Discuss the growth of its lending and borrowing activities and indicate its possible impact on the credit markets.

# Selected Bibliography for Further Reading

*Books and Monographs*

COMMISSION ON FINANCIAL STRUCTURE AND REGULATION, *Report* (Washington, D.C.: U.S. Government Printing Office, 1972).

COMMISSION ON MONEY AND CREDIT *Money and Credit: Their Influence on Jobs, Prices and Growth* (Englewood Cliffs, N.J.: Prentice-Hall, 1961).

FEDERAL HOME LOAN BANK BOARD, *38th Annual Report 1970* (Washington, D.C.: U.S. Government Printing Office, 1971).

GOLDSMITH, RAYMOND, *Financial Institutions* (New York: Random House, 1968).

HART, ALBERT GAILORD, and PETER B. KENEN, *Money, Debt and Economic Activity*, 3rd ed. (Englewood Cliffs, N.J.: Prentice-Hall, 1961).

## Articles

BRILL, DANIEL H., and ANN ULREY, "The Role of Financial Intermediaries in U.S. Capital Markets," *Federal Reserve Bulletin*, Jan. 1967, pp. 18–31.

EHRLICH, EDNA E., "International Diversification by United States Pension Funds," *Quarterly Review*, Federal Reserve Bank of New York, Autumn 1981, Vol. 6, No. 3, pp.1–14.

KAUFMAN, GEORGE G., and ELEANOR ERDEVIG, "Improving Housing Finance in an Inflationary Environment: Alternative Residential Mortgage Instruments," *Economic Perspectives*, Federal Reserve Bank of Chicago, July-Aug. 1981, Vol. V, Issue 4, pp. 3–23.

KEEN, HOWARD, JR., "Thrifts Compete with Banks: Getting a Clearer View of a Changing Picture," *Business Review*, Federal Reserve Bank of Philadelphia, Sept.-Oct. 1979, pp. 13–29.

LAPORTE, ANNE MARIE, "The New Federal Financing Bank," *Business Conditions*, Federal Reserve Bank of Chicago, May 1974, pp. 9–15.

LIGHT, JACK S., "Increasing Competition Between Financial Institutions," *Economic Perspectives*, Federal Reserve Bank of Chicago, May-June 1977, pp. 230–231.

MORGAN GUARANTY TRUST COMPANY OF NEW YORK, "A $48 Billion Bank Without Vaults or Tellers," *The Morgan Guaranty Survey*, Sept. 1977, pp. 9–15.

O'LEARY, JAMES J., "The Institutional Saving-Investment Process and Current Economic Theory," *The American Economic Review*, May 1954, pp. 455–470.

RESEARCH DEPARTMENT, FEDERAL RESERVE BANK OF CHICAGO, "The Depository Institutions Deregulation and Monetary Control Act of 1980," *Economic Perspectives*, Federal Reserve Bank of Chicago, Sept.-Oct. 1980, pp. 3–23.

SMITH, WARREN L., "Financial Intermediaries and Monetary Controls," *Quarterly Journal of Economics*, Nov. 1959, pp. 533–553.

U.S. LEAGUE OF SAVINGS ASSOCIATIONS, *Savings and Loan Fact Book '80*, Chicago, Ill., 1980.

# PART 4

# COMMERCIAL
# BANKING
# PRACTICES

# 12

# CHAPTER

# Bank Portfolio Management and Its Regulation

Traditionally, banks were expected to have short-term assets (either loans or investments) to be able to meet the possible cash drains resulting from a very short-term liability position (i.e., demand deposits). Only to the extent that banks had lower turnover deposits in the form of time or savings deposits were they enabled to acquire long-term earning assets such as mortgages.

In the two decades since early 1960 increasing emphasis has also been placed on innovations in liability management. These innovations have given bank management more freedom in managing their asset portfolio. Various periods of credit restraint such as 1973–1974 and 1981–1982 have nevertheless made clear to managers of all kinds of financial institutions the risks involved in borrowing short and lending long. Interest rates on short-term deposits in such periods rise faster than the average rate on longer-term assets, which can create a liquidity squeeze for some institutions.

In general, in the period since World War II banks have changed their composition of assets from those consisting primarily of reserves and U.S. government securities to one consisting largely of loans to the private sector and increasing amounts of securities of state and local governments. At the same time that low-risk and low-yield assets have been reduced, banks have acquired more high-risk and high-yield assets.

The percentage of time deposits to demand deposits has also greatly increased in this period, reducing somewhat the risk of borrowing short and lending long, which was always a danger when demand deposits were much larger than time deposits. The great growth in time deposits by commercial banks has largely been acomplished by aggressive bank managements paying ever higher interest rates on such deposits to avoid the dangers of disintermediation or nonintermediation in the face of rising money market yields. In turn, the higher costs of time deposits have increased the necessity of finding higher-yielding earning assets.

## TRADITIONAL ASSET MANAGEMENT

In the period just after World War II, demand deposits, or checking accounts, were three times the amount outstanding of time and savings accounts. Banks were not permitted after 1935 to pay interest on their demand deposits, and interest payable on time and savings deposits was restricted to that permitted by the interest rate ceiling set by Regulation Q of the Federal Reserve Board. (Such limitations on interest rates on time and savings accounts will be phased out by March 31, 1986, as a result of the 1980 banking law.) The purpose of banks, it was then thought, was to receive deposits, if the public wished to make them, but the active role assigned to banks was to control the composition of their assets, i.e. **asset management.**

Banks usually preferred to make loans, particularly short-term, self-liquidating business loans. Whenever suitable bank loans could not be made, banks would rather increase their holdings of U.S. government securities, say, than have idle reserves. During World War II ordinary business credit needs were reduced. At the same time, the need for increaed bank credit was very strong on the part of the federal government in order to finance the war. The banking system responded by making large purchases of government securities, made possible by the Federal Reserve's substantial expansion of bank reserves.

At the end of World War II, it appeared almost as if the major function of commercial banks was to hold government debt rather than to extend loans. Table 12–1 shows that $90.6 billion of U.S. government securities was held by commercial banks at the end of 1945, as compared with only $26 billion in loans. Thus 73 percent of total loans and investments of commercial banks was in government securities and only 21 percent of the total was in loans. The remaining 6 percent was in other securities.

By 1981, as shown in Table 12–1, the relationship of government securities and loans was reversed. Only about 9 percent of total loans and investments was in the form of U.S. government securities, whereas 74 percent of the total was in loans and 17 percent in other securities. The banks were clearly back in their primary business of making loans.

The same point is made in Table 12–2, which contains data for the period 1977–1981 inclusive. The three major categories of **bank loans**—commercial and industrial (business), real estate, and to individuals—all increased significantly over this period. Business loans were nearly one fourth of bank credit in 1977 (23.6 percent) and were well over one fourth (27.1 percent) in 1981. This type of **bank credit** showed the strongest growth in the late 1970s and early 1980s. Real estate loans grew somewhat over this period, whereas bank loans to individuals in the late 1970s were clearly growing strongly as they expanded from 15.4 percent in 1977 to 16.2 percent of all bank credit in 1979.

But in 1980 and 1981 such loans to individuals experienced a sharp decline in relative importance, largely because of the special credit controls put on the banking system by the Federal Reserve in mid-March

**Table 12–1  Loans and Investments for All Commercial Banks, 1945–1981 (In billions of dollars)**

| Date (end of December) | Loans and Investments | | U.S. Government Obligations | Other Securities |
| --- | --- | --- | --- | --- |
| | Total | Loans | | |
| 1945 | 124.0 | 26.1 | 90.6 | 7.3 |
| 1947 | 116.3 | 38.1 | 69.2 | 9.0 |
| 1950 | 124.7 | 51.1 | 61.1 | 12.4 |
| 1953 | 143.1 | 66.2 | 62.2 | 14.2 |
| 1957 | 166.4 | 91.5 | 56.9 | 17.9 |
| 1960 | 197.4 | 116.7 | 59.5 | 20.8 |
| 1964 | 272.4 | 172.9 | 60.8 | 38.7 |
| 1967 | 352.0 | 231.3 | 59.4 | 61.3 |
| 1970 | 435.5 | 291.7 | 57.9 | 85.9 |
| 1975 | 775.8 | 546.2 | 84.1 | 145.5 |
| 1976 | 826.4 | 576.0 | 101.2 | 149.2 |
| 1977 | 931.6 | 673.4 | 98.9 | 159.3 |
| 1978 | 1,023.8 | 755.4 | 94.6 | 173.9 |
| 1979 | 1,143.0 | 855.4 | 95.0 | 192.3 |
| 1980 | 1,240.7 | 919.5 | 111.0 | 215.2 |
| 1981 | 1,327.5 | 985.8 | 111.4 | 233.1 |

SOURCE: Board of Governors of the Federal Reserve System, *Federal Reserve Bulletin*, July 1964, p. 864; Dec. 1969, p. A19; Feb. 1970, p. A19; Feb. 1974, p. A18; Feb. 1979, p. A16; March 1981, p. A15; March, 1982, p. A15.

**Table 12-2** **Composition of Bank Credit (percentage of total loans and investments, 1977–1981)**

| Date (end of December) | Loans[a] | | | | Investments | | |
|---|---|---|---|---|---|---|---|
| | Total | Commercial and Industrial | Real Estate | Individuals | Total | U.S. Treasury | Other[b] |
| 1977 | 70.9 | 23.6 | 19.5 | 15.4 | 29.0 | 11.2 | 17.8 |
| 1978 | 73.8 | 24.2 | 20.5 | 16.1 | 26.2 | 9.2 | 17.0 |
| 1979 | 74.8 | 25.6 | 21.2 | 16.2 | 25.1 | 8.3 | 16.8 |
| 1980 | 73.4 | 26.1 | 21.0 | 14.1 | 26.0 | 8.8 | 17.2 |
| 1981 | 74.2 | 27.1 | 21.5 | 14.0 | 25.9 | 9.3 | 17.5 |

[a]Total loans excludes loans to commercial banks.
[b]Other securities held by banks include state and local government securities and securities issued by government agencies and private housing agencies.

SOURCE: Computed from *Federal Reserve Bulletins*, March 1981, p. A15; March 1982, p. A15.

1980, even though they were removed in late July. The recession of 1981–1982 also adversely affected such loans. U.S. Treasury holdings of banks as a percentage of total bank credit declined noticeably, as shown in Table 12–2, while other securities held by banks declined modestly and then recovered in this period. The decline in the percentage of investments, particularly highly liquid Treasury securities held by banks, indicated some deterioration in the liquidity position of banks, as did the rise in loan-deposit ratios in the 1970s and early 1980s.

## HIGHER LOAN-DEPOSIT RATIOS
## AT LARGE BANKS

By the end of 1981, large banks in the United States had an average **loan-deposit ratio** of 85 percent as compared with 76 percent for all commercial banks. This was true whether one considered the 134 large banks with $1 billion or more of assets, as of the end of 1977, or the 170 commercial banks with assets of $750 million or more on the same date. It should further be noted that loan-deposit ratios were higher for all categories of banks as compared with those a decade earlier.

All banks a decade earlier at the end of 1970 had an average loan-deposit ratio of only 65 percent; twelve New York City banks had a loan-deposit ratio of 70 percent; nine Chicago banks had a loan-deposit ratio of 74 percent; whereas 156 other large banks had a ratio of 68 percent. Considering that an increase in bank loan-deposit ratios means that bank liquidity has declined, even though bank profits should increase, these higher ratios at the end of 1981, as compared with 1970, are of considerable significance. It should be further noted that the loan position of many commercial banks was even tighter than suggested by these ratios, because much of their holdings of Treasury securities was not available for further liquidity requirements. Some Treasury securities had to be held against certain categories of deposits, such as tax and loan accounts and those of other governmental authorities.

This considerable decline in liquidity of the portfolio because of an aggressive search for higher bank profits was in contrast with earlier traditional ideas held by banks concerning portfolio management. It was formerly thought that if banks increased their holdings of risk assets (i.e., loans), they were also expected to increase their holdings of cash (primary reserves) and low-risk, low-yielding assets such as U.S. government securities of short maturities (secondary reserves) in order to preserve their liquidity. There were, then, three major considerations expected to govern prudent portfolio management: (1) liquidity, (2) asset quality, and (3) income. These three objectives might also be condensed into the two opposed objectives of maximum profits and maximum safety. The latter two objectives are clearly opposed, because the asset giving the greatest return is ordinarily the one with the greatest risk of default, whereas the safest asset is usually one yielding a low rate of return. Using the threefold classification of objectives, let us now consider liquidity.

## ASSET LIQUIDITY

The liquidity of an asset can be defined as the ease and certainty with which it can be turned into money. The most liquid asset of all, therefore, must be money itself. The next most liquid assets are near-money, or secondary reserves, as contrasted with primary cash reserves. Secondary reserves are money market assets, such as Treasury bills, which have no credit risk and little market risk. That is, these assets will be turned into money within a year by reason of a short-term maturity date. If they need to be sold before maturity, there is little capital loss involved inasmuch as the market price is not subject to wide fluctuations. All banks need such secondary reserves to protect against either regular or unexpected cash withdrawals. Furthermore, the higher the proportion of term loans (business loans of over one-year maturity) in the loan portfolio of a bank, the more urgent the necessity, it was thought, for that bank to have an adequate amount of highly liquid assets in the investment portfolio.

# BANK LIQUIDITY

For certain purposes, it may also be desirable to measure the liquidity of a given bank, or a group of banks, and the changes in its liquidity over time. In this event both primary and secondary reserves should be combined and the ratio of these liquid assets to demand deposits less collection items, or to total deposits, can then be computed. What are some of the factors that affect the liquidity needs of a particular bank? One important factor is the kind of deposit drain to which a given bank may be subject. Demand deposits have a much higher turnover than time deposits; and the ratio of demand deposits to total deposits varies widely from one bank to another. A bank with more demand deposits than another bank will therefore have a greater liquidity requirement, whether this need is recognized by the monetary authorities in the form of higher legal reserve requirements or not.

The deposit structure of the bank needs to be kept in mind in the provision of bank liquidity, because some deposits are likely to be more volatile than others. Interbank deposits and public deposits, for example, tend to be more volatile than other categories of demand deposits. Hence banks with heavy deposits in these categories need to be particularly well protected in their holdings of liquid assets so that they can meet any unexpected heavy deposit withdrawal. Likewise, those banks that cater to large companies that have a substantial nationwide business may be subject to large cash drains.

*Bank Lending and Liquidity*    The pattern of a bank's lending business, as well as the character of its deposits, also helps determine its needed liquidity ratio. The economic structure of the community in which the bank is located will affect both the seasonal and the cyclical nature of loan demands that converge on the bank in question. The composition and maturity pattern of a bank's loan portfolio, as well as the character of its investment portfolio, greatly influence the liquidity needs of a particular bank. A bank that has a loan portfolio with well-spaced maturities of loans, or a bank that has a high proportion of government notes or bonds falling due within a year or two, may feel less need for a higher ratio of liquid assets to deposits than another bank not so fortunately situated.

*Management Attitudes*    Certain management attitudes or predilections may also determine the felt liquidity needs of a particular bank. Some bank managements simply have more risk aversion or are more conservative in their attitudes than others. We would expect a more conservative bank management to wish to hold a higher proportion of liquid assets than another bank with a somewhat less conservative management. Also, the attitude of a given bank's management toward borrowing from the regional Reserve Bank is important. Member banks willing to borrow whenever necessary and possible would presumably need a somewhat lower liquidity ratio than banks that borrow seldom, if at all, from the Federal Reserve.

*Larger and Smaller Banks*     The level of primary reserves that is legally required may also help explain certain differences between, say, larger and smaller banks. Those financial institutions such as banks that have a greater amount of transactions accounts than smaller institutions have always had higher legal reserve ratios imposed on them by the Federal Reserve System than have financial institutions with a smaller total of transactions accounts. Hence after the banking act of 1980 there was a 3 percent reserve ratio imposed on transactions accounts under $25 million but a 12 percent ratio imposed on such accounts above $25 million. The downward pressures on bank profits that these higher reserve requirements imply may help explain a seemingly greater interest on the part of larger banks in investing a higher proportion of the available resources in higher-yielding assets in the maturity and risk area beyond those of the most highly liquid assets. Furthermore, such larger banks, as we have already indicated, tend to have a low level of excess primary reserves.

# BANK DEPOSITS

Liquidity of commercial banks is related not only to the amount of primary and secondary reserves that they hold but also to their demand and time deposits (i.e., **bank deposits**). In fact, changes in a bank's liquidity ratio are often directly connected with changes in its deposits. If there is a net withdrawal of deposits from a bank, that bank will surely lose cash to other banks. The cash, of course, does not disappear from the banking system, but for an individual bank a loss of deposits means a loss of cash, just as an increase in deposits provides added loanable funds for the bank receiving the deposits.

## Losses and Gains in Deposits

When a bank loses deposits, the initial impact is ordinarily a reduction in the amount of its primary reserves—usually either vault cash or deposits in the Federal Reserve System. If the loss of reserves results in a deficiency in legal reserves, the bank will probably borrow from either the Reserve Bank or another commercial bank, perhaps a correspondent bank. If the decline in deposits proves to be more than temporary, the bank suffering the loss will have to reduce its secondary reserves and perhaps, ultimately, its loan portfolio.

The reverse process occurs when a bank gains deposits. When deposits rise, certain liquid assets, particularly excess reserves, also increase. Therefore, in the short run at least, an increase in deposits may be associated with an increase in the liquidity ratio, just as a decline in deposits may be expected to be associated with a decline in the liquidity ratio. Subsequently, we would expect the bank with added excess reserves to employ these in acquiring such earning assets as loans or U.S. government securities, particularly in the intermediate maturity range so preferred by commercial banks.


## LIABILITY MANAGEMENT

Thus far, we have discussed the traditional attitudes of bank managements toward liquidity through management of the kinds and amounts of assets held by banks. Since 1961, at least, liability management has also become accepted by large banks as a principal strategy for adjusting their lending capabilities. In tapping the pool of short-term investible funds in the money market for the purpose of liability management, large negotiable certificates of deposit (CDs) have proved to be even more important to banks than trading in federal funds or engaging in repurchase agreements (RPs) for Treasury bills. In general, large banks "buy" such deposits when their business loan demand is rising and such CDs decline when business loan demand is falling. Banks can thus not only convert assets into cash but can also acquire new liabilities to meet their cash needs. Successful liability management consists of choosing between these alternatives on the basis of their relative cost.

The impressive growth and the important variations in such growth of large CDs from 1961 to 1977 inclusive is shown in Figure 12–1. Here it can be noted that the expansion of CDs in the early 1960s was rapid and steady. In 1969, however, the Federal Reserve Board refused to raise the interest rate ceiling on bank time deposits as governed by Regulation Q, and the banks lost some $12.8 billion in such CDs. The reason was that the business firm holding a large bank CD would simply invest the funds at maturity in some other money market instrument, such as Treasury bills, where it could receive a larger return.

**Figure 12–1    Large Negotiable Certificates of Deposit Outstanding at All Commercial Banks (not seasonally adjusted), 1961–1977**

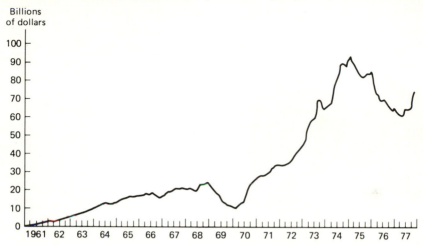

SOURCE: Federal Reserve Bank of New York, *Quarterly Review*, Winter 1977–78, p. 25.

In June 1970, however, the Federal Reserve Board suspended the Regulation Q ceiling rate on large CDs maturing in thirty to eighty-nine days. In May 1973, it suspended the ceiling on all large CDs. Hence with business loan demand at banks growing from 1970 through 1974, the banks were aggressive in their purchase of time deposits through the issuance of bank CDs, which were quite competitive in their yield with other money market instruments. However, the serious recession of 1973–1975 resulted in falling business loan demand at banks, which persisted until 1977. The result was the anticipated response from banks, who let their outstanding CDs fall until business loan demand began to revive in 1977. In the late 1970s and early 1980s, such large CDs resumed their strong growth of the early 1970s. By 1981, they totaled well over $200 billion, or more than double that of four years earlier.

More aggressive attitudes toward profit maximization have also resulted in the economizing of low-yield liquid assets (i.e., the reduction of bank excess reserves and a smaller proportion of U.S. government securities in the total of bank earning assets), as well as in the acquiring of more volatile time deposits to meet bank liquidity needs although such short-term deposits were often very expensive for the banks relying heavily on them as sources of funds. The strong growth of financial institutions such as savings and loan associations, the more permissive attitudes of the Federal Reserve in the raising of the interest rate ceiling

(Regulation Q) on time deposits in the 1960s, and the eventual suspension of much of time deposits subject to Regulation Q in the 1970s made a more aggressive search for more bank funds necessary and possible. Buying of bank deposits, both large and small, could become even more costly later in the 1980s, as Regulation Q must be phased out by March 31, 1986.

---

**Table 12–3    Maximum Interest Rates Payable on Time and Savings Deposits at Federally Insured Commercial Banks (percent per annum)**

| Type and Maturity of Deposit | In effect Dec. 31, 1980 |
|---|---|
| | *Percent* |
| Savings .......................................... | 5¼ |
| Negotiable order of withdrawal accounts ............. | 5¼ |
| Time accounts | |
| *Fixed ceiling rates by maturity* | |
| 14–89 days...................................... | 5¼ |
| 90 days to 1 year................................ | 5¾ |
| 1 to 2 years .................................... | 6 |
| 2 to 2½ years................................... | |
| 2½ to 4 years................................... | 6½ |
| 4 to 6 years .................................... | 7¼ |
| 6 to 8 years .................................... | 7½ |
| 8 years or more ................................. | 7¾ |
| Issued to governmental units (all maturities) ........ | 8 |
| Individual retirement accounts and Keogh (H.R. 10) | |
| plans (3 years or more)[a] ........................ | 8 |
| | |
| *Special variable ceiling rates by maturity* | |
| 6-month money market time deposits[b] .............. | ([c]) |
| 2½ years or more ................................ | ([d]) |

[a]Effective January 1, 1980, commercial banks are permitted to pay the same rate as thrifts on IRA and Keogh accounts and accounts of governmental units when such deposits are placed in the new 2½-year or more variable ceiling certificates or in 26-week money market certificates regardless of the level of the Treasury bill rate.

[b]Must have a maturity of exactly 26 weeks and a minimum denomination of $10,000, and must be nonnegotiable.

[c]Commercial banks, savings and loan associations, and mutual savings banks were authorized to offer money market time deposits effective June 1, 1978. The ceiling rate for commercial banks on money market time deposits entered into before June 5, 1980, is the discount rate (auction average) on most recently issued six-month U.S. Treasury bills.

[d]Effective Jan. 1, 1980, commercial banks, savings and loan associations, and mutual savings banks were authorized to offer variable-ceiling nonnegotiable time deposits with no required minimum denomination and with maturities of 2½ years or more. The maximum rate for commercial banks is ¾ percentage point below the yield on 2½-year U.S. Treasury securities; the ceiling rate for thrift institutions is ¼ percentage point higher than that for commercial banks. Effective March 1, 1980, a temporary ceiling of 11¾ percent was placed on these accounts at commercial banks; the temporary ceiling is 12 percent at savings and loan associations and mutual savings banks.

SOURCE: Board of Governors of the Federal Reserve System, Jan. 1981, p. A9.

## INTEREST RATE CEILINGS AND
## TIME DEPOSIT GROWTH IN THE 1980s

Despite the phaseout of interest rate ceilings by 1986, the early 1980s were still years of interest rate ceilings, as shown in Table 12–3. The new negotiable orders of withdrawal (NOWs), or checking accounts paying interest, had a ceiling of 5¼ percent when first introduced as of December 31, 1980. Although NOW accounts grew by about $50 billion in the first year (1981) after they were authorized, about half of these new accounts involved funds switched from savings accounts. In addition, about one third of total deposits at financial intermediaries were six-month money market time deposits (about $200 billion) or certificates for 2½ years or more (about $35 billion)—both of these certificates paying an interest rate tied to the yield on relatively short-term U.S. government securities.

By 1982, the rapid growth of time deposits as compared with demand deposits and other checkable deposits over more than three decades had led to commercial banks having more than twice as many time and savings accounts as demand deposits. But much of their time and savings accounts growth had involved a sharp growth in costly, and sometimes volatile, deposits, because three fourths of such accounts were small and large time deposits and only one fourth were the more traditional savings accounts. Higher interest rate ceilings had thus enabled banks to attract ever more funds but had also increased their costs of operation.

In the early 1980s, then, some banks discovered that they had a "mismatch," or an excess of interest-sensitive liabilities over interest-sensitive assets. Hence some banks like the Bank of America had some quarters of decline in profits from the year earlier for the first time in a number of years. Inevitably this meant high interest rates for those borrowing from banks. When the interest rate ceilings were removed altogether, it seemed likely that interest rates would also remain high, both for banks as borrowers and as lenders.

## GREATER RELIANCE BY BANKS ON LARGE
## CDs AND FEDERAL FUNDS

The relative decline of demand deposits, as already noted, which was the traditional source of bank funds, is shown in Table 12–4. Such demand deposits provided only 30.9 percent of total bank liabilities in 1972–1975 as compared with 62.4 percent in 1952–1955. Time deposits, minus large

**Table 12-4  Composition of Commercial Bank Liabilities,[a] Percentages of Total Liabilities, 1952-1975**

| | Traditional Sources | | | Purchased Funds | | | | Capital | | | Misc. |
|---|---|---|---|---|---|---|---|---|---|---|---|
| | Total[b] | Demand Dep., Net | Time, Excl. Large CD's | Total[c] | Large CD's[d] | Federal Funds, Net[e] | Euro-dollars | Total | Equity | Debt | |
| 1952-1955[f] | 89.3 | 62.4 | 26.3 | 0.3 | 0.0 | 0.0 | 0.3 | 8.0 | 8.0 | 0.0 | 2.4 |
| 1956-1959 | 88.0 | 57.7 | 29.5 | 0.1 | 0.0 | -0.1 | 0.2 | 8.7 | 8.7 | 0.0 | 3.2 |
| 1960-1963 | 85.5 | 51.0 | 33.6 | 2.3 | 1.9 | 0.0 | 0.4 | 9.1 | 9.1 | 0.0 | 3.2 |
| 1964-1967 | 82.0 | 42.4 | 38.9 | 5.7 | 4.6 | 0.4 | 0.7 | 8.8 | 8.4 | 0.4 | 3.4 |
| 1968-1971 | 79.0 | 37.2 | 41.0 | 7.3 | 4.8 | 1.0 | 1.4 | 8.5 | 8.0 | 0.5 | 5.2 |
| 1972-1975 | 73.8 | 30.9 | 42.4 | 12.2 | 9.3 | 2.1 | 0.4 | 8.1 | 7.5 | 0.6 | 5.9 |

[a]Liabilities are net of interbank deposits and interbank federal funds purchases.

[b]Includes borrowing from Federal Reserve Banks and Federal Reserve float, not shown separately.

[c]Includes loans sold to holding companies, loans from foreign banking agencies, and time accounts at foreign banking agencies, not shown separately.

[d]Negotiable CD's over $100,000.

[e]Consists of security RPs and float on commercial bank interbank loans.

[f]Averages of year-end outstandings.

SOURCE: Jack Beebe, "A Perspective on Liability Management and Bank Risk," *Economic Review*, Federal Reserve Bank of San Francisco, Winter 1977, p. 17.

CDs, another traditional source, provided 42.4 percent of bank funds in 1972–1975 as compared with 26.3 percent n 1952–1955. But large bank CDs, which did not even exist until early 1961, provided some 9.3 percent of bank liabilities in 1972–1975, whereas federal funds, another new source, provided another 2.1 percent. Clearly bank liability management had discovered important new sources of bank funds, even before the late 1970s and early 1980s.

The same point is made graphically in Figure 12–2, which shows the postwar growth in commercial bank liabilities. The higher rate of growth in such liabilities after 1960 is the result of the newer use of such sources of bank funds as large CDs and federal funds. Greater reliance by banks on such borrowed funds did increase somewhat the uncertainties of bank portfolio managers, because these kinds of liabilities furnished by the money market can be more volatile than traditional sources of bank funds.

With the strong growth in such new sources of bank funds (e.g., time deposits and federal funds), higher yielding bank assets could be acquired in larger amounts. State and local government securities have increased both absolutely and relatively in bank portfolios. Consumer-type loans, such as consumer installment loans, including bank credit cards, have also grown enormously. Traditional bank loans, such as

**Figure 12–2    Growth in Commercial Bank Liabilities**ᵃ **(year-end outstandings, 1946–1975)**

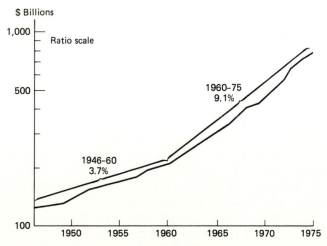

ᵃGrowth rates are annual compound rates between initial and terminal years. Liabilities are net of commercial bank interbank deposits and federal funds purchases.

SOURCE: Jack Beebe, "A Perspective on Liability Management and Bank Risk," *Economic Review*, Federal Reserve Bank of San Francisco, Winter 1977, p. 17.

business loans, have also increased substantially but as a proportion of total earning assets have declined somewhat in relative importance.

This changed bank behavior has undoubtedly had a positive impact on bank profits, and it has also increased the risk to individual banks and to the banking system as a whole. In the severe credit restraint period of 1973–1974, several banks failed, and all banks were experiencing increasing difficulties associated with a general decline in bank liquidity. In 1982 nearly thirty banks failed. The bank and other financial institutions "mismatch" of liabilities and assets in the 1981–1982 credit restraint period led to a decline in profits for a number of institutions and a reduction in liquidity for virtually all of them. This resulted in some movement back toward the older doctrine of bank liquidity being met by certain kinds of assets. Both bank reserves (primary) and secondary reserves (i.e., money market assets) were still seen to play an important part in bank liquidity, even with the newer emphasis on liability management. (Vigorous efforts were also made to reduce costs, particularly through greater reliance on automation.)

## BANK RESERVES

Bank reserves were originally required by various states before the Civil War to provide for convertibility or redeemability of bank notes. Following the panic of 1857 and the National Bank Act of 1863, a number of regulatory agencies required reserves against both bank notes and bank deposits. These required reserves could be either in the form of lawful money or in correspondent balances in other banks. Some states also permitted banks to include certain securities, such as federal government securities and certain state and local government securities, in their legal reserves.

Regardless of the form of bank reserves, they were invariably regarded as being necessary to maintain bank liquidity. In other words, banks in their search for profits had to be prevented by the regulatory authorities from an overextension of bank credit, wherein particular banks might be unable to satisy the claims of their creditors in an emergency period. Today, however, it is recognized that liquidity for the banking system as a whole depends ultimately upon the ability and willingness of the Federal Reserve to supply additional funds to the banking system when needed. Reserve requirements now are regarded as a fulcrum, or pressure point, whereby the monetary authorities can make effective their desired monetary-credit policies. However, this fulcrum of legal reserve requirements applies only to a certain amount of the primary, or cash, reserves of a bank.

## Primary Bank Reserves

Primary bank reserves are simply cash held by the bank, whether in its vaults or in deposits of other banks. The Federal Reserve System, however, does not permit its member banks to include in their legal reserves interbank deposits in other commercial banks, though it does include deposits in regional Reserve Banks. Nevertheless, for many purposes other than meeting legal reserve requirements, deposits in other banks meet all the requirements of ready cash.

The amount of primary, or cash, reserves available to a given bank depends upon two major factors: (1) deposit flows in or out of the bank, and (2) the prevailing Federal Reserve policy, including changes in such policy. The Federal Reserve, of course, has ultimate control over the amount of bank reserves available to the banking system. In addition to the amount of cash reserves available, the primary reserve position of the bank or the entire banking system also depends on the amount of reserves that are required. These required reserves depend not only on the amount of bank deposits but also on their distribution between time and demand deposits. Legal reserve requirements also affect the amount of required reserves.

***Member Bank Reserve Requirements***     In 1935 Congress gave the Board of Governors of the Federal Reserve System the power to impose reserve requirements on both demand and time deposits within a certain range on each set by Congress. At that time legal reserves of member banks were defined as only deposits in the Federal Reserve Banks. In 1959 Congress again amended the basic Federal Reserve Act to permit vault cash as well as deposits in Federal Reserve Banks to be included in legal reserves.

*Lagged Reserve Accounting*     The required reserve base for all depository institutions is computed against average daily deposits for the weekly reserve period, which runs from Thursday to Wednesday inclusive. In 1968 the Federal Reserve introduced lagged reserve accounting so that required reserves for the current reserve week were based on average deposits in the period two weeks earlier. Furthermore, depository institutions were permitted to carry forward into the next reserve week either excess or deficiencies averaging up to 2 percent of required reserves.

In 1982, the Federal Reserve asked for public comment on a proposal to eliminate such lagged reserve accounting and to lengthen the reserve period to two weeks. It was hoped that a return to contemporaneous reserve accounting would increase the control over the money supply by the Federal Reserve.

## The 1972 Reform of Reserve Requirements

Early in 1972 the Federal Open Market Committee (FOMC) decided to place more emphasis on controlling the growth of bank reserves, especially reserves available to support private deposits (RPD), which is total reserves minus reserves needed to support government and inter-bank deposits. Later in the same year, the Board of Governors inaugurated a substantial reform of reserve requirements applying to member banks. Rather than basing reserve requirements partially on the location of the member bank and partially on its size (under or over $5 million in net demand deposits prior to late 1972), a system of graduated reserve requirements was instituted as of November 9, 1972, to apply to all member banks. The first $2 million or less of net demand deposits would require legal reserves of only 8 percent. Larger amounts of net demand deposits required a higher percentage of legal reserves until the maximum reserve requirement of 17½ percent was reached on all net demand deposits of a bank over $400 million. As part of a program of credit restraint in 1973, the Board of Governors increased these legal reserve ratios as of July 19, 1973, by ½ percent for all demand deposits above the first $2 million. In 1975, and again in 1976, these requirements in some deposit intervals were reduced. The reserve requirements in effect before 1980 are given in the first part of Table 12–5.

## The Monetary Control Act of 1980

Under the **Monetary Control Act of 1980,** passed on March 31, 1980, all financial institutions having transactions accounts (except initially those with less than $2 million in assets) were subjected to the same reserve requirements. These can be seen in the second part of Table 12–5, which indicates that initially reserve requirements were 3 percent on transactions accounts under $25 million, whereas reserve requirements were 12 percent for such transactions accounts above $25 million. (In future years, average reserve requirements may be lowered by raising the dollar amount of transaction accounts subject to the 3 percent requirements, that is, from $25 million to $26 million.) Nonperson time deposits less than four years also were required to have a 3 percent reserve, whereas those that are four years or more have no reserve requirements. These new reserve requirements are, of course, much simpler and lower on average than those that prevailed before the 1980 law for member banks, but are, on the average, somewhat higher for those financial institutions that previously did not have to meet reserve requirements set by the Federal Reserve Board.

    These changes in reserve requirements behind transactions accounts, which are used as money to buy goods and services and repay debt, changed the monetary multiplier, so that an increase in reserves results in a much larger increase in money. (The process of money creation, including monetary multipliers, was discused in Chapter 4.) After the Monetary Control Act of 1980, there was some increase in the actual monetary multiplier. The Federal Reserve Bank of Philadelphia (see Selected Bibliography at end of chapter) estimated that the monetary multiplier in early 1979 was about 8¾ and in early 1981 was about 10½. In short, average legal reserve ratio requirements for financial institutions creating transactions accounts were somewhat lower after 1980 than before.

It should be specifically noted, however, that the purpose of imposing reserve requirements on financial institutions is purely for monetary control by the Federal Reserve System. Reserve requirements are *not* used for the purpose of protecting depositors in such institutions such as commercial banks. Safety of depositors in banks, for example, is provided instead by the Federal Deposit Insurance Corporation. For federally chartered savings and loan associations, the safety of depositors is guaranteed by the **Federal Savings and Loan Insurance Corporation** (FSLIC).

## SAFEGUARDING BANK DEPOSITS: THE FEDERAL DEPOSIT INSURANCE CORPORATION

Prior to the Banking Act of 1933, which established the Federal Deposit Insurance Corporation (FDIC) as of January 1, 1934, each bank had to take its own steps to safeguard its depositors. The various reserve requirements established by state laws, the National Banking Act of 1863, and finally the Federal Reserve Act of 1913 all had as underlying philosophy the idea that depositors would be protected by banks carrying reserves, as well as by preventing an overextension of bank credit in speculative ventures. After 1913, the possibility of rediscounting eligible paper by the member banks at the various Federal Reserve Banks also seemed to offer reassurance to depositors that, if they wished to withdraw their money, the member banks could secure the needed cash.

Nevertheless, these safeguards did not prove sufficient. The high casualty rate of commercial banks in the 1920s and 1930s has already been described. In the widespread bank runs of the Depression days of the early 1930s, even sound banks were sometimes forced to close their doors because of an inability to meet the heavy cash withdrawals of their panicky depositors. As a result, bankers have gained the reputation for being conservative and cautious in their lending and investing activities.

**Table 12-5  Depository Institutions[a] Reserve Requirements, Percent of Deposits**

| Type of Deposit, and Deposit Interval in Millions of Dollars | Member Bank Requirements Before Implementation of the Monetary Control Act | | Type of Deposit, and Deposit Interval | Depository Institution Requirements After Implementation of the Monetary Control Act[a] | |
|---|---|---|---|---|---|
| | Percent | Effective Date | | Percent | Effective date |
| *Net demand*[b] | | | *Net transaction accounts*[e] | | |
| 0–2 .............. | 7 | 12/30/76 | $0–$25 million............. | 3 | 11/13/80 |
| 2–10 ............. | 9½ | 12/30/76 | Over $25 million......... | 12 | 11/13/80 |
| 10–100 .......... | 11¾ | 12/30/76 | *Nonpersonal time deposits*[f] | | |
| 100–400 ........ | 12¾ | 12/30/76 | By original maturity | | |
| Over 400........ | 16¼ | 12/30/76 | Less than 4 years.......... | 3 | 11/13/80 |
| | | | 4 years or more ........... | 0 | 11/13/80 |
| *Time and savings*[b,c] | | | | | |
| Savings.............. | 3 | 3/16/67 | *Eurocurrency liabilities* | | |
| Time | | | All types................. | 3 | 11/13/80 |
| 0–5, by maturity | | | | | |
| 30–179 days.............. | 3 | 3/16/67 | | | |
| 180 days to 4 years........ | 2½ | 1/8/76 | | | |
| 4 years or more .......... | 1 | 10/30/75 | | | |
| Over 5, by maturity | | | | | |
| 30–179 days.............. | 6 | 12/12/74 | | | |
| 180 days to 4 years........ | 2½ | 1/8/76 | | | |
| 4 years or more .......... | 1 | 10/30/75 | | | |

[a]Under provisions of the Monetary Control Act, depository institutions include commercial banks, mutual savings banks, savings and loan associations, credit unions, agencies and branches of foreign banks, and Edge Act corporations.

[b](a) Requirement schedules are graduated, and each deposit interval applies to that part of the deposits of each bank. Demand deposits subject to reserve requirements are gross demand deposits minus cash items in process of collection and demand balances due from domestic banks.

(b) The Federal Reserve Act as amended through 1978 specified different ranges of requirements for reserve city banks and for other banks. Reserve cities were designated under a criterion adopted effective Nov. 9, 1972, by which a bank having net demand deposits of more than $400 million was considered to have the character of business of a reserve city bank. The presence of the head office of such a bank constituted designation of that place as a reserve city. Cities in which there were Federal Reserve Banks or branches were also reserve cities. Any banks having net demand deposits of $400 million or less were considered to have the character of business of banks outside of reserve cities and were permitted to maintain reserves at ratios set for banks not in reserve cities.

(c)Effective Aug. 24, 1978, the Regulation M reserve requirements on net balances due from domestic banks to their foreign branches and on deposits that foreign branches lend to U.S. residents were reduced to zero from 4 percent and 1 percent, respectively. The Regulation D reserve requirement on borrowings from unrelated banks abroad was also reduced to zero from 4 percent.

(d) Effective with the reserve computation period beginning Nov. 16, 1978, domestic deposits of Edge corporations were subject to the same reserve requirements as deposits of member banks.

[c](a) Negotiable order of withdrawal (NOW) accounts and time deposits such as Christmas and vacation club accounts were subject to the same requirements as savings deposits.

(b) The average reserve requirement on savings and other time deposits before implementation of the Monetary Control Act had to be at least 3 percent, the minimum specified by law.

[d]For existing nonmember banks and thrift institutions, there is a phase-in period ending Sept. 3, 1987. For existing member banks the phase-in period is about three years, depending on whether their new reserve requirements are greater or less than the old requirements. For existing agencies and branches of foreign banks, the phase-in ends Aug. 12, 1982. All new institutions will have a two-year phase-in beginning with the date that they open for business.

[e]Transaction accounts include all deposits on which the account holder is permitted to make withdrawals by negotiable or transferable instruments, payment orders of withdrawal, telephone and preauthorized transfers (in excess of three per month), for the purpose of making payments to third persons or others.

[f]In general, nonpersonal time deposits are time deposits, including savings deposits, that are not transaction accounts and in which the beneficial interest is held by a depositor which is not a natural person. Also included are certain transferable time deposits held by natural persons, and certain obligations issued to depository institution offices located outside the United States. For details, see section 204.2 of Regulation D.

NOTE. Required reserves must be held in the form of deposits with Federal Reserve Banks or vault cash. After implementation of the Monetary Control Act, nonmembers may maintain reserves on a pass-through basis with certain approved institutions.

SOURCE: Board of Governors of the Federal Reserve System, *Federal Reserve Bulletin*, Jan. 1981, p. A8.

Many senior bankers in their own lifetimes have seen what happened to less prudent bankers. Each bank, therefore, and properly so, has felt it necessary to be concerned with its own liquidity requirements and hence with the safety of its deposits.

## Establishment of the Federal Deposit Insurance Corporation

With the establishment of the FDIC in 1934 an important institution concerned not only with the safety of depositors but with the overall stability of the banking industry came into existence. When the FDIC was organized, all member banks of the Federal Reserve System were required to join. Noninsured state banks were given the option to apply to the corporation for admission to insurance. A sufficient number of these state banks, along with those banks in the Federal Reserve System, did apply for insurance, so that more than 90 percent of all commercial banks have been covered by this depositor insurance since January 1, 1934. Since March 31, 1980, each account has been insured up to $100,000.

*Most Commercial Banks Are Insured*    In 1979, the FDIC insured 14,608 commercial and mutual savings banks with total assets of $1.7 trillion. These banks accounted for 97 percent of all banks in the United States.

*Bank Application for Insured Status*    Most newly established banks apply, even before they open their doors, for such deposit insurance. When a bank applies to the FDIC for insured status, the FDIC considers the following factors: the financial history and condition of the bank, the adequacy of its capital structure, its future earnings prospects, the general character of its management, the convenience and needs of the community to be served by the bank, and the consistency of the bank's corporate powers with the purposes of the Federal Deposit Insurance law. Although most banks applying for insurance are likely to be newly organized banks, some banks already in operation but hitherto not insured also make such applications. In 1978, for example, the FDIC approved applications for deposit insurance of 130 banks and denied only 4 applications. In 1979, 167 applications were approved; only 2 were denied.

## Protection of the Depositor and Problem Banks

In addition to protecting depositors against loss, the FDIC makes such deposits promptly available in the event of bank failure. In most cases, in ten days to two weeks after the closing of the bank the depositors receive a substantial proportion of their insured deposit directly from the FDIC. If the distressed bank has been placed in receivership, the remainder of the depositor claim is paid after certain assets of the bank have been liquidated.

***Loss Record of the FDIC***     An examination of the loss record of the FDIC for the forty-six years from January 1, 1934, to December 31, 1980, reveals an amazingly small net loss. Although the corporation disbursed more than $5.7 billion in this period to protect depositors in 568 failing banks, it recovered $5.4 billion for a net loss of only $300 million for all its insurance transactions. Part of this good record may be a result of the corporation's policy to encourage a distressed bank to merge, whenever feasible, with a sound bank.

In the decade of the 1970s, for example, even though there was an upsurge in bank failures (see Figure 12–3), there were still very small net losses for the FDIC. In that decade, there were seventy-six insured bank failures involving assets of about $8 billion and 2.1 million depositors with about $5 billion in deposits. The FDIC policy was to convert the assets of the closed banks to cash as soon as possible in order to realize maximum recovery for distribution to creditors and stockholders.

In 1980, although ten insured banks with deposits of $216.3 million failed, other banks on the verge of bankruptcy were merged with new or existing banks. Seven such insured banks in 1980 with deposits of $199.8 million were subject to such mergers. In cases of bank failure, some 99.9 percent of depositors had received or were assured of payment up to the legal limit by the end of 1980.

At times as during the 1970s there has been a substantial increase in the number of **problem banks**, which were closely scrutinized by the FDIC in order to reduce the likelihood of still more bank failures. These banks had asset problems resulting from mismanagement and/or insider abuses, poor earnings, inadequate capital, and insufficient liquidity. Such problem banks peaked at 385 in November 1976 and declined thereafter to only 217 at the end of 1980. The decrease in such problem banks was attributed by the FDIC to improvements both in the real estate sector and in local economic conditions following the severe 1973–1975 recession. Problem banks at the end of 1980 represented only about 1.5 percent of all insured banks.

Cease-and-desist orders are issued by the FDIC when it finds that an insured bank has been conducting its business in an unsafe or unsound manner or has violated a law, rule, or regulation, or any agreement with a condition imposed in writing by the FDIC. The problem list contained banks that were only 2½ percent of all insured banks, so that those banks experiencing difficulties in the 1970s were a very

**Figure 12–3    Insured Bank Failures, 1934–1980**

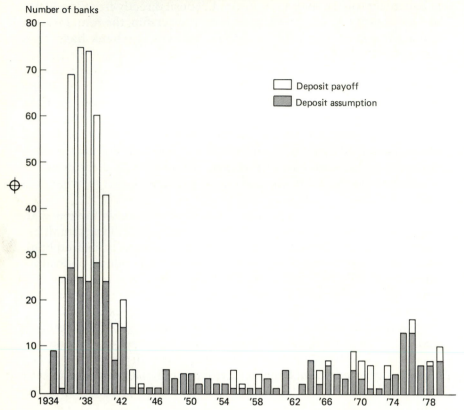

SOURCE: Federal Deposit Insurance Corporation, *1980 Annual Report*, 1981, p. 18.

small part of the total banking industry as compared with those banks in trouble in the 1920s and the 1930s before the advent of the FDIC. One may argue, therefore, that the FDIC itself has apparently made a notable contribution to greater stability in the commercial banking industry.

***Bank Examination***    The contribution of the FDIC to sound banking practice is made not only by its careful consideration of whether or not an applying bank shall be admitted to the insured status but also through its frequent bank examinations. Of the more than 14,700 banks and trust companies in the United States, more than one third are examined by and report to the comptroller of the currency. These consist of 4,600 national banks. Although 9,012 banks are subject to state regulation, the 1,128 state banks that are members of the Federal Reserve System are examined by and submit reports to the Federal Reserve Bank in their district.

The FDIC regularly examines insured banks that are not members of the Federal Reserve System and reviews reports of examination of national banks and state bank members of the Federal Reserve. Banks regularly examined by the FDIC comprise 7,882 banks of deposit, or more than half the nation's banks, which hold about one fifth of the total deposits in insured banks. Examinations of state nonmember banks are made annually, usually in conjunction with examinations conducted by the state supervisory authority. On occasion, the FDIC may even examine bank members of the Federal Reserve System. Total bank examination activities of the FDIC were 19,769 in number in 1980, which were down slightly from 19,914 in 1979. The breakdown of bank examinations in 1980 was: (1) safety and soundness examinations, 6,562; (2) compliance examinations, 6,373; (3) examinations of departments, which were trust departments and data-processing departments, 2,450; (4) investigations, 1,697; and (5) application reviews, 2,687. Because of its rising work load with problem banks, the FDIC in 1974 entered into agreements with three states (Georgia, Iowa, and Washington) whereby most of the nonproblem insured banks would be examined by the state examiners. The FDIC hoped that it could subsequently extend this program to other states, so that most of the nonproblem banks would be examined by state and FDIC examiners on an alternate-year basis.

Whenever unsafe and prohibited practices are reported by the examiners, the corporation undertakes corrective action. Usually the offending bank cooperates in this procedure so that quick remedies are obtained; but whenever the insured bank continues to engage in unsound practices, the corporation has the authority and responsibility to institute proceedings for termination of the insured status of the bank. In the first thirty-five years of its operation, the corporation did initiate termination proceedings in 198 cases. In about 40 percent of these cases, corrective action by the offending bank was subsequently taken; in another third of the cases the banks were absorbed by other banks; in forty-eight cases the banks suspended operations or their insurance was terminated.

## Sources of Income for the Federal Deposit Insurance Corporation

Having considered earlier the amount of disbursements by the corporation to depositors when banks have failed, it might be well to consider the sources of income and financial status of the FDIC. Insured banks have been required since 1935 to pay an assessment rate of 1/12 of 1 percent of their assessable deposits. The 1980 bank law provided for a credit against current assessment, which amounted to 60 percent of the prior year's net assessment income. After receiving assessment credits, the net assessment on assessable deposits of insured banks was only 1/30 of 1 percent in 1979, and was 1/27 of one percent in 1980.

From these assessments and investment income, after deducting losses and operating expenses, the corporation was able by the end of 1980, to build up an asset position of $11.6 billion, of which $9 billion was in U.S. Treasury notes and bonds. An additional $1.7 billion was in short-term Treasury bills. Net FDIC revenues were $1.3 billion in 1980, of which $863 million came from investments in U.S. Treasury securities, $431 million in net assessments paid by banks for deposit insurance, and $17 million from interest no notes receivable and other sources.

In the event of future insurance losses the FDIC not only can draw on these accumulated investment assets but is also authorized to borrow from the Treasury up to an additional $3 billion if needed. So far the latter borrowing authority has never been used, because the income received by the FDIC has been far more than adequate to pay all expenses, including losses of failing banks insured by it.

# Questions for Discussion

1. Discuss traditional asset management. What type of earning assets do banks prefer? Why?
2. What important relative changes were there in the composition of bank credit in the four years from 1977 to 1980 inclusive? Why did such changes occur?
3. Why have the banks in the larger cities, such as New York and Chicago, tended to have higher loan-deposit ratios than banks in smaller cities? What effect on bank liquidity does the move toward higher loan-deposit ratios have? Is this "good" or "bad?"
4. Discuss bank liquidity and asset liquidity and indicate how they can be safeguarded both by bank managements and through regulation by the Federal Reserve and the Federal Deposit Insurance Corporation.
5. Discuss the newer principles of liability management. Contrast these with the more traditional principles of asset management. What led to the greater emphasis on liability management? (Hint: Consider changes in regulations of banks as well as changes in management attitudes.)
6. How did the raising of interest rate ceilings on bank deposits (Regulation Q) in the 1960 and their suspension on large CDs in the early 1970s affect the growth of time deposits? What impact on commercial banks do you believe the elimination of Regulation Q altogether in 1986 will have?
7. How significant as sources of bank funds are the issuance of certificates of deposit and the purchase of federal funds? When did such liabilities became of increasing importance? What were the impacts on the banks of the "mismatch" of assets and liabilities in the early 1980s?
8. What was the original justification for imposing reserve requirements on

commercial banks? Why were higher reserve requirements put on larger city banks as compared with smaller country banks?

9. What changes had the Board of Governors of the Federal Reserve System made in categories of member banks for reserve purposes beginning in 1972?

10. What happened to reserve requirements for all depository institutions after the passage of the 1980 act? What did this do to the monetary multiplier?

11. Discuss the role of the Federal Deposit Insurance Corporation in aiding the stability of the commercial banking system. Why has the amount of bank deposit insured been progressively increased up to $100,000? To what extent may the FDIC affect entry conditions in the banking industry? Briefly discuss the financing of the FDIC and indicate its profit and loss record.

# Selected Bibliography for Further Reading

AMERICAN BANKERS ASSOCIATION ECONOMIC POLICY COMMISSION, *Member Bank Reserve Requirements* (New York: American Bankers Association, 1975).

BOARD OF GOVERNORS OF THE FEDERAL RESERVE SYSTEM, *Federal Reserve Bulletin*, Washington, D.C. (See latest issue for most recent data on bank reserves and bank deposits.)

BREWER, ELIJAH, "Bank Funds Management Comes of Age—A Balance Sheet Analysis," *Economic Perspectives*, Federal Reserve Bank of Chicago, May-June 1981, Vol. IV, Issue 3, pp. 13–23.

FEDERAL DEPOSIT INSURANCE CORPORATION, *Annual Report*, Washington, D.C. (Examine latest annual report for summary data of recent insurance and loss experience of FDIC.)

FRIEDMAN, B.M., and V. V. ROLEY "Investors' Portfolio Behavior Under Alternative Models of Long-Term Interest Rate Expectations: Unitary, Rational or Autoregressive," *Econometrica*, **47**:1495–1497 (Nov. 1979).

HAVRILESKY, THOMAS M., and JOHN T. BOORMAN, eds., *Current Perspectives in Banking Operations, Management and Regulation* (Arlington Heights, Ill.: AHM Publishing, 1976).

KNIGHT, ROBERT E., "Reserve Requirements Part 1: Comparative Reserve Requirements at Member and Nonmember Banks," *Monthly Review*, Federal Reserve Bank of Kansas City, April 1974, pp. 3–20.

LANG, RICHARD W., "Managing the Money Stock: A Time of Transition," *Business Review*, Federal Reserve Bank of Philadelphia, March-April 1981, pp. 3–13.

PROCHNOW, HERBERT V., and HERBERT V. PROCHNOW, JR., eds., *The Changing World of Banking* (New York: Harper & Row, 1974).

UNITED STATES CONGRESS, *Member Bank Reserve Requirements*, Hearings Before the Committee on Banking and Currency, United States Senate, March 23 and 24, 1959 (Washington, D.C.: U.S. Government Printing Office, 1959).

It was the duty of the banks, they seeemed to think, to lend for as long
a time, and to as great an extent as they might wish to borrow.

**THE WEALTH OF NATIONS**

# 13
## CHAPTER

# Bank Lending Policies

Traditionally, one of the main functions of a bank has been to make loans, particularly short-term self-liquidating business loans. To be sure, in World War II the banks added tremendously to their holdings of U.S. government securities while their loans outstanding rose rather modestly. After World War II, however, the proportion of bank loans to total loans and investments rose steadily, until it exceeded 73 percent by the 1980s.

At the same time that the proportion of earning assets in the form of loans increased steadily decade by decade, the composition of the **loan portfolio** changed in significant ways. Although the traditional commercial and industrial (business) loan was not neglected by commercial banks, the percentage of total loans in this form has remained consistently under 40 percent, whereas nontraditional loans to individuals in the postwar period increased so that they now usually make up more than 20 percent of the loan portfolio. All types of bank loans have grown importantly in dollar amount in the postwar period, as banks have sought maximum profits consistent with the requirements of bank liquidity.

## IMPORTANCE OF BANK LOANS

Bank loans are, of course, not made in the same amount by the banking system every year. The extension of additional loans depends upon (1) the available loanable funds of the banking system, which, in, turn, depends importantly upon Federal Reserve policy, and (2) the demand for bank credit by prospective borrowers, especially business firms. This loan demand depends not only on business needs for outside funds but also on the availability of credit and equity capital from nonbank sources.

Data on bank loans for more than twenty-five years are shown in Table 13–1. These data indicate that in the decade of the 1950s total bank loans rose by more than $68 billion, an increase of 163 percent. The growth of commercial and industrial (business) loans nearly kept pace with total bank lending by rising by 137 percent.

In the decade of the 1960s bank lending also more than doubled from $110.8 billion to $286.7 billion—an increase of 158 percent. Commercial and industrial lending more than kept pace as it jumped by 169 percent. As a result, as can be seen in Table 13–1, commercial and industrial lending was 37.8 percent of total bank lending in 1969 as compared with 36.1 percent in 1959.

In the decade of the 1970s, total bank lending rose even faster as it nearly tripled from $286.7 billion to $855.7 billion. Business lending by banks in the 1970s also nearly tripled, rising from $108.4 billion in 1969 to $286.7 billion in 1979. Business lending, as did total bank loans, also rose strongly in 1980 and 1981. Both inflation and increases in real output partly account for these strong increases in bank lending in the 1970s and early 1980s. Difficulties in selling new corporate bonds in the severe credit restraint period of 1981–1982 also led to heavy business borrowing at commercial banks in order to secure needed external funds.

## KINDS OF BANK LOANS

As total bank lending has increased, the need to maintain a diversified loan portfolio (both for profitability and liquidity) has continued. The importance of the major types of bank loans is shown in Table 13–1.

***Business Loans***    It can be noted from Table 13–1 that traditional **business loans** continue to be the largest part of the loan portfolio. As recently as 1981, such loans accounted for 36.7 percent of total loans. This percentage of total loans was noticeably down from the 39.7 percent of 1949, and from the 37.8 percent of 1969. Business loans of more than $360.8 billion in 1981, however, are still a major source of bank profits.

***Real Estate Loans***    The second most important kind of bank loan, as Table 13–1 shows, is **real estate loans** or mortgage loans, which increased from $11,405 million in 1949 to $286.3 billion in 1981. Furthermore, the

**Table 13–1  Loans of Commercial Banks by Four Major Categories, 1949–1981 (In billions of dollars)**

| Date (end of year) | Total Dollar Amount | Commercial and Industrial | | Real Estate Loans | | Loans to Individuals | | Financial[a] | |
|---|---|---|---|---|---|---|---|---|---|
| | | Dollar Amount | Percentage[b] | Dollar Amount | Percentage[b] | Dollar Amount | Percentage[b] | Dollar Amount | Percentage[b] |
| 1949 | 42.5 | 16.9 | 39.7 | 11.4 | 26.8 | 6.0 | 14.1 | 3.1 | 7.2 |
| 1954 | 70.6 | 26.9 | 37.9 | 18.4 | 25.9 | 14.8 | 20.8 | 4.5 | 6.2 |
| 1959 | 110.8 | 40.2 | 36.1 | 28.1 | 26.1 | 24.2 | 21.7 | 7.9 | 7.0 |
| 1963 | 150.0 | 52.9 | 33.9 | 39.1 | 25.0 | 34.6 | 22.1 | 21.0 | 13.3 |
| 1967 | 237.2 | 88.4 | 37.2 | 58.5 | 24.6 | 51.6 | 21.7 | 29.0 | 12.1 |
| 1969 | 286.8 | 108.4 | 37.8 | 70.0 | 24.4 | 63.3 | 22.4 | 17.6 | 6.1 |
| 1971 | 327.7 | 118.5 | 36.1 | 81.6 | 24.9 | 74.5 | 22.7 | 32.5 | 8.3 |
| 1973 | 460.1 | 159.4 | 34.6 | 118.0 | 25.6 | 99.9 | 21.7 | 40.7 | 8.8 |
| 1975 | 507.2 | 179.3 | 35.3 | 134.8 | 26.5 | 106.4 | 20.9 | 42.2 | 8.3 |
| 1977 | 638.3 | 212.6 | 33.3 | 175.5 | 27.4 | 139.0 | 21.7 | 54.1 | 8.4 |
| 1978 | 755.4 | 248.2 | 32.8 | 210.9 | 27.9 | 164.8 | 21.8 | 55.7 | 7.3 |
| 1979 | 855.7 | 292.4 | 34.1 | 242.9 | 28.4 | 186.2 | 21.7 | 59.9 | 6.9 |
| 1980 | 919.5 | 325.3 | 35.4 | 261.4 | 28.4 | 176.2 | 19.1 | 61.5 | 6.6 |
| 1981 | 983.0 | 360.8 | 36.7 | 286.3 | 29.1 | 186.5 | 18.9 | 53.9 | 5.4 |

[a]Financial loans by banks include security loans, lease financing receivables, and loans to nonbank financial institutions.

[b]This is the percentage of total loans.

SOURCE: Board of Governors of the Federal Reserve System, *Federal Reserve Bulletins*, Feb. 1952, p. 163; April 1961, p. 434; July 1964, p. 868; Mar. 1964, p. 446; Feb. 1966, p. 228; April 1970, p. A24; March 1972, p. A24; Aug. 1973, p. A22; June 1974, p. A18; Sept. 1975, p. A16; Sept. 1976, p. A16; July 1977, p. A18; Feb. 1981, p. A15; March 1982, p. A15.

percentage of total bank loans in the form of real estate loans rose somewhat. In 1949, such real estate loans were 26.8 percent of total loans and in 1981 they were 29.1 percent.

*Loans to Individuals*    The type of loan called **Loans to Individuals** in Table 13–1 is quite different, however. Bank loans to individuals have jumped importantly, not only absolutely but relatively as well, though there has been only a little relative growth in this type of bank lending since the late 1950s. Such loans rose from $6 billion in 1949 to $186.2 billion in 1979, which also represented an increase in their percentage of total loans from 14 percent in 1949 to 21.7 pecent in 1979.

It can be noted, however, in this table that total bank loans to individuals, as well as the percentage of such loans to total bank loans, fell sharply in 1980. This was the result of a short but sharp recession in the second quarter of that year and considerable credit restraint applied by the Federal Reserve both before and after the recession. Hence at the end of 1981, such loans totaled only $186.5 billion, almost the same as two years earlier, as Table 13–1 indicates. Individuals, nevertheless, are much more important customers of commercial banks now than they were earlier. When individuals borrow from commercial banks, they borrow for many reasons, but particularly to buy durable goods, especially automobiles.

## BUSINESS LENDING BY BANKS

Why do business firms borrow from commercial banks? A nationwide sample survey conducted by the Survey Research Center of the University of Michigan shows that business firms mainly borrowed to secure either working capital or funds for capital expenditures. Borrowing for working capital includes such purposes as building up or carrying inventories, seasonal credit, borrowing for financing sales or credit to customers, discounting receivables, and the like. The latter purposes all fall within the traditional doctrines of the proper use of bank credit whereas the use of bank credit to finance capital expenditures does not.

### Working Capital Loans

Nevertheless, the Survey Research Center discovered that borrowing exclusively for working capital occurs most frequently among medium-sized firms. A sizable number of such firms, however, borrow from banks for both working capital and capital expenditures. Among large firms a much smaller percentage borrowed exclusively for working capital, whereas nearly one fifth borrowed only to finance capital expenditures. An additional one fifth of large firms borrowed for both working capital and capital expenditures.

***Short-Term, Self-Liquidating Business Loans***    Banks are clearly interested in satisfying the credit needs of business firms as the sharp increase in the postwar period in the dollar amount of industrial and commercial loans, as shown in Table 13–1, indicates. Although these business loans may be written with maturities to fit the need of the borrowing firm, the traditional type of business loan favored by banks was supposed to be the short-term, self-liquidating loan. This is the type of loan that a retail business might secure from a bank to buy inventory before the heavy selling season prior to Christmas or Easter.

*Real Bills Doctrine*    The desirability of having commercial banks heavily specialize in this type of business lending was elaborated into a doctrine of banking both in England and the United States. In England it was called the **real bills doctrine,** whereas in the United States it was called the **banking school theory,** or the commercial loan theory. When the Federal Reserve was established in 1913, the banking school theory was in evidence inasmuch as the act required that eligible commercial paper presented by the banks to a Federal Reserve Bank for discount not have a maturity longer than ninety days.

 The economic justification for the real bills doctrine was that the price level would tend to be stable if commercial banks restricted themselves to such inventory loans. As the money supply expanded with bank lending, so too would real goods production be increased to permit the expansion of business inventories. The ***pari passu*** expansion of goods with money would make impossible, it was thought, any general rise of prices caused by "too much money chasing too few goods."

## TERM LOANS

An ordinary **term loan** has a formal loan agreement in which the period of maturity is specified at more than one year, although repayment may be either in a lump sum or in periodic installments. Other types of business loans may also be term loans, even though they appear superficially to be short-term loans with a maturity of less than one year. Such may be the case with bank credit extended under revolving credit or standby agreements. Even though the note may be drawn originally with a maturity as short as ninety days, the loan agreement may permit the borrower to renew the note at maturity so that the credit may remain on the books of the lending banks for periods as long as two years or more.

## Purposes of Term Lending

Term loans are extended by commercial banks for two somewhat different purposes. First, banks make intermediate-term loans (five to eight years in initial maturity) that are repaid from the borrower's earnings or other internal sources. Second, banks extend interim credits with typical maturities of one to two years, which are then repaid from the proceeds of new bond or stock issues in the securities markets. In either case, a great advantage of this type of borrowing is that a bank term loan can be tailored to the specific needs of the individual borrower through direct negotiation with the lending bank, so that the borrower can have more freedom in determining the repayement schedule, thus permitting more efficient use of the proceeds of the loan.

## Importance of Term Lending

Many short-term loans are in effect term loans, because they are more or less routinely renewed whenever they come to maturity. Likewise, businesses may borrow from banks on a pledge of business property with the intention of using such loan proceeds to finance capital expenditures, or additions to permanent working capital. In the reported statistics, however, such loans would not be reported as term loans but would be identified instead as real estate loans. In short, reported figures on term lending invariably understate the importance of term lending, even though the reported figures show an impressive growth in this kind of bank lending. By the end of 1981, such term loans at large commercial banks (the 134 large weekly reporting commercial banks with assets of $1 billion or more as of Dec. 31, 1977) totaled $85 billion. This was nearly half of the $175 billion total of commercial and industrial domestic loans at these same large commercial banks. New York City banks, which account for about a third of business loans of weekly reporting banks ($56.2 billion at the end of 1981), have an even higher proportion of business loans outstanding as term loans.

## Term Revolving Credit

In some instances, short-term business borrowing is replaced with term revolving credit. An example of this occurred in 1981 when International

Harvester, a major manufacturer of trucks and agricultural machinery, reached an agreement with eight banks to replace short-term borrowings of $3.4 billion with a three-year revolving credit arrangement. Previous to this new agreement, the company and its credit corporation subsidiary had relied on notes due in thirty, sixty, and ninety days. The eight banks included three foreign banks and three New York City banks, a well as Bank of America and Continental Illinois National Bank and Trust Company.

*Large Corporations Desire Term Loans*    The demand for term loans centered heavily on New York City banks in the 1970s and 1980s, not only because they had enough funds to satisfy most of these demands but also because New York City banks cater particularly to large corporations. These large firms normally finance most of their operations from internal sources and from the capital businesses.

In periods of high-level capital expenditures, large business firms turn with greater frequency to large commercial banks. Partly it is to use bank financing as a supplement to other sources of funds and partly as a temporary substitute for capital market credit when yields are rising in the financial markets.

*Term Lending as Interim Financing*    It has been estimated that nearly half the total expenditures of public utilities ultimately financed in the capital markets are initially financed by commercial banks. For manufacturing industries such interim financing by banks is equal to about one fourth of the capital expenditures ultimately financed by capital market flotations. The effect of both interim financing at banks plus term lending that remains with the banks until final repayment is that very large sums of money are being loaned by banks for more than one year.

## MORTGAGE OR REAL ESTATE LOANS BY BANKS

Mortgages are also important earning assets for commercial banks, as evidenced by the fact that total assets in this form are second only to business loans. As indicated earlier, a fairly steady proportion of about one fourth of total bank loans has been in mortgages throughout the postwar period. Commercial banks are a considerable but not the primary source of funds for the mortgage market as a whole. As mortgage lenders, commercial banks are exceeded in importance by savings and loan associations, life insurance companies, and mutual savings banks. Commercial banks now account for more than 14 percent of total mortgages held by all institutions. This proportion has also remained fairly constant in the postwar period.

## Countercyclical Fluctuation of Bank Mortgage Lending

Commercial banks, like life insurance companies, are more interested in mortgage lending during certain phases of the business cycle than during others. In the upswing of the cycle, when loanable funds are scarce in relation to the demand for them, banks prefer to satisfy business borrowers first and mortgage borrowers later. But when business activity turns downward and the demand for bank loans among businesses usually slackens, banks exhibit much greater interest in mortgage loans. The interest rate ceiling on government guaranteed mortgages and the relative inflexibility of mortgage rates generally affect the flow of funds into mortgages as compared with other possible earning assets. It is this "stickiness" of interest rates on mortgages that helps account both for the usual lack of interest on the parts of banks and other lenders in making mortgage loans in the upswing of the cycle and for their greater interest in making such mortgages in the downswing.

*Mortgage Lending by Banks in Credit Restraint Years*    The impacts of changing monetary-credit policy by the Federal Reserve on commercial bank mortgage lending behavior in the latter part of the 1960s (with about a year lag) are clearly revealed in Federal Reserve data. In 1965 and 1966, commercial banks increased their holdings of mortgages by $5.7 billion each year. After considerable credit restraint in 1966, however, bank mortgage lending was only $4.7 billion in 1967, or about $1 billion less than in the previous year.

In 1968, after a lessening of credit restraint after midyear, there was a sharp increase in bank mortgage lending. Commercial banks loaned $6.6 billion in mortgage funds that year, which was $2 billion more than in the previous year. In 1969, a year of even more severe credit restraint than 1966, the serious adverse effects on bank mortgage lending were experienced both that year and in the following year. Bank mortgage lending in 1969 was $1.7 billion less than in 1968, and such mortgage lending declined another $2.4 billion in 1970.

In the 1973–1974 period of credit restraint, when interest rates reached new peaks not attained in either 1966 or 1969, bank mortgage lending held up relatively well. Bank mortgage lending by commercial banks actually rose by $13 billion in 1973 over the 1972 pace, but it fell by $5.3 billion in 1974 and declined another $9 billion in 1975 from the earlier date. Bank mortgage lending, however, rose by $2.6 billion in 1976.

## Renewed Bank Mortgage Lending

Some commercial banks, which had begun to curtail their mortgage lending in 1973 and 1974, resumed considerable interest in this type of lending in the late 1970s. Certainly there was a wariness on the part of the banks in making an excessive amount of loans on condominiums or townhouses because of their earlier difficulties in this loan market, but the single-family detached dwelling (usually built or purchased by higher-income families who were better credit risks) again became an attractive outlet for banks with more funds to lend.

In both 1978 and 1979, real estate loans of banks rose by more than $30 billion each year—$35.4 billion in 1978 and $32 billion in 1979. In 1980, however, a year of alternating credit restraint and ease (and a sharp recession in the second quarter), real estate lending of banks fell to only $18.5 billion but rose by $24.9 billion in 1981. Because of inflation in housing prices and a decline in mortgage lending by other institutions, this amount of mortgage credit financed a smaller number of housing starts than would have been true even a few years earlier. There were only 1.3 million housing starts in 1980 and 1 million in 1981 as compared with 1.7 million in 1979 and 2 million in 1978.

Some growth in the relative importance of commercial banks in the mortgage loan market in the fifteen years from the mid-1960s to 1980 is indicated in Table 13–2, which shows that commercial banks, which accounted for only 14.3 percent of nationwide aggregate mortgage loans outstanding on one- to four-family nonfarm homes in 1965, increased their participation rate in this market to 17.2 percent by 1975. In 1980, commercial banks held 16.7 percent of the mortgages outstanding on one- to four-family homes. The three other major types of private financial intermediaries—savings and loans, mutual savings banks, and life insurance companies—all also had some slippage in their relative importance. The really big growth in mortgage lending was by federally supported agencies, which rose from only 3 percent in 1965 to a significant 12.8 percent in 1975 and to an even larger 19 percent in 1980.

In some cases, large commercial banks would make Federal Housing Administration (FHA), Veterans Administration (VA), or con-

**Table 13–2  Nationwide Aggregate Mortgage Loans Outstanding on One- to Four-Family Nonfarm Homes (percent)**

|                              | 1965  | 1975  | 1980  |
|------------------------------|-------|-------|-------|
| Savings and loans            | 44.3  | 40.6  | 43.3  |
| Commercial banks             | 14.3  | 17.2  | 16.6  |
| Mutual savings banks         | 14.1  | 10.3  | 6.6   |
| Life insurance companies     | 13.9  | 4.0   | 3.0   |
| Federally supported agencies | 3.0   | 12.8  | 19.0  |
| Others                       | 10.4  | 5.1   | 11.5  |
|                              | 100.0 | 100.0 | 100.0 |

SOURCE: Federal Reserve Bank of Chicago. *Economic Perspectives*, May-June 1977, p. 27; Board of Governors of the Federal Reserve System, *Federal Reserve Bulletin*, May 1981, p. A39.

ventional mortgage loans with the intention of reselling them in the secondary market (e.g., to Fannie Mae—Federal National Mortgage Association—or Ginnie Mae—Government National Mortgage Association). By selling such mortgages originated by the bank, the bank could reinvest in additional mortgage loans. The advantages of this arrangement were that the bank collected on servicing loans, had a continued availability of money, and could develop additional income through origination fees. Furthermore, servicing of such accounts kept the bank in contact with these mortgage customers and could lead to selling these customers additional services, such as checking and savings accounts, automobile loans, home improvement loans, and trust business.

## BANK FINANCING OF CONSUMER INSTALLMENT CREDIT

The third most important kind of commercial bank loan volume consists of Loans to Individuals, which accounted for $186.5 billion of bank earning assets in 1981, as shown earlier in Table 13–1. Nearly two thirds of these individual loans were in the form of installment credit, which thus suggests that one should examine the specific role of commercial banks in the extension of **consumer installment credit.**

*Higher Proportion of Installment Credit from Banks*    Total installment credit held by commercial banks at the end of 1981 amounted to $149.3 billion out of total installment credit of $333.3 billion held by all holders of such credit. The proportion of such credit held directly by commercial banks at the end of 1981 was 44 percent as compared with 37.7 percent at the end of 1960, 36.6 percent at the end of 1955, and only 26.3 percent in 1940. Of the installment credit held directly by commercial banks, about $59 billion in 1981, or about two fifths of installment credit supplied by banks, was in the form of automobile paper, whereas the remaining amount was used to finance purchases of other consumer goods, for repair and modernization of homes, and for personal purposes such as vacations or the payment of unexpected medical expenses. In addition, about $10.3 billion in 1981 financed the purchase of mobile homes.

## *Bank Credit Card and Check Credit Plans*

One way in which banks have expanded their participation in consumer installment credit is through the extension of credit card and check credit plans to many of their customers. After the mid-1960s, **bank credit card** and check credit plans were the most dynamic growth components of total consumer credit offered by commercial banks. Some smaller banks had tried these plans earlier, and some larger banks initiated them in the late 1950s, but it was not until around 1965 and later that these plans grew significantly across the country.

## Bank Credit and Debit Cards

Although about 200 independent bank credit cards are operated mostly by small banks, there is a "big two" in the bank credit card field. Master Charge, issued by an association of banks called Interbank, is the largest bank card operation. National BankAmericard is second. In 1977, National BankAmericard changed the name of its card to Visa. Nearly 95 percent of all bank card credit outstanding is generated by these two systems. By the 1980s, nearly 9,000 banks were offering credit cards to their customers. Citicorp, the largest bank in New York City, is the largest bank card issuer, with about 7.5 million cards outstanding.

Despite the widespread use of bank credit cards, many banks have had difficulty in generating a profit from them owing to customer fraud, theft, default on account payments, mismanagement, collusion by merchants, and the high cost of processing records of transactions. Since many card holders pay their full balance owed each month, credit card issuers are deprived of interest payments. As a result of these problems, banks issuing credit cards suffered some losses in the 1970s and early 1980s.

Because of losses on conventional bank credit cards, the two large systems offering such cards added a debit card in the early 1980s. MasterCard called its debit card MasterCard II and had about 200 banks issuing such cards in 1981. Visa had nearly 300 bank issuers in 1981.

A **bank debit card,** unlike a credit card, merely transfers funds already held in the bank by the customer. A credit card, on the other hand, involves a loan of bank funds to the customer. Interest rates in 1982 were also increased, typically to 21 percent, on consumer installment debt incurred in using credit cards. Some banks also instituted annual fixed charges for each card.

*Check Credit Plans*   Check credit plans are basically a form of installment credit connected with a bank checking account, with one out of ten banks offering such a service. In a variety of forms, these check credit plans combine elements of cashier's checks, travelers' checks, overdraft banking, and check-guarantee programs. One type of check credit provides the individual with a prearranged automatic line of credit, which is activated the moment the individual's account is overdrawn. The individual uses a regular checking account and regular checks. This means that regular checks are honored that otherwise would be returned to the sender.

The other major type of check credit involves plans in which a prearranged line of credit is activated by employing a special checking account and special checks provided by the bank. This is a more prevalent type of check credit than the overdraft type of check credit. About 1,621 banks by the 1980s offered some such bank check credit plan.

## Bank Revolving Credit

Both bank credit cards and check credit plans are a form of revolving credit offered by commercial banks and were combined in the data published by the Federal Reserve after 1976. Such **bank revolving credit** rose by $4 billion in 1977, spurted another $6 billion in 1978, and rose again by $5.5 billion in 1979. In 1980, however, because of a controversial credit control plan imposed by the Federal Reserve Board in mid-March and not lifted until late July, there was virtually no growth in such credit at all. Such revolving bank credit was $29.8 billion at the end of 1979 and $30 billion at the end of 1980.

## FINANCIAL LOANS

In addition to business and commercial loans, real estate loans, and other loans to individuals, including bank credit card and check credit plans, loans by banks to various financial institutions increased in the 1970s and early 1980s. As Table 13–1 indicates, these financial loans, which averaged only 7.2 percent of total bank loans in 1949, had jumped to 13.3 percent of total bank loans by 1963. More than a decade later—at the end of 1975—such loans had fallen to some 8.3 percent of total bank loans and were only 5.4 percent in 1981. This category of financial loans thus continued to be the smallest of the four major categories of bank loans.

## BANK CREDIT LINES AND COMPENSATING BALANCES

Having considered the four most important kinds of bank loans, it may now be well to consider some of the mechanics of bank lending, particularly as pertains to business loans. When large business firms establish a regular relationship with a large commercial bank, it is quite likely at some time that a credit line will be established.

## Nature of Credit Lines

A **credit line** is generally an informal understanding between the borrower and the bank as to the maximum amount of credit that the bank will provide the borrower at any one time. Although this arrangement is not a binding contract, most banks endeavor to honor the credit line unless some very unusual circumstance develops in the affairs of the would-be borrower. The usual duration of the credit line is one year or less, with a careful review of the borrower's situation by the bank at the end of the period.

*Seasonal Borrowing Needs and Credit Lines*   Credit lines are often extended to borrowers who have large and recurring seasonal needs for bank credit. Such credit lines may be associated also with revolving credit and floor-plan financing, inventory and equipment financing, and construction activity. Business firms that often secure such lines of credit include sales finance companies, manufacturing and mining companies, commodity dealers, and trade and construction firms. All these kinds of businesses rely importantly on bank credit to help finance their seasonal needs for working capital.

Furthermore, many businesses with large credit needs find it necessary to establish multiple credit lines (i.e., credit lines at a number of banks). Firms sometimes have multiple credit lines so that they can meet the annual loan cleanup requirement of banks by securing a new loan from a new bank to pay off an outstanding loan at another bank.

*Compensating Bank Balances*   When they set up a credit line for a business borrower, most banks also establish a required minimum deposit balance. The range for this minimum balance typically seems to be 10 to 20 percent. When credit is tight the minimum balance required may be increased, whereas a greater availability of credit may be reflected in a lowering of the bank's minimum balance requirement. For sales finance companies, which are important users of bank credit lines, the most common minimum balance requirement, or **compensating balance,** seems to be 10 percent of the credit line when not borrowing and 20 percent when borrowing. This reduces the funds available for the borrower to use. For example, a borrower who pays 8 percent on a loan but must keep 20 percent of the loan on deposit with the bank is receiving only 80 percent of the loan. Hence the borrower is really paying an effective rate of 10 percent of the money that can be used. In computing the average minimum balance maintained, the bank is usually willing to relate this requirement to the average deposit over the entire year, although sometimes a bank insists that this minimum deposit be maintained at all times.

## BANK RATES ON LOANS

Bank rates tend to vary with the overall demand for credit as compared with the availability of loanable funds. When borrowers such as business firms need more outside funds to expand working or fixed capital to meet increased demand for their product or service, they may turn to any one of a number of sources of loanable funds, almost certainly including commercial banks. When the credit needs of a number of important borrowers tend to increase, the price of such credit, which is the interest rate, also tends to rise.

### The Prime Rate

The **prime rate** was originated by commercial banks in 1933 and since then it has had to serve three major functions: (1) it is the interest rate applicable to a bank's most creditworthy customers, (2) it is a base rate to which are tied, either formally or informally, the higher interest rates on nonprime bank loans, (3) it is an index rate for floating-rate bank loans, which are often term loans of more than one year in which interest rates vary up and down with short-term market rates as represented by the prime rate. All these functions are quite important, but the floating-rate function of the prime has become of ever greater importance in the last two decades as interest rates have become increasingly volatile. By the decade of the 1980s, at least half of the dollar volume of business lending at most large banks was made under floating-rate provisions.

### The Floating Rate Formula Experiment in the 1970s

Not only does the prime rate serve as a base on which to float other bank interest rates for other than very short-term business loans, but the determination of the prime rate itself in the 1970s was given over to a formula that allowed the prime rate to float (i.e., to change as key interest rates in the money market changed). This experiment was begun in late 1971 and 1972 by a number of large money market banks, especially by Citibank, which is the largest bank in New York City, where the money market is centered. In 1980, however, the experiment in establishing the prime rate by formula was abandoned as money market interest rates became increasingly volatile.

When the formula for a **floating prime rate** was in use, it was usually set about 150 basis points (1½ percent) above the dealer rate on high-grade commercial paper due in ninety days. In a few cases, the base selected was the interest rate on large ($100,000 or more) short-term CDs offered by large commercial banks. The reason for usually preferring the rate on commercial paper was that this was a common method of short-term borrowing for large business borrowers to sell commercial paper (unsecured IOUs) in the money market. This was increasingly resorted to if they could not get an attractive rate on their borrowing at commercial banks.

## Undercutting the Prime Rate

Whether the prime rate is set by formula as in the 1970s, or administratively as it was earlier and is again in the 1980s, it still turns out that some customers can get a lower rate than the posted prime rate. This price cutting by the banks for selected good business customers has taken place over a number of years but became particularly noticeable in periods of sharp declines in interest rates, as in the second quarter of 1980, when concessions of as much as 4 percent under the posted prime rate were given. The fundamental reason for banks giving such concessions on their posted prime rate is that there are a small number of very large national corporations that have a number of alternative sources from which they can secure business credit. Commercial banks are only one such source for these business borrowers.

Other alternatives for securing borrowed funds for giant corporations include issuing commercial paper or borrowing in Eurocurrency credit markets. Such corporations thus have considerable bargaining power and can exact price concessions from large commercial banks. In effect, therefore, we often have two prime rates.

The posted prime rate obtains for most business customers, either because that is the rate at which they can borrow or the rate at which they borrow is based on this posted prime rate. The other prime rate(s) is based on bargaining between the bank and a few select large business customers and may, in fact, be significantly below the posted prime rate. This negotiated prime rate might even be called a "super prime rate."

## Determining the Posted Prime Rate

Determining the posted prime rate is part of the decision-making process involved in managing a bank's balance sheet. Three major types of market rates are considered in making this particular decision: (1) rates on nonloan bank assets (e.g., yields on U.S. government securities), (2) rates on bank-acquired liabilities (i.e., the rate banks pay when they "buy" deposits in the form of certificates of deposit), (3) the rate on corporate debt claims issued in place of bank borrowing (e.g., yields in the commercial paper market). The effect of a change in the demand for nonprime loans, as well as prime loans, must also be considered when the prime rate is changed, because a change in this key bank lending rate often leads to changes in other bank lending rates. Figure 13–1 shows the close relationship between the prime rate and the commercial paper rate during an important part of the floating prime rate period from 1974 to 1977. Even before the floating prime rate was introduced, when the prime rate was set administratively, it tended to be related to money market rates, though not quite so closely as after the floating principle was established. In the 1980s, important changes in money market rates are still likely to lead to changes in the posted prime rate.

## Changes in the Prime Rate

Table 13–3 gives the annual average posted prime rate for selected years from 1945 through 1980. This table shows a marked trend for higher

**Figure 13–1    The Prime Paper Rate Spread, 1974–1977**

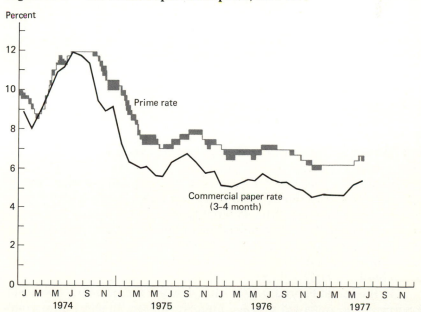

SOURCE: Federal Reserve Bank of Chicago, *Economic Perspectives*, July–Aug. 1977, p. 18.

Table 13–3  Commercial Bank Prime Rate, 1945–1980 (annual average percent)

| Year | Rate | Year | Rate |
|------|------|------|------|
| 1945 | 1.50 | 1973 | 8.02 |
| 1950 | 2.07 | 1974 | 10.80 |
| 1955 | 3.16 | 1975 | 7.86 |
| 1960 | 4.82 | 1976 | 6.83 |
| 1965 | 4.54 | 1977 | 6.82 |
| 1970 | 7.91 | 1978 | 9.05 |
| 1971 | 5.70 | 1979 | 12.66 |
| 1972 | 5.25 | 1980 | 15.26 |

SOURCE: Federal Reserve data.

levels in the prime rate in the thirty-five years for which data are presented. From a low of 1.50 percent in 1945, the prime rate rose to a high average annual level of 10.80 percent in 1974 because of a high demand for bank credit and a Federal Reserve policy of credit restraint. The prime rate rose to 12 percent in mid-1974.

Thereafter some declines in the prime rate occurred in 1975, 1976, and 1977 as a result of the severe recession of 1973–1975 and an accommodating Federal Reserve policy in 1975 and 1976. In 1978, 1979, and 1980, the prime rate rose to ever higher levels until it reached a record average annual level of 15.26 in 1980. It actually hit a peak of 21.5 percent in December 1980.

In addition to the steady rise in the prime rate over time to the high levels of 1980, there has been considerable fluctuation in this key bank lending rate. If every change in the prime rate were shown rather than annual average percent, the variability would be more noticeable. Furthermore, after the move toward a floating prime rate in 1971, the amount of variability increased even more in the 1970s than in previous decades. This variability continued into the 1980s.

## New Survey in 1977 of Terms of Bank Lending

In February 1977, the Federal Reserve enlarged its previous survey of lending at 120 large commercial banks to a new sample of 340 banks. This sample still included the 48 large money center banks, which account for about half of all bank lending to business, but it also included 100 nonmember banks in addition to the 240 member banks. Data could now be collected that would represent all of the more than 14,700 commercial banks.

In the initial February 1977 survey, when the prime rate was still 6¼ percent, the weighted average interest rate on all short-term commercial and industrial loans was 7.98 percent. At the same time, the weighted average interest rate on long-term commercial and industrial loans was 9.25 percent. The survey further confirmed the view that a high proportion of lending by banks, particularly large banks, was now being made at floating rates. Some two thirds of short-term business loans were made in 1977 at floating rates, whereas three fourths of long-term business loans utilized the device of floating rates.

## Bank Interest Rates in a Credit Restraint Period (1981)

Bank interest rates, as taken from this new survey of the terms of bank lending, are shown in Table 13–4 for a period of severe credit restraint, from August to November 1981. Although not shown in this table, all of these interest rates are significantly higher than they were a year earlier. For every size of borrower in August 1980, they are fifty percent or more higher than in August 1981. By November 1981, however, as shown in Table 13–4 there was some easing in interest rates from the August peaks. The Federal Reserve, though still maintaining its basic policy of credit restraint, did ease somewhat in the second half of 1981 because of the economic recession which began then and continued into 1982.

One of the notable things about the data in this table is the virtually flat (high) interest rate curve for all sizes of borrowers in August 1981. Almost all loans were being made at about 21 percent interest rates. By November, however, the traditional advantage of the larger borrower reappeared, so that, in general, the larger the amount borrowed the lower was the interest rate charged. Hence, those borrowing a million dollars or more in November paid 16.73 percent as compared with the higher interest rates charged for all smaller borrowers.

*Lower Interest Rates for Large Borrowers*    The lower interest rates associated with large-size loans as shown in Table 13–4 can be partly attributed to the fact that larger business firms tend to borrow in larger amounts from commercial banks than do smaller firms. These firms often are a smaller credit risk than smaller firms and hence deserve a lower interest rate. Furthermore, the administrative cost associated with processing business loans is not likely to be much more for a large loan than for a small loan, which means that the unit cost per dollar loaned is smaller for larger loans and hence, again, justifies the lower interest rate.

Finally, and perhaps most important of all, large business borrowers have a number of alternative sources from which they can secure funds. They can borrow from some other commercial bank; they can borrow from a nonbanking financial institution such as a life insurance company, particularly if they wish to issue bonds; they may be able to

Table 13–4   Terms of Lending at Commercial Banks, Survey of Loans Made, August 3–8, 1981, to November 2–7, 1981 (size of loan in thousands of dollars)

| | All Sizes | | 1–24 | | 25–49 | | 50–99 | | 100–499 | | 500–999 | | 1,000 and over | |
|---|---|---|---|---|---|---|---|---|---|---|---|---|---|---|
| | Aug. | Nov. | Aug. | Nov. | Aug. | Nov. | Aug. | Nov. | Aug. | Nov. | Aug. | Nov. | Aug. | Nov. |
| **Short-term commercial and industrial loans** | | | | | | | | | | | | | | |
| Weighted average maturity (months) | 1.6 | 1.6 | 3.1 | 3.0 | 3.5 | 2.8 | 3.1 | 3.9 | 3.4 | 3.4 | 3.2 | 3.0 | 1.2 | 1.2 |
| Weighted average interest rate (per cent per annum) | 21.11 | 17.23 | 20.76 | 19.95 | 21.18 | 19.19 | 21.36 | 19.65 | 21.37 | 19.13 | 21.85 | 18.64 | 21.06 | 16.73 |
| **Long-term commercial and industrial loans** | | | | | | | | | | | | | | |
| Weighted average maturity (months) | 20.62 | 37.6 | | | 26.9 | 29.4 | | | 39.2 | 34.0 | 48.7 | 37.1 | 63.5 | 41.8 |
| Weighted average interest rate (per cent per annum) | 20.62 | 18.94 | | | 19.77 | 19.60 | | | 20.70 | 21.22 | 21.45 | 18.52 | 20.65 | 17.55 |

SOURCE: Board of Governors of the Federal Reserve System, *Federal Reserve Bulletins*, Dec. 1981, p. A26; March 1982, p. A26.

issue commercial paper in the money market; or they may issue long-term debentures in the capital markets. The large firm with more alternatives has better bargaining power than the small firm with few credit alternatives; so it should not be surprising that the larger business borrower tends to receive a lower bank rate than the smaller business borrower.

## Foreign Lending of U.S. Banks

In addition to the domestic lending of U.S. banks, which has been emphasized in this chapter, large American banks in recent years have also greatly expanded their lending abroad, either from their home offices or from foreign branches. Such foreign lending has greatly increased because (1) the dollar is the major international unit of account, (2) international trade more than quadrupled from the 1960s to the 1980s, and (3) foreign lending was so profitable that it often accounted for half or more of the profits of large and very large American banks. At the end of 1980, total claims on foreigners of domestic offices and foreign branches of U.S. banks amounted to $350 billion, most of which was held by foreign branches. This was an increase of 50 percent in only four years.

Slightly over half of this total was to the highly developed countries in Europe, Japan, Australia, South Africa, and Canada. Despite the risk in making any kind of loan and the special "country risks" (balance of payments difficulties and the risk of social or political upheavals) in making foreign loans, such loans had a lower loss record than domestic loans. The loss ratio on international loans of the seven largest U.S. banks is only about one third of the loss ratio on the total loan portfolio. In addition to the contribution to total bank profitability of these foreign loans, the great bulk of funds to make these loans is secured from foreign sources (i.e., deposits in branches of U.S. branches abroad). This means that these foreign loans are not being made at the expense of would-be domestic borrowers.

# Questions for Discussion

1. Discuss the importance of loans for commercial banks. Discuss the growth of such bank loans in the period from 1949 to 1980 inclusive, as shown in Table 13–1.
2. Discuss the different types of bank loans with an ordering of their relative importance. Which types of bank loans have been growing most rapidly in

recent years? Which types of loans have remained relatively constant as a proportion of total bank loans?

3. Discuss the importance of business lending for commercial banks. Why do business firms borrow from banks?

4. Why has term lending by banks been growing so rapidly in recent years? Discuss the advantages and disadvantages of such term lending insofar as commercial banks are concerned. What do you think will happen to term lending in the rest of the 1980s? Why?

5. What are some of the factors affecting bank mortgage lending? (In particular, what happens to bank mortgage lending in periods of credit restraint?) Do banks generally prefer conventional or government-guaranteed mortgages? Why? How important are commercial banks in the entire mortgage market? Why have banks increased their servicing of mortgage loans by the 1980s?

6. How interested do banks appear to be in consumer installment credit? How important is bank credit, directly and indirectly, in this area of consumer finance? Are there important differences between banks in their concern with this kind of lending? Why?

7. Discuss the entry of a number of banks into the bank credit card and check credit field after the mid-1960s. How do you account for the rapid growth in this type of consumer installment credit furnished by banks? Discuss the difficulties involved in generating a profit in this kind of bank lending. Do you expect a further growth in this type of bank lending in the late 1980s? Why?

8. Discuss financial lending by the banks in the 1980s as compared with the 1960s and 1970s.

9. What is a line of credit? What kind of borrowers might qualify for lines of credit? What factors would a commercial bank consider in deciding the size of a line of credit for a particular borrower? How often is a line of credit regularly reviewed? Why?

10. What is the key bank interest rate? How is this prime rate determined? What causes this key interest rate to move up or down? How variable are bank interest rates as compared with market interest rates? Why? Discuss the relationship between the prime rate and other short-term rates in the 1970s and 1980s.

11. Discuss the implementation of the floating prime rate in late 1971. What was the experience with this kind of a prime rate? Why do you think that increasing numbers of, but not all, commercial banks adopted this particular system of setting the prime rate in the 1970s? Why did they abandon it in 1980? Why do business borrowers, not eligible for the prime rate, often pay a "floating rate" based on the prime rate?

12. Discuss some of the important factors that result in different bank borrowers being charged different interest rates. Do you think that it is fair that different borrowers pay different interest rates, or should all borrowers pay the same interest rate when borrowing from the same bank? Defend your answer. Briefly summarize the results of the latest Federal Reserve survey of the terms of bank lending.

13. Discuss the growth of foreign lending by large U.S. banks in recent years. What are some of the advantages and possible disadvantages of such lending? What differences are there between U.S. loans to other developed countries and those to less developed countries?

# Selected Bibliography for Further Reading

## Monographs

BOARD OF GOVERNORS OF THE FEDERAL RESERVE SYSTEM, *Bank Credit-Card and Check-Credit Plans* (Washington, D.C.: Board of Governors of the Federal Reserve System, July 1968).

JACOBY, NEIL H., and RAYMOND J. SAULNIER, *Business Finance and Banking* (New York: National Bureau of Economic Research, 1947).

KATONA, GEORGE, *Business Looks at Banks* (Ann Arbor, Mich.: The University of Michigan Press, 1975).

ROBINSON, ROLAND I., *The Management of Bank Funds*, 2d ed. (New York: McGraw-Hill, 1962).

## Articles

FEDERAL RESERVE BANK OF CHICAGO, "Bank Credit Cards," *Business Conditions*, July 1972, pp. 8–16.

FEDERAL RESERVE BANK OF NEW YORK, "Term Lending by New York City Banks in the 1960's," *Monthly Review*, Oct. 1967, pp. 99–203.

MERRIS, RANDALL C., "The Prime Rate," *Business Conditions*, Federal Reserve Bank of Chicago, April 1975, pp. 3–12.

——, "The Prime Rate Revisited," *Economic Perspectives*, Federal Reserve Bank of Chicago, July-Aug. 1977, pp. 17–20.

——, "Prime Rate Update," Federal Reserve Bank of Chicago, May-June 1978, pp. 14–16.

——, "Business Loans at Large Commercial Banks: Policies and Practices," *Economic Perspectives*, Federal Reserve Bank of Chicago, Nov.-Dec. 1979, Vol. III, Issue 6, pp. 15–23.

PRELL, MICHAEL J., "Part II Index-Linked Loans," *Monthly Review*, Federal Reserve Bank of Kansas City, Nov. 1971, pp. 9–20.

WALLICH, HENRY C., "Statement on International Lending of U.S. Banks," Before Subcommittee of Committee on Banking, Finance and Urban Affairs of U.S. House of Representatives, March 23, 1977, *Federal Reserve Bulletin*, April 1977, pp. 362–366.

> It is chiefly by discounting bills of exchange, that is by advancing
> money on them before they are due, that the greater part of banks and
> bankers issue their promissory notes.
>
> THE WEALTH OF NATIONS

# 14
# CHAPTER

# Bank Investing Policies

Commercial banks have placed increasing emphasis on liability management in recent years. This has meant that the banks' traditional concern with asset management, including the acquisition of various investments such as U.S. government securities, has assumed a secondary role. The banks, however, have not neglected entirely the importance of an adequate and diversified investment portfolio. In 1969, banks had cut their holdings of U.S. government securities in half, from $90 billion held at the end of World War II to $45 billion.

But by mid-1976, banks had rebuilt their holdings of U.S. government securities to the $90 billion that they held at the end of World War II. By the end of 1981, banks held about $110 billion in such securities. This amount of securities in 1980 represented a smaller percentage of bank earning assets than the same dollar amount in 1945, but the banks felt an urgent necessity to rebuild their reduced liquidity, because such liquidity had been reduced to very low levels in the credit restraint periods of 1973–1974, and 1981–1982. **Bank investing policies** are thus still important.

## THE LIQUIDITY PROBLEM

The need for bank liquidity was discussed earlier. Nevertheless, liquidity is such an important matter for commercial banks, and the subject of liquidity is so germane to portfolio management, that it should be mentioned here again. The basic problem that bank managements face is that they are borrowing short and lending long (i.e., most of the earning assets of banks have a longer maturity than the demand deposit and time deposit liabilities of banks). This fundamental characteristic of the asset-liability structure of a bank's balance sheet, along with the danger of disintermediation (i.e., a sudden withdrawal of deposits by the public to invest in higher-yielding debt instruments in periods of credit restraint such as 1966, 1969, 1973–1974, and 1981–1982), makes it imperative that banks pay particular attention to their liquidity needs.

Because of earnings considerations, banks prefer to hold as little excess cash as possible over and above the amount of cash reserves needed to fulfill the legal reserve ratio requirements of the monetary authorities. This means that temporarily surplus funds will be invested primarily in short- and intermediate-term government securities. All banks therefore have such government securities in their investment portfolio and well over four fifths of such government securities have a maturity of fewer than five years.

These government securities particularly help provide for needed bank liquidity, because they can be readily sold, or run off at maturity, with little market rise as to price fluctuations. In the early 1980s, a nearly flat yield curve on U.S. government securities prevailed, so that short- and intermediate-term government securities yielded as much, and in some cases more, than long-term government securities.

Regardless of yield, short- and intermediate-term government securities are preferred because of their higher liquidity. The longer the maturity, of course, the greater the possibility of price and yield changes, which in turn cause changes in the capital value of the securities of the portfolio. Let us now consider the various kinds of government securities available for inclusion in the bank portfolio.

## UNITED STATES GOVERNMENT SECURITIES

Securities issued by the federal government are almost always considered suitable for banks. However, these securities are of various types, not all of which are available for bank investment. The major type of security excluded is encompassed by the term savings bonds, which are designed for the small individual investor. In addition, other government securities, such as those special issues designed for the government trust funds or for the Federal Reserve, also cannot be acquired for bank portfolios. But most of the very large marketable federal debt is available for bank acquisition, even though particular maturities and types of government securities are particularly preferred by banks.

## Types of Marketable Government Securities

Marketable government securities are either Treasury bills, notes, or bonds. Treasury bills are of four types: cash management bills, which are fewer than 30 days in maturity (e.g., 15-day or 24-day Treasury bills, first issued in 1975, 91-day Treasury bills, first issued in 1929, 182-day Treasury bills, first issued in December 1958, and 1-year Treasury bills, first issued in December 1958). Treasury notes range from two to ten years in maturity, whereas bonds are usually over ten years to maturity at the time of issue.

***Treasury Bills Sold at a Discount***   Unlike other government securities, which usually have a common rate established by the Treasury, all Treasury bills are sold at a discount at an auction (i.e., the price, and consequently the yield, on these securities is set by the bidders rather than by the Treasury). Cash management bills are sold by the Treasury just before periods when it expects large receipts, as it does around April 15. For example, on March 25, 1981, the Treasury sold $6 billion of 22-day cash-management bills.

The 91-day and 182-day Treasury bills are sold every Monday and dated the following Thursday in an amount aggregating around $10.0 billion, and about $5 billion in 1-year bills are sold every month on a Friday and dated the following Tuesday. By the end of 1980, $216 billion of all kinds of Treasury bills were outstanding, which was an increase of $52 billion of Treasury bills in only four years. Commercial banks may submit tenders for their own account in these bill auctions or they may bid for their customers.

## Treasury Notes

**Treasury notes** are also of great importance in the bank portfolio, because they are in the intermediate maturity area of two to ten years and usually yield a somewhat higher return than Treasury bills, which are all one year or less in maturity. At the end of 1981, there were a greater amount of Treasury notes ($375 billion) outstanding than of Treasury bills ($245 billion). Quarterly Treasury refundings usually contain substantial amounts of notes.

## Marketable Bonds

For many years prior to 1971, the Treasury was unable to issue any new marketable bonds because the coupon rate on such bonds by law was not permitted to exceed 4¼ percent. After Congress permitted the Treasury to issue a limited amount of marketable bonds outside that statutory ceiling (now up to $100 billion), some new bonds were issued. Each quarter, the Treasury engages in a refunding operation involving both notes and bonds. For example, on May 15, 1981, the Treasury sold $3 billion in three-year notes, $1.75 billion in ten-year notes, and $2 billion in thirty-year bonds. Some $2.1 billion of this borrowing operation involved new cash borrowing.

Commercial banks, however, do not show much interest in such new bonds. As shown in Table 14–1, commercial banks hold only $2.3 billion of government securities with maturities in excess of ten years. The small amount of such longer-term government securities is largely the residual of bond issues bought by the banks some years ago.

## Bank Holdings of Marketable Governments

Commercial banks at the end of 1981 held a total of approximately $109 billion in marketable government securities. In the Treasury Survey of Ownership for December 1981, which covered 5,350 commercial banks, a total of $77.6 billion in government securities held by banks was classified by kind and maturity, as shown in Table 14–1. Of this total, some $25.5 billion matured within one year, which was down somewhat from the $31.2 billion at the end of 1976 but still up markedly from the $15.1 billion of more than a decade earlier at the end of 1969. At the end of 1981, a substantial amount, more than half the total or some $39 billion, was in Treasury securities maturing in one to five years, which was a rise of 10 percent in five years and represented nearly a doubling from eleven years earlier. Holdings in the five- to ten-year category were down somewhat, but there was an increase in the holdings over ten years.

Importantly, of course, banks hold government securities for

**Table 14–1    Marketable Government Securities Held by Commercial Banks, 1969, 1976, and 1981 (In billions of dollars)**

| Maturing | December 1969 | December 1976 | December 1981 |
|---|---|---|---|
| Within 1 year | 15.1 | 31.2 | 29.5 |
| 1–5 years | 24.7 | 40.0 | 39.0 |
| 5–10 years | 4.4 | 6.3 | 4.5 |
| Over 10 years | 1.0 | 0.8 | 1.6 |
| Total | 45.2 | 78.3 | 74.6 |

SOURCE: Board of Governors of the Federal Reserve System, *Federal Reserve Bulletins*, Feb. 1970, p. A43; Feb. 1977, p. A33; March 1982, p. A33.

liquidity purposes, but in other cases such securities are bought for residual purposes (i.e., new credit-worthy demands are not high enough to absorb all of bank reserves available). Sometimes, as shown in Table 14–1, both of these motives, and that of profitability too, can be seen. Bank liquidity was severely reduced in the credit restraint years of 1973 and 1974. Thus by December 1976, it was necessary for banks to increase substantially their holdings of virtually all maturities of government securities but particularly those maturing in less than one year.

However, as a result of credit restraint in 1973 and 1974, business loan demand fell and the Federal Reserve subsequently increased bank reserves in the following period of credit ease in 1975 and 1976, so that banks had more reserves with which to buy more governments. Seeking higher profits, as well as more liquid assets, they bought ever larger amounts of securities maturing in one to five years. It can be noted in Table 14–1 that this category recorded substantial increases by December 1976 and remained at about this level in December 1981. When profitability in investments is the most important consideration, however, banks are especially likely to add to their holdings of **municipal securities**, rather than government securities.

## MUNICIPAL SECURITIES HELD BY COMMERCIAL BANKS

Because of this great stress on bank profitability, the largest amount of securities held by all commercial banks consists of municipals, or debt obligations of state and local governments, which the 1980s have averaged about half of all investments of banks, as shown in Table 14–2. For large city banks these state and local securities are an even higher proportion of investments. This is because such large city banks are aggressive in their desire to maximize their profits, and state and local government securities yield a larger after-tax return than do federal government securities. (The term *municipal* should be understood as applying to debt obligations of any state or local government authority (e.g., a toll road authority or a school district) and is not limited to a city government. The term *tax-exempt* is a synonym for municipal.

Purchasers of state and local government securities thus buy one principal feature: exemption of the interest income from the income taxation of the federal government and sometimes even exemption from income taxation of the state of issue. Because of this tax-exempt feature, individuals falling within the high-income bracket are important buyers of this particular kind of security. Commercial banks, however, rank second only to individuals as holders of municipals.

**Table 14–2    Investments of All Commercial Banks in the United States, 1949–1981 (In millions of dollars)**

| Date (end of year) | All Investments | U.S. Government Obligations | State and Local Government Obligations | Percentage of State and Local Obligations to All Investments | Other Securities[a] |
|---|---|---|---|---|---|
| 1949 | 75,793 | 65,820 | 6,400 | 8.4 | 3,574 |
| 1959 | 79,438 | 58,937 | 16,958 | 21.2 | 3,127 |
| 1969 | 126,050 | 54,709 | 59,483 | 46.0 | 12,158 |
| 1970 | 147,860 | 61,742 | 69,637 | 47.0 | 16,481 |
| 1971 | 169,634 | 64,930 | 82,420 | 49.0 | 22,284 |
| 1972 | 184,111 | 67,028 | 89,504 | 49.0 | 27,579 |
| 1973 | 188,852 | 58,277 | 95,145 | 50.3 | 35,429 |
| 1974 | 194,949 | 54,453 | 100,032 | 51.3 | 40,098 |
| 1975 | 229,622 | 84,119 | 102,029 | 44.4 | 43,474 |
| 1976 | 235,836 | 91,420 | 102,994 | 43.6 | 41,258 |
| 1977 | 257,353 | 100,213 | 113,834 | 43.5 | 43,209 |
| 1978 | 262,199 | 95,068 | 121,260 | 46.1 | 45,776 |
| 1979 | 285,600 | 93,800 | 143,600[b] | 50.3 | 48,276[b] |
| 1980 | 324,600 | 110,700 | 163,100[b] | 50.3 | 50,776[b] |
| 1981 | 344,500 | 114,400 | 180,900[b] | 52.5 | 52,230[b] |

[a]Includes loans to farmers directly guaranteed by Commodity Credit Corporation (CCC), Export-Import Bank portfolio fund participations, and corporate stock. Most of these, however, are U.S. agency obligations.

[b]Estimated.

SOURCE: Board of Governors of the Federal Reserve System, *Federal Reserve Bulletin*, April 1956, p. 360; April 1961, p. 434; March 1966, p. 372; Feb. 1970, p. A19; May 1973, p. A22; June 1974, p. A18; June 1975, p. A16; June 1976, p. A16; June 1977, p. A16; June 1978, p. A18; Sept. 1980, p. A18; May 1982, p. A15. Percentages were computed.

It is the search for increased profitability rather than a desire to increase liquidity that has led banks to increase their holdings of debt obligations of state and local governments to an amount larger than their holdings of U.S. government securities. But even here, there has been considerable variability in such holdings. This is shown in Figure 14–1. The relative decline in the early 1970s was caused by an upsurge of bank loans to business firms. Subsequently, there was a greater growth in the holdings of U.S. government securities.

*Importance of Municipals to Commercial Banks*    Table 14–2 shows how important municipals are to commercial banks as compared with other securities held in the investment portfolio. This table shows that not only has the absolute amount of municipals held by commercial banks increased greatly in the postwar period but also that the percen-

**Figure 14–1    Commercial Bank Holdings of Municipal Bonds, 1965–1975, Municipal Obligations as a Percent of Total Loans and Securities (all commercial banks)**

SOURCE: Federal Reserve Bank of Philadelphia, *Business Review*, July–Aug. 1976, p. 13.

tage of such municipal securities to total investments rose sharply until a decline in relative importance in 1975 and 1976, although the percentage rose again by the early 1980s.

## The Tax-Exempt Feature

One important factor accounting for this great interest in municipals on the part of banks is the higher rate of income tax that banks have had to pay in the postwar period as compared with the prewar period. Greater investment in municipal securities is one way of reducing this tax liability and securing a higher net return. The average market yield on all general obligations of state and local securities was only 10.43 percent in 1981 as compared with 12.87 percent on long-term federal government securities. Nevertheless, the after-tax yield on these municipal securities was substantially higher than the after-tax yield on government securities, and even higher than the return on loans.

Mutual savings banks and savings and loan associations are exempt from federal income taxation until their capital funds exceed 12 percent of liabilities and so these institutions have shown little interest in tax-exempts. (This special tax treatment for these thrift institutions, incidentally, is a major reason why banks have charged unfair competition as the reason for the rapid growth of these competitors.) Life insurance companies also enjoy relatively low marginal and average tax rates but nevertheless acquire municipals, though they do not play the relatively important role in the investment portfolio of life insurance companies that they do for commercial banks.

## Underwriting of Municipals by Commercial Banks

Another reason why commercial banks seem increasingly attached to municipal securities is that they can underwrite and deal in **general obligation bonds** of states and municipalities. The Banking Act of 1933 denied them the right to underwrite and deal in corporate securities or to operate subsidiaries that engage in this business. State and local government obligations, however, are exempt from this prohibition. The important money market banks, therefore, combine the operation of large investment portfolios of such securities with underwriting and dealing of the broadest sort. The role of underwriter gives such banks the chance of securing new offerings on a most advantageous basis. Furthermore, the dealer role allows such a bank a greater liquidity for its holdings of municipal securities, because they can be sold off, if desired, more quickly and easily by the bank than by holders who must resort to outside dealers.

*More Revenue Bonds Floated*    Regulatory authorities have generally ruled that the more risky **revenue bonds** of state and municipalities, in which a specific tax is pledged behind the bond, could not be underwritten by commercial banks. In recent years the proportions of new revenue bonds as compared with general obligation bonds has nevertheless increased. In Table 14–3, variations in the percentage of revenue bonds in the total obligations of state and local governments in the fifteen years from 1966 to 1980 inclusive can be noted. In this period, the proportion of revenue bonds sold by state and local governments to their total debt flotations rose from more than one third (34.2 percent) in 1966 to more than 70 percent in 1980. This fifteen year period was also one of substantial increase of both general obligation and revenue bonds with total bond flotations, which quadrupled from $11.4 billion in 1966 to $48.4 billion in 1980.

*Decline in Bond Flotations in 1969 and 1979*    In 1969, however, as Table 14–3 shows, both general obligation and revenue bonds of state and local governments declined sharply from the previous year, though the decline was particularly abrupt for revenue bonds. The same was

Table 14–3   **New Issues of State and Local Governments, 1966–1980 (In millions of dollars)**

| Period | Total[a] | General Obligations | Revenue | Percentage Revenue Bonds to Total State and Local Government Obligations[b] | Other Issues[c] |
|--------|---------|---------------------|---------|------------------------------------------------------------------------------|-----------------|
| 1966 | 11,405 | 6,804 | 3,955 | 34.2 | 637 |
| 1967 | 14,766 | 8,985 | 5,013 | 34.0 | 811 |
| 1968 | 16,596 | 9,269 | 6,517 | 39.1 | 810 |
| 1969 | 11,881 | 7,923 | 3,556 | 29.6 | 402 |
| 1970 | 18,164 | 11,850 | 6,082 | 33.1 | 234 |
| 1971 | 24,962 | 15,220 | 8,681 | 34.9 | 1,062 |
| 1972 | 23,652 | 13,265 | 9,332 | 39.5 | 1,018 |
| 1973 | 23,969 | 12,257 | 10,632 | 44.3 | 1,080 |
| 1974 | 24,315 | 13,563 | 10,212 | 41.3 | 540 |
| 1975 | 30,607 | 16,020 | 14,511 | 47.3 | 76 |
| 1976 | 35,313 | 18,040 | 17,140 | 48.5 | 133 |
| 1977 | 46,769 | 18,042 | 28,655 | 61.2 | 72 |
| 1978 | 48,607 | 17,854 | 30,658 | 63.0 | 95 |
| 1979 | 43,490 | 12,109 | 31,256 | 71.8 | 125 |
| 1980 | 48,462 | 14,100 | 34,267 | 70.7 | 95 |

[a]All issues, new and refunding.

[b]Percentages were computed.

[c]Includes bonds sold pursuant to the 1949 Housing Act, which are secured by contract requiring the Housing Assistance Administration to make annual contributions to the local authority, and also includes loans made directly by the U.S. government to a state or subdivision.

SOURCE: Board of Governors of the Federal Reserve System, *Federal Reserve Bulletins*, Feb. 1970, p. A45; June 1973, p. A45; Feb. 1977, p. A36; June 1978, p. A36; April 1981, p. A34.

true in 1979, although revenue bonds did not decline as much as they had a decade earlier. Not only are revenue bonds somewhat more risky than general obligations bonds but they are often subject to legal interest rate limitations imposed by states and municipalities. In a period of severe credit restraint, such as 1969, the going market yields often exceed these legal limitations and prevent the sale of new municipal bonds. Nevertheless, the dollar amount of revenue and general obligation bonds floated in 1969 was more than the amount sold in 1963 and 1964, whereas revenue bonds sold in 1969 were equal to the amount floated in 1964.

In 1972, a smaller decline in state and local government bond flotations occurred than had taken place in 1969. Furthermore, contrary to the experience of three years earlier, there was a moderate rise in revenue bonds, with all the decline in such flotations taking place in the general obligation issues. Unlike 1969, the year 1972 saw the greatest increase in the money supply (9 percent) permitted by the monetary authorities of any year since World War II. This made it much easier to sell revenue bonds than in the credit restraint year of 1969. The large increase in new issues of state and local governments in 1975 (over $6 billion) was largely induced by credit ease during the recession of 1973–1975.

In 1973–1974, even greater credit restraint was applied than in 1969 and, perhaps oddly enough, there were no declines in total flotations of state and government securities. However, during the ensuing recession, which hit bottom in 1975, the swing to credit ease by the Federal Reserve led to lower interest rates in financial markets and an outpouring of new security issues by state and local governments. (Some of these new issues had been postponed during the prior period of credit restraint.)

Thereafter in the 1970s, there was an increase in the flood of new municipals coming to market each year, except for a decline in 1979, as a result of some increased credit restraint that year. Perhaps the most notable point, therefore, evident from the data in Table 14–3 is the tremendous growth over time of new municipal flotations, which reflects in part the strong interest of commercial banks in buying such new municipal bond issues.

***Gaining Municipal Deposits***    Even smaller banks have a special interest in state and local government securities because they can originate and deal in them. Local pride often means that local banks can be counted upon to put in a bid for new issues of municipal securities originating in their own area. Furthermore, a desire to secure and maintain deposits of these local governmental units also provides an incentive for a hometown bank to purchase local tax-exempts.

It might almost be said that a kind of customer relationship often tends to develop between such a bank and the local government, instead of the impersonal relationship that we often tend to think of in connection with the capital markets. Of course, this kind of a personal relationship has its disadvantages for the bank as well as its advantages. It usually is quite difficult for a bank to dispose of local or state government securities once they have been acquired. Outsiders might conclude that there were hidden difficulties confronting these governmental units that induced the local bank to dislodge its holdings. Hence most bankers treat their holdings of state and local government securities as having no greater liquidity than that possessed by local loans.

***Quality of Municipals Varies***    Information on the quality of municipals held by banks is quite scant. In some cases small municipal issues are not even rated by the rating services, although an expert in this field is likely to be able to make a close judgment on what the approximate rating would be. Supervisory authorities, however, seem to be unrelenting in urging high standards on banks for their municipal bond portfolio. The Federal Deposit Insurance Corporation has been particularly interested in keeping insured banks aware of the necessity of great care in acquiring this type of security. One way, of course, that commercial banks try to protect themselves is by restricting their major buying interest to the shorter maturities of the new offerings. Because municipal securities, unlike some other debt obligations, are ordinarily offered in serial form (i.e., offered in a series of maturities in the same offering), it is possible for banks to buy new debt of a particular governmental unit only in the shorter-maturity area.

*Countercyclical Bank Demand for Municipals*   The demand of commercial banks for municipals is nevertheless normally quite countercyclical. The purchases of commercial banks tend to be concentrated heavily during those periods when banks have large amounts of reserves available for investment. These periods are usually during economic recession, when the demand for bank credit is falling and the Federal Reserve is giving the banks more reserves. In the opposite situation, in periods of business upswing, reserves tend to be in shorter supply because of the restraint usually imposed by Federal Reserve policy. Such credit restraint and an increase in business loan demand mean that banks are sometimes loaned up in periods of business upswing. Under these conditions, bank purchases of municipals tend to be cut back sharply. Banks are sufficiently important buyers of municipals that state and local governments therefore often find themselves forced to postpone contemplated flotations during the advanced period of the business upswing.

The postponed municipal securities, however, are usually then floated during the following economic recession, when bank demand is strong. The strength of bank demand for municipals in recession periods is because factors opposite to those operating in the upswing now appear. Federal Reserve policy usually switches from credit restraint to **credit ease**, and bank reserves are supplied with more liberality. Furthermore, business loan demand usually declines sharply in a recession. For these recession periods, municipal securities are much more attractive investments to commercial banks.

Table 14–4, which shows twenty-three years from the mid-1950s to the 1970s, indicates this countercyclical behavior of commercial banks in acquiring municipal securities. In the credit restraint periods of 1955–1956 and 1959–1960, well under ten percent of the municipal securities floated were acquired by commercial banks. (The small percentage

**Table 14–4  Net Acquisition of Municipal Bonds by Commercial Banks, 1956–1978 (In millions of dollars)**

| Period | Net Bank Acquisition | Total Municipal Bonds Floated | Percentage of Commercial Bank Acquisitions to Total Flotations[a] |
|--------|---------------------|-------------------------------|-------------------------------------------------------------------|
| 1956 | 203 | 5,446 | 3.7 |
| 1957 | 1,014 | 6,926 | 14.4 |
| 1958 | 2,590 | 7,526 | 34.6 |
| 1959 | 480 | 7,697 | 6.2 |
| 1960 | 585 | 7,292 | 8.0 |
| 1961 | 2,775 | 8,566 | 32.5 |
| 1962 | 4,410 | 8,845 | 50.0 |
| 1963 | 5,031 | 10,538 | 47.6 |
| 1964 | 3,747 | 10,847 | 34.2 |
| 1965 | 5,122 | 11,329 | 45.1 |
| 1966 | 2,348 | 11,405 | 20.1 |
| 1967 | 9,003 | 14,766 | 61.2 |
| 1968 | 8,564 | 16,596 | 51.8 |
| 1969 | 613 | 11,881 | 5.1 |
| 1970 | 10,454 | 18,164 | 57.5 |
| 1971 | 12,783 | 24,962 | 51.2 |
| 1972 | 7,084 | 23,652 | 29.9 |
| 1973 | 5,641 | 23,969 | 23.4 |
| 1974 | 5,252 | 24,315 | 21.4 |
| 1975 | 5,023 | 30,607 | 16.4 |
| 1976 | 965 | 35,313 | 2.7 |
| 1977 | 10,840 | 46,769 | 23.1 |
| 1978[b] | 9,901 | 48,607 | 20.0 |

[a]Percentages are computed.

[b]Data not available for following years separating bank acquisition of municipals from "other securities."

SOURCE: Board of Governors, *Federal Reserve Bulletins*, Feb. 1962, p. 333; March 1962, p. 318; April 1964, p. 468; April, 1965, p. 580; March 1967, p. 412; April 1968, p. A22; Oct. 1969, p. A45; Feb. 1970, p. A24; Dec. 1972, p. A24; June 1973, p. A22; July 1974, p. A18; July 1975, p. A16; July 1976, p. A16 and p. A37; June 1977, p. A16; Aug. 1978, p. A16; Nov. 1978, p. A16; Sept. 1980, p. A18.

of municipals bought by banks in 1976 is difficult to explain because it was not a credit restraint year, although it was one of increased business loan demand.) On the other hand, in the credit ease years of 1954 and 1958, which were years of economic recession, the banks bought 26 percent and 34.6 percent, respectively, of the new borrowings of state and local governments. Likewise, in the recession years of 1974 and 1975, the banks bought 21.4 percent and 16.4 percent of municipals sold.

*Importance of Bank Participation in the Municipal Bond Market*    After 1960, banks became extremely important in the municipal bond market. In no year in the decade of the 1960s other than 1969 did they buy less than 20 percent of the new bond offerings, and in a number of years they bought around half or more of the new municipals sold. In the 1970s, there were three years in which banks bought less than 20 percent of municipals sold, though in every year except 1976 they were an important part of this market. Nevertheless, the eagerness of the banks to buy municipal securities is still usually influenced considerably by the prevailing monetary-credit policy of the Federal Reserve.

*Credit Restraint Reduces Bank Purchases of Municipals*    In the credit restraint year of 1966, as can be noted in Table 14–4, bank participation in the municipal bond market fell sharply from 45.1 percent in the previous year to a low figure of 20.1 percent. When the Federal Reserve somewhat eased its monetary policy the next year because of a slowdown in the rate of economic growth, the percentage of commercial bank purchases of municipals rose sharply to 61.2 percent of total municipal bond flotations in 1967. In 1968, however, even when the Federal Reserve was adding somewhat less total bank reserves than in 1967, the banks still purchased more than half the state and local obligations floated that year.

In 1969, a period of severe credit restraint similar to 1966, net acquisition by banks of new municipal bond flotations fell sharply to .05 percent from the 51.8 percent of 1968. In the next two years, however, commercial banks came back into the municipal bond market and purchased in each year one half or more of all new municipal bonds floated. From 1972 to 1975, banks bought $5 billion or more municipals each year, though the percentage bought of total flotations fell somewhat.

## Quasi-Governmental Securities

In only three years, from the end of 1969 until 1972, commercial banks more than doubled their holdings of "other securities," which are primarily notes and bonds of government agencies and government-sponsored credit agencies (i.e., quasi-governments). At the end of 1969 such bank holdings of "other securities" totaled only $12.1 billion, whereas by the end of 1972 this category of bank-held securities reached a total of $27.6 billion. Furthermore, the percentage of such "other securities" rose from only 9 percent of total securities held by all banks to more than 16 percent in the same period. This category of bank investments includes such miscellaneous items as loans to farmers directly guaranteed by the CCC, Export-Import Bank portfolio fund participations, and corporate stock. But for the most part this category of investments consists of bonds and debentures issued by various instrumentalities of the federal government or government-sponsored credit agencies. At the end of September 1978, securities issued by U.S. government agencies and held by commercial banks totaled over $40 billion, and securities issued by government-sponsored agencies and held by commercial banks totaled an additional $5.7 billion. It is evident that banks have continued to add to their holdings of such securities.

## Federal Home Loan Banks

Another government-sponsored credit agency that taps the money and capital markets for funds from time to time is the Federal Home Loan Bank System, established in 1932 to help the sagging home-building industry; it became privately owned, though still government-sponsored, after World War II. It is composed of twelve Home Loan Banks, which have about 4,600 savings and loan associations as members that can secure credit from the parent banks.

It is thus organized similarly to the Federal Reserve System, which has commercial bank members who can borrow from their regional banks. Unlike the Federal Reserve System, however, the Federal Home Loan Bank System issues notes and bonds in the financial markets, which may be purchased by commercial banks for their investment portfolio. To attract buying interest, the Federal Home Loan Bank Board (FHLB) offerings of notes or bonds are at a higher yield than comparable Treasury issues because they are not fully guaranteed by the Treasury. At the end of 1981, it had sold debt securities totaling some $58 billion, which was up sharply from only $16.8 billion debt outstanding at the end of 1976.

## Fannie Mae Debentures and Ginnie Mae Obligations

Another former government agency that issues substantial amounts of **debentures** from time to time, which can be purchased by commercial banks, is the Federal National Mortgage Association (Fannie Mae). Fannie Mae sells notes with maturities up to three years. It became a private association in September 1968. New financial arrangements involved the establishment of a $150 million line of credit with 124 commercial banks. Hence credit extended to Fannie Mae, which formerly was classified under "other securities," now moved to the loan portfolio, although Fannie Mae debentures continued to be classified under other securities. Fannie Mae had some $58.7 billion of debt outstanding at the end of 1981, as compared with only $30.5 billion outstanding at the end of 1976.

In September 1968, the Government National Mortgage Association (GNMA, or Ginnie Mae) was created. Under the mortgage-backed security program, GNMA guarantees the timely payment of principal and interest on both pass-through and bond-type securities, which are backed by a pool of mortgages. These quasi-government securities have been purchased in substantial amounts by commercial banks and other institutional investors.

### Other Government-Sponsored Credit Agencies

Other government-sponsored credit agencies include the Federal Intermediate Credit Banks (twelve in number) and the Banks for Cooperatives (also twelve in number). Each of these federal credit systems issues debentures. The Federal Intermediate Credit Banks usually issue nine-month debentures, whereas the Banks for Cooperatives usually issue six-month debentures. Both types of debentures are eligible for commercial bank purchase.

### Department of Housing and Urban Development (HUD)

The Department of Housing and Urban Development (HUD) also issues securities that, unlike securities issued by other federal instrumentalities, are originally obligations of local governmental authorities but are directly guaranteed by the credit of the federal government. Prior to 1965 such housing offerings were handled by the Public Housing Administration (PHA). Such obligations take the form either of short-term notes with original maturities of one year or less, or of longer-term bonds with maturities running as high as forty years. These HUD obligations are essentially the debt of various local public housing authorities created by statutes in the various states. Nevertheless, HUD, under a contractual financial arrangement, agrees to provide sufficient money for the local authorities to pay interest and principal when due, if this proves to be necessary.

The Department of Housing and Urban Development, in turn, can secure funds if needed from the Treasury. These HUD obligations could also be mentioned under municipal securities, because interest income from them is exempt from federal income tax. These securities, like those of other federal instrumentalities, are approved for bank investment. The comptroller of the currency has ruled that national banks may invest in such obligations of federal instrumentalities and government-sponsored credit agencies without regard to statutory limitations applicable to investment securities.

Changing bank preferences for different types of securities (e.g., governments, municipals, or quasi-governments) depends in part on changes both in the level and structure of interest rates. What happens to the level of interest rates in the various financial markets is influenced importantly by Federal Reserve Policy. Central banking, the Federal Reserve System in the United States, is the subject of Part 5, which follows.

# Questions for Discussion

1. List and discuss the major objectives of portfolio management. Can you think of any portfolio objectives in addition to those listed in this chapter? In what respects may these objectives conflict with one another? How can the bank officer in charge of the investment portfolio resolve these seeming conflicts? In what respect are funds employed in an investment portfolio used in a residual way?
2. What types of securities would a bank be particularly interested in acquiring for a bank portfolio if it placed major emphasis on liquidity considerations? What type of securities would the bank be interested in if it placed major emphasis on income?
3. List the major categories of U.S. government securities. How important is each in bank portfolios? Why have both Treasury bills and Treasury notes increased so much in their dollar amount outstanding in the 1970s and the 1980s?
4. What changes in the postwar period have occurred in bank holdings of different maturities of government securities? Why? What is the purpose of holding Treasury bills for a commercial bank? How does the bank's holdings of government securities relate to its concern for bank liquidity?
5. Discuss the growth of holdings of state and local obligations by commercial banks in recent years. Why are banks so interested in acquiring such securities? Why do banks acquire more of such securities in some years than in others?
6. What has happened to the relative participation of banks in this bond market as a result of the growth of revenue bond flotations by states and municipalities? What may happen to the municipal bond market, in your judgment, in the early 1980s?
7. Discuss the growth in the issuance of quasi-government securities and the reason for commercial bank interest in such securities.

# Selected Bibliography for Further Reading

BANKS, LOIS, "The Market for Agency Securities," *Quarterly Review*, Federal Reserve Bank of New York, Spring 1978, Vol. 3, No. 1, pp 7–19.
COMPTROLLER OF THE CURRENCY, *Annual Reports*, Washington, D.C.

EINSTEIN, MAJOR B., *Investing for Banks* (St. Louis, Mo.: First National Bank in St. Louis, 1959).

JOHNSON, RODNEY, "A Fresh Look at the Municipal Bond Market," *Business Review*, Federal Reserve Bank of Philadelphia, July–August 1976, pp. 11–12.

KASRIEL, PAUL L., "The Federal Debt and Commercial Banks," *Business Conditions*, Federal Reserve Bank of Chicago, Oct. 1975, pp. 3–9.

LYON, ROGER A., *Commercial Bank Investment Portfolio Management* (Rutgers, N.J.: Rutgers University Press, 1961).

ROBINSON, ROLAND I., *The Management of Bank Funds*, 2d ed. (New York: McGraw-Hill, 1962).

——, *Postwar Market for State and Local Government Securities*, National Bureau of Economic Research (Princeton, N.J.: Princeton University Press, 1960).

ROLEY, V. V., "Role of Commercial Banks' Portfolio Policy in the Determination of Treasury Bill Yields," *Journal of Money, Credit and Banking* 12: Special Issue 367–369 (May 1980).

——, "The Role of Commercial Banks' Portfolio Behavior in the Determination of Treasury Security Yields," *Journal of Money, Credit and Banking*, Vol. xii, No. 2: 353–369 (May 1980).

UNITED STATES SAVINGS AND LOAN LEAGUE, *Savings and Loan Fact Book* (Chicago: Annual).

WATSON, RONALD D., "Bank Bond Management: The Maturity Dilemma," *Business Review*, Federal Reserve Bank of Philadelphia, March 1972, pp. 23–29.

# PART 5

# CENTRAL BANKING

The trade of Scotland has more than quadrupled since the first erection of the two public banks at Edinburgh, of which the one, called The Bank of Scotland, was established by act of parliament in 1695; the other, called The Royal Bank, by royal charter in 1727.

THE WEALTH OF NATIONS

# 15
## CHAPTER

# Structure and Functions of the Federal Reserve System

When the Federal Reserve Act was passed in December 1913, and the twelve Federal Reserve Banks opened their doors in November 1914, the most important part of the money supply was *not*, as it is in the 1980s, demand deposits of commercial banks and other transactions accounts of commercial banks and other financial intermediaries. The United States had been on the *de facto* gold standard for much of the nineteenth century (from 1834 to 1861 and from 1879 to 1900) and on the full *de jure* (legal) gold standard from 1900 on (until 1933). Gold coins and gold certificates were important parts of the money supply.

So, too, were the national bank notes issued by the national banks after 1863. This money supply, however, including the national bank notes, was often seen to be inelastic, or unresponsive to the needs of trade and commerce. Hence one of the first major responsibilities of the new Federal Reserve System, as indicated in the preface to the act, was to provide for an elastic money supply. This was to be accomplished primarily though the discount window of each Federal Reserve Bank and its branches. In this manner, the new central bank would be a **"lender of last resort"** and the ultimate provider of liquidity for the entire financial system.

This liquidity function of the new central bank, and the injunction on it to provide for a flexible money supply, was also joined with regulatory and service functions assigned to the new system. The three major functions of all central banks, including the Federal Reserve System, are (1) to be a bankers' bank (i.e., holding reserves and regulating various activities of its member banks, as well as being a lender of last resort to them); (2) to be a bank to the national government, acting as a fiscal agent to the government in the sale and redemption of government securities, holding government deposits, and even advising the government when asked and assisting in representing the government in foreign monetary conferences; (3) to control bank reserves and the money supply and to influence the level of interest rates.

## THE EARLY FEDERAL RESERVE SYSTEM

The original Federal Reserve Act expressed the intentions of establishing this new system of Reserve Banks in order to furnish a more elastic currency, provide for a means to rediscount eligible commercial paper, and provide a more effective supervision of banking in the United States. The first members of the Federal Reserve System were to comprise all national banks and certain eligible state banks. All member banks in the original act were supposed to subscribe to the capital stock of the Federal Reserve Bank in their district a sum equal to 6 percent of the paid-up capital and surplus of the member bank. So far, however, member banks have been required to pay only half of their prescribed capital subscription. On this Federal Reserve stock the member banks receive a 6 percent dividend each year.

## STRUCTURE OF THE FEDERAL RESERVE SYSTEM

Because Congress, rather than the executive branch, has the constitutional responsibility to regulate the money supply, the new Federal Reserve System was required to report annually to Congress. The Federal Reserve, in effect, was to be the agent of Congress. As such, it would have a good deal of "independence" from the executive branch, even though originally the comptroller of the currency and the secretary of the Treasury were members of the Federal Reserve Board.

The 1935 amendments to the Federal Reserve Act, however, removed these two persons from the Federal Reserve Board. The remaining seven members of the Board of Governors were still to be appointed by the president of the United States, including the chairman, with the advice and consent of the Senate. However, for the term of their office (fourteen years for each governor and four years for the chairman), the president could not remove them. Figure 15–1 provides an overview of the structure of the Federal Reserve System.

***Number of Federal Reserve Banks***     The original Federal Reserve Act provided that no fewer than eight nor more than twelve cities should be known as Federal Reserve cities located in the same number of Federal Reserve districts. These districts did not have to be coterminous with any

**Figure 15–1     The Federal Reserve System**

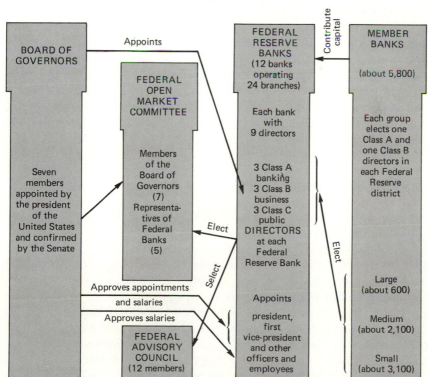

SOURCE: Adapted from Board of Governors of the Federal Reserve System, *The Federal Reserve System Purposes and Functions* (Washington, D.C., 1974), p. 18.

state or states. As it turned out, twelve Federal Reserve Banks were established in twelve districts. The cities of Boston, New York City, Philadelphia, Richmond, Atlanta, Cleveland, Chicago, St. Louis, Dallas, Minneapolis, Kansas City, and San Francisco were each given a Federal Reserve Bank. Twenty-five other large cities have had Federal Reserve branches established in them. Boston and Philadelphia do not have any branches and New York, Chicago, and Minneapolis have only one each. Atlanta has the largest number, five, whereas San Francisco is second with four branches.

*Directors of Federal Reserve Banks*    The **Board of Directors** for each **Federal Reserve Bank** is divided into three equal groups of A, B, and C directors. The A and B directors are elected by the member banks in the district. The A directors are commercial bankers representing, respectively, the large, medium-sized, and small member banks of the district. The B directors are actively engaged in commerce, agriculture, or some other industrial pursuit; they may not be bankers. The Class C directors are chosen by the Board of Governors of the Federal Reserve System to represent the public. One of the C directors is designated by the board to serve as chairman of the Board of Directors and act as Federal Reserve agent. Although the Board of Directors of each Reserve Bank appoints the officers of each bank, the choice of president and first vice-president of each bank must be approved for their five-year terms by the Board of Governors in Washington. The Board of Directors of each Reserve Bank also selects a representative of the district, usually a commercial banker, to serve on the Federal Advisory Council, which confers at least four times a year with the Board of Governors.

## Board of Governors of the Federal Reserve System

The Board of Governors of the Federal Reserve System, as already noted, is composed of seven members appointed by the president of the United States, with the advice and consent of the Senate. The term of office for board members is fourteen years and no member of the board can be reappointed after having served a full fourteen-year term, although a member may serve part of an unexpired term and then be appointed to a full term. Until February 1, 1936, the secretary of the Treasury and the comptroller of the currency served as ex officio members of the board, but with the passage of the 1935 amendments to the Federal Reserve Act they were dropped from the board.

The chairman and vice-chairman are each named by the president to serve in their offices for four years. The Board of Governors receives income sufficient to pay its expenses by semiannual assessments on the Federal Reserve Banks. The board makes an annual report of its operations to Congress. After the system pays its expenses out of its gross earnings, the remaining amount of net earnings is paid to the Treasury. The Federal Reserve paid $14 billion of such earnings to the Treasury in 1981. Gross earnings in 1981 totaled $15.5 billion, a 21 percent increase from a year earlier.

## The Federal Open Market Committee

The Federal Open Market Committee (FOMC) was not made a formal part of the structure of the Federal Reserve System until the amendments of 1933 and 1935. In the spring of 1922, the Reserve Banks established a Committee of Governors of four banks (later increased to five) to coordinate individual bank purchases and sales of government securities. A year later, the Board of Governors took charge of this new weapon of open market operations by establishing the committee as one to be appointed by the board and to be under its general supervision. Thus the committee normally met in Washington and submitted its findings to the board for approval or disapproval. It was not until 1935, however, that the members of the Board of Governors were considered members of this committee.

   With the statutory establishment of the Federal Open Market Committee in 1935, the twelve members of the FOMC consisted of the seven members of the Board of Governors, along with five representatives of the Federal Reserve Banks who were to be either presidents or first vice-presidents of the Federal Reserve Banks. The New York City Bank was to be permanently represented, whereas the other Reserve Banks were combined in such a way that representatives of the various banks would be rotated in a fixed cycle. The presidents of the Chicago and Cleveland banks alternate every other year. The nine remaining Reserve Banks are combined into three groups, each of which is on a three-year cycle of rotating membership, so that each Reserve Bank president serves at least one year out of three on the FOMC.

   The Federal Reserve Act provides that the FOMC shall meet at least four times a year. After the abolition of the Executive Committee of the FOMC in June 1955, the full Open Market Committee met regularly about every month through 1980. Beginning in 1981, however, the FOMC started meeting about twice each quarter. These meetings, usually lasting all day Tuesday, are attended in Washington by every president or first vice-president of a Reserve Bank, plus additional staff economists invited to the meetings. Although the *de jure* membership of the FOMC is only twelve, the *de facto* membership is nineteen (i.e., the seven members of the Board of Governors plus the twelve Reserve Bank presidents).

## Members of the Federal Reserve System

Originally all national banks, as already noted, were required to become **members of the Federal Reserve System,** whereas state banks were permitted to join if they met the rigid standards of the Federal Reserve. Most state banks never wanted to join, however, because legal reserve ratio requirements of the various states were invariably lower than those of the Federal Reserve. Lower reserve ratios meant the possibility of greater bank profits.

By the end of 1979, fewer than 4,500 national banks and fewer than 1,000 state banks were still members of the Federal Reserve System. A number of state banks had left the system in the 1970s to enjoy lower state reserve requirements. This attrition of membership led to a decline in the proportion of all bank deposits accounted for by member banks, from 80 percent in 1970 to 70 percent at the beginning of 1980.

In its *Annual Report 1979*, published in 1980, the board recommended applying reserve requirements to *all* depository institutions. "To enable the Federal Reserve to maintain disciplined control of the money supply and to meet its other responsibilities for protecting the safety and soundness of the banking system, the Board recommends legislation that would apply reserve requirements to all depository institutions on a universal and mandatory basis."[1] The Federal Reserve Board had made this request almost annually to Congress since 1964. A proposed Financial Institution Act granting this request was first considered by Congress in 1973.

Finally, in 1980 Congress enacted The Depository Institutions Deregulation and Monetary Control Act of 1980, signed into law by President Carter on March 31, 1980. This law imposed universal reserve requirements on all depository institutions. At the same time, such depository institutions would have access to a number of services provided by the Federal Reserve Banks (at a price), as well as being able to borrow, if necessary, at one of the discount windows maintained at each Federal Reserve Bank and branch.

## Governance of the Federal Reserve System

General supervision over the entire Federal Reserve System has always been exercised by the Federal Reserve Board. The operations at each Federal Reserve Bank, with their branches, if any, are under the supervision of a president, first vice-president, and other officers and employees. These operating officers are overseen by nine directors of each

[1]Board of Governors of the Federal Reserve System, *Annual Report 1979*, Washington, D.C., 1980, p. 254.

Federal Reserve Bank. As shown earlier in Figure 15–1, the three Class A banking directors and the three Class B business directors are elected by the member banks in each Federal Reserve District. The three Class C directors, who must be nonbankers like the Class B directors, are selected to represent the public by the Board of Governors in Washington.

Regulatory responsibilities (e.g., bank examination and approval or disapproval of proposed bank mergers) are assigned by statutory law and regulations issued by the Federal Reserve Board in part to the board and in part to the various Federal Reserve Banks. Bank examinations, for example, are conducted by the various Federal Reserve Banks. The same Federal Reserve Banks and their branches make discounts and advances (through the discount window) to member banks and other depository institutions. The interest rate on these loans (the **discount rate**) is recommended by the Board of Directors of each Federal Reserve Bank.

The Board of Governors in Washington, however, has the power to review and determine these discount rates. The Board of Governors also has the power under the 1935 amendments and the 1980 Monetary Control Act to establish within guidelines set by Congress the reserve ratio requirements applicable to various sizes of depository institutions. The Board of Governors has been given a number of other powers by statute over bank mergers, bank holding companies, and the like.

The most important power of the Federal Reserve System, however, has always been determining monetary policy. And that power for the most part is employed by the FOMC in establishing policy for open market operations. The FOMC, as already noted, includes both the Board of Governors and representatives of the twelve Federal Reserve Banks.

## FUNCTIONS OF THE FEDERAL RESERVE SYSTEM

### Federal Reserve Control of Monetary and Credit Policy Tools

A schematic presentation of the control of monetary and credit policy tools is shown in Figure 15–2. The tools, the way in which they are used, and the objectives toward which they are applied have all changed in the nearly seventy years since the Federal Reserve was established. The three present major tools of quantitative monetary and credit policy are (1) changes in reserve requirements of depository institutions, (2) changes in the discount rate, and (3) open market operations. Changes in margin requirements, shown by the Figure 15–2, are also tools of Federal Reserve policies, as are other qualitative controls such as Regulation Q. (We have already pointed out that as a result of the Monetary Control Act of 1980, Regulation Q, determining maximum rates on time deposits, will be phased out by 1986.) Another Federal Reserve weapon is moral suasion, which involves suggestions to financial institutions relating to their extension of credit, such as slowing down added bank loans to businesses during a period of inflationary pressures.

As an "independent" agency reporting to Congress, the Federal Reserve has always had a good deal of latitude in employing its particular instruments of monetary and credit control. Some critics of the Federal Reserve have felt that it had too much latitude, especially in controlling the rate of growth in the money supply. The fact is that the Federal Reserve does have considerable discretion in employing the powers granted it by Congress, even though it is required to follow congressional intent.

## Determining Reserve Requirements

Some of the historical development of requiring cash reserves for banks has already been discussed, so that will not be repeated here. Suffice it to recall that the original purpose of having reserve requirements was to ensure the safety of banks, the redeemability of bank notes, and the availability of bank deposits on demand. This purpose was replaced by the needs of controlling the money supply after the Federal Reserve System was established in 1913, and the FDIC was established twenty years later in 1933.

Once the Federal Reserve System was in place, there was a "lender of last resort" that was supposed to ensure liquidity for the entire financial system, even though this function did not seem to work well in the early days of the Great Depression of the 1930s. The support role of the Federal Reserve was buttressed, however, in 1933 by the establishment of the FDIC, which guaranteed repayment up to a limit to depositors in all member banks of the Federal Reserve System and other insured state banks. Even if a bank went into bankruptcy, insured depositors would still receive their deposits. The amount insured originally was $2,500 but was raised progressively to its current $100,000. The new insurance for bank deposits reduced the likelihood of "bank runs," which had caused even some sound banks to close their doors in 1932 and early 1933.

In 1935, the Federal Reserve System was greatly strengthened by amendments to the Federal Reserve Act. As already noted, the secretary of the Treasury and the comptroller of the currency were removed from

**Figure 15–2     The Federal Reserve System—Relation to Instruments of Credit Policy**

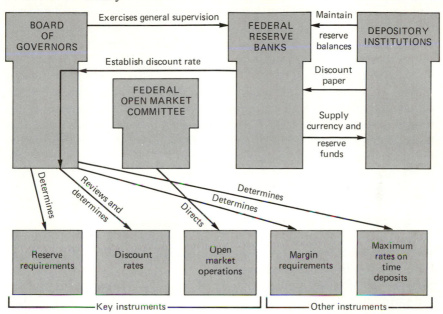

SOURCE: Adapted from Board of Governors of the Federal Reserve System, *The Federal Reserve System Purposes and Functions* (Washington, D.C., 1974), p. 50.

the Federal Reserve Board. The FOMC, which had been operating on an informal basis for ten years, was now made a statutory part of the structure of the Federal Reserve System. **Margin requirements,** first imposed in 1934, on stock market credit were instituted and given to the Federal Reserve Board to determine. Interest on bank demand deposits was forbidden and the Federal Reserve Board was given the power to set a ceiling on interest rates payable on time and savings deposits. This was the origin of Regulation Q of the Federal Reserve Board.

## *Federal Reserve Discretion in Varying Legal Reserve Ratios*

The Federal Reserve Board was also given the power to vary the legal reserve ratio of the three categories of member banks—central reserve city, reserve city banks, and country banks. The first were downtown banks in New York City and Chicago. The second category were member banks in other designated large cities, and the third category was all other member banks.

The range of reserve ratios to be applied to demand deposits was 13 to 26 percent for central reserve city banks, 10 to 20 percent for reserve city banks, and 7 to 14 percent for country banks. Time and savings deposits had a range of 3 to 6 percent. This range of reserve requirements gave substantial discretionary power to the Federal Reserve Board in its power to determine the money supply.

Changes in reserve ratio requirements also, incidentally, had an impact on member bank profits (i.e., a lowering of required reserve ratios tended to increase bank profits while an increase in such ratios tended to reduce bank profits). Perhaps partly because of this impact on bank profits and the official doctrine of the Federal Reserve that changing such reserve ratio requirements was a "blunt and cumbersome instrument," changes in legal reserve ratios were not made often but did occur occasionally.

In some periods of credit restraint (i.e., slower growth of the money supply and higher interest rates), legal reserve ratios were increased somewhat, and in some periods of credit ease they were reduced somewhat. In general, in the period after World War II such legal reserve ratios tended to be reduced over time. This instrument of Federal Reserve policy often seemed to be more of a secular (long-run) instrument for promoting long-run growth in the money supply, rather than a countercyclical (short-run) instrument for changing the rate of growth in the money supply.

Changes in the law and regulations of the Federal Reserve Board changed the rules of the game from time to time. In 1959, as already noted, the Federal Reserve Act was amended to permit member banks to include vault cash as well as deposits in Federal Reserve Banks in their legal reserves available to satisfy the legal reserve ratios imposed on their demand deposit base. The category of central reserve city banks was also combined with that of reserve city banks. In 1968, lagged reserve accounting was introduced by regulation of the Federal Reserve Board. In 1972, the board established a new system of progressive reserve ratios for all member banks, which significantly modified the earlier system, which was largely based on the location of member banks in particular cities.

## Universal Reserve Requirements on All Depository Institutions in 1980

The present system of legal reserve ratios was established by the Monetary Control Act of 1980, compared by some commentators in importance to the original Federal Reserve Act and by others to the significant 1935 amendments to the Federal Reserve Act. However it is described, this is a very significant act for the entire financial system. After 1980, universal reserve requirements were imposed on *all* depository institutions. The long-time recommendations of the board to Congress were finally accepted. Furthermore, the board continued to have considerable flexibility in applying reserve ratio requirements to depository institutions.

Congress still set minimum reserve ratio requirements, but once again it gave a range of discretion to the Federal Reserve Board in applying reserve requirements. A reserve of 3 percent was to be maintained by all depository institutions with transactions accounts (those on which a check could be written) of $25 million or less. For transactions accounts in excess of $25 million, the reserve ratio range was 8 to 14 percent, with an initial ratio of 12 percent. In addition, each depository institution was required to maintain reserves against nonpersonal time deposits in an amount ranging from zero to 9 percent, with an initial ratio of 3 percent. **Depository institutions** were defined, for the purpose of the act, to include commercial banks, mutual savings banks, savings banks, savings and loan associations, and credit unions if federally insured or eligible for federal insurance. Although reserve requirements must be uniformly applied to all transactions accounts at all depository institutions, the Federal Reserve Board was permitted to vary reserve ratios applicable to nonpersonal time deposits depending on the maturity of such deposits.

Beginning December 31, 1981, the board was required each year to index the $25 million breakpoint on transactions accounts of individual depository institutions. It was to issue a regulation that would increase or decrease the $25 milion figure by 80 percent of the increase or decrease in total transactions accounts of all depository institutions between June 30 of that year and June 30 of the preceding year. This legal requirement seemed likely to reduce the average reserve ratio requirement for depository institutions over time by increasing the amount of transactions accounts to which the 3 percent legal reserve requirement applied.

In general, after all the provisions of the 1980 law became applicable, the average reserve ratio requirement for member banks would be reduced, whereas that for nonmember depository institutions would be increased from the prior lower state requirements. As we have already noted, a change in legal reserve ratio requirements has an impact on the profitability of the financial instituton. To minimize any adverse impact on earnings, there was to be an eight-year phase-in of the new reserve requirements. After this transitional period, member bank required reserves (based on existing deposit levels) would decline from about $32 billion to about $14 billion. This would, of course, minimize the profitability motive for banks to give up membership in the Federal

Reserve. Furthermore, competition between the various financial institutions for deposits and earning assets would be on much more even terms than before, because they would have similar reserve requirements.

### Contemporaneous Reserve Requirements Proposed in 1982

Another important possible change in reserve requirements, after the 1980 act, was the proposed return to contemporaneous reserve requirements (CRR) in 1982. In 1968, the Federal Reserve Board had instituted lagged reserve accounting (LRA) in which required reserves for this week (Thursday-Wednesday) for each member bank was based on the average daily deposit level of two weeks earlier. Critics of this regulation had argued that the Federal Reserve had partly lost control over the money supply, because it was forced to "accommodate" the banks' needs for reserves this week either through open-market operations or at the discount window. With CRR, they argued, the Fed would have much tighter control over the money supply in any given week or other reserve period.

When the Federal Reserve Board proposed in 1982 to return to contemporaneous reserve requirements, it proposed that reserve requirements would then be maintained over a two-week period, which would still end on Wednesday, as had been true for the reserve week. Furthermore, CRR would apply only to reserve requirements on transactions accounts for medium-sized and large depository institutions, or those with total deposits of $15 million or more. The 1982 proposal takes effect on February 2, 1984. Although interest rates were expected to be somewhat more volatile, it was expected that swings in the money supply would be moderated.

For those institutions affected by contemporaneous reserve requirements, required reserves would be computed on the basis of average deposit levels over a two-week period ending on Monday. There would then be a two-day interval to compute the required reserves needed in the two-week period ending on Wednesday. Vault cash would still be counted as a reserve and continue to be lagged. It would be equal to vault cash holdings during a computation period ending seventeen days before the beginning of the maintenance period.

No change would be made in the prior limit of plus or minus 2 percent of daily average required reserves that would apply to carryover of reserve surpluses or deficiencies into the next reserve week. Lengthening the reserve period to two weeks, however, would have the same effect as doubling the carryover limit with a one-week period.

## The Discount Rate and Discount Window

Another major tool of Federal Reserve monetary policy consists of changes in the discount rate and the administration of the discount window. When the Federal Reserve was first established, it was thought that this was the major tool of a central bank. After all, the Federal Reserve was to be a "lender of last resort" and as such the provider of ultimate liquidity to the financial system. Added cash reserves could always be obtained at the Federal Reserve at a price (the discount rate), if the bank were following proper procedure in making short-term self-liquidating loans and therefore had "eligible" paper to rediscount at the Federal Reserve.

By the mid-1920s, open market operations was beginning to displace some of this central function of providing reserves to the banking system through the discount window, although the bulk of reserves were still loaned to banks in the 1920s. As a result of the 1935 amendments, open market operations began to assume a more dominant role. It was unnecessary for the banks to borrow at the discount window anyway from the early 1930s until the early 1950s because of a substantial amount of excess bank reserves.

Once the Federal Reserve regained its independence after the March 4, 1951, accord with the Treasury, which is discussed in the next chapter, the discount window began to resume some of its former importance. It never quite regained the dominant role of the 1920s, however, so that it is now generally regarded as an adjunct to open market operations. If the Federal Reserve does not supply all the reserves desired by the financial system through open market operations, temporary borrowing of added reserves is possible at the discount window.

The regulation governing such borrowing of reserves is appropriately named **Regulation A,** because it was the first regulation issued by the board. This regulation was revised after March 4, 1951, to stress that member bank borrowing was to be regarded as a "privilege" and not a right. This made it possible for the Federal Reserve to utilize nonprice rationing at the discount window as well as changes in the discount rate (the interest rate paid when borrowing). Access to the discount window is discussed in more detail in Chapter 18.

Regulation A was revised again as of September 1, 1980, to take account of the changes brought about by the Monetary Control Act of 1980. The new regulation said in part, "Federal Reserve credit is available to a depository institution under such rules as may be prescribed to assist the institution, to the extent appropriate, in meeting temporary requirements for funds. . . ."[2] The Federal Reserve still thinks of bor-

---

[2]Board of Governors of the Federal Reserve System, *Federal Reserve Bulletin*, Sept. 1980, p. 756.

rowing as a privilege that may be restricted if the borrowing is not appropriate.

Nevertheless, smaller depository institutions may have different needs than medium-sized or larger depository institutions. Hence the revised regulation noted that "Federal Reserve credit is available for periods longer than those permitted under adjustment credit to assist smaller depository institutions. . . ."[3] Such longer-term needs are considered seasonal and must persist for at least four weeks.

Federal Reserve credit may also be available to depository institutions "where similar assistance is not reasonably available from other sources, including special industry lenders."[4] This, of course, could apply to savings banks and savings and loan associatons. Finally, in unusual circumstances a Reserve Bank, after consulting with the board, could extend emergency credit to individuals, partnerships, and corporations, which are not depository institutions.[5]

## Open Market Operations

The most important tool of monetary policy, as already noted, is open market operations, discussed in Chapter 17. Still, we would be remiss if we did not stress here the importance of open market operations (OMO). Open market operations were discovered in the mid-1920s, when the twelve Federal Reserve governors (as the heads of the Federal Reserve Banks were then called) assembled in New York City under the leadership of Governor Benjamin Strong of the Federal Reserve Bank of New York.

The purpose of the governors was to invest surplus funds safely in the government securities market, but they soon discovered that their operations were having effects on market yields and even on bank reserves and the money supply. The Board of Governors in Washington invited them to meet there so that the board could help oversee these new operations. But in the 1920s the amount of government debt outstanding was small and the magnitude of OMO was also small compared with the amount of bank reserves supplied through the discount window.

After the 1935 amendments to the Federal Reserve Act establishing the formal Federal Open Market Committee (FOMC), the amount of OMO increased, as did the amount of government debt outstanding. The two grew in importance in World War II, when the government engaged in very large deficit financing as part of the war effort and the Federal

[3]*Ibid.*
[4]*Ibid.*
[5]*Ibid.*

Reserve "supported" the prices of government securities at par through OMO. This made it possible for the banks to buy government debt, which could not be sold to the public.

These Federal Reserve operations, of course, had the effect of increasing bank reserves and the money supply, but the major inflationary impact was not felt until all price controls were removed by Congress in June 1946. Unfortunately, the Federal Reserve continued most of its support operations in the government securities markets, which meant that it had largely lost control of the money supply, until the Korean War beginning in June 1950 made that support policy increasingly inflationary. Finally, on March 4, 1951, after its accord with the Treasury, the Federal Reserve regained its independence.

In the more than three decades since then, Federal Reserve OMO have increased in size and subtlety. In addition to outright purchases and sales of government securities, the **Trading Desk** of the Federal Reserve Bank of New York, which conducts all OMO for the FOMC, has added short-term supplying of banking reserves (repurchase agreements) and short-term subtractions of reserves (**matched sale-purchase agreements**) to its arsenal of weapons. Some RPs are even extended on bankers' acceptances, and the debt of some government agencies is sometimes purchased. The Federal Reserve, however, has firmly rejected any proposals that it purchase state and local debt, and it has never considered buying private debt.

At times in past decades, the major purpose of OMO seems to have been influencing, if not determining, the level and variability of various key interest rates. These have usually been very short-term rates such as the federal funds rate and the Treasury bill yield. This is so because OMO directly affect the supply of bank reserves and hence the yield on excess bank reserves (federal funds), which are traded in the money market. Also, most of the operations of the Trading Desk are in the Treasury bill market, although some longer-term issues are also bought. This concern with interest rates in the market was particularly evident in the 1960s, although it was not absent in the 1970s.

After the accord of March 4, 1951, the Federal Reserve had tried to avoid directly influencing interest rates, though it was aware that its moves toward credit tightening or easing did affect interest rates. By the 1980s, however, after the historic FOMC meeting of October 6, 1979, great stress was placed on providing reserves for the financial system to attain targeted ranges of growth on various measures of the money supply. Interest rates were allowed to swing rather freely in the market, though there was a broad range of federal funds rates thought to be consistent with the desired monetary targets. Moreover, the main emphasis of monetary policy in the early 1980s was a reduction in the inflation rate, which was to be attained by reducing the rate of growth of the money supply.

## Qualitative Controls Exercised by the Federal Reserve

The three major monetary policy tools already discussed are quantitative weapons of control. These tools affect the total amount of monetary reserves and the total amount of the money supply, however defined. These quantitative controls are exercised through varying the rates of growth of bank reserves and the money supply. No matter which one of these weapons is used, there is no attempt to encourage or discourage particular types of credit. Monetary policy may thus be distinguished from credit policy. Nevertheless, in 1934 and 1935 during the Great Depression, Congress gave the Federal Reserve two qualitative credit controls: margin requirements on stock market credit and the power to set maximum interest rates on time and savings deposits.

The Securities Exchange Act of 1934 provided that the Board of Governors should regulate the extension of stock market credit. This act was passed because it was then believed that excessive credit fueling the stock market speculation of the late 1920s had led ultimately to the 1929 stock market crash and the ensuing Depression. Under this law, the board issued Regulation T, which governs the extension of credit by brokers and dealers on listed securities, and Regulation U, which prescribes how much banks can loan on stocks. Under both regulations the limit on the amount of credit that can be extended on a security is indicated by the maximum loan value. This loan value is a specified percentage of its market value at the time of extension. Margin requirements are the difference between the market value (100 percent) and the maximum loan value. In 1982, margin requirements, which had been in effect since January 3, 1974, were 50 percent under both regulations

Maximum interest rates on time and savings deposits since the mid-1930s have been set by Regulation Q. The ceiling has been raised over time, and in 1970 for certain maturities, and again in 1973 for the other maturities, it was suspended for large certificates of deposit ($100,000 or more). The ceilings in effect in the early 1980s were given in Chapter 9. Although Regulation Q was of importance in various past credit restraint periods, especially in 1969, the Monetary Control Act of 1980 specified that it will be removed gradually until it disappears in 1986.

## Pricing of Federal Reserve Services After 1980

In addition to employing its different major monetary policy tools and its less important credit policy tools, the Federal Reserve System supplies many services to the financial system. Prior to 1980, most of these services such as the transport of cash were free to the member banks in order to give them some benefits to offset the cost of membership. But after 1980 the average reserve requirements were lower than those imposed earlier on member banks. Furthermore, with greater access to services of the system for all depository institutions, who included many more thousands of additional financing institutions than before, Congress required the Federal Reserve to charge a price for its services.

Pricing of services was to offset in part the loss of revenue to the Treasury from lower reserve requirements (i.e., the Federal Reserve would not need to buy as many government securities to provide needed monetary reserves on which it would receive an interest rate). Net profits of the Federal Reserve are each year returned to the Treasury. In addition to offsetting the loss of revenue, Congress believed that pricing for **Federal Reserve services** would encourage competition and efficiency in the provision of such services.

The Federal Reserve services on which prices were to be established were eight: (1) transportation of currency and coin, and coin wrapping, (2) check clearing and collection, (3) wire transfer of funds, (4) use of Federal Reserve automated clearinghouse facilities, (5) net settlement of debits and credits affecting accounts held by the Federal Reserve, (6) book entry, safekeeping, and other services connected with the purchase or sale of government securities, (7) noncash collection—the receipt, collection and crediting of accounts of depository institutions in connection with municipal and corporate securities—and (8) the cost to the Federal Reserve of float—the interest on such items, usually the dollar value of checks, credited by the Federal Reserve to one depository institution before being collected from another. Interest on **Federal Reserve float** was to be charged at the current market rate for federal funds, whereas other fees were to be based on all direct and indirect costs of providing such services. In addition there was to be an initial markup of 12 percent as the private sector adjustment to the Federal Reserve's cost of providing services. This adjustment would be reviewed annually.

## PREVIEW OF MONETARY POLICY

Whereas this chapter has focused on the broad structure of the Federal Reserve System and its major functions, the following four chapters focus particularly on monetary policy. Chapter 16 considers the major goals of monetary policy, the main weapons used to attain these goals, and some major experiences with different types of monetary policy. At the end of that chapter, we consider the current focus on controlling the growth of the monetary aggregates. Monetary aggregates and the major weapon of open market operations are discussed in Chapter 17. The adjunct weapons of changes in the discount rate and the administration of the discount window are considered in Chapter 18. Chapter 19 looks at the coordination of the various weapons of monetary policy and their different impacts on the economy.

## Questions for Discussion

1. Summarize the three major functions of central banks, including the Federal Reserve System. Which one of these functions was stressed in the Federal Reserve Act of 1913 and why?
2. Discuss the overall structure of the Federal Reserve System. Indicate the functions played by each part of this system.
3. Discuss the Board of Directors of each Federal Reserve Bank. How are the three different types of directors selected? What responsibilities do the directors have?
4. Discuss the composition and selection of the Board of Governors of the Federal Reserve System. What are their major powers and duties?
5. Discuss the composition and function of the Federal Open Market Committee (FOMC). How often does this committee meet? What part in the formulation of monetary policy does the FOMC have? Why?
6. Discuss the governance of the Federal Reserve System with emphasis on powers given to the Federal Reserve Board, on the one hand, and to the Federal Reserve Banks, on the other.
7. What were the original purposes of requiring legal reserve ratios for banks? Why do we have legal reserve ratios for all depository institutions now? How much discretion does the Federal Reserve Board have in setting these reserve ratios under the Monetary Control Act of 1980?
8. Why did the Federal Reserve Board propose returning to contemporaneous reserve requirements (CRR) in 1982? What were the disadvantages of lagged reserve accounting in effect since 1968? Why was the proposed move in 1982 from a one-week reserve period to a two-week reserve period?
9. What is the general role of the discount rate and the discount window, as compared with other monetary policy weapons? Why have the discount window at all?
10. How have the open market operations of the Federal Reserve changed over time? Why is this the most important monetary policy tool? Why are these conducted only by the Federal Reserve Bank of New York?
11. Briefly discuss the qualitative controls exercised by the Federal Reserve. Why is Regulation Q gradually being phased out?
12. Why did the Federal Reserve begin charging a price for its services after 1980? Which services were included? What were the major principles underlying its pricing?

# Selected Bibliography for Further Reading

BOARD OF GOVERNORS OF THE FEDERAL RESERVE SYSTEM, *The Federal Reserve System Purposes and Functions* (Washington, D.C.: 1974).

——, "The Depository Institutions Deregulation and Monetary Control Act of 1980," *Federal Reserve Bulletin*, June 1980, pp. 444–453.

FEDERAL RESERVE BANK OF BOSTON, *Controlling Monetary Aggregates, Proceedings of a Conference Held in June 1969* (Boston: 1970).

——, *Controlling Monetary Aggregates II: The Implementation, Proceedings of a Conference in September 1972* (Boston: 1973).

FEDERAL RESERVE BANK OF CHICAGO, "The Depository Institutions Deregulation and Monetary Control Act of 1980," *Economic Perspectives*, Sept.-Oct. 1980, pp. 3–23.

FEDERAL RESERVE BANK OF NEW YORK, *Essays in Domestic and International Finance* (New York: 1969).

MAYER, THOMAS, *Monetary Policy in the United States* (New York: Random House, 1968).

PROCHNOW, HERBERT, ed., *The Federal Reserve System* (New York: Harper & Row, 1960).

Also, see latest *Annual Reports* of the Board of Governors and of the Federal Reserve Bank of New York.

The stability of the Bank of England is equal to that of the British government. . . . It acts, not only as an ordinary bank, but as a great engine of state.

THE WEALTH OF NATIONS

# 16
# CHAPTER

# Central Banking Policy in the United States and Great Britain

Central banks play a more important role in influencing and carrying out government policy today than they did in the late eighteenth century. As the role of central banks increased in importance, it also increased in complexity. At every step of the way much public controversy has surrounded the operations of central banks.

Should a central bank, such as the Federal Reserve System in the United States, merely carry out national priorities as determined by the administration in power, or should it assume an independent policy role not only for itself but as an adviser on overall macroeconomic policy of the administration? Should national policy emphasize domestic policy goals, such as full employment or price level stability, or should more attention be paid to the value of the dollar in foreign exchange markets and even to the market price of gold?

Which domestic policy goal is the more important, price level stability or full employment? And which set of monetary variables should the central bank emphasize, interest rates or the growth in monetary aggregates such as the money supply as it is variously defined? Even the implementation of monetary policy tools such as the conduct of open market operations is subject to controversy. Our concern here is to focus our discussion on the major alternative goals and ways of implementing monetary policy, as well as some consideration of the recent actual record of monetary policy in the United States and Great Britain.

# MONETARY INDICATORS AND MONETARY POLICY TOOLS

A change in Bank Rate by the Bank of England or a change in the discount rate by the Federal Reserve Banks in the 1920s was commonly thought to be the major policy tool used by central banks in those countries, and in other countries as well. In this period, three fundamental propositions underlay much of the theory of central banking: (1) a change in the central bank interest rate would assure a generally corresponding change in interest rates at commercial banks; (2) a change in the level of interest rates could be summarized as being a change in "the" interest rate, because it was assumed that there would be a synchronous change on yields on comparable debt instruments of all maturities; and (3) whenever interest rates changed as a result of central bank acquisition, there would be changes in the amount of funds offered by lenders and changes in saving by consumers out of income.

Some sixty years later in the 1980s, a much greater stress is placed on controlling the growth of the money supply with less emphasis on deliberate variations in central bank lending rates (e.g., the discount rate). The preferred instrument of monetary policy is now open market operations and direct control over the growth in bank reserves, and the growth in the money supply is implemented through the purchase and sale of government securities.

A change in the discount rate is now looked upon as a "signal" of the intentions of the monetary authorities to carry out a particular monetary policy of credit ease or credit restraint rather than a major tool in and of itself. Furthermore, the use of market interest rates as an indicator of monetary policy is subject to considerable measurement error because of the impact on such interest rates of many influences other than monetary policy (e.g., a change in the budget deficit or a variation in business loan demand).

There is also increasing empirical evidence that changing rates of growth of the money supply do have a significant impact on both the price level and the rate of growth of real output. Hence more observers put increasing emphasis on judging the intentions of the monetary authorities by weekly, monthly, quarterly, and annual data on the growth of the money supply. Although some variation in the growth of the money supply may be the result of forces other than those of monetary policy, ultimately the control of the growth of the money supply is in the hands of the monetary authorities. However, insofar as the central bank controls the money supply, it is through its control over bank reserves.

## STABILIZING SHORT-RUN FLUCTUATIONS IN INTEREST RATES

Traditionally, most central banks have tended to put a strong emphasis in their open market operations on stabilizing short-run fluctuations in interest rates, though this approach in the United States was largely abandoned after the "Saturday Night Special" of October 6, 1979. The Federal Open Market Committee at that time strongly emphasized controlling the rate of growth of monetary aggregates rather than determining interest rates

Central banks still tend to operate in the money market and hence often prefer a certain amount of money market stability. Central banks also play an important role in the debt management operations of their governments, which gives them another reason for concern about the stability of the financial markets. If you sell government securities for your Treasury, as does the Bank of England, you wish the market to be receptive to your offerings. A long-run downward drift in the price of such government securities can be tolerated, but excessive short-run fluctuations in price and yield are to be avoided.

Unfortunately, such market stabilizing behavior by central banks whenever indicated tends to promote some procyclical growth in the stock of money in a period of economic expansion. When the economy is expanding rapidly, credit demands are also rising, which tends to produce upward pressure on interest rates. To prevent interest rates from rising rapidly, the central bank must then increase the monetary base (bank reserves) and the money supply.

This tends to feed the fires of inflation. During a recession, when credit demands fall, interest rates fall, and the money supply tends to decline, the central bank is still likely to increase bank reserves and the money supply still further to stimulate the economy. Thus the central bank often seems to exhibit a proinflationary rather than an antiinflationary bias because of its great concern with minimizing interest rate fluctuations. It also seems to want to reduce or hold down the level of interest rates.

In the earlier gold standard period, which ended in Great Britain in 1931 and in 1933 in the United States, it was expected that central banks would also influence money market rates by varying the Bank Rate, or the discount rate, as already indicated. When a deficit in the balance of payments developed and gold flowed out of the country, higher interest rates at home would restrain capital outflows and gold outflows and perhaps even attract some capital or gold from abroad. As a result of the Great Depression of the 1930s and the publication of *The General Theory of Employment, Interest and Money* by John Maynard Keynes in 1936, the emphasis shifted to the necessity of the central bank's lowering long-term interest rates to stimulate investment and thereby increase real output and the level of employment. After World War II, central banks tended to hold down long-term interest rates to assist economic recovery in a recession period and to assist in stimulating higher rates of economic growth over a period of a decade or more.

## Monetary Aggregate Targets

It was not until the 1970s in both the United States (in January 1970 and again on October 6, 1979) and in Great Britain that greater emphasis was placed on the necessity of the central bank's establishing annual, quarterly, and even bimonthly target ranges for the growth of the money supply in its various definitions. By this decade it was widely recognized that excessive growth in the money supply could result in general price inflation, though there were still vocal advocates of monetary stimulus to promote increases in real output.

Control of the various monetary aggregates was often given primacy in the menu of central bank intermediate goals. Nevertheless, stabilizing the money market (minimizing fluctuations in short-run interest rates) was still among the instructions given by the monetary authorities to those who actually carried out open market operations. Sometimes, indeed, money market considerations were given a higher priority than attainment of a given growth in the money supply. This was particularly likely to be the case if the Treasury were embarking on a large-scale debt management operation in the market.

## MONETARY POLICY GOALS

In the Federal Reserve Act passed in 1913 the attainment of "an elastic currency" was one of the goals of this new central bank. The National Banking System then in effect had as one of its major defects an inelastic currency (i.e., a currency that would not expand and contract with the needs of trade). In subsequent years, however, particularly after the economic debacle of the early 1930s and the emphasis on full employment and economic growth in the post-World War II period, broader and more sophisticated economic goals were assumed by the Federal Reserve System.

## Four Major Goals

There appear to be four major policy goals of this central bank in the 1980s: (1) to preserve the value of the dollar over time (i.e., minimize inflation of the price level), (2) to maintain full employment (i.e., keep unemployment from rising much above 4 to 5 percent), (3) to achieve a significant rate of economic growth (i.e., to help maintain a real growth rate of output of 5 to 6 percent per year), and (4) to help achieve equilibrium in the American balance of payments. It should not be thought that the Federal Reserve System has imagined that it could achieve even one of these goals solely by the manipulation of the monetary policy weapons at its disposal. It is fully understood in the Federal Reserve System that the achievement of any or all of these public policy goals requires a coordinated effort by many governmental agencies.

## Monetary Policy in 1981

To illustrate specifically these goals of monetary policy in the decade of the 1980s, we might quote from a report to Congress by the Federal Reserve Board in early 1981: "The growth of money and credit will have to be slowed to a rate consistent with the long-range growth of the nation's capacity to produce at reasonably stable prices. Realistically, that rate must be approached over a period of years to avoid severe contractionary pressures on output and employment."[1] This report notes that monetary policy targets for 1981 "imply a significant deceleration of growth in the monetary aggregates from the rates of 1980 and other recent years."[2]

   The years prior to 1981, particularly from 1973 on, had often been years of high and accelerating rates of inflation. Double-digit inflation rates were even recorded in several different periods. A contributing factor to this unfortunate inflation experience may well have been excessive growth in the monetary aggregates under the control of the Federal Reserve System. It also appeared that chronic and sometimes increasing budget deficits was also a significant inflationary factor.

   [1]Paul A. Volcker, Chairman, Federal Reserve Board, *Monetary Policy Objectives for 1981*, Feb. 25–26, 1981, p. 3.
   [2]Ibid., p. 3.

*Fiscal Policy Versus Monetary Policy*     In the case of a budget deficit, the powerful demand effects of fiscal policy can overwhelm even the appropriate restraining effects of monetary policy.[3] Then inflation of the price level can continue, even though interest rates are still rising (e.g., as in 1973–1974 and again in 1981–1982). On the other hand, assuming that the Federal Reserve is successful in its deflationary efforts, some undesirable side effects may occur. Although the desired goal of credit restraint by the monetary authorities is to slow down or eliminate inflation, a slowdown in output and employment may also result.

*The Phillips Curve*     The trade-off between unemployment and the price level can be summarized in a *Phillips curve*, named after the English economist who first performed the critical empirical research. Studies not only in England but in the United States as well have shown that money wages and indeed the price level tend to rise more rapidly when unemployment is reduced, and vice versa. Hence part of the cost of restraining inflation may be to have rising unemployment.

Price stability and full employment are thus seen to be incompatible, conflicting goals. Nevertheless, some economists and some policy makers in the 1970s came to believe that a permanently lower unemployment rate could be achieved by paying the price of some constant rate of inflation, and that wage-price guideposts and/or labor power policies could shift the Phillips curve toward the origin and thus reduce the amount of inflation related to any given unemployment rate. Other economists, especially Milton Friedman, argued that inflationary expectations would render any such trade-off policy ineffective.

Friedman believed that there was a **"natural rate of unemployment,"** which was the equilibrium rate for the economy. Temporarily, workers might have an expected rate of inflation below the actual rate of inflation and thereby permit their real wages to be reduced, so that employers would hire more workers and thus reduce the unemployment rate. Believing, however, that workers would not suffer a "money illusion" in the long run, the ultimate effect of public policies to reduce the unemployment rate would be a return to the "natural rate of unemployment," but at a higher rate of inflation than formerly.

Most economists came to agree that there were families of short-run Phillips curves, and that these curves could shift to alter the inflation-unemployment relationship. **Stagflation** in some years in the 1970s, when *both* inflation and unemployment increased, seemed to a number of economists to indicate that Friedman was right after all. Nevertheless, many economists still believed that there was such a

---

[3]It is also possible for credit ease to offset the effects of fiscal restraint. The classic example of this is the buildup of inflationary pressures in the economy after mid-1968 because of an easing in credit restraint by the Federal Reserve after a 10 percent tax surcharge took effect July 1, 1968.

trade-off in the long run, though the price of full employment might be a high (or even unacceptable) rate of price inflation, whereas the price of price-level stability might be a high or even unacceptable rate of unemployment. This controversy is summarized in the article cited in the bibliography at the end of the chapter.

*Adverse Effect of Inflation on Balance of Payments*    Inflation at home is also unlikely to be compatible with a satisfactory equilibrium in a country's **balance of payments**, which is the accounting statement that records all the flows of goods, services, and capital between one country and the rest of the world. An increase in export prices more rapid than that of one's major foreign competitors would likely lead to a diminution of growth in exports and a rise in imports. An inflationary growth of income in a country thus has both price and income effects on that country's balance of payments. A rise in prices of most goods also results in a rise in prices of goods exported, which will tend to adversely affect exports. Also, the rise in income will tend to increase imports. If the country already has an equilibrium in its balance of payments, a deficit in the balance of payments will now result

*Goal of Economic Growth*    An emphasis on **economic growth** as a major concern of the monetary authorities in the United States did not develop until the late 1950s and early 1960s. By that time, the Soviet Union was seen as an important economic as well as ideological competitor of the United States. Hence the United States came to look at its rate of economic growth as compared with that of the Soviet Union. By the early 1960s, the Federal Reserve, as already noted, along with other parts of the federal government, was determined to assist in the attainment of a higher rate of noninflationary economic growth.

*Higher Prices and Economic Growth*    Until the mid-1960s, it seemed that a higher rate of economic growth and a lower unemployment rate might be compatible with stable prices or at least a slowly rising price level. After the Vietnam War escalation began in 1965, government military expenditures began to rise sharply and welfare spending also increased. The subsequent added rise in private investment expenditures and consumer expenditures also increased the fuel feeding the inflationary fires that were earlier ignited. After several years of strong economic growth, the unemployment rate was finally reduced below 5 percent in late 1973. Unfortunately, as the unemployment rate fell, the rate of inflation accelerated.

In 1973, consumer prices rose more than 6 percent. In 1974 and 1975 they rose in many months at double-digit rates. Prices, which rose by 12 percent or more in 1974, increased on the average by 9.3 percent in 1975. It took the severe recession of 1973–1975, which produced higher unemployment rates not only then but also in 1976 and 1977, to reduce the inflation rate to more acceptable levels. In 1976 prices rose at an annual rate at the retail level in excess of 5 percent and in 1977 about 6.5 percent. In 1978, inflation accelerated to a 9 percent rate and rose still more in 1979 and 1980 to double-digit levels. In 1979, consumer prices on average rose by 13.3 percent and in 1980 by 12.4 percent. Not until 1981 did the inflation rate fall below double-digit rates, when it increased 8.9 percent.

By the 1970s, therefore, a higher rate of economic growth with the low rates of unemployment accompanying it was also seen as somewhat incompatible with price-level stability. The trade-off problem for the monetary policymakers had become clearly established, both for the United States and Great Britain.

## THE BANK OF ENGLAND

Before considering some of the recent changes in central banking techniques in the United States (i.e., in the operations of the Federal Reserve System), it may be useful to consider an older central bank still in operation today, the Bank of England. The **Bank of England** was organized under an act of Parliament and Royal Charter of 1694. By the late eighteenth century, the Bank of England was already operating in close concert with the British government, but it was not until the act of 1946 that it was nationalized. Under this act the governing Court of Directors was to consist of the governor, deputy governor, and sixteen directors, all of whom were to be appointed by the Crown. The term of office of both the governor and deputy governor was five years and that of the directors four years. All were to be eligible for reappointment.

In Britain "the monetary authorities—a wider term embracing the Bank and Treasury under the political leadership of the Chancellor of the Exchequer—and major policy decisions as being determined by the government as a whole"[4] is a different concept than in the United States, where it might properly be restricted to the Federal Reserve System. The actual operations of the Bank of England are clearly influenced by the fact that overall monetary policy is being made by the government in power.

Hence, as the Bank of England clearly states: "In their operations in the money markets the Bank have three aims: first to ensure that short-term finance is available to meet government expenditure; second to implement government monetary policy, particularly in relation to

---

[4] Charles A. E. Goodhart, "Monetary Policy in the United Kingdom," *Monetary Policy in Twelve Industrial Countries*, ed. by Karel Holbik (Federal Reserve Bank of Boston, 1973), pp. 467–468.

short-term interest rates; and third to maintain the liquidity of the banking system."[5] The stress on interest rates indicated here is much greater than in the United States. In recent years in the United States more emphasis has been placed on controlling the rate of growth of monetary aggregates.

To the extent that the Bank of England is concerned with controlling the rate of growth of the money supply, it still does so through its influence on interest rates. A higher rate of interest (lower price) on gilt-edge stocks (bonds) will induce more buyers for such long-term debt. This thereby permits the bank to reduce the amount of Treasury bills outstanding.

When the Treasury runs a deficit, it must sell more securities through the bank, which handles debt management operations. But if the bill issue expands, so does the monetary base of the banking system and, subsequently, so does the stock of money. Only by reducing Treasury bills outstanding by selling more bonds can the bank control the growth in the money stock. Incidentally, in Britain all purchases and sales of government securities by the bank are made through the government broker, who is in constant contact both with the bank and the market.

As is typical of all central banks, the government's main accounts are held with the Bank of England. For operational purposes, the Bank of England has eight branches—at Birmingham, Bristol, Leeds, Liverpool, Manchester, Newcastle, Southampton, and at the Law Courts in London. The key commercial bank accounts are those of the London clearing banks. Mergers in 1968–1969 reduced the number of these London clearing banks from eleven to six.

The money market, however, with which the Bank of England (through the government broker) conducts open market operations and to which it is the lender of last resort, consists of eleven discount houses that are members of the London Discount Market Association. The weekly tender for Treasury bills is always covered in full by these discount houses, with each house bidding for a proportion of the total tender related to its capital and resources. The discount houses also provide an active market for commercial bills.

In the fall of 1972, the Bank of England changed the way in which it determined its rate on loans to the discount houses. Furthermore, the traditional term **"bank rate"** was abandoned. The minimum lending rate (MLR) of the Bank of England to the discount houses was now tied to the average rate on the latest weekly bill tender. Like the traditional bank rate, the MLR was also set above the money market yields, but it is now floated week to week.

[5]Bank of England, *"The Functions and Organization of the Bank of England,"* May 1975, p. 6.

## Competition and Credit Control

In September 1971, the Bank of England made a number of reforms in its techniques of monetary policy. The new arrangements had three fundamental characteristics: (1) the abandonment of ceilings on bank and finance house lending, (2) a more general application of monetary policy, relying more heavily on changes in interest rates to control the growth of money and credit, and (3) the replacement of deposit banks' liquid assets and cash ratios by a reserve ratio applicable to all deposit holding institutions. The new ratio was set at 12.5 percent for banks and 10 percent for finance houses. These reserve ratios were supposed to provide a firm basis for open market operations by the Bank of England and for calls for special deposits. (These are, in effect, temporary increases in the ratios, because they drain funds from the banks.)

Unfortunately, the several years after the September 1971 reforms in Great Britain were years of rapid increases in bank credit and in the money supply, which in turn led to double-digit inflation in 1974–1977. Using a broad definition of the money supply ($M_3$) and considering the growth in total banking sector assets and total banking sector advances, we see that these three variables increased at compound annual rates of 27.4 percent, 41.4 percent, and 47.7 percent, respectively, from October 1971 through December 1973. Long-term growth rates were correspondingly only 4.7 percent, 3.9 percent, and 3.8 percent for the period 1891–1966.[6] This rapid growth in these monetary aggregates led to accelerating inflation by 1974–1975, when 24 to 25 percent annual rates of growth in consumer prices each month were common. In 1976, the inflation rate was nearly 15 percent and it was still running at double-digit levels in the late 1970s and early 1980s.

A chronic deficit in the Treasury's budget and undoubted subordination of monetary policy as conducted by the Bank of England to the needs of the Treasury is probably the major explanation for this destabilizing behavior of the monetary aggregates. The much greater independence of the Federal Reserve System in the United States makes this particular experience less likely, even though the Federal Reserve has certainly made mistakes in its monetary policy from time to time that have had destabilizing effects on the economy.

## The Changing Role of the Federal Reserve System

In addition to having a more independent role within the government in formulating monetary policy, especially since 1935 when the secretary of

---

[6]A.D. Chesher, D.K. Sheppard, and J. Whitwell, "Have British Banks Been Imprudent?" *The Banker*, pp. 31–33, Jan. 1975.

the treasury and the comptroller of the currency were removed from the Board of Governors of the Federal Reserve System, the Federal Reserve also does not have to be as concerned with the interest rate and exchange rate implications of being an "open economy" in quite the same way as does the Bank of England. Although the importance of foreign trade as a percentage of gross national product has risen in recent years in the United States, it is still possible for the major focus of monetary policy in this country to be on domestic policy. This was even truer in earlier years.

*Optimism About Central Banking in the 1920s*    In the 1920s, after the re-establishment of central banking in the United States with the passage of the Federal Reserve Act in 1913, there was considerable optimism among economists and businessmen that the mere existence of such a central bank would reduce the likelihood of another American financial panic and depression. The flexible tools at the command of the Federal Reserve seemed to many of these observers to be adequate to preserve the basic liquidity of the American banking system, even in the face of any possible lack of public confidence in banks or in our monetary system. The existence of such a financial bulwark, which could be a lender of last resort for member banks and a creator of additional money as needed, would provide, it was believed, financial stability.

*Pessimism About Monetary Policy in the 1930s*    Optimism about monetary policy in the 1920s vanished in a wave of deep pessimism about the stabilizing powers of central banking in the 1930s. Keynes, in 1936 in his *The General Theory*, voiced openly and in theoretical terms many of the reservations about the powers of central banks to prevent or overcome depressions that many observers already shared. The Keynesian liquidity trap seemed to explain why central banks appeared to be completely powerless to restore prosperity once a country had fallen into the deep trough of a serious depression.

## The Keynesian View

Keynes believed that the power of a central bank to influence economic activity had to be exerted through its ability to vary the long-term rate of interest. Only if the central bank could lower that rate sufficiently to stimulate enough additional investment to raise the level of national income and employment to the full employment level could the central bank be regarded as puissant in its stabilizing activities.

The interest rate, however, could not fall to the necessary level to restore full employment equilibrium, because a barrier to a further decline in the interest rate would be reached at some low interest rate such as 2 percent. At this level, individuals and institutions supposedly would be willing to absorb in their cash balances all the additional money provided by the central bank. They would accumulate cash at this low interest rate rather than increase spending on securities or goods and services.

*Low Interest Rates and Borrowing Demand*     Even if the holders of cash did not interpose such a barrier to the necessary downward adjustment of the long-term rate of interest, such a low interest rate would not likely do much good in stimulating the needed investment borrowing and spending anyway. In other words, the early Keynesians believed that the investment demand for borrowed funds was generally inelastic. Furthermore, because of a depression-induced "collapse" of the marginal efficiency of capital schedule, perhaps only a negative rate of interest (implying government subsidies) would be adequate to stimulate needed investment, even if such investment demand were more sensitive to changes in the rate of interest than the Keynesians believed.

*Emphasis on Fiscal Policy*     With such a gloomy attitude toward the ability of central banks to cope with the economic paralysis of the 1930s, it is not surprising that economists, public officials, and even the electorates of many countries should look elsewhere than toward central banking to help their countries secure high-level employment and income once again. The magic solution seemed to lie in **fiscal policy,** wherein the central government would manipulate tax rates and government expenditures so that prosperity could be attained and maintained. In a deep depression such as the one of the 1930s, it seemed desirable to engage in large-scale, deficit-financed government expenditures, though full-scale resort to such devices was not made until after the outbreak of World War II.

## THE SUPPORT POLICY OF THE FEDERAL RESERVE, 1941–1951

The only role assigned to the central bank, then, was to assist the Treasury in its financing and **debt management** problems. In fact, the Federal Reserve System did this so ably during World War II that this war has sometimes been called the "3 percent war" in indication of the low rate of interest on new government bonds during this conflict.

Although this "junior partnership" role of the Federal Reserve was undoubtedly appropriate for the large-scale, war financing needs from 1941 to 1945, it can be doubted that this same subservient position was appropriate in the postwar period. Once the war was over and the structure of wartime controls was dismantled—as was largely accomplished in the United States by June 1946—strong inflationary pressures manifested themselves in the American economy. The wartime scarcities of goods and services had led both consumers and businessmen to develop a backlog of unsatisfied demands.

## Accumulated Liquid Assets After War

The substantial amount of personal and business saving accumulated during the war was now available in the form of large amounts of liquid assets, which could be turned into money to try to obtain goods and services that had previously been available only in limited quantities. These goods and services were still relatively scarce in the early postwar period, so that the inevitable effect of strong increases in final and intermediate demand was to push up prices. The demand pressures of the early postwar years were soon joined by wage pressures from strong unions, so that a number of wage-price rounds were added to the inflationary pressures already evident.

***The Federal Reserve as an Instrument of Inflation***    Strangely enough, in such an inflationary environment the Federal Reserve allowed itself to become a passive instrument of inflation. The wartime policy of supporting government bond prices at par was continued in the early years after World War II partly because of uncertainty as to what might happen to the large government debt, which had swollen to the unprecedented total of $278.7 billion at the end of the war, as compared with $64.3 billion at the beginning of the war. There was much worry as to what might happen if the Federal Reserve let the price of marketable federal debt be determined solely by private market forces. Any possible decline in the price of such debt would mean a rise in interest rates. This would not only increase the cost of servicing the large government debt but might also bring on a postwar depression.

*Bank Selling of Government Securities*    The commercial banks took advantage of this support policy in the early postwar years and unloaded large amounts of government securities that they had purchased during the war. The banks sold billions of dollars of government bonds to make the more profitable business loans that business enterprises were then requesting from their banks. When the Federal Reserve bought substantial quantities of these bonds—to prevent their prices from falling sharply—bank reserves were created. The newly created bank reserves were used by the banks to make still more loans, which expanded the money supply. An increase in the money supply under these conditions inevitably fueled inflation, so instead of restraining inflation the American central bank was actually feeding it.

*Inflationary Pressures of the Korean War*     With the outbreak of the Korean War in June 1950 and the quick involvement of the United States in this conflict, the government added strong demand pressures to an economy already unable to satisfy all the demands of consumers and businesses. In fact, both consumers and businesses increased their spending sharply in the second half of 1950. Further price increases were naturally to be expected, when spending was growing faster than productive capacity could be increased. Although some limited war controls were reimposed on the economy, it became increasingly evident that the Federal Reserve would have to follow a somewhat different monetary policy than it had followed in World War II and the early postwar period.

## THE MONETARY POLICY RENASCENCE AFTER THE ACCORD OF MARCH 4, 1951

After some months of intensive discussion between Federal Reserve and Treasury officials, an **accord** was announced on March 4, 1951, whereby the Federal Reserve was given its "independence" to establish its own economic priorities. Furthermore, the Federal Reserve was to stop supporting the price of government securities at par and refurbish its traditional major weapon of monetary policy in the form of dynamic open market operations. Even the discount window, which had been virtually unused since the early 1930s, was now to play an important role in the new arsenal of Federal Reserve weapons. In the more than two decades since the accord of March 4, 1951, various other new techniques of Federal Reserve policy have also been developed.

### The Bills Only Doctrine in the 1950s

In the 1950s the Federal Reserve was absorbed in much internal discussion as to how the powerful weapon of open market operations was to carry out monetary policy so that it would not simply be the tail to the kite of Treasury debt management. This internal discussion spilled over into academia, and the technical economic journals of these years are filled with numerous articles on the **"bills only"** controversy. In 1952, the Open Market Committee adopted the recommendations of its Ad Hoc Subcommittee, which had suggested that open market operations should normally be restricted to the buying and selling of Treasury bills, then only of ninety-one-day maturity, to avoid the possibility of the Federal Reserve's trying to establish or support a given pattern of open market yields.

## OPERATION NUDGE OF THE EARLY 1960s

With the inauguration of John F. Kennedy as president, and the arrival in Washington of a new set of economic advisers from the academic community, the scales tipped against the bills only advocates. The doctrine was publicly abandoned in February 1961 after a conference in the White House of leading Federal Reserve officials meeting with top Treasury officials and the new members of the Council of Economic Advisers. The new approach then inaugurated came to be called "operation nudge" or "operation twist," which gave much more importance to the influence of the central bank on the interest rate structure than had been given by the monetary authorities in the 1950s.

It appeared to the new administration officials in early 1961 that the United States was faced with two opposing public policy problems in the economic sphere. At home, there was still a mild economic recession, while the years of the 1950s as a whole had been marked by relatively low real rates of economic growth. The new administration wanted very strongly to increase this real rate of economic growth, as well as to move out of the recession. A vigorous monetary policy to assist fiscal policy efforts would have involved considerable credit easing and lowering of interest rates.

By 1961 there was also a serious problem in the American balance of payments. Despite a sizable favorable balance of trade (i.e., excess of exports of merchandise goods over imports of merchandise goods) there was still an overall deficit in the American balance of payments. This deficit existed because of government grants and loans abroad, either for military assistance to allies or to encourage economic growth in some of the developing nations, and because of a considerable outflow of private capital. Some of this outflow was for making direct investments in other countries and some of it was for short- or long-term investments in the money and capital markets of foreign countries.

### Higher Short Rates and Lower Long Rates

The answer seemed to be to drop the bills only doctrine and try to "nudge" short-term rates up and to "nudge" long-term bond yields down. Critics of this policy believed that this was an attempt to "twist" the interest rate structure into a pattern contrary to that which could be expected from the operation of normal market forces. The Treasury, however, cooperated with the Federal Reserve in its effort to push up Treasury bill yields by increasing the amount of the weekly bill tenders. From December 1960, when the amount of Treasury bills outstanding totaled $39.5 billion, until December 1965, when the total outstanding was $60.2 billion, the increase in Treasury bills was $20.7 billion, a rise of more than 50 percent. This amounted to two thirds of the increase in gross federal debt in this period, which increased by $31 billion.

At the same time that the Treasury bill rate was being pushed up for balance of payments reasons, the long-term end of the interest rate structure was being held down. The Federal Reserve assisted in this objective by providing much of the desired increase in bank reserves by buying coupon government securities, rather than concentrating all its purchases in the Treasury bill market. The purchase of government notes and bonds helped to push up their prices and thus lower their yields, as well as to give the banks more reserves. The banks could then purchase more government securities and make more loans.

## CREDIT RESTRAINT IN THE LATTER HALF OF THE 1960s

The monetary-credit policy of the Federal Reserve, which was desirous of encouraging low long-term interest rates during the business expansion of the first half of the 1960s, turned toward a policy of credit restraint as American involvement in the war in Vietnam escalated during the spring and summer of 1965. Furthermore, until fiscal year 1969, the federal government financed much of the rising military expenditures through budget deficits, which necessitated large Treasury borrowings in the money and capital markets. In fiscal year 1968 alone, the budget deficit totaled more than $25 billion and resulted in the government's borrowing more than $23 billion in that fiscal year. The government's need for borrowed funds was superimposed on the private borrowing needs of an already expanding economy.

### High Interest Rates in 1966

In an effort to curtail some less urgent borrowing needs in an increasingly inflationary environment, the Federal Reserve began curtailing the growth of bank reserves and the money supply. The American central bank also took steps to increase the cost of borrowing by permitting interest rates to rise. Total bank reserves, which had risen by 5 percent in

1965, were held down to a small 1 percent increase in 1966, which proved to be a year of considerable credit restraint. The money supply likewise grew by only 2 percent in 1966, which was far below the 5 percent growth rate of 1965.

## Higher Interest Rates in 1969–1970

Five years after the escalation in Vietnam in 1965, the level of interest rates on all kinds of borrowing for all maturities was sharply higher and at new record levels. The prime rate for the best business borrowers at commercial banks, which had remained at 4½ percent from August 1960 to December 1965, was subsequently increased a number of times until it reached 8½ percent in June 1969. The discount rate of the Federal Reserve itself, which had fallen to 3 percent in September 1960, began a process of upward adjustment in mid-1963. By April 1969, it had reached 6 percent.

The ninety-one day Treasury bill rate, which was still slightly below 4 percent in September 1960, was yielding 8 percent by early 1970. The prime commercial paper rate was 9 percent in early 1970. Long-term government securities were yielding 7 percent, and the average yield for all corporate bonds was about 8 percent. Federal funds traded at a rate of over 9 percent in early 1970. Credit restraint was finally beginning to bite.

## Severe Credit Restraint in 1969

The signal for the new period of credit restraint had been given in early December 1968, when the Federal Reserve Banks raised their discount rates to 5½ percent. The discount rate rose again in April 1969 to 6 percent and reserve requirements of member banks were hiked. By the late spring of 1969, negative free reserves had reached the $1,250 million level and interest rates moved to record-high levels. The renewed credit restraint that had begun in late 1968 in response to an acceleration of inflationary forces in the economy of 1968 and 1969 thus became quite severe in the second quarter of 1969. This move toward credit restraint in late 1968 had been necessitated by the quickened pace of price increases, which during 1968 rose about 4.7 percent at the retail level.

## ALTERNATING EASE AND RESTRAINT IN THE 1970s

Alternating periods of credit ease and restraint continued in the 1970s, as they had in the 1950s and 1960s. A greater emphasis on controlling the growth of monetary aggregates after January 1970 did not lessen the concern of the monetary authorities with changes in interest rates. The high levels of interest rates and slow growth in the money supply of the severe period of credit restraint in 1969 were replaced by lower interest rates and a greater expansion in bank reserves and the money supply in 1970.

The easing in 1970 from the severe restraint of 1969 took the form both of easing in the money market (lower interest rates) and moderate growth in money and bank credit (i.e., higher rates of growth in these monetary aggregates than in 1969). The money stock grew at an annual rate of 5.4 percent in 1970, as compared with 3.2 percent in 1969, and bank credit expanded at a strong 7.4 percent, as compared with a growth of only 4 percent the previous year. The credit restraint "stop" of 1969 was followed by the credit ease "go" of 1970.

Further growth in the money supply at a substantial rate occurred in the 1970s. The first three years of the decade saw an acceleration in the rate of growth of the money supply (M1, or currency plus demand deposits of commercial banks) from 5.4 percent in 1970 to 6.2 percent in 1971 and 8.4 percent in 1972. In the years 1973–1975, the rate of growth in the money supply fell each year to 6.2 percent, 5 percent, and finally to the low rate of 4.4 percent in 1975.

From 1976 to 1978, money growth again accelerated to 5.7 percent, 7.9 percent, and 8.2 percent, respectively. (Data for 1978, 1979, and 1980 are for the redefinition of the money supply to M-1B, which is currency plus all transactions accounts plus nonbank travelers' checks.) In 1979 and 1980, the rate of growth fell somewhat to 7.7 percent and 7.3 percent, respectively; these were still very high rates of growth of money. Because the velocity of money also increased in the second half of the 1970s, it is not surprising that the rate of inflation in the price level increased again to double-digit levels in 1979–1980 as it had earlier in 1973–1974.

## EMPHASIS ON MONETARY AGGREGATES IN THE 1970s AND 1980s

Despite the often unfavorable outcome for the economy of high rates of inflation in the 1970s, the Federal Reserve usually expressed its intention of reducing inflationary forces. Early in the decade, the Fed abandoned its policy of focusing on interest rates in the money market, which had been typical of the 1960s, in favor of emphasizing controlling the growth rate of key monetary aggregates such as various definitions of the money supply, bank reserves, and bank credit. The FOMC in both the 1970s and early 1980s formulated its instructions to the Trading Desk (the Securities Department of the Federal Reserve Bank of New York) mainly in the form of a range of desired rates of growth in these various monetary aggregates because it believed there was a direct linkage between these aggregates and the price level and other macroeconomic aggregates, such as total output, total employment, and total income.

***FOMC Meeting of January 15, 1970***    On January 15, 1970, the FOMC specifically announced that it would henceforth put greater emphasis on controlling the rate of growth of key monetary aggregates. "The Committee concluded that in the conduct of open market operations increased stress should be placed on the objective of achieving modest growth in the monetary aggregates, with about equal weight being given to bank credit and money stock."[7] Throughout the decade this greater stress on controlling monetary aggregates was followed, though sometimes this meant controlling bank reserves, adjusted, so that only reserves required for private deposits were considered; sometimes it meant unborrowed bank reserves; and at other times it meant various definitions of money (e.g., M1, M2, or later M1-A or M1-B).

***FOMC Meeting of October 6, 1979***    Despite this professed desire to stress control of the growth of various monetary aggregates, the Federal Reserve still desired to control certain money market rates, especially the federal funds rate, which is the interest rate on excess bank reserves traded between banks for periods as short as twenty-four hours. But at the end of the decade, on October 6, 1979 ("Saturday Night Special"), the Fed decided to permit much greater fluctuations in the federal funds rate in order to try to curb the excessive inflationary pressures that had developed after the mid-1970s. This meant still greater stress on controlling monetary aggregates. As the minutes of the FOMC showed, "most members strongly supported a shift in the conduct of open market operations to an approach placing emphasis on supplying the volume of bank reserves estimated to be consistent with the desired rates of growth in monetary aggregates, while permitting much greater fluctuations in the federal funds rate than heretofore."[8]

***Key Monetary Aggregates by 1980s***    By the early 1980s, the Federal Reserve had targets for six monetary aggregates, which are shown in Figure 16–1 for 1979 and 1980. Despite substantial ranges for targeted growth for these monetary aggregates in 1980, this figure shows that the Federal Reserve had considerable difficulty in hitting these targets.

M1-B, for example, the most commonly used definition of money

[7]Board of Governors of the Federal Reserve System, *Annual Report 1970*, pp. 96–97.
[8]Board of Governors of the Federal Reserve System, *Annual Report 1979*, p. 202.

**Figure 16–1    Targets and Growth in the Monetary Aggregates, 1979–1980**

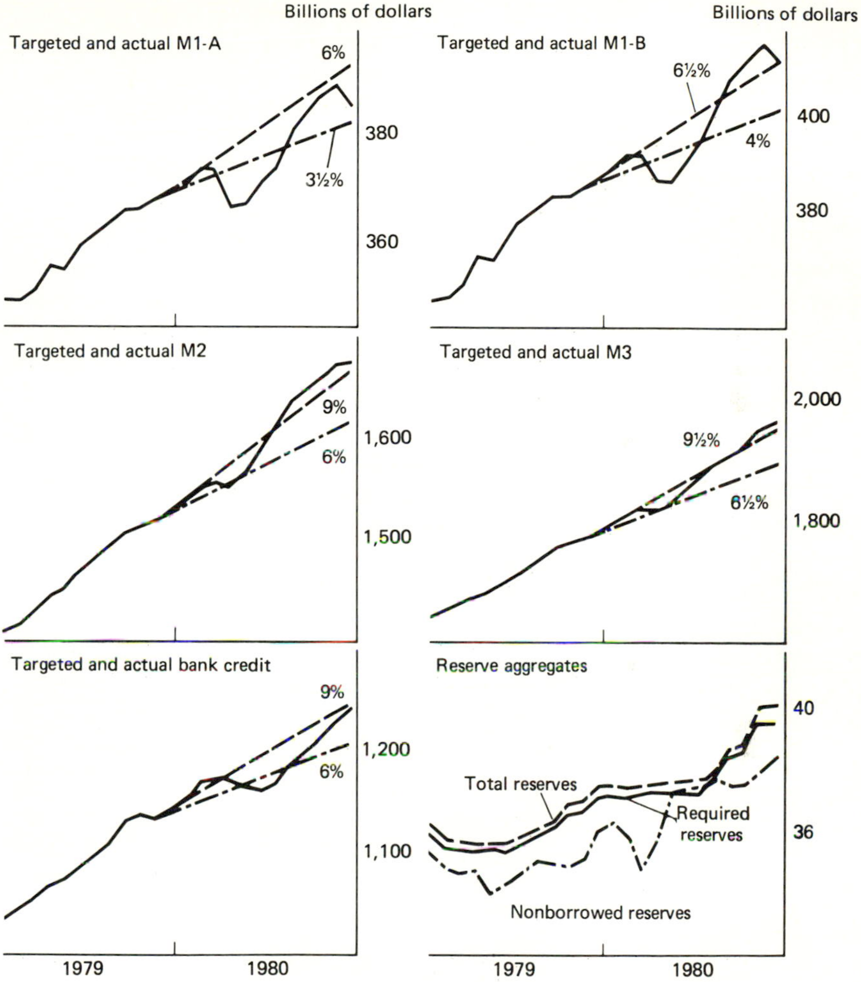

SOURCE: Board of Governors of the Federal Reserve System, *Annual Report 1980*, p. 17.

until M1 replaced it in 1982, grew both at a sharply lower rate than the target in the second quarter of 1980 and at a sharply higher rate in the second half of the year. The average rate of growth for the year was 7.3 percent, which was clearly outside the desired ceiling of 6.5 percent. The other monetary aggregates also seemed quite difficult to control within the very short run, though some of them (e.g., M2) seemed to have an average rate of growth for the entire year that was closer to their targeted range than the results for M1-B.

Similar information regarding the growth of the various monetary aggregates is shown in Table 16–1, although the targets for these aggregates are not shown. Data are given for 1978, 1979, and 1980 and by quarters for the last quarter of 1979 and the four quarters of 1980. Perhaps the most striking thing about these data is the considerable variability in growth of the monetary aggregates. Even by year this is true, though the quarter-to-quarter variability in some cases is almost startling.

The most commonly used concept of money in this period, M1-B, shows a deceleration in growth rate in 1978, 1979, and 1980 from 8.2 percent, to 7.7 percent, to 7.3 percent. But in 1980, the quarterly changes in the rate of growth of this measure of money are quite substantial. A slow growth rate in M1-B of 4.9 percent in the fourth quarter of 1979 and of 5.8 percent in the first quarter of 1980 turned into a drop of 2.6 percent in the second quarter. In the third and fourth quarters, on the other hand, very strong growth rates of 14.6 percent and 10.8 percent, respectively, were recorded. The other measures of money in Table 16–1 exhibited similar variability in their rates of growth.

**Table 16–1   Reserves and Monetary Aggregates (based on seasonally adjusted data unless otherwise noted, percents)[a]**

| Item | 1978 | 1979 | 1980 | 1979 Q4 | 1980 Q1 | Q2 | Q3 | Q4 |
|---|---|---|---|---|---|---|---|---|
| Member bank reserves[b] | | | | | | | | |
| Total...................... | 6.2 | 2.6 | 7.1 | 11.6 | 4.3 | .4 | 6.7 | 16.5 |
| Nonborrowed............... | 6.3 | .3 | 7.8 | 5.1 | 3.3 | 7.4 | 12.4 | 7.2 |
| Required .................. | 6.3 | 2.4 | 6.8 | 10.4 | 5.1 | .7 | 5.8 | 15.2 |
| Monetary base[c] ............. | 9.2 | 7.8 | 8.8 | 9.3 | 7.8 | 5.2 | 9.9 | 11.2 |
| Concepts of money[d] | | | | | | | | |
| M1-A....................... | 7.4 | 5.0 | 5.0 | 4.5 | 4.6 | −4.4 | 11.5 | 8.1 |
| M1-B....................... | 8.2 | 7.7 | 7.3 | 4.9 | 5.8 | −2.6 | 14.6 | 10.8 |
| M2......................... | 8.4 | 9.0 | 9.8 | 7.2 | 7.3 | 5.6 | 16.0 | 9.1 |
| M3......................... | 11.3 | 9.8 | 9.9 | 9.1 | 8.0 | 5.8 | 13.0 | 11.6 |
| Nontransaction components of M2 | | | | | | | | |
| Total (M2 minus M1-B) ....... | 8.5 | 9.4 | 10.7 | 7.9 | 7.9 | 8.3 | 16.4 | 8.5 |
| Small time deposits......... | 16.2 | 23.1 | 15.3 | 25.8 | 17.4 | 23.7 | 1.0 | 16.3 |
| Savings deposits ........... | −.5 | −11.9 | −4.6 | −21.4 | −20.3 | −23.3 | 27.8 | −.9 |
| Money market mutual funds shares (n.s.a.) .......... | 163.9 | 324.2 | 90.3 | 120.0 | 151.9 | 82.7 | 75.7 | −15.5 |
| Overnight RPs and overnight Eurodollar deposits (n.s.a.) .............. | 25.4 | 17.2 | 21.8 | −33.1 | 9.0 | −57.4 | 135.6 | 15.4 |

---

**Table 16–1** *(Continued)*

| Item | 1978 | 1979 | 1980 | 1979 Q4 | 1980 Q1 | 1980 Q2 | 1980 Q3 | 1980 Q4 |
|---|---|---|---|---|---|---|---|---|
| MEMO (change in billions of dollars) | | | | | | | | |
| Managed liabilities at commercial banks . . . . . . . . . . . . . . . . . . . . . . | 77.8 | 57.7 | 12.4 | 10.5 | 11.3 | −3.3 | −12.5 | 17.0 |
| Large time deposits, gross . . . . . | 50.4 | 19.6 | 22.0 | 10.7 | 6.3 | 6.2 | −4.3 | 13.8 |
| Nondeposit funds . . . . . . . . . . . | 27.4 | 38.1 | −9.6 | −.2 | 5.0 | −9.5 | −8.2 | 3.2 |
| Net due to foreign related institutions . . . . . . . . . . . . . . | 6.9 | 25.1 | −23.4 | 0 | −2.3 | −8.6 | −11.5 | −1.0 |
| Otherᵉ . . . . . . . . . . . . . . . . . . . . | 20.5 | 13.0 | 13.8 | −.2 | 7.3 | −.9 | 3.2 | 4.2 |
| U.S. government deposits at commercial banks . . . . . . . . . . | 3.3 | 1.5 | .6 | −4.0 | 1.6 | −1.6 | 2.9 | −2.3 |

ᵃChanges are calculated from the average amounts outstanding in each quarter.

ᵇAnnual rates of change in reserve measures have been adjusted for regulatory changes in reserve requirements.

ᶜConsists of total reserves (member bank reserve balances in the current week plus vault cash held two weeks earlier), currency in circulation (currency outside the U.S. Treasury, Federal Reserve Banks, and the vaults of commercial banks), and vault cash of nonmember banks.

ᵈM1-A is currency plus private demand deposits net of deposits due to foreign commercial banks and official institutions. M1-B is M1-A plus other checkable deposits (negotiable order of withdrawal accounts, accounts subject to automatic transfer service, credit union share draft balances, and demand deposits at mutual savings banks). M2 is M1-B plus overnight repurchase agreements (RPs) issued by commercial banks, overnight Eurodollar deposits held by U.S. nonbank residents at Caribbean branches of U.S. banks, money market mutual fund shares, and savings and small time deposits at all depository institutions. M3 is M2 plus large time deposits at all depository institutions and term RPs issued by commercial banks and savings and loan associations.

ᵉConsists of borrowings from other than commercial banks through federal funds purchased and securities sold under repurchase agreements plus loans sold to affiliates, loans sold under repurchase agreements, and other borrowings. 1980 Q4 estimated.

**n.s.a. Not seasonally adjusted.**

SOURCE: Board of Governors of the Federal Reserve System, *Annual Report 1980*, p. 15.

---

# EVOLUTION OF MONETARY POLICY

As we have seen in this chapter, monetary policy, as determined and executed in Great Britain by the Bank of England and in the United States by the Federal Reserve System, has changed from decade to decade. It has also changed from year to year and sometimes even from month to month. The monetary policy problems of the 1930s were not the same problems faced by these monetary authorities during World War II. Likewise, the problems of the 1960s, 1970s, and 1980s have differed from decade to decade. In the 1960s the earlier problems of stability were replaced by a greater concern for economic growth. By the 1970s, the trade-off problem between greater growth and lower rates of unemployment, on the one hand, and the stabilization of the price level, on the other, seemed very important to the monetary authorities. By the 1980s, both lower inflation rates and higher real growth rates were being sought.

As the policy orientation changed, so too did the use of short-run objectives in the use of open market operations. In particular, in the 1980s there has been a greater emphasis on seeking to attain the desired rate of growth in various monetary aggregates, or various definitions of the money supply, such as M1 and M2. Concern with stability in the money market and a day-by-day concern with certain key money market rates such as the federal funds rate since October 6, 1979, has been regarded as less important by the monetary authorities.

## Questions for Discussion

1. Discuss some of the important indicators of monetary policy. Which group of indicators has come to be regarded as the most important in the 1980s? Why?
2. Why was minimization of variation in short-term interest rates traditionally regarded as a responsibility of central banks? What is the major problem with focusing monetary policy on this particular intermediate goal?
3. Discuss and define the different monetary aggregates used as targets by the Federal Reserve in the 1980s. Which aggregate would you recommend to the monetary authorities? Why?
4. Discuss the four major policy goals of the Federal Reserve System and indicate the nature of the "trade-off" problem. Which goals, do you think, are most important? Why?
5. Discuss some of the difficulties in achieving price-level stabilization by the Federal Reserve in the 1970s and 1980s. Illustrate by giving examples (e.g., 1973–1974 and 1979–1980).
6. Discuss the modern organization of the Bank of England. What does the term *"monetary authorities"* mean in Great Britain? Why does the Bank of England control the money supply through its control over interest rates?
7. What were the purposes of the reforms of monetary policy in September 1971 by the Bank of England called Competition and Credit Control? Why weren't these reforms completely successful?
8. Discuss the role of the Federal Reserve System in the 1920s. Why was there so much optimism that this new American central bank would prevent another financial panic and depression?
9. What, in your opinion, accounted for the inability of the Federal Reserve to prevent, or reverse, the Depression of the 1930s, which began in the fall of 1929? (Include in your discussion the Keynesian diagnosis of the failure of central banking in the 1930s.)

10. Discuss the consequences of the Federal Reserve continuing its World War II policy of supporting the price of government securities into the postwar period. Why do you think that this policy was continued into the postwar period? Do you think that this support policy was justified?
11. What led to the accord of March 4, 1951, between the Treasury and the Federal Reserve System? What implications did this new accord have for American central banking?
12. Contrast the "bills only" doctrine of the 1950s with "operation nudge," which followed in the early 1960s. Discuss these two policies critically in the light of different economic policy problems as perceived by the central bank in these two different periods.
13. Why was the expansionary credit policy of the Federal Reserve during the first half of the 1960s changed to one of credit restraint in most of the second half of the decade? What were some of the effects of this latter policy of credit restraint?
14. Discuss the important similarities and differences of the policy of credit restraint in 1973–1974 with the "credit crunch" of 1966 and the even more severe credit restraint of 1969. To what extend do you believe that these earlier experiences affected the monetary policy posture of 1973–1974? Why and when did this period of credit restraint end?
15. Discuss the conduct of open market operations since the "Saturday Night Special" of October 6, 1979. How do you account for the extreme variability in the growth of monetary aggregates in 1980 and also of interest rates in that year? Why was the experience somewhat better in 1981?

# Selected Bibliography for Further Reading

## Books and Monographs

THE AMERICAN ASSEMBLY, COLUMBIA UNIVERSITY, *United States Monetary Policy,* 2d ed. (New York: Praeger, 1964).

BOARD OF GOVERNORS OF THE FEDERAL RESERVE SYSTEM, *Monetary Policy Objectives for 1981* (Washington D.C.: Feb. 25–26, 1981).

——, *Monetary Policy Objectives for 1981, Midyear Review of the Federal Reserve Board* (Washington D.C.: July 21, 1981).

CONRAD, JOSEPH W., *An Introduction to the Theory of Interest* (Berkeley, Calif.: University of California Press, 1959).

HANSEN, ALVIN H., *Monetary Theory and Fiscal Policy* (New York: McGraw-Hill, 1949).

JOHNSON, HARRY G., *Essays in Monetary Economics* (Cambridge, Mass: Harvard University Press, 1967).

MAYER, THOMAS, *Monetary Policy in the United States* (New York: Random House, 1968).

## Article

Humphrey, Thomas M., "Changing Views of the Phillips Curve," *Monthly Review*, Federal Reserve Bank of Richmond, 59, No. 7 (July 1973), pp. 2–13.

## Federal Reserve Publications

See also the annual reports of the Board of Governors and the Federal Reserve Bank of New York for comprehensive summaries of monetary policy each year. For other discussions, see the *Federal Reserve Bulletin* of the Board of Governors and the monthly or quarterly reviews of each of the twelve Federal Reserve Banks.

Money is more readily advanced upon them than upon any other species of obligation; especially when they are made payable within so short a period as two or three months after their date.

**THE WEALTH OF NATIONS**

# CHAPTER 17

# Open Market Operations and Monetary Aggregates

The most important weapon at the disposal of the monetary authorities in controlling the rate of growth of the monetary aggregates in order to influence the level of output, employment, and the price level is open market operations. When the Federal Reserve buys or sells government securities (e.g., Treasury bills) in the money market, there is an impact on the price, and thus on the yield, of such money market instruments. In the 1980s, the major emphasis in the conduct of open market operations is on the control of the rate of growth of monetary aggregates through their linkages with the growth in nonborrowed bank reserves directly affected by open market operations. The tone and functioning of the money and credit markets (stressed so much in the 1960s) is now given relatively little weight by the Open Market Committee and the Trading Desk.

The Trading Desk usually simply offsets the effects of other factors on bank reserves when it engages in direct purchases or sales of government securities or when it temporarily supplies added reserves through repurchase agreements or temporarily reduces bank reserves through matched sale-purchase agreements. At other times, the Federal Reserve is concerned with slowing down or speeding up the rate of growth of the monetary aggregates. Such changes in the availability of added bank reserves from the Federal Reserve have an initial impact on the price of excess bank reserves being loaned (the federal funds rate). Subsequently, the impact of the changed availability of bank reserves affects other interest rates and bank lending and investing.

The growth of various monetary aggregates such as M1 and M2 is thereby varied because the total of bank liabilities such as demand and time deposits changes when the total of bank earning assets changes. Before examining the details of open market operations, however, let us first discuss the structure and functioning of the group that makes policy for open market operations. This is the Federal Open Market Committee, the chief policymaking group of the Federal Reserve System, because, as noted, open market operations is the major tool for implementing monetary policy.

## THE FEDERAL OPEN MARKET COMMITTEE

The Federal Open Market Committee, or the FOMC as it is more commonly known, was formally established by statute when the Federal Reserve Act was amended in 1935. At that time, it was provided that the seven members of the Board of Governors of the Federal Reserve System in Washington, D.C., should be members, along with five presidents or first vice-presidents chosen from the twelve Federal Reserve Banks. It was provided by law, as amended in 1942, that the method of selection should be as follows:

> One by the board of directors of the Federal Reserve Bank of New York; one by the boards of directors of the Federal Reserve Banks of Boston, Philadelphia, and Richmond; one by the boards of directors of the Federal Reserve Banks of Cleveland and Chicago; one by the boards of directors of the Federal Reserve Banks of Atlanta, Dallas, and St. Louis; and one by the boards of directors of the Federal Reserve Banks of Minneapolis, Kansas City, and San Francisco.[1]

---

[1]Board of Governors of the Federal Reserve System, *The Federal Reserve Act As Amended Through December 31, 1956* (Washington, D.C.: 1957), p. 41.

## Members of the Federal
## Open Market Committee

The selection procedure has worked out in practice so that the president of the Federal Reserve Bank of New York is always a member of the FOMC, whereas the presidents of the Banks of Chicago and Cleveland alternate as official FOMC members every other year. The remaining nine Banks, which are grouped together into three groups, are on a three-year regular cycle. The remaining nine presidents either are officially on the FOMC this year, were last year, or will be next year. This applies to the five Federal Reserve Bank *de jure* members, as indicated. The "year" for FOMC membership begins on March 1. All twelve presidents of the twelve Federal Reserve Banks, or the first vice-presidents in those instances when the president of the Bank involved is unable to go, attend all the meetings of the FOMC and participate as full *de facto* members. Formal voting, however, is restricted to the five members from the Federal Reserve Banks and the seven members of the Board of Governors.

*Meetings of the FOMC*    Whereas the law provides only that the FOMC should meet at least four times a year, it became customary, after the executive committee of the FOMC was abolished in June 1955 until the end of 1980 for the full *de facto* membership of the FOMC (nineteen officials ) to meet in Washington approximately every month on a Tuesday for an all-day meeting. During the twenty years from 1936 to 1955 that the FOMC had an executive committee, the full membership of the FOMC usually met only the requisite four times a year. One important implication of the abolishment of the executive committee was that thereafter the attendance of a representative of each Federal Reserve Bank was required at a meeting in Washington every month to consider the appropriate national monetary policy that should prevail in the weeks and months ahead.

About a year after the much greater stress on controlling monetary aggregates by the FOMC at its meeting of October 6, 1979, the FOMC decided to hold about eight regular meetings each year, with telephone conferences when needed. In 1981, the FOMC began to meet regularly twice a quarter, one meeting near the beginning of the quarter and the other in the middle. The first quarterly FOMC meeting (e.g., in late December for the first quarter of the new year) establishes short-run quarterly targets for the monetary aggregates M1 and M2 and an appropriate range of federal funds rate. The midquarterly meeting, plus any telephone conferences if needed, can make any corrections in these short-run targets.

For example, at its meeting of February 2–3, 1981, the FOMC noted: "If it appeared during the period before the next regular meeting that fluctuations in the federal funds rate, taken over a period of time, within a range of 15 to 20 per cent were likely to be inconsistent with the monetary and related reserve paths, the Manager for Domestic Operations was promptly to notify the chairman, who would then decide whether the situation called for supplementary instructions from the Committee"[2] A federal funds rate consistently near the bottom, or at the top, of the specified range could lead to such a notification, which might result in a telephone conference of the FOMC to determine whether any supplementary instructions to the Trading Desk were needed. If not ,the short-run targets would be routinely reviewed anyway at the next regular FOMC meeting.

Two of the eight regular FOMC meetings are particularly important. The regular meeting in early February of each year decides upon fourth-quarter to fourth-quarter targets for the monetary aggregates, even though those targets may have been discussed at the prior meeting. The FOMC meeting in midsummer (early July) confirms the annual targets for that year and even sets preliminary targets for the next year.

Updated economic forecasts are prepared for the FOMC meetings by the board staff but are particularly important for the February and July meetings. For the July meeting, a six-quarter forecast must be available, whereas a four-quarter forecast is enough for the February meeting. Updated **quarterly forecasts** are also needed throughout the year. Each forecast for the period ahead is conditional upon assumed rates of growth of the various monetary aggregates. A separate set of short-run financial forecasts, which associate interest rates with alternative paths of growth of the monetary aggregates, is also prepared by the staff for the FOMC.

Data covering the major economic and financial developments in recent weeks are organized into three major detailed staff reports distributed to members of the FOMC ahead of the meeting, which are then supplemented and brought up to date by oral briefings during the meeting. The three written staff reports focus on (1) key developments in domestic business, (2) recent changes in domestic financial markets, and (3) recent developments in the U.S. balance of payments.

***Procedures of the Open Market Committee***   Before these three oral reports by members of the staff of the Board of Governors are given to the FOMC meeting, reports have been made by the special manager of the system's open market account in charge of foreign currency operations and by the manager of the open market account. After each of

[2]Board of Governors of the Federal Reserve System, *Federal Reserve Bulletin*, April 1981, p. 317.

these reports by operating managers for the FOMC, the committee is asked to "approve, ratify, and confirm" what has been done since the previous FOMC meeting. Then the detailed staff reports on recent economic and financial conditions are given.

After these oral staff reports are presented, each board member and bank president—nonvoting as well as voting—presents his views in turn around the table. The first comments are always made by the president of the Federal Reserve Bank of New York. The order of subsequent comments is changed from meeting to meeting, except that the chairman of the Board of Governors always speaks last. In addition to comments on current economic and financial conditions at the national level, each president reports on any significant recent economic developments in his district. Furthermore, each committee member (both presidents and board members) presents his views on monetary policy by indicating whether he believes that money market conditions and the volume of reserves available to member banks should be kept unchanged, or changed in a particular direction.

References to pressures on interest rates, the rate of expansion of bank credit and growth in other liquid assets, as well as the latest price indices, unemployment data, and the index of industrial output, with their implications for overall monetary policy, are also often referred to by committee members. After the other committee members have spoken in turn, the chairman of the committee, who is also the chairman of the Board of Governors of the system, summarizes the points of view presented, along with what appears to be the consensus on open market policy.

***The FOMC Domestic Policy Directive to the Trading Desk***     After this summary by the chairman, attention is directed to any change in the current directive of the FOMC to the Trading Desk at the Federal Reserve Bank of New York, where all actual open market operations for the entire system are conducted. It is not uncommon for the **domestic policy directive** to be modified a number of times throughout the year. Before this directive is changed, however, all points of view are discussed. Then the voting members of the committee signify their approval or disapproval of any proposed change. An especially close review of all continuing directives and operating procedures is made by the FOMC at its annual organization meeting in early March, when the new *de jure* members formally become part of the FOMC.

The main purpose of the domestic policy directive is to establish guidelines for the Account Manager to follow in day-to-day operations in affecting the availability of bank reserves and the degree of ease or firmness desired in the money market until the next committee meeting, normally in four weeks. It is not feasible or desirable for the FOMC to direct the manager as to the exact dollar volume of securities he should buy or sell in the market until the next meeting.

The committee determines the appropriate quarterly, or annual, growth rates of M1 and M2 and so instructs the **Manager for Domestic Operations** in New York City. A path of nonborrowed reserves appropriate for the selected targets of M1 and M2 is then prepared by the staff because the amount of monetary reserves available to depository institutions ultimately determines the growth rate of the monetary aggregates. A range of federal funds rate, as already noted, is also selected by the committee to include in its instructions to the Trading Desk. The range of federal funds rates serves to monitor developments on the path of nonborrowed reserves and M1 and M2, rather than serving as a target as was true before October 6, 1979.

### Move from an Accommodative Money Market Policy to an Emphasis on Monetary Aggregates

The greater emphasis on the control of monetary aggregates in the 1980s was anticipated in part in the 1970s. This was first indicated in January 1970, but an even stronger emphasis on controlling monetary aggregates was decided upon at the FOMC meeting of October 6, 1979. When it emphasized interest rates and credit conditions in the money market in the 1960s, the Federal Reserve had acted in a passive manner designed to accommodate changes in the demand for money and credit. The other possibility, which was emphasized particularly in the 1970s and early 1980s, was that of aggressively trying to influence monetary variables that would ultimately be linked to real output, employment, and the price level.

Under the **accommodative policy,** increases in interest rates caused by higher borrowing demands resulted in the Federal Reserve's increasing bank reserves. The borrower would then be determining growth in both bank reserves and bank deposits. This permitted the money supply to grow in a manner desired by the users of money. Under these conditions, as in the 1960s, it was difficult to argue that Federal Reserve monetary policy was really an **exogenous policy** (i.e., external to forces operating in the economy).

Even when the Federal Reserve moved toward a more conscious impact on the money supply, rather than on market interest rates, it had to realize that it did not control the money stock directly. What the Federal Reserve could control was unborrowed bank reserves. Even total bank reserves could be changed by variations in member bank borrowing, which in turn was not directly controlled by the monetary authorities.

Both the Federal Reserve and various market forces interact to determine the money supply at any given time. The Treasury, foreigners, banks, and the nonbank public all interact with the Federal Reserve to determine the actual stock of money and the short-run growth in the money supply. Over a period of time longer than a week or a month, however, the impact of the Federal Reserve can be more decisive. The Federal Reserve does have the tools, especially in open market operations, to offset other factors impacting on member bank reserves and the growth in the money supply.

It is quite practical, then, for the Federal Reserve to chart and control the growth in the money supply over a period of several quarters or even a year. The longer the time period, the easier it is for the Federal Reserve to offset other influences, including its own misjudgments of earlier forces, in order to get the desired result. In the very short run, such as a **reserve week** (Thursday to Wednesday), or two weeks after February 2, 1984, an operating target such as the federal funds rate on unborrowed bank reserves prior to October 6, 1979, was used as a **proxy** for the desired growth in the money supply. After October 6, 1979, greater stress was put on short-run control of unborrowed reserves.

If the amount of unborrowed reserves that the Trading Desk supplies to the banking system is not what is desired by the banking system, individual banks will be forced to borrow reserves in the federal funds market from other banks with excess reserves or from the regional discount window of a Federal Reserve Bank. Federal Reserve restraint, or ease, then is directly reflected in the availability and cost of reserves for depository institutions. Such variability can be seen in the two graphs shown in Figure 17–1, which shows the extreme volatility in the federal funds rate and in **member bank borrowing** for thirteen months—the twelve months of 1980 and January 1981. Let us now turn to the implementation of open market operations by the Trading Desk.

# THE FEDERAL RESERVE TRADING DESK

The Trading Desk is the operating arm of the FOMC and does the actual buying and selling of government securities. In carrying out these open market operations, the Manager of the System Account, who is a vice-president of the Federal Reserve Bank of New York, must have some latitude in developing tactical or operational policies. After he has secured advice from other officers in the department and discussed his plans with at least one member of the FOMC, the manager of the account actually decides whether the Trading Desk will buy or sell government securities in what amount on a particular day. On some days the decision is to neither buy nor sell, but that decision requires as much considera-

**Figure 17–1    Money Market Conditions and Borrowed Reserves**

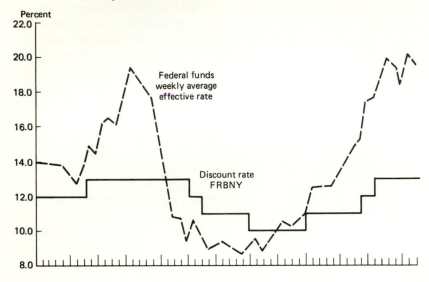

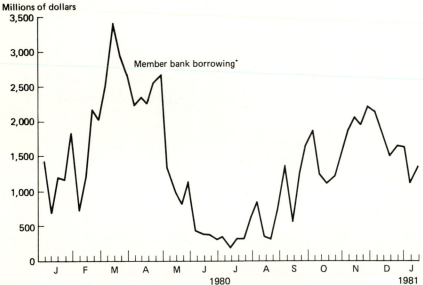

\* Excludes emergency borrowing by one large
regional bank.

SOURCE: Federal Reserve Bank of New York, *Quarterly Review*, Summer 1981, p. 71.

tion as one involving a direct buying or selling of government securities. In every case, the manager of the Trading Desk tries to stay within the range of the monetary aggregate targets provided by the FOMC.

One fundamental difficulty in the Trading Desk's hitting precisely any of the targets formulated for it by the FOMC is that the only variable completely and directly under the control of the Open Market Account Manager is the size and composition of the account's portfolio. But for various reasons, operating instructions have never been formulated exactly in these terms. Hence, trying to hit the specified monetary aggregate growth rate targets means that the Trading Desk must adjust its portfolio to offset the effects of noncontrolled items (e.g., Federal Reserve float on money market conditions or the money supply). Other short-run factors that affect the money and credit markets and must also be considered by the Federal Reserve Bank of New York in order to avoid churning the money and credit markets include the following: (1) the intensity of the demand for, and the depth of supply of, federal funds; (2) the amount of money needed by government security dealers and their sources and costs of financing; and (3) day-to-day trends in market prices and yields for Treasury securities.

Only if the Trading Desk could forecast the uncontrolled variables with complete accuracy could it hit its targets precisely in the short run. Because such precise forecasts are not possible, a range is invariably specified by the FOMC for the target variable and even that is not always achieved. Far more accurate results seem to have resulted in the 1970s from the Trading Desk's control over the federal funds rate than its control over the growth of monetary aggregates. This was true because the Trading Desk can control rather precisely the margin of available bank reserves in the banking system and the money market through outright transactions, repurchase, or matched sale-purchase agreements. Nevertheless, the FOMC abandoned the federal funds rate target on October 6, 1979.

Growth in bank credit, however, and the resultant growth in both M1 and M2 are affected not only by changes in the demand for bank credit but also by changes in the demand for money (which determines the velocity or turnover of money) and by changes in bank demand for excess bank reserves. Participants in the money market such as government securities dealers also have varying rates of change in the demand for credit and even for federal funds.

Sometimes the sum of these random, or unforecast, disturbances in the money market is referred to as "statistical noise." In any event, such uncontrolled factors can seriously distort the Federal Reserve's efforts to control precisely the growth of the money supply in a short-run period such as a week, a month, or a quarter. Over a six-month period and certainly over a period as long as a year, however, the Federal Reserve can be held responsible for the resulting growth in the monetary aggregates. This should be the result that the Federal Reserve wanted, or at least permitted, to happen.

## *Data on Changes in Reserves of Depository Institutions*

Like the FOMC, the Trading Desk relies heavily on collecting and analyzing current data before making its operational decisions. The horizon of the Trading Desk must cover at least the current one-week reserve period because required reserves, excess reserves, and unborrowed reserves are calculated on a daily average basis for this period. Regular reserve projections are developed, however, not only for the current reserve week but for the following several reserve periods as well. The period between regular FOMC meetings is thus bridged by projections on the major factors expected to affect unborrowed reserves. These projections include estimates on such factors as (1) Federal Reserve float, (2) currency in circulation, (3) Treasury operations, (4) gold and foreign account, and (5) other items affecting unborrowed reserves.

Each morning, the daily and weekly estimated factors affecting reserves are revised on the basis of the actual reserve figures then available for the preceding business day. Data are available, for example, for each major depository institution in New York City, Chicago, and some other large cities, showing their borrowings and reserve positions. From these figures some calculations can be made as to the distribution of reserves among these institutions. Daily data are also collected on transactions in the federal funds market by a sample of large money market banks, which help provide information on the demand for and supply of excess reserves, which in turn are affected by the current demand for bank credit. Aggregate daily data showing current inventories, volume of trading, and sources of financing for the government securities dealers are also available to the Trading Desk.

*Trading Desk Influences Depository Institutions' Borrowing*    If monetary policy is not to be changed in the immediate period ahead, open market operations will seek to maintain reasonably stable daily average borrowing of institutions for the current reserve period. If firmer money market conditions and a slower growth in monetary aggregates such as unborrowed reserves and the money supply are desired by the FOMC in order to implement greater credit restraint, open market operations will not completely offset factors tending to reduce reserves, so that the federal funds rate for excess bank reserves will rise. Depository institutions will have to resort to the discount window of their regional Reserve Bank more often for larger amounts. Contrariwise, a move toward credit ease in open market operations implies that a larger amount of reserves will be supplied to the financial system, which will make it possible for many borrowing institutions to repay some of their borrowings from the Federal Reserve and for the monetary aggregates to grow more rapidly.

*Marginal Demand for Reserves of Depository Institutions*     The Manager of the System Account essentially makes judgments each day about the marginal demand for bank reserves, which will be unsatisfied in the federal funds market, and so will likely result in increased borrowings by depository institutions at the various discount windows. Although the manager has forecasts for daily levels of unborrowed reserves for at least four weeks ahead, he focuses first on the expected behavior of such reserves during the current statement period. For a given day, developments in the federal funds market reflect with considerable accuracy the marginal availability of and demand for bank reserves. In effect, the degree of firmness in the federal funds market and depository institutions' borrowing from the Federal Reserve are opposite sides of the same coin.

***The Feel of the Money Market***     The Trading Desk can also develop the feel of the money market through frequent daily conversations with various dealers. Before the market opens each morning, one of the large dealers will make a personal visit to the Federal Reserve Bank of New York and give an evaluation of money market trends. Throughout the trading day, frequent telephone contacts with dealers results in a great deal of additional information on current rate and price quotations in the money market, as well as estimates of customer offerings and demands in the market for federal funds and for government securities. This information received orally helps in the interpretation of the data and projections available on factors affecting bank reserves. Some judgment as to market expectations can also be gained from these frequent contacts with dealers.

***Daily Procedures of the Trading Desk***     Each day, the account manager decides on the course of action in the following sequence of events. At 10 A.M. information is provided on the Treasury's plans for the day. If, for example, the Treasury plans to reduce its balances at Federal Reserve Banks to pay for government expenditures, depository institutions' reserves will be increased, which may require offsetting action by the Trading Desk. Estimates of other uncontrolled factors affecting depository institutions' reserves such as changes in the Federal Reserve bank float (due to uncollected bank checks) and changes in currency outstanding, as well as data on foreign reverse repurchase agreements to be executed in the next few days, are also available. Using this information, the desk constructs an estimate of the supply of reserves expected to be available during this and the next statement period.

The account manager compares this estimate of reserves with the targeted path of various monetary aggregates such as M1 and M2. A preliminary decision is then made on whether to add or drain reserves today and, if so, by how much and for how long. This decision is influenced by the "tone and feel" of the money market during the morning. Finally, the Desk must consider which day this is in terms of the entire statement period, because the market often behaves differently on different days.

The proposed operations for the day may include **outright transactions,** which are usually purchases or sales of Treasury bills, though sometimes Treasury notes or bonds are bought. If reserves are to be supplied temporarily to the market, repurchase agreements with government security dealers are executed, whereas a temporary withdrawal of reserves involves matched sale-purchase agreements wih the same dealers. The open market program recommended by the manager is reviewed during a conference call at about 11 A.M. between Desk staff members, senior officers at the Board of Governors, and a Reserve Bank president currently a voting member of the FOMC. When agreement is reached on the day's open market operations, the transactions, if any, are initiated by about 11:30 A.M.

During the conference call, the account manager first gives a summary of conditions in the money and capital markets as they have developed during the first hour of trading. A summary of reports from the dealers of their volume of trading and their position at the close of business on the preceding day is also presented. Then a review of reserve positions of depository institutions throughout the country, with particular attention paid to the money market banks in New York City and Chicago, is outlined. Finally, after giving a review of other pertinent developments expected during the day, the account manager outlines his proposed operations for that trading day. The other participants in the call may then make any comments they consider appropriate, such as calling attention to other developments they may regard as relevant. After the call is completed, a detailed summary of the telephone conference is placed on the desk of each member of the Board of Governors with the same information telegraphed to the presidents of all the Reserve Banks. This rapid dissemination of information makes it possible for members of the FOMC to make comments or suggestions if they desire to do so.

*Frequent Reports From the Trading Desk*   During the day, hourly reports are made to the Board of Governors on prices and interest rates on government securities. The reports also indicate what operations in the market were undertaken by the Trading Desk during the previous hour. After the market closes at 4:00 P.M. a summary of the day's developments is telephoned to the board. A written summary is prepared daily after the market has closed, which is sent to the Board of Governors and to interested officers of other Reserve Banks. (This daily report is called the "board letter" at the New York Bank and is called the "New York Bank letter" at the board and the other Reserve Banks.)

At the end of each statement period, a detailed report on account operations as well as developments affecting unborrowed reserve positions, the money market, government securities market, and capital market is also sent to the top nineteen officials of the system who are the *de facto* members of the FOMC. Similar reports are prepared up to the close of business on Monday night preceding the Tuesday morning meeting of the FOMC. Full and complete information on the background against which open-market operations are conducted, as well as the details of the operations themselves, is available at all times to all the top officials in the Federal Reserve System responsible for formulating the policy governing the operations of the Trading Desk.

## MONETARY TARGETS FOR OPEN MARKET OPERATIONS

The Federal Reserve operates directly (day by day or at least week by week) in the financial markets to purchase and sell securities (outright, or through repurchase, and matched sale-purchase agreements), which in turn affects interest rates, bank reserves, and the money supply. In order to guide such open market operations, the Federal Reserve needs to select short-run policy targets that will connect actions in the financial markets with ultimate goals (e.g., price-level stability and high rates of real economic growth). Federal Reserve actions, however, have an indirect rather than a direct or immediate impact on output and prices.

In general, as is discussed in detail in Chapter 21 on **macroeconomics,** real output and the average level of prices are determined by the aggregate demand for and the aggregate supply of goods and services. When the Federal Reserve reduces the rate of growth of bank reserves and the money supply, this puts upward pressure on interest rates. In turn, many would-be borrowers are expected to be deterred in their borrowing and spending plans by the higher interest rates, which will result in lower real output and put downward pressure on prices. This deflationary process may take some time before it has an impact on all, or most, of the major sectors of the economy.

### Implementation of Monetary Policy

In the development and implementation of its monetary policy, the Federal Reserve in the late 1970s and early 1980s tended usually to select monetary aggregates (e.g., or M1-A or M1-B or M1 and M2) as intermediate targets. A desired growth path with minimum and maximum rates of growth for the next quarter or two, even for the next year, was established for the selected monetary aggregates.

To provide a short-run "operating target" for the Trading Desk, the FOMC typically provided a growth path for unborrowed bank reserves. In addition, a broad range of federal funds rates was also specified that was believed to be consistent with the monetary aggregate targets. These policy choices were somewhat controversial, because some economists preferred only interest rate targets, while others preferred only monetary aggregate targets. The FOMC choice has been often somewhat of a compromise between opposing viewpoints, though the stress in the 1980s has been on monetary aggregates.

The traditional view of the major function of monetary policy has been to regard it as offsetting disturbances in the economy that come either from the **financial sector** or the **real sector.** Because the major type of disturbance to the American economy in the late 1970s and early 1980s was generally believed to be inflationary (i.e., resulting from excessive borrowing and spending either by the government or private sectors), the preferred short-run and intermediate targets were the monetary aggregates. The FOMC was quite aware, however, that a slower rate of growth of the monetary aggregates as in 1981 would result in higher levels of interest rates and greater difficulty in borrowing funds, both of which are characteristic of periods of credit restraint.

## Monetary Aggregate Targets for 1982–1983

In its midyear review on July 21, 1981, the Federal Reserve Board first released its monetary aggregate targets for 1982. As in 1981, when the target ranges were lowered from those of 1980, the new target announced for 1982 for the narrowest definition of money was lower than that in effect for 1981. Furthermore, the FOMC reinstated the term M1, which was to be used in 1982 with the same coverage as that of M1-B in 1981. For the period covering the fourth quarter of 1981 to the fourth quarter of 1982, the projected targets were to be (1) M1, 2½ to 5½ percent, (2) M2, 6 to 9 percent, (3) M3, 6½ to 9½ percent, and (4) commercial bank credit, 6 to 9 percent. The target range for M1 for 1982 was reduced by about ½ percent from that prevailing for M1-B in 1981, but the range was also widened by ½ percentage point. The target ranges for M2 and M3 were left unchanged. On February 10, 1982, these monetary aggregate targets of 1982—selected seven months earlier—were confirmed as the official 1982 targets.

In its midyear review on July 20, 1982, the Federal Open Market Committee decided that there was no need to change the previously announced targets for 1982, although it was prepared to accept growth around the top of the ranges for the various aggregates. Furthermore, it decided that the ranges then in effect should be adopted as preliminary targets for 1983. This decision was made because of the serious economic recession then underway and because substantial progress had been made in reducing the rate of inflation.

## Difficulties with Interest Rate Targets

One of the important reasons for shifting from a monetary target emphasizing interest rates to one emphasizing growth in the monetary aggregates was that holding to an interest rate target would mean automatically supplying enough reserves to accommodate shifts in the demand for money. In an expansionary period in the economy, when the demand for bank credit was increasing, this would result in a higher level of bank deposits and required reserves. Bank needs for more funds for further lending and to accommodate higher levels of required reserves would induce the banks to sell Treasury bills in the money market, which tended to push up the level of yields on such Treasury bills.

Banks would also buy more federal funds (excess reserves held by other banks), which would force up the federal funds rate. To prevent such an increase in money market yields, if maintaining a given level of yields were the target for open market operations, would require the Trading Desk to inject more reserves into the money market. This increase in the supply of reserves in response to higher levels of demand for borrowed funds would lead to a further increase in the money supply with the likelihood of inflationary consequences for the economy.

On the other hand, sole emphasis on controlling the rate of growth of the money supply, however defined, resulted in greater instability in money market conditions than had been experienced previously. In late 1979, 1980, and 1981, there was considerable instability in both the money and capital markets.

## Selecting Intermediate Targets

When the Federal Reserve develops monetary strategy for its open market operations, as already noted, it must select some intermediate target such as the growth rate of the money supply or a key interest rate for which there is empirical evidence to link it to the output, price, and employment goals of the monetary authorities. Some econometric model must be used to generate quarterly forecasts of the economy into which alternative growth rates of money, for example, and varying levels of the federal funds rate can be inserted. The Open Market Committee can then select the growth path that it believes to be most likely and/or most preferable.

However, a great number of monthly and even quarterly patterns of growth in the money supply can generate the desired annual rate of increase. Because of this fact and the difficulty of offsetting all the random factors in the money market affecting the growth of the various monetary aggregates, the FOMC invariably provides the Trading Desk with a range for each month and quarter. Even then, the Trading Desk often has great difficulty in hitting the assigned range of the target.

Most open market operations consist simply of offsetting, more or less, the effects on bank reserves of changes in these other money market factors in a given reserve week. Rather than being concerned directly with the gross volume of open market operations, the committee is more interested in the net supply of reserves that will be available in the weeks ahead to the whole banking system. In this way the desired growth in bank credit and the other monetary aggregates can be adequately supported.

## *Difficulties in Hitting Monetary Aggregate Targets, 1979 and 1980*

Tolerance ranges of rates of growth of the various monetary aggregates are established by the FOMC for the guidance of the Federal Reserve Bank of New York in performing open market operations. Annual growth ranges for the two-year period of the fourth quarter of 1980 to the fourth quarter of 1981 are shown in Table 17–1, which shows that both the lower and upper limits of M2 and M3 are invariably higher than those for M1-A and M1-B (M1 in 1982), whereas the desired range for bank credit is the same as that for M2.

This table also shows that the FOMC had great difficulty hitting its targets in 1980, because all of the annual growth rates (except the growth in bank credit) were higher than the upper limits set by the committee. M1-A and M1-B are within the target ranges only after adjusting for higher than expected growth of automatic transfer service accounts (savings accounts that were automatically transferred as needed into checking accounts). The very rapid growth of the monetary aggregates in 1980 helped contribute to a high inflation rate that year and lower rates of growth for the monetary aggregate targets for 1981.

How well the Federal Reserve Bank of New York succeeded in hitting the M1-A and M1-B targets for 1979 and 1980 can be seen in Figure 17–2. M1-B, the most widely used definition of money in 1979–1980 (M1 in 1982), seemed particularly difficult for the Federal Reserve to control. The actual growth rate of M1-B was substantially below the target band in the second half of 1979 and substantially above it in the second half of

**Table 17–1  Federal Open Market Committee's Annual Growth Rates and Target Ranges for the Aggregates, Fourth Quarter to Fourth Quarter, 1980–1981 (percentages)**

| Aggregates | 1980 Annual Target Ranges | Annual Growth Rates | 1981 Annual Target Ranges |
|---|---|---|---|
| M1-A............................... | 3.5–6.0 | 5.0 (6.3)[a] | 3.0–5.5[b] |
| M1-B............................... | 4.0–6.5 | 7.3 (6.7)[a] | 3.5–6.0[b] |
| M2................................. | 6.0–9.0 | 9.8 | 6.0–9.0 |
| M3................................. | 6.5–9.5 | 9.9 | 6.5–9.5 |
| Bank credit........................ | 6.0–9.0 | 7.9 | 6.0–9.0 |

[a]Adjusted for the more rapid than expected growth of ATS accounts in 1980. This adjustment assumes that two thirds of the unexpected growth of other checkable deposits during 1980 resulted from shifts of funds out of demand deposits and one third from shifts out of savings accounts.

[b]After adjusting for the effects of nationwide NOW accounts.

SOURCE: Federal Reserve Bank of New York, *Annual Report 1980,* 1981, p. 14.

1980. As noted in Chapter 15, the Federal Reserve Board considered eliminating lagged reserve accounting in 1982 in favor of contemporaneous reserve accounting, which, it was hoped, would give the Fed greater control over the money supply. Let us now consider the actual conduct of open market operations.

**Figure 17–2   M1-A and M1-B Levels and Targets, 1979–1980**

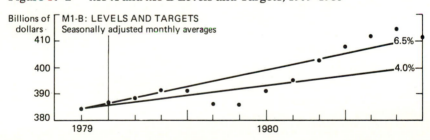

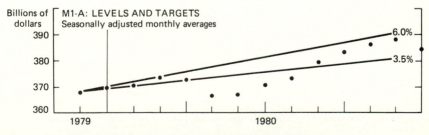

SOURCE: Federal Reserve Bank of New York, *Annual Report 1980,* 1981, p. 16.

## OPEN MARKET OPERATIONS IN THE LATE 1970s AND EARLY 1980s

The amount and type of Federal Reserve open market operations in the late 1970s and early 1980s are shown in Table 17–2. Several important generalizations about open market operations can be drawn from this table. The use of repurchase agreements, whereby the Trading Desk

**Table 17–2  Federal Reserve Open-Market Transactions, 1978–1981 (In millions of dollars)**

|  | 1978 | 1979 | 1980 | 1981 |
|---|---|---|---|---|
| **U.S. government securities** | | | | |
| *Outright transactions* | | | | |
| *All maturities* | | | | |
|   Gross purchases | 24,591 | 22,325 | 12,232 | 16,690 |
|   Gross sales | 13,725 | 6,855 | 7,331 | 6,769 |
|   Redemptions | 2,033 | 5,500 | 3,389 | 1,816 |
| *Treasury bills* | | | | |
|   Gross purchases | 16,628 | 15,998 | 7,668 | 13,899 |
|   Gross sales | 13,725 | 6,855 | 7,331 | 6,746 |
| *Matched transactions* | | | | |
|   Gross sales | 511,126 | 627,350 | 674,000 | 589,312 |
|   Gross purchases | 510,854 | 624,192 | 675,496 | 589,647 |
| *Repurchase agreements* | | | | |
|   Gross purchases | 151,618 | 107,051 | 113,902 | 79,920 |
|   Gross sales | 152,436 | 106,968 | 113,040 | 78,733 |
| **Federal agency obligations** | | | | |
| *Outright transactions* | | | | |
|   Gross purchases | 301 | 853 | 668 | 494 |
|   Gross sales | 173 | 399 | 0 | 0 |
|   Redemptions | 235 | 134 | 145 | 108 |
| *Repurchase agreements* | | | | |
|   Gross purchases | 40,567 | 37,321 | 28,895 | 13,320 |
|   Gross sales | 40,885 | 36,960 | 28,863 | 13,576 |
| **Bankers' acceptances** | | | | |
| Outright transactions, net | 0 | 0 | 0 | 0 |
| Repurchase agreements, net | −366 | 116 | 73 | −582 |
| Net change in system account | 6,951 | 7,693 | 4,497 | 9,175 |

SOURCE: Board of Governors of the Federal Reserve System, *Federal Reserve Bulletins*, May 1981, p. A10; March 1982, p. A10.

gives temporary reserves to the banking system and the money market (gross purchases) or temporarily absorbs such reserves in matched transactions, is far larger than outright transactions in each year. By 1981, such operations were more than ninefold the dollar amount of outright transactions. Matched sale-purchase agreements, wherein the Trading Desk temporarily absorbs funds from the money market, have grown even more enormously and are now nearly sixfold the dollar amount of RPs. In both RPs and matched sale-purchase agreements, the contracts by the Trading Desk are typically for one to seven days in duration.

A marked decline in outright transactions occurred in 1980 after the change in open market policy of October 6, 1979. Nevertheless, as Table 17–2 shows, such outright transactions, which are primarily in Treasury bills, resumed their growth in 1981. Repurchase agreements executed in 1981, however, declined sharply from the annual levels of the late 1970s. Matched transactions, however, declined only moderately in 1981.

Whenever the Federal Reserve is buying government securities, *ceteris paribus*, bank reserves are increased by that amount, but whenever they are selling government securities, *ceteris paribus*, bank reserves are decreased by that amount. However, a number of other factors also influence the amount of bank reserves available to the banking system. The cost and availability of bank reserves by borrowing at the regional discount windows of the Federal Reserve Banks are examples of such added factors affecting bank reserves. The terms, discount rate, and willingness of the Federal Reserve to extend such borrowed reserves to depository institutions are also often considered adjuncts to open market operations. Discount rate and discount window policy are discussed in the next chapter.

# Questions for Discussion

1. Discuss the composition of the Federal Open Market Committee. Why do you think that the amendments to the Federal Reserve Act in 1935 provided that a majority of the FOMC should consist of members of the Board of Governors? What were the implications for monetary policymaking of the elimination of the Executive Committee in 1955?
2. What are the basic monetary policy goals of the Federal Reserve System? Why may controversies develop within the system itself over which goal should be emphasized during a given period of time? What divisions of opinion have occurred recently within the Federal Reserve System? Why?
3. Discuss the accommodative "money market strategy" of the Federal Reserve in the 1960s and contrast it with the great emphasis on controlling the rate of growth of various monetary aggregates in the 1970s and 1980s. Relate

these changes in the strategy of monetary policy to the monetary indicator problem.

4. How important is it to specify "links" between the various monetary aggregates and interest rates and how important is it to link such variables with aggregate variables such as real GNP and employment? What is the connection between the monetary policy strategy followed by the Federal Reserve in selecting short-run targets and intermediate indicators and the level of prices?

5. How does the FOMC phrase its Domestic Policy Directive to the Trading Desk? Why are ranges specified for the various monetary aggregates instead of a single number? What is the significance of specifying a range of federal funds rates for the Trading Desk? What are the exact divisions of responsibility between the FOMC and the Trading Desk?

6. Discuss some of the procedures of the Trading Desk. How does the manager of the system account make sure that he is following the policy guidelines laid down by the Federal Open Market Committee?

7. Discuss the use of repurchase agreements and matched sale-purchase agreements by the Trading Desk. What are the advantages of these types of open market operations as opposed to outright purchases and sales of Treasury bills or coupon issues?

8. What is the nature of the feedback from the Trading Desk to the members of the Open Market Committee?

9. Discuss the conduct of open market operations by the Trading Desk in carrying out the changing policies of the Open Market Committee since the FOMC changes of October 6, 1979. Do you believe that these changes in open market operations have contributed to greater stability in the financial and real sectors or not?

10. Discuss some of the difficulties the Trading Desk has experienced in the 1980s in trying to achieve the rate of growth in the monetary aggregates specified by the FOMC. How successful has the FOMC been in achieving its ultimate goals relating to price stability and the growth of real output? What part have exogenous changes including changes in the velocity of money played in these difficulties? Would a time period longer than a quarter help the Trading Desk achieve its goals? Why?

# Selected Bibliography for Further Reading

AHEARN, DANIEL S., *Federal Reserve Policy Reappraisal 1951–1959* (New York: Columbia University Press, 1963).

AXILROD, STEPHEN H., "Monetary Policy, Money Supply, and the Federal Reserve's Operating Procedures," *Federal Reserve Bulletin*, Jan. 1982, pp. 13-24.

BECK, DAVID C., "Excess Reserves and Reserve Targeting," *Quarterly Review*, Vol. 6, No. 3 (New York: Federal Reserve Bank of New York, Autumn 1981), pp. 15–22.

BERKMAN, NEIL G., "Open Market Operations Under the New Monetary Policy," *New England Economic Review* (Boston: Federal Reserve Bank of Boston, Mar.-Apr. 1981), pp. 5–20.

BOARD OF GOVERNORS OF THE FEDERAL RESERVE SYSTEM, *The Federal Reserve Act As Amended Through December 31, 1956* (Washington, D.C.: 1957).

——, *Fifty-Fifth Annual Report Covering Operations for the Year 1968* (Washington, D.C.: 1969).

——, *Open Market Policies and Operating Procedures—Staff Studies* (Washington, D.C.: July 1971).

——, *Monetary Policy Objectives for 1981* (Washington, D.C.: Feb. 25–26, 1981), pp. 3–15.

——, *Monetary Policy Objectives for 1981, Midyear Review of the Federal Reserve Board* (Washington, D.C.: July 21, 1981), pp. 1–10.

——, *Monetary Policy Objectives for 1982* (Washington, D.C.: Feb. 10, 1982), pp. 2–14.

——, *Monetary Policy Objectives for 1982, Midyear Review of the Federal Reserve Board* (Washington, D.C.: July 20, 1982), pp. 1–14.

CARLSON, KEITH, and SCOTT E. HEIM, "Monetary Aggregates as Monetary Indicators," *Review*, Vol. 62, No. 9 (St. Louis: Federal Reserve Bank of St. Louis, Nov. 1980), pp. 12–21.

FEDERAL RESERVE BANK OF NEW YORK, *Monetary Aggregates and Monetary Policy* (New York: Oct. 1974).

——, *Glossary: Weekly Federal Reserve Statements* (New York, 1972).

GILBERT, ANTO R., and MICHAEL E. TREBING, "The FOMC in 1980: A Year of Reserve Targeting," *Review*, Federal Reserve Bank of St. Louis, Vol. 63, No. 7, Aug.-Sept. 1981, pp. 2–22.

GUTTENTAG, J. M., "The Strategy of Open Market Operations," *Quarterly Journal of Economics*, Feb. 1966, pp. 1–30.

HOLMES, ALAN, "The Problems of the Open Market Manager," *Controlling Monetary Aggregates II: The Implementation* (Boston: Federal Reserve Bank of Boston, 1973), pp. 61–68.

JORDAN, JERRY L., "FOMC Policy Actions in 1972," *Review* (St. Louis: Federal Reserve Bank of St. Louis, March 1973), pp. 10–24.

LOMBRA, RAYMOND and F. STRUBLE, "Monetary Aggregate Targets and the Volatility of Interest Rates: A Taxonomic Discussion," *Journal Money, Credit and Banking*, **11** (Aug. 1979), pp. 297–300.

LOMBRA, RAYMOND E., and RAYMOND G. TORTO, "The Strategy of Monetary Policy," *Economic Review*, Vol. 61 (Richmond, Va.: Federal Reserve Bank of Richmond, Sept.–Oct. 1975), pp. 3–14.

MEEK, PAUL, *Discount Policy and Open Market Operations* (New York: Federal Reserve Bank of New York, Feb. 26, 1968).

——, "Open Market Operations and the Monetary and Credit Aggregates—1971," *Monthly Review*, Vol. 54, No. 4 (New York: Federal Reserve Bank of New York, April 1972), pp. 79–94.

——, "Open Market Operations in 1972," *Monthly Review*, Vol. 55, No. 5 (New York: Federal Reserve Bank of New York), pp. 102–114.

ROOSA, ROBERT V., *Federal Reserve Operations in the Money and Government Securities Markets* (New York: Federal Reserve Bank of New York, July 1956).

SELLON, GORDON H., JR., and RONALD L. TEIGEN, "The Choice of Short-Run Targets for Monetary Policy Part I: A Theoretical Analysis," *Economic Review*, Vol. 66, No. 4 (Kansas City, Mo.: Federal Reserve Bank of Kansas City, April 1981), pp. 3–16.

——, "The Choice of Short-Run Targets for Monetary Policy Part II: An Historical Analysis," *Economic Review*, Vol. 66, No. 5 (Kansas City, Mo.: Federal Reserve Bank of Kansas City, May 1981), pp. 3–12.

*Treasury-Federal Reserve Study of the U.S. Government Securities Market*, Report and Staff Studies (Washington, D.C.: U.S. Government Printing Office, 1969).

VOLCKER, PAUL A., "A Broader Role for Monetary Targets," *Quarterly Review*, Spring 1977, Vol. 2 (New York: Federal Reserve Bank of New York), pp. 23–28.

This bank was more liberal than any other had ever been, both in granting cash accounts, and in discounting bills of exchange.

THE WEALTH OF NATIONS

# 18
## CHAPTER

# Federal Reserve Discount Rate and Discount Window Policy

The oldest instrument of central banking is called the "Bank Rate" in Great Britain and the discount rate of the Federal Reserve Banks in the United States. When a central bank changed the interest rate on its loans of reserves to the discount houses (in Great Britain) or to depository institutions such as commercial banks (in the United States), all other key interest rates such as the prime rate were also expected to change. However, this traditional view of the great importance of the discount rate has changed in recent years. Open market operations are now seen as the most powerful and flexible instrument of the central bank. The discount rate and discount window administration are now largely regarded as adjuncts to open market operations.

In the United States the discount rate, which depository institutions are charged when they borrow reserves from their regional Reserve Bank, is often allowed to get out of touch with key money market rates (e.g., the federal funds rate), which is the interest rate banks charge one another for lending and borrowing excess reserves. Because the discount

371

rate is often changed only intermittently—sometimes remaining constant when other interest rates are rising—there is a separate problem of administering loans of reserves to depository institutions. If the discount rate were always a "penalty rate" (i.e., higher than the federal funds rate and the Treasury bill rate), it would never be necessary to use nonprice rationing of would-be borrowing of reserves from the Federal Reserve Banks. In fact, the discount rate is sometimes below these key interest rates, so that the Reserve Banks are compelled to emphasize to borrowing financial institutions that this is a privilege rather than a right and therefore subject to administrative as well as price rationing.

## LEGAL PROVISIONS AND MECHANICS GOVERNING BORROWING BY DEPOSITORY INSTITUTIONS

The Federal Reserve Act provides that

> Any Federal Reserve Bank may make advances for periods not exceeding fifteen days to its member banks on their promissory notes secured by the deposit or pledge of bonds, notes, certificates of indebtedness, or Treasury bills of the United States. . . . All such advances shall be made at rates to be established by such Federal Reserve Banks, such rates to be subject to the review and determination of the Board of Governors of the Federal Reserve System.[1]

This act was amended on March 31, 1980, to extend the borrowing privilege to all financial institutions with transactions accounts. In practice in recent years, those depository institutions that are member commercial banks have held a sufficient quantity of government securities at their regional Reserve Bank for safekeeping, so that these securities have been readily available as collateral for any needed bank borrowing from the Reserve Bank.

### Mechanics of Depository Institution Borrowing

The usual mechanics of such borrowing are that a responsible officer of the depository institution, or member bank, simply makes a telephone call to the discount window department of the regional Reserve Bank and readily secures the needed temporary accommodation as an ad-

---

[1]Board of Governors of the Federal Reserve System, *The Federal Reserve Act As Amended Through December 31, 1956* (Washington, D.C.; 1957), p. 46.

vance secured by U.S. government securities. As indicated, the interest rate on these reserves on a string is the prevailing discount rate of the Reserve Bank. Usually all twelve Reserve Banks have the same discount rate, though occasionally a split-discount rate may prevail, as was true from April to August 1956, when ten Reserve Banks had a 2¾ percent rate and two Reserve Banks had a 3 percent discount rate. The different discount rates from January 15, 1973, to May 5, 1981, are shown in Table 18–1.

## Changes in the Discount Rate

For the nine years shown in this table, the strong trend for the discount rate was upward. The discount rate on short-term adjustment credit from the Federal Reserve Banks was only 4½ percent at the end of 1972. For many months in 1981, the basic discount rate was 14 percent, to which was added a 4 percent **penalty surcharge** for large depository institutions making frequent use of the discount window. But in late 1981 this surcharge was gradually eliminated. In August 1982, the discount rate was at 10 percent.

In addition to the upward trend for the discount rate until the peak of 14 percent in 1981, the data in Table 18–1 are notable in that they show the frequency of adjustment in the discount rate. There were seven changes in the discount rate in 1973, two in 1974, four in 1975, and two in each year of 1976 and 1977. There were seven changes, however, in 1978, three in 1979, and seven again in 1980, with the first imposition ever of a penalty surcharge in late 1980. There was only one increase in the discount rate in 1981, in early May, but it raised the basic rate to the record level of 14 percent with an added penalty rate of 4 percent for large, frequent borrowers. For the first half of 1982, the discount rate remained unchanged at 12 percent, though it was cut to 11 percent in July and 10 percent in August. Regarding such changes in the discount rate as a signal of Federal Reserve policy, one can see the progressive tightening and then gradual easing as mirrored in changes in the discount rate. Stability in policy, of course, tends to be associated with an unchanged discount rate.

## Decline in Use of the Discount Window

In the early days of the Federal Reserve System it was thought that the discount mechanism would be the major instrument of the Federal Reserve in providing an elastic currency. The provision of discounting facilities at the Federal Reserve Banks, commonly called the discount

**Table 18–1  Federal Reserve Bank Discount Rates, 1973–1982 (percent per annum)**

| Effective Date | | | Range (or level) —All F.R. Banks[a] | F.R. Bank of N.Y.[a] | Effective Date | | | Range (or level) —All F.R. Banks[a] | F.R. Bank of N.Y.[a] |
|---|---|---|---|---|---|---|---|---|---|
| 1973 | Jan. | 15 | 5 | 5 | 1978 | Jan. | 9 | 6–6½ | 6½ |
| | Feb. | 26 | 5–5½ | 5½ | | | 20 | 6½ | 6½ |
| | Mar. | 2 | 5½ | 5½ | | May | 11 | 6½–7 | 7 |
| | Apr. | 23 | 5½–5¾ | 5½ | | | 12 | 7 | 7 |
| | May | 4 | 5¾ | 5¾ | | July | 3 | 7–7¼ | 7¼ |
| | | 11 | 5¾–6 | 6 | | | 10 | 7¼ | 7¼ |
| | | 18 | 6 | 6 | | Aug. | 21 | 7¾ | 7¾ |
| | June | 11 | 6–6½ | 6½ | | Sept. | 22 | 8 | 8 |
| | | 15 | 6½ | 6½ | | Oct. | 16 | 8–8½ | 8½ |
| | July | 2 | 7 | 7 | | | 20 | 8½ | 8½ |
| | Aug. | 14 | 7–7½ | 7½ | | Nov. | 1 | 8½–9½ | 9½ |
| | | 23 | 7½ | 7½ | | | 3 | 9½ | 9½ |
| 1974 | Apr. | 25 | 7½–8 | 8 | 1979 | July | 20 | 10 | 10 |
| | | 30 | 8 | 8 | | Aug. | 17 | 10–10½ | 10½ |
| | Dec. | 9 | 7¾–8 | 7¾ | | | 20 | 10½ | 10½ |
| | | 16 | 7¾ | 7¾ | | Sept. | 19 | 10½–11 | 11 |
| 1975 | Jan. | 6 | 7¼–7¾ | 7¾ | | | 21 | 11 | 11 |
| | | 10 | 7¼–7¾ | 7¼ | | Oct. | 8 | 11–12 | 12 |
| | | 24 | 7¼ | 7¼ | | | 10 | 12 | 12 |
| | Feb. | 5 | 6¾–7¼ | 6¾ | 1980 | Feb. | 15 | 12–13 | 13 |
| | | 7 | 6¾ | 6¾ | | | 19 | 13 | 13 |
| | Mar. | 10 | 6¼–6¾ | 6¼ | | May | 29 | 12–13 | 13 |
| | | 14 | 6¼ | 6¼ | | | 30 | 12 | 12 |
| | May | 16 | 6–6¼ | 6 | | June | 13 | 11–12 | 11 |
| | | 23 | 6 | 6 | | | 16 | 11 | 11 |
| 1976 | Jan. | 19 | 5½–6 | 5½ | | July | 28 | 10–11 | 10 |
| | | 23 | 5½ | 5½ | | | 29 | 10 | 10 |
| | Nov. | 22 | 5¼–5½ | 5¼ | | Sept. | 26 | 11 | 11 |
| | | 26 | 5¼ | 5¼ | | Nov. | 17 | 12 | 12 |
| 1977 | Aug. | 30 | 5¼–5¾ | 5¼ | | Dec. | 5[b] | 12–13 | 13 |
| | | 31 | 5¼–5¾ | 5¾ | | | 8 | 13 | 13 |
| | Sept. | 2 | 5¾ | 5¾ | 1981 | May | 5 | 13–14 | 14 |
| | Oct. | 26 | 6 | 6 | | May | 8 | 14 | 14 |
| | | | | | | Nov. | 2 | 13–14 | 13 |
| | | | | | | Nov. | 6 | 13 | 13 |
| | | | | | | Dec. | 4 | 12 | 12 |
| | | | | In effect  Feb. 28, 1982 | | | | 12 | 12 |

[a]These discount rates are for short-term adjustment credit.

[b]Effective Dec. 5, 1980, a 3 percent surcharge was applied to short-term adjustment credit borrowings by institutions with deposits of $500 million or more that borrowed in successive weeks or in more than four weeks in a calendar year. On May 5, 1981, this penalty was increased to 4 percent. On September 21, 1981, the surcharge was returned to 3 percent; on October 12 it was reduced to 2 percent. It was eliminated on Nov. 17, 1981.

SOURCE: Board of Governors of the Federal Reserve System, *Federal Reserve Bulletins,* June 1981, p. A7; March 1982, p. A7.

window, was originally intended as a service to member banks for selling (i.e., discounting) eligible ninety-day commercial paper to the Reserve Banks in order to secure added reserves. In recent years, however, commercial banks and other depository institutions have secured direct advances from the Federal Reserve, with government securities as collateral, rather than rediscounting commercial paper.

This instrument has now come to be regarded as playing a secondary role to open market operations. In the 1920s, about 60 percent of Federal Reserve credit was supplied through the discount window, whereas by the 1980s only a minor part of Federal Reserve credit was being supplied in this fashion. Nevertheless, the discount window in the 1970s and early 1980s was a much more important weapon of the Federal Reserve than it had been in the 1930s and 1940s. In fact, from the early 1930s to the early 1950s, member bank borrowing from the Federal Reserve was almost nonexistent.

## *Revival of Member Bank Borrowing After 1951*

After the Federal Reserve accord with the Treasury on March 4, 1951, all this was changed. The Federal Reserve gradually abandoned its support policy with the result that banks were forced to show a loss on their books if they sold government securities in order to make more loans. Furthermore, the monetary authorities deliberately embarked on countercyclical policies that called for credit restraint in periods of economic upswing accompanied by possible inflationary dangers. The result was that short-run reserve adjustments of commercial banks were increasingly accomplished by resort to the discount window.

## BORROWING OF DEPOSITORY INSTITUTIONS FROM THE FEDERAL RESERVE

The borrowing of depository institutions from the Reserve Banks supplies an important marginal part of reserves in periods of credit restraint. One of the important ways that the Federal Reserve makes such a policy of credit restraint effective is by forcing financial institutions to resort to borrowing from the Federal Reserve Banks when they need additional reserves. This increase in borrowing ordinarily takes place in a period of economic expansion when credit demands on banks and other financial institutions are rising.

As commercial banks and other depository institutions increase their loans and investments outstanding, they find that previously held unused or excess reserves have now been used up. Under such conditions, these financial institutions are forced to find additional sources of loanable funds. If the additional loanable funds are needed for a substantial period of time, the institutions are expected to sell some of their investment securities, particularly short-term government securities, in order to secure these needed funds. Short-term reserve needs, however, are met by federal funds purchases or borrowing at the discount window.

### *"Reluctance to Borrow" by Depository Institutions*

Since the mid-1920s, Federal Reserve officials have assumed that member banks were "reluctant" to borrow from the discount window, because the member banks were supposed to be under pressure to repay the borrowings whenever they were secured. This "tradition" has been reinforced by Federal Reserve officials following the revival of member bank borrowing after the accord of March 4, 1951. The revision of Regulation A in 1955 stressed in the preface that member bank borrowing was a privilege and not a right.

     After the Monetary Control Act of 1980, many more new depository institutions were eligible to use the discount window than before. That the borrowing was a privilege, which should ordinarily be exercised within a tradition of **reluctance to borrow**, had to be re-emphasized for the new would-be borrowers. Because the Federal Reserve has always regarded itself as a "lender of last resort," it expected that depository institutions would make reasonable efforts to secure borrowed funds from usual sources, including industry lenders, before turning to the discount window.

## NEW DEPOSITORY INSTITUTIONS BORROWING

Nevertheless, for those institutions who still needed added liquidity, credit would be available from the Federal Reserve for periods extending up to twelve months and even beyond, if necessary. Such credit had to be fully collateralized with collateral valued at 90 percent of its estimated market price. How much credit could be received would depend upon a careful evaluation of the needs of a borrowing institution. In order to encourage prompt repayment of such credit, when liquidity pressures on the institution eased, the Federal Reserve required a written plan that detailed how the institution expected to strengthen its financial position and encourage an inflow of funds from other sources.

The detailed administrative attention at the discount window is not only focused on the newer depository institutions but even on those commercial banks that were members of the Federal Reserve System before the 1980 act. It was very tempting for banks as profit maximizers and cost minimizers to resort to the discount window when a "cheap" discount rate prevailed as compared with the cost of borrowing federal funds in the money market. This was often the case in the 1970s and early 1980s, when the discount rate was typically below the federal funds rate.

This was true, for example, in the severe credit restraint period of 1974, when the discount rate was 8 percent and the federal funds rate soared to 13 percent. It was also true in the even more severe credit restraint period of 1981–1982. In mid-February 1982, for example, the discount rate was 12 percent and the federal funds rate was fluctuating typically between 14 and 15½ percent. The variation in heavy borrowing by depository institutions at the discount window is shown in Table 18–2. Borrowing, which was relatively low for the first eight months of 1980, became heavy in late 1980 and throughout 1981 until November and December.

## THE NEW SEASONAL BORROWING PRIVILEGE AFTER 1973

The typical depository institution is permitted to borrow reserves from the discount window for adjustment credit reasons for two weeks, with the possibility of renewing the loan if need be. The smaller depository institutions, however, can now borrow for up to ninety days to satisfy seasonal needs for credit in their communities.

A **seasonal borrowing privilege** was proposed in 1968, but it was not until April 19, 1973, that such borrowing for periods of up to ninety days was available to member banks. However, this new use of the discount window was primarily intended for those 2,000 small member banks that then had less than $50 million in total deposits. These small depository institutions lack reasonably reliable access to national money markets. Financial institutions eligible for seasonal borrowing are expected to provide part of their own seasonal needs up to 5 percent of their average total deposits in the preceding calendar year. Additional seasonal needs can be met by borrowing from the Federal Reserve.

Prior to the provision for seasonal borrowing, 75 to 80 percent of the smaller member banks did not borrow even once a year from the Federal Reserve. On the other hand, the larger city banks usually borrowed occasionally during any given year.

**Table 18–2 Borrowings of Depository Institutions at the twelve Federal Reserve Discount Windows (In millions of dollars)**

| Month | 1978 | | 1979 | | 1980 | | 1981 | |
|---|---|---|---|---|---|---|---|---|
| | Total[a] | Seasonal[b] | Total[a] | Seasonal[b] | Total[a] | Seasonal[b] | Total[a] | Seasonal[b] |
| Jan. | 481 | 32 | 994 | 112 | 396 | 11 | 1,405 | 120 |
| Feb. | 405 | 52 | 973 | 114 | 318 | 8 | 1,278 | 148 |
| Mar. | 344 | 47 | 999 | 121 | 348 | 7 | 1,004 | 197 |
| Apr. | 539 | 43 | 897 | 134 | 215 | 5 | 1,343 | 161 |
| May | 1,227 | 93 | 1,777 | 173 | 332 | 5 | 2,154 | 259 |
| June | 1,111 | 120 | 1,396 | 188 | 354 | 5 | 2,038 | 291 |
| July | 1,286 | 143 | 1,179 | 168 | 629 | 7 | 1,751 | 248 |
| Aug. | 1,147 | 188 | 1,097 | 177 | 659 | 10 | 1,408 | 220 |
| Sept. | 1,068 | 191 | 1,344 | 169 | 1,311 | 26 | 1,473 | 222 |
| Oct. | 1,261 | 221 | 2,022 | 161 | 1,335 | 67 | 1,149 | 152 |
| Nov. | 722 | 185 | 1,908 | 141 | 2,156 | 99 | 695 | 79 |
| Dec. | 874 | 134 | 1,454 | 81 | 1,617 | 116 | 642 | 53 |

[a]Data are averages of daily figures within the month.

[b]Effective April 19, 1973, the board's Regulation A, which governs lending by Federal Reserve Banks, was revised to assist smaller member banks to meet the seasonal borrowing needs of their communities.

SOURCE: Board of Governors of the Federal Reserve System, *Federal Reserve Bulletins*, Aug. 1978, Feb. 1979, Aug. 1979, Feb. 1980, Aug. 1980, July 1981, Jan. 1982.

# BORROWING BY DEPOSITORY INSTITUTIONS IN A PERIOD OF CREDIT RESTRAINT

Both total depository institution borrowing and seasonal borrowing are shown for the four years 1978 to 1981 inclusive in Table 18–2. These years were selected because they illustrate the use of the discount window by depository institutions in a period of credit restraint. In such a period, loan demand in the credit markets and at depository institutions increased because of rising economic activity and rising prices. (Double-digit inflation occurred in 1979 and 1980 but inflation rates fell in 1981.)

But the inflationary forces that encourage more borrowing also lead the Federal Reserve to slow down the growth in reserves of depository institutions and in the money supply. There is a growing shortage of the supply of loanable funds in relation to the demand for them and also an increase in required reserves because of larger dollar amounts of transaction accounts resulting from previous lending. These pressures lead the depository institutions to search for additional reserves.

In addition to buying more federal funds, which are excess reserves sold by other banks for twenty-four hours, large commercial banks in particular also often find it necessary to go to the discount window of their regional Reserve Bank more frequently for increasingly larger amounts of borrowed reserves. This symptom of a period of credit restraint is illustrated clearly in Table 18–2, which shows that average monthly levels of borrowings of $1 billion to $2 billion typically occurred in 1979–1981.

Seasonal borrowing throughout this period, however, never reached monthly levels higher than $291 million. This suggests that the pressures of credit restraint were felt more intensely by the larger depository institutions than by the smaller ones. In periods of credit ease, of course, there is less pressure on the reserve position of all depository institutions and, correspondingly, a decline in borrowing of reserves at the twelve discount windows.

# EXTENDED CREDIT PROGRAM OF 1981

In addition to regular or seasonal borrowing at the discount window, the discount window is also available to institutions under sustained liquidity pressures. Such institutions may even borrow if necessary for sustained periods. This privilege was established after the passage of the

Monetary Control Act of 1980 but imposes a higher interest rate than the basic discount rate. On August 20, 1981, the interest rates were established for such **extended credit** to institutions under liquidity pressures. The new rate was the basic discount rate of 14 percent for the first sixty days of borrowing, 15 percent for the next ninety days, and 16 percent thereafter.

In establishing this new program of lending, the Federal Reserve stated, in part, "When conditions warrant, extended credit is available to assist institutions (including those with longer-term asset portfolios) that may be having difficulties adjusting to changing money market conditions. These advances may be extended over a longer period than contemplated in the use of **adjustment credit**, particularly at times of deposit disintermediation."[2]

This new extended credit program was designed to help commercial banks, savings and loan associations, savings banks, and credit unions adjust to sustained liquidity pressures. By late August 1981, the most severe credit restraint program ever imposed by the Federal Reserve had been in existence nearly ten months since early November 1980. This resulted in high, rising interest rates and severe disintermediation problems, particularly for the thrift institutions.

## Continuous Borrowing and Surveillance

Initial requests for Federal Reserve credit from the regional discount window by depository institutions, whether in a period of credit restraint or credit ease, are invariably accommodated promptly with little or no discussion. Subsequent requests for credit, however, particularly if large continuous borrowing appears to be involved, may lead to "**surveillance**" of the borrowing institution. The process of surveillance may involve a determination of whether the borrowing request is for an appropriate or an inappropriate purpose (i.e., for need or for profit). If it is determined that the borrowing request is inappropriate, then "administrative counseling" of the depository institution may be invoked by the discount department of the Reserve Bank. Surveillance and counseling are part of the process of nonprice rationing and moral suasion at the discount window.

Initially, surveillance takes place through the collection and analysis of data on the operations of borrowing institutions. Some of these data may be secured by direct inquiries to the institution, whereas other data on amounts and periods of borrowing are already available within the discount department. The tentative decision that depository

---

[2]Federal Reserve Board Press Release, August 20, 1981.

institution borrowing, which has continued over some time, is inappropriate is dependent on such factors as (1) the amount being borrowed, (2) the previous borrowing record of the institution, (3) the stated purpose of the borrowing, (4) the borrowing institution's management of its assets and liabilities, and (5) the duration of borrowing.

## Inappropriate Borrowing and Counseling

If the determination that the borrowing is inappropriate is made, administrative **counseling**, or "discipline," is undertaken. A depository institution such as a commercial bank that has frequently or extensively borrowed from the discount window will receive a request to come to a conference with a Reserve Bank official. At this conference additional information about the circumstances causing the institution to borrow heavily or frequently will be solicited. In some cases, then, the depository institution will be counseled that continued frequent borrowing is inappropriate.

If the borrowing nevertheless continues, further conferences involving higher-level officials take place. As a final measure, it may be necessary to indicate that the depository institution's request for a renewal of credit will not be honored. All these conferences take place within the framework of the proper purposes of depository institution borrowing as prescribed by Regulation A of the Board of Governors. This regulation says in part,

> Federal Reserve credit is generally extended on a short-term basis to a member bank in order to enable it to adjust its asset position when necessary because of development such as a sudden withdrawal of deposits or seasonal requirements for credit beyond those which can reasonably be met by use of the bank's own resources.[3]

This is the phraseology of Regulation A, referring to member banks before March 31, 1980.

*Appropriate Borrowing from the Federal Reserve*     What, then, are the conditions under which it is appropriate for a depository institution to borrow from its regional Reserve Bank? The basic condition is that an individual depository institution has suffered an unanticipated—or larger than anticipated—loss of reserves through the clearing process. Ordinarily, depository institutions such as commercial banks are likely to expect that reserves lost through adverse clearing will be offset by

---

[3]Board of Governors of the Federal Reserve System, *The Federal Reserve System Purposes and Functions* (Washington, D.C.: 1963), p. 43.

reserves gained through favorable clearings, but occasionally a bank may suffer an unexpected large reserve drain through the clearing process. This may well occur in a period when the money market is under pressure from the Federal Reserve, because the system is not willing through its open market operations to provide all the reserves that could be used by money market banks. When these reserve losses suffered by a bank in the clearing process are expected to last only for a very short time (a few days or weeks at most), the bank or other depository institution may borrow appropriately from its regional Reserve Bank.

***Inappropriate Borrowing for Profit***    Losses in reserves that may occur because of more or less predictable seasonal movements in trade, or because the particular large depository institution is growing more rapidly than other financial institutions and therefore may suffer reserve losses through withdrawals of some of its large depositors, are ordinarily not good reasons for borrowing from the Federal Reserve. (After April 19, 1973, smaller depository institutions were able to utilize a new seasonal borrowing privilege for periods of up to ninety days.) When a large depository institution can reasonably be expected to be able to foresee reserve losses, the institution is expected to provide for such contingencies ahead of time.This may be accomplished in periods when customer credit requirements are low by accumulating such highly liquid investments as Treasury bills, which can then be liquidated in periods of rising demand for customer credit accommodation.

Also, the Federal Reserve would undoubtedly look most unkindly on any borrowing for profit, as distinguished from borrowing for need. For instance, the type of borrowing wherein a depository institution borrowed reserves from the Federal Reserve System because the discount rate was lower than the Treasury bill rate and could therefore make a profit through such borrowing would be actively discouraged through the administrative procedures of the discount window.

*Reluctant Borrowing*    If depository institutions did not observe the principle of being reluctant borrowers and, in fact, utilized the discount window for regular, heavy, and continuous borrowing of reserves, then of course any efforts at credit restraint through Federal Reserve open market operations would be completely nullified. Attempts by the Federal Reserve to prevent reserves going out the front door (open market operations) in order to prevent an inflationary increase in bank credit and the supply of money would be completely frustrated by having reserves go out the back door (discount window), with undesirable inflationary consequences. The existence of the discount window facilities, is, however, designed simply to provide a safety valve for Federal Reserve credit restraint policies.

All depository institutions will not be affected equally by the initial impacts of any move toward greater credit restraint. When the Federal Reserve is applying more pressure generally on reserve positions of depository institutions, it is quite appropriate for individual institutions to have a short period of adjustment until their portfolios can be readjusted to the change in monetary policy. When an institution borrows reserves from its regional Reserve Bank, it is in effect buying time to readjust its loan and security portfolio, but this time is not expected to be unlimited

## Large Depository Institutions Borrow More Often

All depository institutions do not resort equally to the facilities of their regional Reserve Bank discount window, even though the number of institutions borrowing rises significantly in periods of credit restraint. In 1969, for example, a period of severe credit restraint, 1,695 member banks borrowed from the Federal Reserve. With an easing of credit conditions in 1970 and 1971 the number of borrowing banks declined to 1,391 in 1970 and to 900 in 1971.[4] These borrowing banks represented 29 percent of member banks in 1970 and only 16 percent in 1971.

Insofar as size of member banks was considered, the data reveal that, among members banks with total deposits of $1 billion or more, 90 percent borrowed from the Federal Reserve in 1969, whereas only 10 percent of member banks with total deposits of less than $3 million engaged in such borrowing.[5] Larger depository institutions seem to find it more necessary to borrow reserves, because they often experience more unstable deposit behavior than smaller institutions. Furthermore, the larger institutions are likely to be more aggressive profit maximizers than smaller institutions and thus more likely to find themselves with a loss of reserves in periods of sharp rises in business lending. As has been noted, however, the Federal Reserve in 1973 revised Regulation A in such a way as to encourage more borrowing from the discount window, particularly when such borrowing seemed likely to assist smaller banks in meeting the seasonal borrowing needs of their communities.

[4]Andrew F. Brimmer, "Member Bank Borrowing, Portfolio Strategy and the Management of Federal Reserve Discount Policy," mimeographed paper given at the Western Economics Association. Aug. 25, 1972, p. 37.

[5]Ibid.

*Summary of Inappropriate Borrowing*    By way of partial summary of borrowing at the Federal Reserve by depository institutions, we may suggest the following categories of **inappropriate borrowing.** (1) Borrowing to finance speculative activities in securities, real estate, or commodities is inappropriate. (2) Borrowing to finance investments, such as borrowing to purchase securities for an institution's own account, is frowned upon. (3) Borrowing from a Reserve Bank to avoid liquidating investments at a capital loss is also discouraged. If depository institutions that in an earlier period purchased longer-term government securities, which are now selling at a discount, wish to avoid selling these securities at a capital loss, they may not appropriately borrow from the Federal Reserve to avoid this undesired capital loss. (4) Continuous borrowing, except in an emergency or some unusual situation, is also inconsistent with Federal Reserve discount window policy. Only borrowing for a short period to make adjustments in earning assets and lending policies is considered to be appropriate. (5) Borrowing from the Federal Reserve was never intended as a source of capital to supplement a depository institution's own resources. (6) Borrowing to earn a rate differential or to gain a tax advantage are other purposes that are considered inappropriate. It should be further pointed out that the principles regulating borrowing from the discount window do not change over the course of the business cycle, even though the discount rate itself is changed by the Federal Reserve in a countercyclical manner.

## Effect of Discount Rate Changes on Depository Institutions Borrowing

Although one might think that changes in the discount rate would tend to discourage or encourage borrowing at the discount window, the effect of changes in the discount rate on such borrowing is exactly a direct relationship. A high discount rate tends to be associated with high levels of depository institution borrowing, whereas a low discount rate tends to be associated with a low level. This apparent paradox can be explained by realizing that when the discount rate is high or when it is being raised, credit restraint on the financial system is being imposed by the Federal Reserve System. The system in such periods is deliberately forcing financial institutions to borrow reserves through the discount window, because these reserves are not being provided for the financial system through Federal Reserve open market operations.

When the discount rate is low or being cut in a given period, the economic problem facing the Federal Reserve is one of recession in economic activity, and the monetary policy followed by the Federal

Reserve is credit ease. That is, in periods when the Federal Reserve is cutting the discount rate, it is also normally supplying substantial amounts of reserves to depository institutions through aggressive open market operations. Furthermore, at such times of credit ease, demands for credit accommodation by would-be borrowers at such institutions are also declining. Thus both from the point of view of the supply of loanable funds, which are being increased by the Federal Reserve, and from the point of view of the demand for these loanable funds, financial institutions are not under pressure to borrow more reserves from the Federal Reserve. Therefore high discount rates are usually associated with high levels of discount window borrowing and low discount rates are usually associated with low levels.

## The Discount Rate and the Interest Rate Structure

A second channel of influence whereby changes in the discount rate are made part of the overall monetary policy of the Federal Reserve is through the impact of such changes in the discount rate on the entire structure of market interest rates. One expects to find a close interrelationship between the level of the discount rate and the level of short-term market interest rates, because depository institutions may use either the money market or the discount window of the Federal Reserve as sources for additional needed reserves. Hence, if the discount rate is above the market rate on Treasury bills and other short-term securities, there is an incentive for commercial banks and other depository institutions needing reserves to sell off some of their short-term investments instead of borrowing from the Reserve Bank.

Whenever the Federal Reserve permits the discount rate to stay below the short-term market rate for any prolonged period, difficult problems of administration in the discount window may arise, because depository institutions needing reserves have a strong incentive to borrow from the Federal Reserve instead of liquidating some of their investments. Whenever the discount rate is markedly below the short-term Treasury bill rate, it might seem apparent that the Federal Reserve is trying to encourage financial institutions to borrow from the discount window.

In some cases, however, the Federal Reserve may simply be reluctant to raise the discount rate to its "normal" position above money market yields, because the Federal Reserve is afraid such a move would tend to push up interest rates generally. The impact of Federal Reserve actions on market expectations must always be considered. A change in the discount rate may thus have an **announcement effect**. Not only participants in the money market but the business community and the public as well tend to interpret changes in the discount rate as a signal of a change in Federal Reserve credit and monetary policy.

## Questions for Discussion

1. Discuss the purpose and functioning of the discount windows of the twelve Federal Reserve Banks. Why is a rise in borrowing at the discount windows associated with increased credit restraint? Discuss the mechanics of borrowing by depository institutions. Why do large depository institutions tend to borrow somewhat more than small institutions?

2. Discuss the proposed reforms in the discount window with particular attention being paid to the proposed "basic borrowing privilege." Why do you think that these reforms were proposed? What results have followed from the new seasonal borrowing privilege of up to ninety days for small depository institutions as inaugurated in April 1973?

3. Under what conditions is it appropriate for institutions to borrow from the Federal Reserve? Would you expect that some depository institutions are more likely than others to use the facilities of the discount window? Why?

4. Discuss the "reluctance to borrow" principle as it affects the use of the discount window by depository institutions. How do the discount window officers enforce this principle? How could many of the administrative problems of the discount window be eliminated or diminished?

5. What are some inappropriate reasons for borrowing from the Federal Reserve? Is borrowing a right or a privilege? How may the Federal Reserve discourage what it regards as inappropriate borrowing?

6. Why does the Federal Reserve change the discount rate from time to time? Illustrate by discussing some of the changes in the late 1970s and early 1980s. Does a change in the discount rate always mean that there has been a change in Federal Reserve policy? Would you expect high discount rates to be associated with high borrowing or low borrowing? Why?

7. Discuss the announcement effect of changes in the discount rate. Does the discount rate lead or lag changes in the prime rate and other interest rates? Illustrate the relationship between the discount rate and the prime rate by giving some examples of the timing of such changes in these key interest rates.

8. Discuss changes in the discount rate in periods of credit ease (e. g., 1970–1971) as "signals" of Federal Reserve policy as compared with changes in the discount rate in a period of credit restraint (e.g., 1978–1982).

9. What is the effect on total reserves of depository institutions of a rise in borrowing at the discount windows of the regional Reserve Banks? To what extent does a discount rate below other key money market rates necessitate administrative counseling of would-be borrowers by discount window officers?

10. Why was the extended credit program inaugurated by the Federal Reserve in late August 1981? Do you believe that such a program was then necessary? How often in the 1980s do you think that depository institutions will have to apply to the Federal Reserve for such extended credit?

# Selected Bibliography for Further Reading

BOARD OF GOVERNORS OF THE FEDERAL RESERVE SYSTEM, *Reappraisal of the Federal Reserve Discount Mechanism Report of a System Committee* (Washington, D.C.: 1968).

——, *Reappraisal of the Federal Reserve Discount Mechanism*, three volumes (Washington, D.C.:Vol. 1, Aug. 1971; Vol. 2, Dec. 1971; Vol. 3, June 1972).

——, *Lending Functions of the Federal Reserve: A History* (Washington D.C.: 1973).

BREWER, ELIJAH, "Some Insights on Member Bank Borrowing," Economic Perspectives (Federal Reserve Bank of Chicago, Nov./Dec. 1978), pp. 16–21.

CACY, J. A., BRYON HIGGINS, and GORDON H. SELLEN, JR., "Should The Discount Rate Be a Penalty Rate?", *Economic Review* (Federal Reserve Bank of Kansas City, Jan. 1981), pp. 3–10.

GILBERT, R. ALTON, "Benefits of Borrowing from the Federal Reserve When the Discount Rate Is Below Market Interest Rates," *Review* (Federal Reserve Bank of St. Louis, March 1979), pp. 25–32.

——, "Access to the Discount Window for All Commercial Banks: Is It Important for Monetary Policy?" *Review* (Federal Reserve Bank of St. Louis, Feb. 1980), pp. 15–24.

KASRIEL, PAUL L., "The Discount Rate—Will It Float?", *Economic Perspectives* (Federal Reserve Bank of Chicago, May/June 1981), pp. 20–23.

SELLON, GORDON H., JR., "The Role of the Discount Rate in Monetary Policy: a Theoretical Analysis," *Economic Review* (Federal Reserve Bank of Kansas City, June 1980) pp. 3–15.

The operations of this bank seem to have produced effects quite opposite to those which were intended by the particular persons who planned and directed it.

THE WEALTH OF NATIONS

# 19
# CHAPTER

# Monetary Policy Coordination and Impacts

The coordination of the various tools of monetary-credit policy under the control of the Federal Reserve system had become especially important by the decade of the 1980s with the increasing emphasis placed on the control of the rate of growth of the various monetary aggregates. This is particularly true because the desired rate of growth of these aggregates sought by the Federal Open Market Committee (FOMC) is to be achieved primarily through the Trading Desk's influence on money and credit market conditions in carrying out the domestic policy directive given it by the FOMC.

Because the members of the FOMC are the seven Boards of Governors and five of the twelve Federal Reserve Bank presidents, the members of this key policymaking group can also consider what use to make of the various adjuncts to open market operations, such as the discount rate and the discount window. If the desired rate of growth in aggregates is to be achieved, all these weapons must be carefully coordinated. Otherwise a slowdown in the rate of growth of the money supply achieved by open market operations could be partly or completely offset by unrestricted access of the member banks to the discount window at a discount rate that well might be below the federal funds rate.

Furthermore, even if the major emphasis is to be on control of the money supply, the effects of open market operations and the other Federal Reserve tools of policy on the costs and flows of funds in the financial markets cannot be ignored. For one thing, a sudden and precipitous tightening of money and credit to slow down the growth in the money supply might have serious adverse effects on prospective or current Treasury borrowing operations. In addition, too sharp a rise in interest rates, again as a consequence of a dramatic slowing in the rate of growth of the money supply, might seriously damage the prospects for economic recovery from a recession. The possible impacts of monetary policy both on the financial markets initially and ultimately on borrowing and spending must thus be taken into account in the formulation of monetary policy and the coordination of its tools.

Nevertheless, the impact of changes in monetary policy are not felt equally by all sectors of the economy. For example, the construction industry, and particularly the residential part of it, is likely to be more adversely affected by monetary and credit restraint than, say, food processors or various service industries. Even so, commercial and industrial construction may be influenced less than residential construction. However, in periods of credit ease, residential construction is stimulated more than many other industries. On the other hand, some types of spending may be affected very little by changes in interest rates and the money supply.

***The Transmission Process of Monetary Policy*** In describing and evaluating how monetary policy affects the financial sector of the economy and then influences or interacts with the various real sectors of the economy, it is first necessary to have some behavioral theory of how monetary policy is supposed to affect economic activity. Regardless of the theoretical approach each theory usually has the following three basic assumptions: (1) the central bank acts initially on member bank reserves, (2) all real and price-variable targets are mutually attainable and may be represented by nominal national income, (3) there is no simultaneous feedback from the target variables to the monetary variables.

***Five Major Models*** Skeleton frameworks for the five major monetary theories may be given as follows: (1) the classical quantity theory is $R \rightarrow M \rightarrow Y$, where $R$ is member bank reserves, $M$ is the stock of money, and $Y$ is nominal national income; (2) the simple Keynesian theory is $R \rightarrow M \rightarrow$ "$i$" $\rightarrow I \rightarrow Y$, where "$i$" is *the* rate of interest and $I$ is real investment; (3) the portfolio adjustment theory is

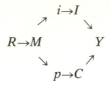

where $i$ is the vector of all market rates of interest (i.e., a variable that shows the direction of change of yields in the money and capital markets, $p$ is a vector of all prices (i.e., a variable that shows the direction of change in prices), and $C$ is consumption; (4) the availability theory is $R \rightarrow i \rightarrow L \rightarrow K \rightarrow Y$, where $L$ is liquidity and $K$ is all credit; (5) the bankers' theory is

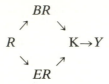

where $BR$ is reserves borrowed at Federal Reserve Banks and $ER$ is excess reserves of member banks. (These simple diagrams were first developed by George G. Kaufman, then an officer of the Federal Reserve Bank of Chicago, for presentation at central banking seminars at that Reserve Bank).

## THE PORTFOLIO ADJUSTMENT MODEL

The most generally accepted theory among most students of monetary economics appears to be the portfolio adjustment theory, which is a more complicated version of simple Keynesian theory, which in turn is a more complicated theory than traditional monetary theory in the form of the quantity theory. In the portfolio approach, when the central bank changes bank reserves either through open market operations or changes in reserve requirements, there is an initial impact on the prices (and yields) of various financial assets, especially government securities. After the price and yield impacts are transmitted throughout the financial markets, there will be impacts on the borrowing and expenditures of various household and business spending units. The changes in spending of these decision-making units also affect the prices of real goods and services.

Changes in the relative prices of newly produced goods, and changes in the prices of existing goods (the wealth effect), induce additional changes in spending on both financial assets and goods. These additional effects occur until a new equilibrium is attained in both the money market and the real goods market. The development of new equilibrium prices will also result in new **equilibrium levels of output** and **employment**. The path to the new equilibrium values, however, may not be smooth or instantaneous.

***Time Lags***     In short, there may be important and variable **time lags** in moving from one equilibrium condition to another equilibrium set of variables as a result of central bank action. Furthermore, there is not complete unanimity among economists as to the preferred theoretical approach. All five theoretical schema have their devoted followers, as well as their persistent detractors. Growing out of the different basic theoretical approaches, there have come to be different views as to the proper role of the central bank in achieving its ultimate goals through its power over various financial variables, especially bank reserves. Regardless of one's theoretical view, it is clear to all monetary economists that one should specify how changes in monetary policy affecting bank reserves and the money supply ultimately have an impact on real output, employment, and the price level.

## CHANGES IN THE MONEY SUPPLY AND IMPACTS ON REAL ECONOMIC SECTORS

After the added emphasis on the direct control of key monetary aggregates at the open market meeting of October 6, 1979, the staff of the Federal Reserve Board and the Federal Reserve Banks conducted research studies to try to determine the quantitative relationships between changes in the money supply and the real sectors of the economy. Governor Henry C. Wallich reported that there were five major conclusions of these studies, which in effect pointed to certain limitations of monetary policy in achieving the goals desired quickly and certainly.

For one thing, the studies revealed that the relationship between the money supply and the real sectors had become looser in the 1970s and the early 1980s than earlier. **Money-demand equations** that had been regarded earlier as quite reliable now quite seriously overpredicted money, given GNP and interest rates. In short, there was a downward shift in the demand for money probably resulting from new **cash-management practices** arising from new high levels of interest rates. This necessitated the formulation of new money-demand equations.

Second, the Federal Reserve studies revealed, as had often been true of earlier studies, a high degree of randomness in any money-supply series. This randomness is often called "**noise.**" Third, because of such randomness in the variation of growth in the money supply, an attempt to return to a target path in a period of less than three months does not in fact greatly improve the actual performance of the money supply in terms of the targeted path. However, any improvement in attaining the path targeted will lead to increasingly greater volatility in interest rates.

Fourth, short-term deviations of the money supply from its target path, which last three to six months, have only minor real sector consequences. It is true that in the unusual year of 1980 over- and undershoots of the monetary targets coincided closely with movements in the economy. That year must be regarded as something of a "sport," however, because there is little or no long-term empirical evidence that confirms a lagless relationship in which an exogenous money supply affects the economy. On the contrary, a more plausible hypothesis is that there is an **endogenous** money supply dominated by economic activity, which can be expected to follow fluctuations of the real sector (perhaps contemporaneously) rather than leading them. Furthermore, when the Federal Reserve focuses on much tighter control of the growth path of the monetary aggregates as in 1980, 1981, and 1982 greater volatility of interest rates is almost inevitable.

Finally, insofar as the impact of higher interest rates on would-be borrowers is concerned, Governor Wallich noted that there is in effect a two-tier structure of borrowers. For business firms with positive profits, the tax deductibility of interest payments means that they are only moderately affected by high nominal rates. For many borrowers in this tier, the real after-tax interest rate may still be negative even with relatively high nominal rates. On the other hand, business firms with losses, or households taking the standard deduction, are not cushioned against the impact of high interest rates. For them, prospective borrowing and subsequent spending may very well be reduced when interest rates are moved up sharply by Federal Reserve credit restraint policies.

## EMPHASIS ON OPEN MARKET OPERATIONS

In influencing the flows of money and credit and the price of such credit in the financial markets, either in a period of credit restraint or the opposite period of credit ease, the Federal Reserve can use an assortment of monetary-credit instruments. The list of chosen instruments depends on the potency of the impact desired, as well as on the nature of the policy problem judged as having currently the highest priority on the scale of values of the monetary authorities. Since 1951 the traditional weapon, which has been used most frequently, is open market operations.

Such open market operations involve the purchase and sale of government securities, either outright or with repurchase agreements or matched sale-purchase agreements, by the Trading Desk of the Federal Reserve Bank of New York. These operations not only directly change the amount of bank reserves by the exact amount of the purchase or sale but also change prices and yields of the money or capital market instruments traded. Because open market operations usually involve Treasury bills, it is not surprising that the Open Market Committee prior to the 1970s was often concerned with maintaining or reaching a particular level of Treasury bill rates.

## Adjunct Role of Discount Window

The discount rate and the administration of the discount window are usually viewed as adjuncts to open market operations. If the Federal Reserve decides not to accommodate all the banking system needs for added reserves through open market operations, it may still be willing to allow depository institutions to borrow needed reserves at their regional Reserve Bank. Because the "reluctance principle" is supposed to be in effect, the depository institutions are presumably under pressure insofar as their liquidity position is concerned when they are in debt to the Federal Reserve.

At times the discount window officers screen borrowing requests of continuous borrowers with some care, but at other times the window seems to be freely open to all borrowing requests. As previously noted, in 1980 and 1981 a penalty surcharge of 3 or 4 percent was added to the basic discount rate for large continuous borrowers. At all times, however, the Federal Reserve frowns on borrowing for profit, or in avoidance of loss, and sanctions only borrowing for need.

Nevertheless, it is true that regardless of the motive, depository institutions' borrowing increases bank reserves and thereby negates to some extent the depressing effect of open market operations on reserves in a period of credit restraint. Hence the discount window can be regarded either as a **safety valve** for depository institutions feeling the restrictive effects of credit restraint or as an escape from credit restraint by the financial system.

## Changing Reserve Ratio Requirements

One major defect of open market operations is that all such operations are concentrated in the central money market in New York City, so that the depressing or easing effects of credit restraint or credit ease are felt first by the major money market banks. Because these are no more than

134 weekly reporting banks out of some 14,700 banks and in practice may be substantially fewer than this number, it may be that in some circumstances it is better to affect directly a larger group of commercial banks. One way to make credit restraint or ease affect all depository institutions with transactions accounts in a given short period of time is to change the legal reserve ratio behind demand or time deposits.

Beginning in the summer of 1966, this weapon of monetary policy was used again in periods of credit restraint and in periods of credit ease. In the next eleven years, legal reserve ratios were changed fourteen times. In five instances the reserve ratios were increased, whereas in nine other cases they were decreased. A number of changes in legal reserve ratios were relatively minor after the November 1972 changes in the structure of legal reserve ratios. (After November 1972, legal reserve ratios were on a sliding scale based entirely on the amount of net demand deposits held by the member banks.) Often one category of deposits would have a changed legal reserve ratio while the other categories were left unchanged. Furthermore, when changes were made they were only in increments of ¼ or ½ of 1 percent.

However, when the Monetary Control Act of 1980 was passed, reserve requirements were simplified by being only two reserve ratios—one applying to transactions accounts under $25 million and the other applying to more than $25 million in transactions accounts. After the passage of this act it appeared that this weapon (i.e., changes in reserve ratio requirements) would henceforth be used infrequently.

## DEVELOPING A CREDIT RESTRAINT POLICY

Let us assume that the various instruments of Federal Reserve policy are being used to carry out a newly determined policy of credit restraint (e.g., after October 6, 1979). Excess demand has already developed in some product markets and is reflected in rising prices. Both consumer expenditures and business expenditures for new plant and equipment are rising markedly. Increased loan demand is being felt at commercial banks and in the financial markets. Interest rates are rising. Inflationary price increases of goods and services became so sharp in 1979–1980 that double-digit inflation often resulted (e.g., nearly an 18 percent annual rate in the first quarter of 1980). In short, this was a typical period of demand-pull inflation.

***Budget Deficit Leading to Inflation***    The original cause of the inflation was a sharp rise in government expenditures in a period of near full employment, including military expenditures, which were not matched by a corresponding rise in tax receipts. National defense spending in fiscal 1980 (October 1, 1979, to September 30, 1980) was $135.8 billion, as compared with $117.7 billion the previous year. Spending for income security likewise rose sharply in the same period, from $160 billion to $193 billion.

A sizable **budget deficit** thus developed and was financed in part by monetizing government debt by the commercial banking system. The budget deficit rose from $27.7 billion in fiscal 1979 to $59.5 billion in fiscal 1980. This sale of new government debt to the banks was aided and abetted in part by the provision of additional bank reserves by the Federal Reserve System.

Even so, the money supply (M1-B) rose only 7.4 percent in 1979 and 6.7 percent in 1980. Higher interest rates from greater borrowing demands by the federal government and many private borrowers also resulted in an economizing of cash balances and thus a higher turnover (velocity) of money. Higher spending rates and the higher turnover of money in the face of slower rates of growth in real output led to the double-digit inflation rates in the general price level in 1979 and 1980.

## Use of Federal Reserve Instruments to Restrain Inflation

This situation induced the Federal Reserve to resort to still greater restraint to try to slow down private borrowing through higher interest rates in hopes of attaining slower growth rates in the monetary aggregates. The main reliance, as usual, was on open market operations. The legal reserve ratio behind transactions accounts of depository institutions was not increased in this period but was instead lowered somewhat after the 1980 act. Discount rates, however, were raised a number of times, and a penalty surcharge was added, as already stated.

The consequence of these restrictive monetary and credit actions by the Federal Reserve was a somewhat slower growth of money in 1980 than in 1979 and much greater volatility in interest rates, as well as a higher level of interest rates. Despite a very sharp recession in the second quarter of 1980 (nearly a 10 percent decline in real output), inflation rates remained at double-digit levels, only slightly lower than the 1979 rates.

## Credit Restraint in 1981

In November 1980, Ronald Reagan was elected President of the United States and his new conservative administration encouraged the Federal Reserve to adopt still more restrictive policies in 1981 to curb what had become chronic inflation. Accordingly, in early February 1981, the FOMC adopted growth paths for the various monetary aggregates, which had ceiling rates markedly below the actual growth rates of these same aggregates in 1980. The most commonly used definition of money then, M1-B, even after adjustment for the impact of ATS and NOW accounts, had grown by 6.7 percent in 1980. In 1981 the target range was to be 3 to 5½ percent.

In the first quarter of 1981, however, the GNP in real terms grew about 8.6 percent, which was much higher than had been generally expected. Moreover, the income velocity of money continued to rise. By April, M1-B was growing at an annual rate of about 14 percent, which was much greater than had been targeted. The result, as might have been expected, was a shift toward much more substantial credit restraint in late April and early May. This greater credit restraint is probably why GNP declined slightly at a 1.6 percent annual rate in the second quarter of 1981, and why a sharp economic recession began in the fourth quarter of 1981.

## Higher Borrowings, Higher Federal Funds Rates, Higher Discount Rates in 1981

The first signs of greater credit restraint came in a jump in depository institution borrowings at the discount windows of the Federal Reserve Banks to a level averaging about $2.4 billion in the two statement weeks ending May 6. In the previous three weeks, such borrowings had averaged only about $1 billion. Clearly, the Trading Desk was not providing as much reserves as the banks and other depository institutions thought they needed.

Further evidence as to greater monetary restraint was provided by looking at the **federal funds rates**. This key interest rate on bank borrowings of excess reserves fluctuated within a range of 17 to 20 percent in the last days of April and the first days of May. In the previous three weeks, it had averaged around 15½ percent.

If there was any doubt that the Federal Reserve had moved toward greater monetary and credit restraint, the signals should have been most clear as to that intent when the **basic discount rate** was raised from 13 to 14 percent on May 4. At the same time, the penalty surcharge for large, continuous borrowers was increased from 3 to 4 percent.

## Impacts of 1981 Credit Restraint

In a telephone conference on May 6, the FOMC confirmed the steps that had been taken towards greater tightening and also permitted the Trading Desk to allow the federal funds rate to move above the range of 13 to 18 percent, which had been set by the Committee on March 31. In the next few days, federal funds typically traded between 18 and 19 percent.

At its regular meeting of May 18, the FOMC confirmed that a posture of restraint needed to be maintained. The committee also lowered the target path for M1-B to an annual rate of 3 percent *or lower* for the period from April to June. The targeted range for the key federal funds rate was now moved up to 16 to 22 percent. Even then the Trading Desk was not expected to take action through open market operations to bring the federal funds rate within this range unless the rate was persistently outside the target range.

Market yields on all maturities of private and public debt rose in 1981, as expected, in response to persistent credit tightening by the Federal Reserve. Not until September 1981 did such market yields reach a peak after earlier apparently peaking in early May. By September, long-term Treasury issues were yielding about 14½ percent, and new mortgages were being extended at effective rates above 17 percent.

All these successive turns of the credit screw by the monetary authorities in 1981 finally seemed to have some desired effects, especially on inflation. The inflation rate in the second quarter as measured by the GNP deflator fell to only 6 percent. The inflation rate of consumer prices for the entire year of 1981 was 8.9 percent, well below the 12.3 percent figure of 1980.

There was, however, a price to be paid in terms of lost real output. The second quarter of 1981 registered a moderate decline in real output. A small increase in final output appeared in the third quarter, but a serious recession began in the fourth quarter, which continued in the first half of 1982. Because of declines in real output, unemployment rates also increased to 9.8 percent by July 1982.

## Higher Interest Rates in Credit Restraint

The effects of Federal Reserve credit restraint on interest rates can be seen in Figure 19–1, not only for the very severe credit restraint period of 1979–1981 but also for the earlier period of 1974. In both cases, double-digit inflation rates led to the Federal Reserve measures that escalated interest rates. Also in both periods, short-term interest rates (top of the graph) were much more volatile than long-term rates (bottom of the graph). Nevertheless, the considerable impacts of credit restraint on long-term rates can also be observed in this figure.

## Corporate and Municipal Bond Postponements in Periods of Credit Restraint

When capital market yields are moving up sharply as they did in late 1979–1981, earlier in 1973–1974, and still earlier in 1966 and 1969, a

**Figure 19–1    Selected Interest Rates, 1974–1980**

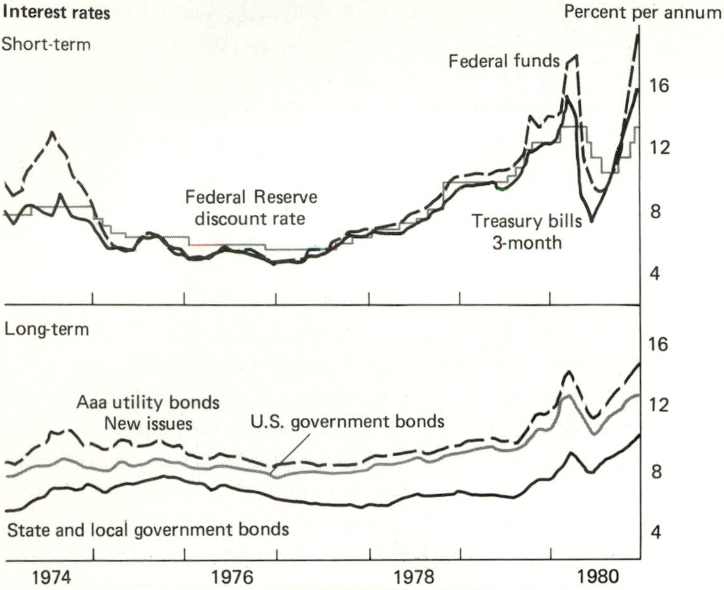

SOURCE: Board of Governors of the Federal Reserve System, *Annual Report 1980*, p. 14.

number of proposed corporate and municipal bond issues are post-poned. Looking first at the period a decade earlier, we find that corporate issues, which reached a high level of $31.9 billion in 1971, as a result of **bond postponements** fell to $27.7 billion in 1972 and fell even more sharply to $22.3 billion in 1973. By 1974, however, corporations apparently felt it necessary to accept the higher levels of borrowing costs in the capital markets, especially because the prime rate at banks had risen sharply and thus increased their bond flotations to $32 billion. When bond yields declined in 1975 and 1976, corporations responded by floating more than $42 billion of bonds in 1975 and again in 1976. More than $40 billion in corporate bonds were sold in 1977 and 1978 and more than $50 billion in 1979.

The restrictive effects of credit restraint on corporate bond sales thus proved to be temporary as corporate needs for external funds have grown over time. Oddly enough, in 1980 corporate bond sales totaled some $73.7 billion, up sharply from the $51.5 billion of 1979. Nevertheless, considerable numbers of proposed bond sales in the first quarter of 1980 were not sold until the second and third quarters of that year. (Actually, credit restraint by the Fed in 1980 peaked in early April, then eased in the second and third quarters, and then became even more restrictive in the fourth quarter and continued in 1981 and 1982). As a result of greater restraint in late 1980, which lasted past mid-1982, corporate bonds sold in 1981 were $8.7 billion less than bond sales in 1980, while municipal bond sales declined by $3.2 billion. Corporate and municipal bond sales remained depressed in 1982, as credit restraint continued.

## Bank and Business Escapes from Credit Restraint

When the Federal Reserve is imposing a policy of severe credit restraint on the banking system—as in 1979–1982 or earlier in 1973–1974—the banks and business firms feeling the squeeze attempt to mitigate the effects of such pressures, if possible. A temporary easing of pressure may be secured by borrowing needed reserves from the Federal Reserve itself. Or if these become unavailable in the quantity desired, commercial banks with deficient reserves may borrow from other banks with excess reserves through the federal funds market. Large American banks may even resort to borrowing in the Eurodollar market by having their London branches remit dollar time deposits to the home office. This may be done even though the interest costs of borrowing such scarce time deposits abroad may soar in a period of credit restraint.

Banks may also attempt to escape the effects of a shortage of loanable funds by setting up one-bank holding companies, which can then sell commercial paper in the money market. Banks may also sell some of their investment portfolio of U.S. government securities and even lighten somewhat their holdings of state and local government securities.

*Economizing on Scarce Money*    Bank customers such as large business firms may further delay the full impacts of credit restraint by various ingenious schemes to economize on scarce money and credit. The commercial paper market may be tapped for funds by such companies as well as traditional sources of bank credit. Firms may also borrow in foreign money and credit markets. Delay in payment of bills due—or a greater use of trade credit—also economizes on scarce money. Any and all of these efforts to create money substitutes inevitably increase the velocity of money. Even though the growth in the stock of money may be curtailed by the monetary authorities, the money flow (MV) can still increase. All these offsets extend the time required for the full impact of credit restraint policies to be felt on the economy.

Hence the inflationary forces leading to price and wage increases were still operative in 1979 and 1980, as they had been earlier in 1973 and 1974, despite the substantial credit restraint that the Federal Reserve had imposed on the economy. In 1980, prices were still rising at double-digit rates and the inflation rates did not fall to the high single-digit rate until 1981. Moreover, the slowdown in borrowing and spending that took place in 1980, 1981 and 1982 did not affect all would-be borrowers equally.

## Measuring Credit Restraint or Ease

Credit restraint or ease may be measured by looking at various key monetary indicators. Which indicator is the most important at any time depends in part on the relative emphasis given by the monetary authorities to various intermediate variables such as the money stock or various interest rates. This in turn depends on which monetary model explaining the supposed "linkages" of these intermediate variables with the final policy goals of full employment or price level stability is most in vogue at the moment.

By the 1980s, as indicated, greater attention was being focused on such monetary aggregates as the money stock (M1, M2, and M3) and various measures of reserves, particularly unborrowed reserves. Nonetheless, the concern of the 1960s with key money market interest rates was not entirely neglected. In all the FOMC meetings in the 1970s, all the major developments in the economy, including interest rate changes in the money and capital markets, continued to be analyzed and in part deliberately influenced.

Even after October 6, 1979, a broad band of federal funds rate was monitored, when open market operations were being conducted by the Trading Desk. Interest rate changes in both the money market and the capital markets are thus always examined by the FOMC and the Trading Desk. Hence it was perfectly proper for the impartial observer to look at a number of indicators of either monetary restraint or ease. In measuring credit restraint or ease, one should consider changes in interest rates as well as changes in the growth rate of the key monetary aggregates.

## CREDIT EASE POLICIES OF THE FEDERAL RESERVE

A period of credit restraint is invariably followed by a period of credit ease. That is, the American economy is subject to variations in business activity.For three or four years there may be an upswing in production and employment, which is likely at some stage to result in inflationary pressures and credit restraint policies by the Federal Reserve. During the upswing in economic activity, distortions in the cost-price structure and excessive inventory accumulation may develop, which eventually lead to a downturn in economic activity. These recessions typically last less than a year and are accompanied by credit easing policies of the Federal Reserve.

In general, in a period of credit ease the Federal Reserve follows the opposite policies to those that it utilizes in a credit restraint period. Hence the instructions by the FOMC to the Trading Desk now call for a faster rate of growth in all monetary aggregates and a decline in the level of the federal funds rate. Even prior to a fall in money market rates, the discount rate sometimes is cut at all twelve Federal Reserve Banks as a signal of the intention of the Federal Reserve to move toward credit ease. Legal reserve ratios in the past have also sometimes been reduced to further stimulate the greater availability of reserves and thus more loanable funds at all member banks.

The intent of these credit easing actions is to reduce the level of all interest rates, particularly long-term rates, and to increase the general liquidity of the economy. In turn, with greater liquidity and lower borrowing costs, it is hoped that business firms and consumers will borrow more and spend more to increase total output and employment. A study supervised by Robert Weintraub in 1976 found that for each 1 percent increase in the money supply, real GNP increased on the average by 0.73 percent the same year. However, a rise in real GNP, which initially accompanies increased money growth, recedes quickly after three years and is about zero after five years. Such money supply growth therefore does contribute to recovery from a recession.

If the Federal Reserve stimulus to rapid growth in the money supply continues too long, significant inflationary pressures can develop that subsequently lead to credit restraint policies by the Federal Reserve. The Weintraub study showed that on the average consumer prices rose 1 percent two years after each yearly increase of 1½ percent in the then narrowly defined money supply, M1. Hence more than 70 percent of the rise in consumer prices in the inflationary 1966–1975 decade can be attributed to excessively rapid money growth. Additionally, increases in the velocity of money even after money growth slows make possible still higher money payments and can add to inflationary pressures in a full employment period.

Despite the dangers of an excessively easy monetary policy by the Federal Reserve, considerable political pressures often urge greater growth in the money supply and lower interest rates. These political pressures become particularly intense in credit restraint periods because of the differential impacts of credit restraint. That is, some sectors of the economy suffer more from credit restraint than others.

# DIFFERENTIAL IMPACTS OF MONETARY POLICY

A major way that the central bank affects the general level of economic activity is by varying not only the quantity of the stock of money but also the level of interest rates, as suggested earlier. All would-be borrowers, however, do not react in the same manner to changes in the cost of borrowing external funds. In technical terms, borrowers have different **elasticities of demand for borrowed funds**. Some borrowers, in short, are more sensitive than others to changes in the cost of borrowed funds. For example, in 1969, when the policy of credit restraint was beginning to take hold, state and local governments were forced by unsettled conditions in the financial markets to postpone or reduce their scheduled borrowings by at least $4 billion to $5 billion. In the same year business loans at large commercial banks rose by $5 billion.

More than a decade later in 1980, when state and local bond flotations were rising only by $5 billion, corporate bond flotations rose very sharply, by $22 billion. For both types of borrowers, however, bond flotations were particularly heavy in the second and third quarters, when the Fed eased, than in the first and fourth quarters, when restrictive monetary and credit policies were in force. In 1981, however, credit restraint was intensified. As might have been expected, all kinds of bond issues declined. Corporate bonds, alone, fell by $8.7 billion in 1981.

## *Industries Most Affected by Credit Restraint*

Whenever the monetary authorities impose a restrictive credit policy on the banking system, we should expect that some sectors of the economy will be harder hit than others. Industries that feel the greatest impact of such a restrictive credit policy are characterized by one or more of the following: (1) a higher percentage of borrowed funds in working and fixed capital than other industries, (2) a higher capital-output ratio than other industries, (3) poorer credit of firms in the industry, perhaps because of the presence of a large number of small firms, (4) production of goods or services for other sectors, which may suffer a reduction in their planned expenditures as a result of credit curtailment, (5) a chronic shortage of working capital, as revealed perhaps by lower liquidity ratios than other industries, (6) traditionally relatively small profit margins, and (7) a small backlog of orders or even working below production capacity. These characteristics of industries that may have difficulty in meeting all of their borrowing requirements in a period of increasing credit restraint do not mean that only declining or stagnating industries experience difficulty in borrowing all that they may wish. Expanding industries, too, may find difficulty in receiving all of the desired credit accommodation. In addition to differences among industries, one might also expect considerable variations among business firms, even in the same industry, in their ability to secure borrowed funds.

***Small Versus Large Firms***    One common allegation often made in a period of tight money is that small business firms are discriminated against by commercial banks in favor of large business firms. The paucity of the right kind of data makes it difficult to respond conclusively to this allegation. What data there are seem to be subject to varying interpretations. Larger-sized bank loans have tended to rise more than small-sized loans in periods of credit restraint. But does this prove there is unfair discrimination in access to bank credit against small business firms? Already by introducing the word "unfair", we have entered the area of value judgments. Furthermore, large numbers of depth interviews would be needed with both business people and bankers to try to answer any such question of fairness. Every period of credit restraint does however bring renewed charges of this type of credit discrimination. Available evidence suggests that commercial banks, like other businesses, tend to prefer to deal with their established customers whenever credit becomes scarcer and has to be rationed. These long-standing customers, of course, may turn out to be large, medium, or small business firms.

***Housing Starts in the 1970s and early 1980s***    In the decade of the 1970s as in earlier decades, **housing starts** with a lag of a few months reflected swings by the Federal Reserve to policies of credit restraint, which were followed by moves to ease credit. Credit restraint in 1969 was followed by credit ease in the first several years of the 1970s. Credit ease in 1971 and 1972 resulted in more than two million housing starts each year, a sharply higher rate than the 1.4 million level of 1970, which resulted from credit restraint in 1969.

Even in 1973 housing starts were at the two-million level, although they were down somewhat from the 2.3 million rate of 1972. But credit restraint in 1973, which became quite severe in 1974, led to only 1.3 million starts in 1974 and an even lower level of 1.1 million in 1975. However, the severe recession of 1973–1975, which was brought on in part by credit restraint, resulted in an easing of credit restraint in late 1974 and all of 1975.

Housing starts began to pick up in 1976, when they reached the 1.5 million level, and rose in 1977 and 1978 until they reached a peak rate, which slightly exceeded two million starts in 1978. Another period of credit restraint that began in late 1979, was relaxed for several quarters in 1980, and then was reapplied with greater vigor in late 1980, 1981 and

1982 had a very severe impact on housing starts. In 1979 housing starts fell to 1.7 million; in 1980 they were about 1.3 million; and in 1981 they were also slightly above 1 million starts.

*Lags in Impact of Monetary Policy*   Part of the difficulty in assessing the impact, differential or otherwise, of monetary policy at any given time is that there is a pronounced lag in the full impact of any change in monetary policy. If, for example, the economy is recovering from a recession and the prevailing climate of monetary-credit policy turns from one of pronounced ease to one of less ease and finally credit restraint, there is bound to be a **monetary lag** before would-be borrowers are really subject to noticeable difficulties in securing credit. The effect on actual spending as indicated in the series of new housing starts takes even longer to show up. For one thing, advance credit commitments are the rule for many mortgage lenders. New housing starts, therefore, can continue to increase even after the monetary authorities have started putting on the brake for new credit extension. Similarly, after a period of downturn in general economic activity has occurred and the monetary authorities have released the brake and accelerated the extension of new

**Figure 19–2    Cumulative Percentage Distributions of the Effects of Various Money Aggregates on GNP**

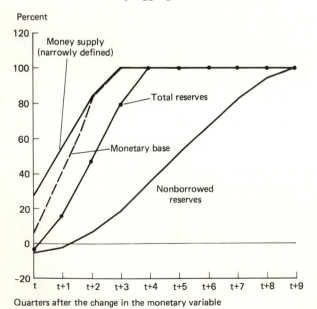

SOURCE: Michael J. Hamburger, "The Lag in the Effect of Monetary Policy: A Survey of Recent Literature," *Monthly Review,* Federal Reserve Bank of New York, Dec. 1971, p. 293.

credit, there is a noticeable lag before the engine of the economy fully responds.

Views among monetary economists differ as to the length of time required for the impact of monetary policy as measured, say, by changes in various key monetary aggregates such as the money supply, bank reserves, and unborrowed reserves to affect the GNP. Some believe that the major impact is very short (i.e., one or two quarters); others believe that it is very long, perhaps as much as two years. (See Weintraub study.) The typical view among monetary economists, however, seems to be that most of the effect is accomplished within four or five quarters, and that important impacts on the GNP can be felt some six to nine months after major monetary policy changes. This consensus viewpoint is summarized in Figure 19–2.

# Questions for Discussion

1. Summarize the five major models of monetary theories and briefly discuss the differences in these models.
2. Discuss the major channels of monetary policy and the problem of lags in the impact of monetary policy on the economy. Indicate the results of simulation studies using econometric models.
3. Discuss the use of the discount window and changes in reserve requirements as Federal Reserve weapons to be coordinated with the use of open market operations. To what extent is the discount window a safety valve or an escape from credit restraint brought about by open market operations? Why might the Federal Reserve wish to accomplish some of a given policy of credit restraint or credit ease through changing reserve requirements rather than entirely through open market operations?
4. Discuss the progressive development of a posture of credit restraint by the Federal Reserve in a period of increasing inflationary pressures. To what extent is gradualism involved in the successive steps likely to be taken by the Federal Reserve? Discuss the coordinated use of the various instruments available to the Federal Reserve.
5. Discuss the impacts on the rate of growth of the monetary aggregates and on interest rates of a policy of increasing credit restraint by the Federal Reserve. To what extent may commercial banks lessen the effects on them of such increasing credit restraint? (*Hint*: Include in your discussion the issuance of commercial paper by bank holding companies, as well as increased resort to the federal funds market. What other ways are available for banks to increase their loanable funds?)
6. Discuss the development of a policy of credit ease by the Federal Reserve, indicating the way in which each weapon is used. What are some of the short-run and long-run effects of such a credit ease policy?

7. Discuss the differential effects of policies of credit ease and restraint on different sectors of the economy. Why do some borrowers seem more sensitive to changes in interest rates than others? Are the same borrowers sensitive to lower interest rates that are sensitive to higher interest rates? Why?
8. Discuss the lags in credit restraint and ease on both lenders and borrowers. Why may a period of some months ensue before lenders start rationing funds or increasing the availability of funds to would-be borrowers? Discuss both price and nonprice rationing by lenders. How effective are increases or decreases in interest rates in slowing down or increasing borrowing demands on commercial banks? Why?
9. Discuss the restraining and stimulating effects of credit restraint and credit ease on the housing industry, using the decade of the 1970s and the early 1980s to illustrate such monetary policy impacts.

# Selected Bibliography for Further Reading

## Books and Monographs

COMMISSION ON MONEY AND CREDIT, *Impacts of Monetary Policy* (Englewood Cliffs, N.J.: Prentice-Hall, 1963).

FEDERAL RESERVE BANK OF BOSTON, *Controlling Monetary Aggregates Monetary Conference June 1969* (Boston: 1969).

JACOBY, NEIL H., ed., *United States Monetary Policy* (New York: Praeger, 1964).

KAUFMAN, GEORGE C., *Current Issues in Monetary Economics and Policy: A Review* (New York: Institute of Finance, New York University, May 1969).

MAYER, THOMAS, *Monetary Policy in the United States* (New York: Random House, 1968).

RITTER, LAWRENCE S., ed., *Money and Economic Activity Readings in Money and Banking*, 3rd ed. (Boston: Houghton Mifflin, 1967).

ROOSA, ROBERT V., *Federal Reserve Operations in the Money and Government Securities Market* (New York: Federal Reserve Bank of New York, 1956).

WEINTRAUB, ROBERT, Staff Director, Subcommittee on Monetary Policy, Committee on Banking, Currency and Housing, House of Representatives, *The Impact of the Federal Reserve System's Monetary Policies on the Nation's Economy* (Washington, D.C.: U.S. Government Printing Office, 1976).

## Articles

BRUNNER, KARL, "The Role of Money and Monetary Policy," *Review*, Federal Reserve Bank of St. Louis, July 1968, pp. 9—24.

HAMBURGER, MICHAEL J., "The Lag in the Effect of Monetary Policy: A Survey of Recent Literature," *Monthly Review*, Federal Reserve Bank of New York, Vol. 53, No. 12, Dec. 1971, pp. 289–298.

WALLICH, HENRY C., "The Limits of Monetary Control," remarks to the Midwest Economics and Finance Associations, Louisville, Kentucky, April 3, 1981, Mimeographed, pp. 1–16.

# PART 6

# MONETARY AND INCOME THEORY

# 20
# CHAPTER

# Traditional Monetary Theory

Much traditional monetary theory once centered around the "quantity" theory of money. Many early economists observed that there seemed to be some connection between the amount of money in a country and its price level. It remained for the neoclassical economists of the nineteenth and early twentieth centuries to formulate these more or less common-sense observations into a theory explaining cause and effect relationships. These quantity theorists invariably emphasized the effect of changes in the supply of money as a factor leading to changes in the price level. In analyzing the interrelationships between money and the prices of goods and services, the early twentieth-century money theorists used some version of the equation of exchange that included the variables of the velocity of money and the price level. These quantity theorists usually assumed, however, that the turnover of money and the volume of transactions and output were constant, so that necessarily and logically any given change in the stock of money was reflected in a similar proportional change in the average prices of goods and services.

Modern quantity theorists, usually called "**monetarists**," do not necessarily make these same simple assumptions, so that recent formulations of the quantity theory are more complex as well as more sophisticated. Furthermore, modern quantity theorists are as much concerned with the demand for money as with the supply. But they still believe that the single most important variable determining nominal money income (and the price level) is the stock of money.

411

## THE TRADITIONAL QUANTITY THEORY OF MONEY

Even the simplest version of the quantity theory represented a kind of aggregate demand theory, though it was not usually presented in these terms. Later economic writers liked to refer to the value of money as determined in much the same way as the value of any given commodity (i.e., by demand and supply). Insofar as the demand for money was involved, however, no rational economic transactor was supposed to want money for its own sake; otherwise the transactor would be suffering a "money illusion."

The only reason that people or institutions were supposed to desire money was to acquire enough purchasing power to buy goods and services. Their total spending on real goods and services, as well as on securities, would determine their "transactions" demand for money. This transactions demand for money occurs because persons, business firms, and governmental units typically all suffer from a lack of synchronization of receipts and expenditures; spending and receipt of money do not occur at exactly the same time. If only spending on currently produced goods and services was involved, then an "income" demand for money was involved. Some writers used the transactions demand for money and the income demand for money as if these terms were readily interchangeable.

If total transactions in the economy increased, or the total income generated in the economy rose, then the demand for money needed to accomplish the higher level of money spending would necessarily increase also. In effect, therefore, the demand for money would be regarded as given, once the level of income or transactions was given. When the economy was in full equilibrium, which would involve full employment of all the available factors of production, a unique aggregate demand for money would be specified. With a given demand for money, it was easy to see that the value of money would be determined by the supply of money. If the supply of money changed (increased), the value of money would also change (fall). This, then, became the central proposition of the quantity theory of money.

## THE EQUATION OF EXCHANGE

In the traditional formulations of the quantity theorists, the celebrated **equation of exchange** was often used. Irving Fisher of Yale developed and presented this equation in his book, *The Purchasing Power of Money*, published in 1911. The equation of exchange states that $MV = PT$. In this equation, $M$ is the stock of money and $V$ is its velocity of circulation. On the other side of the equation, index numbers are commonly used, so that $P$ represents the price level as measured by a price index and $T$ stands for the physical volume of transactions as measured by an index. In some versions of this equation, $O$ or $Q$ is substituted for $T$, meaning that only the current output of goods and services is considered. A more complicated version of the equation developed by Fisher separated money into components of currency and bank deposits, whereas the turnover of each was treated separately. This equation was $MV + M'V' = \Sigma pQ$, where $M$ was the currency component, $M'$ was bank deposits, $V$ and $V'$ were the velocities of currency and deposits, respectively, and $\Sigma$ was the sum of all prices $p$ times the physical volume of trade $Q$.

Regardless of the form of the equation, it is a definition or a truism. The equation is saying that the same dollar payments may be looked at from different points of view. Whether we consider the dollar expenditures of buyers or the dollar receipts of sellers, the aggregate dollars involved are the same amount in either case. As in demand and supply analysis, the amount sold is necessarily equal to the amount bought.

Using some version of this equation of exchange, economists could easily expound a quantity theory of money that, unlike the equation of exchange, can be tested as to validity by reference to statistical data. This simple version of the quantity theory states that a given change in the quantity of money will result in a proportional change in the price level. This means that a given change in $M$ cannot result in an inverse change in $V$ or have the effect of raising real output. The level of real output was often assumed to be a given constant, which would have to be explained by other factors. The turnover of money was determined by the demand for money to hold, which was usually assumed to be a constant or closely related to a fixed level of total transactions.

# THE FISHER FORMULATION
# OF THE QUANTITY THEORY

In addition to developing the equation of exchange, Fisher made other important contributions to the quantity theory tradition. He believed that the general price level, which determined the purchasing power of money, was determined by five separate variables: (1) the quantity of money, (2) the quantity of bank deposits, (3) the velocity of money, (4) the velocity of bank deposits, and (5) the volume of trade.[1] By "money" Fisher meant the number of dollars in circulation, which could be either

[1]Irving Fisher, *The Purchasing Power of Money* (New York: Augustus M. Kelley, Reprints of Economic Classics, 1963), p. 149.

gold or silver coins and paper money. Many modern economists would be inclined to combine (1) and (2), which does not, however, change the main thrust of the Fisher analysis.

Fisher, like most economic theorists, was interested ultimately in developing causal hypotheses that would be helpful in explaining the nature of economic phenomena and in aiding public policymakers. Examining the six variables of the more complicated equation of exchange, Fisher argued[2] that the effect of doubling currency, or money in circulation, normally would also result in the doubling of bank deposits, because deposits normally have a fixed ratio to money in circulation. Fisher's formulation of the quantity theory would be the same whether one uses a narrow or a broad definition of money. More important, however, Fisher believed that a doubling, say, in the money supply would normally not affect $V$, $V'$, or $Q$. The only effect of a change in the stock of money would be to change the price level.

***Velocity Assumed Constant***    The assumed constancy of the **velocity of money** is ascribed to technical conditions (i.e., the preferences of various individuals and institutions for money balances) that should not change simply because the total quantity of money has changed. This also assumes that the **demand for money** is entirely a transactions demand, which, moreover, is perfectly inelastic with respect to the rate of interest. This is implied in the assumption of a constant velocity of money, because a rise in the price level resulting from a larger supply of money could lead to rising profits and expectations of continued price increases. Under these conditions of inflationary expectations and rising profits, businesses might reasonably be expected to wish to borrow more funds from the lending institutions, such as commercial banks.

***Change in Cash Balances***    A rise in loan demand, with a given supply of loanable funds, should lead to an increase in interest rates. If money balances are interest elastic, the higher opportunity cost of holding such money balances would lead to efforts to reduce them, which in turn would result in a higher turnover, or velocity, of money. Because the demand for money balances was supposed to be in real terms, a rise in the price level should actually increase the demand for nominal cash balances rather than reduce it. In any event, if one believes that the transactions velocity of money is constant, one also necessarily believes that the transactions demand for money is interest inelastic.

Fisher's view on the velocity of money was that ". . . doubling money, deposits and prices would necessarily leave velocity quite unchanged . . . The ratio of money expended to money on hand would not

---

2Ibid., pp. 151–154.

vary."[3] Fisher believed that an increase in the quantity of money would mean that most people would have more money and deposits on hand than they desired. In an attempt to get rid of this surplus money by buying goods, services, or securities, the price of such goods, services, and securities would increase until money balances were reduced to the desired level. The rise in spending and the inflationary increase in the price level would not reach a new equilibrium level until the price level had increased in the same proportion as the rise in the stock of money. Only at that time would the initial velocity of money and ratio of cash balances to transactions be restored to the original desired levels.

## CAMBRIDGE CASH-BALANCE EQUATION

In Cambridge, England, in the late nineteenth century, the quantity theory of money held full sway. A somewhat different equation from the equation of exchange (which was popular among American ecnomists) was developed by Professor Alfred Marshall and is variously known as the Marshallian equation or the Cambridge **cash-balance equation**. The Marshallian version of the equation to be used with the quantity theory may be expressed as $M = kY$. If we substitute for $Y$ (national income) the variables $PO$, where $P$ represents the price level and $O$ represents real output, the equation becomes $M = kPO$. Another way of writing the Cambridge equation is $P = M/kO$. In this equation, $k$ is that fraction of real income that people wish to hold command over in the form of money balances. Algebraically, the Cambridge equation can be translated into the equation of exchange or vice versa. (This assumes that the money market is in equilibrium, so that $M_d = M_s$.) That is, $V = 1/k$, or $k = 1/V$. The demand for money and the velocity of money are simply reciprocals of each other. When the neoclassical economists talked about an increase in hoarding, they were also saying that the velocity of money had declined.

Even though the $V$ of the equation of exchange, stated as $MV = PO$, and the $k$ of the Cambridge equation, $M = kY$, are simply reciprocals of each other, it should not be concluded that it makes no difference which equation is used. In the equation of exchange, the emphasis is on the supply of money, whereas in the Cambridge equation the emphasis is on the demand for money. Therefore $V$ was often held to be constant by those quantity theorists using the equation of exchange, whereas quantity theorists using the Cambridge equation felt called upon to explain the factors affecting the demand for money.

[3]Ibid., p. 153.

*The Value of Money and the Quantity of Money*   Being quantity theorists, Marshall and his Cambridge disciples believed that the value of money varied inversely with its quantity. As Marshall put it, ". . . an increase in the volume of a country's currency, other things being equal, will lower proportionately the value of each unit. In fact, if that increase threatens to be repeated, the value of each unit may fall more than in proportion to the increase already made."[4] Marshall here added the influence of price expectations as an influence on the value of money. The demand for money was considered to be in real terms and was a constant proportion of income and property. Most money balances were needed for transactions purposes, but some could be held as part of the wealth of the money holder.[5]

## PROPORTIONAL CHANGES IN MONEY AND PRICE LEVEL

Assuming that other things remain equal, a given proportional increase in the volume of currency, or money, say, a rise of 10 percent, would have the same proportional effect on the price level. Thus the quantity theorists in the United States and England came to essentially the same conclusion about the effect on the price level of a change in the stock of money, even though they were emphasizing a somewhat different equation. A quarter of a century before he wrote the statement quoted, Marshall testified before Parliament's Committee on Indian Currency and gave a simple, classic statement of the quantity theory. On January 11, 1899, he said, "I hold that prices vary directly with the volume of currency, if other things are equal; but other things are constantly changing."[6] Marshall wants to modify it in the very sentence that he states as the quantity theory to make it correspond more nearly with economic reality as he saw it to be. In the same testimony, Marshall quotes some statistics from "one of the ablest of the younger school of American economists, Mr. Fisher of Yale."[7]

Unlike Fisher, Marshall seemed at times to be almost as concerned with the possible variability of the factors subsumed under "other things being equal" as he was with the static formulation of the quantity theory in the form of a simple equation. Marshall noted that the factors that had to remain equal included: (1) population, (2) the amount of business transacted per head of the population, (3) the percentage of

[4]Alfred Marshall, *Money Credit and Commerce* (London: Macmillan, 1924), p. 38.
[5]Ibid., p. 44.
[6]Alfred Marshall, *Official Papers* (London: Macmillan, 1926), p. 267.
[7]Ibid., p. 271.

that business effected directly by money, and (4) the efficiency of money or the average rapidity of the circulation of money.[8]

## REAL FACTORS AND MONETARY FACTORS

Marshall was so cognizant of the possibility of **real factors** affecting the level of prices, as well as inflationary or deflationary influences arising from changes in the monetary base in the form of changes in the amount of gold and silver held by a country, that he took specific account of this possibility in his 1887 testimony before the Royal Commission on the Values of Gold and Silver. He stated, "So a great rise of prices is possible without a change in the supplies of gold and silver, provided that there is a sufficient change in the methods of business."[9]

A similar emphasis on real factors was placed by Marshall in this same testimony when he gave his views about the effect of a change in the stock of money on the money rate of interest (the rate of discount), as compared with the effect of a change in the stock of capital goods on the real rate of interest (the profitableness of business). "The rate of discount, in my opinion, is merely the ripple of the wave on the surface, the average level is the rate of interest which can be got for the investment of capital and this is being lowered by the rapid and steady growth of capital . . . ."[10]

In this distinction between the money rate of interest (the rate of discount) and the real rate of interest (profitability of capital), Marshall anticipated the writings of Knut Wicksell by a decade and the writings of his student J. M. Keynes by a half a century. Money is essentially "neutral" in its effect on a real price (the rate of interest), because the supply and demand for real capital basically determine the rate of interest. The money rate of interest may differ from the real rate temporarily if the economy is not in complete equilibrium, but normally the money rate of interest simply fluctuates around the real rate.

*Marshall's Demand for Money*  Although Marshall expressed the typical quantity theory of money point of view in his opinion, other things being equal, that a change in the stock of money would be reflected in a proportionate change in the price level, he was also aware that the demand for money depended on the price level. This interdependent view of the demand and supply of money and the price level,

---

[8]Op. cit., p. 48.
[9]Op. cit., p. 40.
[10]Ibid., p. 49.

given certain technical conditions (habits), is expressed in the following statement: "I do not say that I think the amount of currency one wants depends entirely on the level of prices. It depends chiefly on one's habits. But the habits remaining the same, it depends on the level of prices."[11]

Marshall also emphasized that the demand for money must be viewed in "real" terms. In his book on money he stated, "A country's demand is not for a certain amount of metallic (or other) currency; but for an amount of currency which has a certain purchasing power."[12] In his Appendix C, Marshall showed that the real demand for money might be viewed as a rectangular hyperbola, which would mean that the coefficient of the elasticity of demand for money would have a value of one everywhere on the schedule.

*Real Balance Effect*    Members of the Cambridge school often argued subsequently that the demand for money balances in real terms had a **unitary elasticity**. The real amount of money demanded to hold would then be the same regardless of the prices of goods and services. The demand for goods and services and the demand for money were viewed as determined independently. This also implies that there is no **money illusion**, or effect on the demand for goods if money prices and money income change proportionally. If these conditions are met, an increase in the supply of money results in increased money expenditures, because the holders of money already have a large enough stock of money in view of their existing preference patterns. Inasmuch as it was always assumed that the existing output of goods and services for sale was fixed, the ensuing higher money expenditures on the part of buyers merely pushed up prices. As the prices of goods and services continue to increase under the pressure of higher consumer demand, the value of each monetary unit would tend to decline. Eventually the larger monetary stock would be voluntarily held, because the increased expenditures, on the one hand, and the fall in the value of money, on the other, would reduce the real value of money balances to the desired level. This effect later came to be called the **real balance effect**, and was emphasized by A. C. Pigou of Cambridge University.

This assumed unitary elasticity of demand for a given amount of money balances in real terms was also supposed to provide a floor for any economic decline, because a decline in the price level, associated with a fall in economic activity, would increase the value of cash balances above the desired level. This increase in the real value of cash balances would lead the holders of cash balances to increase their spending and would therefore bring about an upswing in economic

[11]Ibid., p. 44.
[12]Op. cit., p. 39.

activity. It did not even matter whether the holders of these redundant cash balances spent them in final commodity markets, in the markets for inputs such as labor, or in the securities markets. If additional bonds were purchased, the interest rate would be reduced, which in turn, it was believed, would increase business borrowing. The added business borrowing would be spent on acquiring additional capital goods or similar forms of real investment, so that the economy would be given an upward surge.

## VALUE OF MONEY AND THE PRICE LEVEL

It might be said that what quantity theorists were really concerned with all along is the value of money. What is it that determines the value of money? The quantity theorists tend to argue that the quantity of the stock of money determines its value, although modern monetarists analyze the demand for money and focus also on the stock of money. By definition, of course, it is the price level that determines the value of money. When the price level changes, the value of money changes. The relationship here is an inverse one, so that when the price level goes up (inflation), the value of money goes down, whereas when the price level goes down (deflation), the value of money goes up. The value of money is determined by its purchasing power.

When prices are low, money buys a certain amount of commodities, and when prices are high, money buys correspondingly fewer commodities. Thus the problem of deciding what determines the value of money is really one of deciding what determines the price level of a country. Referring to the equation of exchange again ($MV = PT$), if velocity of money and the total volume of physical transactions are held constant, it follows logically that an increase in the stock of money will increase the price level, which in turn lowers the value of money. The empirical problem then becomes one of deciding whether the velocity of money and the physical volume of transactions are constant, either in the short run or in the long run.

### *Income Velocity of Money*

The income velocity of money is defined in the equation $V = GNP/M$. (GNP is gross national product, which is the market value of all final goods and services produced in a given time period, such as a year.) The Marshallian $k$, from the Cambridge cash-balance equation, is just the reverse of this, so that $k = M/Y$. ($Y$ here is defined as being alternatively national income or gross national product.) Alvin Hansen made a long-term study of the income demand for money, or $k$, extending from 1800 to 1947. Hansen's data revealed a strong upward trend of $k$, or decline of $V$. However, in some decades $k$ rose rapidly, whereas in others it rose slowly. Hansen concluded, "There appears to be no dependable or fixed trend in the ratio of $M$ to $Y$. . . . The money supply holds no dependable constant relation to the national income."[13] Hansen defined the money supply as currency plus demand and time deposits. A more recent study by Lawrence Ritter, over a shorter period of time, shows a similar variability in the velocity of money. Ritter concludes, "The record also reveals that short-run fluctuations in velocity have been frequent, with velocity generally rising when GNP has been rising and falling when GNP has been falling."[14] The money supply definition used by Ritter is that of demand deposits adjusted plus currency outside banks.

Another study by Richard Selden on income velocity agrees with the conclusions independently reached by Hansen and Ritter. Selden's conclusions are that income velocity has clearly declined over a long period of time, most notably in the period from 1829 to 1939, and that any controversey over this empirical conclusion derives from investigators' using different definitions. Selden prefers, as did Hansen, to include time deposits along with demand deposits and currency in the definition of money and to use national income rather than total money transactions as the numerator in the equation defining income velocity. For the short run, Selden concludes as did Ritter that income velocity generally rises during business expansions and falls during contractions. Furthermore, Selden discovered that there tends to be a seasonal low in income velocity in the first quarter of the year and a seasonal high in the last quarter.

## STABILITY OF VELOCITY VERSUS MULTIPLIER

Despite this variability in the velocity of money, a study by Milton Friedman and David Meiselman for the independent Commission on Money and Credit argued strongly for retaining the quantity theory of money approach as contrasted with the income-expenditure approach. Their study involved regression coefficients of consumption expenditures with both autonomous expenditures and the stock of money, respectively, utilizing various leads and lags. Autonomous expenditures

---

[13]Alvin Hansen, *Monetary Theory and Fiscal Policy* (New York: McGraw-Hill, 1949), p. 3.
[14]Lawrence Ritter, "Income Velocity and Monetary Policy," *American Economic Review*, (March 1959), p. 121.

were defined by Friedman and Meiselman as net private domestic investment plus net foreign balance plus government deficit on income and product account, whereas the stock of money was defined to include time deposits as well as demand deposits and currency outside banks.

After making their statistical calculations, Friedman and Meiselman conclude that "Velocity is impressively stable over cycles by comparison with the **multiplier**." [15] Furthermore, they argue that their findings "indicate that the quantity-theory approach to income change is likely to be more fruitful than the income-expenditure approach." [16] These investigators do *not*, however, claim that the empirical data show that the velocity of money is constant. In fact, they admit that "there is every reason to seek to understand the changes in velocity that do occur." [17]

***Instability of Velocity***  The great body of empirical evidence that points clearly to a substantial amount of instability in the velocity of money appears to render most unwise any rigid use of the quantity theory of money, which depends importantly on a relative constancy of such velocity. It would seem that the monetary authorities, operating as they must in the short run, would not be able to depend on any simple relationship between a change in the money supply and a change in the price level. Over a long-run period, it seems more likely that there will be a similar direction of change in the quantity of money and the price level.

That is, if there were a substantial expansion (contraction) in the money supply, we should not be surprised to find an increase (decrease) in the price level. Even then, we should have no expectation of finding a one-to-one change in the supply of money and the price level, inasmuch as empirical studies have demonstrated that there are long-run as well as short-run shifts in the velocity of money. None of these caveats on the quantity theory should be interpreted as denying that money is a strategic variable in the economy, but they do suggest the need for both further theorizing and further empirical study.

## THE TOTAL VOLUME OF TRANSACTIONS

The other assumption of the crude quantity theorists, which relates to an assumed level of real total transactions, poses equal if not greater

---

[15]Milton Friedman and David Meiselman, "The Relative Stability of Monetary Velocity and the Investment Multiplier in the United States 1897–1958," *Stabilization Policies*. Prepared for the Commission on Money and Credit (Englewood Cliffs, N.J.: Prentice- Hall, 1962), p. 215.

[16]Ibid., p. 213.

[17]Ibid., p. 215.

difficulties. There is no room under this assumption for existing inventories of goods to take care of any increase in demand until production can be increased. It must be taken for granted that these theorists believed that the supply curve for most commodities and services was highly inelastic, with sharply rising costs of production accompanying any increase in production beyond the present level of output. Modern cost curve studies have cast considerable doubt on this assumption as representing typical conditions in modern manufacturing. Furthermore, administered prices fixed by a few large manufacturing firms, as a typical condition over large sections of the economy, were certainly not considered in this earlier monetary theory.

Where these conditions of a high degree of market power concentration exist in the form of a few large sellers (**oligopoly**), it may even be that long-run considerations such as fear of trust-busting or similar interference by governmental authorities, or even an adverse public opinion, may result in any price increases being less than those immediately warranted by the increase in consumer demand. Such a situation existed in the United States immediately after World War II, when sharp increases in consumer demand could not be fully met immediately by the existing level of output of goods and services. Even where price increases did occur, as in the automobile industry, the price adjustments were not made completely up to the equilibrium price, which would have obtained in a purely competitive market. Some unsatisfied consumer demand thus prevailed in the short run, even though it was eventually satisfied as expansion in productive facilities proceeded apace.

***Full Employment Assumption***    It may be evident, by implication at least, that the quantity theorists often assumed full employment of all resources. If there is full employment of all resources in an economy, any increase in the stock of money is more likely to be reflected in price increases than if there are substantial unused productive capacity and substantial amounts of unemployed resources, such as idle workers. This assumes, in any case, that a given increase in the stock of money will be fully reflected in increased spending (i.e., no decline in the velocity of money).

The empirical question relating to the constancy of real $T$, or $O$, is how typical is such a condition of full employment? The answer seems to be that the American economy has been, and continues to be, subject to cyclical fluctuations in employment and national income. Sometimes we are at full employment and sometimes we are not. Furthermore, some of the downturns in economic activity are quite severe, as in the 1930s, and some are quite mild, as was true in the United States after World War II until 1981–1982. In short, the assumption of $T$ as a constant at full employment might sometimes be relatively accurate, and sometimes it might be wide of the mark. When the economy has substantial reserves of unused resources, an increase in spending brought about, say, by an increase in the stock of money increases not only $P$ but to some extent real $T$ and $O$.

# FLEXIBILITY OF PRICES

If a manufacturer with a substantial unused productive capacity suddenly finds that his orders have increased, he is not immediately likely to hike his prices sharply. In the very short run, he may not change his prices at all. Subsequently, if orders continue to increase and the output of his factory approaches its rated capacity, the manufacturer may decide to increase his list prices. An increase in list prices is particularly likely if the increased demand conditions affecting his particular firm are being experienced by business firms throughout the economy. In this event, the manufacturer will find in time that some of his raw material costs have increased as well as some components of his labor costs. As output rises, business firms are forced to hire less productive workers, while labor unions are usually demanding higher wages. Overtime costs and higher maintenance on machines used more intensively also add to the costs of production. It may even become more difficult to buy some of the materials needed in the productive process. All these conditions are typical of bottleneck situations in which price increases often occur.

# ELASTICITY OF SUPPLY AND INVESTMENT

The technical answer to the question of the impact on $T$, or $O$, and $P$, respectively, of an increase in spending is that it depends partly on the **elasticity of supply** of goods and services. The price elasticity of supply at a point on the supply schedule $E_s = dQ/Q \div dP/P$ of a given product indicates how much of a percentage increase (decrease) in output can be expected with a given percentage increase (decrease) in price. The percentage increase in output in turn depends on such considerations as the amount of unused productive capacity, mobility of the factors of production, and ease or difficulty of entry of new firms into a particular industry. Furthermore, the elasticity of supply varies widely from industry to industry. For some industries it is relatively easy to expand output, especially if there are unused productive facilities, whereas for other industries it is much more difficult.

For example, when the demand for medical services increases, it is not easy for the supply of physicians to expand as readily as the demand for their services. Under these conditions, we should not be surprised to see medical fees rising. It takes a great deal of time to train new physicians, so that their supply, in the short run, tends to be relatively inelastic. It may even be difficult to increase the output of medical services of a given physician who has already developed a large practice. It is a general principle that the supply of virtually everything is more inelastic in the short run than in the long run. Hence the longer the time period over which the increased demand extends, the more likely there will be some expansion of output.

When demand increases to the point at which factories are operating at or near capacity, we should expect businesses to start thinking about plans to expand their productive facilities. This principle is the **accelerator** relation, which tells us that new real investment is affected by changes in the level of output, which in turn is affected by the level of demand. This relation has been confirmed to some extent by American experience in the period since World War II. This period of ever increasing final demand has also been characterized by a great boom in the capital goods and construction industries. With few exceptions, most sectors of the economy have been forced to embark on expansion of their productive facilities. In the long run, therefore, as well as sometimes in the short run, an expansion of demand tends to increase real $T$, or $O$, as well as $P$.

When the dynamic element of expectations is introduced, which seems to be needed in any complete theory of investment, a number of economists believe that an increase in $P$ itself may stimulate investment expenditures. It has long been noted, for example, that inventory accumulation tended to be stepped up in periods of price increases. If you expect the price of raw material or a finished commodity to be higher a few weeks or a few months from now, why not buy it now? For businesses that must always hold some inventories to fulfill their economic function, the temptation must be very strong at times to vary inventory policy somewhat depending upon price expectations.

Even construction expenditures can be influenced by the expectation of price increases in the future. When sales of the goods produced by a factory are not high enough to operate at full capacity, the managers of the factory may still decide to expand if both demand and prices are expected to rise in the future. Why not build now when construction costs are lower than they will be in the future? Hence an anticipated as well as an actual rise in $P$ may also lead to a future rise in real $T$, or $O$, which may then lead to a decline in $P$ when increased production rolls off newly finished production lines. It might therefore be argued that it is very difficult if not impossible to predict the final effect on the price level of any given change in the stock of money.

# TRADITIONAL INTEREST RATE THEORY

Traditional interest rate theory is discussed in some detail in Chapter 24. Suffice it to note here that the interest rate for traditional monetary theorists was determined as is any price by demand and supply. Furthermore, as a relative price for the use of capital as compared with the relative price for the use of other factors of production, it was in "real" or nonmonetary terms.

Traditional monetary theorists, however, recognized that the money interest rate in the financial markets might well diverge from the real rate of interest. The primary reason for this was that the value of money as measured by the price level was not always constant. Hence if the price level were rising or falling, the market rate of interest in money terms would diverge from the real rate of interest.

As Irving Fisher put it, "That is, when prices are rising, the rate of interest tends to be high but not so high as it should be to compensate for the rise; and when prices are falling the rate of interest tends to be low, but not so low as it should be to compensate for the fall." [18] Thus in a country now experiencing a higher rate of inflation than in the recent past, lenders would add an "inflation premium" to their rate of interest. Then market rates of interest would rise, even if the real rate of interest remained constant.

Some economists such as Knut Wicksell, a late nineteenth-century Swedish economist, even explained the business cycle in terms of the difference between the market rate of interest (which included a premium for expected inflation) and the real rate of interest. If the market rate of interest were below the real rate of interest plus the rate of inflation, then lenders would not have correctly anticipated future price inflation, so that borrowers would gain a profit by borrowing cheap and selling dear. Even if lenders did not correctly anticipate the actual amount of future inflation one would nevertheless expect interest rates to increase when there was a general rise in the price level. Thus the problem of inflation of prices was always of concern to the traditional monetary theorists, even when they were particularly concerned with interest rates.

# THE STOCK OF MONEY AND WOULD-BE BORROWERS

The emphasis of most traditional monetary theory, as expressed in the quantity theory, was on the effect of a change in the supply of money on

---

[18]Irving Fisher, *The Theory of Interest* (New York: Macmillan, 1930), p. 43.

money expenditures and thence on the price level. Keynes, after 1936, and his followers, however, emphasized changes in the demand for money. Keynes placed great weight on the elasticity of the demand for money to hold in the form of cash balances at various rates of interest, with a completely elastic demand for such idle cash prevailing at a very low rate of interest.

***Elasticity of Demand for Borrowed Funds***     In addition to the problem of the elasticity of demand for cash to hold, there is a similar problem of the elasticity of demand for borrowed funds. Just as the Keynesian critics of the quantity theory have claimed that the holders of cash balances are sensitive to the rate of interest, even to the extreme condition when they would be willing to hold unlimited idle cash balances at some low rate of interest, some critics of the quantity theory have also claimed that would-be borrowers of funds are not very sensitive to the rate of interest. In other words, if the monetary authorities manage to increase the stock of money so that financial institutions such as commercial banks now have more loanable funds, it is alleged that would-be borrowers are not likely to be very tempted to borrow, even if the interest rate at which they can borrow is lower than it had been before. In the 1930s it was often said in criticism of an easy money policy having much effect on the desire of businesses to borrow, "You can lead a horse to water, but you can't make him drink," or "You can't push on a string."

In technical terms, it was said that the demand schedule for borrowed funds was **interest inelastic.** It was argued that profit expectations was the main factor influencing the desire of businesses to borrow. In this event, an increased stock of money created by the central bank was bound to be offset by a decline in the velocity of money, because credit-worthy borrowers would not turn up at the desks of bank lending officers to ask for the loans that banks could then give. This criticism seemed to be particularly relevant to the experience of the 1930s, when the banks had considerable excess reserves and interest rates were very low, but bank lending ability continued to be greater than actual lending. Part of the depressed condition of bank lending in the 1930s may have been the reluctance on the part of businesses to borrow, even at very low rates of interest, and part may have been the result of the reluctance on the part of banks to increase their risk assets.

***Money Supply May Be Passive***     Some economists have even argued that the stock of money is a passive variable rather than an active one. Contrary to the quantity theory, which regarded $M$ as the ultimate determinant of the level of money wages and money prices, these economists invert the relationship and regard wages and prices as the determinants of the quantity of money. By the 1980s, some monetary economists pointed to a "feedback" from changes in income to changes in the stock of money (i.e., a rise in business activity would increase the demand for borrowed funds from banks, which, when granted, would increase bank demand deposits).

In the period following World War II, which was marked by early rounds of the wage-price spiral, some commentators asserted that the monetary authorities were forced by political circumstances to validate higher wages and prices negotiated by powerful unions and powerful business firms. If the money supply were not permitted to increase in the wake of an important series of wage-price settlements, the labor force would be bound to face higher rates of unemployment, because **aggregate demand** would not be sufficient to purchase the full output of American industry at the higher level of administered prices. The political necessities, at least since the Employment Act of 1946 and the Humphrey-Hawkins Act of 1978, have been that the various instrumentalities of the federal government, including the Federal Reserve System, are committed to promoting a policy of maximum employment. Under these conditions it might seem to be politically unwise for the Federal Reserve to refuse to let the money supply grow and instead let unemployment in the economy increase.

## EQUILIBRIUM STOCKS AND FLOWS

Although much traditional monetary theory focused on the *stock* of money, it was not too difficult to move to a consideration of the *flow* of money. The flow of money could be obtained by taking the average stock of money over a given period of time and multiplying this average stock by the turnover, or velocity, of the amount of money available. This **money flow** of spending on goods and services would be exactly equal to the value of goods, services, and securities sold during the given time period if total transactions were being considered. If only current income or output were examined, the total money flow of expenditures would exactly match the money value of current income or output. This view of money flow involves a truism. The value of aggregate demand must necessarily be equal to the value of aggregate supply in this instance, because the value of goods purchased is always equal to the value of goods sold.

Assuming that a given stock of money is in fact that desired by the economic transactors, so that the flow of money income generated is likewise in equilibrium with the flow of output valued in money terms, we may regard the monetary economy as being in equilibrium. Now, if some external factor such as the central bank operating on the banking system disturbs this equilibrium by increasing the stock of money, an adjustment process is called for. All those who hold money cash balances will discover that they now have higher average balances than they desire. To get rid of some of the unwanted cash, these transactors will increase their spending on goods, services, and securities.

The higher level of money flows operating on the limited quantity of real goods and services available will tend to increase the market prices of these commodities. This in turn reduces the real value of each unit of nominal money until eventually all the increased stock of money is willingly held by economic units. Any increased spending on securities, say, bonds, by raising the price of these securities will also reduce the yield on them.

The lower levels of interest rates result in some disequilibrium conditions in the markets equating saving and investment. Borrowing for investment expenditures will tend to rise faster than voluntary saving because of the inducement to borrow from the banking system offered by easier credit conditions symbolized by lower interest rates. Increased investment expenditures mean higher prices in the capital goods industries and a shift in real resources from the consumer goods industries to the capital-producing industries. The resulting increase in the general price level results in some "forced saving" because (1) the rise in prices deprives the general public of some consumption goods and services they had expected to purchase at the lower level of prices, and (2) the rise in prices reduces the real value of the public's cash balances, so that the public will voluntarily refrain from some consumption in order to build up their desired cash balances.


## NEUTRAL MONEY AND BUSINESS FLUCTUATIONS

Thus to the extent that the economy is in equilibrium, money will have no effect on real prices, output, or even the allocation of resources between competing ends. Under these circumstances, money can be said to be "neutral." Because the standard economic theory models of the neoclassical economists were equilibrium models, **neutral money** was commonly assumed in this traditional theory.

If the quantity of money were arbitrarily (and overnight) doubled, the price level would also be doubled, so that each unit of nominal money would be valued in real terms at exactly half of what it was worth before. This change in the stock of money and the general price level, however, was not expected to have any effect on relative prices (e.g., the price of apples in terms of nuts). If these relative prices remained unchanged and consumer and producer preferences remained unchanged, then the role of money was strictly that of a unit of account, or **numéraire.**

# SUMMARY OF TRADITIONAL QUANTITY THEORY

The essence of the traditional quantity theory of money was that the stock of money was the main determinant of the price level. But this theory also consisted of a set of interrelated propositions or postulates that supported that conclusion. These propositions were that (1) *P* will vary in exact proportion to changes in the quantity of *M* (i.e., a given percentage change in the stock of money will result in the same percentage change in the prices of goods and services); (2) the direction of causation runs from *M* to *P*, that is, money is the active variable and prices are the passive or dependent variable, so that monetary changes precede and cause price level changes; (3) except for transitional adjustment periods, monetary changes exert no influence on real economic variables such as total output, product mix, and total employment, because these are determined by such real variables as taste, technology, and amounts of the factors of production; (4) not only do changes in the stock of money affect only the price level but monetary factors, rather than nonmonetary disturbances in the real sector of the economy, are the principal cause of any price level instability; and (5) the nominal stock of money is an exogenous variable (determined entirely by the central bank) rather than being determined endogenously within the economic system as a result of changes in the demand for money. For the central bank to have complete exogenous control of the nominal money supply, there must be stable links between the base of high-powered money created by the central bank and the transactions, or deposit money created by the depository institutions. In short, the monetary multiplier must be constant.

The real stock of money, on the other hand, depends not only on the nominal stock of money but also on the price level. In the short run, changes in the public's holdings of nominal money will be reflected in public spending and the level of prices of goods and services. This in turn affects the real value of money. Many of these propositions are still held by the modern quantity theorists, or the monetarists. These propositions are compared with the views of the neo-Keynesians in Chapter 22 after the discussion of macroeconomics in the next chapter.

# Questions for Discussion

1. Discuss some of the major concerns of traditional monetary theory. Indicate the importance of money in affecting certain economic variables.
2. Discuss the simple quantity theory of money using the equation of exchange.

Be sure that you spell out the basic assumptions of this theory in terms of the variables of the equation of exchange. What explanation did Fisher give for his assumption of a constant velocity of money?

3. Distinguish between the Fisherian and the Marshallian approach to the quantity theory of money. What is the difference between emphasizing the velocity of money, on the one hand, and emphasizing the demand for money, on the other?

4. Discuss the major elements in the Marshallian or Cambridge cash-balance approach. What is the relationship in this approach between monetary and real factors?

5. What is the real balance effect? Does this presumed effect have any relationship to the fluctuations of national income and employment over the business cycle? What critical assumption must be made before the real balance effect is operative?

6. Briefly discuss the difference between the nominal, or market, rate of interest and the real rate of interest in traditional monetary theory. What part does the expected rate of inflation play in affecting these rates of interest, or in the differential between them?

7. What do you think determines the value of money? In what sense might it be said that the quantity theory is a theory of the value of money? Could anything else besides the stock of money be responsible for variations in the value of money? In recent years when the value of money has changed (i.e., in periods of inflation) what do you think have been the major factors responsible?

8. What is the income velocity of money? How stable is it? How would you explain any variability in money velocity? What implications do the empirical studies on the velocity of money have for the validity of the quantity theory of money?

9. How realistic is it to assume that $T$ in the equation of exchange, which is the total volume of transactions, is constant? Why did quantity theorists, in earlier periods at least, assume that $T$ could be regarded as constant? What bearing on the question of the constancy of $T$ does the elasticity of supply have? Is it more realistic to assume that $T$ is relatively more constant in one stage in the business cycle than in other stages?

10. What are some of the questions that have been raised about the effects of changes in the stock of money on would-be borrowers? How valid, in your opinion, are the criticisms that have been raised in this connection about the effectiveness of monetary policy? Are any such criticisms perhaps more valid in certain stages of the business cycle than in others?

12. Briefly summarize the major propositions of the traditional quantity theory of money. How valid do you think each of these propositions is?

# Selected Bibliography for Further Reading

FISHER, IRVING, *The Purchasing Power of Money* (New York: Augustus M. Kelley, Reprints of Economic Classics, 1963).

——, *The Theory of Interest* (New York: Macmillan, 1930).

FRIEDMAN, MILTON, ed., *Studies in the Quantity Theory of Money* (Chicago: The University of Chicago Press, 1956).

——, "A Theoretical Framework for Monetary Analysis," *Journal of Political Economy*, **78**, No. 2 (Mar.-Apr. 1970), pp. 193–238.

——, and DAVID MEISELMAN, "The Relative Stability of Monetary Velocity and the Investment Multiplier in the United States 1897–1958," *Stabilization Policies*. Prepared for the Commission on Money and Credit (Englewood Cliffs, N.J.: Prentice-Hall, 1962).

HANSEN, ALVIN, *Monetary Theory and Fiscal Policy* (New York: McGraw-Hill, 1949).

HART, ALBERT GAILORD, *Money, Debt and Economic Activity* (Englewood Cliffs, N.J.: Prentice-Hall, 1953).

HUMPHREY, THOMAS M., "The Quantity Theory of Money. Its Historical Evolution and Role in Policy Debates," *Economic Review*, Federal Reserve Bank of Richmond, Vol. 60, May-June 1974, pp. 2–19.

KURIHARA, KENNETH K., *Monetary Theory and Public Policy* (New York: Norton, 1950).

LUCAS, ROBERT, JR., "Two Illustrations of the Quantity Theory of Money," *American Economic Review*, **70**, No. 5 (Dec. 1980), pp. 1005–1014.

MAKINEN, GAIL E., *Money, The Price Level and Interest Rates: An Introduction to Monetary Theory* (Englewood Cliffs, N.J.: Prentice-Hall, 1977).

MARSHALL, ALFRED, *Money Credit and Commerce* (London: Macmillan, 1924).

——, *Official Papers* (London: Macmillan, 1926).

PATINKIN, DON, *Money, Interest, and Prices: An Integration of Monetary and Value Theory*, 2d ed. (New York: Harper & Row, 1965).

TOBIN, JAMES, "Friedman's Theoretical Framework," *Journal of Political Economy* (Sept.-Oct. 1972) pp. 852–863.

WEINTRAUB, SIDNEY, *Classical Keynesianism, Monetary Theory and the Price Level* (Philadelphia: Chilton Book Company, 1961).

> ... the wealth of nations as consisting not in the unconsumable riches of money, but in the consumable goods annually reproduced by the labour of the society ...
>
> **THE WEALTH OF NATIONS**

# 21
# CHAPTER

# Macroeconomics

The Great Depression of the 1930s resulted in an agonizing reappraisal of the traditional received doctrines of economic theory. The neoclassical synthesis had led economists to expect **full employment** of all resources once the economy reached equilibrium. If the economy were not always at full employment, it was certainly supposed to be tending in that direction. If some people found themselves out of work, they could easily discover jobs somewhere if they would only accept a cut in their money wages. Involuntary **unemployment** was therefore thought to be nonexistent.

One of the economists who went through this searching re-evaluation of traditional economic beliefs was an English economist, John Maynard Keynes, a Fellow of King's College, Cambridge University. Keynes had been one of the outstanding students of Alfred Marshall, who had contributed to bringing about the neoclassical synthesis of economic theory. Keynes specialized in monetary theory, as had his teacher Marshall. For most of his professional life, Keynes believed in, taught, and wrote using the concepts of traditional monetary theory. In short, Keynes believed in the doctrines of the quantity theory and accepted the other major doctrines of neoclassical economics.

By 1936, however, the trauma of the **Great Depression** had forced him to re-examine his premises and beliefs. Out of this deep introspection, brought on by the widespread and prolonged unemployment of workers and machines on both sides of the Atlantic, came a new book that has already become something of a classic of twentieth-century economics. This book, published in 1936, is *The General Theory of Employment, Interest and Money*. From this book developed the new branch of economic theory called macroeconomics, which explains the factors determining the equilibrium level of national output and employment.

## KEYNES ON THE QUANTITY THEORY OF MONEY

Before considering the new approach of macroeconomics, it may be useful first to discuss Keynes's attitude toward the central piece of traditional monetary theory (i.e., the quantity theory). As has been noted, Keynes believed in this quantity theory all of his professional life. By the 1930s, however, his attitude toward this traditional doctrine had become somewhat jaundiced. In Chapter 21, "The Theory of Prices" in *The General Theory*, Keynes made his new views on this matter quite clear. Although he was critical insofar as the simple quantity theory was considered, he did not reject all its propositions outright. What he expounds here is a kind of modified quantity theory.

***The Simple Quantity Theory of Money***     In the simple quantity theory "it seems that the elasticity of supply must have become zero and demand proportional to the quantity of money. . . ."[1] These conditions might be largely met, Keynes believed, when full employment of all resources prevailed. In the new Keynesian macroeconomic approach, however, equilibrium of the economic system might often be attained far short of full employment. In an unemployment equilibrium situation, there may still be some influence on effective demand if the quantity of money is increased.

***The Liquidity Trap***     This is true, however, only if we are not in the "**liquidity trap**," where all increases in the money supply remain in idle money hoards. Such a trap may develop because the rate of interest is too low to tempt investors to buy interest-bearing securities. Other than that condition of monetary stalemate, "the increase in effective demand will, generally speaking, spend itself partly in increasing the quantity of employment and partly in raising the level of prices. Thus instead of constant prices in conditions of unemployment, and of prices rising in proportion to the quantity of money in conditions of full employment, we have in fact a condition of prices rising gradually as employment increases."[2]

[1]John Maynard Keynes, *The General Theory of Employment, Interest and Money* (London: Macmillan, 1936), p. 292.
[2]Ibid., p. 296.

*Production Bottlenecks and Price Increases*   Somewhat later in his discussion, Keynes suggested, by implication at least, that as the economy moved closer and closer to the desired goal of full employment, the assertions of the quantity theorists were more likely to be a closer approximation to economic reality. As output increases generally throughout the economy in the upswing of the business cycle in response to rising aggregate demand, certain production **bottlenecks** are likely to be reached, so that the supply of certain products and services becomes less elastic than heretofore. Any increase in the money supply, then, is likely to further increase aggregate demand and result in some sharp rises in particular prices and an increase in the overall price level. As Keynes put it, "But as soon as output has increased sufficiently to reach the 'bottlenecks,' there is likely to be a sharp rise in the price of certain commodities."[3]

*Complementarity of Macroeconomics and Microeconomics*   Thus it appears, contrary to the impressions of some, that Keynes did not totally reject all the teachings of traditional economic theory, even including the quantity theory. His theoretical emphasis, however, was quite different from that of a number of his intellectual predecessors. Furthermore, to sharpen the differences between himself and the neoclassical economists, and in particular to note the different premises involved, Keynes often stated his argument in a form calculated to make it appear diametrically opposed to the traditional wisdom.

The macroeconomic approach of Keynes and the microeconomic approach of the neoclassical economists are now realized to be complementary. When full employment is reached, the old concern with the distribution of the product among the factors of production, and even the use of a modified form of the quantity theory, seem much more relevant than when the economy is suffering from mass unemployment. Nevertheless, in certain major respects the Keynesian theory differs importantly from what preceded it.

## THE APPROACH OF MACROECONOMICS

The new approach to economic theory offered by Keynes, which is now generally called macroeconomics, or national income analysis, differs from traditional economic theory mainly in its approach to the whole economic system. Keynes emphasized aggregate demand, whereas his neoclassical predecessors had emphasized aggregate production. Eco-

[3]Ibid., p. 300.

nomic theorists in the nineteenth century and early twentieth century were largely concerned with the shortage of material resources available to satisfy the unlimited wants of humankind. The **"economizing problem"** seemed to them to involve the study of how these scarce material resources could be properly and efficiently allocated to satisfy the unlimited and competing demands of humankind. The major concern of economics, therefore, had to be on production or supply. If production could be increased, there would undoubtedly be plenty of unsatisfied human wants, which could easily absorb the increased production of goods and services.

## Say's Law

One of the early classical economists in France, Jean Baptiste Say, had developed a Law of Markets that subsequently came to be called **Say's Law.** Simply stated, this law argued that supply creates its own demand. No one would contribute to the process of production, Say and many other economists believed, unless he desired to obtain real goods and services.

Although money would be accepted in payment for the services furnished by the different factors of production, the money so obtained was simply viewed as a medium of exchange useful in acquiring the real goods and services desired. In effect, the supply of a factor of production simply represented the demand for other real goods. Furthermore, all the value generated in the process of production would be paid out to the various factors of production (land, labor, and capital), so that supply would generate its own demand.

## Aggregate Demand

A few of the early economists such as Thomas Malthus argued that adequate aggregate demand should not be taken for granted, but David Ricardo and other early nineteenth-century economists argued more persuasively that general **"under consumption"** was impossible. For a hundred years or more, the major focus in economic theory was therefore on production—its creation and distribution among the factors of production. Not until the Great Depression made almost impossible the neglect of total demand did Keynes come along to challenge the prevailing orthodoxy in economic theory.

The older theory had focused virtually all its attention on the individual decison-making units entering into the market system, such as the household and the firm, whereas Keynes was more concerned with aggregate demand. This newer approach thus focused on the behavior of broad aggregates such as consumption, saving, and investment. Keynes's major contribution to economic theory was first to ask what determines the general level of output, or income, and employment, and second to provide a theoretical answer in terms of the fluctuations in aggregate demand. Say's law was turned inside out. Instead of supply determining demand, it almost seemed that Keynes was saying that aggregate demand determined aggregate supply.

## THE KEYNESIAN SYSTEM OF MACROECONOMICS

This theoretical explanation of the determination of the equilibrium level of national income was the core of Keynes's argument in *The General Theory*, with great stress being placed on the relationship between investment and saving as the key element. In price theory, or microeconomics, demand and supply schedules are the two basic theoretical tools employed, and equilibrium price and output are the two key variables to be explained. In the Keynesian macroeconomic system, the supply of saving schedule and the demand for saving (investment) schedule are the two basic theoretical tools designed to explain the determination of equilibrium income-output and equilibrium saving-investment.

### Investment and Saving

Not only was the relationship between aggregate supply and aggregate demand reversed but so too was the relationship between saving and investment. For many of the neoclassical economists, saving was the active factor and investment was the more passive factor, whereas for Keynes the reverse was true. In neoclassical economics saving was a function of the rate of interest, whereas for Keynes saving was a function of real income. In the traditional view, therefore, saving could be stimulated by raising the rate of interest or retarded by lowering it.

For Keynes, the rate of interest could be used to stimulate or retard the rate of investment, which in turn affected the level of income. As income changed, so too did saving. Keynes, like his neoclassical predecessors, defined investment and saving in his national income equations in such a way that they are necessarily equal. Assuming a closed economy and ignoring government expenditures, aggregate real consumption plus aggregate real investment equals aggregate real income, or output ($c + I = Y$).

Hence aggregate real investment is equal to total output, after subtracting that part of output that is devoted to consumption goods and services ($I = Y - C$). On the other hand, aggregate consumption plus aggregate saving also equals aggregate income, or output ($C + S = Y$). So aggregate saving can be determined by subtracting aggregate consumption from aggregate income ($S = Y - C$). By a rule of logic, if two things are equal to a third, they are equal to each other. Because $I = Y - C$ and $S = Y - C$, it is necessary that $I = S$.

The neoclassical economists thought that the prudent and frugal individual could be induced by a reward in the form of the payment of interest to refrain from some present consumption. This would make it possible for resources to be transferred from consumption goods to capital goods industries. The saver's willingness to practice abstinence thus made it possible for investment to take place.

In certain instances some "forced saving" might take place, as when business borrowed newly created money from the banking system. This new business spending would bid up the prices of the needed factors of production so as to move them through the market mechanism from consumer to capital goods industries. In general, however, it was believed that additions to the stock of capital goods depend largely on the willingness of prudent individuals to save, assuming, of course, that they are properly rewarded for their abstinence from present consumption.

For Keynes, however, saving represented "not consuming," and thus represented a gap in aggregate demand. This was true because the people and institutions doing the saving are not necessarily the same as the people and institutions doing the real investing. Moreover, the motives for saving and investing are different. Saving, for example, is related mainly to the level of income, whereas investment is determined by expected profits. The relationship of saving and consumption to income is given by the Keynesian **propensity to consume schedule.**

## The Propensity to Consume Schedule

This concept of Keynes is generally regarded as his most important contribution to economic theory. It is a simple concept, but it posits a relationship that had been largely overlooked by most traditional economists. Keynes phrased it in these words: "The fundamental psychological law, upon which we are entitled to depend with great confidence both *a priori* from our knowledge of human nature and from the detailed facts of experience, is that men are disposed, as a rule and on the average, to increase their consumption as their income increases but not by as much as the increase in their income."[4]

[4]Ibid., p. 96.

*The Savings Ratio*    The way in which *all* consumers divide their disposable personal income (personal income minus income taxes) into consumption expenditures and into saving is an important factor for total economic activity. Even a slight rise in the aggregate **savings ratio** brings a considerable decline in consumption expenditures, which in turn means that business firms are suffering a loss in previous or expected sales. A temporary decline in sales may be temporarily offset by a rise in **inventory accumulation** (sometimes unintended), but eventually a lower level of sales will mean a reduction in output and employment throughout the economic system.

Some consumers may spend more than their total income by relying on past saving or by going into debt in reliance on future income and saving. Other consumers tend to save at least part of their disposable income. In general, most personal saving is done by income recipients who are in the higher brackets of income distribution. When we aggregate all personal spending and personal saving (whether positive or negative), we can then obtain a relationship or function between disposable personal income and personal saving.

*Measuring Aggregate Consumption and Income*    There are, however, different ways of measuring aggregate consumption and aggregate income. The simplest way to look at total consumption and disposable personal income, which is personal income after personal taxes, is in current dollars year by year in a given country. It may be more useful, however, to adjust these current dollar figures for price changes to put them in real terms. For other purposes, it may even be useful to adjust the data to a per capita basis in order to remove the effect of population growth. Real per capita consumption and real per capita disposable personal income are then attained. Different functional relationships may still be postulated between aggregate consumption and aggregate income.

**Four Different Consumption Relationships**    Figure 21–1 shows four different possible relationships between national income and consumption. In graph A, consumption plus investment ($C + I$), which is also equal to aggregate spending, is measured along the vertical axis in billions of dollars, whereas national output, or income ($Y$), is measured along the horizontal axis in billions of dollars. The 45-degree line $OY$, which bisects the 90-degree angle at the origin, is a guiding line in order to make it easier to read from the graph the difference between intended consumption and income, which is intended saving.

The $OY$ line also shows aggregate output. The guiding line $OY$ has a slope of 1, which means that at any point on this line a perpendicular dropped to both the $x$ axis and the $y$ axis will give the same number of

**Figure 21–1    The Consumption Function***

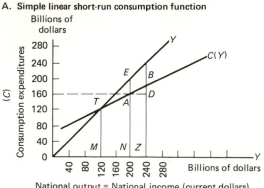

A. **Simple linear short-run consumption function**

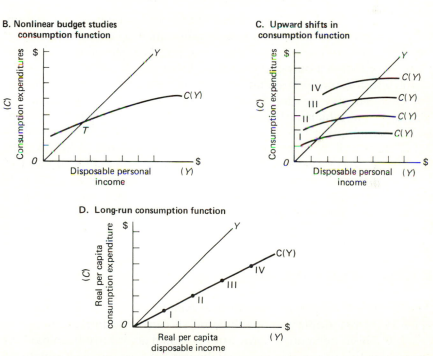

B. **Nonlinear budget studies consumption function**

C. **Upward shifts in consumption function**

D. **Long-run consumption function**

*Consumption, as a dependent variable, may be related to different kinds of income as an independent variable. Three kinds of income are shown here.

dollars. For example, at point *T*, national income is $120 billion on both axes, so the value of aggregate spending is equal to the value of aggregate output.

Graph A shows the relationship between aggregate consumption and total national output in a current short-run period. In most years, two thirds of GNP is made up of the production of consumer goods and services. Although the consumption function is drawn here as a straight line for pedagogical purposes, the consumption function should be shown shifting upward over time, as in graph C, if the ratio of consumption to income remains constant over time, as most time series data seem to suggest. At a given moment, however, graph B may be more representative of the relation of consumption to income than graph A or graph C. In graph B, the percentage of added consumption to added income declines as income increases. With a given income distribution, budget studies show that higher-income recipients do save more, both absolutely and relatively, than those with lower incomes. This is shown in graph B.

*The Consumption Function*    The consumption schedule or function, *C(Y)*, regardless of its shape, shows how much will be consumed at different levels of income. To return to graph A, at the level of national income, or national output, *ON* ($200 billion), *AN* or $160 billion will be devoted to consumption spending. The difference between the *C(Y)* line and the 45-degree guiding line *OY* gives the amount of aggregate intended saving, which in this case is *AE*, or $40 billion. The positive slope of the consumption function *C(Y)* suggests that at higher levels of income there will be a greater amount of consumption expenditures, whereas at lower levels of income there will be a smaller amount of consumption spending. Thus consumption spending in this concept is determined largely by income, though in the short run there will be some consumption even at zero income.

## INCOME AND SAVING

The income that is most directly relevant to individual consumption spending is **disposable personal income,** shown on the horizontal axis of graph B. This is personal income after personal taxes have been paid. As the level of this disposable personal income rises, so too does consumption. This is the basis of the common observation that rich families spend more than poor families. Of course, rich families also save more than poor families, because as income is increased part of it goes not only to increased consumption spending but also to increased saving. The patterns of consumption and saving for a given income level in the general population are determined not simply by the dollar income, even adjusted for price changes, but more importantly by the income level of a group relative to other income groups in the economy. In short, the consumption-saving patterns of other people affect one's own consumption-saving pattern.

The difference between income and consumption spending, as already indicated, is nonspending, or saving. This saving, which is the difference between the C(Y) line and the guiding line OY in both graphs A and B, becomes larger as income rises. Larger savings are shown graphically by the gap between these lines becoming wider at higher levels of income. In graphs A and B, at point T, the C(Y) line crosses the guiding line OY, which indicates that at this level of national income all income is utilized for consumption purposes. Here, then, saving is zero. To the left of point T, saving becomes negative. When consumption spending is higher than income, there is dissaving.

## The Marginal Propensity to Consume

When a given relationship between income and consumption has been established (the consumption function), not only can total income be divided into consumption and saving but also any increase in income can be divided into added consumption and added saving. The fraction dividing added income into consumption is called the **"marginal propensity to consume"** *(MPC)*, which is equal to added consumption divided by added income, or $MPC = \Delta C/\Delta Y$.

When income rises, consumption should rise too, though not by as much as the rise in income. Hence $\Delta C/\Delta Y$ is positive and less than unity. In graphic terms, *MPC* is the slope of the *C(Y)* lines in the four different graphs in Figure 21–1. If the consumption function is drawn as a straight line, as in graph A, the marginal propensity to consume will be constant at all levels of income.

Keynes believed that the slope of the consumption function would become less steep at higher levels of income, as shown in graph B of Figure 21–1. He believed that people (nations) at higher levels of income would save a higher percentage of their added income than they would at lower levels of income. In this case, the marginal propensity to consume would decline at higher levels of income while the marginal propensity to save would increase. This would have the effect not only of increasing the saving "gap," which investment expenditures, or government spending, would have to fill to maintain national income at the full employment level, but also would lower the value of the multiplier coefficient, which is discussed shortly. Full employment would thus become more difficult to attain and maintain for these two interrelated reasons.

The increase in thriftiness at higher levels of income suggested by graph B of Figure 21–1 does appear to be characteristic of wealthier persons with higher levels of income as distinguished from those with lower levels. This is why it is designated as a budget studies consumption function. However, as the national income in a country such as the United States grows over time, it does not appear that the percentage of savings to national income continues to grow, as would be the case if the entire population had a declining marginal propensity to consume as income increased. It appears that the average percentage of savings out of disposable personal income is remarkably stable over time, even though from quarter to quarter it may exhibit considerable variability.

## Constant Proportion of Consumption and Saving

To reconcile the fact that the percentage of national income saved has not become larger over time, as both graphs A and B would suggest, but has remained roughly constant over time, the consumption function can be shown shifting upward over time, as in graph C. The long-run stability in the ratio of consumption and saving to income is indicated graphically by a straight-line consumption function drawn from the origin, as in graph D in Figure 21–1. In graph D, price effects and the effect of a growing population have been removed statistically from the data. The relationship, then, of real per capita consumption to real per capita income is the most significant long-run consumption relationship.

   With a **proportional consumption function,** as shown in the long-run consumption function (graph D), the same percentage of income is devoted to consumption at all levels of income. Furthermore, as income rises the proportion of added consumption to added income (the marginal propensity to consume) remains the same. Because the multiplier is calculated from the marginal propensity to consume, it remains the same at all levels of income. The average propensity to consume, $APC$ $(C/Y)$, is also equal to the marginal propensity to consume, $MPC = \Delta C/\Delta Y$, so that the multiplier can be calculated directly from statistical data relating total consumption and total income.

*The Multiplier*    This marginal propensity to consume fraction is important in national income analysis, because from it we derive the multiplier, $k$, sometimes call the *"investment multiplier."* The multiplier $k$ is defined as the reciprocal of 1 minus the marginal propensity to consume, or $k = 1/(1 - MPC)$. Because the marginal propensity to consume and the marginal propensity to save are fractions that add up to 1, we can also say that $k$ is the reciprocal of the marginal propensity to save. The value of the multiplier, derived from the slope of the consumption function, necessarily changes if the slope of the consumption function changes (i.e., $k$ changes if spending and saving habits change).

We can also calculate the marginal propensity to consume, and hence the multiplier, from Figure 21–1. Moving from *ON* level of national income on graph A ($200 billion) to *OZ* level of national income ($240 billion), we find that the increase in national income ($\Delta Y$) is *NZ* = *AD* = $40 billion. Total consumption at *ON* level of national income was *AN*, or $160 billion. At the higher level of national income, *OZ*, total consumption expenditures are now $180 billion, so that the increase in consumption expenditures, *DB*, is $20 billion. Thus *MPC* = $\Delta C/\Delta Y$ = $20 billion / $40 billion = ½. Inserting this marginal propensity to consume into the formula for the multiplier, we find that $k$ = $1/(1 - $ ½) = 2.

What is the significance and use of the multiplier in national income analysis? The multiplier shows that any increase in one of the important components of national income, such as investment spending or government spending, has a magnified effect on national income. Because national income is an aggregate or total of its spending components, it is expected that an increase in spending in any component, assuming that the other components of spending are unchanged, will increase total spending or total national income. The multiplier, however, shows that any such increase in spending in one component will raise national income by *more* than the spending, because the persons receiving the added spending as added income will in turn spend part of the increase in income as well as saving part of it.

The question then becomes not why is there a multiplier but why is it not infinite? The answer to this question is that the multiplier would indeed be infinite if everyone spent every bit of any and all increases in income. Under these conditions, any increase in spending by any component of spenders would explosively (and inflationarily) expand money income for the country infinitely, as every recipient of additional income resulting from the new spending quickly respent the added dollars received, which in turn would be quickly respent by the next person receiving them as income, and so on.

The fact is, however, that some persons will save part of any increase in income, so that the multiplier actually is finite rather than infinite. It is this fact—that added income is partly saved—that acts as a brake on income expansion arising from added spending. If only a very small part of added income goes into saving, the multiplier will be large, whereas if a large part of added income is saved, the multiplier will be small. At the extremes, as already indicated, if there is no national saving out of an increase in national income, the multiplier will be infinite. If all of an increase in national income is saved, the multiplier is 1 (i.e., national income will rise only by the amount of the increase in spending of one of its components).

## The Investment Function

Before the equilibrium level of national income can be determined, it is necessary to have an investment schedule as well as a saving schedule. This function is shown in Figure 21–2, where the **marginal efficiency of investment**, $r$, is plotted on the vertical axis and the amount of investment, $I$, is plotted on the horizontal axis. The shape and level of this investment function are determined by profit expectations. It is not the actual level of profits last year that determines this year's investment expenditures by business firms but the level of profits expected in future years from investments made this year. The rate of discount that should be applied to the expected future stream of profits accruing to the new investment was termed by Keynes the "marginal efficiency of investment" (MEI) and is shown as $r$ on the vertical axis of Figure 21–2.

*Rise or Fall in Investment*    In Figure 21–2, $i$, the long-term rate of interest, is plotted on the vertical axis as well as $r$. Both of these, of course, are in percentage terms. This diagram implies that more investment expenditures will be made at a lower cost of securing borrowed funds. If the market rate of interest $OR$ is subsequently lowered to $OS$ as a result of credit easing by the monetary authorities, we would expect investment expenditures to increase from $OM$ to $ON$. The **equilibrium** amount of investment expenditures is $ON$, with a lowered interest rate, because stopping short of this amount of investment expenditures by the business firm would mean foregone profit by the firm. In the case of capital inputs, as with any input of a factor of production, the firm maximizing its profits will continue to utilize added units of the input until the marginal value product of the input is exactly equal to the price of the input. The firm would thus borrow funds and increase its investment expenditures as long as the market rate of interest is below the marginal efficiency of investment. Increasing the rate of new investment would drive down the marginal efficiency of investment until it is equal to the market rate of interest. At that time the firm would be in equilibrium insofar as its investment expenditures are concerned.

The investment function will shift upward as a result of any development tending to increase the expected profits of the firm, whereas the schedule will shift downward if profit expectations are reduced. Such real factors as technological change reducing per unit costs of production or an increase in product demand can shift the schedule upward, as well as a growth in confidence about the future. The schedule may move downward sharply if confidence is suddenly destroyed or if factors emerge that increase unit costs of production or cause a decline in product demand. Keynes believed that a panic and severe depression

**Figure 21–2    The Investment Function**

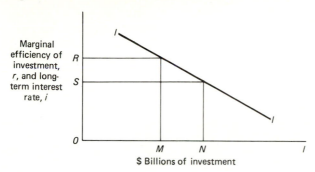

such as in 1929–1933 was characterized by a collapse of the marginal efficiency schedule.

*Real Investment and Expectations*    This investment spending in national income analysis means real investment—purchases of newly produced capital goods, factories, apartment buildings, and the like. When businesses invest in such produced goods used for further production, they are hoping for a profit over the life of the asset. A decision to invest or to acquire a new capital asset means that investors expect a flow of income over the life of the asset that will cover the supply price of the asset and the costs of operating the asset. The asset must also yield a net return at least equal to the rate of interest they would have had to pay if they borrowed the money to buy the asset. Alternatively, we may say that the present value of the asset (i.e., the discounted value of future expected income) must equal or exceed the supply price of the asset.

The anticipated future income of a given asset depends importantly upon the state of **business expectations** about the future. Their expectations in turn are likely to be significantly affected by the trend of sales and profits in their business firm and their industry generally in the recent past. Because trends in business sales, costs, and profits are subject to considerable variations from time to time, expected profits in the future, and real investment based on such expected profits, may also shift substantially from one period to another.

*The Accelerator*    Investment spending may also be viewed in relation to changes in national income. Two possibilities of the relationship between investment and national income are shown in Figure 21–3. In graph A, investment is determined independently of short-run changes

**Figure 21–3    Autonomous and Induced Investment**

A. Autonomous investment

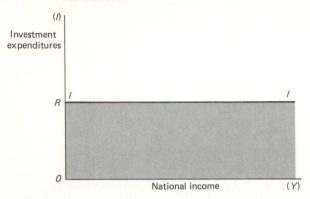

B. Induced and autonomous investment

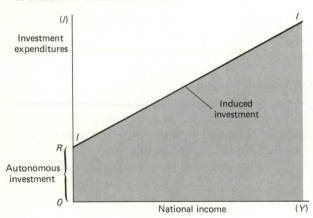

*OR* of Graph A = *OR* of Graph B.

in national income. The profit expectations of business are here determined by the long view. Technological and population changes over a
period of time, rather than short-run variations in national income and
sales, determine plans for business additions of capital equipment or
the construction of new factories. In graph B, some such autonomous
investment is still shown, but in addition investment expenditures are
determined by past and expected future changes in national income
and sales. Investment dependent upon changes in income is referred
to as induced investment, whereas the relationship between changes in
national income leading to changes in investment is called the
"accelerator."

***The Supermultiplier*** As previously noted, the relation showing the reverse direction of causation from changes in investment to changes in national income is called the *"multiplier."* When the effects of changes in national income on investment are added to the original effects on national income of a change in investment spending, we have a magnified effect on national income that is termed the **"supermultiplier."** The multiplier receives its value as a coefficient from the slope of the consumption function. Where $c = a + by$, $b$ is the slope of the function, or the marginal propensity to consume, whereas $a$ is the vertical intercept of the function. The ordinary multiplier, as already noted, is defined as $k = 1(1-b)$. The equation for investment, including both autonomous and induced investment, is $I = e + fy$, where $f$ is the slope of the investment function and indicates the dependence of induced investment on changes in income and $e$ is the vertical intercept.

The supermultiplier is $K = 1/(1-b-f)$. $K$ is always larger than $k$, as illustrated by an arithmetical example. If the slope of the consumption function is .6 or $^3/_5$, the ordinary multiplier $k$ is 2½. If the slope of the investment function is .2, or $^1/_5$, we must then subtract $^4/_5$ from 1 in the denominator of the supermultiplier equation before inverting and multiplying to arrive at the reciprocal of this fraction. The supermultiplier in this case is 5, which is double the value of the ordinary multiplier. This mutual interaction between rising levels of national income and rising levels of investment expenditure means that any increase in a component of aggregate spending, assuming the other components remain unchanged, can have a powerful expansionary effect on increasing national income. Of course, both the multiplier and the supermultiplier work in a downward direction when spending is falling and in an upward direction when spending is rising.

## INTENDED INVESTMENT AND SAVING

Not only do investment and income interact, both when income is rising and when it is falling, but **intended investment** and **intended saving** interact. In fact, the interaction between the schedules of investment and saving determines the equilibrium level of income. In effect, there is a tug of war between investors and savers, because the acts of investing and saving are largely performed by different groups of people for different reasons.

What people wish to save out of their current income and what businesses wish to invest need not be equal at all. People save for a variety of reasons, such as making provisions for a "rainy day," putting aside funds for a desired vacation, saving for a child's college education, or similar reasons. Investors, on the other hand, buy new capital equipment or authorize the construction of new factory or apartment buildings simply because they *expect* to receive a profit.

## The Savings and Investment Schedules

Intended saving may be visualized as a schedule relating different dollar amounts of saving to different dollar levels of income. Likewise, investment expenditures may be viewed as related to different levels of income by a schedule. Viewed in this manner, it may become clearer why it should be unlikely that intended saving and intended investment would be equal, because they can be expected to have different relationships to different possible levels of income. The relationship between the saving and the investment schedules can be seen graphically in Figure 21–4.

If, however, what persons want to save at a given level of income and what businessess want to invest at a given level of income are different, it will be necessary for the level of income to change until intended saving and intended investment are equal. Income is then in an equilibrium relationship, because the force tending to push it up (investment) is balanced by the force tending to push it down (saving). Investment tends to push income up, because investment is a form of spending, whereas saving depresses income because it is nonspending.

*The Investment Schedule*    In Figure 21–4 the investment schedule as a function of the marginal efficiency of investment is drawn first in graph A. In graph B, the saving schedule, which is the mirror image of the consumption function, because $S = Y - C$, is drawn and intersects the investment schedule at $E$. (If the consumption function is drawn concave from above so that MPC declines as national income rises, the saving function would be convex from below, showing that MPS would be rising as national income increases.) Equilibrium national income with these graphed linear schedules is $OM$, whereas equilibrium saving and investment are indicated by $OR$.

Each point on the investment schedule represents a given amount of investment spending associated with a given level of national income, whereas each point on the saving schedule gives an amount of saving associated with a given level of national income. Only at the equilibrium level of national income do these two schedules intersect, so that intended investment is equal to intended saving. If intended investment were greater than intended saving, the level of income would necessarily be less than $OM$, but it would rise to that higher level of national income because that is the equilibrium level of income. If intended investment were less than intended saving, the existing level of national income

**Figure 21–4    Saving and Investment Schedules**

A. The investment schedule

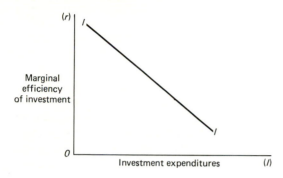

B. Saving and investment

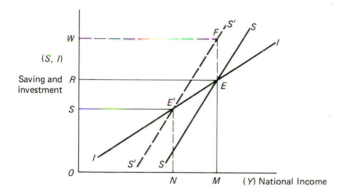

would be higher than *OM*, but income would tend to fall to that equilibrium level.

If actual income is different (higher) than equilibrium income, actual inventories are different (higher) than intended inventories. A disequilibrium level of national income thus implies that actual investment is different (higher, say) than intended investment and will be changed (reduced) in order to reach the desired equilibrium position.

***The Saving Schedule***    In graph B we can also observe the paradox of thrift. This condition arises when people try to save more than they are currently saving but actually end up saving less than their current amount of saving. In graph B, when the SS schedule shifts upward and to the left as S'S', people now try to save *MF* = *OW* amount of saving, which is higher than the equilibrium saving of *OR* at *OM* national income. With a higher saving schedule (*S'S'*), the intersection between the saving and investment schedules is at $E'$, which is a new lower level of equilibrium national income. Income has thus fallen from $OM$ to $ON$ and actual saving has fallen from $OR$ to $OS$. Hence the attempt to save more ends up with less savings, because national income falls and actual savings are largely determined by actual national income.

Because saving tends to be determined fairly closely by income, whereas investment expenditures can vary considerably from time to time depending on the outlook for future profits, it is possible that the tendency to save can exceed the tendency to invest. Under these conditions, people might be unwilling to consume a high enough percentage of their income, so that what they wish to save can be greater than what businesses wish to invest. This was true in the Great Depression of the 1930s, although it does not appear to be the case in the 1980s. This can mean, under those depressed circumstances, that more saving could be regarded as a social vice, even though it continues to be an individual virtue because the leakage of saving from the income stream could result in the equilibrium level of income declining, if the flow of new investment is not enough to oflset the subtractions from spending.

## Falling Levels of Income

When income declines, real output and employment also drop so that the number of workers and machines unemployed rises. This was the major explanation that Keynes gave for the Great Depression of the 1930s. It was not that actual saving was greater than actual investment, because that was impossible the way the concepts were defined. It was not even that actual saving was higher in the 1930s than in the 1920s. Quite the contrary; because saving depends on income and income fell, actual saving declined too.

Not only did intended saving fall because actual income fell but the saving schedule shifted upward as the desire to spend in a period of great uncertainty declined. At the same time that households were wishing to save more—or spend less—businesses wished to cut back their investment expenditures. This meant that the investment schedule was declining during a period when the saving schedule was increasing. Hence at the full employment level of income, intended saving was greater than intended investment.

This made it impossible to be at the full employment level of income. Because of the excess of desired savings over desired investment at full employment, income fell until intended saving and intended investment were equal. Although the aggregate desire to invest was very weak, the aggregate desire to save was very strong, so there was a very low level of national income and high levels of unemployment.

## Growth in Output and Employment

On the other hand, when real income (output) is high and growing, we would expect to see high and expanding levels of employment. The nearly forty years after World War II have been characterized generally by such more favorable conditions, as compared with the depressed 1930s prior to World War II. Nevertheless, this postwar period has seen years of excessive aggregate demand, which were years of inflation (e.g., 1972–1973 and 1979–1980), even though output was still expanding, whereas other years have witnessed declines in output and employment when the economy suffered an economic recession.

After the early postwar recession of 1948–1949, there were seven other major recessions, in 1953–1954, 1957–1958, 1960–1961, 1969–1970, 1973–1975, a one quarter recession in 1980 and a recession in 1981–1982. After the trough of each recession was reached, there were generally years of strong recovery in both real output and employment. In some recovery periods, however, a strong growth in the labor force has tended to make the unemployment rate sticky at a high level.

## Actual and Potential Output

The sluggishness in the rise in employment in recovery periods and the persistence of unemployment levels over the "full employment" rate may also be considered as a gap between actual and potential gross national product. Actual and potential GNP over a twenty-two-year period are shown in Figure 21–5. (Potential GNP is that gross output that would occur if utilization of capital is 86 percent and the unemployment rate is 4.9 percent.)

As seen in this figure, except for the late 1960s and 1973, the gap between actual and potential GNP has tended to be chronic, though variable. Even in 1972, a year of strong economic growth, a gap of nearly $40 billion existed in the fourth quarter of that year. Of course in recession periods like 1975 and 1980, the gap between actual and **potential output** widened. Although actual output in 1974 was only 2.3 percent below such potential output, it rose sharply to 6.6 percent in 1975. It fell again to 4.7 percent in 1976, to 2.8 percent in 1977, and down to a very low gap of only 1.5 percent in 1978 and 1.4 percent in 1979. In 1980, however, with a sharp recession in the second quarter, it rose to 4.4 percent.

Aggregate demand, rather than the potential output of goods and services in traditional macroeconomic analysis, thus determines how many goods and services will actually be produced and how many workers will be employed to produce those goods and services. Although showing strong growth, aggregate demand has fluctuated over time,

**Figure 21–5   Gross National Product, Actual and Potential**

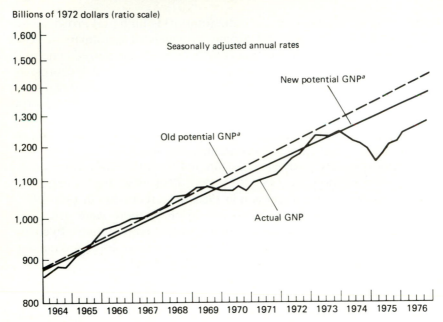

Billions of 1972 dollars (ratio scale)

[a] Old potential GNP was estimated to rise 3.9 percent per year, whereas new potential GNP is estimated to be 3.6 percent per year.

SOURCE: *Economic Report of the President, January 1977* (Washington, D.C.: U. S. Government Printing Office, 1977), p. 55.

whereas potential output has steadily increased as a result of a constant increase in the productive facilities of the economy. These productive facilities, which represent the sum of all past net real investment, though not increasing at the same rate each year, have nevertheless increased year after year in the postwar period.

## *Supply-Side Economics*

Like all revolutions, the Keynesian revolution finally inspired a counter-revolution. Though it was some years in developing, this counterrevolution reached full flower in the early 1980s, when it was embodied in the new macroeconomic policies of the Reagan administration, which came to office on January 20, 1981. The basic thrust of these new macroeconomic policies came from economic theories that are usually called **"supply-side economics"** and "monetarism." Because monetarism is discussed in the next chapter, we ignore it here, but supply-side economics will now be summarized.

There was an apparent early success of demand management policies clearly based on Keynesian and post-Keynesian theories in the early period after World War II. They seemed to run into great difficulties in the late 1960s, however, and throughout the decade of the 1970s. Demand management policies relied on monetary and fiscal policies to stimulate aggregate demand and thereby increase output and employment when actual output was markedly below potential output. When output increased, of course, total employment should also increase and the unemployment rate should fall. And all of these happy results should occur without an undue increase in the inflation rate. But in the decade of the 1970s stagflation often seemed to be the prevailing economic malaise, in which inflation and unemployment increased simultaneously. This happened either in spite of, or partly as a result of, demand management policies.

The times thus seemed ripe for a return to the lessons of classical economic theory (i.e., pre-1936 economic theory). This in fact is what supply-side economists would have us do. Before the Great Depression, economists generally had believed that government could increase the level of output and employment only by implementing policies that increased financial, or market, incentives to produce. Higher rates of return to labor and capital, these traditional economists believed, should result in more labor being offered to the market and more saving taking place and thus more investment in capital occurring.

Government, then, should abandon its emphasis on demand management policies (though the monetarists had some injunctions for monetary policy) and instead emphasize cuts in tax rates on labor and capital income. These tax cuts would increase output by increasing the supply of labor and by increasing the incentives to save and invest. This supply-side economics therefore provided the theoretical underpinning for the Reagan administration's budget recommendations to Congress in 1981. This new budget emphasized cuts in planned civilian government spending, and loosened government regulations of private businesses for the years ahead, as well as business and personal tax cuts over a period of three years. It remained to be seen whether these new public policies emphasizing the supply-side approach would work better than the demand management policies they were designed to replace.

# Questions for Discussion

1. Discuss Keynes's attitude toward the traditional quantity theory of money as given in his *General Theory* of 1936. Discuss his modified quantity theory.
2. What different approach to the problems of an economic system is taken in

the macroeconomic approach as distinguished from the more traditional microeconomic approach?

3. Discuss the importance of saving and investment in the Keynesian macroeconomic system. Which variable is active and which is passive? Why? In what sense are saving and investment equal and in what sense may they be unequal?

4. Explain carefully the nature of the concept of the consumption function. Graph this function and show how different amounts of aggregate consumption and aggregate saving can be read from this curve. Where, and why, is aggregate saving zero?

5. What is the difference between a straight-line, short-run consumption function and one in which the consumption function is flatter at higher levels of national income? Which one is the more consistent with budget studies?

6. Why is the long-run consumption function different from the short-run consumption function? How can the long-run and short-run consumption functions be interrelated?

7. Define the multiplier and tell how its value is derived from the consumption function. What is the significance and use of the multiplier in national income analysis? Define and discuss the supermultiplier.

8. Define, graph, and discuss the investment function. What is the marginal efficiency of investment and how is it related to the level of investment expenditures? How does the rate of interest affect investment expenditures? What is the difference between autonomous investment and induced investment?

9. Discuss the derivation, shape, and level of the investment and saving schedules. What factors can cause shifts in these schedules? Demonstrate graphically how the investment and saving schedules determine the equilibrium level of national income. Show how a change in one, or both, of these schedules leads to a new equilibrium level of income.

10. Discuss and graph the possible gap between actual and potential output. What do you think the gap, if any, will be in the 1980s? Why?

11. Discuss the challenge to traditional aggregate demand macroeconomic policies of the newer supply-side economics of the early 1980s. Discuss some of the policies based on these theories in this period. Analyze their effectiveness. How would you evaluate these theories?

# Selected Bibliography for Further Reading

ACKLEY, GARDNER, *Macroeconomics: Theory and Policy* (New York: Macmillan, 1978).

GLAHE, FRED R., *Macroeconomics Theory and Policy* (New York: Harcourt Brace Jovanovich, 1973).

HANSEN, ALVIN, *Monetary Theory and Fiscal Policy* (New York: Norton, 1949).

KEYNES, JOHN MAYNARD, *The General Theory of Employment, Interest and Money* (London: Macmillan, 1936).

LINDAUER, JOHN, *Macroeconomics*, 2d ed. (New York: 1971).

PRESIDENT'S COUNCIL OF ECONOMIC ADVISERS, *Economic Report of the President* (Annual).

PROTOPAPADAKIS, ARIS, "Supply-Side Economics: What Chance for Success?" *Business Review*, Federal Reserve Bank of Philadelphia, May-June 1981, pp. 11–23.

TATOM, JOHN A., "We Are All Supply-Siders Now!" *Review*, Federal Reserve Bank of St. Louis, May 1981, Vol. 63, No. 5, pp. 18–30.

> What is the proportion which the circulating money of any country bears to the whole value of the annual produce circulated by means of it, it is, perhaps, impossible to determine. It has been computed by different authors at a fifth, at a tenth, at a twentieth and a thirtieth part of that value.
>
> THE WEALTH OF NATIONS

# 22 CHAPTER

# Money and Income: Monetarism Versus Neo-Keynesianism

Macroeconomics became clearly distinguished as a separate branch of economic theory after the publication of the *General Theory* by Keynes in 1936. Although new views about the role of money and income became popular, the more traditional views of monetary theory did not become extinct. In the 1960s and 1970s the disciples of traditional monetary theory labeled themselves as monetarists and included such academic economists as Milton Friedman, Karl Brunner, Allan Meltzer, and a group of economists at the Federal Reserve Bank of St. Louis. This group might also be called neo-Marshallians or neo-Fisherians, after Alfred Marshall and Irving Fisher, respectively.

An even larger group of economists that considered themselves to be **neo-Keynesians** included such economists as James Tobin, Paul Samuelson, Franco Modigliani, Gardner Ackley, Lawrence Klein, and Walter Heller. After years of debate between these two groups, a certain amount of consensus appears to have emerged. Nevertheless, significant differences of emphasis in theory and different policy recommendations still remain to differentiate the thinking of these two groups.

456

# THE MONETARISTS

In many ways the basic theoretical structure of the monetarists resembles that already discussed in Chapter 20, Traditional Monetary Theory. It may be recalled that traditional monetary theory accompanied the theoretical structure of neoclassical analysis. In general, economic theory prior to 1936 stressed long-run equilibrium analysis in which real factors determined real output and employment. Individual prices were also in real terms (i.e., in relative price terms).

The role of money was simply to determine the general price level. A change in the quantity of money was not thought to have any impact either on the velocity of money or the quantity of output. In some simple theoretical versions, both velocity and output were regarded as constant. In all cases, they were thought to be stable. Velocity was determined by technical conditions such as timing of receipts and expenditures. Output, under equilibrium conditions in the entire economy, would be at the full employment level and was determined by real, or relative, prices. Money was thus regarded as neutral in its impact on output.

Like traditional economists, the monetarists regard the real economy as essentially stable or tending toward full employment equilibrium whenever it is displaced from that balanced position. The balance of the economy, however, may be disrupted by poor public policies, especially in the management of the money supply by the central bank.

The excesses of the business cycle, according to this group of economists, are largely the result of excessive or variable rates of change in the money supply. Changes in the growth rate in the money supply are regarded as under the firm control of the Federal Reserve System. Any changes in the growth rate of money will cause changes in nominal income and nominal interest rates. In the short run, such changes in the growth of money may even result in changes in real output.

Leonall C. Andersen, an economist at the Federal Reserve Bank of St. Louis, has succinctly summarized the views of the monetarists as to the effect of changes in the stock of money on nominal and real income.

> Changes in the trend growth of money are considered the dominant, not the exclusive, determinant of the trend of nominal GNP and the price level. Long-run movements in output are little influenced by changes in the growth rate of money. . . . In the short run, however, changes in the trend growth of money or pronounced variations around a given trend exert a significant, but temporary, impact on output.[1]

---

[1]Leonall C. Andersen, "The State of the Monetarist Debate," *Review*, Federal Reserve Bank of St. Louis, Vol. 55, No. 9, Sept. 1973, p. 3.

Both the short-run and long-run impacts of money on the economy are summarized in this statement.

In the long run, little if any change in real output can be expected from such money manipulation, and both real interest rates and the unemployment rate will return to their normal equilibrium levels, if they have been displaced from them. The long run is still dominated by the real factors in the economy, even if the economy experiences the economic effects of monetary manipulation in the short run. The proper monetary policy, therefore, should encourage a stable rate of growth in the supply of money consistent with the growth rate in real output, so that a stable price level can be maintained. Fiscal policy, if used at all, is regarded simply as a way of transferring real resources from the private to the public sector.

## FRIEDMAN ON MONETARY POLICY

One of the better known monetarists is Milton Friedman, formerly of the University of Chicago. In his presidential address to the American Economic Association in December 1967, Friedman enunciated some of his views on monetary policy. In talking about what monetary policy cannot do, he stated: "We are in danger of asking it to accomplish tasks that it cannot achieve. . . ." Later he indicated: "(1) It cannot peg interest rates for more than very limited periods; (2) It cannot peg the rate of unemployment for more than very limited periods."[2]

Friedman argues that monetary policy cannot peg the rate of unemployment because there is a **"natural rate of unemployment"** determined by general equilibrium in the economic system. Any market rate of unemployment can be reduced only temporarily below the natural rate and it can be kept there for a while only at the price of accelerating inflation. Similarly, Friedman believes that the market rate of interest can be kept only temporarily below the natural rate of interest and again only by paying the price of accelerating inflation.

Friedman believes that to avoid being a source of instability in the economy itself, the monetary authorities should avoid sharp swings in monetary policy. Furthermore, the authorities should choose some fixed rate of expansion of the money supply, such as 3 to 5 percent, and stick to that rate. He argued: "It would be better to have a fixed rate that would on the average produce moderate inflation or moderate deflation, provided that it was steady, than to suffer the wide and erratic pertur-

[2]Milton Friedman, "The Role of Monetary Policy," *The American Economic Review*, **63**, No. 1, (March 1968), p. 5.

bations we have experienced."[3] Underlying all of Friedman's policy recommendations, as is true for other monetarists, is the theoretical view that real growth in the economy is determined by real factors such as technology and growth in the stock of capital and the supply of labor. Changes in the money supply, because they are thought to affect only the price level, are essentially neutral in their effects on real output.

***Rules Versus Discretion*** Distrusting the ability of policymakers accurately to forecast economic activity and believing that government actions tend to destabilize the economy, the monetarists thus strongly recommend fixed **monetary** rules rather than discretion in policy. Although they emphasize the importance of a fixed rate of growth of the money supply, they also recommend that taxes and spending of the federal government be set so that the budget is balanced at full employment. Since the monetarists believe that private economic fluctuations tend to be mild, they would not have the government attempt any countercyclical variations in aggregate demand through policy changes. Real factors determine real output, and the money supply is neutral on real output in the long run, as noted.

## THE NEO-KEYNESIANS

The neo-Keynesians, on the other hand, believe that the money supply is not necessarily neutral, even in the long run. The rate of growth in the money supply, they believe, should be increased in periods of unemployment in order to increase real output then and subsequently over time. This group also believes that the demand for money is relatively interest elastic, so that higher interest rates will reduce the amount of cash balances desired and thereby increase the velocity, or turnover, of money. This view contrasts with the traditional belief in constant, or at least very stable, rates of velocity of money. However, the neo-Keynesians do not generally believe that the investment demand for borrowed funds is very interest elastic, so that the ability of the monetary authorities to increase investment and output through reducing interest rates is limited.

Public policy therefore needs to focus on fiscal policy, which will increase aggregate demand and output by cutting taxes or increasing government spending on goods and services in periods of less than full employment. The opposite fiscal policy is recommended in periods of inflationary pressures (i.e., reducing government spending, or at least

[3]Ibid., p. 16.

reducing the rate of increase of such government spending, and increasing tax revenues as a result of growth in money income in such a period, or even by including an increase in tax rates).

The private market-oriented economy is often viewed by many neo-Keynesians as inherently unstable. Offsetting monetary and fiscal policies are thus necessary to correct the destabilizing variations in private aggregate spending over the business cycle. Such stimulus may also be needed to promote long-run noninflationary economic growth.


## CHANNELS OF MONETARY POLICY

As noted earlier, present-day monetarists are intellectual heirs of the quantity theory tradition. In the cash balance equation version of the quantity theory ($M = kY$) favored in Great Britain by the students of Marshall, any change in the money supply by the central bank would result in holders of cash balances having a higher ratio of cash ($k$) than the desired, or equilibrium, cash ratio. In such circumstances, the means by which the central bank's control of the money supply affected the economy was by inducing holders of cash balances to spend the added undesired cash balances on goods and services. If the economy were at the equilibrium full employment level, such increased money spending would raise the price level rather than increase output or employment.

As Keynes summarized this traditional quantity theory of money in *The General Theory*, "It seems that the elasticity of supply must have become zero and demand proportional to the quantity of money."[4] Keynes's own modified version of the quantity theory was that "we must first consider the effect of changes in the quantity of money on the quantity of effective demand; and the increase in effective demand will, generally speaking, spend itself partly in increasing the quantity of employment and partly in raising the level of prices."[5] Contrary to some critical summaries of what Keynes said in *The General Theory*, he did not neglect the impact of an increase in the quantity of money on the price level. Nevertheless, unlike his more traditional predecessors, Keynes did point out that an increase in the quantity of money may also increase real output and therefore the level of employment.

The monetarists, as did Marshall before them, emphasize the direct influences of changes in the money supply on the real sector, the price level, and nominal income through the efforts of holders of cash

[4]John Maynard Keynes, *The General Theory of Employment, Interest and Money* (London: Macmillan, 1936), p. 292.
[5]Ibid., p. 296.

balances to return to their desired or equilibrium ratio of cash to real income when the central bank increases, or decreases, the nominal supply of money. Changes in the price level may also affect the demand for money (the real balance effect of A. C. Pigou), because the demand for money balances to hold is not in nominal terms but rather is a fraction of real income demanded in money balances.

## *The Importance of the Demand for Money*

Modern monetarists and Keynesians, along with traditional monetary theorists, have always put a great deal of emphasis on the importance of understanding the factors that determine the demand for money. Part of any difference of opinion as to the relative importance of controlling the money supply, say, by the monetary authorities arises over the importance and stability of the demand for money. The traditional quantity theorists particularly placed a great deal of stress on the importance of a relatively stable demand for money. Milton Friedman, for example, has argued that "The quantity theory is, in the first instance, a theory of the demand for money. It is not a theory of output, or of money income, or of the price level."[6] Likewise Keynes noted that after individuals have decided how much of their present income they want to save, they must make a further decison. "Does he [the saver] want to hold it in the form of immediate, market command (i.e., in money or its equivalent)?"[7]

## THE KEYNESIAN DEMAND FOR MONEY

The previously accepted view of money prior to Keynes's *General Theory* was that it was demanded for transactions purposes (i.e., to provide funds needed by households or businesses for spending from one receipt of money to another). Only those suffering from a money illusion, the neoclassical economists believed, would seem to desire money for its own sake. Keynes, on the other hand, noted that money has the great utility of being the most liquid of all assets. At times the demand for this asset might rise sharply. In order to secure money, many investors would sell their other assets to become liquid at all costs. This would be a liquidity crisis or financial panic, in which the desire for money as an asset might reach very high levels.

---

[6]Milton Friedman, "The Quantity Theory of Money—A Restatement," *Studies in the Quantity Theory of Money*, ed. by Milton Friedman (Chicago: The University of Chicago Press, 1956), p. 4.
[7]Keynes, op. cit., p. 166.

## Two Demands for Money

The demand for money can be regarded as having two parts: (1) transactions demand, and (2) asset demand. Let $L$ = total demand for money, which is made up of $L_1$ and $L_2$. Transactions demand, or $L_1$, is shown in Figure 22–1. The **transactions demand for money** is thus seen as a positive function of income, so that as income, production, and sales rise, there is greater need for money to serve as a medium of exchange and temporary store of value.

Keynes, however, was concerned with the store of value function of money, not as an alternative to holding goods, but as an alternative to holding debt instruments that would yield an interest rate. His demand for money thus was a function of the interest rate rather than of income. This liquidity preference schedule, as he called the asset demand for money, sloped downward from left to right, showing that a greater amount of money would be demanded for cash balances at a lower than at a higher interest rate; at a very low rate of interest, say, 2 percent, the demand for money becomes perfectly elastic. This schedule is shown in Figure 22–2. This schedule is the $L_2$ schedule, or the asset, or speculative demand for money. This is what Gottfried Haberler calls liquidity preference proper. Thus $L_2$ is a different demand for money than $L_1$, which is the transactions demand for money and is a function of the level of income.

**Speculative Demand for Money**   The pure quantity theorists earlier ignored any demand for money other than the transactions demand and later assumed that the speculative or **asset demand for money** was inelastic with respect to the rate of interest. If persons have a fixed amount of money in real terms that they wish to hold, or if their desire to hold money is unaffected by changes in the rate of interest, then it follows that any increase in the stock of money brought about by the monetary authorities will be reflected in increased expenditures. This is the "real balance effect" of A. C. Pigou, which was criticized by Keynes. If, on the contrary, the desire to hold idle money is affected by the rate of interest on government securities, as Keynes assumed, then an increase in the stock of money by the monetary authorities may go in part, or entirely, into these idle hoards rather than be spent on goods or services.

**Hoarding of Money**   This speculative motive was largely ignored by most monetary economists prior to 1936. As it turns out, this is the most volatile component of the demand for money, because it is the part that is most sensitive to changes in the rate of interest (i.e., it is interest elastic). Whenever the earlier economists referred to this type of behavior at all, they were likely to use the term **"hoarding."** Hoarding often proved to be difficult to define because it was used variously to

**Figure 22–1    Transactions Demand for Money**

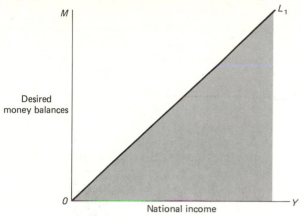

mean not-spending, or saving, as well as desiring to accumulate stores of wealth in the form of money. Some writers also used hoarding to mean the inverse of the velocity of money, so that an increase in hoarding could be defined simply as a decline in the velocity of money, whereas a decrease in hoarding was reflected in an increase in the velocity of money.

It was not always clear, to the ordinary reader at least, that the public could not hoard more money than the monetary authorities were willing to provide for them. It is most ironic that in periods of financial crisis, when the desire to hoard money was likely to increase the most, the quantity of money generally would tend to decline rather than increase. This desire for greater liquidity on the part of most businesses, financial institutions, and the like, therefore, could not possibly be satisfied.

**Figure 22–2    Liquidity Preference Schedule**

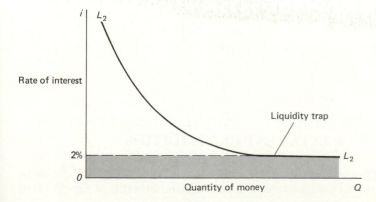

## *The Liquidity Trap*

The reasons for the Keynesian **liquidity preference schedule** being perfectly elastic at some low rate of interest are (1) the opportunity cost of hoarding is lower the more the rate of interest declines on alternative forms of holding wealth, and (2) the lower the rate of interest, the less the likelihood that it will fall even lower and the greater the probability that it will rise in the future. Therefore, as Figure 22–2 shows, at some very low rate of interest such as 2 percent, the demand for idle cash becomes perfectly elastic. This has often been called the liquidity trap.

After this low rate of interest has been reached, the monetary authorities can do virtually nothing more to stimulate economic activity by increasing the stock of money. This perfect elasticity of demand for money might be encountered in a deep depression such as the 1930s, when monetary policy did not seem to be especially significant in inducing recovery. (Some recent empirical studies relating to the 1930s have raised doubts, however, as to whether the liquidity trap existed even then).

*Factors Determining Liquidity Preference*   Attitudes about the future are particularly important in determining the level of the liquidity preference schedule. Because our knowledge of the future is at best uncertain and subject to rumors, speculation, and other emotional factors, so too is the desire to hold money for this reason likely to be highly variable. Persons who are bearish (i.e., pessimistic) about the future course of prices of securities, goods or services want to become more liquid now. That is, **bears** will sell some of their other assets now in order to increase their cash holdings in the expectation of being able to purchase income-bearing assets at a cheaper price in the future. (Likewise, investors at the same time are likely to be pessimistic about the expected flow of profits on new investment so that the present rate of real investment is reduced.) **Bullish speculators,** who expect the future prices of assets to be higher than they are now, will prefer to reduce their present holdings of cash to the bare minimum required by transactions and precautionary motives. Bulls thus speculate by holding assets bearing an interest or profit return rather than speculating by holding money as an asset.

## SUMMARY OF THEORY OF MONETARISTS AND KEYNESIANS: INTEREST ELASTICITIES

Much of the preceding discussion centering on the theories of the monetarists and the Keynesians may be summarized in terms of the different interest rate elasticities assumed by each group. As a result of different assumed interest rate elasticities, different policy recommendations emerge, because each group has a different view on how monetary policy affects the economy.

In general, traditional monetary theorists as represented by the monetarists believe that the demand for money is interest inelastic. That is, a change in interest rates will not affect the amount of money desired in real cash balances. As a result of this insensitivity to changes in interest rates, the velocity of money will not change either when interest rates change. As demonstrated earlier in the chapter on traditional monetary theory, the demand for real money balances ($k$) is the reciprocal of $V$ in the equation of exchange, when the money market is in equilibrium. The monetarists largely disregard the asset demand for money.

The Keynesians, on the other hand, believe that the demand for money is interest elastic. In the liquidity preference schedule of Keynes, which focuses on the asset demand for money, there is some low rate of interest (say, 2 percent) at which the demand for money might become perfectly elastic. (Even in the depressed 1930s, however, the long-term rate of interest only fell to 3 percent.) Even the transactions demand for money, however, has some interest rate elasticity for Keynesians. Because the demand for money is interest elastic, it is to be expected that rising rates of interest will lead to higher velocity or turnover rates of money. Holders of money will economize more on money holdings at higher interest rates, because the money now has a higher opportunity cost in terms of interest forgone on alternative asset holdings (e.g., U.S. government securities).

In keeping with traditional economic theory, the monetarists also believe that, contrary to the demand for money, the demand for borrowed funds as represented by the investment schedule is interest elastic. (The same was also true for traditional economists concerning the interest elasticity of the savings schedule. This position is not generally held today, however, because nearly all economists believe that savings is largely a function of income.) If the investment schedule is interest elastic, then any change induced in interest rates by monetary policy will have a significant impact on the economy. In a period of recession, lower interest rates induced by an increase in the money supply will stimulate investment and help revive the economy. In a period of inflation, higher interest rates induced by credit restraint policies will reduce borrowing and investment spending and thereby curb inflationary pressures. The monetarists also believe that different amounts of money balances may directly affect spending without the necessity of changes in interest rates. Many monetarists, however, do not stress a **countercyclical** type of monetary policy, because they prefer a steady growth in the money supply.

Keynesians, on the other hand, generally believe that the investment schedule is interest inelastic. Actual investment expenditures, they believe, are largely the result of profit expectations, which, in turn, are volatile over the business cycle. Hence they are often quite pessimistic about the prospects of monetary policy contributing significantly to a stabilization of the economy. Fiscal policy, which involves changes in government spending and tax revenues, is instead relied upon to provide the needed stabilization policies.

Another important theoretical difference between these two groups is that the monetarists seem to believe that the macro supply of goods and services is more price inelastic than do the Keynesians. At "full employment" the supply of aggregate goods and services is price inelastic and this was usually the assumed equilibrium position of the economy for traditional theorists. Keynesians, on the other hand, are often concerned with positions of "unemployment equilibrium" when there are substantial amounts of unused resources. In such circumstances, increases in aggregate demand will have substantial impacts on increasing employment and output and only minor effects on the price level. When the economy is at full employment, however, an increase in aggregate demand will have most of its impact in the form of inflation of the price level and increase real output very little.

## INTEREST RATE CHANGES INDUCED BY MONETARY POLICY AFFECT THE ECONOMY

The neo-Keynesians also usually prefer to emphasize an indirect mechanism, whereby changes in the money supply induced by central bank actions such as open market operations influence the economy through changes in the nominal rate of interest. A portfolio theory has been developed by neo-Keynesians such as Tobin of Yale and Baumol of Princeton to explain how changes in interest rates influence portfolio holders to shift the composition and amount of their asset holdings and thereby transmit the monetary impulses to the rest of the economy. Although this modern theory has been elaborately developed, a precursor of such a theory stressing the indirect influence of the central bank on the economy through changes in interest rates was developed in the late nineteenth century by Knut Wicksell of Sweden. As a result of the great popularity of the Keynesian idea, Wicksell has been rediscovered by a number of economists.

Wicksell argued that an increase in the money supply by the central bank would depress the market rate of interest below the real rate of interest, which is determined by the productivity of real capital.

With the borrowing cost of funds below the real return on investment, businesses are encouraged to borrow and thereby step up their rate of investment. As businesses borrow increasing amounts of funds from the banking system, the nominal or market rate of interest charged by the banks increases while the real rate of return on capital declines because of the **law of diminishing returns.** This explains why one would expect a decline in the profit rate as the proportion of capital to the other factors of production rises.

Eventually, the favorable differential between the market rate of interest and the real rate of interest disappears, so that the borrowing and investing activities of businesses decline sharply. The sharp decline in investment spending leads to a downturn in overall business activity and a recession or depression ensues. Finally, the process is repeated all over again. A greater accumulation of loanable funds by the banking system in a period of recession leads to a fall in the market rate of interest. Then a greater shortage of capital relative to the other factors of production returns the real rate of interest to a higher level than before. A new upsurge of borrowing and investing by businesses next takes place with the same consequences as before for the business cycle.

## HIGHER VELOCITY OF MONEY RESULTS FROM HIGHER INTEREST RATES

One of the consequences of higher interest rates is that the velocity of money is likely to increase. This is because idle money now has a higher opportunity cost in terms of forgone interest on alternative monetary assets. Furthermore, a great growth of money substitutes such as Treasury bills and other money market assets in the period after World War II also encourages the rise in velocity.

This tendency for the velocity of money to increase in periods of rising interest rates—either cyclical or secular—has been confirmed in numerous empirical studies. One of these completed in 1977 at the Federal Reserve Bank of Chicago concluded: "A major economic factor influencing the postwar rise in velocity is the general rise in interest rates that has occurred."[8] The significant increase in the income velocity of money that took place over the thirty years from 1947 to 1977 is shown in Figure 22–3, which shows that the income velocity of money had nearly a threefold increase in this thirty-year period.

Although it is not easy to see in Figure 22–3, the velocity of money

[8]Anna Marie Laporte, "Behavior of the Income Velocity of Money," *Economic Perspectives*," Federal Reserve Bank of Chicago, Sept.-Oct., 1977, p. 9.

**Figure 22–3    Velocity, 1947–1977, Has Been on a Rising Trend**

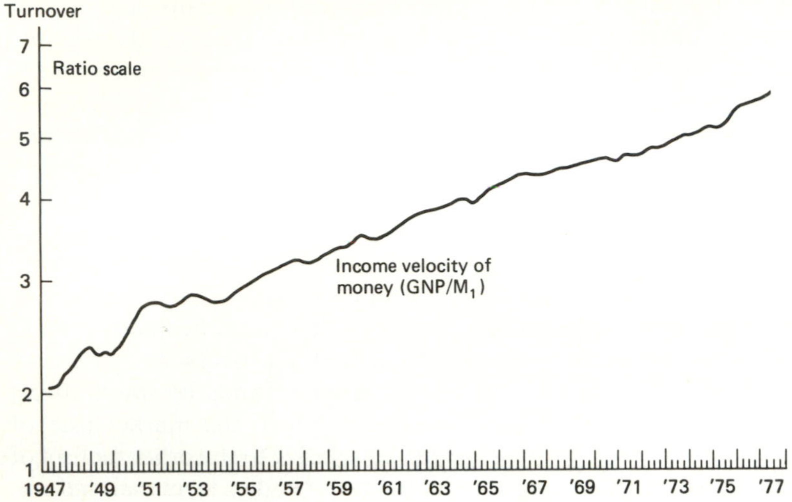

Turnover

SOURCE: Anna Marie Laporte, "Behavior of the Income Velocity of Money," *Economic Perspectives*, Federal Reserve Bank of Chicago, Sept.–Oct. 1977, p. 9.

also has a tendency to rise in the upswing of the business cycle and to fall in the downswing. Again, we might attribute this behavior largely to increases in interest rates in the upswing of the cycle and declines in interest rates in the downswing. The significance of such velocity changes is that money flows tend to increase more in the upswing of the cycle, when the Federal Reserve often slows down the growth in the money supply. On the other hand, when the Federal Reserve is trying to stimulate the growth of the money supply in the downswing of the cycle, the tendency of the velocity of money to fall as interest rates fall means that money flows will not rise as much as policymakers desire.

That the velocity of money not only has a rising trend but is quite variable from quarter to quarter can be seen in Figure 22–4. In this figure, the 1980–1981 definition of money (M1-B) is used and its velocity is measured as a ratio to Gross National Product. In the six years from 1975 through 1980 shown in this figure considerable short-run variability in velocity is apparent.

In addition to the important impact of variation in interest rates on the velocity of money, various institutional changes in recent years have also tended to contribute to rising, and variable, velocity. The great growth in various **money substitutes** such as Treasury bills and money market mutual funds has already been noted. Continued growth of various types of money substitutes—some of which are sometimes even included in one or another definition of "money"—occurred in the 1980s

**Figure 22–4    Quarterly Changes in the Velocity of Money**

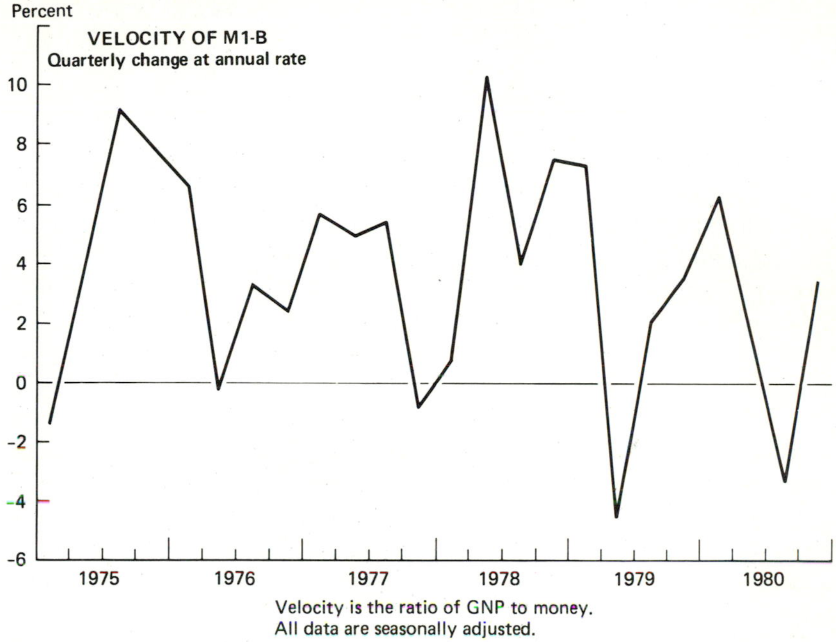

Velocity is the ratio of GNP to money.
All data are seasonally adjusted.

SOURCE: Federal Reserve Bank of New York, *Annual Report 1980*, p. 20.

as many financial institutions took advantage of the liberalized provisions of the Depository Institutions Deregulation and Monetary Control Act of 1980. The variability of velocity is particularly troublesome to the monetary authorities, because the same rate of growth of the monetary aggregates will have different impacts on inflation and real output if velocity varies in an unpredictable manner.

## The Income Demand for Money

The demand for money has often been formulated by monetary theorists as a function of income or transactions needs. (The asset demand for money reflected in the "liquidity trap" of Keynes is either disregarded by these theorists or, in some cases, thought to be nonexistent.) The transactions demand for money is a positive function of income. (This was shown in Figure 22–1.) Therefore as income rises, the dollar amount of nominal money held for transactions purposes increases even if the proportion of transactions cash balances to income remains constant. Hence if the central bank is unwilling to increase the nominal supply of money *pari passu* as the level of income rises, the interest rate, or the opportunity cost of holding money, will necessarily rise.

## The Demand for Real Cash Balances

Although the money supply, which was illustrated in Figure 22–1, is the *nominal* quantity of money, modern quantity theorists are usually concerned with the demand for the *real* money supply (i.e., the stock of money adjusted for changes in the price level). These monetary theorists also assume that there is a fairly definite real quantity of money that people wish to hold in particular circumstances.[9]

If there is a disequilibrium between actual and desired money balances such that actual money balances are greater than desired, people seeking to reduce their actual real balances will spend more on securities, goods, and services, or repay debt. The effect of this increase in money spending should be that prices, and perhaps output as well, will rise until the desired equilibrium in real money balances is reached. Changes in prices and nominal money income thus can arise from the existence of an excess supply or an excess demand for real money balances.

*Cost of Idle Money Balances*　Philip Cagan argues that the cost of holding idle money balances as part of one's stock of wealth must be measured "solely by the change in the real value of a given nominal cash balance—the rate of depreciation in the real value of money."[10] This particular **opportunity cost** of holding cash differs from the Keynesian cost, which is the interest rate that could have been earned on such funds if they had been invested in long-term government securities, or consols. In the Cagan approach, an inflationary period in which the real value of money is declining should lead to a reduction in money balances relative to income (i.e., a rise in the velocity of money). The total cost of holding idle money should include both the opportunity cost, or interest yield on an alternative monetary asset, and a discount rate for the expected future real decline in the value of such idle money.

*Decline in Money Balances and Inflation*　Hence a decline in money balances would occur in an inflationary period, because money holders would not wish to continue suffering this decline in the real value of their money in the future. This flight from currency could under certain

---

[9]For an excellent summary of the quantity theory on this and other points, see Milton Friedman, "Quantity Theory of Money," *The International Encyclopedia of the Social Sciences*, Vol. 10 (New York: Free Press, 1968), pp. 432–446.

[10]Philip Cagan, "The Monetary Dynamics of Hyperinflation," in *Studies in the Quantity Theory of Money*, ed. by Milton Friedman (Chicago: The University of Chicago Press, 1956), p. 31.

circumstances even lead to "runaway inflation," or at least to some increase in the future rate of inflation as a result of self-justifying expectations of continued inflation. Inflationary expectations can become self-justifying when they lead to increased spending on goods and services and a corresponding reduction in the present demand for money balances.


## THE DEMAND FOR MONEY AS
## A FUNCTION OF WEALTH

When the demand for money is regarded as depending largely on the transactions motive for holding money and thus is a function of the level of income, money is viewed as one of the major items used by the household and business sectors as a kind of "shock absorber" affected by transitory components of income. For the Friedman school of quantity theorists, however, money is regarded as a "durable consumer good held for the services it renders and yielding a flow of services proportional to the stock."[11]

The appropriate constraint on money holdings then becomes the expected yield on wealth. Because wealth is difficult to measure, a proxy for wealth in the form of "permanent income" is used. This analysis implies that the demand for money, and hence the velocity of money, would be relatively stable, assuming that the preference for money as compared with other forms of wealth is in equilibrium in the long run.

*Long-Run Equilibrium Relationships*     In emphasizing "permanent income" or wealth, Friedman remains clearly in the neoclassical theoretical tradition, which focused on **long-run equilibrium** relationships rather than concerning itself largely with short-run equilibrium, or even disequilibrium, states. Keynes, on the other hand, in his *General Theory* of 1936, emphasized short-run equilibrium states for the entire economy.

The great advantage of using the long-run equilibrium approach is that a monetary theory can thus be integrated into neoclassical value and distribution theory.[12] Stress can also be placed on long-run variables, which show a reasonable amount of statistical stability. One such variable, which the Friedman school believes has such stability over a long-run period, is the velocity of money, or the cash-balance relationship to income.

---

[11]Milton Friedman, "The Demand for Money: Some Theoretical and Empirical Results," *The Journal of Political Economy*, **67:**327–351 (Aug. 1959).

[12]For such an integrative approach, see Don Patinkin, *Money, Interest, and Prices*, 2d ed. (New York: Harper & Row, 1965).

*Services Rendered by Money*    The expected rate of return on money and other assets can then be considered as the analogue to the prices of commodities in the theory of consumer choice. Problems of substitutes and complements would also have to be considered here as they are in the theory of the household. The various variables bearing on the utility of money must be given particular attention. If the services rendered by money are considered as "necessary," increases in money holdings will not be proportionate to rises in income. In this case, the velocity of money would rise as income rises, which in fact it generally does.

If the services rendered by money are considered "luxuries," money holdings will rise more than income rises. Then the velocity of money would fall as income increases. (This, however, is contrary to the record of the period since World War II.) The degree of economic stability expected in the future by the holders of money today must also affect their demand for money. When uncertainty as to the future increases (e.g., when a financial crisis develops or when war threatens), the demand for money will rise and velocity will fall. Any increase in uncertainty—including expectations as to the future course of interest rates—will particularly increase the Keynesian asset or speculative demand for money.

## Sources of Asset Demand for Cash

Although the asset or speculative demand for money arises from uncertainty as to the future course of interest rates, it is some function of present interest rates compared with those expected in the future. Hence if future interest rates are expected by most or all major money managers to be higher than present interest rates, the demand for asset money at some low interest rate becomes perfectly elastic with respect to this low present interest rate on long-term bonds (i.e., the liquidity trap develops).

The preference for cash now, rather than other monetary assets that yield some rate of return, is the result of an inelasticity of expectations of future interest rates. This type of expectations about future interest rates means that investors hold an ideal of a "normal" interest rate to which they expect the rate of interest to return. Falling interest rates, in this case, do not generate expectations that interest rates will continue to fall to zero. Instead, investors believe that interest rates will rise in the future to a more normal level. Holders of cash for asset purposes then receive "utility" in the form of a reduction in risk and inconvenience, even though they pay a "cost" in the form of some forgone yield on an alternative monetary asset.

Keynes considered only one kind of substitute (government

bonds, or more precisely, **consols**) for money balances, whereas more recent formulations in the Keynesian tradition (the portfolio approach) have sometimes substituted other financial assets for bonds. The number of variables has also sometimes been increased from the traditional two. The modern quantity theorists emphasizing the cash balance approach would stress, on the other hand, the substitution between money and real goods and services. In any event, when the demand for money as an asset must be evaluated, the opportunity cost (i.e., the rate of return on some other financial asset), must be set against the useful services provided from holding money, whereas the uncertainty of the future must also be explicitly or implicitly considered, as well as the transactions costs incurred in switching from one financial asset to another.

## MEASURING THE DEMAND FOR MONEY

In his monograph on the demand for money David Laidler, after surveying the literature of empirical studies on the demand for money, concludes, "There is an overwhelming body of evidence in favor of the proposition that the demand for money is directly related to the rate of interest.[13] This means that the velocity of money is directly related to the rate of interest, because any reduction in money holdings as a proportion of income would be reflected in a rise in the income velocity of money.

This is consistent with the **"square root rule"** of Baumol, which asserts that the proportion of money held declines as real income rises. Because interest rates also tend to rise as real income increases, a high inverse correlation of money holdings and the rate of interest would be expected.

*The Use of Scale Variables*    A number of empirical studies[14] of the demand for money have emphasized not only the importance of the cost of money in terms of some interest rate, or a number of interest rates, but also include some "scale" variables such as income, total transactions, or a wealth measure to explain much of the variation over time in the amount of money held by the public. Actual money stocks are often assumed to be those desired, so that theorizing can be restricted to adjustment in equilibrium stocks. DeLeeuw's findings are consistent

---

[13]David E. W. Laidler, *The Demand for Money: Theories and Evidence*, 2d ed. (Scranton, Pa.: International Textbook Company, 1977), p. 97.

[14]See, for example, Frank DeLeeuw, "The Demand for Money: Speed of Adjustment, Interest Rates, and Wealth" in *Monetary Process and Policy: A Symposium*, ed. by George Horwich (Homewood, Ill.: Richard D. Irwin, 1967), pp. 167–186.

with the inventory theory of money demand (the Baumol-Tobin approach). This theory suggests that the current volume of transactions and current interest rates on risk-free assets (e.g., Treasury bills) influences not only the desire for money balances but the actual volume of such balances.

***Problems in Choosing Best Interest Rate***     DeLeeuw had some uncertainty as to which was the "best" interest rate to use, because he found no clear statistical preference, based on correlation analysis, as to use of a long-term interest rate, on the one hand, and some combination of rates of Treasury bills and time deposits, on the other hand. The difficulties in making a choice arise from colinearity problems (i.e., it is generally expected that both long- and short-term interest rates will move in the same direction because of similar causal factors such as credit ease or restraint by the Federal Reserve).

***Yield on Nonbank Intermediary Liabilities***     T. H. Lee's empirical results[15] were that the yield on nonbank intermediary liabilities was the most significant interest rate variable affecting the demand for money. This yield was regarded as the most significant since Lee discovered that the closest substitute to money was savings and loan shares, whether money was defined either to include or exclude time deposits.

## MONEY SUBSTITUTES

The demand for money is thus affected by the availability and cost of money substitutes. These substitutes include not only liquid assets, which can be readily turned into cash through early maturity or through easy marketability, but also access to credit. Marketable liquid assets include such money market instruments as certificates of deposit of commercial banks, Treasury bills, banker's acceptances, commercial paper, and money market mutual funds. (All these were discussed in some detail in Chapter 6.) Access to credit means that one has a good "credit rating," or ability to borrow funds when needed. Certainly, the ability to borrow funds on short notice will reduce the amount of cash needed in present balances, as well as the possession of a stock of liquid assets, which can be turned into cash as needed.

[15]Tong Hun Lee, "Alternative Interest Rates and the Demand for Money: The Empirical Evidence," *The American Economic Review*, **57**, No. 5: 1168–1181 ((Dec. 1967).

## *The Degree of Substitutability of Monetary Assets*

The degree of substitutability of monetary assets generally depends on the following objective factors: (1) costs of asset exchange, (2) predict-ability of real and money asset values at various future dates, (3) cor-relations among asset prospects, (4) liquidity of an asset, or the time it takes to realize its full value, (5) reversibility of the asset, or the pos-sibility and cost of simultaneously buying and selling an asset, and (6) timing and predictability of the investor's expected needs for wealth. In a sense, these needs for wealth may be considered to be related to the planning horizon for spending and saving in relation to expected future income. This planning horizon depends fundamentally on the time preference pattern of the investor toward consumption goods and services.

## *Cost of Money Substitutes and Scale Variables*

In addition to the availability of money substitutes affecting the demand for money, the cost of these substitutes and any complements to money as well affect the shape and level of the demand for money. In demand theory the cost of substitutes and complements must be considered in explaining the shape and level of the demand function for any given product. Insofar as the lender of money is concerned, the cost of money substitutes may be considered to be the interest rate differential between the interest rate prevailing on short-term loans as compared with that existing on long-term loans. If lenders invest some of their supply of cash in short loans, the cost of acquiring such a money substitute is the rate that they could have obtained on long loans.

From the borrowers' point of view, this rate differential represents the cost of money complements and is negative, because borrowers can save on their interest rate (usually) by borrowing short rather than long. Considering both borrowers and lenders, a widening of this short-long differential implies an increase in the cost of money substitutes (for lenders) and a decrease in the cost of money complements (for bor-rowers). For both parties, the demand for money balances will rise.

## MONETARISM AND MONETARY POLICY

Although the focus in this chapter is on monetary theory—both tradi-tional monetary theory in the form of monetarism today and neo-

Keynesianism, it should be noted that whatever theory is embraced has policy implications. Furthermore, if one favors a particular public policy, it almost surely has a theoretical basis to it. It should not be surprising, therefore, that in inflationary periods such as the late 1960s, all of the 1970s, and the early 1980s, monetarism, which stresses the importance of controlling the growth in the money supply, should have received increased attention both by theorists and by practitioners of public policy.

In general, most of the historical and statistical studies of the monetarists focus on the relationship between changes in the money supply, or the monetary base behind the money supply, and changes in the price level over rather long periods of time. The close correlations thus derived are usually translated into theoretical propositions to the effect that an externally caused change in the money supply by the monetary authorities results in the observed changes in the price level. Ergo, in order to control the price level (e.g., to reduce the rate of inflation), it is necessary only for the monetary authorities to exercise more discipline. As already noted, this should preferably be through rules imposed on them, but if not there should be lower target rates of growth for the key monetary aggregates.

It was this monetarist point of view that first led to the greater emphasis on monetary aggregates in January 1970, still greater stress on controlling such aggregates on October 6, 1979, and the severe credit restraint period of 1981 to 1982. (In 1981, M1-B, adjusted, grew at an annual rate of only 2.3 percent, which was sharply down from 1980 and even below the low target rate of 3.5 percent.) M2 in 1981, by way of contrast, grew at a 9.4 percent rate, which was somewhat above the high end of its target range of 9 percent.

The Federal Reserve, however, does not directly control the growth rate of M1-B, M2, or any other definition of the money supply for that matter. What the Federal Reserve does control is bank reserves, both total and unborrowed, because every time it buys or sells government securities in its open market operations, bank reserves are increased or decreased.

In order for the money supply to be subsequently affected, there must be a dependable monetary multiplier linking the change in bank reserves with a change in the money supply. Then, for a change in the money supply to have the desired impact on the price level, there must be a dependable demand for money, or a stable velocity of money. We have already noted the changes in the velocity of money, both over the long- and short-run.

Economists at the Morgan Guaranty Bank in New York City plotted changes in the monetary multipliers for both M1-B and M2 for the sixteen years from 1965 through 1980. The results are shown in Figure 22–5, where it can be seen that there is considerable volatility in such

**Figure 22–5   Changes in the Monetary Multipliers (compound annual rates)**

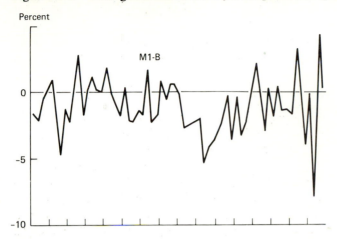

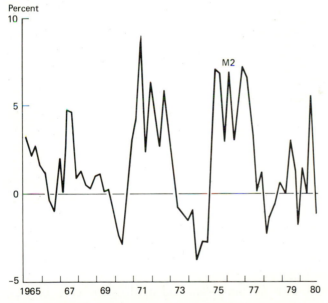

NOTE:   Multipliers are calculated as ratios of the respective monetary
aggregates to the adjusted monetary base (consisting of currency and adjusted total reserves) as published by the Federal
Reserve Bank of St. Louis. Plottings are quarterly.

SOURCE: The Morgan Guaranty Bank, *The Morgan Guaranty Survey*, Feb. 1981, p. 12.

monetary multipliers from quarter to quarter. Finally, it should be noted
that although most of the monetarist studies focus on long-run correla-

tions between money and other macro aggregates, monetary policy as presently constituted is targeted on a quarterly basis (and is sometimes changed even within the quarter). The Federal Open Market Committee thus operates in the very short run. Perhaps it is not surprising that the monetary authorities have not been willing to commit themselves to a single monetary theory and have often instead been quite eclectic in their theories and quite pragmatic in their policies. This approach of the Federal Reserve in turn has provoked considerable controversy.

## CONTROVERSY OVER APPROPRIATE PUBLIC POLICIES

As a result of the developments in monetary theory in recent years that have been discussed, there is now widespread agreement among economists that the supply of money is a very important variable in affecting both nominal and real aggregate demand. There are still some differences over the short-run and long-run impacts of changes in the stock of money, but most of the remaining differences of opinion among economists really center upon the appropriate set of public policies (i.e., monetary and fiscal policy) that should be utilized.

The monetarists believe that there should be a constant rate of growth in the nominal money supply and that the rate of growth in nominal money should correspond to the long-run increase in real output of the economy, so that monetary policy will not contribute to inflationary pressures. Both interest rates and the unemployment rate, though subject to short-run changes arising from significant changes in the rate of growth of the money supply, are really determined by real factors in their long-run equilibrium model. Because the economy tends toward equilibrium in the long run, any monetary policy deviating from a modest constant rate of growth in the nominal money supply will simply contribute to instability in the economy.

The neo-Keynesians by the 1980s had made significant concessions to the monetarist point of view. In many ways a synthesis of some of the positions of different monetary theorists had been achieved. But the neo-Keynesians were not willing to concede the full case of the monetarists and, in particular, they were not willing to accept the position of the monetarists on appropriate public policies. Franco Modigliani of MIT, a leading neo-Keynesian, put the position of this group very clearly in his presidential address to the American Economic Association in 1976.

The monetarists have made a valid and most valuable contribution in establishing that our economy is far less unstable than the early Keynesians pictured it and in rehabilitating the role of money as a determinant of aggregate demand. They are wrong, however, in going so far as asserting that the economy is sufficiently shockproof that stabilization policies are not needed.[16]

Modigliani does agree that stabilization policies can at times be destabilizing, but he also argues very forcefully that maintaining a constant rate of growth in the nominal money supply in and of itself will not guarantee stability of the economy if it is subjected to significant exogenous shocks. Modigliani points to two periods of about four years each in which the economy was quite unstable despite a relatively smooth growth in the nominal money supply. For nearly four years, beginning in the first quarter of 1971, the money supply grew relatively smoothly at about a 7 percent average rate, generally in a range from 6 to 8 percent. The deviation from the mean was only 0.75 percent. Nevertheless, this period was unstable with sharp fluctuations in output and in the rate of change in prices.

An earlier period of stable growth in the money supply was the four-and-a-half-year period from the beginning of 1953 to the middle of 1957. The average rate of growth in the money supply during this period was a low 2 percent with the average deviation from the mean again being only 0.7 percent. This period, too, had considerable instability in real output with a recession in 1953–1954, a sharp recovery in 1955, and another recession beginning in the second half of 1957 that lasted until the spring of 1958. This contraction of output and employment was the most serious in the period after World War II until the even sharper decline of 1973–1975.

Although Modigliani agrees that "fine tuning" the economy is neither possible nor desirable, he does believe, as do most neo-Keynesians, that there is still a very considerable role for both monetary and fiscal policy in minimizing instabilities originating in the real sector of the economy. The problem for both neo-Keynesians and monetarists is to avoid either monetary or fiscal policy that will in and of itself be a source of instability. Difficulties in forecasting the exact future course of the economy, along with substantial and variable leads and lags in such policy impacts on the private economy, make the development and implementation of such a menu of public policies difficult, though not impossible.

Arthur Burns, who was chairman of the Board of Governors of the

[16]Franco Modigliani, "The Monetarist Controversy, or Should We Forsake Stabilization Policies," *The American Economic Review*, **67**, No. 2:17 (March 1977).

Federal Reserve System from January 1970 to January 1978, agrees with Modigliani that discretionary public policy is necessary and desirable and disagrees with the fundamental propositions of the monetarists, even though Milton Friedman was a student of his at Columbia University. Burns has been a life-long student of the business cycle and he is quite critical of the monetarist belief that the American economy is fundamentally stable. "Monetarists recognize this. They believe that most economic disturbances tend to be self-correcting. . . . But neither historical evidence nor the thrust of explorations in business-cycle theory over a long century gives support to the notion that our economy is inherently stable."[17]

Burns is very positive when he comments on the use of discretionary economic policy, such as monetary policy. "Discretionary economic policy, while it has at times led to mistakes, has more often proved reasonably successful. . . . Flexible fiscal and monetary policies, therefore, are often needed to cope with undesirable economic development."[18]

Burns notes that in the short run the rate of change in the money supply is quite erratic and therefore not necessarily representative of the prevailing monetary policy. However, judging from Federal Reserve staff studies he argues: "The experience of the past two decades suggests that even an abnormally large or abnormally small rate of growth of the money stock over a period of up to 6 months or so has a negligible influence on the course of the economy—provided it is subsequently offset."[19] It is clear from the tenor of his comments that Burns is fairly optimistic about the use of monetary policy and fiscal policy.

# Questions for Discussion

1. Summarize the major tenets of the monetarists. How are these views similar to, or different from, those of traditional quantity theorists? Is money regarded as completely "neutral" in its impact on the real economy for monetarists?
2. Summarize the major theoretical policy views of the neo-Keynesians. How do these differ importantly from the views of the monetarists?
3. Discuss rules versus discretion in monetary policy. Why do the monetarists so strongly emphasize rules?
4. Discuss the channels of monetary policy as developed by the quantity theo-

---

[17]Arthur Burns, "Money Supply in the Conduct of Monetary Policy," *Federal Reserve Bulletin,* **59**:791–798 (Nov. 11, 1973).

[18]Ibid., pp. 792–793.

[19]Ibid., p. 795.

rists such as Marshall and Pigou and those emphasized by the neo-Keynesians.

5. How important are interest rate changes for neo-Keynesians? (Distinguish between changes in the level of interest rates and changes in the structure of interest rates.) Summarize the Wicksellian schema that placed great emphasis on the differences in market and natural rates of interest.

6. What importance would you attach to considering the various factors that determine the demand for money? How important are these factors for quantity theorists? In considering the demand for money, does it matter how one defines "money?"

7. Discuss the "income demand" for money and contrast it with the "wealth demand" for money. Which theoretical approach do you prefer? Why?

8. Discuss the demand for money as part of the theory of the demand for wealth. If wealth cannot be measured directly, which surrogate is commonly used? How are substitutes and complements for money incorporated into this theory?

9. Discuss the Keynesian demand for money. What are the important differences between the Keynesian transactions, or income, demand for money and the Keynesian speculative, or asset, demand for money? In each case, discuss the possibilities with respect to the interest elasticity of the demand for money. Graph the more important possibilities.

10. Discuss the alternatives available to individuals wishing to change their money balances (i.e., either increase or decrease these balances).

11. Briefly discuss the relevance of the velocity of money for the theory of the demand for money. How stable do you believe the velocity of money to be both in the long run and the short run? Why? What implications does your answer have for the demand for money?

12. Discuss "incomes, tastes, and expectations" insofar as they relate to the demand for money. In particular, discuss the question of whether money should be regarded as an "inferior" or "superior" good. What difference does this make in the demand for money as income changes? How may expectations, say, of future changes in the level of prices affect the demand for money?

13. Discuss the nature and costs of money substitutes and money complements. To what extent does the cost and availability of these related commodities to money affect the demand for money itself?

14. Discuss the theoretical and statistical problems involved in determining the cost of money. That is, which interest rate, or adjusted average interest rate, do you believe best measures the cost of money? Why?

15. Discuss the major proposals of monetarism with respect to monetary policy. What are some of the difficulties in implementing these proposals?

16. Summarize some of the major differences in the public policy approach of the neo-Keynesians and the monetarists. In what respect does Modigliani, a leading neo-Keynesian, make concessions to the monetarist position and in what respects does he continue to deviate from it? What are your own views? Defend your position.

17. Summarize the views of Arthur Burns on the use of discretionary monetary and fiscal policy. Why does he disagree with the monetarist position?

# Selected Bibliography for Further Reading

## Books

FRIEDMAN, MILTON, ed., *Studies in the Quantity Theory of Money* (Chicago: The University of Chicago Press, 1956).

KEYNES, JOHN MAYNARD, *The General Theory of Employment, Interest and Money* (London: Macmillan, 1936).

LAIDLER, DAVID E. W., *The Demand for Money: Theories and Evidence*, 2d ed. (Scranton, Pa.: International Textbook Co., 1977).

MAKINEN, GAIL E., *Money, The Price Level and Interest Rates: An Introduction to Monetary Theory* (Englewood Cliffs, N.J.: Prentice-Hall, 1977).

PATINKIN, DON, *Money, Interest, and Prices*, 2d ed. (New York: Harper & Row, 1965).

## Articles

ANDERSEN, LEONALL C., "The State of the Monetarist Debate," *Review*, Federal Reserve Bank of St. Louis, Vol. 55, No. 9, Sept. 1973, pp. 2–8.

BURNS, ARTHUR, "Money Supply in the Conduct of Monetary Policy," *Federal Reserve Bulletin*, Vol. 59, No. 11, Nov. 1973, pp. 791–798.

FEIGE, E. L., and D. K. PEARCE, "Casual, Causal Relationship Between Money and Income; Some Caveats for Time Series Analysis," *Review of Economics and Statistics*, Vol. LXI, No. 4, Nov. 1979, pp. 521–533.

FRIEDMAN, MILTON, "Quantity Theory of Money," *The International Encyclopedia of the Social Sciences*, Vol. 10 (New York: Free Press, 1968), pp. 432–446.

———, "The Role of Monetary Policy," *The American Economic Review*, Vol. LVIII, No. 1, March 1968, pp. 1–17.

JOHNSON, HARRY G., "The Keynesian Revolution and the Monetarist Counter-Revolution," *The American Economic Review*, Vol. No. 1, LXI, May 1971, pp. 1–14.

LAPORTE, ANNE MARIE, "Behavior of the Income Velocity of Money," *Economic Perspectives*, Federal Reserve Bank of Chicago, Sept.-Oct., 1977, pp. 1–9.

LEE, TONG HUN, "Alternative Interest Rates and the Demand for Money: The Empirical Evidence," *The American Economic Review*, Vol. 57, No. 5, Dec. 1967, pp. 1168–1181.

MODIGLIANI, FRANCO, "The Monetarist Controversy, or Should We Forsake Stabilization Policies," *The American Economic Review*, Vol. 67, No. 2, March 1977, pp. 1–19.

MORGAN GUARANTY TRUST COMPANY, "The Pitfalls of Mechanical Monetarism," *The Morgan Guaranty Survey*, Feb. 1981, pp. 8–13.

MULLINEAUX, DONALD J., "On Active and Passive Monetary Policies: What Have We Learned from the Rational Expectations Debate?" *Business Review*, Federal Reserve Bank of Philadelphia, Nov.–Dec. 1979, pp. 11–19.

PESTON, MAURICE, "The Integration of Monetary, Fiscal and Income Policy," *Lloyds Bank Review*, No. 141, July 1981, pp. 1–13.

SELDEN, RICHARD T., "Inflation: Are We Winning the Fight?" *The Morgan Guaranty Survey*, Morgan Guaranty Trust Company, Oct. 1977, pp. 7–13.

As the quantity of stock to be lent at interest increases, the interest, or the price which must be paid for the use of that stock, necessarily diminishes. . . .

THE WEALTH OF NATIONS

# 23
## CHAPTER

# Monetary Equilibrium: *IS-LM* Analysis

The condition for monetary equilibrium is that the demand for money is equal to the supply of money. The previous chapter discussed in some detail the various theoretical factors that influence the demand for money. The supply of money is assumed by some monetary theorists to be exogenously determined by the central bank. When the money market is in equilibrium, the demand for money and the supply of money are equal to each other and may be shown as an *LM schedule.* This *LM* schedule relates different rates of interest and different levels of national income where the demand and supply of money are in equilibrium.

If the real commodity markets are in equilibrium, the investment demand for internal and external funds and the internal and external supply of saving, both in real terms, must also be equal to each other. (Initially, the government and foreign sectors are ignored.) This equilibrium condition in the commodity markets may be summarized in an *IS schedule.* The *IS* schedule, like the *LM* schedule, relate different rates of interest and different levels of national income, though the necessary condition is that there is an investment-saving equilibrium relationship.

Both the *LM* schedule and the *IS* schedule, because they connect the same two variables, may be drawn on the same graph. In this way, the unique rate of interest and the unique level of national income that are consistent with equilibrium in *both* the money and commodity markets may be determined. If any of the underlying real or monetary factors determining these schedules change, a shift in either or both schedules will change the conditions of general equilibrium.

## NEUTRAL MONEY AND THE CONDITIONS FOR MONETARY EQUILIBRIUM

In the neoclassical economic theory tradition prior to 1936, money was largely neglected, so that money market equilibrium was given little attention by most theorists. The determination of value took place through demand and supply in real terms for various commodities and services, because money was neutral in its effect on the relative exchange value of goods and services. When money was introduced, it was only as a *numéraire*, or arbitrary measure of exchange value. All market transactors were assumed to act rationally in their own economic interest.

Because money was barren of any return, unlike capital or paper securities, no rational person should desire such a commodity, except for its use as an intermediary between the sale of a given commodity or service and the purchase of another commodity or service. Money was desired only for facilitating transactions. The value of money, as measured by an index of the price level of all real goods and services, would be determined by the aggregate demand for money for such transations purposes as compared with the total money stock. The stock of money was regarded as determined by the monetary authorities acting through the commercial banking system.

*The Rate of Interest*    In any event, the demand for and the supply of money did not determine the rate of interest, because the price of borrowed capital, like any price in the neoclassical system, was determined by the relevant demand and supply functions (i.e., the investment function and the saving function), both of which were related to the rate of interest. An increase in the rate of interest was thought to increase the amount of voluntary saving forthcoming and was also expected to depress the rate of investment. A decline in the interest rate, on the other hand, was expected to stimulate investment and to decrease the amount of saving generated. Obviously, only a given equilibrium rate of interest, where these two schedules intersect, would satisfy the requirements of both given functions.

*Money as a Veil*    Because money was regarded as a veil through which one should peer to discover real values as determined by the relative exchange ratios of goods and services, no rational person or institution would suffer a money illusion, or desire money for its own sake. (Persons were suffering a money illusion if their demand for goods and services changed when their nominal income and all prices changed at the same time in the same proportion.) With these assumptions, money was neutral with respect to real values in the economy. A change in the quantity of money could affect neither the real price of a commodity nor the amount of that commodity that could be produced.

**Flexible prices** (including wages) were expected to reflect any changes in consumer preferences or any changes in the techniques of production. Assuming rationality and such flexible prices, full employment of all resources was inevitable once long-run equilibrium of the system was attained. A change in the quantity of money could only affect the value of money itself (i.e., the price level of real goods and services).

## The Keynesian View of Money

When Keynes undertook his revolution of economic theory in 1936, some changes in the role of money ensued. For one thing, Keynes argued that in the real world, many prices, particularly wages, tend to be relatively sticky and often operate on a **ratchet effect**—they are easier to push up than they are to push down. Furthermore, Keynes believed that in a world of great uncertainty, and given very low rates of interest (high bond prices), many individuals and institutions would prefer to hold almost unlimited quantities of money rather than risk a future loss of capital value. If interest rates rose in the future, bond prices would decline, and holders of bonds would suffer a capital loss.

Money was assigned by Keynes a much more significant role than his neoclassical predecessors had been willing to give to it. Keynes believed that the modern economy was a monetary economy in which changes in the quantity of money could affect not only its own value but even the amount of real goods and services produced, as well as the employment of available labor power. Money therefore was no longer viewed as neutral. The demand for and supply of money for Keynes determined the equilibrium rate of interest.

## THE KEYNESIAN MODEL OF THE MONEY MARKET

The Keynesian model of the money market focuses on the asset demand for money (the liquidity preference function) as it intersects the supply of money function (minus the stock of money absorbed in transactions balances), and thereby determines a monetary rate of interest. This rate of interest is held to be a long-term rate of interest; hence it can be properly related to the investment function, as it subsequently is. This liquidity preference model of the money market, first presented by Keynes in 1936, focuses on the excess demand for or excess supply of money.

*The Loanable Funds Doctrine*    A more recent monetary theory, which has been labeled the **"loanable funds doctrine,"** analyzes instead the differences in the supply of and demand for bonds. Although this is apparently somewhat different from the liquidity preference approach, it can be demonstrated that the two approaches are essentially different ways of saying the same thing.[1] Both of these approaches, however, can be contrasted with the more traditional monetary theory, which emphasized the excess demand and supply of goods as determining the real rate of interest, which in turn determines the rate of investment, saving, and consumption. Here, however, the purely monetary rate of interest approach of the Keynesian model is followed by utilizing the equilibrium demand-supply of money (*LM*) schedule. This model was developed originally by John R. Hicks.[2]

## *A Graphic Analysis Using the* LM *Schedule*

Figure 23–1 shows the derivation of the equilibrium *LM* schedule from the asset and transactions demand for money. (All variables are in real terms.) The asset demand for money $L_2$ is shown in graph A, where the interest rate (for Keynes this was the yield on government bonds in perpetuity, or consols) is plotted on the horizontal axis. In graph B the equilibrium condition specified is that the total demand for money (both the asset and transactions demand) must be equal to the total money supply. In graph C the transactions demand for money, shown as the dependent variable, is a function of the independent variable, national income. Finally, graph D illustrates the final equilibrium of the money market, where the *LM* function is graphed.

   If we assume an initial interest rate of 4 percent, which is *OR* on the vertical scale on graph A, there would be *OM* amount of money demanded for asset purposes. This can be read off graph A by drawing a horizontal line from *OR* to point *a* on the $L_2L_2$ line and then dropping a perpendicular line to the horizontal axis.

[1]On this point see the excellent article by Don Patinkin, "Liquidity Preference and Loanable Funds: Stock and Flow Analysis," *Economica*, **25**, No. 100:300–318 (Nov. 1958).
   [2]See John R. Hicks, "Mr. Keynes and the Classics," *Econometrica*, **5**, No. 2:147–159 (April 1937).

**Figure 23–1    Equilibrium of the Money Market: The *LM* Schedule**

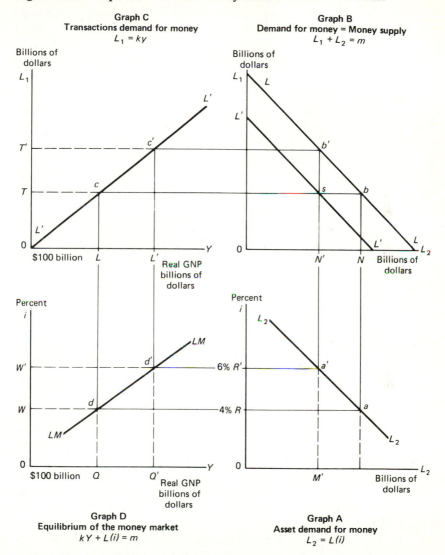

Graph C
Transactions demand for money
$L_1 = ky$

Graph B
Demand for money = Money supply
$L_1 + L_2 = m$

Graph D
Equilibrium of the money market
$kY + L(i) = m$

Graph A
Asset demand for money
$L_2 = L(i)$

***The Demand for Money***    Subsequently, one can extend another line vertically upward from *a* to *b* on the *LL* schedule, which represents the total demand for money equal to the total supply of money. Where the line *ab* intersects the horizontal axis on graph B at *ON* is the amount of money demanded for asset purposes. (*ON* on graph B = *OM* on graph A.) Dropping a perpendicular line from *b* on *LL* to the vertical axis gives an intercept of *OS*, which is the amount of money demanded for transactions purposes. $ON + OS$ must equal the total stock of money at any one time (i.e., the total amount of money available is held either for asset or transactions purposes).

Following the horizontal line $Sb$ to graph C, the point on the $L_1L_1$ schedule intersected is $c$. Continue the horizontal line to the $Y$ axis of graph C to the intercept $OT$. This is the amount of money $L_1$ demanded for transactions purposes ($OT = OS$). Dropping a perpendicular line to the real GNP horizontal axis of graph C yields an intercept of $OL$, the level of real GNP associated with a transactions demand for money of $OT$.

Continuing the perpendicular line of $cL$ down to the $LM$ schedule in graph D, we arrive at $d$ on that schedule. Dropping the perpendicular line still further to the horizontal axis of graph D, we have $OQ$ level of national income ($OQ = OL$). This is the equilibrium level of real GNP, which is associated with $OW$ equilibrium rate of interest ($OW = OR = 4$ percent). The initial rate of interest, given the demand for and the supply of money, thus indicates what level of equilibrium real GNP will be possible.

## Different Interest Rates Associated with Different National Income Levels

If the initial rate of interest is assumed to be 6 percent ($OR$ on graph A), the chain of effects—traced through graphs B and C to graph D—will lead to a different, higher level of real income. That is, to have the higher rate of interest as an equilibrium rate of interest, the level of real income must be higher. If the demand for money schedules remains unchanged, a higher interest rate would thus result only if real factors pushed the level of real income higher. This would mean that the amount of money held in idle asset balances would decline from $OM$ to $OM'$ in graph A and from $ON$ to $ON'$ in graph B, whereas active transactions balances needed at the higher level of income would rise from $OS$ to $OS'$ in graph B, or from $OT$ to $OT'$ in graph C.

On the other hand, if the supply of money is reduced from $LL$ to $L'L'$ in graph B, the rate of interest would also rise from 4 to 6 percent in graph A, assuming that income is unchanged. With the higher interest rates increasing the opportunity cost for holding idle asset money balances, such balances, as shown in graphs A and B, would fall. Likewise, the transactions balances of money would decline. Since the $OQ$ equilibrium level of income in graph D remains unchanged, the income velocity of money has necessarily increased.

With the use of these graphs we can thus trace out the interrelationships between the rate of interest and the level of real income-output. When real national income rises because of a shift to the right of the *IS* schedule, more money is needed for transactions purposes, as shown in graph C, and the interest rate therefore increases. The movement of part of the fixed supply of money into active transactions balances leaves less money balances available to satisfy the asset demand for money. A reduction in the amount of cash for such asset money purposes implies a higher rate of interest and a movement upward along the liquidity preference schedule.

## Interest Rates and the LM *Curve*

Graph D of Figure 23–1 shows that the equilibrium rate of interest in the money market is low when real national income is low but rises when real national income rises. How sensitive the rate of interest is to such changes in the level of national income is shown graphically by the *LM* curve. The steeper this curve, the faster will interest rates increase when *Y* rises, whereas the more horizontal the *LM* curve, the less will interest rates respond to such changes in national income. The upward slope of the *LM* curve as shown in Figure 23–1 thus implies some elasticity between rising real national income and rising interest rates.

Graph A of Figure 23–1 shows some interest elasticity of the asset demand for money. This means that at higher interest rates asset holders of money are willing to release some of their cash balances for transactions purposes. This permits real national income to rise, even though the money stock may be constant. An increase in the stock of money by the monetary authorities implies a shift of the *LM* schedule to the right. This would make possible a given increase in real national income without any corresponding rise in interest rates.

## Shifts in the LM *Schedule*

The *LM* schedule could also shift to the right because of a decline in the demand for money, either for asset or transactions purposes. Regardless of the factors leading to such a shift in the *LM* schedule, subsequent increases in national income caused by a downward shift along the *IS* schedule (assuming a negative slope for the *IS* function) would result both in a higher level of real national income (as a result of larger investment expenditures) and lower interest rates. If this higher level of real national income is still insufficient for policy purposes, say, to achieve full employment, the monetary authorities will be called upon to lower interest rates still further to stimulate still higher levels of real investment and economic activity.

## THE MODEL FOR THE COMMODITY MARKETS

The equilibrium investment-saving *IS* schedule is derived from a simple Keynesian model of the commodity markets. (All variables are in real terms.) In this model, which was discussed in Chapter 21, the government and foreign sectors are ignored initially. There are, then, four basic variables of (1) investment expenditures *I*, (2) saving out of income *S*, (3) the interest rate *i*, and (4) the level of national income *Y*. Two of the four basic equations are $I = I(i)$ and $S = Y - C(Y)$.

$C(Y)$ is the familiar consumption function. In the saving equation, saving is equal to national income minus consumption expenditures. It is also necessary for *I* to equal *S* at equilibrium, or for intended investment to be equal to intended saving, in order for an equilibrium level of national income to be attained.

The final equation showing the equilibrium of the product market is $I(i) = Y - C(Y)$. When this equation is graphed, the *IS* curve demonstrates how equilibrium interest rates and equilibrium real national income levels are interrelated in the commodity markets. These four equations are shown graphically in Figure 23–2, where the derivation of the *IS* curve can be traced out.

### *Graphing the* IS *Schedule*

In graph A of Figure 23–2 investment expenditures are shown as a function of the rate of interest. Because this *II* schedule is drawn like any ordinary demand curve, sloping downward from left to right, at lower interest rates a greater amount of investment expenditures will be undertaken by business firms. Similarly, at higher interest rates a decline in such borrowing and such investment expenditures can be expected.

In graph B, saving *S* is plotted on the vertical axis and investment *I* is plotted on the horizontal axis—both in billions of dollars. A 45-degree line is drawn from the origin. Any such 45-degree line has a slope of 1 and will give the same reading for both variables at any and all points on the line (i.e., a perpendicular dropped from a point on this line will yield the same value on the horizontal axis as will a perpendicular dropped from the same point to the vertical axis). This 45-degree line shows planned investment as equal to planned saving at all values, which is a necessary condition for income *Y* to be in equilibrium.

*Saving as a Function of National Income*    In graph C, saving *S* is shown as a function of real national income *Y*. This saving function is the mirror image of the consumption function discussed earlier in Chapter 21. If the

**Figure 23–2    The *IS* Schedule**

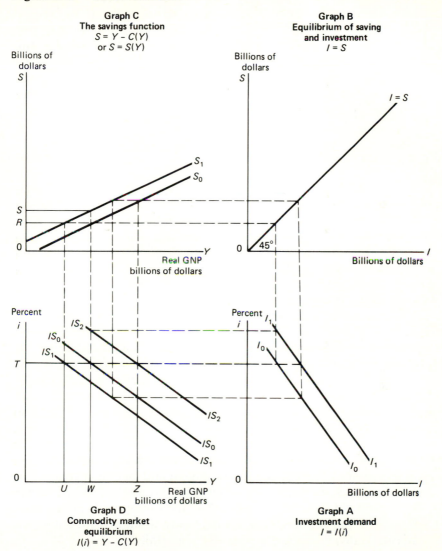

consumption function is linear, so too will be the saving function; if the consumption function is concave from above, the saving function will be convex from below.

*Product Market Equilibrium*    In graph D the final condition of product market equilibrium is shown in the *IS* schedule. This shows us, given the assumptions discussed, all the combinations of interest rates and levels of real national income that are consistent with equilibrium in the commodity markets. As might be expected, graph D suggests that a lower rate of interest will result in a higher level of real national income. This result follows because, as graph A indicates, a lower rate of interest will result in higher investment expenditures. When investment expenditures rise, so too does national income through the multiplier relationship previously discussed.

## Saving and the Rate of Interest

Graph C also indicates that when real national income rises so does national saving. In part, this conclusion differs from one of the conclusions of neoclassical economics, which argued that a lower rate of interest would result in a smaller amount of savings, whereas higher savings could be obtained only by raising the rate of interest. However, in that type of analysis the level of income was taken as given, so that a redistribution of income occurred between consumption and saving as the price of saving (the interest rate) changed.

In the Keynesian analysis, however, the level of income is to be determined rather than simply assumed to be at a full employment equilibrium level. Furthermore, what the level of income will be is determined by the relationship between the investment and saving schedules, with the dominant active factor usually expected to be investment. Saving is regarded as usually more passive because it is expected to change only when the level of income changes, rather than varying directly with the interest rate.

The fact that the *IS* schedule slopes downward from left to right indicates that the marginal efficiency of capital, which is determined by the expected rate of profit, falls as investment and income increase. This should be expected because the original investment (*II*) schedule also slopes downward from left to right. Only the multiplier is in operation here, because the accelerator is in effect only when investment expenditure rises (falls) when national income rises (falls).

## Shifts in the Schedules Change Equilibrium National Income

The *IS* schedule not only gives the value of real national income *Y* as the rate of interest *i* varies, the forms of the saving and investment functions being specified, but it also shows how *Y* varies with a given interest rate if either the saving or the investment schedules shift. In graph C, with national income held constant at $QW$, let the saving schedule shift to the left from $S_0$ to $S_1$. In this case, the amount of desired national saving increases from $OR$ to $OS$. Such an upward shift of the saving function leads to a decline in the equilibrium $IS$ schedule in graph D. The original $IS$ schedule of $IS_0$ thus shifts to the left to $IS_1$. With a given interest rate of $OT$, national income then falls from $OW$ to $OU$.

On the other hand, if the investment schedule of graph A shifts to the right from $I_0I_0$ to $I_1I_1$ because of an increase in profit expectations that may result from, say, an innovation, then the original $IS$ schedule $IS_0$ could shift to the right to $IS_2$. The amount of this shift would be determined by the autonomous change in investment times the multiplier. With such a rightward shift of the $IS$ schedule, the equilibrium level of income increases from $OW$ to $OZ$, assuming that interest rates remain constant.

## The Shape of the IS Schedule

The $IS$ schedule may have any given shape (i.e., it is not necessary that this schedule be drawn as a straight line, as has been done in Figure 23–2). The precise shape of this equilibrium schedule depends on the shapes of the underlying investment and saving functions. The shapes of these functions depend upon such empirical matters as the degree of responsiveness (the elasticity) of these functions with respect to changes in the rate of interest or changes in the level of income.

If the investment schedule is elastic with respect to the rate of interest, the schedule will tend to be more horizontal than the one drawn here. If this schedule is interest inelastic, the schedule will be more vertical than it is depicted here. The $IS$ schedule thus could be either more horizontal or more vertical than shown here. Similarly, the savings schedule need not be linear in the manner shown, or it may be linear in a different way (e.g., it may originate at the origin rather than cutting the horizontal axis to the right of the origin). If the savings schedule intersects at the origin, however, there would be no possibility of dissaving. Any change in the saving schedule from that depicted would likewise affect the final shape of the equilibrium $IS$ schedule.

## Simultaneous Equilibrium in Both the Commodity and Money Markets

The derivation and meaning of both the $IS$ schedule, which summarizes equilibrium in the commodity markets, and the $LM$ schedule, which summarizes equilibrium in the money markets, have been examined.

These two schedules can now be combined to illustrate the conditions for simultaneous equilibrium in both these markets. Because a **two-sector model** is specified for the entire economy, equilibrium for the entire economy will then be determined. What makes possible the integration of the models of these two markets into one model is that ultimately both the *IS* schedule and the *LM* schedule are functions connecting the same two variables of the interest rate *i* and the level of real national income *Y*.

The *IS* schedule alone shows that there are a number of interest rates and different levels of real national income consistent with equilibrium in the commodity markets. Likewise, the *LM* curve shows that a number of interest rates and levels of real national income are consistent with equilibrium in the money markets. However, when the two schedules are combined, there is but one intersection point, so there is only one equilibrium rate of interest and only one equilibrium level of real national income consistent with simultaneous equilibrum in both these markets.

In Figure 23–3, the *IS* curve and the *LM* curve intersect each other in a familiar demand-supply cross. In this diagram, only a 3 percent rate of interest and only a $450 billion level of national income are consistent with equilibrium in both markets. This rate of interest and this level of national income are stable values for these two particular *IS* and *LM*

**Figure 23–3    Simultaneous Equilibrium in the Commodity and Money Markets: The *IS-LM* Schedules**

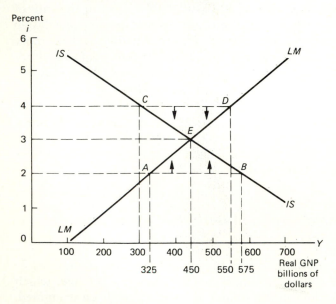

functions. This can be demonstrated by arbitrarily assuming other rates of interest either lower or higher than the equilibrium rate of 3 percent, or other levels of national income.

## STABLE EQUILIBRIUM AT INTERSECTION OF *IS* AND *LM* SCHEDULES

Let us assume that a market rate of interest of 2 percent is now arbitrarily given. In this instance, more real investment and real saving would tend to be generated, because business firms would prefer to borrow more and spend more on investment by acquiring additional capital goods such as machine tools than they did at the higher rate of interest. A higher expected level of investment expenditures would also lead to a higher expected level of national income (real GNP). As can be seen in Figure 23–3, a rate of interest of 2 percent would intersect the *IS* curve at *B*. A perpendicular dotted line from *B* to the horizontal axis gives an expected national income of $575 billion, as compared with the lower level of national income of $450 billion at the higher interest rate of 3 percent.

*Lower Interest Rate Results in Higher National Income*    However, the new rate of interest of 2 percent intersects the *LM* schedule at *A*. A perpendicular line from *A* to the horizontal axis gives an expected national income of only $325 billion, which is lower than the equilibrium national income of $450 billion, and $250 billion lower than the level of national income predicted by the *IS* schedule. Hence, it should be obvious that any higher level of national income temporarily achieved in this instance by lowered interest rates would be unstable. Although business firms are desirous of acquiring additional funds to finance the increased flow of new investment desired, the monetary authorities, the commercial banking system, and private holders of money balances are all unwilling to provide the additional funds desired at this lower rate of interest.

*Higher Demand for Funds Pushes Up Interest Rate*    The monetary authorities may be unwilling to increase the money supply, which would shift the *LM* schedule to the right, because of their belief that such a sharp increase in investment expenditures and such a sharp rise in national income would be too inflationary. Financial institutions and private individuals might be unwilling to provide the additional funds desired, because the lower rate of interest appears too low to compensate them for the sacrifice of liquidity involved. Under these conditions of conflicting desires and behavior, the market system will force the rate of interest back to the equilibrium level of 3 percent, which then reduces the amount of desired investment, on the one hand, but increases the flow of funds to the financial markets on the other hand.

## Increasing the Rate of Interest

If another arbitrary rate of interest, say, 4 percent, is assumed, which is higher than the equilibrium rate of interest, forces contrary to those previously described come into play. The 4 percent rate of interest intersects the *IS* schedule at *C*. A perpendicular line from this point to the horizontal axis gives an expected level of national income of only $300 billion, as compared with the equilibrium level of $450 billion. This lower level of national income would result from the discouragement of borrowing for the purposes of making investment expenditures. The decline in investment expenditures through the multiplier coefficient would then have a multiple decreasing effect on national income.

On the other hand, the higher interest rate of 4 percent intersects the *LM* curve at *D*. Dropping a perpendicular from this point to the horizontal axis gives us a predicted value of national income of $550 billion. This does not mean that a national income of $550 billion would be reached, but it does mean that an increased flow of financial funds, equivalent to that which would be generated at a national income level of $550 billion, would tend to be forthcoming.

Many lending institutions would be willing to loan larger amounts at the higher interest rate than they were at the lower, and many institutions and individuals would be willing to reduce some of their asset money balances because of the higher opportunity cost of holding idle funds. This greater flood of loanable funds, as the downward arrows from the dotted line *CD* indicate, would push down the interest rate to *E*, where the equilibrium rate of interest prevails. Hence only at *E* in Figure 23–3, where the rate of interest is 3 percent and the level of national income is $450 billion, does a stable equilibrium prevail.

## STOCKS AND FLOWS OF MONEY

At *E* there is a **unique equilibrium set** of output of goods and services and an equilibrium rate of interest, so that both the commodity markets and the money markets are in simultaneous equilibrium. The amount of money stock demanded in a given time period through the sale of products and services and borrowing will thus be equal to the aggregate stock of money supplied from the purchase of goods and services or money loaned. Hence, the demand and supply of money stocks must be in equilibrium.

Because the excess demand for money as a stock is identical with the excess demand for money as a flow,[3] both the demand and supply of money flows, as well as the demand and supply of stocks, will be in equilibrium. For the determination of the rate of interest, only the system of excess demand equations is relevant because of the accounting identity that the stock at the end of a period must equal the stock at the beginning plus the net inflow during the period. The reason for analyzing changes in money flows ultimately, rather than simply changes in the stock of money, is that national income itself is a flow concept because it refers to the net production of goods and services within a given time period.

## Real and Monetary Factors Affecting Equilibrium

One great value of using a model with *IS* and *LM* curves is that one can sort out analytically different factors having an impact on equilibrium values in the commodity and money markets. In particular, this theoretical approach may help distinguish between changes in monetary and real factors insofar as they affect conditions of equilibrium. As indicated earlier, rightward shifts in the *IS* schedule, assuming a constant *LM* schedule, result not only in higher levels of national income but higher levels of interest rates as well.

Hence when both interest rates and national income are rising, it is quite likely that the common cause of both is a rightward shift in the *IS* schedule caused by real factors. Although a rise in interest rates can be caused by a leftward shift in the *LM* schedule, in this case national income will fall rather than rise. Similarly, the particular behavior of interest rates and national income may imply not only shifts in the schedules but even a particular shape in these schedules.

## Elasticity of the **LM** Schedule

This latter point is illustrated in Figure 23–4, where the *LM* schedule is drawn as highly interest elastic at low levels of income and quite interest inelastic at higher levels of income. This kind of **curvilinear** *LM* schedule is what would be expected if the asset demand for money had

---

[3]Patinkin, op. cit.

**Figure 23–4    Shifting the _IS_ Schedule with a Constant Curvilinear _LM_ Schedule**

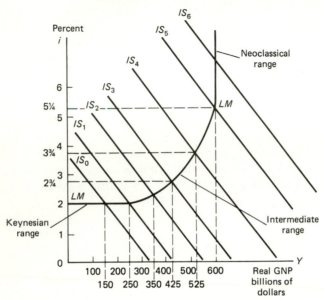

the shape postulated for it by the Keynesian liquidity preference schedule. Therefore at low levels of income a rightward shift in the _IS_ schedule, either as a result of a shift in the investment demand function or of rising government expenditures financed by a budget deficit, will raise national income, though interest rates remain unaffected. Once a certain level of real GNP is reached, which is assumed to be about $300 billion in Figure 23–4, further upward shifts in the _IS_ schedule have the normal effect of raising both national income and interest rates.

## Fiscal Policy and Shape of **LM** Schedule

As already noted, fiscal policy either in the form of tax cuts or rising government expenditures can increase the _IS_ curve. The effect on real output and employment and on interest rates of any given fiscal policy depends importantly on the characteristics of the demand for money as reflected in the _LM_ curve. If the asset demand for money is perfectly elastic, as Keynes believed, then the resulting _LM_ curve will also be flat. This horizontal part of the _LM_ curve in Figure 23–4 is thus labeled the Keynesian range.

When interest rates are very low, say, 2 percent in a depression, then the liquidity trap exists, because holders of money are willing to forgo the 2 percent interest return. In such a period they are certain that bond prices will fall (interest rates will rise) in the future. Hence fiscal policy resulting in a higher *IS* curve is effective. An increase from $IS_0$ to $IS_1$ in Figure 23–4 increases real income by the amount of the added government spending times the multiplier. If the *IS* schedule increases as a result of a cut in taxes, the *IS* schedule moves up a somewhat smaller amount because part of the increase in disposable income will be saved.

In the neoclassical part of the *LM* curve, the curve is completely vertical. Then, we can see graphically in Figure 23–4 that fiscal policy can still increase the *IS* schedule (from $IS_5$ to $IS_6$) without an increase in real output and employment, because we are already at full employment. Instead, the rate of interest increases and the price level also increases (not shown in Figure 23–4). Thus under these conditions fiscal policy becomes ineffective in achieving the desired result of increasing output and employment.

On the other hand, in the more typical intermediate range an increase in the *IS* schedule caused by a stimulative fiscal policy, which shifts the *IS* schedule from $IS_3$ to $IS_4$, will increase both real income and the rate of interest. (Some increase in the price level is also to be expected.)

## Monetary Policy and the IS-LM Schedules

In Figure 23–5, the **effectiveness of monetary policy** is seen to depend on the shape of the *LM* schedule and possible shifts in the *IS* schedule. This *LM* schedule has an infinite elasticity at a low rate of interest because of the liquidity trap in the asset demand for money schedule. If the *IS* schedule is at the low level of $IS_0$, no matter what the monetary authorities may try to do to increase the money supply in order to lower the rate of interest and thus to stimulate investment expenditures and raise the level of national income, their efforts are doomed to failure. **Real GNP** will stagnate at the $300 billion level, which may be so low that substantial amounts of unemployment are involved.

*Shift in the* IS *Schedule*     Such unemployment can be reduced only if the $IS_0$ schedule can somehow be shifted rightward to the substantially higher level of $IS_1$, either through programs designed to stimulate private investment or through a rise in government expenditures. In this event, an increase in the *LM* schedule in Figure 23–5, say, from $LM_0$ to $LM_1$, could increase real GNP still further from the $450 billion level to a higher level of $525 billion.

*Increase in the* LM *Schedule*    The increase in the *LM* schedule would thus have a favorable decreasing effect on interest rates, because the effective part of the *LM* schedule at this higher level of national income is not plagued with the high elasticity (liquidity trap) of the lower levels of national income. When the *IS* schedule is shifted from $IS_0$ to $IS_1$ in Figure 23–5, national income increases from $300 billion to $450 billion, but the equilibrium rate of interest also increases from 2 to 3 percent. If the monetary authorities were to increase the money supply schedule so as to shift the *LM* schedule to the right, they could push interest rates back down to 2½ percent. This would stimulate a further rise in real GNP from $450 billion to a higher level of $525 billion.

Monetary policy, which is denied effectiveness at lower levels of income because of the high elasticity of the *LM* schedule, once more has a significant role to play when a higher *IS* schedule raises real national income. At these higher levels of national income, any given *LM* schedule has an area of lower interest elasticity. Hence there are greater effects in reducing interest rates and in increasing real national income when the *LM* schedule is increased.

## NEOCLASSICAL ECONOMICS AND THE REAL BALANCE EFFECT

Neoclassical economists have not usually been able to accept the Keynesian version of the *IS-LM* framework. In the first place, they usually believe that there can be a lasting unemployment equilibrium only under the most special circumstances. Prices would have to be downwardly rigid and the quantity of money fixed at an amount inadequate to provide for a full employment level of aggregate demand. Because they believe in a stable velocity of money, such economists hold that it is sufficient to reach a full employment output either by a great enough increase in the supply of money or an adequate decline in prices, which are generally held to be flexible.

The most trenchant criticism from such neoclassical economists comes, however, from their emphasis on the real balance effect in connection with the demand for real money balances. This tradition, which follows from Alfred Marshall ($M = kY$) and one of his students, A. C. Pigou, argues that the presumed **dichotomy** of the financial and product markets must be rejected.

Hence an increase in the real quantity of money will also cause consumption to shift upward as a function of income (i.e., an increase in the *LM* schedule also causes an increase in the *IS* schedule). Once the *IS*

**Figure 23–5    Shifting the *IS* and *LM* Schedules**

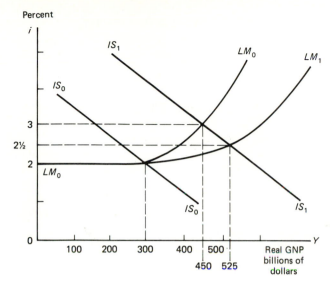

schedule is permitted to shift in response to changes in the money supply, the Keynesian flat range of the *LM* function ceases to operate as a liquidity trap preventing any increase in the stock of money from increasing aggregate demand. In the neoclassical system, consumer wants are regarded as unlimited. **Involuntary unemployment** therefore cannot exist in equilibrium if the money supply is increased enough. This, then, is the real balance criticism of the *IS-LM* paradigm.

*Neoclassical Analysis and Full Employment*    When unemployed resources are eliminated by the device of reaching "full employment," the **neoclassical analysis** clearly comes back into its own. Under these conditions, an increase in the quantity of money will simply decrease its exchange value (i.e., raise the price level of goods and services), and will not affect the real output of goods and services. The monetary authorities earlier may have been most concerned about facilitating real economic growth by a judicious expansion of the money supply through shifts in the *LM* schedule, so as to increase aggregate demand for, and aggregate output of, goods and services. The authorities will now have to be concerned that the supply of money (and the *LM* schedule) not rise in a disequilibrating fashion. Further increases in the *IS* schedule may necessitate the monetary authorities holding the *LM* schedule constant, even though some increases in interest rates occur, and even though some slowdown in the rate of expansion of national income may take place.

# Questions for Discussion

1. Why was money assumed to be neutral in its effect on real prices by the neoclassical economists? If money is neutral and the stock of money is changed, what effect will this have on any economic variables?
2. Discuss the role assigned to money by Keynes as differentiated from that in neoclassical economic theory. Briefly compare the interest rate theories of Keynes and neoclassical economics.
3. Discuss and graphically demonstrate the derivation of the equilibrium *LM* schedule. Indicate the major variables in real terms considered in this model of the money market.
4. Discuss the factors affecting the shape and elasticity of the liquidity preference function. What different behavioral assumptions about individuals and institutions participating in the money market are involved in different elasticities of the liquidity preference function at different rates of interest? What do you think is the elasticity of the relevant portion of the liquidity preference function today?
5. Discuss and graphically demonstrate the derivation of the equilibrium *IS* schedule. Indicate the major variables in real terms considered in this model of the commodity markets.
6. Graph the intersection of the *LM* and *IS* schedules. Discuss the significance of the equilibrium rate of interest and the equilibrium level of real national income that result from the intersection of these two schedules. Graphically demonstrate that this is a stable equilibrium condition.
7. Graph and discuss shifts in the *IS* and *LM* schedules. Shift only one schedule while holding the other constant, and show the effect on the equilibrium values. Then shift the two schedules simultaneously in such a manner as to offset the effect on one variable, say, the equilibrium interest rate, of the shift of the first schedule. Is it possible to shift the second schedule in such a manner as to offset effects on *both* equilibrium values of a shift in the first schedule?
8. Discuss some of the major underlying monetary and real factors that may change in a manner calculated to shift either the *IS* schedule or the *LM* schedule, or both. To what extent may changes in such underlying variables be the result of private market forces or governmental public policies? Discuss the effects of each kind of change.
9. Discuss the implications for both fiscal and monetary policies of the shape and level of the *IS* schedule and the *LM* schedule, assuming a governmental commitment to stable economic growth. How can public policies affect the shape and level of these equilibrium schedules?
10. Discuss the real balance effect emphasized by neoclassical economists in their criticism of the *IS-LM* model.

# Selected Bibliography for Further Reading

## Books and Monographs

AMERICAN ECONOMIC ASSOCIATION, *Readings in Monetary Theory* (New York: Blakiston, 1951).

HAHN, F. H., and F. P. R. BRECHLING, eds., *The Theory of Interest Rates* (London: Macmillan, 1965).

HANSEN, ALVIN, *Monetary Theory and Fiscal Policy* (New York: McGraw-Hill, 1949).

HICKS, SIR JOHN, *Critical Essays in Monetary Theory* (Oxford: Clarendon Press, 1967).

JOHNSON, HARRY G., *Essays in Monetary Economics* (Cambridge, Mass.: Harvard University Press, 1967).

PATINKIN, DON, *Money, Interest, and Prices*, 2d ed. (New York: Harper & Row, 1965).

WICKSELL, KNUT, *Interest and Prices* (New York: Augustus M. Kelley, Reprints of Economic Classics, 1962).

WONNACOTT, PAUL, *Macroeconomics* (Homewood, Ill.: Richard D. Irwin, 1978).

## Articles

HICKS, JOHN, R., "Mr. Keynes and the Classics," *Econometrica*, **5**, No. 2 (April 1937), pp. 147–159.

PATINKIN, DON, "Liquidity Preference and Loanable Funds: Stock and Flow Analysis," *Economica*, **25**, No. 100 (Nov. 1958), pp. 300–318.

> During the reign of Queen Anne, the market rate of interest had fallen from six to five per cent, and in the twelfth year of her reign five per cent was declared to be the highest rate which could lawfully be taken for money borrowed upon private security.

THE WEALTH OF NATIONS

# 24
## CHAPTER

# The Theory of Interest: Level and Structure of Interest Rates

Monetary theory has not only emphasized the effects on the price level, and on economic activity generally, of changes in the stock of money, but has also stressed the important role of the interest rate in affecting decisions to invest and save. It is not always clear, however, which interest rate is being referred to, because in the real marketplace there are many interest rates. Sometimes this difficulty is avoided by referring to a pure interest or a normal interest rate. But monetary theorists have not always been perfectly clear on this matter. The difficulties are further confounded for serious students when they discover that some monetary theorists are mainly concerned with the short-term interest rate, whereas others tend to concentrate on the long-term interest rate. In either case, the writer may discuss factors determining "the" interest rate.

      This chapter discusses the theories of interest rate determination that relate to the level of interest rates, whether the focus be on a short-term or long-term rate, as well as the term structure of interest rates. What is a normal pattern of interest rates on debt obligations as we move from very short maturities to those of the intermediate-term and then long-term bonds? Does this pattern change over time (e.g., over the business cycle), and if so, in what way? What effect does a change in the level of interest rates, on the one hand, or a change in the **structure of interest rates,** on the other hand, have on economic activity? Is it possible to change the level of interest rates without affecting the structure of interest rates? In each case, what are the implications for public policies, such as monetary policy or the debt management policies of the Treasury?

In this discussion, various important alternative theoretical positions are presented as impartially as possible. There are differences of opinion and much unfinished business in this area of monetary theory. Nevertheless, what people think about public policies depends importantly on the kind of theoretical views they hold. For this reason students must understand the important theories of interest, whether they relate to the level or the structure of interest rates, so that they can better evaluate different public policy proposals concerning monetary and fiscal matters.

## THE PURE THEORY OF INTEREST

The neoclassical monetary theorists in the late nineteenth and early twentieth centuries were concerned with the development of a **pure theory of interest** that would explain certain questions about the rate of interest. The three major questions with which they were concerned were (1) why can interest be paid? (2) why must interest be paid? and (3) how much interest will be paid? In general their answers were that (1) interest can be paid because capital is productive; (2) it must be paid because most people suffer a disutility in saving (i.e., they have positive time preference), so that they prefer present to future goods; and (3) the demand and supply of saving will determine the price (interest rate) of borrowed funds. In making their contributions to interest rate theory, these traditional monetary theorists wished to develop a pure theory of interest that would be abstracted from the imperfections of the marketplace. Their desire was to have a real theory of interest uncomplicated by states of expectations, the illusion of the money veil, and the like.

### *The Price of Borrowing Money*

The architects of this neoclassical theory of interest were economists such as Eugen Boehm-Bawerk of Austria and Irving Fisher of the United

States. For them the interest rate was simply a price determined like any other price. Instead of a commodity being bought and sold, however, the price was for the service of using someone else's money for a certain period of time. Nevertheless, demand and supply determined this price, as they did other prices. Fisher took particular note of the necessity of the lender to include an **"inflation premium"** to take account of future expected inflation in determining the long-term rate of interest required by the lender. Money lent could have been used by lenders for their own consumption instead of being used to increase the supply of savings. On the side of lenders, therefore, the rate of interest was the price they received for saving rather than consuming. In this manner abstinence was rewarded.

*Positive Time Preference for Income*    This abstinence from present consumption was held to depend importantly on the time preference pattern relating to income. At a zero interest rate, the person who prefers more present than future income is said to have **positive time preference,** whereas one who prefers more future income is said to have negative time preference. People who prefer neither present nor future income are said to have zero time preference. In this latter case, the people are indifferent to the shape of their income over time.

In neoclassical economics, it was generally assumed that most persons would have positive time preference (i.e., that most persons would prefer to consume real goods and services in the present rather than in the future). A person having such positive time preference for income could be described as **myopic** (i.e., shortsightedness as to future income needs). Positive time preference played an important role in the traditional pure theory of interest in justifying a higher rate of interest as necessary to bring forth greater savings. The unusual person with a **negative time preference,** on the other hand, would be willing to pay interest for the privilege of saving money (i.e., such a person would be willing to accept a negative rate of interest).

## The Problem of Time

One difficulty in the neoclassical theory of interest, which was not always successfully resolved, was the problem of time. Some economists in this school asserted that interest would be paid even in a **static society** with pure and perfect competitive markets. Joseph Schumpeter, on the other hand, argued in his theoretical schema that productive interest could be neither earned nor paid in such a static circular economy. His argument rested upon the lack of development or technological change in such a society. Net real savings would not be needed in this system, because the existing stock of capital would merely need to be maintained. The additional reason for the absence of interest in a static economy is that no change over time is permitted.

The future is certain in a static society, so consumers need not put aside present income to meet their future contingencies. Furthermore, with no net capital formation, business firms would not be bidding for possible savings by being willing to pay higher interest rates. Time preference, either positive or negative, should not exist in such an economy. When interest exists, time enters in most importantly, because the interest rate is one way of comparing future needs and wants with present needs and wants. (The social importance of time preference as a way of comparing present and future income has become of considerable importance in the 1980s. In this decade, **underdeveloped countries** seek to grow faster and therefore need a higher rate of savings.)

*Comparing Present with Future Income*     When an interest rate is given for a dynamic system, each person can decide, in a price context linking the present and the future, the most rational disposition of his or her income by weighing the satisfying of present wants with the satisfying of future wants. Part of present income can be put aside in the form of savings and placed into any asset earning an interest return up to the point where income in both the present and future yields the maximum utility. With a given time preference pattern and a given interest rate, one can either lend or borrow in such a way as to maximize total satisfaction over time. When desired lending and desired borrowing are brought into equilibrium at a given interest rate, desired saving and desired investment are also equated. If disequilibrium occurs, the rate of interest must change until a proper balance is attained. It follows logically, likewise, that the higher the rate of interest, the more potential lenders will be willing to save while they are consuming less.

*Borrower is Willing to Pay for Present Funds*     On the other hand, borrowers are willing to pay a price for receiving present funds because of the higher value they might place on present as compared with future consumption, if they wish to borrow to increase their present level of consumption expenditures. The more typical borrowers, however, are thought to be the businesses that borrow not to increase present consumption but rather to invest, or to increase their stock of capital goods. A new machine is more productive than an old machine or an old method of production, which in turn tends to increase the profits of the business firm engaged in this kind of investment.

*Productivity of Capital Goods*     The productivity of new capital goods thus largely determines the level and shape of the demand for savings.

This schedule then indicates the price that the business firm is willing to pay for borrowing these savings to expand or to make more efficient existing productive facilities. At some particular rate of interest, a balance or equilibrium will be reached between the amount of savings that an individual or a group of persons is willing to put aside out of present income in order to receive an interest return and the amount of funds that firms wish to borrow to increase productivity and, presumably, their profits.

*No Money Illusion*    This is a real rate of interest and is not complicated by a money illusion created by changing money incomes or changes in the stock of money. The rate of interest is thus simply determined by the willingness or reluctance of persons to save, on the one hand, and the expected productivity of new capital equipment that could be secured with these savings, on the other hand. Although it might seem implicit that the rate of interest under discussion is the long-term rate of interest, the time period of the loan does not seem to be critical for this kind of analysis. The length of the possible maturity of the loan enters in only to the extent that savers need a higher inducement (i.e., a higher rate of interest), to forgo consumption for a longer period than they do for a short period.

*Normal Interest Rate Structure*    Thus a normal structure of interest rates would apparently contain a real long-term interest rate that is higher than the short-term interest rate in order to induce savers to withhold consumption over a greater time period. Furthermore, the neoclassical theorists always argued that a more roundabout method of production (i.e., using more capital goods), would be more productive and therefore more profitable than a simpler production method. Consequently, the business firm should be perfectly willing to pay a somewhat higher price to secure the hire of savings over a longer period inasmuch as the savings could be used for more capitalistic (i.e., more productive) production processes. So the pure theory of interest not only gives the major factors determining the level of interest rates but implies interest rate differentials, or a structure of interest rates, as well.

## Graphical Analysis of the Pure Interest Rate

After the amount of savings people wish to retain out of their income and the amount of funds demanded by business firms for capital expansion are determined, the two sides of the factors determining the rate of interest can be graphed in familiar demand and supply form. Figure 24–1 illustrates the theory of interest rate determination in neoclassical

**Figure 24–1    The Interest Rate As Determined by the Supply of Savings and the Investment Demand for Savings**

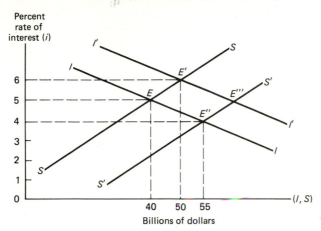

economics. On the vertical axis is the rate of interest $i$; on the horizontal axis is the amount of saving supplied $S$ and the amount of saving demanded for real investment $I$. The equilibrium rate of interest $i$ is determined where the supply of saving schedule ($SS$ curve) intersects the investment demand for saving ($II$ curve). The schedules assume a particular relationship between the supply of saving and the rate of interest, on the one hand, and the demand for saving for real investment and the rate of interest, on the other hand.

As the rate of interest is increased, people are willing to increase the amount of saving they supply out of current income. At higher rates of interest, however, business people wish to invest a smaller amount because of the higher cost of borrowing money. At lower rates of interest, they wish to borrow more, but savers will provide a smaller amount of saving. There is only one rate of interest, at $E$, at which the willingness to save and the willingness to invest are in equilibrium with each other, where the saving $S$ and investment $I$ schedules intersect. The equilibrium rate of interest with the original schedules is 5 percent, and the amount that will be saved and invested is $40 billion.

This analysis results in some similar, and some different, results from that involving the $IS$ and $LM$ schedules discussed in the previous chapter. If the investment schedule is shifted upward in Figure 24–1, the interest rate will rise, as is true when the $IS$ schedule is shifted upward. In Figure 24–1 the amount of savings increases immediately, whereas an increase in the $IS$ schedule increases income first and savings only second.

The greatest difference between these two theoretical approaches involves the supply schedules. In the *IS-LM* approach the supply schedule is the supply of money, whereas in the neoclassical theory of interest the supply schedule is the supply of savings. The Keynesians typically believe that the supply of savings is interest inelastic, because saving is depicted as depending solely on the level of income. The neoclassical analysis as shown in Figure 24–1 suggests that a rise in the interest rate should call forth a larger amount of saving, whereas a decline in the interest rate would lead to a decline in the amount saved. The *IS-LM* analysis comes to the reverse conclusion, because a lower interest rate leads to more investment, a higher level of income, and a larger amount of savings.

*Increase in Demand for Goods and Services*    Returning to the traditional analysis, we find that if the demand for final goods and services increases permanently, business borrowing will increase in order to expand productive capacity and thus take profitable advantage of higher demand. Also, if the cost of some other factor of production such as labor is increased as a result of higher wages and salaries, firms may wish to borrow even more savings to acquire still more capital equipment in order to substitute a relatively cheaper input, capital, for the more expensive labor input. It is even possible where the elasticity of demand for a product is high that a reduction in the price of labor will still stimulate demand for borrowed capital—not to substitute capital for labor but to use increased quantities of all the factors of production to produce more items at a cheaper cost to satisfy the market demand for a lower-priced item. In any of these events, firms must be willing to pay more for their borrowed funds or else a greater supply of saving will not be forthcoming. This situation is shown in Figure 24–1, when the *II* curve is shifted to *I'I'* to illustrate a higher investment demand for saving. The equilibrium rate of interest then moves upward from 5 to 6 percent and is indicated by the new intersection of the demand and supply schedules at *E'*. At the higher rate of interest, consumers are willing to save more, so that the amount of real saving increases from $40 billion to $50 billion.

*Change in Time Preference Pattern*    If, on the other hand, we assume that the time preference pattern of consumers for present versus future income changes, so that the amount of saving that they are willing to make out of present income increases, then we should expect the rate of interest to decline. This is also shown in Figure 24–1, when there is a shift in the saving schedule from *SS* to *S'S'*. The new equilibrium point now is *E''*, where the *II* schedule and the *S'S'* schedule intersect. Increased saving by consumers results in a decline in the rate of interest to 4 percent. At the lower rate of interest, business firms are willing to borrow more funds and thus increase their desired rate of capital accumulation to $55 billion.

In each instance of a change in one schedule, it is assumed that the other schedule remains unchanged. If both the supply of saving schedule and the demand for saving schedule increase (decrease) at the same time, it is possible that the rate of interest will be unchanged even though real saving and investment will increase (decrease). In Figure 24–1, when the *II* schedule increases to *I'I'* and the *SS* schedule increases to *S'S'*, the 5 percent rate of interest at *E* is unchanged at *E'''*.

If the schedules move in opposite directions at the same time, the effect of changes in the schedules on interest rates is magnified. The sensitivity of either the supply schedule or the demand schedule to changes in the rate of interest depends on the assumed shape of the schedules (elasticity of the curves), so that one can reach almost any desired result depending on one's assumptions. The critical question is what determines the real shape and level of these schedules of the supply and demand for saving. Monetary theorists have different points of view on this matter.

## Saving: Voluntary and Forced

The saving with which neoclassical economists were usually concerned was saving made voluntarily by consumers out of their disposable personal income. There are, however, other sources of saving as well. Business firms generate a substantial amount of gross saving in most years from internal sources. These funds include retained profits, depreciation allowances, and taxes accrued but not yet paid. Governmental units also provide saving to the economy when the level of their expenditure is less than the amount of receipts from taxes, so that there is a budget surplus. Another kind of saving to which the neoclassical economists gave a great deal of attention, however, was often called **"forced saving."**

Forced saving was thought to arise from an increase in the quantity of money. Whether the new money resulted from an expansion of bank loans by the commercial banking system or from government deficit financing, the result was usually held to be an increase in the price level, or inflation. (This explanation is clearly the quantity theory of money already discussed.) Because of generally rising prices of goods and services, it would be necessary for many consumers to cut back on their acquisitions of real goods and services.

If consumers decide to acquire the same bundle of commodities as they had before the price increases, they would have to spend more money for them. Many business firms would find that their money income for the same amount of real production had increased. Costs of labor and other factors of production tend to be somewhat "sticky," so that an inevitable result of higher money income for business firms would be a higher level of profits. That part of profits retained by the firm has already been defined as saving, so that the result of an inflation of the price level ensuing from a greater quantity of money was forced saving by consumers.

The public policy implications of this line of theoretical reasoning seemed clear to the neoclassical school. To secure for the market mechanism the function of allocating scarce savings among the competing investment demands of business firms, the monetary authorities of the government should aim at a level of interest rates that would ensure a neutral or equilibrium rate of interest. Under these conditions, the rate of interest prevailing would properly equate saving and investment without any resort to forced saving. The prevention of those disequilibria conditions giving rise to inflation and forced saving seemed best achieved by a relatively constant quantity of money. It seemed to many of these economists that the "root of all evil" was not just money, or the love of it, but rather an increase in the quantity of it. This kind of analysis is not concerned with business cycle fluctuations or the adequacy of economic growth, because these problems were ignored by the traditional assumption of full employment of all resources under pure and perfectly competitive markets.

## The Fisher Effect

Irving Fisher of Yale University, who was himself a neoclassical monetary economist, developed a theory of interest that carefully distinguished between the nominal, or market, rate of interest and the real rate. The real rate of interest was determined by the marginal productivity of physical capital, which in turn was related to the savings behavior of individuals and the state of technology. This real rate was the fundamental rate of interest, whereas the nominal rate of interest was essentially an adjunct to the real rate. The nominal rate incorporated an inflation premium that reflected the dominant view as to the expected rate of inflation. This came to be called the **"Fisher effect."**

Therefore, if nominal interest rates were high, as in 1973–1974 and 1981–1982, the most effective way to reduce them was to reduce the actual and expected rate of inflation. The somewhat paradoxical policy conclusion of this theory was thus that a slower rate of growth in the supply of money (by reducing the actual and expected rate of inflation) would lead eventually to a lower market rate of interest. On the other hand, a higher rate of growth in the supply of money, by generating more inflationary expectations, would actually lead to higher interest rates.

## A MONETARY THEORY OF INTEREST: LIQUIDITY PREFERENCE

In the neoclassical tradition, the rate of interest was thus explained basically in real or nonmonetary terms. Money was only a veil to penetrate in order to analyze the real factors at work. One of these factors, as already indicated, was the presumed time preference of most consumers for present income, so that a price in terms of a rate of interest had to be paid to them in order to induce them to postpone the enjoyment of some of their present income (i.e., to save). The other major factor was the expected productivity or profitability in real terms of new investment. Businesses were willing to hire money only if they expected to increase their profits thereby.

This kind of analysis of the determinants of the rate of interest came to be challenged by several important economists. As early as 1898, Knut Wicksell in Sweden distinguished between the **natural rate of interest** and the market rate; Irving Fisher also emphasized the differences between the real and nominal rate of interest. The market rate of interest, for Wicksell, was determined by the interplay of monetary factors, as differentiated from the productivity of capital, which determined the natural rate of interest. Somewhat later, Joseph Schumpeter stated that his theory of interest was a monetary theory, claiming that "this money form is not shell but kernel."

As discussed earlier, one of the three basic Keynesian functions is liquidity preference. For Keynes, the rate of interest was a purely monetary phenomenon determined by the demand for money (liquidity preference) and the supply of money determined by the monetary authorities. The uniquely Keynesian demand for money is an asset demand that exists because of an expected future fall in bond prices. This can be contrasted with the traditional demand for money for transactions purposes.

## *Loanable Funds Theory*

A post-Keynesian theory of interest that has attracted a good deal of attention among modern monetary theorists is called the "loanable funds theory." It combines the real factors of neoclassical theory with the monetary factors emphasized by Keynes. In this theoretical formulation, the equilibrium rate of interest is at the level that equates the demand and supply of loanable funds. Another way of saying the same thing is to refer to the demand and supply of debt claims, or interest-bearing securities. Both formulations can be used interchangeably. This approach specifically includes net hoarding and net changes in the quantity of money as well as real saving and real investment. Monetary factors in the loanable funds theory are not regarded as a veil to penetrate or otherwise disregard but rather as factors of some causal significance in themselves.

A great advantage of the loanable funds theory in considering the supply and demand for securities is that a single rate of interest on all securities, regardless of risk or maturity, does not have to be assumed. Each security can be regarded as having its own supply and demand and therefore its own yield. Furthermore, the supplies and demands can be looked at as stocks or flows. Most loanable funds theorists use a frame of reference suitable for a flow analysis. This might be called a kind of sources and uses analysis, because the sources of funds that go into securities are indicated and the types of securities using such available funds are identified. A complete sources and uses analysis would point out for what purposes the funds secured are being used (e.g., working capital or fixed capital). Conventional loanable funds theory ordinarily tends to discuss securities in general rather than in particular.

*The Demand for Loanable Funds*    The demand for loanable funds consists of (1) consumer borrowing to spend future income now—often for acquiring durable consumer goods such as automobiles—but it may also be for obtaining certain services such as medical services or a vacation now; (2) demand for borrowed funds by governments, otherwise known as deficit financing; and (3) demand for money capital on the part of business firms—this includes in a complete analysis all that is obtained from internal sources, from borrowing and from the sale of stock. It is often said that most borrowing demands are insensitive or inelastic to changes in the rate of interest. Nevertheless, some evidence suggests that certain types of borrowing demands may indeed be influenced by the terms on which borrowed funds are available.

Household spending, for example, appears to be affected by the terms on which households can secure mortgages. The terms of mortgage lending relate not only to the stated interest rate but to the percentage of downpayment and the maturity of the loan as well. Local governments, too are sometimes affected by conditions in the capital markets in their **bond flotation** efforts. School district bonds have often been postponed when interest rates are rising in the capital markets. These bonds, however, are usually later brought to market when interest rates have declined and borrowing conditions are more propitious for bond flotations. Even the Treasury will find it more difficult to float long-term issues, because it must compete with long-term private borrowers willing to pay high rates of interest. The Treasury then may be forced into the short end of the market instead.

Certain kinds of business firms, particularly public utility firms, that rely heavily on borrowing large sums of outside capital for long periods of time may well be affected by the conditions prevailing in the capital markets. These conditions include the level of interest rates and the direction of change in interest rates, as well as the amount of funds available for the purchase of various types of securities. In general, the demand of business firms for borrowed funds is dependent, like the demand for the output produced by the firm. Whenever consumer demand for the firm's product or service increases, the firm's demand for all the factors of its production will increase. As the firm's output nears its rated production capacity, the management will often start thinking about capital expansion plans, which in turn often involve the securing of outside capital. The terms on which this outside financing is available may have some influence on the amount the business firm finally decides to borrow at a given time.

When the firm, or a local governmental unit, does go into the capital market and borrow a sizable sum of money, the funds thus secured are not likely to be spent immediately. Money from a large bond or stock flotation is likely to go partly into increased bank balances, or even into the money market into such short-term earning assets as Treasury bills, because disbursements for new construction or new capital equipment will be made over a somewhat more extended period. Hence the demanders of borrowed funds in one segment of the loan market may be suppliers of loanable funds in another segment of the loan market.

***The Supply of Loanable Funds*** The supply schedule of loanable funds in general is composed of saving out of income received in the prior time period, plus dishoarding of idle balances and net additions to loanable funds from increases in the money stock permitted by the monetary authorities and the commercial banking system. Because the saving portion depends on the level of income, the total supply of loanable funds is not completely determined until a level of national income is given. Dishoarding (hoarding) of idle balances is the same thing as an increase (decrease) in the velocity of money.

*Components of Loanable Funds* The major components of loanable funds, as related to GNP, are shown in Figure 24–2. Here both commercial banks in their lending and investing activities and consumers in their

**Figure 24–2    Sources of Loanable Funds**

A. **Financial institutions**

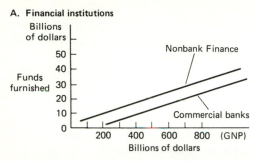

B. **Nonfinancial sources**

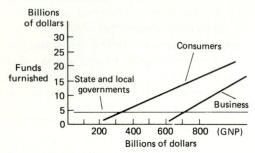

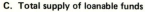

C. **Total supply of loanable funds**

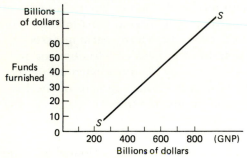

personal saving are major contributors to the total loanable funds in the economy. In both cases as national income rises, so does the amount of saving furnished. Consumers, as might be expected, are somewhat more sensitive than commercial banks to changes in income in the provision of saving.

The contribution of financial institutions, including banks, is shown in graph A of Figure 24–2. The reason banks increase their loanable funds as GNP rises is not only that the demand for such funds is greater on the part of would-be borrowers but also that the Federal

Reserve usually increases bank reserves in such a period in order to continue economic growth.

In graph B of Figure 24–2, the most sensitive saving source as income rises is clearly business firms. Consumers also increase their funds available to borrowers as income rises. State and local governments, however, seem to furnish about the same amount of loanable funds to the credit markets regardless of the level of GNP.

## Aggregate Supply of Funds

The supply schedules of graphs A and B are aggregated in graph C of Figure 24–2, which shows the total supply of loanable funds. This graph indicates that such loanable funds rise substantially with an increase in GNP. Higher levels of economic activity, which bring forth greater demands for loanable funds, also help to satisfy these demands, because higher levels of income generate a greater volume of saving of all kinds. Some of the factors affecting the availability of such loanable funds such as change in the supply of money and the turnover in such money stock are not directly shown here, though the influence of such factors is reflected in these supply schedules. Some of these factors are in part autonomous of income change. For simplification, these saving schedules are assumed to be linear in relation to income.

## Supply of Money May Be Exogenous or Endogenous

The supply of money may for some theoretical purposes be assumed as an exogenous factor inasmuch as the stock of money in the economy at any one time is determined ultimately by monetary policy acting on commercial bank reserves. In other theoretical schema such as those developed by monetary economists in the post-Keynesian tradition, the supply of money is regarded as an endogenous factor determined within the economic system. Variations in the level of demand deposits of commercial banks are the direct result of changes in the earning assets of banks, which include both securities and loans. Business loans of banks, an important component of earning assets, depend on the demand for loans, which tend to rise as income rises. Hence if the stock of money is growing as a result of an increase in bank loans, the supply of money may be regarded as an endogenous factor.

On the other hand, whether the banking system increases its liabilities—demand deposits and time deposits—by making loans or buying government securities is a matter of indifference. Normally we expect commercial banks to acquire some kind of earning asset whenever the Federal Reserve System increases bank reserves. If business loan demand is lacking and the Federal Reserve increases bank reserves, the banks will acquire government securities or state and local securities. Under these circumstances, because the money supply still increases, it may be considered as exogenously determined by the Federal Reserve System.

## Exchange of Existing Assets

The exchange of existing assets, such as transactions in old securities, is excluded from the supply of loanable funds. Both the supply and demand for loanable funds in the market for these outstanding claims balance each other out, so these transactions can be disregarded. The same may be said for transactions in real assets as opposed to claims. If we wish to consider **implicit rates of interest,** as well as market rates of interest, we would have to add the reinvestment of earnings retained in the business firm to the supply of loanable funds, even though the supply of these funds is also neatly balanced by the demand for the amount of such internal funds on the part of these firms.

In focusing on the factors affecting the market rate of interest alone, we can safely disregard such internal transactions because they do not directly affect activity on the loan market. As for equilibrium in the loan market itself, all the factors affecting the total demand for borrowed funds can be assembled and balanced against the factors making up the total supply of borrowed funds. In the unlikely event that *ex ante* (anticipated) demand for funds is equal to *ex ante* supply of funds, there will be no change in the market rate of interest.

***Equilibrium Conditions in the Credit Markets*** Realistically, there is usually some disequilibrium between *ex ante* demand for funds and *ex ante* supply of funds, so that the market rate of interest is often tending to move up or down. In the upswing of the business cycle the demand for loanable funds, whether for consumption or real investment, is often greater than the supply of voluntary saving that is forthcoming at the given level of disposable income. Under these conditions, part of the gap between the demand for loanable funds and the supply of loanable funds may be met by increasing the supply of money.

As already indicated, this increase in the supply of money may result in forced saving through the inflationary route. At the same time, it should be expected that an excess of the demand for borrowed funds in relation to the present quantity of funds for hire would result in a rise in the price (interest rate) of such borrowed funds. Such an increase in the rate of interest may enlarge the amount of voluntary saving, as the neoclassical economists believed, but it is almost certain to result in an increase in the velocity of money.

*Opportunity Cost of Cash*   With higher interest rates, the opportunity cost of idle cash balances is increased. Any given state of preference for liquidity is then likely to be at least partially overcome, so that some holders of idle cash balances are willing to give them up for earning assets that now bear a much more attractive rate of interest. The loanable funds doctrine would thus lead one to expect that an increase in the level of demand for borrowed funds, by resulting in a higher level of interest rates, would lead to a somewhat greater quantity of loanable funds supplied at the higher interest rate. We are not asserting that demand creates its own supply. We are merely suggesting that the supply schedule of loanable funds is tilted upward from left to right, as the ordinary supply schedule is, so that at a higher interest rate the *ex post* (actual) amount of loanable funds forthcoming would be larger.

*Indeterminate Factors*   Although the loanable funds theory may provide a simple analytical framework that is useful in analyzing determinants of the rate of interest—even proving helpful in examining the structure as well as the level of interest rates—there are a number of indeterminant or unexplained factors. For one thing, the level of national income must be given, because the amount of voluntary saving is heavily dependent on this variable. In addition, the supply of money and changes in the supply of money must be regarded as given. The loanable funds theory *per se* does not explain the factors affecting a given monetary policy, which in turn determine what the stock of money shall be. Changes in the velocity of money are not really explained, except for the hypothesis that an increase in the level of interest rates is likely to result in a higher velocity of money.

## THE TERM STRUCTURE OF INTEREST RATES

Previously, the discussion has been of what might be called a "general theory" of interest rates, in that the major theories concerning the determination of "the" interest rate have been examined. But what is "the" interest rate? It may be an average of all interest rates, a particular short-term rate, a particular long-term rate, or some abstract interest rate to which there is no exact correspondence in terms of actual interest rates.

The more realistic situation is a variety of interest rates. In what sense are these different interest rates functionally related to each other so that we can refer to a structure of interest rates? In trying to answer this question, let us start with traditional neoclassical theory, which is an **expectations theory** which involves a number of simplifying assumptions. We will only gradually dispense with some of these assumptions as we approach the greater complexities of the marketplace.

*Classical Assumptions of Term Structure Theory*   First, various institutional factors involving such specifics as tax laws, call features, and rights are not considered. Second, all securities are assumed to be risk-less insofar as payment of interest and principal are concerned. Third, it is assumed that the given set of expectations concerning short rates is held with complete confidence into the indefinite future. Fourth, **arbitrage** under pressure of the profit motive is possible without restraint among maturities of different terms. Under these particular assumptions the yield to maturity of any long-term security should be approximately equal to an average of the short-term rates expected to rule over the remaining life of the security.

The use of these assumptions means that the effective rate of return for any given period will be the same on securities of all maturities as long as capital gains and losses, as well as interest income, are included in the calculated effective rate of return. For example, if the present rate on loans with one-year maturity is 2 percent, and if the market confidently expects a 4 percent rate on one-year loans one year from now, the rate for two-year loans now must be approximately 3 percent. Under these conditions, no one would buy a two-year security yielding very much less than 3 percent now, because he or she could buy a one-year maturity now yielding 2 percent and one year hence buy another security with a maturity of one year yielding 4 percent. Likewise, no one would pay more than 3 percent to borrow money for a term of two years now, because the alternative would be to borrow funds now for one year at 2 percent and refund at the end of the first year for an additional maturity of one year at the then prevailing rate of 4 percent. Through arbitrage, therefore, an equilibrium rate of 3 percent would be established now for loans with a maturity of two years.

*Three Different Term Structures of Interest Rates*   In Figure 24–3, three different possible term structures of interest rates are shown, depending on the present set of expectations concerning future short-term interest rates. In graph A a simple monotonically increasing term structure of interest rates is pictured. Graph A shows that interest rates are higher as the maturity of the debt is longer. Longer maturities are associated with higher interest rates because of the present set of ex-

**Figure 24–3    The Term Structures of Interest Rates**

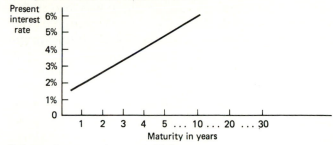

A. Higher short-term rates expected in future

B. Lower short-term rates expected in future

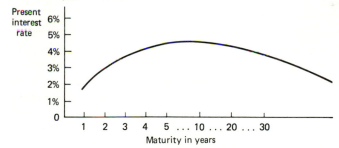

C. The humped interest rate curve

pectations as to future interest rates. This graph corresponds to a present one-year rate of 2 percent and a 4 percent rate expected to prevail one year from today. Furthermore, it is assumed that short-term rates will continue to increase in the future. Such a set of expectations may exist in a period of rising income and rising interest rates.

In Graph B of Figure 24–3 the contrary set of expectations is indicated. Here short-term rates are high, as in 1929, but future short-term rates are expected to be lower than present short-term rates. With these expectations, the present long-term rate is lower than the present short-term rate.

Graph C of Figure 24–3 shows a **humped interest rate curve** of the kind that existed for several years in the 1950s. Short-term rates were expected to be somewhat higher in the next several years but thereafter were expected to decline again. In the late 1960s there was also such a hump in the yields on government debt, though interest rates on private debt had a downward sloping curve, as shown in graph B. Neither graph B nor graph C is considered normal by some observers, though they are just as possible as graph A. In the mid-1960s the interest rate curve was nearly horizontal, because the longest rates were only slightly higher than the shortest rates. In the second half of 1973 and early 1974 the humped interest rate curve reasserted itself in the government securities market with one-year yields lower than yields on three- and six-month bills, whereas yields on three- to five-year issues were lower than those on one-year issues.

***Interrelationship of Short and Long Rates***    Inasmuch as there is an equality in effective returns over any given time period, it can be concluded that the yields to maturity of long-term debt instruments will be approximately that of the average of short rates over the intervening time, whatever the shape of yield curve. This conclusion, however, does not imply that short rates in any sense cause long rates. All interest rates are caused by the present and expected future supply and demand for loanable funds and the factors underlying these supply and demand schedules.

Long-term rates thus depend on the various supply and demand conditions prevailing throughout the time period until the security reaches maturity. If it is said that today's long-term rate will equal the average of future short-term interest rates, the assertion is simply being made that today's long-term rate is determined by present and future schedules of demand and supply of loanable funds. The same claim could be made for the determination of today's short-term interest rate.

*Importance of Short-term Rate*    The procedure of making simplifying assumptions in order to isolate certain major features of price determination is a familiar analytical technique of neoclassical economics. In the case of the theory of the term structure of interest rates, the traditional monetary theorists found that the most efficient way to understand the real determination of the many interest rates in the marketplace was to focus attention first on short rates. It should be understood, that these short rates are not simply interest rates on short-term securities but are interest rates on all securities within the same very short period of time. Interest rates can be so volatile in response to changes in demand and supply that some very short period of time is needed in which no change in interest rates could be expected.

Furthermore, the short-term rate considered is usually that on short-term government securities, because these securities hold no risk of default for the borrower. The yield on other securities must be sufficiently higher than this rate to cover a **risk premium** against the danger of default. The short-term interest rate on government securities already has a premium to take care of the possibility of market changes in the price of the security before maturity. This market risk is felt directly by lenders only if they wish to sell the debt instrument before maturity. Nevertheless, the ability to sell an asset with little risk of capital loss (liquidity of an asset) must be considered in managing a portfolio. Therefore any such risk must be paid for by the borrower in the original interest rate set at the time of floating the debt instrument.

## Uncertainty and Market Segmentation

At a later stage of analysis, as the approach is made closer to the actual structure of interest rates, it will be necessary to introduce the greater complexities involved in uncertainty and **market segmentation.** Furthermore, in some time periods uncertainty regarding the future will be greater than at other times, though market participants live and work day by day with at least some uncertain expectations about the future. At times when cyclical turning points are occurring or some dramatic shift in public policy occurs, such as the development of a large budget deficit that had not been expected, the prevailing state of expectations may change very rapidly.

In short, although the received doctrine of interest rate determination is static, the actual interest rates that develop in the money and capital markets are the result of dynamic forces. Also more variables need to be included to develop a theoretical model better adapted to explain interest rate changes in modern financial markets. Moving from the assumption of perfect arbitrage for various maturities of debt contracts to the more realistic hypothesis of a complex of separate, somewhat imperfect markets for borrowed funds is similar to moving from the theories of pure and perfect competition to the theories of monopolistic competition and oligopoly in the area of price theory. The relaxation of the assumption of perfect certainty of expectations is also analogous to moving from static to dynamic analysis.

## Difficulty of Perfect Arbitrage

Whenever the realities of uncertainty and market segmentation in the actual operation of the money and capital markets are considered, it becomes more apparent that perfect arbitrage is virtually impossible. Thus the effects of changes in one sector of these loan markets become fully reflected throughout the entire complex of loan markets only after a time lag. In some cases the time lag may be so long that other new factors come into the markets and cancel out the effect of the original change. Arbitrage in these markets may also be prevented or impeded because of the cost and inconvenience of investment and disinvestment in securities, particularly for very short-term securities.

The cost of moving in and out of the market frequently includes not only the actual money outlay in the form of a commission or a dealer's spread but also the cost of maintaining a highly skilled staff to watch the market closely for any possible profit opportunities. As a result of these costs, many persons whose funds can be used for only a brief period of time would prefer to hold idle cash. Hence only large financial institutions and some of the very large nonfinancial institutions with ample funds available for temporary employment in the money market are likely to build up the skilled staff necessary for such participation in the market.

Market separation between securities of different terms also occurs, because many investing institutions are likely to place their funds in investments whose maturities are similar to the life of their own liabilities. Life insurance companies thus typically buy long-term securities, commercial banks often prefer short and intermediate government securities, and so on. These institutional preferences provide an important explanation of market segmentation. Even within a given investing institution, certain proportions of the total investment portfolio may be assigned to different maturity ranges with the power to change these proportions vested only in a top management committee whose decisions to change may not come as rapidly as changes in the market. Finally, market imperfection arises from the fact that certain sectors of the market, particularly the long end of the market, tend to have fairly **thin markets.**

As a result of this kind of a thin market, money market institutions find it virtually impossible to make large-scale exchanges of certain securities in particular periods, even when profit considerations might seem to indicate the desirability of such swaps. Regular participants in the market have a strong preference for market stability and hence would not deliberately seek to cause undue churning in the market for a possible small profit gain. In some cases in a deteriorating market, an institution might also encounter reluctance on the part of the security dealers to buy a large block of securities offered, so that the sale could be consummated only at the expense of a substantial drop in the price of the security being sold.

# EMPIRICAL EVIDENCE ON THE TERM STRUCTURE OF RATES

When the possibility of such market imperfections as segmentation and uncertainty are admitted, the likelihood of any firm conclusions from empirical evidence about causal influences determining the market pattern of interest rates may seem remote. Nevertheless, Joseph Conard of Swarthmore did make such an empirical study of the term structure of interest rates in the 1950s and reached certain firm generalizations. Conard concluded that though we may generally expect rate movements on securities of different term usually to move in the same direction, this is not always so. Similarities in movements of market yields seem to be greatest for long-term securities in that different issues appear to respond typically in a similar manner to changed market expectations. Diverse rate movements among short-term securities, or between shorts and longs, should not be regarded as unusual, however.

Short- and long-term interest rates may even change in opposite directions at times because of a desire on the part of investors to avoid a capital loss or to make a capital gain. If a substantial segment of the market comes to expect declining interest rates in the future, this, of course, suggests that security prices in the future will rise. Inasmuch as the prices of long-term securities fluctuate more in response to a given change in market yield than do short-term securities, it may be that the market will sell shorts and buy longs, which in turn would cause yields of shorts and longs to move in opposite directions.

## *Expectations Theory Confirmed by Empirical Evidence*

Other empirical studies have tended generally to confirm the major propositions of the traditional academic expectations theory, rather than confirming the market segmentation theory held by a number of participants in the financial markets. For example, David Meiselman found that annual data taken from the 1901–1954 period are consistent with the expectations theory when these data are combined with a hypothesis that revisions of expectations of future short-term rates are linear functions of past errors in predicting short-term rates. Burton G. Malkiel used three different sets of interest rate time series and several alternative time periods and reached conclusions that corroborated Meiselman's findings that expectations play a major role in determining the interest rate structure.

If the segmented markets theory is correct—and debt assets in different parts of the financial markets are imperfect substitutes for one another—then changing the supply of different maturities of debt, assuming that demand remains unchanged, should have the effect of changing the maturity yield differentials. Yet empirical studies have not shown this to be the case. Changing the relative supplies of securities with different maturities seems to have only small effects on maturity yield differentials. This not only casts considerable doubt on the validity of the market segmentation theory but also appears to support the expectations theory.

Even if loans of different maturities are perfect substitutes to investors in the aggregate, it is not necessary to argue that all such loans are perfect substitutes for each type of institutional investor. Although various institutional investors may have strong preferences for certain types of debt assets (in order to match the maturity of these assets with the maturity of their outstanding liabilities), these different investor groups may also overlap considerably in the financial markets.

In that event, the structure of yields will be adjusted in the same manner, as if each investor believed that all securities were perfect substitutes. Moreover, in addition to risk-averter institutions with possible overlapping demand for debt assets, there appears to exist a group of traders who are indifferent to the maturity of the various debt issues. These traders, then, help to ensure that changing expectations in one maturity of the debt markets are reflected in yield changes in other debt maturities.

## FORECASTING INTEREST RATES

One would think that choosing the right theory of interest rates would help in the difficult yet very important job of **forecasting interest rates.** All private financial institutions, who are lenders, and the nonfinancial corporations, who are borrowers, are interested in what future interest rates may be. The Federal Reserve and the Treasury too, as well as the Office of Management and Budget, are likewise concerned about future movements in interest rates. Unfortunately, no one has yet developed a foolproof method of forecasting interest rates—particularly since the important changes by the Federal Reserve in open market policy and operations of October 6, 1979. In the two years after that change, the financial markets experienced very great volatility of interest rates. Nevertheless, financial economists do have to make interest rate forecasts, and when they do they look at certain relationships that often held in the past.

One such relationship we have already noted under our discussion of the Fisher effect, which is the relationship between interest rates and inflation. Although the Fisher findings were specifically for long-term interest rates, the relationship also seems to hold for short-term interest rates. Changes in the price level and the rate on three-month Treasury bills from 1960 to 1980 were shown in Figure 1–1. Technically, of course, it was inflationary expectations that Fisher related to interest rates, but the present rate of inflation is often used as a proxy for such expectations of inflation.

Another such relationship that often proved to be meaningful is that between the business cycle and interest rates. As economic activity improves, the demand for loanable funds should rise, and because there is only a finite supply of such loanable funds, the price of these funds, or the interest rate, should rise. This relationship is shown in Figure 24–4, where it does seem to hold, at least loosely, for both three-month Trea-

**Figure 24–4    Interest Rates and the Business Cycle**

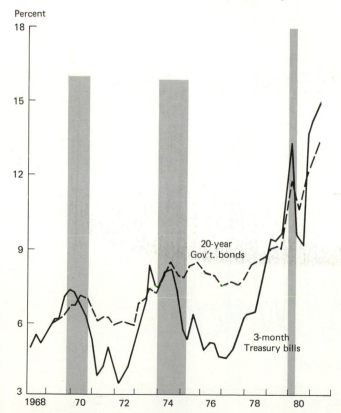

SOURCE: Morgan Guaranty Trust Company of New York, *The Morgan Guaranty Survey*, Sept. 1981, p. 2.

sury bills and twenty-year government bonds. Economic recessions are shown by the shaded part of the graph. It appears that interest rates peak after the onset of the recession and continue to fall even after the economic recovery has begun.

Finally, we can see in Figure 24–5 the relationship between monetary policy and interest rates. This relationship seems closer than the two previous graphs. Here, the two decades from 1960 to 1980 are pictured with **free reserves** on the left scale and the federal funds rate on the right scale. Free reserves consists of excess bank reserves minus bank borrowing at the Federal Reserve Banks. When such bank borrowing rises, the banks are supposed to be under pressure and to liquidate marketable assets or restrain their lending until they reduce their debt.

Conversely, when the Federal Reserve is supplying substantial amounts of reserves through open market operations, such borrowing falls. Interest rates rise when free reserves are negative, yet they fall when free reserves are positive. Interest rates are here represented by the

**Figure 24–5    Interest Rates and Monetary Policy**

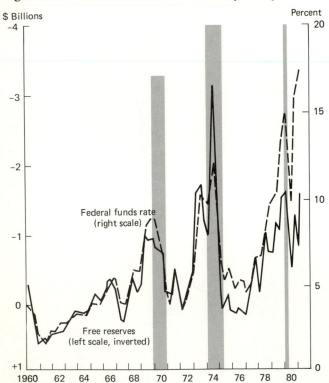

SOURCE: Morgan Guaranty Trust Company of New York, *The Morgan Guaranty Survey,* Set. 1981, p. 3.

federal funds rate, which is the interest rates on excess reserves that banks lend to one another for twenty-four hours. When the federal funds rate changes, other money market rates also tend to change.

# Questions for Discussion

1. What are the major assumptions of the neoclassical theory of interest insofar as saving is concerned? An increase in saving might come about as a result of changes in what factors? (Contrast the neoclassical determinants of saving with those in the Keynesian formulation.) What is forced saving? Graphically illustrate the neoclassical theory of interest.
2. What are regarded as the major determinants of the demand for saving? What would ordinarily be the effect on the interest rate of an increase in the demand for saving?
3. Would an increase in the rate of interest be associated with an increase or a decrease in the rate of real investment, or would this depend on what happened to the schedules? Defend your answer.
4. How important were monetary factors in the neoclassical theory of interest? What conclusions relating to monetary policy were often reached by the holders of the general theory of interest of the neoclassical school?
5. Discuss the Fisher effect and indicate the effect of an increase in the rate of inflation on the price level. If nominal interest rates are too high, how can they be reduced, assuming that real rates are unchanged?
6. What is meant by hoarding? In what way, if at all, does an increase in hoarding affect the stock of money? Would you expect the desire to hoard money to be different in different time periods? Why?
7. What are the major differences between the loanable funds theory and the Keynesian theory of interest rate determination? What is the relationship between the loanable funds theory and the neoclassical general theory of the interest rate?
8. What are the major kinds of demand for loanable funds? What are the major sources of supply of loanable funds?
9. What is the term structure of interest rates? What kind of interest rate is emphasized in the neoclassical theory of the structure of interest rates? Why?
10. How are interest rates for loans of different maturities interconnected? List the major assumptions underlying this particular interest rate theory. How valid do you think these assumptions are?
11. What are the conclusions of empirical studies concerning the validity of the traditional expectations hypothesis of the term structure of interest rates as compared with the more recent theory of market segmentation? What difference does it make to the monetary authorities, or to participants in the financial markets, which theoretical explanation appears to be the more correct?

12. What are some major relationships between interest rates and other variables that can be helpful in forecasting interest rates? Why have interest rate forecasts often gone astray? What do you think will happen to interest rates in the next year? Why?

# Selected Bibliography for Further Reading

## Books

CONARD, JOSEPH W., *An Introduction to the Theory of Interest* (Berkeley, Calif.: University of California Press, 1959).

DUE, JOHN F., and ROBERT W. CLOWER, *Intermediate Economic Analysis* (Homewood, Ill.: Richard D. Irwin, 1961).

FISHER, IRVING, *The Theory of Interest* (New York: Macmillan, 1930).

HANSEN, ALVIN H., *Monetary Theory and Fiscal Policy* (New York: McGraw-Hill, 1949).

———, *A Guide to Keynes* (New York: McGraw-Hill, 1953).

HART, ALBERT GAILORD, and PETER B. KENEN, *Money Debt and Economic Activity* (Englewood Cliffs, N.J.: Prentice-Hall, 1961).

KEYNES, JOHN MAYNARD, *The General Theory of Employment, Interest and Money* (London: Macmillan, 1936).

KURIHARA, KENNETH K., *Monetary Theory and Public Policy* (New York: Norton, 1950).

MALKIEL, BURTON G., *The Term Structure of Interest Rates* (Princeton, N.J.: Princeton University Press, 1966).

MEISELMAN, DAVID, *The Term Structure of Interest Rates* (Englewood Cliffs, N.J.: Prentice-Hall, 1962).

PATINKIN, DON, *Money, Interest, and Prices*, 2d ed. (New York: Harper & Row, 1965).

## Articles

LEROY, STEPHEN F., "Interest Rates and the Inflation Premium," *Monthly Review*, Federal Reserve Bank of Kansas City, May 1973, pp. 11–18.

MORGAN GUARANTY TRUST COMPANY OF NEW YORK, "Forecasting Interest Rates: Some First Principles," *The Morgan Guaranty Survey*, Sept. 1981, pp. 1–7.

WOOD, JOHN H., "Interest Rates and Inflation," *Economic Perspectives*, Federal Reserve Bank of Chicago, May-June 1981, Vol. V, Issue 3, pp. 3–12.

# PART 7

# PUBLIC POLICY

The Public funds of the different indebted nations of Europe, particularly those of England, have by one author been represented as the accumulation of a great capital, by means of which its trade is extended, its manufacturers multiplied, and its lands cultivated and improved much beyond what they could have been by means of that other capital only.

THE WEALTH OF NATIONS

# 25
# CHAPTER

# Fiscal Policy and Debt Management

Interest rates are influenced not only by investor preferences, as indicated in the preceding chapter, but also by the amount and type of borrowing in the various credit markets. The most important borrower of funds—especially in the money market—is the federal government. It has been alleged by some economists that when the Treasury runs a large budget deficit, the Federal Reserve is forced to induce a large expansion in the supply of money because of its concern with stabilizing the level of interest rates.

There can be little doubt that changes in the level of aggregate demand are importantly affected by changes in total government expenditures and total tax revenues. Such changes in aggregate demand in turn affect total output and employment and the level of prices. These are some of the reasons why a course in money and banking needs to have some concern with fiscal policy.

## FISCAL POLICY

The term "fiscal policy" has been in common currency only about 45 years and therefore is a much newer concept than, say, monetary policy.

That government expenditures and taxes have significant impacts on the private sectors of the economy has been known for many years. But it remained for the advocates of the new theories of fiscal policy in the 1930s to argue that such expenditures and tax revenues should be deliberately managed to affect the total level of national income and employment of the entire economy.

If the aggregate level of private demand is too low so that resources are unemployed, the use of fiscal policy would require the federal government to increase its level of spending while holding tax rates constant or possibly even cutting taxes. This deficit in tax revenues related to government expenditures would then mean that the government was spending more in the income-spending stream than it was withdrawing. On the other hand, if the economy were generating such a full head of steam at full employment that inflationary pressures threatened to push up the price level substantially, the proper fiscal policy of the government would be to cut government expenditures or else raise tax rates, so that a surplus of tax revenues over expenditures would result. The government would then be taking more funds out of the income stream than it was putting in and thus would provide a drag to help offset the stimulus to price increases coming from rising private expenditures.

Fiscal policy, then, may be defined as being the conscious variation of the total level of government expenditures and tax receipts to affect the level of income, employment, and the price level. In the 1970s and the 1980s, fiscal policy has been used not only to deal with the inflationary excesses of a high employment economy but also to promote noninflationary economic growth. The proponents of fiscal and monetary policy have shifted their main concern from stabilization of aggregate demand over the business cycle to the long-run promotion of higher rates of real economic growth. There have been only three years since 1957 that the budget has had a surplus. Nevertheless, if the budget deficit is being reduced, there is fiscal restraint on the economy.

At times, this means that fiscal and monetary policy together may exercise enough restraint on the economy in an inflationary period (e.g., 1969–1970, 1973–1974, and 1981–1982), that the real rate of economic growth will decline for some quarters in a recession period, such as in 1973–1975 or 1981–1982. Regardless of the type of fiscal policy, it is essential that it be coordinated with monetary policy. However, since so much attention has already been devoted to the discussion of monetary policy, most of the discussion here is on fiscal policy alone.

In **countercyclical fiscal policy** it was often thought possible and desirable that any increase in government debt incurred in a depression period as a result of deficit spending should be offset by a surplus in the budget in a period of rising levels of economic activity accompanied by rising levels of tax revenues. In the 1980s, however, increasing acceptance may be given to the possibility of a gradually rising level of government debt, rather than one that would be stationary. Attention has now come to be directed at the relative size of the debt to income, and of increases in debt to increases in income (e.g., the absolute size of the federal debt might increase somewhat even though the relative size of the debt in terms of income might be falling).

The burden of the debt of the federal government, like the burden of private debt, is thus viewed as depending on this relative relationship of debt and debt service to income rather than on some arbitrary quantitative limit of debt. Even in this new view, it is possible for debt to increase too fast or too slowly for proper fiscal stabilization policy. The emphasis, in any case, is on rates of change rather than merely on levels. This is as true for government expenditures and tax revenues as it is for debt.

## FISCAL POLICY AND THE SUPPLY OF MONEY

It has often been argued that a large and rising budget deficit may contribute to inflationary pressures, particularly if the economy is in a period of strong upswing in economic activity. This is true not only because of the increase in aggregate demand associated with growing government expenditures financed by a budget deficit but also because the Federal Reserve is likely to increase the money supply as a result of a growing budget deficit. If the Federal Reserve did not increase the money supply, interest rates would sharply increase, as in 1981. The increase in the money supply, according to this argument, would increase still more with any inflationary pressures. This argument depends importantly on the assumption that the major concern of the Federal Reserve is with the stabilization of interest rates.

The money market strategy of the 1960s did indeed seem to be focused on the relative stability of the credit markets. In that decade the Federal Reserve often tended to increase bank reserves and the money supply when market forces were pushing up interest rates. In the 1970s and 1980s the open market policy of the Federal Reserve shifted to a concern with controlling the rates of growth of various key monetary aggregates (i.e., the narrowly defined money supply and various broader defined money supplies (M1, M2, and M3).

A study by an economist at the Federal Reserve Bank of Kansas City, which was published in 1975 and involved a regression analysis for the 1970–1974 period, did not support the belief that the Federal Reserve now responds to a budget deficit by increasing the money supply so as to prevent interest rates from rising. The narrow definition of money, M1, was even found to be negatively correlated with the budget. The Federal Reserve economist concluded: ". . . the Federal Reserve apparently did not respond to the deficit by taking actions that affected money. Rather, it appears that the Federal Reserve allowed the deficit to change interest rates."[1]

There is one technical circumstance in which a budget deficit will still increase the money supply, and that is where the Treasury finances a deficit, in whole or in part, not by borrowing but by drawing down balances it holds at commercial banks or at Federal Reserve Banks. In that event, privately held money balances rise as money balances held by the government decline. Because deposit balances held by the Treasury are not included in any definition of the money supply, the supply of money will rise. There is, however, a finite limit to the effect of such an operation on the money supply, because the Treasury only holds a certain amount of money balances. Furthermore, most of these balances are needed so that the Treasury can pay its bills when presented. Hence one would normally expect that a rising budget deficit will generally be financed by increased borrowing.

If the Treasury sells government securities to the banking system, which has some excess reserves, or if the Treasury sells securities to the public who pays for these securities by borrowing from the banking system, then the money supply can still increase. Once again, however, there is a real limitation to how far either development can take place. The banking system in the 1980s does not typically tend to carry much excess reserves. Furthermore, the securities sold by the Treasury are not usually so attractive to the public that the public is likely to do much borrowing from the banking system to finance such purchases.

Beyond such limited effects on the supply of money, the Federal Reserve must increase the reserves of the banking system in order for the money supply to grow as the budget deficit increases. By the 1980s, there was a greater awareness of the inflationary implications of such a policy, along with a preoccupation with controlling the growth of monetary aggregates rather than simply stabilizing interest rates. Hence it does not appear that the Federal Reserve would finance a growing budget deficit by expanding bank reserves and the money supply.

## THE BUDGET

### Purposes of the Budget

Whenever we talk about fiscal policy we are talking about government expenditures and tax revenues. Both expected government expenditures

---

[1]J.A. Cacy, "Budget Deficits and The Money Supply," *Monthly Review*, Federal Reserve Bank of Kansas City, June 1975, p. 7.

and expected tax revenues are encompassed in the budget document sent to Congress each January by the president. The four basic purposes of any national budget are (1) the depiction of a proposed allocation of resources to serve national objectives between the private and public sectors, and within the public sector, (2) the taxing and spending stabilization policies of the government, (3) the president's requests to Congress for appropriations and changes in tax legislation, and (4) a report to Congress and the public on past tax receipts and expenditures. No single budget concept can satisfy completely all these purposes.

The budget now is designed to provide a unified picture of the federal government's finances and has taken the place of the earlier administrative budget, designed to focus on project requests of the various agencies, and the consolidated cash budget, which incorporated the transactions of the growing trust funds along with the operations of the administrative budget. The national income accounts budget, which focuses on the federal sector of the national income accounts and presents budget estimates in national income terms, is still useful, however.

## The Unified Budget

In January 1968, the president sent Congress the first unified comprehensive summary budget statement, for the fiscal year 1969. This new budget was based on the major recommendations of the President's Commission on Budget Concepts, which reported on October 10, 1967. The new **unified budget** encompassed all programs of the federal government and its agencies. Outlays and deficits were divided between the expenditure account and loan accounts and receipts were set off against outlays, regardless of the funding structure at any particular time. Payments between funds were eliminated from the totals.

***Earlier Budget Concepts*** The older administrative budget had covered receipts and expenditures of funds owned by the government. In the administrative budget, receipts and expenditures were shown gross, except for refunds, although certain receipts were offset against expenditures. This older budget for many years was regarded as the principal financial plan for the federal government.

In the period since World War II the budget was supplemented by the **consolidated cash budget,** which sought to reflect all transactions between the government and the public. Its totals were basically on a checks-paid basis, as distinguished from the checks-issued basis of the administrative budget. The inclusion of the trust funds in the consolidated cash budget and the growing importance of such trust funds led economists to be more concerned with the economic impact of the government as measured in the former cash budget than in the even older administrative budget.

In terms of coverage, the new unified budget is very similar to the former consolidated cash budget, although total receipts and total expenditures are somewhat smaller in the new budget than in the older cash budget, and expenditure totals are on a checks-issued basis. There is also a greater netting of receipts against expenditures in the new budget than in the cash budget. Receipts and expenditures are also usually somewhat lower in the new budget than in the national income accounts budget.

## Budget Deficits in the 1970s

Larger budget deficits in the 1970s and 1980s, as can be seen in Table 25–1, became chronic. However, the budget deficits in fiscal year 1975 and thereafter were substantially larger than they had been in the early 1970s or in the 1950s or 1960s. From 1975 through 1982, in no year was the deficit less than $40 billion and deficits of $100 billion or so were expected for several years beginning in 1982. Even as a percentage of a larger GNP, federal budget deficits reached higher levels from the mid-1970s on.

## Tax and Budget Cuts in 1981

After a decade of budget deficits, slow real economic growth, and several periods of **double-digit inflation** (1973–1974 and 1979–1980), the newly elected Reagan administration (November 1980) persuaded Congress in early August 1981 to enact a three-year tax cut program and severe budget cutbacks in civilian spending programs, while sharply increasing military spending. President Reagan promised a balanced budget by fiscal year 1984 with declining budget deficits each year from fiscal year 1982 until then.

The tax cut enacted in 1981 included a 25 percent across the board cut in personal income tax rates in three installments—5 percent October 1, 1981, 10 percent July 1, 1982, and 10 percent July 1, 1983. Substantially faster depreciation write-offs for business firms were also put in law at the same time, retroactive to January 1, 1981. Also, there were tax breaks for persons who put money into various kinds of savings accounts; a substantial reduction in the 1980 "windfall" tax on oil revenues and royalties, and the near elimination of estate taxes. As a result of these sweeping tax cuts, tax revenue was to be reduced $36.3 billion in fiscal 1982, $95.2 billion in 1983, $148.7 billion in 1984, and $195 billion in 1985.

At the same time that tax rates were cut, nonmilitary government

**Table 25–1   Total Federal Budget and Off-Budget Surplus or Deficit and Gross National Product, Fiscal Years, 1970–1987 (In billions of dollars)**

| Fiscal Year | Total Federal Budget and Off-Budget Surplus or Deficit (−) | |
|---|---|---|
| | Amount | As Percent of GNP |
| 1970 ......................................... | −2.8 | −.3 |
| 1971 ......................................... | −23.0 | −2.2 |
| 1972 ......................................... | −23.4 | −2.1 |
| 1973 ......................................... | −14.9 | −1.2 |
| 1974 ......................................... | −6.1 | −.4 |
| 1975 ......................................... | −53.2 | −3.6 |
| 1976 ......................................... | −73.7 | −4.5 |
| 1977 ......................................... | −53.6 | −2.9 |
| 1978 ......................................... | −59.2 | −2.8 |
| 1979 ......................................... | −40.2 | −1.7 |
| 1980 ......................................... | −73.8 | −2.9 |
| 1981 ......................................... | −78.9 | −2.8 |
| 1982[a] ......................................... | −118.3 | −3.8 |
| 1983[a] ......................................... | −107.2 | −3.1 |
| 1984[a] ......................................... | −97.2 | −2.6 |
| 1985[a] ......................................... | −82.8 | −2.0 |
| 1986[a] ......................................... | −77.0 | −1.7 |
| 1987[a] ......................................... | −62.5 | −1.3 |

[a]Estimates.

SOURCE: Council of Economic Advisers, *Economic Report of the President 1982*, Feb. 1982, p. 98.

spending was also being cut. Some $35 billion was cut in fiscal year 1982 alone. Over four years from fiscal year 1981 through 1984, the cuts were expected to total about $135 billion. Military spending, however was stepped up sharply. President Reagan upped military spending some $7 billion in fiscal year 1981 over that of his predecessor, President Carter. In fiscal 1982, there was a further increase of $26 billion. For fiscal years 1983–1986, the Reagan administration in 1981 planned military cumulative increases of some $200 billion over that of the Carter administration. There was to be a $36 billion increase in 1983 and the increase would culminate in a $68 billion increase in 1986.

The administration's budget projections in mid-1981 for the five fiscal years 1981–1985 were as follows. Tax receipts were expected to rise from $605.7 billion in fiscal 1981 to $832.5 billion in fiscal 1985. Tax receipts were expected to rise despite the sharp tax cuts because real economic growth was expected to accelerate from the stimulus of tax cuts, while the inflation rate at the same time was expected to fall. Total government spending was expected to rise from $661.2 billion in fiscal 1981 to $834.6 billion. The budget deficit, however, because of the optimistic forecast growth in tax receipts, was expected to show a slight surplus in fiscal year 1984 and only a slight deficit in fiscal year 1985. These years contrasted with the $55.5 billion deficit expected in fiscal year 1981.

Six months later—in February 1982—the expected budget deficits had already been revised upwards by the President's Council of Economic Advisers, as shown earlier in Table 25–1. Congress and private forecasters were expecting even larger deficits than these, unless Congress sharply cut projected government expenditures and raised some taxes to offset some of the tax revenues lost from the 1981 tax cuts. In August 1982, Congress raised taxes by $98.3 billion over a three-year period. Even then, high budget deficits for several years seemed likely.

These fiscal policies of the Reagan administration in 1981 were based on supply-side economics rather than on aggregate demand management, which was the typical form of fiscal policy prior to 1981. Supply-side economics asserted that changes in marginal tax rates (i.e. cuts) could lead to an increase in the labor supply and increased productivity by those already in the labor force. Furthermore, by increasing real disposable income (income after taxes in constant dollars), saving would be increased. This in turn would lead to more investment in real plant and equipment, which would also increase productivity and total real output. Furthermore, it was expected that the inflation rate and market rates of interest would also decline.

It remained to be seen whether all the recommended budgetary changes for fiscal 1983 and thereafter would be enacted by Congress, and it was also unclear whether the budgetary changes enacted into law would have all the beneficial economic effects claimed for them. Because of the newness of these new fiscal theories and uncertainties as to what changes in budgetary policies might in fact be made during fiscal years 1983–1987, most of our discussion in this chapter is based on the more traditional demand management view of fiscal policy.

## Effective Fiscal Policy

If the federal government is taking in more money from the private sectors of the economy in the form of tax receipts than it is returning to them in the form of government expenditures, the effective fiscal policy of the government is restrictive on further growth in the private sectors. This would be true whether the growth in the private economy is viewed in terms of private spending or output of goods and services for private consumption. If the government is taking in less money in the form of tax receipts from the private sectors than it is returning to these sectors in the form of government spending, the overall impact of this fiscal policy is stimulating to private spending and output. This in turn might result in an increase in real output of goods and services if unused real factors of production were available, or it might result in inflation of the price level if the economy were operating at or near full employment.

Recognizing that government expenditures represent an important part of aggregate demand, whereas taxes represent an important subtraction from private aggregate demand, the advocates of fiscal policy often recommend that changes in government spending and tax rates should be made for stabilization and growth purposes. If private demand seems inadequate for full production of goods and services and substantial numbers of unemployed men and women are in evidence, then changes in the budget position of the government should be undertaken to correct this shortfall in private demand.

This could be accomplished by a rise in government expenditures and/or a cut in taxes. In either case, aggregate demand should be increased. If aggregate demand appears to be greater than aggregate supply at current prices, and the price level is therefore rising, efforts should be made to cut aggregate demand. This could be done through fiscal policy by a cut in government expenditures and/or a rise in tax rates.

## DISCRETIONARY VERSUS AUTOMATIC FISCAL POLICY

Advocates of **discretionary fiscal policy,** whether for countercyclical or growth purposes, would thus recommend changes from time to time in tax rates and government spending, depending on the stage of the cycle or the rate of economic growth. In this view, whenever the number of employed was judged to be too low or the rate of unemployment too high, tax rates should be cut and expenditures by the federal government increased. Whenever inflationary pressures threatened, tax rates should be increased and government expenditures decreased. The only difficulty with this approach is persuading Congress to do what *seems* to be the appropriate thing under the circumstances.

Delays in Congress, sometimes up to two years and in no case fewer than many months, seem to make it difficult to change tax rates quickly to deal with cyclical problems of employment or price stability. Furthermore, Congress has strenuously resisted or ignored various suggestions that it give up certain of its powers to change tax rates to some board in the executive branch. Congress did delegate some of its constitutional powers over money management to the Federal Reserve Board in 1913, but it seems unlikely in the near future to delegate any of its powers over tax rates to a fiscal board in the executive branch. Proper use of the power to change tax rates, either to stimulate the rise of income or to reduce upward pressure on the price level, would imply some ability to forecast the near future in economic activity. There are differing opinions about the present reliability of such forecasting. (There is also a theoretical challenge to this view of proper fiscal policy in the form of supply-side economics, which has already been noted.)

## Automatic Fiscal Policy

Recognizing the difficulties in changing tax rates and expenditures at the proper time, along with the inevitable lag in their full impact on the economy, some proponents of fiscal policy have recommended a stabilizing budget policy that would contain certain automatic features. This kind of policy would circumvent the weaknesses of the managed compensatory budget policy both as to frequent discretionary changes and the difficulties of forecasting. The basic objective of a stabilizing budget would be to set tax rates to balance the budget, and possibly even provide some surplus to apply to debt retirement, at an agreed high level of employment and national income. Once these tax rates were decided upon, they would have to be left alone, unless national policy changed or there were basic changes in the economic system.

**Tax Receipts Rise and Fall with National Income**    The basic point about setting a single tax rate and leaving it alone is that tax receipts vary not only according to changes in tax rates but also as taxable income changes. Thus as national income rises, tax collections also increase, whereas as national income falls, collections from taxes decline. In the first instance, the fiscal drag of increased tax receipts tends to slow down the rate of increase in national income and thereby reduce any tendency for increases in spending to outrun increases in the productive capacity to generate added goods and services and thus result in inflation. On the other hand, a slowdown in economic activity would be automatically offset in part, because the federal government would be taking fewer funds out of the income stream as tax collections decline with falling income. In both cases the automatic changes in tax receipts flowing to the government would have some countercyclical effects on economic activity.

*Government Expenditures Change over the Cycle*     There are also certain automatic changes in government expenditures over the business cycle, without the necessity of specific new congressional action. For example, when unemployment increases, as it does during a downswing in economic activity, then a rise in unemployment compensation payments results in an increased cash flow from the government to the public. Old-age pension payments under Social Security also rise during a downswing as more older workers elect to retire. Even payments under the agriculture programs of the federal government increase in an economic downswing as softness in farm prices brings greater support activity from the government under existing legal programs.

Other kinds of government spending may be varied somewhat over the cycle without specific new congressional action. A speedup in dividends to holders of National Service Life Insurance policies may be ordered in a recession. An increase in construction of new post offices and other public works may occur under existing authorization from Congress. Even military orders may be increased somewhat under outstanding obligational authority without asking Congress to pass new appropriations. Somewhat the reverse actions may be taken if the real danger seems to be inflation, rather than an increase in unemployment and a decline in national income.

The built-in stabilizers thus provide an important line of defense against recessions. As the various Social Security programs have expanded in size and coverage, they have in fact increased the strength of this automatic defense against the possibility of recessionary forces becoming cumulative in a downward spiral, as in 1929–1933. These built-in stabilizers thus provide valuable time not only for the private economy to develop corrective actions but also for the possible need of discretionary government actions to be considered. Furthermore, these automatic stabilizers reverse direction as economic trends change direction, so they dampen somewhat a possible excess of speculative exuberance as an economic upswing moves strongly into a boom of major proportions.

## UNCONTROLLABLE BUDGET OUTLAYS

Although certain government expenditures tend to move inversely to the general level of economic activity, many other expenditures have become insensitive to such changes in output and employment. Furthermore, the percentage of relatively uncontrollable budget outlays (e.g., **entitlement programs** such as various parts of the Social Security System, have been rising in recent fiscal years). By FY 1981, more than two thirds of government outlays might have been so categorized.

Some of these outlays might change in a stabilizing manner, but many other types of government expenditures simply rise year after year. This is true not only for the various entitlement programs but is especially true for interest rate payments on the government debt. These have risen in recent years not only because of large and rising budget deficits, but also because of rising market rates of interest. The greatest amount of reliance on automatic fiscal policy must therefore be placed on the substantial variation in tax revenues, as personal and corporate income change in response to changes in economic activity.

***Framework for Stabilizing Fiscal Policy*** If major reliance were placed on a stabilizing budget policy as the major tool of fiscal policy, certain changes from present budgetary practice would be necessary. Estimates of tax revenue, whether from existing taxes or proposed new taxes, would have to be based on full employment income rather than the present forecasts of expected national income in the fiscal year ahead. It would also have to be generally agreed that a certain modest surplus in the budget would be the target for a full employment level of economic activity.

Some reform for the generation of income for the government might also be undertaken, so that a greater reliance would be placed on progressive taxes, such as the progressive income tax and less reliance placed on regressive taxes such as the various excise taxes and import duties. Although three-fifths of all tax revenue accruing to the federal government in the 1980s comes from corporation and individual income taxes, two fifths of the federal revenue comes from taxes less sensitive to changes in income. A truly stabilizing budget policy should utilize to the maximum income taxes, which would increase tax revenue substantially to the government in a period of rising income and result in substantial declines in tax revenues in periods of declining national income. Both personal and corporate income taxes do have this characteristic in common.

## Discretionary Fiscal Policy Still Needed

Despite the attractiveness of the foregoing automatic stabilizer approach, there may be conditions when it is necessary to use a discretionary approach to fiscal policy, particularly if the policy orientation is not simply full employment in the business cycle sense but rather attainment of as high a rate of economic growth as possible for the economy without inflationary excesses. Inasmuch as it may prove impossible to predict exactly the growth in private consumer and investment demand over a long period, even if population forecasts and forecasts of the rate of new family formation prove to be reasonably accurate, it may be necessary to introduce discretionary tax changes from time to time in order to continue a period of noninflationary economic expansion already underway.

This was the justification for the tax cuts enacted by Congress in the spring of 1964. The economy was not then in a period of economic recession, nor did it appear that it would be soon. In fact, the period was one of substantial economic growth. There was a danger, however, that this rate of economic growth might slow down if some fiscal policy stimulus were not provided. Rather than increase the level of government expenditures, which was one possibility, the administration of President Johnson chose to recommend to Congress a two-stage income tax cut that would benefit both consumers and business firms. This fiscal policy experiment seems to have been successful in retrospect, inasmuch as the long upswing then underway was continued. New vigor in spending was injected in the boom. Not until 1965 did the unemployment rate fall to such a low level that production was pressing against capacity in a number of industries. Under these conditions, various industries posted price increases.

## Inflation Led to 1968 Surtax

The rate of inflation continued to increase after 1965, as government expenditures rose to supply military requirements for an expanded American role in Vietnam. Nonmilitary government spending also increased. Tax revenues were increasing as a result of higher levels of national income, but these revenues were not increasing as rapidly as government spending. This rising gap between spending requirements and tax revenues resulted in the large budget deficit of more than $25 billion in FY 1968.

Finally, Congress acceded to presidential recommendations and passed a temporary 10 percent surcharge on income taxes as of July 1, 1968. This surcharge, curbs on rising government spending, and the continued growth in tax revenues in a growing economy helped to bring about a small budget surplus in FY 1969, though the inflationary pressures that had been generated earlier were not thereby quickly eliminated because of lags between the new policies and their full economic impacts. Both the lag problem and the potency of impact problem were recognized in a number of studies in the late 1960s.

## FISCAL POLICY IMPACTS

One of these studies was in the form of an elaborate **econometric model** developed by the staff of the Board of Governors of the Federal Reserve System (FRB) and academic economists under the leadership of Professors Albert Ando and Franco Modigliani of the Massachusetts Institute of Technology (MIT). This model was constructed after the mid-1960s to measure the role of monetary and fiscal policies in the determination of gross national product. This FRB-MIT model, now called the Social Science Research Council—MIT—Penn, or SMP model, revealed that an increase in federal government purchases of goods and services not accompanied by increased tax rates produces an increase in GNP of roughly three to four times the rise in federal spending.

The same model estimated that a 4 percent rise in the money supply brought about by Federal Reserve open market operations resulted in a 1 percent rise in current dollar GNP in one year, a 2½ percent increase in two years, and a nearly 3 percent increase in three years. Slower-changing fiscal policy had a quicker impact on the economy than monetary policy. The FRB-MIT model revealed a significant impact of such fiscal policy on GNP even in the first quarter following a fiscal action.

Although government spending in any phase of the business cycle has a significant impact on current dollar GNP, its effects on real GNP depend on the amount of unused productive capacity. If there is widespread unemployment and factories are not operating at their rated capacity, an increase in aggregate demand stimulated by a rise in government spending tends to have a substantial impact on real output and a smaller effect on the level of prices. If, however, the economy is already operating near full employment, a further rise in government spending has more inflationary impacts than in a recessionary period. In order to measure the probable impact of fiscal policy on the economy, it is thus necessary to look at the full employment, or high employment, budget surplus.

## HIGH EMPLOYMENT BUDGET SURPLUS

By the 1980s it was generally realized among students of fiscal policy that the amount of fiscal stimulus provided to the economy cannot be accurately measured by the realized budget surplus or deficit. Instead, it became necessary to estimate the budget position at a noninflationary, high employment level of the economy. Some discussions of this concept refer to it as the "full employment surplus," which would be the amount of the budget surplus if only 4 percent of the labor force were unemployed. Because the unemployment rate had dropped below 4 percent in the second half of the 1960s, the term **"high employment budget surplus"** was often substituted.

By estimating the expected budget surplus of different budget structures at a noninflationary high employment level of economic activity, it is possible to analyze the expected impact on the economy of such a planned total of tax revenues and government expenditures. One budget program can be regarded as more expansionary to the economy than another budget program if it has a smaller high employment budget surplus. If, for example, a projected tax structure and planned government expenditures would yield a surplus of $20 billion at a high employment level of income, this would mean that the government would be withdrawing $20 billion more from the income stream than it was putting back into it.

The dampening effects of such a high level of tax rates would make it difficult actually to reach the projected level of high employment income, unless private demand were strong. If private demand were weak, such a high employment budget surplus would mean that the actual budget surplus would be much smaller, or perhaps even in a deficit position. The expected level of tax revenues at high employment would be reached only if private demand were strong enough to take the economy to that level in the face of a restrictive budget policy.

If the high employment surplus is too large relative to expected private expenditures on goods and services, then production of goods and services, and hence real income, falls short of the productive potential of the economy. Thus a gap may develop between actual production and potential production. Furthermore, because of the shortfall in the productive performance of the economy, an actual deficit rather than a surplus may occur in the budget, because the economy never achieves full employment. On the other hand, too small a high employment surplus may result in inflationary overheating of the economy.

Inasmuch as the levels of GNP necessary to sustain full employment increase over time, both because of the growth in productive capacity resulting from continued real investment by business firms and because of a growth in the labor force, the high employment surplus has a tendency to increase over time. We should thus expect either a reduction in federal tax rates or an increase in federal expenditures to prevent serious fiscal drag developing over time that would result in a much lower growth rate than is possible by the productive capacity of the economy. Whatever the degree of fiscal drag, the Treasury must engage in debt management operations in each fiscal year.

## Treasury Debt Management Operations

The Treasury has run a generally growing budget deficit since fiscal year 1970, as noted already in Table 25–1. In virtually every fiscal year the Treasury must thus enter the credit markets for substantial amounts of new cash borrowings and it must also refund the large amounts of old debt falling due each year. Table 25–2 shows the consequences of many years of budget deficits, which was typical in most years even before the 1970s, in terms of the total debt and the amount of the various kinds of Treasury securities.

In the seven years shown in this table, the total government debt nearly doubled from the $532.1 billion at the end of 1975 to the $1,013.3 billion at the end of 1981. As a result of the large growth in the total debt, all types of government securities increased. Treasury bills outstanding rose from $128.6 billion in 1975 to $245.0 billion in 1981. Notes increased from $150.3 billion to $375.3 billion, while bonds outstanding rose from $36.8 billion to $99.9 billion. Marketable issues, on which the going market rate of interest must be paid, more than doubled from $315.6 billion in 1975 to $720.3 billion in 1981, while nonmarketable issues increased by only 50 percent, from $216.5 billion in 1975 to $307.0 billion in 1981.

## Selling Marketable Securities

Because nearly two thirds of the federal debt consists of **marketable securities,** let us now focus our discussion on these types of securities and on techniques of selling them in the credit markets. The three types of marketable Treasury securities, bills, notes, and bonds, are distin-

**Table 25–2   Public Debt Securities Outstanding (In billions of dollars)**

| End of year | 1975 | 1976 | 1977 | 1978 | 1979 | 1980 | 1981 |
|---|---|---|---|---|---|---|---|
| Total interest-bearing debt | 532.1 | 619.3 | 718.2 | 782.4 | 844.0 | 928.9 | 1,027.3 |
| Nonmarketable issues | 216.5 | 226.7 | 255.3 | 294.8 | 313.2 | 305.7 | 307.0 |
| Marketable issues | 315.6 | 392.6 | 459.9 | 487.5 | 530.7 | 623.2 | 720.3 |
| Treasury bills | 128.6 | 161.2 | 161.1 | 161.7 | 172.6 | 216.1 | 245.0 |
| Notes | 150.3 | 191.8 | 251.8 | 265.8 | 283.4 | 321.6 | 375.3 |
| Bonds | 36.8 | 39.6 | 47.0 | 60.0 | 74.7 | 85.4 | 99.9 |

SOURCE: Board of Governors of the Federal Reserve System, *Federal Reserve Bulletins*, July 1977, p. A30; Sept. 1980, p. A32; Aug. 1981, p. A30, March 1982, p. A32.

**Table 25–3   Issues of Marketable Treasury Securities, 1970–1976 (In billions of dollars)**

| Fiscal Years | 1970 | 1971 | 1972 | 1973 | 1974 | 1975 | 1976 |
|---|---|---|---|---|---|---|---|
| | *Gross Amounts Issued (Par Value)* | | | | | | |
| Total marketable securities | 226.1 | 252.2 | 278.2 | 277.3 | 285.2 | 356.4 | 447.7 |
| Treasury bills | 191.4 | 209.2 | 243.6 | 244.2 | 262.9 | 295.2 | 367.0 |
| Regular weekly (3- and 6-month) | 155.3 | 172.4 | 211.3 | 218.4 | 224.7 | 253.4 | 317.9 |
| Regular monthly (52-week) | 19.4 | 20.4 | 20.4 | 21.2 | 23.4 | 26.5 | 38.8 |
| All other | 16.7 | 16.4 | 11.9 | 4.5 | 14.8 | 15.7 | 10.3 |
| Cash management | — | — | — | — | — | — | 8.3 |
| Notes and bonds | 34.7 | 42.9 | 34.6 | 33.2 | 22.3 | 61.1 | 80.7 |
| Yield auctions | — | — | — | — | — | 43.9 | 64.9 |
| Price auctions | — | 4.3 | 16.2 | 17.4 | 22.3 | 17.3 | 2.6 |
| Subscription offerings | 10.7 | 3.4 | — | — | — | — | 13.2 |
| Exchange offerings | 24.0 | 35.2 | 18.4 | 15.7 | — | — | — |
| | *Net Funds Raised* | | | | | | |
| Total marketable securities | 6.4 | 12.8 | 11.8 | 5.8 | 3.6 | 49.0 | 77.0 |
| Treasury bills | 7.8 | 10.4 | 8.0 | 5.4 | 5.0 | 23.6 | 32.6 |
| Regular weekly (3- and 6-month) | 5.2 | 7.4 | 11.6 | 3.1 | 2.2 | 19.8 | 21.6 |
| Regular monthly (52-week) | 0.8 | 1.0 | 0 | 2.5 | 0.2 | 4.9 | 12.3 |
| All other | 1.8 | 2.0 | –3.6 | –0.2 | 2.6 | –0.9 | –1.6 |
| Notes and bonds | –1.3 | 2.4 | 3.8 | 0.4 | –1.4 | 25.5 | 44.3 |
| Yield auctions | — | — | — | — | — | 22.2 | 38.2 |
| Price auctions | — | 4.3 | 7.2 | 3.5 | –0.4 | 4.0 | 1.6 |
| Subscription offerings | 2.2 | 2.3 | — | — | — | — | 5.5 |
| Cash redemptions | –3.6 | –4.3 | –3.5 | –3.2 | –1.0 | –0.8 | –0.9 |

SOURCE: Federal Reserve Bank of Kansas City, *Monthly Review*, July–Aug. 1977, p. 16.

guishable mainly by their period to maturity at the time of issuance. All Treasury bills are one year or less at original maturity and are either from less than one month in maturity (cash management), three-month, six-month, or 52-week. Notes are U.S. government coupon issues, which have an original maturity from two to ten years. Bonds are long-term issues with an original maturity of more than seven years from the date of issue.

The amount of marketable Treasury securities outstanding and the amount of net funds raised from 1970 to 1976 is given in Table 25–3. Despite the steady growth in such securities outstanding, it was not until fiscal year 1975 that the amount of Treasury financing reached really large proportions. As a result of borrowing needs in 1975 and 1976 (see Table 25–3), the gross amount of Treasury bills issued rose from the $191.4 billion in 1970 to $367 billion in 1976. Notes and bonds issued likewise rose sharply from the $34.7 billion issued in 1970 to $80.7 billion in 1976. It was the decline in tax revenues as a result of the severe recession of 1974–1975, and the continued rise in government expenditures that resulted in such large borrowing needs in 1975 and 1976.

The federal government continued to have large borrowing needs for the rest of the 1970s and into the 1980s, though net borrowing varied from year to year. In 1976, the government borrowed some $61.3 billion, which was down from 1975. In 1977 there was a further decline to $44.1 billion. After that, however, borrowing resumed its strong upward growth. Whereas only $51.3 billion was borrowed in 1978, a very large amount, $87.9 billion, was borrowed in 1979. This was even larger than the previous high in the 1970s of $75.7 billion in 1975. In 1980, however, the amount rose to $85 billion and soared to $98.5 billion in 1981. The other early years of the 1980s also looked as if they would be years of heavy government borrowing.

When the Treasury issues these marketable securities, they can be purchased directly from the Treasury or from its fiscal agents, the Federal Reserve Banks and branches. After the original issue, securities can be purchased from one of the government security dealers. Smaller purchases (less than the $1 million multiples typically traded in the government securities market) can usually be arranged through a commercial bank.

## INNOVATIONS IN DEBT MANAGEMENT

In order to raise the large sums of money needed, the Treasury in 1975 and 1976 adopted several policies designed to improve market reception of its new issues in the years ahead. The Treasury regularly informed the market of its estimates of financing needs and offered an even wider spectrum of maturities of debt on a regular basis. The Treasury was even able in 1976 to increase the average maturity of the debt outstanding, the first time since 1964 that the debt had been extended.

One of the reasons that it has always been difficult to increase the maturity of the debt is a law passed by Congress in 1919 that set a 4¼ percent interest rate ceiling on bonds. As a result of sharp rises in interest rates in 1966 and again in 1969, it became impossible to sell marketable bonds under this interest rate ceiling. Without being able to offer new longer maturities of debt, the average maturity of the debt outstanding would thus decline each year, which would ultimately greatly increase the problems of debt management for the Treasury.

As a result of this plight of the Treasury, Congress in 1971 passed a law exempting $10 billion of the total amount of government bonds from this ceiling. In 1976, the ceiling was raised to $30 billion and in 1982 to $100 billion. By January 31, 1977, the Federal Reserve Banks and government investment accounts held $11 billion of such bonds with coupon interest rates above 4¼ percent. Hence more than $40 billion of such marketable bonds were outstanding in early 1977.

In 1976 the maximum maturity of Treasury notes, which are not subject to the interest rate ceiling, was extended from seven to ten years. The greater freedom in the issuance of coupon securities led to greater use of these securities by the Treasury in its debt management operations. Hence monthly offerings of two-year notes began in February 1975 and later quarterly sales of four-year and five-year notes were added to the **financing schedule.** The Treasury continued to add to its offerings of Treasury bills, which are sold at a discount.

In 1976, for the first time in six years, the Treasury also made use of fixed price subscription issues, in which the coupon rates are set by the Treasury and the obligations are sold at par. In that year, one issue of seven-year notes and two issues of ten-year notes were offered in minimum denominations of $1,000, whereas Treasury bills are offered in a minimum amount of $10,000. The small amount of the minimum issue and the attractive coupon rates attracted a great diversity of buyers. Because the issues were heavily oversubscribed, the Treasury was able to raise $18.5 billion of funds, which was $7.5 billion more than the amount originally planned.

Another important innovation in Treasury debt management was the first issuance of cash management bills with a maturity of less than one month, in August 1975. These bills are also called federal funds bills or short-dated bills. Somewhat earlier, in December 1974, the Treasury discontinued its prior practice of issuing tax anticipation bills (TABs) and using additional issues of strips of outstanding series as a means of raising short-term funds in the bill market.

The cash management bill offering is announced one to ten days prior to the auction and only competitive tenders are invited. The offering is usually an additional amount of an outstanding issue with an original maturity of six months, although some additional amounts have been issued for original fifty-two-week maturity bills. The minimum acceptable bid is $10 million with increments of $1 million over that amount. Tenders are accepted only at Federal Reserve Banks and branches and in some cases may be submitted by wire or telephone.

The time between the auction and the date of issue ranges from one to five days. Payment must be made in immediately available funds (federal funds) on the date of the issue. Denominations issued, calculation of interest, and determination of acceptable competitive bids are all similar to the characteristics of a regular bill issue.

## HOLDERS OF TREASURY SECURITIES

The major holders of Treasury securities from 1972 to 1976 inclusive are shown in Table 25–4. Although households were the largest category

**Table 25–4** Holdings of Treasury Securities, 1972–1976 (In billions of dollars, at the year end)

| Sector | 1972 | 1973 | 1974 | 1975 | 1976 |
|---|---|---|---|---|---|
| Nonfinancial corporate business | 8.5 | 3.2 | 5.3 | 14.3 | 22.5 |
| Commercial banks | 68.0 | 59.2 | 56.6 | 85.4 | 102.8 |
| Thrift institutions | 9.2 | 6.2 | 5.6 | 10.1 | 13.4 |
| Savings and loan associations | 5.7 | 3.2 | 3.1 | 5.4 | 7.5 |
| Mutual savings banks | 3.5 | 3.0 | 2.6 | 4.7 | 5.9 |
| Households | 77.6 | 94.6 | 103.9 | 114.3 | 111.4 |
| Savings bonds | 57.7 | 60.4 | 63.3 | 67.4 | 72.0 |
| Other Treasury | 19.9 | 34.2 | 40.5 | 47.0 | 39.3 |
| Private pension funds and state and local government retirement funds | 6.5 | 5.6 | 4.7 | 10.1 | 16.0 |
| Insurance companies | 6.7 | 6.3 | 6.2 | 9.5 | 12.6 |
| State and local government general funds | 26.2 | 26.1 | 24.3 | 30.6 | 41.3 |
| Foreign | 54.4 | 54.8 | 58.4 | 66.5 | 76.6 |
| Federal Reserve | 69.9 | 78.5 | 80.5 | 87.9 | 97.0 |
| Other[a] | 4.5 | 5.0 | 5.9 | 8.6 | 13.0 |
| Total | 331.5 | 339.4 | 351.5 | 437.3 | 506.4 |

[a]The category "Other" consists of investment companies, money market funds, securities brokers and dealers, credit unions, and federally sponsored credit agencies.

SOURCE: Federal Reserve Bank of New York, *Quarterly Review*, Spring 1977, p. 22.

holding Treasury securities in each year, more than 60 percent of their holdings were in the form of savings bonds. Of the holders of marketable securities, the Federal Reserve ranked first in four of the five years, but in 1976 commercial banks regained their position as the largest holder of such securities. Foreign holders increased their portfolio of government securities each year, but in 1975 and 1976 nonfinancial corporate businesses, pension funds, and insurance companies all added to their holdings of Treasury securities.

Similar information for holders of Treasury securities for the later period 1977–1980 inclusive is shown in Table 25–5. It should be noted, however, that the data here, which are taken directly from a *Federal Reserve Bulletin* are organized somewhat differently. Some detail in the earlier table was reported differently for the later years (e.g., nonfinancial corporate business holdings are reported as "other companies").

In the four years from 1977 to 1980 shown in Table 25–5, there seems to have been less volatility in holdings of Treasury securities for the different categories of holders than was evident for the five earlier years presented in Table 25–4. Some increase and decrease in holdings of such securities did occur for commercial banks, mutual savings banks,

Table 25–5    Holdings of Treasury Securities, 1977–1980 (In billions of dollars, at year end)

| Sector | 1977 | 1978 | 1979 | 1980 |
|---|---|---|---|---|
| Private investors | 461.3 | 508.6 | 540.5 | 616.4 |
| Commercial banks | 101.4 | 93.1 | 91.5 | 104.7 |
| Mutual savings banks | 5.9 | 5.0 | 4.7 | 5.8 |
| Insurance companies | 15.1 | 14.9 | 14.8 | 15.2 |
| Other companies | 22.7 | 21.2 | 24.9 | 24.6 |
| State and local governments | 55.2 | 64.4 | 67.4 | 74.7 |
| Individuals | 105.3 | 111.0 | 116.1 | 128.9 |
| Savings bonds | 76.7 | 80.7 | 79.9 | 72.2 |
| Other securities | 28.6 | 30.3 | 36.2 | 56.7 |
| Foreign and international | 109.6 | 137.8 | 123.8 | 134.3 |
| Other miscellaneous investors[a] | 46.1 | 58.2 | 97.4 | 127.9 |

[a]Includes savings and loan associations, nonprofit institutions, corporate pension trust funds, dealers and brokers, certain government deposit accounts, and government-sponsored agencies.

SOURCE: Board of Governors of the Federal Reserve System, *Federal Reserve Bulletin*, Aug. 1981, p. A30, 1.41.

and even for the large category of foreign and international investors in this period. Interest rate differentials between the interest rate prevailing on new marketable government securities and that available on corporate and other debt, of course, determined the relative desirability of holding these alternative interest-earning assets.

But for most categories of Treasury security holders, each year recorded approximately the same or a larger amount held than the year before. Commercial banks at the end of the period held approximately what they held at the beginning of it, which was also true for mutual savings banks, insurance companies, and other companies. Private investors, on the other hand, held nearly 50 percent more in 1980 than they did in 1977. The same was approximately true for state and local governments. Foreign investors held nearly 20 percent more, whereas other miscellaneous investors had nearly tripled their holdings.

In general, one would attribute the strong growth in holdings of Treasury securities by many holders to the substantial increase in the government debt in this period. There were also much higher interest rates paid on this marketable debt at the end of the period, as contrasted with the lower interest rates in the mid-1970s, before total government debt began to expand so rapidly. Let us now turn to various principles governing the sale of new marketable Treasury securities in a year when the budget is in deficit.

## OBJECTIVES OF DEBT MANAGEMENT

One basic problem of debt management obviously is to be able to sell enough new kinds of securities in a period of budget deficit in order to accomplish the cash financing needed. Another basic requirement is to refund old debt falling due, when there is no budget surplus or the surplus is inadequate to pay off debt at maturity. At the same time, the Treasury wishes its cash financing and refunding operations to be consistent with public policies of stabilization and growth pursued by the Federal Reserve and other parts of the federal government. Therefore both marketing and public policy considerations must govern the principles of debt management followed in any given period by the Treasury.

Orthodox debt management principles prescribe that a federal budget deficit in a recession period should be financed by the issuance of Treasury bills or other short-term government securities. In a boom period, the debt should be funded both by having the Treasury use a budget surplus to retire short-term debt, especially that held by commercial banks and the Federal Reserve, and by issuing long-term securities in refunding operations. If these principles of countercyclical debt management are followed, debt operations reinforce the drag of a fiscal surplus desired in an inflationary period and increase the liquidity of the economy in a period of recession, thus assisting the stimulating effects of a budget deficit. The reverse of such countercyclical debt management policies would mean that some of the potency would be taken out of the employment of countercyclical fiscal policies.

### *The Least-Cost Objective*

Although one objective of debt management can be the stabilization and growth of the overall economy, sometimes the Treasury may appear to be narrowly focused on its particular problems of selling new debt issues in the most economical and efficient way possible to minimize the technical borrowing problems of the Treasury. Whenever the Treasury is concerned only with financing itself at the least cost, the greatest possibilities exist that the Treasury's debt management operations will be **procyclical** rather than countercyclical. The least-cost criterion would mean that the Treasury would concentrate on offering short-terms in the upswing of the cycle and long-terms in the downswing, even though this cyclical pattern of debt management will not conform with the objectives of a stabilizing fiscal policy. Furthermore, such procyclical debt management also conflicts with countercyclical monetary policies usually followed by the Federal Reserve.

*Adverse Cyclical Effects of Least-Cost Debt Management*    Whenever private borrowing demands are high and rising, as they typically are in the upswing of the business cycle, the likelihood is that interest costs too will increase. This is particularly so if the Federal Reserve does not continue to expand the bank reserve base of bank credit in the expansionary way that it probably did in a prior slower period of economic growth or decline in economic activity. Therefore if the Treasury is to avoid the costly competition of meeting the higher interest rates in the long area of the market, as profit-oriented companies are willing to do in a period of expanding sales, it should refrain from offering long-terms in the upswing of the cycle and restrict itself to the short or money market part of the credit markets. If, however, the Treasury follows this kind of policy for its own convenience and economy in selling its debt, it will be sharply increasing the supply of liquid instruments—Treasury bills—at the very time that the Federal Reserve is desirous of restraining a growth in such highly liquid assets to prevent inflationary tendencies from developing in the economy. Also, by withdrawing from the capital markets, the Treasury is also removing a pressure for increasing long-term interest rates, which, again, may be contrary to Federal Reserve desires of increasing long-term interest rates as an anti-inflationary device.

On the other hand, during a period of economic decline and falling private demand for borrowed funds, the resulting decline in interest rates in all areas of the market, including the long end, may tempt the Treasury to force its bonds onto the market at a time when it appears that conditions for selling them at a low net cost to the Treasury are good. When this kind of cost minimization is a dominant factor in the thinking of the Treasury's debt managers, the result may be quite costly to the stabilization efforts of the Federal Reserve and other parts of the federal government.

## Lengthening the Federal Debt

For much of the period since World War II the Treasury has seemed desirous of trying to lengthen the maturity of the outstanding federal debt at all times when it could be accomplished. This can be attributed in part to a preference for making as few refunding trips to the market as could be arranged and in part to the fact that the mere passage of time is always working to shorten the debt. In the Treasury Survey of Ownership, for example, at the end of 1980, $297 billion of marketable federal debt, or nearly half of the $623 billion gross federal debt reported in the Treasury Survey, was in securities maturing within one year. And when the Treasury is running a deficit, as it usually seems to do, new cash borrowings must also be undertaken. It is no wonder that the Treasury would like to reduce somewhat the volume and strain of these frequent borrowings. The Treasury must refund short-term debt falling due as well as sell new debt to finance the ongoing budget deficit.

Part of the pressure operating toward always trying to lengthen the debt can be reduced somewhat when the Treasury places as much of the short-term debt as possible on a regular schedule of **bill "rollovers."** Much progress in recent years in this direction has been achieved.

### Regular Treasury Financings

Regular Treasury borrowings are needed, therefore, both for refunding outstanding debt falling due as well as new cash borrowings needed to finance current budget deficit requirements. Hence, by mid-1982, the Treasury was borrowing nearly $10 billion each week in equal amounts of 91-day and 182-day Treasury bills sold at a Monday auction and dated the following Thursday. Each month about $5 billion was being sold in an auction of 52-week Treasury bills.

Each quarter there is a combined offering of notes and bonds. In May 1981, for example, the Treasury sold $3 billion in three-year notes, $1.75 billion in ten-year notes, and $2 billion in thirty-year bonds. Although the amounts sold each quarter change, there is a common pattern. In anticipation of tax revenue to be received, the Treasury also sells varying amounts of very short maturities (less than thirty-days) of cash-management bills each quarter. The maturities can vary from fifteen or sixteen days to twenty to twenty-two days. For example, on March 30, 1982, the Treasury sold at auction $8.02 billion of twenty-day cash-management bills. These bills were dated April 2 and matured April 22. The two prior sales of such cash-management bills were the end of December and the end of August respectively.

## TREASURY DEBT MANAGEMENT OPERATIONS AND TREASURY–FEDERAL RESERVE INTERRELATIONSHIPS

In the conduct of debt management operations, either for new cash financing or in the refunding of outstanding debt, the Treasury and the Federal Reserve interact to influence the policies of each other. The market environment existing in the money and capital markets is largely established by the prevailing Federal Reserve policy of credit ease or restraint. The Treasury must compete in its borrowings with all other borrowing needs without direct underwriting assistance from the Federal Reserve. The Treasury, then, must adapt its offerings in respect to rate of interest, maturity, and offering techniques to the availability and cost of funds in the market as determined by the Federal Reserve and by private sources and uses of funds. Even if the Federal Reserve is regarded as being a marginal participant in this total complex of credit markets, it can still be a decisive influence if it desires.

On the other hand, it must be admitted that the Federal Reserve in establishing its monetary and credit policies is unavoidably influenced by Treasury debt policies. Because the Treasury may at times be the principal demand factor in the credit markets, the credit-supplying function of the Federal Reserve will in these instances necessarily be affected by Treasury financings. The Federal Reserve prefers to try to follow an **"even keel" policy** immediately preceding and during periods of a Treasury financing operation. This even keel policy means that the Federal Reserve will not change its prevailing monetary policy during such periods of Treasury financings. The Treasury often comes to market four or five times a year with large refunding operations, with occasional cash financing trips interspersed in the intervening months. Hence it is likely to be a rare quarter of the year that the timing or implementation of Federal Reserve policies is not affected by Treasury debt management decisions.

## Federal Reserve Financing Aid to Dealers

To avoid a permanent commitment of added reserves to the banking system, the Federal Reserve may extend repurchase agreements to government security dealers needing additional credit accommodation during a sizable government financing operation. For the week ending July 22, 1981, as an example, the Federal Reserve supplied about 50 percent of the dealers' total financing requirements in this way, and during a large Treasury borrowing operation the percentage may run even somewhat higher. In a sense, therefore, one might argue that the Federal Reserve sometimes indirectly underwrites a Treasury financing operation through the credit assistance extended to the government security dealers who directly buy, and then resell, the new debt offerings of the Treasury.

When the Federal Reserve does extend such repurchase agreements to the dealers, the maturity of such an agreement over a period may range from one to fifteen calendar days. U.S. government securities that mature in two years or less or bankers' acceptances maturing in six months or less are acceptable collateral for such contracts. The interest cost paid by the dealer for such credit is usually the discount rate at the New York Reserve Bank, because it may not be lower than the discount rate of that Bank or the issuing rate on the latest issue of three-month bills, whichever is the lower.

## Underwriters of New Treasury Issues

In the issuance of new short- and intermediate-term Treasury issues for cash, and sometimes in long-term cash issues, commercial banks are the principal **underwriters,** whereas the government security dealers are more likely to perform the principal underwriting for the Treasury's refunding operations. In such Treasury cash financings, therefore, the commercial banks may sometimes be given the privilege by the Treasury of crediting part of the cost of a new short-term cash purchase of new Treasury securities to the tax and loan accounts maintained by the Treasury with most of the commercial banks in this country. When this crediting privilege is not available for a given issue and undue pressure builds up in the money market, member commercial banks can resort to the discount window of their regional Reserve Bank to ease the pressure on bank reserves.

In providing such funds to banks, the Federal Reserve System is acting in an indirect way as a partial underwriter of new Treasury borrowings. Occasionally, the system will even anticipate the possibility of some pressures building up in the money market during a large Treasury financing and provide some added ease to the banking system in the several weeks prior to such an operation. No matter how pure its intentions or how independent its motives, the Federal Reserve cannot escape the impact of large-scale debt management operations conducted by the Treasury on the formulation and execution of its monetary policies.

### Possible Conflicts Between Debt Management and Monetary Policy

Inappropriate debt management policies by the Treasury can, moreover, partly offset the intended countercyclical monetary policies of the Federal Reserve. If the Treasury relies heavily on increased bill tenders in the upswing of the business cycle, the increase in the stock of near-money assets thus furnished, as earlier indicated, may provide the total economy with more liquidity than is desirable, even though the Federal Reserve may be slowing down the rate of growth of the most liquid asset of all, money. On the other hand, attempts of the monetary authorities to splash the economy with more cash in order to bottom out a recession period may be partly thwarted. This can happen if the Treasury insists on offsetting policies of reducing the liquidity characteristics of its outstanding debt by shifting the term structure of the debt more into the long-term area by forcing the capital markets with substantially increased new bond issues. Possible conflict between these two institutions may also arise if each is following a different set of policies as to the appropriate acquisition or retirement of government debt as between banks and nonbanks.

A budget surplus in the upswing of the business cycle is usually regarded as having a dampening effect on possible inflationary forces, but it is sometimes overlooked that retirement of outstanding Treasury debt releases to the capital market funds that would not otherwise be available. If the Federal Reserve is putting pressure on bank reserve positions, it is likely that it will be bank-held debt that is reduced, thus providing the banks with additional loanable funds. On the other hand, the new Treasury securities issued to finance a budget deficit in a period of economic recession will probably largely find their way into bank portfolios, because the Federal Reserve is invariably providing the banking system with new reserves in recession periods.

If the Treasury runs a deficit in the upswing of the cycle, as well as in the downswing, the addition of net Treasury demand for credit to that already existing on the part of private and other public borrowers could force the Federal Reserve either to permit a greater increase in money and credit than it would like to see, or else to permit a greater restriction on the availability of funds to these other borrowers than is justified by economic conditions at that time. The Treasury will always be able to secure the borrowed funds it needs, whereas this is not always true of every unit of state and local governments, which are often subject to legal interest rate ceilings, and it is also not true for all private borrowers. The Treasury itself, as earlier noted, is subject to a legal ceiling of 4½ percent on its new bonds, but there is no ceiling on the interest rate that it can pay for obligations of ten years or under. Inasmuch as a potential market demand for these highly liquid securities always exists, the Treasury by one financing technique or another can always finance whatever budget deficit there is.

***Treasury Debt Mix Affects Velocity of Money***     The change in the mix of Treasury securities outstanding may also have impacts on the velocity of money that are not desired by the central banking authorities. For instance, a slowdown in the expansion of the money supply called for by restrictive anti-inflationary policies of the Federal Reserve could be partially offset if an expansion in near-money is permitted by the Treasury. An increase in the amount of Treasury bills outstanding, by increasing the supply of close money substitutes, permits economizing on the use of the available stock of money for both transactions and asset purposes.

Any economizing in the use of money balances, as revealed in a decline in such money balances to total transactions, is reflected in a greater turnover of money balances. Hence the flow of money expenditures can remain constant or even increase in a period of restraint on the growth of the stock of money. Contrariwise, in a period when the central bank wishes greater liquidity and a larger amount of money expenditures in the total economy, an increase in the stock of money can be partially offset by a decline in its velocity, if the total amount of money substitutes is also declining. Although there are other near-money assets besides those provided by the Treasury, an important form of near-money is short-term government securities, so that an important influence over the velocity of money is in the hands of the debt managers of the Treasury.

## Questions for Discussion

1. Discuss the concept of fiscal policy and indicate how it has developed in complexity in recent years as it has moved from stabilization over the business cycle to the promotion of economic growth.
2. Discuss the relationship between fiscal policy and the supply of money. How does this relationship change if the Federal Reserve shifts from controlling interest rates to controlling the rate of growth of the monetary aggregates?
3. Discuss the four basic purposes of any national budget. Indicate how stress on different purposes at different times has led to different budget concepts being developed.
4. Discuss the coverage and basic purpose of the unified budget, first introduced in FY 1969. In what respects did it outmode earlier budget concepts?
5. Why do you believe budget deficits became so chronically large beginning in the mid-1970s? What impact on the budget deficit did the Reagan tax and budget cuts of 1981 have? What do you expect the budget deficit to be in the following years of the 1980s?
6. Discuss the basic principles of supply-side economics and their implementation in the budget changes of 1981. How do you expect that these newer fiscal policies will work in practice?
7. From the viewpoint of more traditional fiscal policy (i.e., aggregate demand management), how may fiscal policy restrain aggregate demand in a period of inflation such as the late 1970s and early 1980s? In what respect did inadequate fiscal policy contribute to a build-up of inflationary pressures in the late 1970s?
8. Discuss the difference between discretionary and automatic fiscal policy after first defining each concept. Why do built-in stabilizers work automatically over the business cycle? Examine these two different types of fiscal policy in some phase of a business cycle, and discuss the lag problem of fiscal policy.
9. Discuss the meaning and use of the full employment or high employment surplus. How does this concept fit in with either automatic or discretionary fiscal policy?

10. Discuss some of the important innovations in the conduct of debt management by the Treasury in the mid-1970s. In what important ways, and why, has the composition of Treasury securities outstanding changed in the last decade or so?
11. How can the Federal Reserve affect the conduct and success or failure of an exchange offer or a cash borrowing by the Treasury? Should the Federal Reserve, directly or indirectly, underwrite the Treasury? Why? How does the liquidity position of the banking system and the borrowing resources of the dealers affect the success of debt management operations?
12. What are the possible impacts of a Treasury surplus or deficit in the budget on the money and capital markets, as distinct from the purely fiscal policy effects on private expenditures of such a surplus or deficit? Explain your answer.

# Selected Bibliography for Further Reading

AHEARN, DANIEL S., *Federal Reserve Policy Reappraised 1951–1959* (New York: Columbia University Press, 1963).

BANYAS, LAWRENCE, "New Techniques in Debt Management Since the Late 1950's," *Treasury-Federal Reserve Study of the U.S. Government Securities Market* (Washington, D.C.: Board of Governors of the Federal Reserve System, mimeographed, 1967).

BEDFORD, MARGARET E., "Recent Developments in Treasury Financing Techniques," *Monthly Review*, Federal Reserve Bank of Kansas City, July–Aug. 1977, pp. 12–24.

BOARD OF GOVERNORS, FEDERAL RESERVE SYSTEM, "Fiscal Policy and Debt Management," *Federal Reserve Bulletin*, Nov. 1965, pp. 1507–1517.

BROCKSCHMIDT, PEGGY, "Treasury Cash Balances," *Monthly Review*, Federal Reserve Bank of Kansas City, July–Aug. 1975, pp. 12–20.

CACY, J.A., "Budget Deficits and the Money Supply," *Monthly Review*, Federal Reserve Bank of Kansas City, June 1975, pp. 3–9.

ECKSTEIN, OTTO, *Public Finance* (Englewood Cliffs, N.J.: Prentice-Hall, 1964).

FEDERAL RESERVE BANK OF KANSAS CITY, *The Federal Budget and Economic Activity* (Kansas City: 1969).

FEDERAL RESERVE BANK OF NEW YORK, *Essays in Domestic and International Finance* (New York: 1969).

GAINES, TILLFORD, *Treasury Debt Management* (New York: Columbia University Press, 1960).

HOTEL, ARLINE, "Financing the Federal Deficit in 1975 and 1976," Federal Reserve Bank of New York, *Quarterly Review*, Vol. 2, Spring, 1977, pp. 19–22.

POLLOCK, STEPHEN H., "Off-Budget Federal Outlays, "*Economic Review*, Federal Reserve Bank of Kansas City, March 1981, pp. 3–15.

The quantity of such commodities, therefore, remaining the same, or nearly the same, while the competition to purchase them is continually increasing, their price may rise to any degree of extravagance, and seems not to be limited by any certain boundary.

**THE WEALTH OF NATIONS**

## 26
# CHAPTER

# The Problem of Inflation

The great challenge to monetary-fiscal policy in the 1980s seems to be facilitating an optimum rate of economic growth that can produce desired low levels of unemployment while at the same time preventing the rate of inflation from exceeding an acceptable rate. In the nearly two decades beginning in 1965, the problem of controlling inflation seemed to be a particularly difficult one for traditional fiscal and monetary tools. Public impatience with annual rates of increase in consumer prices, which averaged about 2.7 percent in the mid-1960s and had accelerated to 12 percent by 1974, led to experimentation with an incomes policy to be achieved by imposing wage and price controls in a series of "phases," which began in mid-August 1971. Even higher rates of inflation were experienced in 1979 and 1980, but the earlier experiment with wage and price controls was not repeated.

Although these direct controls seemed initially to have some success in restraining the upward movement of prices, by the time that Phase III and Phase IV were introduced in 1973, the increase in consumer prices had accelerated to an annual rate of 8 percent for the twelve months ending in December 1973. Wholesale commodity prices were rising at a rate of 18 percent, so that the rate of inflation in 1973 was worse than before the imposition of direct controls in 1971. In 1974, the inflation rate rose to 12 percent. Although the inflation rate did cool off somewhat in 1975 and 1976, when it fell to 7 percent and 4.8 percent, respectively, it was still uncomfortably high in terms of past experience. Furthermore, consumer prices rose by 6.8 percent in 1977 and by 9 percent in 1978. The years 1979 and 1980 had double-digit inflation rates of 13.3 percent and 12.4 percent, respectively. Not until 1981 did the inflation rate fall again below the double-digit level to an 8.9 percent rate.

The problem of inflation seemed to be a chronic one likely to trouble all the 1980s, even though the early years of the decade had lower rates of inflation than was typical of some years in the 1970s. An understanding of the causes of inflation, even before an analysis of the proposed cures, thus seems in order for the student of monetary economics. Inflation affects not only the value of money but also the banking system and other financial institutions, the balance of payments, and, indeed, it seems intertwined with almost all macroeconomic problems.

## FIVE INDICATORS OF INFLATION

One of the leading observers of inflation in the United States is Geoffrey H. Moore, the Director of Business Cycle Research at the National Bureau of Economic Research. In an article published in 1977, Moore summarized certain little-known facts about inflation. The first major point is that inflation is closely related to the business cycle. When real output of goods and services is increasing, so too is the rate of inflation. When there is a recession in economic activity, or sometimes even a slower rate of growth in real output, then the rate of inflation tends to decline. The price level is always increasing every year, largely because of a shift in the mix of goods and services toward an increasing emphasis on services; but the rate of increase in prices varies substantially from year to year.

Second, food price inflation is also closely related to the business cycle. When employment is rising and the unemployment rate is falling, more food is being purchased at the retail level and prices on such food tend to rise. The reverse is true when employment is falling, because a smaller number of employed workers buy less food. Even though unemployed workers still usually receive some income and even food stamps, their weekly spending on food will be less than when they were employed. In technical economic terms, the supply of food is relatively inelastic, whereas the demand for food is income elastic.

Third, the average index of **producer prices** (PPI) is *not* a good forecaster of future consumer prices. Only about 30 percent of the PPI is directly related to prices paid by consumers. Furthermore, the increasingly important component of the **Consumer Price Index** (CPI), which is services, is not even included in the PPI. That part of the PPI which is most useful as a leading indicator for the consumer price index is the PPI for crude materials, excluding foods, feeds, and fibers.

Fourth, the employment ratio is a better indicator of inflationary pressures than is the unemployment rate. The employment ratio is the percentage of the population of working age that have jobs. The unemployment rate can even rise on occasion when the employment ratio is rising if more people decide to enter the labor force (i.e., look for jobs). If the number of people employed rise, the price level is likely to rise also, because the labor market is now tighter. This is true even though the unemployment rate might seem to be high as compared with past experience.

Finally, forecasts, even by economists, of the future rate of inflation have not been notably accurate. The best first approximation of the inflation rate for next year is that it will be the same rate as this year. (This is the same principle of predicting that the weather tomorrow will be the same as the weather today.)

Nevertheless, this kind of a forecast, which is based on inertia in economic forces, will almost invariably miss the turns in the rate of inflation. If the inflation rate accelerates or decelerates next year, such a forecast will be clearly wrong. Summaries of inflation forecasts after World War II show that they typically lag turns in the inflation rate by about six months.


## EXCESS AGGREGATE DEMAND AND INFLATION

The traditional explanation of inflation is that it is caused by **excess aggregate demand** when the economy is operating at a level of high employment. This is sometimes summarized as "too many dollars chasing too few goods." In this classic **demand-pull inflation,** an increase in the quantity of money resulting from a budget deficit, or from a multiple expansion of demand deposits by the banking system, is almost always a contributory factor. The quantity theory of money is an example of such a demand-pull theory of inflation, as is the inflationary gap hypothesis in Keynesian economics.


### Cash Balances and Money Spending

Because traditional economic theory expected the economy to be at the full employment level if it was in general equilibrium, it would follow that any increase in money spending could only increase the general level of money prices. Furthermore, if the various sectors of the economy are in equilibrium, they would already have the cash balances in relation to income that they desired. Any increase in the stock of money, therefore, would mean that households and business firms would have redundant cash balances. To reduce their cash balances to the desired portfolio level, spending units would increase their money expenditures.

Such a rising flow of money spending would increase the prices of final goods and services and would also subsequently increase the prices of the various inputs needed to produce these goods and services. This would follow, because the demand for the factors of production is derived from the demand for the final product, and prices and wages were assumed to be flexible in the upward directon. If the output of goods and services is already being produced by the economy in maximum amounts (full employment), then inevitably an increase in the money supply will be reflected rather quickly in an inflation in the price level. Hence the value of the individual unit of money was inversely related to its quantity, because an increase in the quantity of money by raising the price level has the effect of reducing the value of each individual unit of money. This also assumes that the velocity of money is constant.

At times it was not always clear how an increased quantity of money found its way into the spending channels of the economic system, but at the hands of later proponents of the quantity theory, these channels were more specifically spelled out. The argument often made was that whenever the banks possessed more lending power, usually through a greater quantity of monetary reserves, they would be more liberal in extending loans to businesses at lower rates of interest. Because it was usually assumed that the typical business firm had a high elasticity of demand for borrowed funds, it was expected that more firms would wish to borrow bank funds when the interest cost on them was lowered.

When the business firm increased its debt at a bank, it was expected that the borrowed funds would be quickly spent. Likewise, when the government increased its spending in excess of its tax receipts (deficit spending), more money in the form of either paper money or demand deposits of banks could be created. With the creation of added money as a result of private or government borrowing, added spending would occur. In either case, however, if more physical output of goods and services is not forthcoming, prices will rise.

## MONEY AND INFLATION

The particular, and often critical, relationship between growth in the money supply and inflation in the price level has been recognized by many economists. For example, Gottfried Haberler states: "Inflation is a monetary phenomenon in the sense that there has never been a serious inflation without an increase in the quantity of money and that a serious inflation cannot be slowed or stopped without restrictions on monetary growth."[1]

A study by Robert Weintraub for a congressional subcommittee released in December 1976 makes the same point using a simple correlation of year-to-year changes in the consumer price level as explained by previous year-to-year changes in M1. For the period from 1953 to 1976 inclusive, about 60 percent of current year inflation could be explained by year-to-year changes in M1 occurring some twenty-three months earlier. In the highly inflationary 1966–1975 decade, more than 70 percent of the inflation experienced can be attributed to excessively rapid money growth.

An even longer lag was found by Richard Selden of the University of Virginia,[2] who found a long-term lag of thirteen quarters between monetary growth and subsequent inflation in the United States. This lag shortened, however, to about nine quarters in the 1970s, as the United States and many other countries seemed to become more sensitive to inflationary pressures.

Part of this increased sensitivity was the result of a strong tendency for the velocity of money to rise sharply, largely in response to high interest rates. Nevertheless, Selden found that monetary growth usually affected output and employment prior to the time that it affected prices. This helps to explain the political attractiveness of more expansionary monetary policies on the part of the central bank.

Although inflation may accelerate, as it did in 1973–1974 and again in 1979–1980, it may also slow down, as it did in 1975–1976 and in 1981–1982. In either case, the Weintraub study argues that it is changes in the money supply that are decisive. "There is a momentum in inflation, but it is not explosive, cumulative, or even constant. It comes to nothing after two years. Rather, no matter what triggers it and however rapid it becomes, money supply changes are decisive to whether inflation accelerates or is checked and subsides."[3]

However, in testimony by top Federal Reserve officials in mid-1974 before the same House Committee on Banking and Currency for which the Weintraub study was performed, a quite different emphasis was placed on the causes of the inflation in the United States since the

[1]Gottfried Haberler, "Some Currently Suggested Explanations and Cures for Inflation," *Institutional Arrangements and the Inflation Problem,* a supplement to the *Journal of Monetary Economics,* 3:143 (1976).

[2]Richard T. Selden, "Inflation: Are We Winning the Fight?", *The Morgan Guaranty Survey,* Oct. 1977, pp. 7–13.

[3]Robert Weintraub, *The Impact of the Federal Reserve System's Monetary Policies on the Nation's Economy* (Washington, D.C.: Staff Report of the Subcommittee on Domestic Monetary Policy of the Committee on Banking, Currency and Housing, House of Representatives, 1976), p. IV.

mid-1960s. President Howard Morris of the Federal Reserve Bank of Boston stated: "I think the primary causal force has been an excessively expansionary fiscal policy, beginning in late '65 and continuing to the present date."[4] Later on in his testimony, Morris indicated that he had had his staff use the St. Louis econometric model to see how much inflation this model would have predicted from the fourth quarter of 1972 to the fourth quarter of 1973 on the basis of the monetary growth rate and the fiscal policy of the government during that year. "The model indicated that we should have had an increase in the GNP deflator of 3.8 percent. The actual figure was 6.8 percent. The other 3 percent came from the shortage of food, the impact of the devaluation which was a major factor, and now the energy crisis."[5]

These Federal Reserve officials emphasized, as other nonmonetarists do, that even a stable growth in the money supply is not enough to guarantee a stable economy, because exogenous disturbances (e.g., the devaluation of 1971 and the energy crisis of 1973) can result in unpredicted inflation. Even so convinced a monetarist as Haberler observed that the relationship between changes in $M$ and $P$ in the equation $MV = PQ$ is not always close and precise, particularly in the short run where policy makers must operate.

"There is in the short run a sizable and variable lag between changes in $M$ and $P$; and there are longer-run structural changes in the correlation. In other words $V$, the velocity of circulation of money, although neither a volatile nor a plastic magnitude as Keynesians assume, is subject to change. It changes cyclically and it seems to have a secularly downward trend; occasionally it displays longer swings."[6] This does not mean that a stable, and lower, rate of growth in the money supply would not result in less inflation. But since inflation does occur in many economies, even if the causes are both monetary and nonmonetary, it is important to consider the effects of such inflation.

## Costs of Inflation

There are numerous **costs of inflation,** as well as some benefits to particular groups in the economy. Holders of cash balances, which are necessary for households and firms for transactions purposes in order to get from one time of receipt of income to another, will find that the real value of these balances has been reduced. Hence the cost in terms of

[4]*Report on Federal Reserve Policy and Inflation and High Interest Rates.* (A summary of interviews with the twelve Reserve Bank presidents and five members of the Board of Governors, submitted to the Committee on Banking and Currency by Robert E. Weintraub, staff economist, July 12, 1974, p. 1.)

[5]Ibid., p. 2.

[6]Haberler, op. cit., p. 143.

benefits of given nominal cash balances has been increased. To avoid the higher cost, cash holders may reduce their real cash balances still further either by purchasing consumer goods and services (reducing their wealth) or by acquiring other assets, such as gold or diamonds, in place of money. Such a "flight from currency" induces still more inflation of prices, at least of the assets (e.g., gold) that are desired in place of legal tender.

A more pervasive cost of inflation is the redistributon of income and wealth that is brought about by a general rise in the price level. Holders of assets denominated in nominal money terms such as mortgage holders and bondholders will find that the real value of these assets has declined. Furthermore, the stream of interest income due to creditors, though constant in nominal money terms, declines in real value as prices rise. Hence income is being redistributed from creditors to debtors.

Persons on fixed, or relatively fixed incomes such as retired persons on private or public pensions and various categories of white-collar workers will also find that they have been "taxed" by inflation. Real resources are being taken away from such groups, whose wages and salaries or interest income are rising at a slower rate than the price level. These resources are being given instead to those groups in society such as profit recipients and workers in strong unions whose nominal money income is rising faster than the inflationary increases in prices.

## Benefits of Inflation

The other side of the coin is that as certain groups in the economy suffer from the ravages of inflation, other groups receive real **benefits from inflation.** Some of the groups to benefit have already been noted in discussing the costs of inflation. Hence though creditors lose in a period of inflation, debtors gain. Furthermore, any economic groups whose money income is increasing faster than prices enjoy added real income in such a period.

The share of national income going to profits is particularly subject to the vagaries of the business cycle. Though such profit share drops sharply in a period of recession, in a period of rising output and rising business sales, which is often marked by general price increases, profits rise sharply not only absolutely but relatively. Also, when strong aggregate demand is generating not only increases in total output but also gains in total employment, organized wage earners are likely to get new collective bargaining agreements, which may result in substantial real gains for the group of workers covered.

A final substantial benefit may be noted as devolving on the poor of the economy. This is the sector of economic society that particularly bears the burden of rising unemployment. When unemployment is falling, as it often does during an inflationary period (the Phillips curve, see pp. 573–574), the added income going to the poor now employed rather than unemployed can be considerable. The poor are also typically debtors, and we have already noted the gains to debtors in an inflationary period. Even the poor receiving welfare payments or old-age assistance are likely in many periods to receive greater percentage increases in money payments than the percentage increase in prices, particularly in mild or moderate inflationary periods, when prices are rising 5 percent or less rather than 8 to 10 percent or more.

## Government Deficit Spending

Serious periods of inflation in the American experience have been typically caused by a wartime expansion of aggregate demand and the money supply and have resulted in substantial increases in the price level either during the wartime or immediately afterward. The proximate cause of the substantial rise in money expenditures and money income is the great increase in government spending that always occurs in war periods. (This was true in World War II from 1941 to 1945, during the Korean War from 1950 to 1953, and during the U.S. military involvement in Vietnam from 1965 to 1973.) If the government increased tax rates, and thereby tax receipts *pari passu* with the increase in government spending, little inflationary effect could be expected. (The balanced budget-multiplier analysis would suggest that some inflation could result, but certainly not as much as typically does occur in wartime.) Ordinarily, however, Congress appears unwilling to increase tax rates sufficiently, so that resort to the printing press is had.

In World War II, or in the Korean or Vietnam conflicts, it was not literally the case that the government simply printed more paper currency to finance the swollen volume of war-induced government spending—as had been true in the Revolutionary War and the Civil War—because most of the money supply by 1941 was in the form of demand deposits of commercial banks. The result of a deficit in the government budget was that whatever funds could not be borrowed out of the voluntary savings of the public came from newly created demand deposits of commercial banks and ultimately then from forced savings, or an inflationary increase in the cost of most goods and services.

Whenever government debt is sold to the banking system, that debt is thereby monetized. The increased money supply put in the hands of the government was immediately spent in a period when the real output of goods and services was already straining at the limit of productive facilities of the economy. Because increases in output are being subjected to diminishing marginal returns, an inevitable rise in prices occurs. Even though money incomes are rising generally, the imposition of direct wage and price controls can postpone much of the inflation until after the war when controls are removed.

***War and Postwar Inflation*** Most of the inflation caused by World War II was thus not felt completely until 1946, 1947, and 1948. In these early postwar years the annual rate of price increases of 7 or 8 percent per year was greater than that experienced during the war itself. Also during this same period, aggressive union leadership succeeded in pushing up wage rates for most union members, so that the forces of cost-push inflation were added to those of demand-pull. This American period of inflation after World War II was, however, nothing compared with the classic postwar period of **hyperinflation** in Germany that culminated in 1923. In that year, wages and salaries were paid twice each day, so that the German wage earners would be able to receive some real income for their efforts in a period when prices were jumping almost hourly. Postwar inflation, then, when direct controls are weak or removed altogether is open inflation, whereas much of the inflation during the war period is repressed by the controls then in effect. In the Korean and Vietnam wars, direct controls by the government were weaker than in World War II, so that there was considerable inflation during these war periods. In either war or postwar inflation, however, a sharp rise in the supply of money occurs, which gives notice of the inflation yet to come.

The increase in aggregate demand during a war period caused by government deficit spending thus not only pushes up prices during the time when the rise in spending occurs but the increase in liquidity in the economy (rise in the stock of money) accompanied by deferred private demand also results in many inflationary pressures being pushed into the postwar period. This pent-up demand after the war means that people have both the desire to consume more of the goods and services that were often not available in adequate amounts during the war and the means to increase private spending. The accumulation of liquid assets in the form of more money balances and government securities acquired during the war period can now be used to accelerate money spending.

This backlog of **unsatisfied demand** is felt by consumers and also by business firms, who were unable to keep their stock of capital as large and as efficient as desired during the war shortages of supplies, parts, and equipment. Once this deferred demand is allowed to spill over into a postwar period, which still has productive limitations on the output of goods and services, an inflationary spiral can get well underway. Rising money expenditures lead to rising product prices, which then contribute to rising prices of the factors of production including labor needed to produce the desired output, which in turn means higher levels of money income, which can complete the upward spiral by leading to rising money expenditures.

## Inflation in the Money Supply

Although it is possible for a sharp rise in the velocity of money to lead to an inflationary increase in the flow of money spending against a limited flow of output of real goods and services, it is much more normal for higher levels of money spending to be associated with a larger stock of money. The money supply in the United States is controlled by the Federal Reserve System. But when the Federal Reserve Act was passed in 1913, the foreword to the act noted that this new central bank was to provide for a more elastic currency. That is, the new central bank was to allow or encourage the money supply to increase when the needs of trade and commerce increase as they do in the upswing of the business cycle.

Like some other central banks, the Federal Reserve has at times had a strong tendency to stabilize fluctuations in interest rates, particularly in the short run, as in the 1960s and in some years in the 1970s. This tends to result in procyclical variations in the money supply. Hence the money supply tends to grow more rapidly in the upswing of the business cycle (contributing to more inflation) and to grow more slowly in recessions.

## COST-PUSH INFLATION

In the early period immediately after World War II, in the United States some economists concluded that the type of inflation of the price level then occurring was not completely explained by the traditional demand-pull theory of inflation. Redundant liquidity inherited from World War II and deferred consumer and business demands for goods not available in sufficient abundance in wartime were readily conceded to be contributing factors to the postwar rise in prices. However, a new dimension was thought to be present in the great power over prices and wages held not only by firms with the ability to set administered prices but also by more dominant unions now able to push up money wages rapidly. Under these conditions of concentration of market power in the hands of a few decision makers, it was possible for periodic wage increases, including fringe benefits, to be substantially greater than the overall average increases in output per man-hour. This was called **cost-push inflation**.

## Wages and Productivity

If wage costs are rising faster than productivity, prices will undoubtedly be pushed up too. However, and this is a critical point, the higher levels of prices cannot be sustained by the prior level of aggregate demand. This means that the aggregate supply of money must be increased enough to validate the higher prices by raising money demand. If this increase in money expenditures does not occur, widespread unemployment is likely to be the price of a substantial wage-price round of inflation. The monetary authorities under these conditions must make a hard choice between permitting some inflationary rise in the money supply or else freezing the present size of the stock of money and perhaps seeing substantial unemployment as the price of this credit restraint. The decision throughout most of this early postwar period was to permit at least mild inflation, though the mood of the monetary authorities was not completely uniform throughout this entire period. Sometimes these authorities seemed much more concerned with fighting inflation than they did at other times.

If wages and prices are rising in a period in which aggregate demand is also rising, it may be difficult to determine which is cause and which is effect. It is surely to be expected that wages and other prices will rise in a period in which demand is pushing hard on available productive capacity. But it is also true that because wages and other prices are sources of income as well as costs of production, an increase in certain key prices may be reflected, partially at least, in the level of aggregate demand. Some observers are prone to argue that monetary policy is relatively impotent in dealing with an inflation that is largely cost-push in nature. Or, at the minimum, such observers tend to feel that the cost of an anti-inflationary policy to deal with inflation that was fundamentally cost-push in causation would be too large an amount of unemployment for most democracies concerned with the political consequences of all public policies, including monetary policies.

***Flexibility of Wages and Prices***    If prices and wages are flexible or sensitive to changes in demand—even if such prices and wages are initially determined by cost factors—then a public policy such as monetary policy designed to dampen aggregate demand could indeed halt the inflation in fairly short order. It might also be that corrective actions could be taken in the area of government fiscal policy (i.e., a cutback in government spending or an increase in tax rates) that could significantly reduce the inflationary potential of the economy without resort to a restrictive money and credit policy by the central bank. Moreover, even if some restrictive credit policy is instituted by the central bank, a policy of self-restraint in the fiscal area may also be needed if the inflationary pressures are serious.

A cost-push inflation need not arise entirely by an autonomous upward push of administered prices or wages. If administered prices are set by applying a constant profit margin to estimated costs, and if wages, after a lag, are pushed upward by labor unions responding to a prior upward movement in the level of consumer prices, any initial general price rise from any cause will tend to become self-perpetuating. Furthermore, the more insensitive prices of products are to excess plant capacity and the more insensitive wages are to the development of unemployment, the greater are the inflationary possibilities in a given situation. Also, the shorter the lag between the adjustment of prices to wages and vice versa, the faster will be the pace of inflation. Finally, the mere fact that wages are rising faster than productivity in a given time period does not, in and of itself, prove that any inflation underway is necessarily of the cost-push type, because even in a pure demand-pull inflation, wages also rise faster than productivity.

## THE PHILLIPS CURVE AND "FULL EMPLOYMENT"

Whether the inflationary pressures originate in demand-pull excess aggregate demand (buyers' inflation) or in cost-push (sellers' inflation), there is much evidence to show that the rate of increase in prices increases as the economy gets closer and closer to "full employment" (4 percent unemployment). In 1958, an English economist, A.W. Phillips, presented evidence for the period from 1861 to 1957 in Great Britain showing that there was a higher rate of increase in money wage rates as the unemployment rate declined. More than two decades ago in 1960, Paul Samuelson and Robert Solow showed that the same relationship existed between changes in prices and unemployment for the prior twenty-five years for the United States. Samuelson and Solow estimated that price stability in the United States would involve about 5½ percent unemployment, whereas a 3 percent unemployment rate would involve a price rise of about 4½ percent. The Samuelson-Solow modified Phillips curve for the United States is shown in Figure 26–1.

In the 1980s the Phillips curve showing the "trade-off" between

**Figure 26–1    Modified Phillips Curve for the United States**

This shows the menu of choice between different degrees
of unemployment and price stability, as roughly estimated
from twenty-five years of American data.

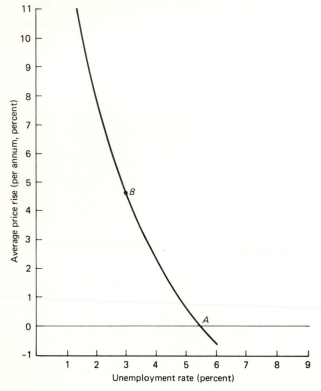

SOURCE: Paul A. Samuelson and Robert Solow, "Analytical Aspects of Anti-Inflation Policy," *American Economic Review*, **50**, No. 2: 192 (May 1960).

unemployment and price level stability has apparently shifted upward
and to the right (i.e., price level stability would involve a higher opportunity cost in the form of a higher rate of unemployment). A given
unemployment rate, say, five to six percent, would also involve a higher
opportunity cost in the form of a higher rate of inflation than had been
true earlier in this country. Structural changes in the labor force involving more teenagers and more women, both of whom have a higher rate
of unemployment than men, are usually advanced as two reasons for the
shift in the Phillips curve. Another reason appeared to be that there were
more general expectations of chronic or secular inflation than had once
been the case.

# THE INFLATION PROCESS IN THE UNITED STATES

A number of empirical studies in the United States have established for this country that changes in the rate of increase in the various price indexes are usually affected mainly by changes in unit labor and material costs. Other influences such as demand conditions, wage and price guideposts or other forms of incomes policies, war, and profit considerations seem to play important but secondary roles to changes in labor costs. The effect of labor costs on prices appears to be characterized by a "ratchet effect" (i.e., increases in labor costs raise product prices), although a decline in labor costs does not usually produce a decline in product prices. This relationship seems to be particularly important for the various manufacturing industries.

Labor costs in turn are affected by wage changes and productivity changes. The single most important factor affecting the rate of wage increases seems to be the level of excess demand as measured, say, by the rate of unemployment. As the rate of unemployment declines, there appear to be successive increments in the rate of increase of wage rates. This is the Phillips curve relationship between unemployment and price increases operating through the effect of changes in money wage rates.

In traditional or neoclassical economic theory, real conditions in the labor market determined real wages, which implies that money wages change proportionally and promptly as prices change. Long-term collective bargaining agreements, which set money wages for three years or more, reduce this linkage between changes in prices and money wages. Some relationship still exists with econometric studies estimating a coefficient of .4–.6, which implies greater price stability in the economy then if every 1 percent change in prices were matched by a 1 percent change in money wages.

Although wage increases are only partly sensitive to price changes in periods of mild inflation, they become more sensitive as the rate of inflation increases and persists over a period of time. The price experience of the prior two years particularly seems important in affecting the expectations of inflation this year, insofar as they are reflected in wage demands of organized labor. Also, if the rate of unemployment falls below 4–4.5 percent, the wage-price mechanism can become explosive. Keeping the unemployment rate below this critical level for a prolonged period of time can result in an accelerated rate of inflation in which past inflation increases lead to inflationary expectations for the future. This set of expectations increases wage demands now. Higher wages then result in higher rates of future price increases. In this sense, inflationary expectations can become self-fulfilling.

## Secular Inflation

Although the rate of inflation varies from time to time, depending in part on how close the economy is to "full employment," many observers in the 1980s have come to believe that the United States has a tendency toward **secular inflation** over the long run. In part, this may be like the converse belief in "secular stagnation" during the deep depression of the 1930s. In any event, the nearly two decades after the mid-1960s has been dominated by a chronic and sometimes even rising rate of inflation. The long-run process of inflation in the United States can be clearly seen in Figure 26–2, which graphs the wholesale price index from 1946 through 1976, inclusive. In the late 1970s and early 1980s, the trend of both wholesale and consumer prices has continued to be upward, despite the earlier stability of wholesale prices in the late 1950s and early 1960s.

Furthermore, there are fundamental reasons for expecting the same trend in the future. In a study published in 1973, G. L. Bach of Stanford University gave six reasons why inflation in the United States will continue: (1) the sanctity of high employment, (2) the impressive demonstrations in World War II that massive government spending can produce such high employment, (3) the increasing political and economic strength of major socioeconomic groups and the increasingly administered structure of prices, (4) increased government responsibility for the welfare of the masses, (5) hot and cold war, and (6) the end of the gold standard. Some of these reasons are obviously overlapping. Nevertheless, it seems apparent not only to Bach but to many other economists as well that there is a strong government commitment to "full employment," which, given the nature of the Phillips curve with its trade-off between unemployment and price stability, make likely the continuance of inflation in the future.

In the past much of the harm to various economic groups in the economy has arisen from **erratic and unanticipated inflation.** If inflation comes to be expected in the future, and if mild or moderate inflation does not become runaway inflation, then greater protection can be given to those groups most disadvantaged by inflation. In 1972, Congress amended the Social Security law to provide for future cost-of-living increases in benefits to retired workers. Many organized workers have for some years had cost-of-living clauses in their collective bargaining agreements. In some countries, though not in the United States, government securities have had escalator clauses guaranteeing that holders of such debt would receive the same amount of purchasing power at the maturity of the bond as they had loaned the government. Variable interest rates have also been used in some countries to protect creditors in periods of inflation.

Not all, however, can have an umbrella erected over them to

**Figure 26–2    Wholesale Industrial Price Index**

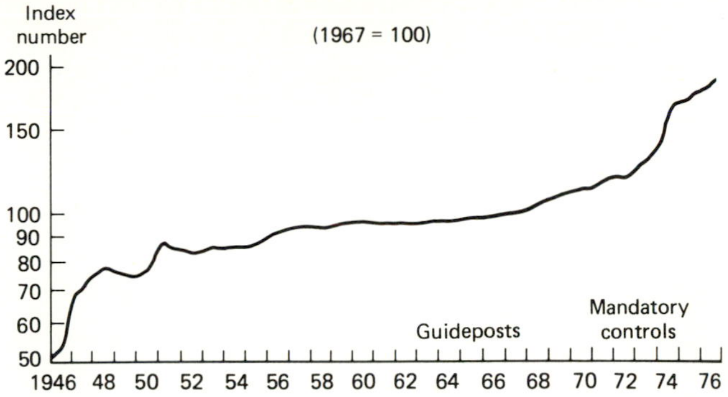

SOURCE: The Morgan Guaranty Bank of New York, *The Morgan Guaranty Survey,* April 1977, p. 10.

protect them from the ravages of inflation. The unorganized or naïve workers are likely to be the most adversely affected in a period of inflation. The shrewd, or those especially protected by cost-of-living clauses, will fare better. Those workers who find employment only because of the "full employment" policies of the government are better off—even in periods of inflation—than if they had no jobs at all or were underemployed in part-time or temporary positions. The trade-off problems of full employment versus inflation thus become ultimately political questions, rather than economic questions that can be resolved through the forces of the marketplace.

## Measurement of Inflation

Although we have referred to inflation of the price level as if it were a single simple concept, there are three major indexes measuring **inflation**, or the average change in the price level. The index to which most newspaper accounts refer is the Consumer Price Index of the Bureau of Labor Statistice (BLS-CPI), which since 1983 has used the year 1977 as its base year. Another price index published by the same government agency is the Producer Price Index (PPI), formerly called the Wholesale Price Index. Finally, the Department of Commerce compiles GNP price deflators, which it uses in converting the money value of current GNP into real terms, such as in constant 1972 prices.

Each of these price indexes is a valid way of measuring the average change in prices, even though the rate of change of prices is often different depending on which index is used. Both the Consumer Price Index and the implicit price deflator for GNP showed that the price level rose about 30 percent in the decade of the 1960s. The Wholesale Price Index, however, showed a rise of only 15 percent. In some years, (e.g., 1958–1964), the Wholesale Price Index showed no increase in average prices at all, even though the Consumer Price Index was rising by 1½–2 percent each year. Because of these differences in measurement, it is important to note certain characteristics of these indexes. Our discussion centers on the Consumer Price Index, because it is the one most often referred to in popular discussions of inflation of the price level.

## THE CONSUMER PRICE INDEX

The Consumer Price Index most commonly used in the United States is that compiled and published by the Bureau of Labor Statistics (BLS-CPI). This index covers prices of everything people buy—food, clothing, automobiles, homes, house furnishings, medical services, beauty care, rent, repair costs, transportation fares, public utility rates, and the like. Inasmuch as the prices are the ones actually charged to consumers, they include such taxes as sales and excise taxes and real estate taxes, but not income or personal property taxes.

### *"Market Basket" Consumer Goods*

The Bureau of Labor Statistics has been calculating the Consumer Price Index for more than half a century. Because buying habits of consumers have changed considerably over this period as new products have been introduced, a number of revisions have been made in the index from time to time. One such change in the weighting of the goods and services included in the index was based on a consumer expenditure survey undertaken by the bureau in 1960–1961 and was first reflected in the index for January 1964. Some 400 items were included in this representative **"market basket,"** as compared with only 325 items in the previous one. Major changes in the Consumer Price Index were made in January 1978 and it was recalculated on the base year 1977 in 1983. Some of the weighting of goods and services was changed, more goods and services were included, more different kind of income earners—including professionals—were included, and more cities were included.

### *Selection of a Base Period*

Changing patterns of consumer expenditures accompanying the rise in real income necessitate changes in the goods and services included in the

BLS-CPI. Also, to keep the **base period** used for comparison purposes up to date, the base period selected must be constantly moved closer to the present year. Until 1970, the base period was 1957–1959. In 1970, however, the base period was moved to the year 1967, so that subsequent index numbers published by the BLS used that base.

In 1982, the Bureau of Labor Statistics announced that beginning with data for January 1983, the base year used in calculating the CPI would be moved from 1967 to 1977. The base period, in fact, is revised approximately every ten years. The year 1977 was chosen for two major reasons: (1) the most recent quiquennial economic censuses were taken in 1977 and many economic series are benchmarked to these censuses, and (2) the continued recovery of the economy in 1977 was relatively balanced from the 1974–1975 recession.

Finally, it should be noted that this particular rebasing of the CPI did not involve any changes in the **weights of index components** nor any other substantive or conceptual changes. In short, it was essentially an arithmetic change to make the index numbers easier to comprehend. Hence the conversion of the annual index numbers for the CPI from a 1967 to a 1977 base simply involved dividing the all items index numbers by the 1977 all items index numbers (181.5) and multiplying by 100. With 1967 as a base, the CPI index numbers for 1967, 1969, 1973, and 1977 were, respectively, 100.0, 109.8, 133.1, and 181.5. The new index numbers for the same years with the 1977 base are 55.1, 60.5, 73.3, and 100.0.

The 1983 changes also reduced the weight given to mortgage interest rates and housing prices. Under the new formula, the housing component was pegged to the cost of renting housing rather than buying it.

## THIRTY-TWO OUT OF THIRTY-FOUR YEARS WERE INFLATIONARY

Annual rates of change in the Consumer Price Index as a whole, for food separately, for commodities less food, and for services, are shown in Table 26–1 for the thirty-four years from 1948 to 1981 inclusive. Changes in the price of energy are shown from 1958 to 1981. In only two years in this long period, both of which were years of recession, did the price index decline. There was a small decline of 1.8 percent in 1949 and an even smaller decline of 0.5 percent in 1954. In the earlier years of this thirty-four year period, only 1950 and 1951, with increases of 5.8 and 5.9 percent respectively, showed significant rates of increase for consumer prices. Most years seemed to be characterized by "creeping inflation," with the steady increase in the price of services year after year the most likely culprit. Commodity prices, for either food or commodity prices less food, showed considerable year-to-year variability with no clear

**Table 26–1  Changes in Consumer Price Indexes, Commodities and Services, 1948–1981 (Percent change. 1967 = 100)**

| Year or Month | All items | | Commodities | | | | | | Services | | Energy[2] | |
|---|---|---|---|---|---|---|---|---|---|---|---|---|
| | | | Total | | Food | | Commodities Less Food | | | | | |
| | Dec. to Dec. | Year to year | Dec. to Dec. | Year to year | Dec. to Dec. | Year to year | Dec. to Dec. | Year to year | Dec. to Dec. | Year to year | Dec. to Dec. | Year to year |
| 1948 | 2.7 | 7.8 | 1.7 | 7.2 | -0.8 | 8.5 | 5.3 | 7.7 | 6.1 | 6.3 | ...... | ...... |
| 1949 | -1.8 | -1.0 | -4.1 | -2.6 | -3.7 | -4.0 | -4.8 | -1.5 | 3.6 | 4.8 | ...... | ...... |
| 1950 | 5.8 | 1.0 | 7.7 | .6 | 9.6 | 1.4 | 5.7 | -.1 | 3.6 | 3.2 | ...... | ...... |
| 1951 | 5.9 | 7.9 | 5.9 | 9.0 | 7.4 | 11.1 | 4.6 | 7.5 | 5.2 | 5.3 | ...... | ...... |
| 1952 | .9 | 2.2 | -.7 | 1.3 | -1.1 | 1.8 | -.5 | .9 | 4.6 | 4.4 | ...... | ...... |
| 1953 | .6 | .8 | -.6 | -.3 | -1.3 | -1.5 | .2 | .2 | 4.2 | 4.3 | ...... | ...... |
| 1954 | -.5 | .5 | -1.4 | -.9 | -1.6 | -.2 | -1.4 | -1.1 | 1.9 | 3.3 | ...... | ...... |
| 1955 | .4 | -.4 | -.4 | -.9 | -.9 | -1.4 | 0 | -.7 | 2.3 | 2.0 | ...... | ...... |
| 1956 | 2.9 | 1.5 | 2.6 | .9 | 3.1 | .7 | 2.5 | 1.0 | 3.1 | 2.5 | ...... | ...... |
| 1957 | 3.0 | 3.6 | 2.6 | 3.1 | 2.8 | 3.3 | 2.2 | 3.1 | 4.5 | 4.0 | ...... | ...... |
| 1958 | 1.8 | 2.7 | 1.3 | 2.3 | 2.2 | 4.2 | .8 | 1.1 | 2.7 | 3.8 | -0.7 | 0.2 |
| 1959 | 1.5 | .8 | .6 | .1 | -.8 | -1.6 | 1.5 | 1.3 | 3.7 | 2.9 | 4.3 | 1.7 |

| Year | | | | | | | | | | | | |
|---|---|---|---|---|---|---|---|---|---|---|---|---|
| 1960 | 1.5 | 1.6 | 1.1 | .9 | 3.1 | 1.0 | −.3 | .4 | 2.7 | 3.3 | 1.5 | 2.6 |
| 1961 | .7 | 1.0 | 0 | .5 | −.9 | 1.3 | .6 | .3 | 1.9 | 2.0 | −1.1 | .2 |
| 1962 | 1.2 | 1.1 | 1.0 | .9 | 1.5 | .9 | .7 | .7 | 1.7 | 1.9 | 2.1 | .3 |
| 1963 | 1.6 | 1.2 | 1.4 | .9 | 1.9 | 1.4 | 1.2 | .7 | 2.3 | 2.0 | −.8 | .3 |
| 1964 | 1.2 | 1.3 | .8 | 1.1 | 1.4 | 1.3 | .4 | .8 | 1.8 | 1.9 | −.2 | −.4 |
| 1965 | 1.9 | 1.7 | 1.6 | 1.2 | 3.4 | 2.2 | .7 | .6 | 2.6 | 2.2 | 2.0 | 1.8 |
| 1966 | 3.4 | 2.9 | 2.5 | 2.6 | 3.9 | 5.0 | 1.9 | 1.4 | 4.9 | 3.9 | 1.8 | 1.6 |
| 1967 | 3.0 | 2.9 | 2.5 | 1.8 | 1.2 | .9 | 3.1 | 2.6 | 4.0 | 4.4 | 1.4 | 2.2 |
| 1968 | 4.7 | 4.2 | 3.8 | 3.7 | 4.3 | 3.6 | 3.7 | 3.7 | 6.1 | 5.2 | 1.7 | 1.5 |
| 1969 | 6.1 | 5.4 | 5.5 | 4.5 | 7.2 | 5.1 | 4.5 | 4.2 | 7.4 | 6.9 | 3.1 | 2.7 |
| 1970 | 5.5 | 5.9 | 4.0 | 4.7 | 2.2 | 5.5 | 4.8 | 4.1 | 8.2 | 8.1 | 4.5 | 2.7 |
| 1971 | 3.4 | 4.3 | 2.9 | 3.4 | 4.3 | 3.0 | 2.3 | 3.8 | 4.1 | 5.6 | 3.1 | 3.9 |
| 1972 | 3.4 | 3.3 | 3.4 | 3.0 | 4.7 | 4.3 | 2.5 | 2.2 | 3.6 | 3.8 | 2.8 | 2.8 |
| 1973 | 8.8 | 6.2 | 10.4 | 7.4 | 20.1 | 14.5 | 5.0 | 3.4 | 6.2 | 4.4 | 16.8 | 8.0 |
| 1974 | 12.2 | 11.0 | 12.7 | 12.0 | 12.2 | 14.4 | 13.2 | 10.6 | 11.3 | 9.3 | 21.6 | 29.3 |
| 1975 | 7.0 | 9.1 | 6.3 | 8.9 | 6.5 | 8.5 | 6.2 | 9.2 | 8.1 | 9.5 | 11.6 | 10.6 |
| 1976 | 4.8 | 5.8 | 3.3 | 4.3 | .6 | 3.1 | 5.1 | 5.0 | 7.3 | 8.3 | 6.9 | 7.2 |
| 1977 | 6.8 | 6.5 | 6.1 | 5.8 | 8.0 | 6.3 | 4.9 | 5.4 | 7.9 | 7.7 | 7.2 | 9.5 |
| 1978 | 9.0 | 7.7 | 8.9 | 7.1 | 11.8 | 10.0 | 7.7 | 5.8 | 9.3 | 8.5 | 8.0 | 6.3 |
| 1979 | 13.3 | 11.3 | 13.0 | 11.4 | 10.2 | 10.9 | 14.3 | 11.7 | 13.7 | 11.0 | 37.4 | 25.2 |
| 1980 | 12.4 | 13.5 | 11.1 | 12.2 | 10.2 | 8.6 | 11.5 | 13.8 | 14.2 | 15.4 | 18.1 | 30.9 |
| 1981 | 8.9 | 10.4 | 6.0 | 8.4 | 4.3 | 7.9 | 6.7 | 8.6 | 13.0 | 13.1 | 11.9 | 13.5 |

SOURCE: *Economic Report of the President, February 1982*, p. 295.

trend evident until 1965 and thereafter. The annual rate of increase for food peaked at a high of 20.1 percent in 1973 while commodities less food rose at 13.2 percent in 1974 and even higher at 14.3 percent in 1979.

The prices of all consumer prices accelerated twice in the decade of the 1970s and reached double-digit rates in both periods. Consumer prices, which increased by only 3.4 percent in 1974, soared to 8.8 percent in 1973 and to 12.2 percent in 1974. The rate of increase subsided for two years, but after 1976 the rate rose again. The 4.8 percent inflation of 1976 was followed by 6.8 percent in 1977, by 9.0 percent in 1978, and peaked at 13.3 percent in 1979. It was still at a double-digit rate of 12.4 percent in 1980, but fell to 8.9 percent in 1981. In early 1982, the rate of inflation was still falling.

The inflation rate was still more than double-digit in 1980, however, at 12.4 percent. In 1981, it fell to 8.9 percent. It can be noted in Figure 26–3 that the rate of increase in consumer prices in late 1981 and early 1982 was considerably less than in 1979 and 1980. This was due to severe credit restraint by the Federal Reserve in 1981–1982. This in turn resulted in a major recession in economic activity in 1981–1982.

Consumer price data for a longer period for the United States are shown in Figure 26–4, where the period from 1967 to mid-1981 is plotted. Although it is clear that there is an upward trend of consumer prices, it is

**Figure 26–3    Consumer Prices, 1979–1982**

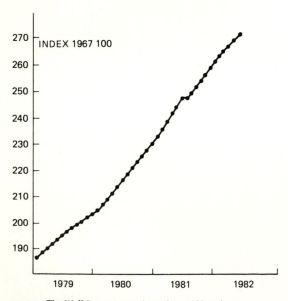

SOURCE: *The Wall Street Journal,* April 26, 1982, p. 1.

**Figure 26–4     U.S. Consumer Price Index, 1967–1981 (12-month percent change)**

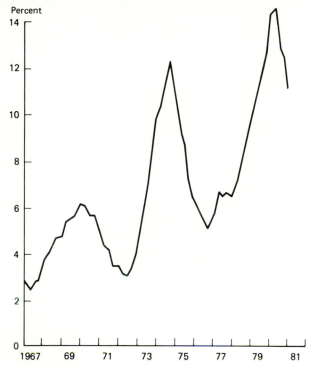

SOURCE: The Morgan Guaranty Bank of New York, *The Morgan Guaranty Survey*, June 1981, p. 2.

also clear that there are substantial fluctuations in the rate of inflation. This instability of prices, as well as the general ratcheting upward of consumer prices over this substantial period of time, is also disconcerting for the ordinary consumer.

The sharp decline in the rate of consumer price inflation, which is so dramatically shown in Figure 26–4, as already noted, continued in 1982. By spring of that year, optimistic forecasts of inflation in 1982 as low as 6 percent were being made. This compared with 8.9 percent in 1981.

## Inflation in Five Industrial Countries

That the problem of inflation is not restricted to the United States may be made clear by the bar diagram shown in Figure 26–5. Here, annual percentage changes in consumer prices are shown for 1980 and 1981 for

**Figure 26–5    Consumer Inflation Rates in Five Industrial Countries, 1980–1981**

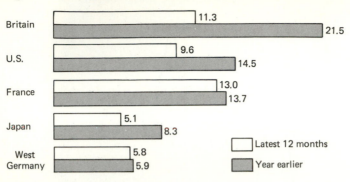

SOURCE: *The Wall Street Journal*, Sept. 18, 1981, p. 48.

the five major industrial countries of the United States, Britain, France, Japan, and West Germany. Although all these five countries did have inflationary problems, they were most serious in the United States, Britain, and France. All three countries had double-digit inflation in 1980, although the United States reduced it to a high single-digit rate (barely) in 1981. Nevertheless, all countries have had some success in containing their inflationary problem, with some achieving better results than others.

***Upward Bias of Index***    One major problem in using a price index to determine the degree of inflation in the United States over a period is the **upward bias** of such indexes. This refers to the fact that improvements in the quality of consumer goods and services may often accompany increases in quoted prices, so that the inflation thus measured is more apparent than real. Furthermore, in some instances new products may be introduced that bear little resemblance to those previously on the market (e.g., television sets as compared with radio sets) that may make price comparisons difficult over time. The Bureau of Labor Statistics is aware of such difficulties and attempts to make the necessary technical adjustments in its index. Even so some upward bias may still remain.

## Inflation in Different Countries in the 1970s and Early 1980s

The inflation record of the United States between the end of 1973 to the spring of 1981 is also compared with that of a number of other major industrial countries in Table 26–2. The United States had a serious acceleration of its rate of inflation in 1973 and 1974 with a consequent

**Table 26-2   Changes in Consumer Prices, 1973–1981**

| Countries | Changes over Twelve Months Ending | | | | | | | | | 1981 |
| | 1973 Dec. | 1974 Dec. | 1975 Dec. | 1976 Dec. | 1977 Dec. | 1978 Dec. | 1979 Dec. | 1980 June | 1980 Dec. | Latest Month |
|---|---|---|---|---|---|---|---|---|---|---|
| | | | | | *In Percentages* | | | | | |
| United States | 8.8 | 12.2 | 7.0 | 4.8 | 6.8 | 9.0 | 13.3 | 14.3 | 12.4 | 10.0[b] |
| Japan | 19.0 | 22.0 | 7.7 | 10.4 | 4.8 | 3.5 | 5.8 | 8.4 | 7.1 | 6.2[a] |
| United Kingdom | 10.6 | 19.2 | 24.9 | 15.1 | 12.1 | 8.4 | 17.2 | 21.0 | 15.1 | 12.0[b] |
| Italy | 12.3 | 25.3 | 11.1 | 21.8 | 14.9 | 11.9 | 19.8 | 20.7 | 21.1 | 19.9[b] |
| Canada | 9.1 | 12.5 | 9.5 | 5.8 | 9.5 | 8.4 | 9.8 | 10.1 | 11.2 | 12.6[b] |
| France | 8.5 | 15.2 | 9.6 | 9.9 | 9.0 | 9.7 | 11.8 | 13.5 | 13.6 | 12.5[a] |
| Sweden | 7.5 | 11.6 | 8.9 | 9.6 | 12.7 | 7.4 | 9.8 | 13.1 | 14.1 | 12.9[b] |
| Germany | 7.8 | 5.8 | 5.4 | 3.7 | 3.5 | 2.5 | 5.4 | 6.0 | 5.5 | 5.6[b] |
| Switzerland | 11.9 | 7.6 | 3.4 | 1.3 | 1.1 | 0.7 | 5.1 | 3.3 | 4.4 | 5.6[b] |
| Belgium | 7.3 | 15.7 | 11.0 | 7.6 | 6.3 | 3.9 | 5.1 | 6.2 | 7.5 | 7.4[b] |
| Netherlands | 8.2 | 10.9 | 9.1 | 8.5 | 5.2 | 3.9 | 4.8 | 6.6 | 6.7 | 6.2[b] |
| Austria | 7.8 | 9.7 | 6.7 | 7.2 | 4.2 | 3.7 | 4.7 | 7.1 | 6.7 | 7.4[b] |
| Denmark | 12.6 | 15.5 | 4.3 | 13.1 | 12.2 | 7.1 | 11.8 | 13.3 | 10.9 | 11.3[a] |
| Finland | 14.1 | 16.9 | 18.1 | 12.3 | 11.9 | 6.5 | 8.6 | 11.2 | 13.8 | 13.1[a] |
| Greece | 30.7 | 13.5 | 15.7 | 11.7 | 12.8 | 11.5 | 24.8 | 26.2 | 26.2 | 24.3[b] |
| Norway | 7.6 | 10.5 | 11.0 | 8.0 | 9.1 | 8.1 | 4.7 | 10.8 | 13.7 | 14.6[b] |
| Ireland | 12.6 | 20.0 | 16.8 | 20.6 | 10.8 | 7.9 | 16.0 | 20.2 | 18.2 | 21.0[c] |
| Spain | 14.3 | 17.9 | 14.1 | 19.8 | 26.4 | 16.6 | 15.5 | 15.9 | 15.1 | 13.8[c] |

[a]March.
[b]April.
[c]February.

SOURCE: Bank for International Settlements, *Fifty-First Annual Report 1st April 1980—31st March 1981*, Basle, Switzerland, June 15, 1981, p. 9.

deceleration of inflation in 1975 and 1976. The pace of inflation picked up again in 1977 and 1978. By 1979 and 1980, inflation in the U.S. was running at an even higher rate than the high rates of 1973 and 1974.

Great Britain also had an acceleration of inflation in 1973 and 1974, which continued into 1975. In 1976 and 1977, double-digit inflation still proved to be stubbornly present in Britain until it eased in 1978. In 1979 and 1980, however, it had almost as high inflation rates as in 1974 and 1975. The same extremely serious inflation problem was present in Italy. In Japan, a rapid acceleration of inflation in 1973 and 1974 was followed by fiscal and monetary restraint such that subsequent inflation rates were half of those in 1973 and 1974. The inflation experience in West Germany was the most favorable of any country, whereas France's record was somewhat worse than that of the United States. The **dispersion of inflation** rates among these major industrial countries was thus still quite high in the spring of 1981, though less than it had been five years earlier.

The Swiss experience with inflation is especially interesting among all highly industrialized countries, because Switzerland had an accelerating rate of inflation in 1972 and 1973, but by 1976 and 1977 it had the lowest rate of inflation of any country listed in Table 26–2. How did the Swiss achieve this economic miracle? The answer is that they endured a severe economic recession brought on by government policy that effectively ended the problem of inflation. In 1973, the Swiss money supply was reduced a little, whereas in 1974 it was shrunk by 1.7 percent. Subsequently, in 1975 real output fell in Switzerland by a very sharp 7.6 percent. (In the United States the drop in real output in 1975 was only 1.8 percent.)

Inflation in the consumer price level in major industrial countries became an even more serious problem after 1977 than it had been before. Figure 26–6 shows the rates of change in consumer prices for seven major industrial countries from 1977 to mid-1981. From 1978 on, as this graph shows, the problem of inflation became increasingly acute. In these seven industrial countries as a group, consumer prices accelerated from a 7 percent rate in 1978 to a 12 percent rate in 1980.

At the same time, there was an increase in the dispersion of individual inflation rates in the different major countries. There was only a 9 percentage point range in 1978, but it had increased dramatically to 22 points at annual rates in the first quarter of 1980. The United States, Great Britain, and Italy all were experiencing very high rates in late 1979 and early 1980, while Germany and Japan had much lower rates. As already noted, this dispersion rate was somewhat lower in 1981. All these industrial countries, however, as Figure 26–6 attests, had substantial variation in their inflation rates over this particular four and a half year period of the late 1970s and early 1980. Concern with reducing high

**Figure 26–6    Major Industrial Countries: Consumer Prices, 1977–June 1981 (percentage changes)**

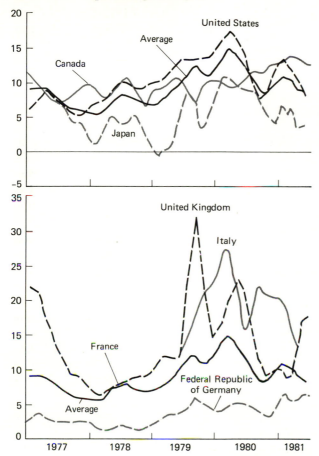

SOURCE: International Monetary Fund, *Annual Report*, 1981, Washington D.C., 1981, p. 6.

inflation rates was inevitably going to be a continuing problem in the decade of the 1980s for most industrial countries.

# Questions for Discussion

1. Discuss the traditional demand-pull type of inflation. Give examples from the recent experience of the United States of this type of inflation. What kinds of public policies can combat it?

2. Discuss the relationship between money and inflation. What kind of lags are there between changes in the rate of growth of the money supply and the rate of growth in the price level?
3. Discuss some of the major costs and benefits of inflation. Which major economic groups are hurt by inflation and which usually benefit by rising prices? How might society offset the cost of inflation that disadvantages particular groups?
4. Discuss the connection between war or postwar periods and inflation in the United States. To what extent does repressed inflation during the war period result in open inflation after the war? How could wartime inflation be further reduced?
5. Discuss the characteristics of cost-push inflation. What are the relationships among money wages, labor costs, and prices in this kind of inflation? What is the "ratchet effect" in cost-push inflation? What kind of public policies might assist in restraining this type of inflation?
6. Discuss the Phillips curve and the trade-off problem. What could be done to shift the Phillips curve downward and to the left, so that a lower rate of unemployment could be accomplished with no higher rate of increase in the price level? What has caused the Phillips curve at such times as in the 1960s and 1970s to shift in the opposite direction?
7. What is secular inflation and why do a number of economists believe that it afflicts the U.S. economy? Is there any likelihood, in your judgment, that long-run factors tending to promote inflation in the United States could be offset by different public policies? Why or why not? Insofar as the impacts of secular inflation are concerned, does it matter whether the inflation is anticipated or unanticipated?
8. Discuss the composition of the Consumer Price Index of the Bureau of Labor Statistics. Why are the base year and the weighting of the various components of the index changed from time to time? (In particular, discuss the changes made in the index in 1983.) How accurate do you believe the BLS-CPI is for changes in the cost of living in your particular area? Why?
9. Discuss the problem of inflation in the United States in the 1970s and early 1980s. What had originally touched off this long period of chronic inflation? Why did the rate of inflation sometimes accelerate and sometimes cool off?
10. Discuss the five indicators of inflation developed by Geoffrey H. Moore at the National Bureau of Economic Research.
11. Discuss the inflation record of other industrial countries in the 1970s and early 1980s. Why did the rate of inflation in these countries accelerate in the late 1970s? How does the record of the United States compare with the inflation records of other countries?

# Selected Bibliography for Further Reading

BACH, G.L., *The New Inflation: Causes, Effects, Cures* (Providence, R.I.: Brown University Press, 1973).

BRUNNER, KARL, and ALLAN H., MELTZER, *Institutional Arrangements and the Inflation Problem*, a supplement to the *Journal of Monetary Economics*, Vol. 3, 1976.

BUREAU OF LABOR STATISTICS, U.S. DEPARTMENT OF LABOR, "Federal Agencies Updating Base Year of Indexes to 1977," *Monthly Labor Review*, Feb. 1981, Vol. 104, No. 2, pp. 75–76.

CAGAN, PHILLIP, "The Non-Neutrality of Money in the Long Run," *Journal of Money, Credit and Banking*, Vol. 1, No. 1, May 1969, pp. 207–227.

——, *Persistent Inflation: History and Policy Essays* (New York: Columbia University Press, 1979), pp. 271–277.

DOMAR, EVSEY D., *Essays in the Theory of Economic Growth* (New York: Oxford University Press, 1957).

ECKSTEIN, OTTO, and ROGER BRINNER, *The Inflation Process in the United States*, a Study Printed for the Use of the Joint Economic Committee Congress of the United States (Washington, D.C.: U.S. Government Printing Office, 1972).

FEDERAL RESERVE BANK OF NEW YORK, *Federal Reserve Readings on Inflation*, New York, 1979.

FOSTER, EDWARD, *Costs and Benefits of Inflation*, Studies in Monetary Economics, Federal Reserve Bank of Minneapolis (Minneapolis, Minn.: March 1972).

HABERLER, GOTTFRIED, *Inflation: Its Causes and Cures* (Washington, D.C.: American Enterprise Association, 1960).

HARROD, R.F., *Towards a Dynamic Economics* (London: Macmillan, 1948).

HIRSCH, FRED, and JOHN H. GOLDTHORPE, eds., *Political Economy of Inflation* (Cambridge, Mass.: Harvard University Press, 1978).

INTERNATIONAL MONETARY FUND, *Annual Report 1981*, Washington, D.C., 1981.

JOHNSON, H.G., *Essays in Monetary Economics* (Cambridge, Mass.: Harvard University Press, 1967).

MOORE, GEOFFREY H., "Five Little Known Facts About Inflation," *The Morgan Guaranty Survey*, Aug. 1977, pp. 12–14.

SAMUELSON, PAUL A., and ROBERT SOLOW, "Analytical Aspects of Anti-Inflation Policy," *American Economic Review*, Vol. L, No. 2, May 1960.

SELDEN, RICHARD T., "Inflation: Are We Winning the Fight?", *The Morgan Guaranty Survey*, Oct. 1977, pp. 7–13.

STEIN, J. L., " 'Neo-Classical' and 'Keynes-Wicksell' Monetary Growth Models," *Journal of Money, Credit and Banking*, May 1969, pp. 153–171.

WEINTRAUB, ROBERT E., *The Impact of the Federal Reserve System's Monetary Policies on the Nation's Economy* (Washington, D.C.: Staff Report of the Subcommittee on Domestic Monetary Policy of the Committee on Banking, Currency and Housing, House of Representatives, 1976).

# 27 CHAPTER

# The American Balance of Payments

Just as fiscal policy and debt management policies affect the monetary policy decisions of the Federal Reserve in certain respects, so too does the existence of a surplus or a deficit in the American balance of payments. In the early 1970s the growing deficit in the balance of payments partly contributed to the central banking posture of credit restraint in 1973–1974. On October 6, 1979, the Federal Reserve tightened monetary policy partly because of concern about adverse developments in the U.S. balance of payments, which had resulted in a decline in the value of the dollar in foreign exchange markets. Subsequently, in late 1980 and in 1981–1982, higher U.S. interest rates led to a stronger dollar in foreign exchange markets.

Higher interest rates in the American financial markets, it was thought, might tend to slow down any possible short-term outflows of capital and might even lead to a recycling of some of the interest-sensitive funds in some instances. This might particularly be the case if the differential between American and Eurodollar interest rates could be narrowed.

# BALANCE OF PAYMENTS AND AMERICAN MONETARY POLICY

Nearly two decades earlier, in the early part of the 1960s, when credit ease policies were promoting economic growth, concern was expressed by the monetary authorities relating to the balance of payments deficit and the gold outflow from the United States. A major justification for dropping the bills only doctrine relating to Federal Reserve open market operations in February 1961 was the necessity of pushing up short-term money market rates for balance-of-payments reasons at the same time that long-term interest rates were prevented from rising. In the years since 1965, when inflationary pressures developed in the American economy, part of the concern with developing public policies for dealing with the inflationary problem has related to the adverse effect that inflation would surely have on the balance of payments.

## *American Balance of Payments Affects Other Countries*

The state of the American balance of payments is important not only in the effect of balance of payments developments on the formulation and execution of monetary and fiscal policy but also in the effect of the American balance of payments on other countries. Because the United States has the most productive economic system in the world, its exports and imports are larger than those of any other nation. Furthermore, the American dollar is still a key international currency. When the United States runs a deficit in its balance of payments, other countries acquire dollars that they can add to their monetary reserves; when there is a positive balance in the American balance of payments, an important source of growth in world monetary reserves is withdrawn. Other countries are therefore vitally concerned with the state of the American balance of payments both because of the effects on them of exports to the United States and of the impacts on international liquidity.

# THE DOLLAR SHORTAGE AND THE MARSHALL PLAN

In the early years after World War II many countries seemed to be suffering from a "dollar shortage." The **monetary reserves** of most countries were inadequate to pay for the large imports of goods needed to rebuild economies damaged by the war. Furthermore, the American balance of payments seemed to be tending toward a chronic surplus on current account, as exports of goods and services were much larger than imports of goods and services. The Marshall Plan, involving large American loans and grants from 1948 to 1951, helped to correct the shortage of dollars in foreign countries.

The success of the Marshall Plan may be gauged by the fact that the persistent surpluses of the American balance of payments of the early postwar period were turned into chronic deficits after 1950, except for 1957 and 1968, when there were small surpluses. These new chronic deficits in the American balance of payments did not reach alarming proportions, however, until 1958. The importance of this new problem for national policy in that year was also underlined by the fact that the United States lost $2.3 billion out of its then large gold stock in that year.

## Gold Outflow from the United States

In the next few years the United States continued to have a net outflow of gold. From a total gold stock of $22.7 billion at the end of 1957, the United States lost $12.4 billion of gold in the next eleven years, so that its stock of gold fell to a level of $10.4 billion at the end of 1968. That was an average **gold outflow** of more than $1 billion a year. From the end of 1968 to the end of 1973, the stock of gold held by the United States remained approximately constant.

The increase in the price of gold in December 1971 and in February 1973 resulted in the value of the gold stock held by the United States at the end of 1973 being increased somewhat, to $11.6 billion. At the end of 1981, the United States still held more than $11 billion at the official price of $42.44 an ounce. At world market prices, however, the value of the United States gold stock was worth more than $120 billion.

## THE CONCEPT OF THE BALANCE OF PAYMENTS

The balance of payments for a country such as the United States shows all the annual transactions in goods, services, and capital flows that result in either (a) an increase in the demand for foreign currencies and an increase in the supply of American dollars, or (b) an increase in the demand for American dollars and an increase in the supply of foreign currencies. Exports of goods and services increase the demand for dollars and/or the supply of foreign currencies, whereas imports increase the demand for foreign currencies and/or the supply of American dollars. Capital outflow as a result of private capital movements or governmental loans and spending abroad increases the supply of American dollars and/or increases the demand for foreign currencies.

All transactions that ordinarily involve payments by foreigners to Americans are considered credit items. Transactions that ordinarily involve payments by Americans to foreigners are considered debit items. Because the balance of payments is a balance sheet, the total of all credits must equal the total of all debits when all transfers of monetary reserves are included.

A deficit or surplus in the balance of payments occurs if the transactions involving foreign trade and capital movements do not in themselves balance out. In this case, certain transactions in transferring money reserves such as a gold flow must be undertaken by the governments of the countries involved in order that the overall total of credits be equal to the overall total of debits.

## Balance on Goods and Services

The oldest balance of payments idea is the merchandise **"balance of trade,"** which is simply the relationship between total exports of goods of a country and that same country's imports of goods. This is shown in Table 27–1 for three decades from 1950 to 1979 inclusive. Although there tended to be a surplus of goods and services throughout this period, except for 1977–1978, the U.S. merchandise trade balance by the decade of the 1970s was invariably unfavorable, with particularly large deficits beginning in 1977.

**Investment income,** however, which represents a return on past large direct and indirect American investments abroad, continued to rise throughout this period. The annual return of investment income was well under $10 billion prior to the 1970s. By the end of that decade it had soared to $32.3 billion. **Financial transfers,** however, were generally negative (i.e., there were usually both short-term and long-term outflows of capital from the United States seeking a higher rate of return abroad).

## THE BUSINESS CYCLE AND THE AMERICAN BALANCE OF PAYMENTS

The effect of the business cycle on the American balance of payments from 1950 to 1979 inclusive can be seen, in part, in the data given shortly

**Table 27-1  Balance of Payments of the United States, 1950–1979 (Annual average, in billions of dollars)[a]**

| Component | 1950–57 | 1958–64 | 1965–69 | 1970–74 | 1975–76 | 1977–78 | 1979 |
|---|---|---|---|---|---|---|---|
| **Goods and services** | **3.6** | **5.5** | **5.4** | **5.3** | **16.3** | **– 8.9** | **5.3** |
| of which: | | | | | | | |
| Merchandise trade balance | 3.1 | 4.5 | 2.8 | – 2.1 | – 0.1 | –32.3 | –29.4 |
| Investment income | 2.7 | 4.0 | 5.5 | 9.9 | 14.4 | 19.8 | 32.3 |
| **Financial transfers** | **–4.5** | **–8.0** | **–5.5** | **+18.6** | **–26.7** | **–26.5** | **–9.8** |
| Unilateral transfers (excluding military) | –2.8 | –2.5 | –3.0 | – 4.4 | – 4.8 | – 4.9 | – 5.6 |
| United States government (excluding reserve assets) | –0.3 | –1.1 | –2.0 | – 1.5 | – 3.8 | – 4.2 | – 3.8 |
| United States banks, net | 0.1 | –0.2 | 3.5 | – 4.1 | –11.6 | –10.4 | 6.6 |
| United States claims reported by United States banks | –0.3 | –1.1 | –0.1 | – 6.6 | –17.5 | –22.2 | –26.1 |
| United States liabilities reported by United States banks | 0.4 | 0.9 | 3.6 | 2.5 | 5.8 | 11.6 | 32.7 |
| Other United States private assets | –2.3 | –4.1 | –6.9 | –11.4 | –22.5 | –22.2 | –32.4 |
| Other foreign private assets in United States | 0.5 | 0.5 | 3.1 | 6.1 | 7.9 | 10.2 | 16.4 |
| Errors and omissions | 0.3 | –0.5 | –0.2 | – 3.2 | 8.1 | 4.9 | 28.7 |
| **Allocation of special drawing rights (SDRs)** | — | — | — | 0.5 | — | — | 1.1 |
| **Allocation of SDRs plus total financial transfers** | **–4.5** | **–8.0** | **–5.5** | **–18.1** | **–26.7** | **–26.5** | **11.0** |
| **Reserve transactions, total** | **0.9** | **2.5** | **0.1** | **12.9** | **10.5** | **35.4** | **–16.3** |
| United States reserve assets (+ = decline) | 0.1 | 1.2 | 0 | 0.7 | – 1.7 | 0.2 | – 1.1 |
| Claims of foreign monetary authorities on United States, (+ = increase) | 0.7 | 1.3 | 0.2 | 12.2 | 12.2 | 35.2 | –15.2 |
| of which: changes in liabilities reported by United States banks | 0.6 | 0.5 | 0.6 | 2.1 | – 0.6 | 3.1 | 6.6 |

[a]Because of rounding, figures may not add to totals.

SOURCE: Federal Reserve Bank of New York, *Quarterly Review*, Summer 1980, p. 24.

in Table 27–1. It can also be seen graphically in Figure 27–1, where the shaded areas represent recession periods. The bottom graph of Figure 27–1 demonstrates that the balance on goods and services for the United States tends to deteriorate prior to a recession and then typically improves dramatically after a recession. When the graph is rising, the balance on goods and services is falling toward zero, or beyond, whereas when the graph is falling the balance on goods and services is improving.

The top graph in Figure 27–1 shows that financial transfers tend to increase prior to, and during, a recession and then fall afterward. The movement of such financial transfers is somewhat similar to that of the balance of goods and services but it is not quite as closely correlated with the business cycle.

## UNITED STATES BALANCE ON CURRENT ACCOUNT

The United States **balance on current account** is shown for the ten years from 1972–1981 inclusive in Table 27–2. This is in many ways perhaps the most significant part of the American balance of payments, because it clearly indicates both changes in the competitive position of American industry vis-à-vis other foreign competitors (exports) and also the high marginal propensity to import of the United States (imports). It can be noted in this table that American exports of merchandise increased in every year from 1972 to 1981, in some years quite strongly. For the entire

**Figure 27–1  Cyclical Movements in the U.S. Balance of Payments**

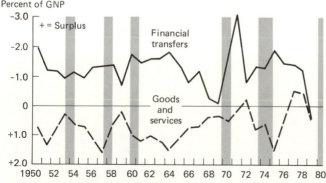

Shaded areas represent periods of recession, as defined by the National Bureau of Economic Research.

SOURCE: Federal Reserve Bank of New York, *Quarterly Review*, Summer 1980, p. 25.

**Table 27-2   U.S. Balance on Current Account, 1972–1981 (In millions of dollars)**

| Credit + or Debits — | 1972 | 1973 | 1974 | 1975 | 1976 | 1977 | 1978 | 1979 | 1980 | 1981[a] |
|---|---|---|---|---|---|---|---|---|---|---|
| Balance on current account | −9,710 | 335 | −3,357 | 18,445 | 4,339 | −15,221 | −14,075 | 1,414 | 3,723 | 6,578 |
| Merchandise trade balance | −6,409 | 955 | −5,277 | 9,047 | −9,353 | −31,059 | −33,759 | −27,346 | −25,342 | −27,817 |
| Merchandise exports | 49,388 | 71,379 | 98,309 | 107,088 | 114,694 | 120,585 | 142,054 | 184,473 | 223,966 | 233,966 |
| Merchandise imports | −55,797 | −70,424 | −103,568 | −98,041 | −124,047 | −151,644 | −175,813 | −211,819 | −249,308 | −264,117 |
| Military transactions, net | −3,621 | −2,317 | −2,158 | −876 | 312 | 1,334 | 738 | −1,947 | −2,515 | −1,943 |
| Investment income, net | 4,321 | 5,179 | 10,121 | 12,795 | 15,933 | 17,507 | 21,400 | 33,462 | 32,762 | 36,757 |
| Other service transactions, net | 2,803 | 3,222 | 3,830 | 2,095 | 2,469 | 1,705 | 2,613 | 2,839 | 5,874 | 6,344 |
| Remittances, pensions, and other transfers | −1,606 | −1,903 | −1,721 | −1,721 | −1,878 | −1,932 | −1,884 | −2,057 | −2,397 | −2,302 |
| U.S. Government grants (excluding military) | −2,173 | −1,938 | −5,461 | −2,894 | −3,145 | −2,776 | −3,183 | −3,536 | −4,659 | −4,460 |

[a]Data for 1981 are preliminary.

SOURCE: Board of Governors of the Federal Reserve System, *Federal Reserve Bulletins*, Feb. 1974, p. A 72; Feb. 1976, p. A 58; Sept. 1978, p. A 54; Aug. 1981, p. A 52; March 1982, p. A 54.

period, exports increased by nearly fivefold from $49,388 million in 1972 to $233,966 million in 1981.

Unfortunately, however, for the merchandise trade balance, imports in the same period also increased by nearly fivefold. Imports rose from $55,797 million in 1972 to $264,117 million in 1981. Because of the considerable growth in real income in the United States in this period, except for the serious recession of 1973-1975, imports increased in almost every year. In some cases, of course, imported products were cheaper than American products, but in other cases the American consumer simply desired the variety offered by a number of foreign products. As a consequence of this strong growth in imports, every year in this ten-year period except for 1973 and 1975 recorded an unfavorable balance of trade (i.e. the merchandise trade balance was negative).

The balance on current account, however, presents a more favorable picture than that shown in the merchandise trade balance. In more than half of the period there was a favorable balance on current account. Much of the good news in the balance on current account was due to high and rising flow of investment income back to the United States on past investment abroad. Investment income actually rose nearly ninefold from 1972 to 1981, as it soared from $4,321 million in 1972 to $36,757 million in 1981. Other service transactions also helped to offset a frequent deficit in the merchandise trade account, as they rose nearly threefold from $2,803 million in 1972 to $6,344 million in 1981.

Data on the United States trade and current account balances for the six years from 1974 to 1979 inclusive are graphed in Figure 27–2. Here it can be seen that the equilibrium in such current account balances in 1974 was replaced by a substantial surplus in the recession year of 1975, primarily because imports always fall in a serious recession period. As the U.S. economy improved in its performance in the second half of the 1970s, the trade and current account balances deteriorated.

There was, however, a substantial move by the current account balance toward equilibrium in 1979, in large part because investment income returned to the United States went up sharply. As can be noted in Table 27–2, such investment income rose some 50 percent in 1979, as it increased from $21.4 billion in 1978 to $33.4 billion in 1979. Let us now examine recent trends in major categories of exports and imports in the U.S. balance of payments.

## MERCHANDISE EXPORTS AND IMPORTS

Looking at the major categories of American exports and imports for 1978, 1979, 1980, 1981, and by quarters for 1981 in Table 27–3, we find that

**Figure 27–2    United States Trade and Current Account Balances**

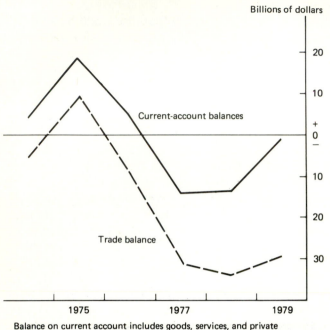

Balance on current account includes goods, services, and private
and government transfers.

SOURCE: Board of Governors of the Federal Reserve System, *Federal Reserve Bulletin*, April 1980, p. 287.

some trends for earlier years are continuing, whereas others are changing. Agricultural exports in particular were booming after the mid-1970s.
This, of course, assisted in narrowing the trade deficit. From the fourth
quarter of 1977 to the fourth quarter of 1978, such agricultural exports
rose nearly 25 percent. In 1979, such exports rose by 18 percent, as can be
seen in Table 27–3. Such exports continued their strong growth by rising
nearly 20 percent in 1980 to a total of $42 billion and rose again somewhat
in 1981 to $44.3 billion. Also in the first quarter, such exports continued to
increase, though they sagged somewhat in the remaining quarters.

Nonagricultural exports also began to grow in 1978, after a slight
decline in 1977. They continued to grow strongly in 1979, 1980, and 1981.
Only in the last two quarters of 1981 was there some sag in such exports.

Imports, as already noted, grew strongly in the 1970s, in part
because of price increases on OPEC oil that caused a larger dollar
amount of imports even for the same volume of imported oil. In fact, the
volume of barrels of oil imported also grew in the 1970s, though such oil
imports declined in the early 1980s. In Table 27–3, the dollar amount of
petroleum imports increased from $60 billion in 1979 to $78.9 billion in

**Table 27–3    U.S. Merchandise Trade, International Transactions Basis, 1978–1981**
**(In billions of dollars, seasonally adjusted annual rates)**

| Item | 1978 | 1979 | 1980 | 1981 | 1981 Q1 | Q2 | Q3 | Q4 |
|---|---|---|---|---|---|---|---|---|
| | | | | | *Value* | | | |
| **Exports** .......... **142.1** | **182.1** | **224.0** | **236.3** | **244.0** | **241.5** | **231.7** | **228.0** |
| Agricultural......... 29.9 | 35.4 | 42.2 | 44.3 | 50.8 | 44.2 | 40.1 | 42.0 |
| Nonagricultural ..... 112.2 | 146.7 | 181.7 | 192.0 | 193.2 | 197:3 | 191.7 | 186.0 |
| **Imports** .......... **175.8** | **211.5** | **249.3** | **264.1** | **262.6** | **269.1** | **259.8** | **265.0** |
| Petroleum .......... 42.3 | 60.0 | 78.9 | 77.6 | 83.1 | 84.7 | 71.6 | 70.9 |
| Nonpetroleum ...... 133.5 | 151.5 | 170.4 | 186.5 | 179.5 | 184.4 | 188.2 | 194.1 |
| **Trade balance** ...... **–33.8** | **–29.4** | **–25.3** | **–27.8** | **–18.6** | **–27.6** | **–28.1** | **–36.9** |

SOURCE: Board of Governors of the Federal Reserve System, *Federal Reserve Bulletins*, April 1980, p. 286; April 1981, p. 270; March 1982, p. 209.

1980, but clearly declined in 1981. The value of such imports rose because of higher prices, whereas the volume of oil imported already declined in 1980, which was continued in 1981. The quarterly data for 1981, moreover, showed a marked decline in the seasonally adjusted annual dollar rates of oil imported for most quarters of 1981. The fourth quarter rate, for example, was some $12 billion below the first quarter rate.

Nonpetroleum imports, in contrast to petroleum, not only increased in the 1970s but continued to increase in the early 1980s. The quarterly movements of such imports in 1981, as shown in Table 27–3, show some variability but no clear sign of decline. Because of this clear tendency of total merchandise imports to increase over time, it seems evident that American exports must likewise grow strongly over time to prevent the merchandise trade deficit from widening.

# UNITED STATES TRADE BALANCE BY GEOGRAPHIC AREAS

In Table 27–4 the United States trade balance by major geographic areas is shown from 1973 to 1980 inclusive. First of all, it can be noted that the total trade balance had been in deficit for most years, with a large jump in the annual trade deficit beginning in 1977. Despite the overall trade deficit, the United States typically runs a trade surplus with Western Europe, which even increased sharply in 1979 and 1980. There were

Table 27–4    United States Trade Balance by Major Geographic Areas[a], 1973–1980
(In billions of dollars)

|  | 1973 | 1974 | 1975 | 1976 | 1977 | 1978 | 1979 | 1980 |
|---|---|---|---|---|---|---|---|---|
| Total trade | 0.9 | − 5.3 | 9.0 | − 9.3 | −30.9 | −33.8 | −29.5 | −27.4 |
| Industrial countries | −0.5 | 3.4 | 10.5 | 4.8 | − 2.3 | −11.2 | 1.2 | 7.4 |
| Western Europe | 1.4 | 3.9 | 9.1 | 8.9 | 5.9 | 2.9 | 12.3 | 20.5 |
| Germany | −1.9 | − 1.6 | − 0.3 | − 0.2 | − 1.4 | − 2.8 | − 2.3 | − 0.9 |
| United Kingdom | 0.2 | 0.6 | 1.1 | 0.9 | 0.9 | 0.8 | 2.8 | 2.8 |
| Canada | −1.0 | − 0.6 | 1.8 | − 0.1 | − 1.1 | − 2.3 | − 2.4 | − 3.2 |
| Japan | −1.3 | − 1.7 | − 1.7 | − 5.3 | − 8.0 | −11.6 | − 8.6 | −10.4 |
| NonOPEC LDCs | 1.6 | 1.5 | 5.0 | − 1.2 | − 6.8 | − 5.7 | − 3.0 | 2.1 |
| OPEC | −1.7 | −11.0 | − 8.9 | −15.8 | −22.9 | −18.4 | −30.5 | −38.2 |

[a]Balance-of-payments basis, excluding military goods.

SOURCE: Continental Bank, *Continental Comment*, April 10, 1981, p. 1.

essentially two reasons for the improvement in trade with Europe for this period: (1) Europe was then enjoying somewhat stronger economic growth than the United States, (2) the devaluation of the dollar in foreign exchange markets in 1977 and 1978 led to improved price competitiveness of United States goods in the two following years.

At the same time that the Untied States was running a trade surplus with most of Europe, it ran a deficit with West Germany, a larger deficit with Japan, and a really big deficit with the OPEC countries, from which the United States continued to import large amounts of oil. Even a 20 percent cut in the volume of petroleum imports was not enough to eliminate the deficit, because the OPEC nations increased the price of oil by 60 percent. Imports from Japan have also increased sharply since 1973. Automotive vehicles represent about 37 percent of imports from Japan and have continued to increase at a somewhat faster pace than imports from Japan generally.

## POSTWAR TRENDS IN EXPORTS
## AND IMPORTS, 1946–1980

Trends in exports and imports for the United States over a longer, thirty-six-year period are shown in Table 27–5 for the years 1946 to 1981 inclusive. In this period there was a surplus of exports over imports in every year until the 1970s. In that decade the traditional merchandise trade surplus gave way to a merchandise trade deficit except for the recession years 1973 and 1975. Only in the recession year 1975 did exports

**Table 27–5   Merchandise Exports and Imports for the United States, 1946–1981 (In millions of dollars)**

| Year | Exports | Imports | Surplus of Exports over Imports |
|------|---------|---------|-------------------------------|
| 1946 | 11,707  | 5,073   | 6,634   |
| 1947 | 16,015  | 5,979   | 10,036  |
| 1948 | 13,193  | 7,563   | 5,630   |
| 1949 | 12,149  | 6,879   | 5,270   |
| 1950 | 10,117  | 9,108   | 1,009   |
| 1951 | 14,123  | 11,202  | 2,921   |
| 1952 | 13,319  | 10,838  | 2,481   |
| 1953 | 12,281  | 10,990  | 1,291   |
| 1954 | 12,799  | 10,354  | 2,445   |
| 1955 | 14,280  | 11,527  | 2,753   |
| 1956 | 17,379  | 12,804  | 4,575   |
| 1957 | 19,390  | 13,291  | 6,009   |
| 1958 | 16,264  | 12,952  | 3,312   |
| 1959 | 16,282  | 15,310  | 972     |
| 1960 | 19,459  | 14,723  | 4,736   |
| 1961 | 19,913  | 14,497  | 5,416   |
| 1962 | 20,945  | 16,389  | 4,556   |
| 1963 | 21,989  | 16,996  | 4,993   |
| 1964 | 25,288  | 18,619  | 6,669   |
| 1965 | 26,285  | 21,492  | 4,793   |
| 1966 | 29,176  | 25,541  | 3,635   |
| 1967 | 30,468  | 26,991  | 3,477   |
| 1968 | 33,626  | 33,226  | 400     |
| 1969 | 36,788  | 36,043  | 745     |
| 1970 | 42,025  | 39,952  | 2,073   |
| 1971 | 42,911  | 45,563  | −2,652  |
| 1972 | 48,419  | 55,583  | −7,164  |
| 1973 | 71,379  | 70,424  | 955     |
| 1974 | 93,310  | 103,679 | −5,369  |
| 1975 | 107,088 | 98,058  | 9,030   |
| 1976 | 114,692 | 123,916 | −9,224  |
| 1977 | 120,816 | 151,689 | −30,873 |
| 1978 | 143,682 | 174,759 | −31,075 |
| 1979 | 184,473 | 211,819 | −27,346 |
| 1980 | 233,966 | 249,308 | −25,342 |
| 1981 | 236,300 | 264,117 | −27,817 |

SOURCE: Economic Report of the President, Jan. 1981, p. 344, *Federal Reserve Bulletins,* July 1981, p. A53, March 1982, p. A 54.

greatly exceed imports. Part of that "favorable" balance of trade was the result of a strong gain in exports but another part was the result of a sharp drop in imports caused by declining aggregate demand in the United States in 1975, as already noted. By the late 1970s and early 1980s, a large chronic unfavorable balance of trade—excess of merchandise imports over merchandise exports—had become characteristic of the U.S. balance of payments.

In the 1960s, on the other hand, there was typically an export surplus. Nevertheless, as shown in Table 27–5, this surplus tended to decline toward the end of the decade as imports grew more than exports. In any case, no year in the postwar period quite matched 1947, in which an export surplus of $10 billion was recorded, though 1975 with its surplus of $9 billion came close. However, the relative surplus was much greater in 1947, because exports totaled some $16 billion as compared with $5.9 billion of imports. In 1975, exports were $107 billion, whereas imports were $98 billion. In 1976, imports rose much more sharply than did exports. The result was a $9.2 billion deficit in that year, which soared even higher to more than $30 billion in 1977. The following three years also had large merchandise trade deficits ranging from $24 billion to $30 billion.

## STRONG RISE IN IMPORTS INTO THE UNITED STATES

The strong increase in American imports in the 1960s, 1970s, and early 1980s can be attributable primarily to the continued secular expansion in aggregate demand within the United States. In 1980, for example, the gross national product rose by 8.8 percent over the previous year, even though there was a small decline in real output. Inflation in both consumer and producer prices in the United States also led to more imports.

The continuing rise in domestic wholesale prices for nearly two decades beginning in 1965 meant that many foreign products now looked more attractive to American buyers. For example in the twelve months from mid-1980 to mid-1981, producer prices for finished goods in the United States rose by 10.2 percent. The same rise in American prices meant that business firms exporting abroad faced more difficulty in pricing their products competitively. The rise in domestic spending levels also absorbed some American products that might have been exported, as well as increased imports from other countries, because often prices on American products were rising faster than prices on foreign products. Imports actually rose faster than domestic expenditures.

## Balancing Items to Offset Deficit

The negative, or unfavorable relationship between merchandise exports and imports is largely offset, as can be seen in Table 27–6 by a positive flow of services in the current account balance. Much of this is investment income returning to the U.S., as a result of large private capital investments made abroad in earlier years.

These earlier private capital outflows, which are negative items in the balance of payments, continued to be so in the 1970s and early 1980s. This is shown, not only in Table 27–6 but also in Table 27–7, which covers the most recent seven years. Government economic and military credits abroad also provide negative entries in these accounts. Some other countries, both OPEC and others, as shown in Table 27–6, have invested each year a substantial amount of capital in the U.S. Let us now focus specifically on capital flows in the balance of payments.

## CAPITAL FLOWS IN THE BALANCE OF PAYMENTS

Exports and imports of goods and services, though accounting for most of the dollar totals in the balance of payments, are not the only items in the balance. Private capital outflows and inflows, as well as government grants, loans, and other financial transactions (including gold flows), are also important. Traditionally, it was often argued that private and government capital and gold flows were simply "balancing transactions." Hence if a country was importing more goods than it was exporting, it could expect to lose gold unless it was able to import capital from abroad. Conversely, if a country exported more than it imported, it would gain gold unless it was willing to make private or government investments abroad.

### Disequilibrating Effects of Capital Flows

Since World War II, there have been a number of years in which such **capital flows** were disequilibrating rather than equilibrating (e.g., in many years the capital outflows from the United States were greater than the surplus on current account). Hence a current account surplus was more than offset by negative items in the balance of payments, so that the overall balance of payments was in deficit.

**Table 27–6    U.S. International Transactions (In billions of dollars capital inflow +)**

| Item | 1980 | 1981 | 1981 Q1 | Q2 | Q3 | Q4 |
|---|---|---|---|---|---|---|
| U.S. current account balance[a]............ | 3.7 | 6.6 | 3.3 | 1.2 | 2.1 | −.1 |
| Trade balance........................ | −25.3 | −27.8 | − 4.7 | −6.9 | −7.0 | −9.2 |
| Other, net .......................... | 29.0 | 34.4 | 8.0 | 8.1 | 9.1 | 9.1 |
| | | | | | | |
| Foreign official capital flows, net ......... | 15.5 | 5.2 | 5.5 | −2.8 | −5.7 | 8.1 |
| Industrial countries................... | 1.0 | −11.9 | .6 | −6.6 | −8.4 | 2.5 |
| OPEC.............................. | 12.7 | 13.4 | 5.4 | 2.7 | 3.1 | 2.2 |
| Other countries ..................... | 1.7 | 3.7 | −.6 | 1.2 | −.4 | 3.4 |
| U.S. government reserve asset flows, net .. | −8.2 | −5.2 | − 4.5 | −0.9 | c | .3 |
| | | | | | | |
| U.S. government credits, net[a] ............ | −5.2 | −5.1 | −1.4 | −1.5 | −1.3 | −1.0 |
| Private capital flows, net ................ | −36.7 | −27.1 | −14.8 | −3.5 | 6.1 | −14.4 |
| Allocations of special drawing rights...... | 1.2 | 1.1 | 1.1 | c | c | c |
| Statistical discrepancy[b] ................ | 29.6 | 24.6 | 10.8 | 7.9 | −1.3 | 7.1 |

[a]Seasonally adjusted.

[b]Net unrecorded inflow = (+).

[c]Less than $50 million.

SOURCE: Board of Governors of the Federal Reserve System, *Federal Reserve Bulletin*, April 1982, p. 208.

The 1960s and 1970s were particularly troublesome in this respect. Capital outflows were not only large but varied considerably from year to year. Furthermore, some areas of the world received more American flows than others. Higher interest rates and higher expected profit rates in Europe attracted substantial amounts of American capital. The great success of the European Common Market in expanding income and output in Europe doubtless increased the magnetic appeal of Europe to American investors.

## Capital Movements

If one studies the data on private capital flows for the period 1975–1980 inclusive as shown in Table 27–6, it is clear that capital flows, like merchandise imports and exports, move on a two-way street. Although United States capital outflows in this period continued in every year to be substantially larger than the foreign capital inflow into the United States, capital flows in and out both grew considerably. Private capital outflows of $96.2 billion in 1981 were nearly four times larger than the $24.4 billion outflow of 1975. On the other hand, foreign capital movements into the United States of $69.1 billion in 1981 were nine times larger than the $7.3

**Table 27-7  Private Capital Flows, 1975–1980 (In millions of dollars; outflow from the United States —)**

| | 1975 | 1976 | 1977 | 1978 | 1979 | 1980 | 1981 |
|---|---|---|---|---|---|---|---|
| Change In U.S. private assets abroad (increase —) | −24,478 | −36,216 | −31,725 | −57,158 | −57,739 | −71,456 | −96,265 |
| Bank reported claims | −13,532 | −20,904 | −11,427 | −33,667 | −26,213 | −46,947 | −84,462 |
| Nonbank reported claims | − 1,447 | − 1,986 | − 1,940 | − 3,853 | − 3,026 | − 2,653 | n.a. |
| U.S. purchase of foreign securities, net | −6,235 | −8,732 | −5,460 | −3,582 | −4,552 | −3,360 | −5,536 |
| U.S. direct investment abroad, net | −6,264 | −4,596 | −12,898 | −16,056 | −23,948 | −18,546 | −6,995 |
| Change in foreign private assets in the U.S. (increase +) | 7,376 | 16,575 | 14,167 | 30,187 | 52,703 | 34,769 | 69,148 |
| U.S. bank reported liabilities | 628 | 10,982 | 6,719 | 16,141 | 32,607 | 10,743 | 41,332 |
| U.S. nonbank reported liabilities | 240 | − 616 | 473 | 1,717 | 2,065 | 5,109 | n.a. |
| Foreign private purchases of U.S. Treasury securities, net | 2,590 | 2,783 | 534 | 2,178 | 4,820 | 2,679 | 2,914 |
| Foreign purchases of other securities, net | 2,503 | 1,250 | 2,713 | 2,254 | 1,334 | 5,384 | 7,078 |
| Foreign direct investment in the U.S., net | 1,414 | 2,176 | 3,728 | 7,896 | 11,877 | 10,853 | 18,664 |

SOURCE: Board of Governors of the Federal Reserve System, *Federal Reserve Bulletins*, June 1978, p. A54; April 1980, p. A54; Aug. 1981, p. A52, March 1982, p. A54.

billion inflow of 1975. It can be noted, however, that capital outflows in 1981 were still larger than capital inflows.

## Growth of Capital Inflows and Outflows

Although United States direct investments had almost tripled in the six-year period from 1975 to 1980 inclusive they still represented one fourth of all United States private assets acquired abroad in 1980, as they had in 1975. Private foreign direct investment in the United States, on the other hand, was a much larger percentage of total foreign acquisitions of assets in the United States in 1980 than had been true only five years earlier in 1975. Such private foreign direct investment was only 19 percent of capital inflows in 1975 but had risen sharply to 31 percent in 1980. Foreign purchases of United States securities, both Treasury securities and others, also rose by 60 percent in this six-year period. American purchases of foreign securities, however, peaked in 1976 and declined sharply thereafter. Such United States purchases of foreign securities in 1980 was only about half of what it had been in 1975.

Some important changes occurred, however, in capital flows in 1981 in contrast with the developments of 1980. Net recorded outflows of private capital, for instance, dropped sharply by nearly $10 billion. The most striking change in private capital flows was a shift in the direct investment category from a net outflow of $8 billion in 1980 to a net inflow of $12 billion in 1981. Direct foreign investment in the U.S. in 1981 totaled $18.6 billion, which was a sharp rise from the $10.8 billion of 1980.

It seems clear after examining these data that private capital flows are quite important in the balance of payments, even though capital outflows are only about one third of the value of imports (both are negative items in the balance of payments). Capital inflows are even less important compared with exports of merchandise, because they are only 11 percent of the value of exports. Both these items are positive in the balance of payments.

## Variability of Private Capital Flows

The variability of private capital flows in the balance of payments over a longer period of time is shown in Figure 27–3 for the period 1952–1979 inclusive. The clear tendency for more capital to flow out of the United States rather than in is clearly seen in this graph as the data show a definite trend toward a larger negative flow (i.e., outflow) of capital over time. Despite this marked trend, there is also considerable volatility of such capital flows over time. Incidentally, these private capital flows

**Figure 27–3    Private Capital Flows in the U.S. Balance of Payments, 1952–1979**

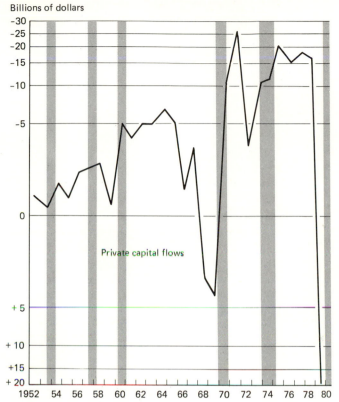

Billions of dollars

"Private capital flows" are the total of changes in the United States private assets abroad, net, other foreign assets in the United States, net, and the statistical discrepancy of the "United States International Transactions".

SOURCE: Federal Reserve Bank of New York, *Quarterly Review*, Summer 1980, p. 27.

include short-term capital flows that are quite sensitive to changes in interest rate differentials from one country to another and to possible changes in official exchange rates of one currency in terms of another.

## FEDERAL RESERVE FOREIGN EXCHANGE OPERATIONS: THE SWAP NETWORK

In order to help changes take place in the value of the dollar in **foreign exchange markets** in a more orderly fashion, the Federal Reserve Bank

**Figure 27–4    The Dollar Against Selected Foreign Currencies**

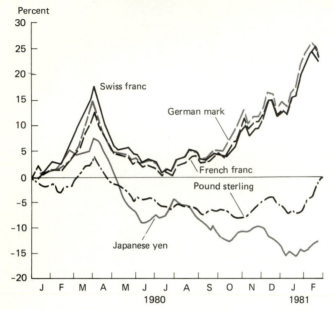

Percentage change of weekly average bid rates for dollars from the average rate for the week of January 2–4, 1980. Figures calculated from New York noon quotations.

SOURCE: Federal Reserve Bank of New York, *Quarterly Review*, Spring 1981, p. 56.

of New York, acting both for the entire Federal Reserve System and the Treasury, intervened in these foreign exchange markets for nearly two decades. Such stabilization operations were abandoned after World War II and not resumed until March 1962. In April 1981, the Treasury after consultation with Federal Reserve officials, announced that "the United States had adopted a **minimal intervention approach**—to intervene only when necessary to counter conditions of disorder in the exchange market."[1]

Prior to this time, however, especially in the late 1970s and in 1980, the Federal Reserve Bank of New York had conducted from time to time substantial operations in the foreign exchange markets. The reason for such intervention was to be found in the great volatility of the dollar's value in these markets in this period. Some idea of this volatility may be gained from Figure 27–4, which shows changes in the value of the dollar for fourteen months in 1980 and early 1981 as measured in terms of the

[1] Board of Governors of the Federal Reserve System, "Treasury and Federal Reserve Foreign Exchange Operations," *Federal Reserve Bulletin*, Sept. 1981, p. 689.

Swiss franc, the German mark, the French franc, the pound sterling, and the Japanese yen.

The Federal Reserve Bank of New York can readily sell dollars in foreign exchange markets if it wishes to offset some of the strength of the dollar, as it did in early 1981. However, it was necessary to borrow currencies from other central banks, if it wished to sell such currencies in order to strengthen the dollar in foreign exchange markets. Such borrowings are called "reciprocal currency arrangements," or "swaps," and the amount of such facilities with the other major central banks for the end of July 1981 are shown in Table 27–8. These **swap arrangements** totaled some $30 billion, some 50 percent more than the total outstanding only four yars earlier. In this same period, a number of these arrangements were heavily used, especially those with the central banks of Germany, Japan, and Switzerland.

## Purposes of the Swap Network

Substantial in-and-out operations were typical of the Foreign Department of the Federal Reserve Bank of New York since its resumption of foreign exchange stabilization operations in 1962, until April 1981, when such major in-and-out operations ceased. Sometimes the swap network

**Table 27–8  Federal Reserve Reciprocal Currency Arrangements (In millions of dollars)**

| Institution | Amount of Facility July 31, 1981 |
|---|---|
| Austrian National Bank | $   250 |
| National Bank of Belgium | 1,000 |
| Bank of Canada | 2,000 |
| National Bank of Denmark | 250 |
| Bank of England | 3,000 |
| Bank of France | 2,000 |
| German Federal Bank | 6,000 |
| Bank of Italy | 3,000 |
| Bank of Japan | 5,000 |
| Bank of Mexico | 700 |
| Netherlands Bank | 500 |
| Bank of Norway | 250 |
| Bank of Sweden | 300 |
| Swiss National Bank | 4,000 |
| Bank for International Settlements: | |
| Swiss francs-dollars | 600 |
| Other authorized European currencies-dollars | 1,250 |
| Total | $30,100 |

SOURCE: Board of Governors of the Federal Reserve System, *Federal Reserve Bulletin*, Sept. 1981, p. 687.

was used to sell foreign currencies against the dollar in the present market; at other times the borrowed foreign currencies were sold in the **forward market.** Often, major stabilization operations were undertaken in concert with foreign central banks. At other times, a foreign central bank would simply draw on its swap agreement with the Federal Reserve to secure dollars so that it could stabilize the value of its currency in various exchange markets.

## Substantial Market Intervention from 1978 to 1981

The two-and-a-half-year period from November 1, 1978, to April 1981 was a particularly active period for Federal Reserve intervention in the foreign exchange markets. On November 1, 1978, President Carter, the U.S. Treasury, and the Federal Reserve announced a series of actions to correct what had become an excessive decline in the value of the dollar in foreign exchange markets. Between early August and the end of October, the dollar had fallen sharply against major foreign currencies. It had depreciated 18 percent in terms of the German mark, 17 percent in terms of the Swiss franc, and 7 percent against the Japanese yen. The dollar had fallen so sharply because of the persistence of large United States trade and current account deficits compared with surpluses in several other industrial countries, and because the inflation rate was rising in the United States, while it was steady or slowly falling abroad.

Large amounts of sales of foreign currencies secured through the swap arrangements were thus made in November and December 1978. A total of some $6.6 billion of foreign currencies was sold in this period. From August 1978 through January 1979, $9.3 billion of such currencies were sold. Some $1.6 billion of German marks were sold in September and October, $2.9 billion in November, and $2.8 billion more in December; these sales of German marks were nearly half of total foreign currencies sold in this six-month period. By early January 1979, the Federal Reserve still had commitments of nearly $5.5 billion with the German Federal Bank, the Swiss National Bank, and the Bank of Japan. By the end of January 1979, however, the Federal Reserve reversed some of these sales and was able to repay some $1.1 billion of indebtedness to foreign central banks.

In early 1979, the value of the dollar continued to sag and the Federal Reserve continued to borrow and sell foreign currencies, especially the German mark. From the end of January to the end of July, the dollar fell a net of 2¼ percent against the continental Western European currencies. Sales of foreign currencies were concentrated in early February and again in June and July. In three trading days through February 8, the Trading Desk of the Federal Reserve Bank of New York sold $507.1 million marks. Some $5.4 billion of foreign currencies was sold in June and July, of which the bulk was German marks.

In the second half of 1979, the dollar continued to decline by a net of 1½ to 5 percent against the German mark and currencies linked to the mark in the European Monetary System, which had been established that spring. Hence to support the dollar the Federal Reserve, acting for itself and the Treasury, sold a total of $5.4 billion of German marks and $67 million of Swiss francs.

## A Stronger Dollar in 1980–1981

From early 1980 through early April, there was considerable demand for the dollar, so U.S. authorities were able to acquire sufficient currencies in the market and from correspondents to repay earlier debt and to build up balances. German marks, Swiss francs, and Japanese yen were thus acquired. Later, when the dollar came under pressure, the Federal Reserve sold off most of these currencies that had been acquired. For the first six months of 1980, the Federal Reserve sold a total of $3.9 billion in foreign currencies, of which $3.5 billion were German marks. By the end of July, however, U.S. authorities were again acquiring foreign currencies in the market to repay swap debt and rebuild balances.

Over the following six-month period—from August 1980 through January 1981—the dollar was in heavy demand in the exchange markets and advanced sharply against other major currencies. In this period the dollar rose by 19 percent against the German mark and by 16 to 20 percent against the other currencies within the joint float of the European Monetary System. This was, of course, in marked contrast to the weakness of the dollar earlier in 1979 and 1980. By the end of October 1980, the Federal Reserve was able to repay in full the remaining $879.7 million owed in swap debt to the German Federal Bank, as well as $166.3 million owed to the Bank of France. For the entire six-month period, the Federal Reserve purchased a total of $7,569.5 million of foreign currencies in the exchange market and sold $368.2 million in the same market.

These heavy trading operations on both sides of the market, which were so typical of the two-and-a-half years from November 1978 to April 1981, came to a halt in April 1981. Before these cessations of operations, considerable intervention occurred in early 1981. On nine trading days in February when the dollar was rising sharply, some $610 million net of marks was purchased in the market and an additional $168.4 million of marks were purchased by correspondents. On March 30, after the assassination attempt on President Reagan, the Trading Desk intervened by selling $74.4 million of marks from balances, which were split evenly between holdings of the Federal Reserve and holdings of the Treasury. The next day, foreign exchange markets quickly returned to more orderly conditions. And in April, as has been noted, the Treasury and the Federal Reserve announced that henceforth they would intervene in the exchange market only if necessary to correct a disorderly market.

The objective of the American authorities after April 1981, as it had been earlier, was to encourage a **"clean" float** of the dollar and other currencies. That is, when developments in the balance of payments of various countries (i.e., a greater surplus or a greater deficit) would tend to lead to changes in the value of that country's currency in the foreign exchange markets, that was supposed to be permitted by the country involved. This, in turn, it was hoped, would lead to self-adjusting developments in trade, services, and capital flows in the country's balance of payments. The main purpose of dollar defenses such as the swap network was to prevent speculators from driving down, or up, the value of the dollar in relation to other currencies when the underlying balance-of-payments situation did not justify such changes in the foreign exchange value of the dollar.

There are still important short-term and long-term capital flows in and out of the United States in the 1980s, as has already been noted. In short, developments in the American balance of payments affect the financial position of other countries. The financial interrelationships among various countries are discussed in the next chapter.

## Questions for Discussion

1. Discuss the likely effects on domestic monetary-fiscal policy and on international monetary relationships if the United States continues to have a persistent deficit in its balance of payments throughout the 1980s, as it had for most of the 1970s. Discuss the causes of this deficit in the 1970s.
2. Discuss the concept of a balance of payments for a country such as the United States. Identify the major credit and debit items.
3. Discuss the balance of trade and the balance of goods and services. Discuss the basic balance in the balance of payments. What has been happening to the surplus in these three accounts in recent years? Why?
4. Discuss the trends in American merchandise exports and imports in the period from 1946–1981 inclusive. Why did imports of goods rise more rapidly than exports of goods in this period?
5. What has been the effect of the business cycle on the U.S. balance of payments in the three decades from 1950 to 1980? (Hint: What happens to the trade deficit in a recession and what happens to it during a recovery period?)
6. Discuss developments in the U.S. balance on current account for the ten years from 1972 to 1981 inclusive. What happened in this period to the merchandise trade balance? Why? What happened to service items in the balance on current account?

7. Discuss the U.S. trade balance by geographic areas. With what area has the United States generally had a trade surplus? Why? With what countries has the United States generally had a trade deficit? Why?

8. Discuss the nature of capital flows in the American balance of payments. What caused these capital outflows to rise from 1975 to 1981 inclusive? Where did most of American capital abroad go? Why? What effect did changes in relative interest rates in the United States and abroad have on this capital flow? Discuss changes in the composition of capital flows (e.g., direct investment).

9. Discuss the nature and operations of the currency swap network. What role does the Federal Reserve Bank of New York play in this network? How did the existence of this swap network assist in stabilizing the value of the dollar in the foreign exchange markets from 1978 to April 1981?

10. Why did the United States cease such foreign exchange operations in April 1981? Do you think it is likely that large in-and-out foreign exchange operations will be resumed? Why?

# Selected Bibliography for Further Reading

BOARD OF GOVERNORS OF THE FEDERAL RESERVE SYSTEM, "Changing Patterns in U.S. International Transactions," *Federal Reserve Bulletin*, April 1976, pp. 283–293.

——, "Treasury and Federal Reserve Foreign Exchange Operations," *Federal Reserve Bulletins*, March 1979, pp. 201–220; Sept. 1979, pp. 720–736; Sept. 1980, pp. 707–725; March 1980, pp. 190–208; March 1981, pp. 209–228; Sept. 1981, pp. 687–706.

——, "U.S. International Transactions in 1980," *Federal Reserve Bulletin*, April 1981, pp. 269–276.

CLARK, STEPHEN V. O., "Perspective on the Untied States External Position Since World War II," *Quarterly Review*, Federal Reserve Bank of New York, Summer 1980, Vol. 4, No. 2, pp. 21–38.

FEDERAL RESERVE BANK OF NEW YORK, *Annual Report* 1981, March 1982.

HELLWELL, J. F. "Balance of Payments: A Survey of Harry Johnson's Contributions," *Canadian Journal of Economics*, Supplement S82–S86, Nov. 1978.

HOLMES, ALAN, AND SCOTT PARDEE, "Treasury and Federal Reserve Foreign Exchange Operations," *Quarterly Review*, Federal Reserve Bank of New York, Spring 1978, pp. 54–70.

INTERNATIONAL MONETARY FUND, *1981 Annual Report* (Washington, D.C.: 1981).

MAYO, ROBERT, "What Is Happening to the U.S. Dollar?" *Economic Perspectives*, Federal Reserve Bank of Chicago, March-April 1978, pp. 10–13.

WESTERFIELD, JANICE M., "Would Fixed Exchange Rates Control Inflation?" *Business Review*, Federal Reserve Bank of Philadelphia, July/August 1976, pp. 3–10.

WOOD, GEOFFREY, AND DOUGLAS R. MUDD, "The Recent U.S. Trade Deficit, No Cause for Panic," *Review*, Federal Reserve Bank of St. Louis, April 1978, pp. 2–7.

> When the exchange between two places, such as London and Paris, is
> at par, it is said to be a sign that the debts from London to Paris are
> compensated by those due from Paris to London.
>
> THE WEALTH OF NATIONS

# 28
## CHAPTER

# The International Monetary System

On August 15, 1971, the United States closed the gold window to foreign
holders of dollars. The inconvertibility of the dollar was accompanied by
a period of weeks and months during which the dollar "floated" on
the foreign exchange markets. In December 1971, the Smithsonian
Agreement was signed in Washington, D.C., which established a new
lower par value for the dollar and raised the official price of gold from
$35 to $38 an ounce. Fourteen months later, in mid-February 1973, the
dollar was devalued again, and the price of gold was raised officially to
$42.22 an ounce.

## INTERNATIONAL MONETARY FUND, 1971–1981

Although the organization and functioning of the **International Monetary Fund (IMF),** which began operations on January 1, 1946, are discussed in detail later in the chapter, it should be noted here that the
unilateral actions of the United States in mid-August 1971 posed a major
challenge to the IMF and the entire international monetary system of
which it is an integral part. At that time the United States prevented
convertibility of the dollar into gold.

The previous monetary system had been established by the Bretton Woods conference of 1944 and was constructed on the principles of stable exchange rates, convertibility of currencies into gold, and the option to borrow short-term reserves by nations suffering a short-run deficit in their balance of payments. Now, some nations such as the United States after 1971 were taking it upon themselves to make their **currencies inconvertible** and to change the par value of their currencies without consulting the IMF in advance. Subsequently, all members of the IMF went even further in abandoning **par exchange rates** by letting their currencies float on international exchange markets for prolonged periods of time.

## Emphasis on Foreign Exchange Markets

When the United States stopped convertibility of officially held dollars into gold or other reserve assets, the major foundation of the par system of relatively stable international exchange rates was abandoned for the market system in which exchange rates would be determined day by day, and sometimes even hour by hour, in the foreign exchange markets in New York, London, and the other major financial centers in the world. Often nations intervened in these markets to protect the value of their currency, as discussed for the United States in the preceding chapter. Nevertheless, there was much more uncertainty as to the future value of any given currency, and speculative movements of capital often anticipated and sometimes brought about significant changes in the value of any one currency. In such a new atmosphere, the role of the IMF was bound to be quite different from what it was originally intended.

In many ways, the twelve years from 1971 to 1982 were a period of transition for the international monetary system and for the IMF itself. It was not always clear what the shape of the new international monetary arrangements would be, but it did seem clear after more than a decade of experience that the foreign exchange markets would be more important than they had been before 1971.

## A New Role for the IMF

This did not necessarily mean that the IMF, with its short-term loans to countries experiencing balance of payments difficulties, would be less important than it had been in the twenty-five years prior to 1971. Membership in the IMF, in fact, was eagerly sought in the decade from the end of 1971 to the end of 1981. Twenty-one additional countries joined the IMF in this decade, bringing membership in this key international organization to 143 countries in 1981. The new members were largely small developing countries, because the major industrial countries were typically members of the IMF from its inception. A larger number of predominantly agricultural developing countries sharpened some of the conflicts of interest that already existed between the rich industrial countries and the poor agricultural countries.

In late 1981, the IMF approved a loan to India that was the largest loan it had ever made. In 1980 India had suffered a $3.3 billion deficit in its balance of payments, owing in part to rising world oil prices. The loan to India was some $5.8 billion, which would be received over a three-year period and would subsequently be repaid over the following four years. The largest previous loan had been made to Great Britain for $3.9 billion in 1977.

Some of the industrial countries in the IMF were not entirely supportive of this shift in emphasis in lending from loans to the industrial to the developing countries. But demands for borrowing from the developing nations were likely to continue, because both Poland and Hungary applied for IMF membership in late 1981. Poland in particular had been running deficits in its balance of payments for some years, largely financed by borrowing from Western countries. At the end of 1981, Poland's external debt was estimated at $27 billion.

It was quite possible for major industrial nations like the United States also to have a serious deficit in their balance of payments. In fact, a chronic and growing deficit in the U.S. balance of payments is what induced the United States to jettison the par system of international exchange rates, which had been jealously guarded by the IMF for twenty-five years. Nevertheless, short-term borrowing from the IMF and policy measures at home (e.g., monetary and fiscal restraint to deal with growing inflationary pressures) could often be counted on to correct balance of payments problems. Changes in the value of the currency also could assist in redressing such problems. Hence a lowered value of the dollar in the early 1970s helped strengthen exports and curbed at least some imports.

Nevertheless, the balance of payments problems of the developing nations seemed more intractable. For major industrial countries and developing agricultural nations the series of oil price shocks administered by OPEC in 1973 and in following years up to the early 1980s posed very serious policy problems. Any inflationary problems of these countries were bound to be aggravated. Any balance of payments deficit was sure to worsen as the price of oil imports soared.

But these problems seemed much worse for many of the developing countries that lacked domestic oil supplies than they did for most industrial countries. An example of the problems facing such developing countries in the early 1980s is given later in the chapter, along with some of the problems that it poses for the IMF. But let us first consider some of the major functions of foreign exchange markets that have always been important but are even more important in the decade of the 1980s than they were before 1971.

## FOREIGN EXCHANGE MARKETS

Although in many ways the world is one market in which goods and services are exchanged, the functioning of this international market is complicated by numerous different political sovereignties. And each country has its own kind of currency, or money, to be used as a unit of account. There are pesos and marks, francs and dollars, pounds and cruzeiros. If the citizens of one country wish to buy goods from another country, they must first acquire the local currency to pay exporters in their own money. When one currency is exchanged for another, the transaction occurs in the foreign exchange market. The price of one currency in terms of another is called the **exchange rate.**

### *Pricing Foreign Currencies in Dollars*

In Table 28–1 the prices of a number of foreign currencies are given in terms of American dollars for May 17, 1982. In other countries, foreign exchange rates would be quoted for their own local currency. After examining this table, for example, it is easy to convert West German marks, which are here quoted at $.4344 each into a measure of the German value of the dollar. That is, the price of $1 in West Germany would be quoted at about 2.3 deutsche marks. In France the dollar was valued at about 6 francs, since the franc was quoted at $.1660.

Table 28–1 also shows that some currencies are worth more in terms of dollars than other currencies. The British pound was valued at $1.8270, whereas some currencies in Latin America have a very low value in terms of the American dollar. What, then, determines the exchange value of one currency in terms of another currency? Or, to ask the same thing, what determines the foreign exchange rate of a given currency in terms of another currency? This question is answered in the following discussion of the New York foreign exchange market and in the discussion of the theory of foreign exchange markets.

### *The New York Foreign Exchange Market*

Traditionally, wherever foreign exchange transactions have taken place, they have tended to be related to the London foreign exchange market.

**Table 28–1   Foreign Exchange Rates**

*Friday, May 14, 1982*

*The New York foreign exchange selling rates below apply to trading among banks in amounts of $1 million and more, as quoted at 3 p.m. Eastern time by Bankers Trust Co. Retail transactions provide fewer units of foreign currency per dollar.*

| | U.S. $ equiv. | | Currency per U.S. $ | |
|---|---|---|---|---|
| Country | Fri. | Thurs. | Fri. | Thurs. |
| **Argentina** (Peso) | | | | |
| Financial .......... | .000071 | .000071 | 14000.00 | 14000.00 |
| **Australia** (Dollar). .... | 1.0618 | 1.0607 | .9418 | .9428 |
| **Austria** (Schilling) .... | .0617 | .0619 | 16.22 | 16.15 |
| **Belgium** (Franc) | | | | |
| Commercial rate ... | .0229 | .0230 | 43.57 | 43.34 |
| Financial rate ...... | .0213 | .0213 | 46.98 | 46.98 |
| **Brazil** (Cruzeiro) ..... | .00644 | .00644 | 155.23 | 155.23 |
| **Britain** (Pound) ...... | 1.8270 | 1.8190 | .5473 | .5498 |
| 30-Day Forward ... | 1.8303 | 1.8226 | .5464 | .5487 |
| 90-Day Forward ... | 1.8349 | 1.8271 | .5450 | .5473 |
| 180-Day Forward ... | 1.8406 | 1.8329 | .5433 | .5456 |
| **Canada** (Dollar) ...... | .8082 | .8070 | 1.2373 | 1.2392 |
| 30-Day Forward ... | .8076 | .8059 | 1.2383 | 1.2408 |
| 90-Day Forward ... | .8064 | .8047 | 1.2401 | 1.2427 |
| 180-Day Forward ... | .8048 | .8029 | 1.2425 | 1.2455 |
| **China** (Yuan) ........ | .5543 | .5588 | 1.8040 | 1.7896 |
| **Colombia** (Peso) ..... | .0161 | .0161 | 62.01 | 62.01 |
| **Denmark** (Krone) .... | .1277 | .1287 | 7.8265 | 7.7700 |
| **Ecuador** (Sucre) ..... | .0303 | .0400 | 33.00 | 25.00 |
| **Finland** (Markka) .... | .2223 | .2235 | 4.4960 | 4.4730 |
| **France** (Franc) ....... | .1660 | .1664 | 6.0225 | 6.0100 |
| 30-Day Forward ... | .1647 | .1656 | 6.0725 | 6.0400 |
| 90-Day Forward ... | .1628 | .1634 | 6.1425 | 6.1200 |
| 180-Day Forward ... | .1604 | .1621 | 6.2325 | 6.200 |
| **Greece** (Drachma). ... | .0159 | .0161 | 62.77 | 62.25 |
| **Hong Kong** (Dollar) .. | .1736 | .1733 | 5.7590 | 5.7650 |
| **India** (Rupee). ....... | .1078 | .1087 | 9.28 | 9.20 |
| **Indonesia** (Rupiah)... | .00158 | .00158 | 652.50 | 652.50 |
| **Ireland** (Pound) ...... | 1.5030 | 1.5075 | .6653 | .6633 |
| **Israel** (Shekel) ....... | .0489 | .0489 | 20.426 | 20.426 |
| **Italy** (Lira). .......... | .000779 | .000779 | 1283.75 | 1283.00 |
| **Japan** (Yen). ......... | .004261 | .004234 | 234.70 | 236.20 |
| 30-Day Forward ... | .004292 | .004263 | 233.00 | 234.55 |
| 90-Day Forward ... | .004345 | .004316 | 230.17 | 231.70 |
| 180-Day Forward ... | .004421 | .004394 | 226.20 | 227.60 |
| **Lebanon** (Pound). .... | .2013 | .2013 | 4.9685 | 4.9685 |
| **Malaysia** (Ringgit). ... | .4353 | .4361 | 2.2975 | 2.2930 |
| **Mexico** (Peso). ....... | .0213 | .0214 | 46.85 | 46.72 |
| **Netherlands** (Guilder) | .3893 | .3906 | 2.5655 | 2.5600 |
| **New Zealand** (Dollar) . | .7735 | .7727 | 1.2928 | 1.2942 |
| **Norway** (Krone). ..... | .1678 | .1687 | 5.9580 | 5.9270 |

**Table 28–1** *(Continued)*

| Country | U.S. $ equiv. Fri. | Thurs. | Currency per U.S. $ Fri. | Thurs. |
|---|---|---|---|---|
| **Pakistan** (Rupee)..... | .0858 | .0858 | 11.65 | 11.6578 |
| **Peru** (Sol) .......... | .00165 | .00165 | 605.01 | 605.01 |
| **Philippines** (Peso).... | .1194 | .1194 | 8.3780 | 8.3780 |
| **Portugal** (Escudo).... | .0142 | .0143 | 70.35 | 69.80 |
| **Saudi Arabia** (Riyal).. | .2916 | .2916 | 3.4295 | 3.4295 |
| **Singapore** (Dollar).... | .4785 | .4780 | 2.09 | 2.0890 |
| **South Africa** (Rand).. | .9430 | .9432 | 1.0640 | 1.0602 |
| **South Korea** (Won) | .00139 | .00139 | 718.30 | 718.30 |
| **Spain** (Peseta) ....... | .00973 | .00979 | 102.70 | 102.10 |
| **Sweden** (Krona)...... | .1733 | .1741 | 5.7690 | 5.7410 |
| **Switzerland** (Franc) .. | .5139 | .5123 | 1.9460 | 1.9520 |
|    30-Day Forward ... | .5198 | .5180 | 1.9240 | 1.9305 |
|    90-Day Forward ... | .5287 | .5274 | 1.8915 | 1.8960 |
|    180-Day Forward ... | .5402 | .5395 | 1.8510 | 1.8535 |
| **Taiwan** (Dollar) ...... | .0262 | .0262 | 38.18 | 38.18 |
| **Thailand** (Baht) ...... | .04348 | .04348 | 23.00 | 23.00 |
| **Uruguay** (New Peso) | | | | |
|   Financial .......... | .0825 | .0825 | 12.124 | 12.1245 |
| **Venezuela** (Bolivar)... | .2329 | .2329 | 4.2937 | 4.2937 |
| **West German** (Mark) . | .4344 | .4329 | 2.3020 | 2.3100 |
|    30-Day Forward ... | .4369 | .4354 | 2.2891 | 2.2970 |
|    90-Day Forward ... | .4410 | .4395 | 2.2674 | 2.2755 |
|    180-Day Forward ... | .4473 | .4457 | 2.2355 | 2.2437 |
| **SDR** ............... | 1.13485 | 1.13952 | .881178 | .87756 |

*Special Drawing Rights are based on exchange rates for the U.S., West German, British, French, and Japanese currencies.*

SOURCE: *The Wall Street Journal*, May 17, 1982, p. 46.

In recent years the foreign exchange market in New York City has come to rival London as the leading center for global foreign exchange dealings. There are several reasons for the rapid growth of the New York foreign exchange market in the late 1970s and early 1980s. For one thing, the United States economy has become more internationalized in recent years. As we noted in the previous chapter, the share of United States exports and imports related to the GNP has grown, as have inflows and outflows of capital.

Second, there has been a dramatic increase in exchange rate fluctuations due to a number of reasons: (1) sharp oil increases after 1973, which have resulted in large surpluses for **OPEC countries,** which in turn have had to be recycled through world financial markets, (2) wide swings in inflation rates and levels of output among the major trading nations, (3) major shifts in monetary and fiscal policies in the major trading countries, including the important technical change in monetary policy in the United States on October 6, 1979, which led to increased interest rate volatility in the New York money market.

Finally, there have been major changes in United States trading practices and conventions involving the foreign exchange markets. In particular, there was a change in 1978 in quotations for currencies, other than the pound sterling, from the former practice in New York of quoting foreign currencies in terms of dollars and cents to quoting them in European terms, that is, foreign currency units per U.S. dollar.

In recent years there has also been a sharp increase in foreign-owned banking offices in New York City. From 1976 to 1979, the number of such offices rose from 139 to 234. Furthermore, these offices represented 48 foreign countries. These foreign banks have traditionally engaged in foreign dealings and they have continued to do so in New York City. This, in turn, has greatly increased the degree of competitiveness in the foreign exchange market in New York City.

In general, the United States foreign exchange market consists of a network of commercial banks, most of which are located in New York City, that buy and sell bank deposits in another currency. There are also several organized exchanges that trade foreign exchange futures contracts. Like the money market, these transactions are over the telephone and there are a relatively small number of major participants. No more than eighty to one-hundred banks actively trade foreign exchange for their own account.

Most of the trading in the New York foreign exchange market is in six major currencies, in order of importance, the German mark, the pound sterling, the Canadian dollar, the Swiss franc, the Japanese yen, and the French franc. The Netherlands guilder, the Belgian franc, the Italian lira, and other foreign currencies are also traded, although with a much lower value of turnover. The eight most active banks in the New York foreign exchange market account for about half of the total transactions.

The twenty most active banks account for roughly three quarters or more of total transactions. Practically all this trading is in **spot transactions.** Because of the high volatility of prices in this market, most participants are reluctant to take a long position. Hence there is a heavy volume of in-and-out transactions, so that the banks participating in the market can even out their positions at the end of the day. This, of course, reduces their inventory holdings of foreign currencies and sharply reduces the risk to them of exchange rate fluctuations over an extended period of time.

# INTERNATIONAL EXCHANGE RATES

As a result of foreign trade and travel, as well as international capital movements, countries need to acquire the currencies of other countries. If the United States, say, is importing British woolens or Americans wish to travel in Great Britain, then Americans will be seeking to acquire British pounds in order to pay for the desired British goods and services. On the other hand, British citizens desire to acquire American dollars if they wish to buy American goods and services. Let us assume no change in the price levels of the two countries and no capital movements. Then, once the relative intensity of desire for goods and services on the part of each country for the goods and services of the other has been established in terms of exports and imports of goods and services, an equilibrium **exchange rate** of pounds in terms of dollars, and vice versa, will be established.

## *Relative Price Levels Affect Exchange Rates*

The demand for goods and services in each country will be affected by the relative price structures of the two countries, which in turn reflects the **comparative advantage** of producing different goods and services in each of the two countries. Any change in the price structure in either or both of the countries will tend to affect the pattern of international trade between them, assuming that the price elasticity of demand is greater than zero in both countries for products entering foreign trade.

If the price elasticity of demand is still greater (i.e., greater than one), then if country A, say, is experiencing inflation of the prices of its goods and services at a more rapid rate than country B, country A will tend to import more goods from country B, whereas the exports of country A to country B will tend to decline. Because country A is offering more of its currency for the currency of country B to acquire more goods from the second country, the value of the currency of country A, if the market for exchange of these two currencies is free, will tend to fall in terms of country B.

Within a given country, the value of its currency is determined by what that currency will buy of real goods and services. Thus when the price level of a country rises, the value of its currency will fall, because a given unit of the currency will now buy less than it did before. Similarly, a country experiencing inflation relatively greater than that of other countries will find that the exchange value of its currency tends to decline in terms of the currencies of other countries.

***Determining a Foreign Exchange Rate***    In general, the value of one country's currency in terms of another country's currency depends on the relative values of each currency as measured by the price level in each country. When the price level, as measured by the price index, is rising, the value of money is falling, and vice versa. If the price levels of all countries remained at the same level, or all went up or down at the same rate, and other conditions remained unchanged, there would be no change in the foreign exchange rate unless there was a change in the demand for foreign goods as compared with domestic goods. Inasmuch as the foreign exchange rates of Latin American currencies, as measured by the dollar, have fallen in recent years, it is not surprising that these countries have had more inflation in their price levels than the United States. On the other hand, the German mark appreciated in value in the late 1970s and early 1980s, especially against the French franc, and at times against the dollar. This suggests clearly that there was less inflation in West Germany than in France and the United States in that period. As already noted, by the fall of 1981 the dollar was valued at 2.24 marks.

***Exports and Imports Determine Demand and Supply of Currencies***    At a given time, the relative value of one currency in terms of another in a free market is determined by the demand for, and supply of, different currencies. If we consider only two countries, say, the United States and Great Britain, the demand for British pounds and the supply of American dollars is determined by the volume of imports into the United States from Britain plus the demand for services from Britain (e.g., American tourists traveling in Britain, plus export of American capital to Britain, plus any governmental grants or loans to Britain). Insofar as the demand for British goods and services is elastic (i.e., the percentage change in the quantity demanded is greater than the percentage change in the quoted price), that part of the demand for British pounds arising from imports of British goods and services is affected by the relative price levels of Great Britain and the United States.

If the price level of Britain plus transportation costs is lower than that of the United States, then imports of British goods into the United States will occur. The demand for British goods is then reflected in American demand for British pounds, and the supply of American dollars, in order to pay British exporters in their own currency. Thus the value of pounds in terms of dollars reflects the relative price levels of the two countries. The reverse is true insofar as American exports of goods and services result in a demand for American dollars on the part of foreigners plus a supply of foreign currencies in the foreign exchange markets.

Trade in goods and services generally goes both ways, so that it is not a matter of the relative price levels of two countries alone. It is the specific price of a given export product of a given country that is relevant, rather than the entire price level of that country. Each country in a free market situation tends to specialize in producing those goods and services in which it has a relative advantage in terms of the costs of production. Often a country can secure a product more cheaply from another country than it can produce the same product at home.

### Capital Movements and Borrowing also Affect the Exchange Rates

Actual foreign exchange rates are not determined only by the demand for, and supply of, currencies arising from imports and exports of goods and services. Private capital flows and government grants and loans that furnish dollars, for example, when the capital flow is from the United States to other countries are also important. Such a strong capital outflow, unless it is matched by an equally strong increase in exports, tends to weaken the value of the American dollar in terms of other currencies, or else leads to a substantial outflow of gold from the United States—at least prior to August 15, 1971. That this is not a purely hypothetical situation is clear from the discussion on the American balance of payments in the previous chapter.

In addition, many countries committed themselves in the postwar period prior to August 15, 1971, to the preservation of their existing exchange rate. Resort was often had in that period to the borrowing facilities of the various international financial institutions, which are discussed later. Such credit was needed particularly when a serious deficit appeared in a country's balance of payments. If the international exchange market were absolutely free to adjust the prices of currencies relative to one another, depending only on the relative demand and supply of currencies arising from international trade, a deficit country would find that the price of its currency in terms of another country's would automatically decline. This has, of course, occurred for many countries in the decade since 1971.

Deficits in a country's balance of payments would then be self-correcting in a completely free international market system if the foreign exchange rates were permitted to vary freely in that the country experiencing a growth in imports relative to its growth in exports would find that a fall in the value of its currency internationally would make imports more expensive and therefore lead to a decline in imports, whereas exports would now be cheaper in price and would tend to increase. Surplus countries, on the other hand, would experience the reverse effects. Such a floating system of exchange rates, though often with some central bank intervention in foreign exchange markets, was used by many countries in the decade after August 15, 1971.

## Stabilizing Around an Adjustable Peg

The system before August 15, 1971, might best be described as an **"adjustable peg" system.** In between major changes in the value of one currency in terms of another, the various central banks of the major countries stabilized the value of these currencies at ± 1 percent of the official price. After the Smithsonian Agreement of December 1971, the range of permissible variation of exchange rates was increased to ± 2¼ percent around the par value of any given currency.

As part of these stabilizing activities, central banks not only bought and sold foreign currencies but also permitted certain gold movements with one another, made "swap" arrangements whereby various currencies are borrowed by one country from another, and bought convertible foreign currencies or obtained **Special Drawing Rights** from the International Monetary Fund. After August 15, 1971, some of these stabilizing activities by central banks were suspended for a time. (The Federal Reserve did not again intervene in foreign exchange markets until July 1973, though these operations were largely suspended again in April 1981.) Most of these activities, except for gold movements, were soon resumed again.

## Exchange Operations by the Central Bank

Earlier technical efforts by the United States to minimize the effects of a persistent balance of payments deficit on the value of the dollar in foreign exchange markets were helpful, but they did not prevent recurrent international monetary crises from developing after 1967. All such technical efforts succeeded in doing was in buying time for the correction of this disequilibrium in the American balance of payments. Other countries had earlier found it necessary to have their central banks intervene to maintain the stability of their currencies in foreign exchange markets. However, it was not until the spring of 1962 that the Federal Reserve Bank of New York resumed the foreign exchange market stabilizing activities that had been abandoned after World War II. This was necessary because the balance of payments deficits for the United States, which first developed in 1950, seemed to be of a larger and more intractable nature beginning in 1958. In the four years prior to 1962, when the exchange rate stabilization began, annual deficits on a liquidity basis averaged $2.3 billion to $3.9 billion.

## Foreign Exchange Operations of the Federal Reserve

Not only the size of the adverse deficit in the American balance of payments but also the backwash of payments flows among third countries sometimes had unfavorable effects on the status of the dollar in foreign exchange markets. It was the importance of protecting this key currency against any such unfavorable effects, including those arising out of the gold outflow from the United States, that led to the resumption of foreign exchange stabilizing operations first by the Treasury and then by the Federal Reserve Bank of New York. As the *Annual Report of the Board of Governors for 1964* put it, "Consequently, the U.S. Treasury and the Federal Reserve have often engaged in exchange operations designed to protect the dollar and the U.S. gold stock from any adverse effects of such payments flows."[1]

## Speculative Pressure in the 1960s

In the 1960s the ability of such operations to protect the value of the dollar in foreign exchange markets was often tested. Not only the American central bank but other central banks as well through cooperative actions were attempting to preserve in broad outlines the existing international monetary system in the 1960s without giving way to the pressures of private speculators. One of the most serious years of such testing of these foreign exchange operations of world central banks was 1968. As Federal Reserve officials put it,

> The central bank defenses developed in recent years to protect the world payments system from disruptive speculative movements of funds were subjected to some of their severest tests in 1968—the March gold crisis, heavy pressures on sterling, a political and economic crisis in France, and massive speculation on a revaluation of the German mark.[2]

This crisis year of 1968 well illustrates the nature of the concerted operations of the central banks of the various major industrial countries to deal with the market pressures on different currencies in that year. For example, in March 1968 the Federal Reserve and U.S. Treasury representing the United States joined with other countries to put together a $900 million package in support of the Canadian dollar. In addition, the United States granted Canada complete exemption from the restraints on U.S. capital outflows, which had been announced by the president on January 1, 1968.

[1]Board of Governors of the Federal Reserve System, *Fifty-first Annual Report of the Board of Governors of the Federal Reserve System Covering Operations for the Year 1964* (Washington, D.C.: 1965), p. 161.

[2]Board of Governors of the Federal Reserve System, *Fifty-fifth Annual Report of the Board of Governors of the Federal Reserve System Covering Operations for the Year 1968* (Washington, D.C.: 1969), p. 275.

## STABILIZING OPERATIONS IN THE 1970s

By the mid-1970s, the Federal Reserve had clearly developed its point of view toward central bank intervention in the foreign exchange markets. In general, the American central bank preferred largely unmanaged floating of exchange rates. If one country had a higher (or lower) rate of inflation than other countries, it was to be expected that its currency would depreciate (appreciate) relative to that of other countries. The different rates of inflation would be reflected in changes in the basic balance of payments of the various trading nations and that in turn should be reflected in the foreign exchange markets. A "dirty float" was thus to be avoided. Intervention to smooth out day-to-day market conditions, especially when speculative pressures tended to disrupt the markets, was considered appropriate, but such central bank trading was not to be conducted to change the total holdings of net official reserves.

This philosophy of central bank intervention in the foreign exchange markets was not shared by all central banks in the 1970s. The single year of 1976 illustrates the diversity of approach. The entire year of 1976 (and early 1977 as well) saw a heavy volume of official intervention in the foreign exchange markets. The Bank of England supported the pound to the amount of about $7 billion. On the other side of the market, Switzerland purchased a total of $7.5 billion in foreign exchange in 1976 to prevent the Swiss franc from appreciating substantially. West Germany likewise bought $4 billion in foreign currencies to prevent the German mark from rising higher than it did on the markets. Japan bought about $4 billion of dollars in 1976, whereas Italy supported the lira to the sum of $2.3 billion. By way of contrast, the Federal Reserve Bank of New York, in the twelve months ending in January 1977, had total interventions of about $1 billion. In the previous chapter the major exchange market operations of the Federal Reserve Bank of New York from 1978–1981 were already discussed, so they will not be repeated here.

### Floating Currencies in the Late 1970s and Early 1980s

Despite rather substantial central bank intervention from time to time, as already noted for 1976, and later from 1978 to the spring of 1981, major currencies were generally on a floating basis in the late 1970s and 1980, and early 1981. The consequences of this floating in terms of the depreciation or appreciation of the value of the currency on the base of the Smithsonian exchange rates of December 1971 for the period between 1977 and 1981 is shown in Figure 28–1. As indicated, the Italian lira and

**Figure 28–1     Effective Exchange Rates 1977–1981 (weekly averages end-June 1977 = 100)**

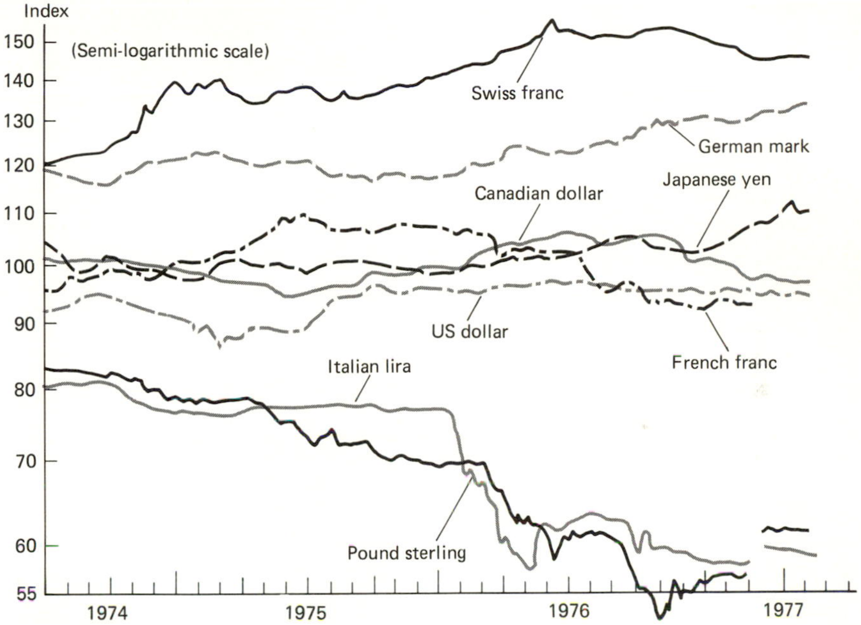

SOURCE: Bank for International Settlements, *Forty-Seventh Annual Report 1st April 1980–31st March 1981*, Basle, Switzerland, 15th June 1981, p. 126.

the British pound both fell substantially in this period—particularly in 1976, despite the intervention of the central banks of these countries. In fact, all of the financial upheavals of the mid-1970s undoubtedly made impossible a managed international financial system similar to that prior to 1971 under the supervision of the International Monetary Fund.

On the other hand, the Swiss franc, the German mark, and to a lesser extent the Japanese yen generally appreciated in this period. The U.S. dollar had its ups and downs but by 1981 it was about back to where it was in early 1977. The Canadian dollar and the French franc showed a downward drift after peaking in 1978.

## The Snake in the Tunnel

One of the new international arrangements on exchange rates developed after August 1971 was among nine members of the Common Market countries in Europe, which called their agreement on agreed-upon European exchange rates the "snake" and the amount of agreed-upon variability "the tunnel." The trick, as noted, was to "keep the **snake in the**

**tunnel,"** which often meant central bank intervention, when the actual market exchange rates threatened to diverge too far from the officially agreed-upon rates.

For the weaker countries in the European community, the strain of maintaining the snake in the tunnel often proved to be too great, because precious foreign exchange had to be offered up to maintain an artificially high exchange rate. As a result, Britain left the snake two months after it was born. Italy withdrew in early 1973 and France went in and out twice, the last time in March 1976. And Sweden, which joined the snake in March 1973, departed in late August 1977. By late 1977, only five countries were still in the snake, a sharp decline from the nine countries that started the arrangement only six years earlier.

### European Monetary System Created on March 13, 1979

The earlier somewhat abortive "snake in the tunnel" efforts in developing more stable exchange rates among the members of the Common Market finally led to the official creation of the **European Monetary System (EMS)** on March 13, 1979. The agreement was to foster "closer monetary cooperation leading to a zone of monetary stability in Europe."[3] The nine countries that established this new monetary system in Europe included Belgium, Denmark, France, the Federal Republic of Germany, Ireland, Italy, Luxembourg, the Netherlands, and Great Britain. Great Britain did not participate initially in the intervention arrangements. The new system established a **European Currency Unit (ECU),** which consisted of a basket of all nine European Community currencies.

Already established credit facilities were enlarged and the former European common margins arrangement, the so called "snake", was retained. The intervention mechanism requires countries to intervene in the foreign exchange markets to prevent movements greater than 2.25 percent around parity in bilateral rates between participants. The currencies of these nine countries could then float freely against nonparticipants to this agreement (e.g., against the dollar of the United States).

An initial supply of ECUs was issued by the European Monetary Cooperation Fund against 20 percent of both the gold and dollar reserves of participating countries. These ECUs were to be used to settle intervention debts in accordance with agreed-upon rules. In addition to increased integration within the European Common Market area because of greater exchange rate stability among the cooperating countries, another principal objective of the EMS was to promote internal financial

---

[3]Quoted in the International Monetary Fund, *Annual Report 1979*, p. 40.

stability. If that were not accomplished, there would inevitably be market pressures on the announced parities of the different exchange rates, which would necessitate a change in par currency rates so typical of the IMF period before August 1971.

## Exchange Rate Changes and Balance of Payments Changes

The adjustments in exchange rates after August 15, 1971 (e.g., the Smithsonian Agreement of December 1971 or those of early 1973), were still thought to be largely in terms of the old par value system. But from the spring of 1973, it was clear that floating, or freely fluctuating, exchange rates were here to stay for some years at least. It was still true, however, that not all countries were fully committed to the new system of freely variable exchange rates.

Only the United States, Canada, and the nations of the European Common Market (considering the value of their countries as a group, that is, the snake) were willing to let forces in the foreign exchange markets arising from changes in their balance of payments affect the relative value of their respective currencies. Many other countries had some kind of a managed exchange rate, sometimes called a **"dirty float,"** wherein the central bank of that country tried to hold the foreign exchange value of the country's currency at about a particular level. Often, however, these pegging efforts were unsuccessful in whole or in part. For example, the Bank of England in 1976 was holding the foreign value of the pound at $1.77 until September 17, 1976, when the cost of lost reserves of foreign exchange (e.g., dollars) became prohibitive. Thereafter the value of the pound fell to about $1.56, though a year later in the fall of 1977 it had regained all its lost ground and was trading again at about $1.77. In early 1978, the pound was valued around $1.86 in the market. By May 1982, as shown earlier in Table 28–1, the pound was valued at slightly more than $1.82 in the exchange market. This was not too different from what it had been three and a half years earlier.

But the success of the various versions of floating exchange rates in the first years of experience with them after August 15, 1971, was somewhat mixed insofar as helping to bring about the needed improvements in the balance of payments. Partly this was because of the various types of intervention in the foreign exchange markets by many countries' central banks, including reliance on official and quasi-official borrowing of foreign exchange to carry out sustained support of a given currency when it was under attack in the foreign exchange markets. Furthermore, the effectiveness of changes in the exchange rate was often undermined by the absence of appropriate domestic demand policies, say, to control inflation.

# THE VICIOUS CYCLE HYPOTHESIS

It was sometimes argued that certain countries with open economies (i.e., economies dependent on both imports and exports) were caught in a **vicious cycle** when their currency was devalued in the foreign exchange markets. When the value of a country's currency, say, the British pound, falls in the foreign exchange markets, the terms of trade now become adverse for that country. The prices of British exports are, in fact, now lower for foreigners, so that British exports should be stimulated and this should thereby help eliminate a current account deficit.

However, the prices of imports into Britain are now also higher. If an important part of past inadequate or even declining exports sales is the result of inflation within Britain, additional inflationary pressures are now created by the devaluation. The cost of raw material imports are now higher and ultimately will lead again to higher export prices. This problem is particularly aggravated if the government is unwilling or unable to exercise the appropriate restraint on domestic demand. This would involve reducing both the growth in the money supply and budget deficits, thereby curbing inflation.

For some other countries, such as West Germany and Switzerland, a **virtuous cycle** may result from changes in the value of their currencies in the foreign exchange markets. Lower rates of inflation in these countries will lead to higher external values for their currencies. This then will improve the **terms of trade,** so that imports are now cheaper than before. Even export sales may not be hurt too much, if domestic costs are kept under control and productivity continues to rise, so that the country gains both abroad and at home.

The possibility of either a vicious or a virtuous cycle of changes in exchange rates affecting domestic inflation is largely a development of the period of freely fluctuating exchange rates since 1971. Prior to 1971, a par system of exchange rates under the supervision of the IMF was the rule. These relatively fixed exchange rates could be changed, but only following consultation with the IMF. Despite the departure from the par system of exchange rates, the IMF still remains an important international financial institution.

# THE INTERNATIONAL MONETARY FUND

The Bretton Woods, New Hampshire, Conference of 1944 brought together financial leaders and experts of various countries of the free world, with a particularly heavy representation from the United States and Great Britain. It was this conference, looking ahead to some of the likely financial problems of the postwar world, that set up both the International Monetary Fund and the World Bank. Whereas the World Bank focused on development loans to the developing countries, the IMF was particularly concerned with minimizing exchange disorders in a postwar period that turned out to have large payments deficits, inconvertible currencies, and persistent inflation among many member countries.

Consultation and international cooperation in the important areas of exchange rates were to be emphasized rather than unilateral actions of a "beggar my neighbor" type. Both loans and technical advice from the fund were available to help countries over short-run liquidity difficulties until disequilibria in their balances of payments could be corrected. Financial order and the promotion of international trade and development were thus assisted in the world, which otherwise might well have been plagued by international financial and economic anarchy. In a real sense the fund and the bank were the economic and financial counterparts of the United Nations.

## Objectives of the Fund

In Article I of the Articles of Agreement establishing the IMF, two of the important objects of the fund were indicated as (1) "to promote exchange stability, to maintain orderly exchange arrangements among members, and to avoid competitive exchange depreciation," and (2) "to assist in the establishment of a multilateral system of payments in respect of current transactions between members and in the elimination of foreign exchange restrictions which hamper the growth of world trade." Achievement of these objectives was held as being essential to shorten the duration, and lessen the extent, of disequilibrium of the international balances of payments of members. Thirty-five countries, including the United States, signed the original articles of agreement in 1945, and four others joined the fund in 1946. By 1981 there were 143 member countries.

**The Gold and Credit Tranches**   Each member country was given a quota, which was in effect a line of credit. Each member could draw up to 25 percent of its quota to secure added reserves for short periods of time. Each member was to pay in gold 25 percent of its quota or 10 percent of its net official holdings of gold and U.S. dollars. The amount of gold furnished the fund was called the *"gold tranche"* position of the member. The remaining 75 percent of the quota was to be furnished, as needed, in the country's own currency. This remaining 75 percent was called the *"credit tranche"* position of the member country.

*Higher Borrowing Quotas*    By 1981 the total quotas of $7.4 billion for the thirty-nine original member countries of 1946 had been raised to more than $60 billion, or more than eight times the original quotas. Furthermore, the quotas are now valued in SDRs, not dollars, and an SDR as shown in Table 28–1 is worth more than $1.13 each. There was also $6.5 billion in additional funds available for the ten major industrial countries through the IMF as a result of the agreement on the **General Arrangements to Borrow,** first concluded in 1962. However, the number of member countries had risen to one hundred and forty-three and the world price level had more than doubled. Hence the increases in world liquidity represented by the rise in fund quotas is not as great as might appear. Furthermore, most of the drawings were only conditionally available as a source of liquidity to countries with balance of payments deficits.

*Conditional Borrowing*    Although drawing on the gold tranche position was automatic, drawing on the credit tranche position was conditional. This meant that the borrowing country could be required to furnish evidence that it was following appropriate economic policies to restore balance to its external payments. One of these conditions relating to member country borrowing is made clear in Article VI of the Fund Agreement, which specifies that "A member may not make net use of the Fund's resources to meet a large or sustained outflow of capital, and the Fund may request a member to exercise controls to prevent such use of the resources of the Fund."

## Special Drawing Rights

In 1970, the IMF created a new kind of international monetary reserves called Special Drawing Rights (SDRs). Initially, SDRs were sometimes called "paper gold" to indicate that they would take their place alongside gold holdings and holdings of hard currencies such as U.S. dollars, Swiss francs, German marks, and Japanese yen in the monetary reserves of the countries belonging to the IMF. At first, the new SDR was related both to gold and the dollar. The unit of value of each SDR was defined as equivalent to .888671 grams of gold, which was the "gold content" of the dollar in 1970. After the dollar was devalued in 1971 and 1973, however, the SDR had a stated value greater than that of the dollar. In 1982, an SDR was worth slightly more than $1.13.

The initial amount of SDRs created totaled $9.5 billion. There were $3.5 billion created in 1970, and $3 billion each in 1971 and 1972. Subsequently in the decade of the 1970s still more SDRs were created, and by 1981, there were nearly SDR 21.5 billion outstanding.

## Governance of the IMF

The governance of the IMF is in the hands of a board of executive directors, partly appointed by individual countries and partly elected by groups of countries, which in turn select a managing director to administer the regular operations of the fund. The five countries that individually appoint an executive director are the United States, Germany, France, and India. These five countries have 45.30 percent of the total voting power in the fund.

The first four countries, together with six other major industrial countries (Belgium, Canada, Italy, Japan, the Netherlands, and Sweden), make up the Group of Ten. Five of these countries, excepting Sweden, in 1968 represented their particular group of four or more countries on the Executive Director's board. The voting power thus represented among the twenty Executive Directors by the Group of Ten is approximately two thirds of the total voting power in the Fund. Thus these ten major countries usually exert effective group leadership for the one hundred and forty-three members of the fund.

## The IMF and Exchange Rates Prior to 1971

The first task of the fund in 1946 was to seek agreement with the thirty-nine member countries on an appropriate structure of exchange rates that would govern most of the international transactions in the world. Ten years later, the eleventh annual meeting of the Board of Governors of the fund noted with satisfaction the progress that had been made thus far. In September 1949, for example, as a result of fund urgings that some readjustments in exchange rates be made, countries accounting for two thirds of world trade had devalued their currencies.

As a result of this devaluation, and progress subsequently made in reconstruction work and control of inflation, the foreign trade of most countries in the world expanded, and the dollar shortage of the early postwar years, as a result of persistent large balances of trade in the American balance of payments, was gradually offset. A number of European countries were even able to turn chronic deficits in their balances of payments into surpluses. The resulting better distribution of gold and dollars assisted in improving the general conditions of international liquidity. Thus from 1960 to 1970 alone, the gold and dollar reserves of the rest of the world outside the United States increased by more than $10 billion. In the 1970s, these global reserves increased enormously by $180 billion.

## DRAWINGS FROM THE FUND

Many member countries came to regard **drawings on the fund** as the equivalent to the use of their own reserves—to be drawn upon as needed and to be replenished after the need passed. Complete freedom was always allowed member countries to draw the equivalent of their gold subscription to the fund, or their gold tranche.

In the late 1970s and early 1980s the heaviest borrowings, or purchases of credit tranches, were by the less developed countries, in contrast to early heavy borrowings by the **highly developed countries,** including the United States. In 1980–1981, total new commitments under standby and extended arrangements reached a peak of SDR 9.5 billion. Total purchases in 1980–1981, which were all made by developing countries, amounted to the equivalent of SDR 4.9 billion. The largest amount was purchased by the People's Republic of China (SDR 450 million), Korea (SDR 384 million), Turkey (SDR 360 million), and Yugoslavia (SDR 376 million).

### *The Case of the Sudan in the Early 1980s*

For some developing countries the availability of borrowings from the IMF is a crucial matter in dealing with continuing deficits in their balance of payments. However, at times the credit of the borrowing country is not as strong as it should be and the IMF is required to impose economic conditions on continued borrowing. A case in point is the African country of the Sudan. During the 1970s, especially late in that decade, the Sudan became a heavy international borrower. Its total international debt by the early 1980s was about $4 billion. The root cause of the Sudan's financial problems in recent years has been its inability to earn enough from agricultural exports to afford its imports of consumer and capital goods. Its trade deficit for 1980 alone was about $1 billion.

This debt was partly to the IMF, the World Bank, other international agencies, and private commercial banks. From 1973 to 1981, the Sudanese borrowed about $400 million from commercial banks alone. Some 115 commercial banks still had outstanding credit to the Sudan in 1981.

For the period from the end of November 1981 to the end of December 1982, the Sudan wanted an additional $220 million from the IMF. This, in turn, would make it possible for an additional $75 million to be borrowed from commercial banks and as much as $150 million from Saudi Arabia. Before the IMF would authorize such additional credits, it required new austerity measures in the Sudan. These included a reduction in the level of government subsidies for food, a ceiling on public-sector borrowing, and a currency devaluation. It is thus clear that strings often are attached to developing countries like the Sudan when borrowing from the IMF.

## United States Official Reserve Position

Before the 1960s, the United States had never exercised its right to drawings from the IMF. During the 1960s, because of a commitment to a fixed value of the dollar in foreign exchange markets and because of some deficits in the U.S. balance of payments, the United States made a number of drawings that totaled about $2 billion. By the mid-1970s, the dollar was floating in foreign exchange markets, so that United States borrowings from the IMF were not necessary to support the external value of the dollar.

Hence although the deficit in the American balance of payments increased to much larger amounts in the 1970s and early 1980s than it had been in the 1960s, official reserve assets of the United States often increased rather than decreased. The increase in United States official reserves in this period was typically due to an increased holding of foreign currencies, though occasionally it was due to its increase in its reserve position in the IMF. From 1977 to 1978, the United States reserve assets fell slightly, from $19,312 million to $18,650 million, because its reserve position in the IMF fell from $4,946 million to $1,047 million. An increase in foreign currencies from $18 million in 1977 to $4,374 million in 1978 did not completely offset this decline, because SDRs from the IMF also fell from $2,629 million to $1,558 million.

In 1979, total reserves increased slightly to $18,928 million, which was largely due to an increase in SDRs to $2,724 million. In 1980, however, official reserve holdings soared to a total of $26,756 million, a sharp rise of $7,800 million in one year. This was mainly due to an increase in holdings of foreign currencies from $3,807 million in 1979 to $10,134 million in 1980. At the same time, the United States reserve position in the IMF increased somewhat from $1,253 million in 1979 to $2,852 million in 1980. By the end of 1981, reserve assets had risen by $3.2 billion to a total of $30 billion.

## Increase in Borrowing Quotas of IMF Member Countries

As international trade has expanded in each decade after World War II, the need for added international monetary reserves to finance such expanded trade has also grown. Also, deficits in various countries' balance of payments also inevitably occur from time to time. The large increase in world oil prices after 1973 put a particularly heavy strain on the balance of payments of nonoil countries, both developed and developing because the cost of total imports, including more expensive oil, has tended to grow faster for many countries than the total value of their exports.

One important way to cope with these growing balance of payments deficits has been to borrow abroad from a variety of private and international lending agencies. The most important international lending agency available to cope with such deficits is the IMF. The fund has responded to this increased need for international liquidity not only by increasing SDRs but also by increasing the borrowing quotas of the member countries. There have been a number of general reviews of quotas, all of which have had to be approved by the IMF members having three quarters of total quotas then outstanding. The Seventh General **Review of Quotas,** which was initiated in 1976 and became effective on November 29, 1980, provided for a general quota increase of 50 percent for all members except the People's Republic of China and Democratic Kampuchea (Cambodia), for which no increases were provided. This new increase in quotas meant an increase from SDR 39.7 billion to SDR 60 billion.

## Sources of Loanable Funds for the IMF

In order for the IMF to provide more borrowing facilities for its member countries it is necessary for it to have more loanable funds. Over the years, as the fund's membership has grown from the original 66 to 143 in 1981, new lending resources were available for the fund because each new member had to provide the fund with a certain amount of gold or hard currencies. We have already noted that the IMF has also created large amounts of new monetary reserves—SDRs—which also provides it with more loanable funds. In addition, the management of the IMF has been ingenious in finding other sources of funds, especially from countries running surpluses in their balance of payments, so that the deficit countries could borrow to cover their deficits. For the world as a whole, there is neither a surplus nor a deficit in its balance of payments. Hence the total value of deficits in balance of payments for individual countries must be equaled in value by countries having balance of payments surpluses.

***The General Arrangements to Borrow (GAB)***    The earliest move to obtain additional lending resources for the IMF was in 1962, when the General Arrangements to Borrow was concluded between the fund and ten major industrial member countries. The original agreement was for four years, but it has been extended a number of times. The latest extension was on October 24, 1980, for a period of five years. The maximum credit available to the fund through the GAB in lenders' currencies is equivalent to about SDR 6.5 billion, of which SDR 5.8 billion was available on April 30, 1981, after adjusting for resources already used. The use of GAB is limited to a participant in the agreement. Hence these funds are obviously not available for nonoil developing countries, for instance.

***The Oil Facility***    Because of the growing number of countries, particularly developing countries, that had even more serious balance of payments difficulties than before in the years after 1973 owing to a series of oil price hikes by the OPEC countries, a special oil facility was established by the IMF in the mid-1970s. An agreement was entered into with the fund in 1974 and 1975 by seventeen lender countries, including Switzerland, to provide it with some SDR 6.9 billion. By April 30, 1981, the fund had repaid the equivalent of SDR 5.4 billion of indebtedness incurred under the oil facility.

***Supplementary Financing Facility***    In 1979, the IMF entered into borrowing agreements with thirteen members and the Swiss National Bank to provide, in different currencies, the equivalent of SDR 7.8 billion as supplementary financing. In 1980–1981, the fund borrowed a total of SDR 1.5 billion under the facility, compared with SDR 502.4 million the previous year. On April 30, 1981, SDR 5.8 billion was still undrawn but had been fully committed under existing standby and extended arrangements.

***Saudi Arabian Monetary Agency***    A large-scale borrowing arrangement was also concluded between the IMF and the Saudi Arabian Monetary Agency (SAMA) on May 7, 1981, whereby the fund's policy of enlarged access also became operative. Under this agreement, the fund could secure from SAMA up to SDR 4 billion in the first year of the commitment period and up to SDR 8 billion in the second year. Balance of payments and reserve positions permitting, the Arabian authorities indicated their intention to consider a further commitment for the third year. Drawings under this borrowing agreement may be made by the fund during a commitment period of six years, each call being subject to a ninety-day notice.

***Bank for International Settlements, Central Banks, and Other Monetary Authorities***    Additional loanable funds were also to be obtained by the IMF in an agreement of August 4, 1981, with central banks or official agencies of sixteen industrial countries, whereby these agencies would make available to the fund the equivalent of SDR 1.3 billion over a commitment period of two years. Of this amount, SDR 675 million was made available under a borrowing agreement with the Bank for International Settlements (BIS). The fund might subsequently enter into other agreements with other member countries or central banks for augmented funds.

## THE INTERNATIONAL MONETARY FUND IN THE 1980s

In the period of more than a decade since the closing of the gold window to the convertibility of the American dollar on August 15, 1971, and the subsequent shift of most countries away from the relatively fixed par value of their currencies to currencies that float in the foreign exchange markets, the role of the IMF has changed substantially. Overseeing proposed changes in par values of currencies is not now a function of the IMF. Even the major emphasis on making short-term (one year or under) loans to the major industrial countries experiencing minor balance of payments difficulties has also given way to a new concern.

***More Intermediate-term Loans***    The major concern increasingly of the IMF seems to be making seven to ten year loans to developing countries that often seem to be experiencing major chronic balance of payments difficulties. To be sure, the financial plight of this group of countries, in particular, was exacerbated by the many rounds of sharp oil price increases by the OPEC nations beginning in 1973. In 1980, OPEC oil revenues were estimated at the large figures of $300 billion. In that same year, the non-OPEC developing countries had an aggregate current account deficit of some $75 billion, which was about two thirds of the collective deficit for the entire world. Moreover, the burden of debt repayment on loans earlier incurred in the developing countries was also becoming even heavier, especially as as interest rates soared in the late 1970s and early 1980s.

***Greater Borrowing Pressures from Developing Countries***   The **World Bank group,** which was established by the same Bretton Woods, New Hampshire, Agreement that set up the IMF, had for years concentrated on assisting the developing countries meet their economic problems. This group, which included the International Bank for Reconstruction and Development (IBRD), the International Development Association (IDA), and the International Finance Corporation (IFC), had made large amounts of low-interest, long-term loans to this group of countries.

From 1945 through 1981, over $92 billion in loans and credit was thus channeled from the developed to the developing countries. In fact, since 1973 the World Bank has considerably increased its lending activities. In fiscal year 1981 alone, over $12 billion was disbursed. But even these large amounts of loans were not enough to satisfy the desires and needs of the developing nations for still more credit. Hence by the 1980s they were urgently turning to the IMF for more help.

***Continuing Balance of Payments Deficits***   What had led to the more urgent search for more external borrowing by the developing countries was their larger balance of payments deficits in the late 1970s and early 1980s. In 1976 and 1977, respectively, the current account deficits of developing countries were $34 billion and $32 billion. But by 1979, the current account deficit for these same countries had risen to $56 billion and in 1980 it soared to around $72 billion. Poor food harvests and the ever increasing price of importing oil had especially exacerbated the problem. Lagging domestic development programs and weaknesses from time to time in their export prices also contributed to balance of payments difficulties for these poorer nations.

***Highly Developed Countries Still Make Policy for IMF***   Despite these pressures from the developing countries for substantially more aid from the highly developed countries through the lending facilities of the IMF, the developed countries in the early 1980s were largely resisting an expanded aid role for this key international lending institution. The highly industrialized countries resisted these pressures even though they often agreed that there had been certain changes in world trade patterns and an undeniable need of the developing countries for more foreign assistance.

Treasury and finance officials of the major industrial countries argued that the fundamental purpose of the IMF was still to promote stability of exchange rates through short-term loans to countries with temporary balance of payments problems, rather than being converted into an international aid agency. To this end, the highly developed countries, who still had the majority of votes in the IMF, resisted still further substantial creation of SDRs or even borrowing by the IMF in world financial markets to increase still further its lending capacity. The traditional source of funds for the IMF thus continues to be the contributions of the member countries plus the creation of new SDRs.

The IMF was still expected to engage in surveillance of central banks and governmental policies so as to discourage some nations from seeking to gain unfair advantages over other nations. In this manner, the *"beggar thy neighbor"* competitive policies of the 1930s were to be avoided. In the 1980s, then, the major emphasis in the evolving international monetary system was away from external imposition of exchange rate stability and toward encouraging responsible policies of the various member countries of the IMF.

## Questions for Discussion

1. How important do you think that gold will be in the international monetary system of the 1980s? Why did the price of gold vary so much in the London gold market after the mid-1970s? What difference did this variable price of gold make?
2. Discuss the determination of exchange rates in the foreign exchange markets. How do developments in the balance of payments of various countries affect the determination of these rates under relatively freely fluctuating exchange rates? How do changes in the price of gold affect exchange rates, or vice versa? (Hint: Be sure to include in your discussion the particular role of the dollar in foreign exchange markets.)
3. What was the purpose of the various "stabilizing operations" by central banks in the foreign exchange markets in the 1960s and 1970s? Contrast the philosophy of the American Federal Reserve System on this matter with that of other central banks, especially after April 1981.
4. Why did the value of the dollar tend to fall in many foreign exchange markets after the mid-1970s? What were some of the consequences of this external decline in the value of the dollar? Why did the dollar recover strongly in 1981? What do you think will happen to the value of the dollar hereafter in the 1980s? Why?
5. Discuss the effect of changes in various exchange rates on the balance of payments of the countries involved. Include in your discussion the experience of "the snake in the tunnel" and the virtuous and vicious cycle hypotheses with examples of several countries to illustrate this latter explanation.
6. What were the major purposes in establishing the IMF in 1946? How successful do you think the fund was in achieving these purposes before August 15, 1971, when the United States suspended convertibility of the dollar? How successful was it in the decade after August 1971?
7. Discuss the creation and use of SDRs in 1970 and thereafter. Why were there

further replenishments of SDRs in the late 1970s and the early 1980s? Do you think the use of SDRs will be expanded later in the 1980s? Why or why not?

8. Why did the developing countries put great pressure on the IMF for additional substantial loans in the early 1980s? Why were the highly developed countries largely resisting this pressure? Do you believe the major functions of the IMF should be or will be changed subsequently in the 1980s?

# Selected Bibliography for Further Reading

ARTUS, J. R., and J. H. YOUNG, "Fixed and Flexible Exchange Rates: A Renewal of the Debate," International Monetary Fund Staff Papers, **26:**694–698 (Dec. 1979).

CHACHOLIADES, MILIADES, *International Monetary Theory and Policy* (New York: McGraw-Hill, 1978).

FEDERAL RESERVE BANK OF CHICAGO, "Special Drawing Rights," *Business Conditions,* Oct. 1969, pp. 6–11.

———, "International Payments—Further Improvements Needed in the System," *Business Conditions,* Feb. 1969, pp. 11–16.

———, *The International Monetary System in Transition,* A Symposium, March 16–17, 1972 (Chicago, 1972).

GOLDSTEIN, M., "Downward Price Inflexibility, Ratchet Effects, and the Inflational Impact of Import Price Changes: Some Empirical Evidence," International Monetary Fund Staff Papers, **24:**609–612, (Nov. 1977).

HANSEN, ALVIN, *The Dollar and the International Monetary System* (New York: McGraw-Hill, 1965).

HODGMAN, DONALD R., *National Monetary Policies and International Monetary Cooperation* (Boston: Little Brown, 1974).

INTERNATIONAL MONETARY FUND, Annual Reports.

KOHLHAGEN, STEVEN W., *Behavior of Foreign Exchange Markets: A Critical Survey of the Empirical Literature,* (Monograph Series in Finance and Economics, 1978–1983 (New York: Salmon Brothers Center for the Study of Financial Institutions, 1978), p. 54 D.

REVEY, PATRICIA, "Evolution and Growth of the United States Foreign Exchange Market," *Quarterly Review,* Federal Reserve Bank of New York, Autumn 1981, Vol. 6, No. 3, pp. 32–44.

SCHADLER, S. "Sources of Exchange Rate Variability: Theory and Empirical Evidence," International Monetary Fund Staff Papers, **24:**293–296 (July 1977).

WARD, RICHARD, *International Finance* (Englewood Cliffs, N.J.: Prentice-Hall, 1965).

YAEGER, LELAND B., *International Monetary Relationships,* 2d ed. (New York: Harper & Row, 1976).

# GLOSSARY

**Accelerator.** The relationship between a change in real income, or real output, and the level of real investment.

**Accommodative policy.** A public policy that responds in a given way to economic events, such as increasing the money supply when the demand for it increases.

**Accord.** On March 4, 1951, the Federal Reserve and the Treasury reached an agreement, or accord, giving the Federal Reserve greater independence.

**Adjustable peg system.** The system of par exchange rates around which small fluctuations were permitted. Sometimes the par or "peg" was changed.

**Adjustable-rate mortgages.** Mortgages that provide for changes in the rate of interest over the life of the mortgage.

**Aggregate.** By adding up the parts of an economic variable, one reaches the total or aggregate.

**Aggregate demand.** The total demand for goods and services in a given period of time, both private and public.

**Announcement effect.** Changes in the Federal Reserve discount rate regarded as a signal of a change in credit and monetary policy.

**Arbitrage.** Buying and selling of different maturities or kinds of financial assets until they yield a comparable return.

**Asset demand for money.** The demand for money as a part of wealth, which increases when prices are expected to fall.

**Asset management.** Acquisition of loans and investments in a portfolio so as to balance profit and liquidity considerations.

**Automatic transfer services.** Funds being automatically transferred from savings accounts to checking accounts, when customers write checks.

**Balance of payments.** The sum total of all financial transactions in and out of a country, which, like a balance sheet, must balance.

**Balance of trade.** The relationship between total merchandise exports and total merchandise imports of a given country.

**Balance on current account.**   The result of total merchandise and service flows in a country's balance of payments.

**Bank assets.**   See *Bank credit.*

**Bank certificates of deposits.**   Time deposits of commercial banks in certificate form with varying maturities from thirty days to one year.

**Bank concentration.**   The percentage of one or more banks' assets in a particular bank marketing area.

**Bank credit.**   The total amount of earning assets (loans and investments) held by banks.

**Bank credit card.**   A card that enables a customer to buy goods and services by borrowing from a bank against an established line of credit.

**Bank deposits.**   Demand deposits, which may be used for third party payments, and time and savings deposits.

**Bank entry.**   The ease or difficulty of existing, or new, banks entering a given market area as controlled by federal and state bank regulators.

**Bank holding companies.**   Companies owning only one bank or 25 percent or more of two or more banks.

**Bank investing policies.**   Bank guidelines regarding the acquisition of federal government securities and state and local government securities.

**Bank liquidity.**   The asset-deposit condition of a bank allowing it to readily convert assets into cash.

**Bank loans.**   Credit extended by banks to their customers.

**Bank merger.**   The acquisition of one bank by another bank.

**Bank of England.**   The central bank for Great Britain founded in 1694 under Royal Charter and nationalized in 1946.

**Bank rate.**   The key interest rate set by the Bank of England on its loans to the London Discount Houses.

**Bank reserves.**   Vault cash, deposits in Federal Reserve Banks and some deposits in correspondent banks.

**Bank reserves, nonborrowed.**   Total bank reserves minus borrowed reserves at the discount window.

**Bank revolving credit.**   Received by customers from banks when they use their bank credit cards or check credit plans.

**Bankers' acceptance.**   Commercial bill of credit used to finance exports or imports of goods and endorsed by a commercial bank.

**Banking school theory.**   The theory that commercial banks should mainly make short-term self liquidating business loans. See *Real bills doctrine.*

**Barter.**   The direct exchange of one good or service for another.

**Base period.**   This is a period set as 100 in constructing price indexes.

**Basic discount rate.**   The interest rate charged for adjustment borrowings by depositary institutions at the Federal Reserve discount window.

**Beggar thy neighbor.**   Policies, common in the 1930's, whereby some countries try to take advantage of other countries through tariffs, subsidies, quotas, and similar trade practices.

**Benefits from inflation.**   See *Inflation benefits.*

**Bears.**   Speculators who expect prices of stock, bonds, or goods to fall.

**Bill rollovers.**   Offerings in a new Treasury bill auction, at least the amount of Treasury bills falling due.

**Bills only.** The doctrine that the Federal Reserve should restrict its open market operations to the buying and selling of Treasury bills.

**Bimetallic standard.** Two commodities, such as gold and silver, are used as money. There must be an official price, or ratio, between these two commodities.

**Bond flotation.** The sale of bonds by state and local governments or corporations in the capital markets.

**Bond postponements.** Corporate and private bonds may be delayed in their prospective sale, when credit conditions are becoming more restrictive.

**Bottlenecks.** Industries where production facilities are strained to meet the demand for goods in the upswing of the business cycle causing prices to rise sharply in these particular industries.

**Branch banking.** A home office of a bank has another full-service facility at a different location.

**Budget deficit.** Government spending is larger than tax revenues in the federal budget.

**Bullish speculators.** Speculators who expect the prices of stocks, bonds, or goods to rise.

**Business expectations.** Ideas about the future, such as the anticipated future income of a given asset.

**Business loans.** Commercial and industrial loans that consist of credit extended by banks to business firms. These are the most important types of bank credit.

**Call loan participations.** Arrangements whereby country banks share in call loans (24-hours or more) by city banks to brokers and dealers in the money market.

**Capital flows.** Short-term or long-term money flowing in or out of a country. An outflow is a negative item and an inflow is a positive item in the balance of payments.

**Capital market.** A long-term credit market which deals in bonds and equities centered in New York City.

**Cash-balance equation.** $M = kY$, where M is the demand for money in real terms, k is the fraction of real income desired, or held in real balances, and Y is real income.

**Cash-management practices.** Money tends to be economized when interest rates rise.

**Central banks.** Financial institutions, such as the Federal Reserve System in the U.S., that act as a banker's bank, a bank to the government, regulate the money supply, and affect interest rates.

**Check clearance.** A bank receiving a check on another bank gets the check cleared by processing it through the local bank clearinghouse, the correspondent banking system, or the Federal Reserve System.

**Clean float.** Foreign currencies should rise or fall in foreign exchange markets without any central bank intervention to determine their market price.

**Commercial banks.** Full-service financial institutions receiving demand and time and savings deposits and making many different types of loans.

**Commercial paper.** Unsecured I.O.U.s of no more than 200 large corporations typically issued for three or four months maturity and traded in the money market.

**Commodity money.** Various useful commodities, which have considerable value in themselves, may be used as a medium of exchange.

**Comparative advantage.** One country can produce a given good relatively cheaper than it can produce another good.

**Compensating balance.** A balance of ten to twenty percent is usually required by commercial banks in extending credit lines and loans to business firms.

**Consolidated cash budget.** Reflects all transactions between the government and the public.

**Consols.** British bonds that have no maturity date.

**Consumer installment credit.** Consumers often get credit from banks and other financial institutions, usually to buy hard goods such as automobiles.

**Consumer price index (CPI).** An average of consumer prices in a given month, or year, as compared to a prior base year as 100.

**Correspondent balances.** Bank deposits in other commercial banks.

**Cost-push inflation.** Higher wages and lagging productivity will result in higher production costs and a higher price level.

**Costs of inflation.** See *Inflation costs*.

**Counselling.** When frequent or extensive borrowing by a bank or depository institution occurs at the discount window, a conference with a Federal Reserve official provides a reminder that such borrowing is a privilege.

**Countercyclical.** Against the business cycle, as in countercyclical monetary policy or countercyclical fiscal policy.

**Countercyclical fiscal policy.** Running a governmental budget deficit in a recession so as to stimulate aggregate demand while running a budget surplus in the inflationary part of the economic upswing.

**Credit.** Lending institutions, such as commercial banks, extend funds to deficit-spending units when they make loans or acquire investments.

**Credit-debt money.** Transaction accounts of various financial institutions are debt of those institutions and are also backed by the credit of those institutions.

**Credit ease.** A condition when the Federal Reserve increases the rate of growth of the money supply and thus lowers interest rates in a period of economic recession.

**Credit line.** Business firms, particularly those having seasonal borrowing needs, secure an informal commitment from a commercial bank, which indicates the dollar amount the firms can borrow.

**Credit restraint.** A slower rate of growth of the money supply, and higher interest rates, as a result of actions by the Federal Reserve in a period of inflation.

**Credit tranche.** The remaining 75 percent (or slice) of a member country's quota in the IMF after paying in 25 percent in gold.

**Credit unions.** Employees of a given business firm may form a financial institution which pools their savings and provides small loans to members.

**Currencies inconvertible.**    After August 1971, the U.S. and most other countries refused to convert their currencies into gold at any official exchange rate.

**Curvilinear.**    Any schedule that is not a straight line.

**De facto.**    The Latin words for *in fact.*

**De jure.**    The Latin words for *legally.*

**De novo.**    The Latin words for *new.*

**Dealer positions.**    The inventory of government securities held by government security dealers.

**Debentures.**    Debt of private or public institutions, typically up to three years maturity, which are sold in credit markets.

**Debt management.**    Management of old debt of the Treasury representing past budget deficits and selling of new debt to finance a current budget deficit.

**Demand deposits.**    Checking accounts of commercial and savings banks are part of the money supply (M1) and are available for third party payments. See *M1.*

**Demand for money.**    Money is desired either for transactions purposes or for asset purposes—either to buy goods and services or to pay debt—or to hold as a part of wealth.

**Demand-pull inflation.**    Too much money chasing too few goods.

**Deposit insurance.**    Most commerical banks and savings banks have their individual deposit accounts insured up to $100,000 by the Federal Deposit Insurance Corporation.

**Depository institutions.**    All financial institutions in the U.S. which accept demand deposits, or NOW accounts.

**Depository Institutions Deregulation Act of 1980.**    Allowed savings institutions to offer transactions accounts and gave them somewhat greater freedom in their lending operations. See *Monetary Control Act of 1980.*

**Dichotomy.**    Dividing the economy into two parts such as the real and financial sectors.

**Dirty float.**    When a central bank of a country has a managed exchange rate.

**Discount rate.**    The interest rate, which depository institutions pay when they borrow reserves from the Federal Reserve discount window.

**Discount window.**    Each Federal Reserve Bank and Branch has a lending department, where depository institutions can borrow monetary reserves when needed.

**Discretionary fiscal policy.**    This involves changes in tax rates and government expenditures by Congress for the purpose of offsetting a decline in private aggregate demand in a recession or an excess of private aggregate demand in a period of inflation.

**Disintermediation.**    When customers move money from depository institutions to the money market in order to obtain a higher yield, usually in periods of credit restraint.

**Dispersion of inflation.**    The difference in inflation rates among the major countries of the world.

**Disposable personal income.**    Income left after subtracting personal taxes from personal income.

**Domestic policy directive.** The summary of monetary policy instructions to the Trading Desk by the FOMC.

**Double-digit inflation.** Inflation rates of 10 percent or more.

**Drawings on the Fund.** Short-term borrowings of member countries from the IMF either on the gold tranche or the credit tranche of the countries.

**Economic growth.** Increases in real per capita income for a country over a period of time, such as a year.

**Econometric model.** Consists of a number of simultaneous equations (based on economic theory) that simulate the entire economy, or part of the economy.

**Economies of scale.** Lower average unit costs resulting when the output of goods and services produced by a given firm increases.

**Economizing problem.** The result of the scarcity of material resources with the infinity of human wants.

**Effectiveness of monetary policy.** The degree of responsiveness of the economy to credit ease or credit restraint.

**Elastic currency.** Currency that expands and contracts with the needs of trade and commerce.

**Elasticities of demand for borrowed funds.** The effect of interest rate changes on the willingness of various business firms and industries to borrow.

**Elasticity of supply.** The percentage change in the quantity of goods and services supplied divided by the percentage change in the price of goods or services.

**Electronic transfer of funds (ETF).** Funds are moved electronically across the country through leased wires and through automated clearinghouse associations.

**Endogenous.** A variable (e.g., money, which results from the internal operation of the economy).

**Entitlement programs.** Government expenditure programs authorized by Congress, such as the Social Security system, that do not involve annual appropriations by Congress.

**Equation of exchange.** $MV = PT$ or $MV = PV$, where M is the stock of money, V is its velocity, P is the price level measured by some price index, and T, or Q, is the real volume of transactions, or the real quantity of transactions.

**Equilibrium.** The best position possible, given the relevant economic factors of the business firm, the household, or the economy.

**Equilibrium exchange rate.** The exchange rate between two countries based on the relative price levels of the two countries.

**Equilibrium levels of output and employment.** The result of the interaction of the consumption function, the investment function, and the liquidity preference function.

**Eurodollars.** Dollar-denominated time deposits in foreign banks or in foreign branches of American banks.

**European currency unit (ECU).** Based on a basket of all nine European community currencies, it is a common reserve currency issued to all members of the European monetary system in 1979 and thereafter.

**European Monetary System (EMS).** A closer system of monetary cooperation to maintain agreed-upon exchange rates by the Common Market after March 13, 1979.

**Even Keel policy.** Monetary policy will not change just preceding or during a major Treasury financing operation.

**Ex ante.** Latin phrase meaning *anticipated*.

**Ex post.** Latin phrase meaning *after the fact*, or *actual*.

**Excess aggregate demand.** When aggregate demand at current market prices is greater than aggregate supply. This subsequently results in inflation of the price level. See *Aggregate demand*.

**Exchange rate.** The price of one country's currency in terms of another country's currency.

**Exogenous policy.** Public policy, such as monetary policy, that may be determined by events external to the economy.

**Expectations theory.** The traditional theory of the term structure of interest rates, which argues that present long-term interest rates are the average of expected short-term rates over the period of maturity of the long-term debt.

**Extended credit.** In 1981, the Federal Reserve permitted depository institutions to borrow—at different higher interest rates—at the discount window for sixty days, ninety days, or beyond ninety days up to one year.

**Favorable balance of trade.** An excess of merchandise exports over merchandise imports in the balance of payments. The reverse is an *unfavorable* balance of trade.

**Federal Deposit Insurance Corporation (FDIC).** The federal agency that insures individual deposits in most commercial and savings banks up to $100,000.

**Federal Financing Bank.** It coordinates the borrowing in credit markets by most federal agencies apart from the Treasury itself.

**Federal funds.** Deposits by member depository institutions in the Federal Reserve Banks, which are bought (borrowed) and sold (loaned) in the federal funds market.

**Federal funds market.** The short end of the money market where primarily large commercial banks buy (borrow) and sell (lend) excess bank reserves for periods as short as twenty-four hours.

**Federal funds rates.** Interest rates on excess reserves, which banks lend to one another or to government security dealers for twenty-four hours or longer.

**Federal Open Market Committee (FOMC).** The Federal Reserve committee which makes open market operations policy. It is composed of the seven Governors and five Presidents of Federal Reserve Banks.

**Federal Reserve Bank Board of Directors.** Every Federal Reserve Bank has nine directors. The three A and the three B directors are both elected by member banks, and the three C directors are appointed by the Board of Governors to represent the public. Only the A directors may be bankers.

**Federal Reserve Bank credit.** Earning assets of the Federal Reserve Banks, which include U.S. government securities, loans to depository institutions, and Federal Reserve float.

**Federal Reserve Banks.**   There are twelve banks in the Federal Reserve System, which make loans to, hold cash for, and process checks for depository institutions.

**Federal Reserve Board of Governors.**   These are seven persons appointed by the President of the U.S. to oversee the Federal Reserve system. Chairman and vice-chairman serve for four years and other members serve for fourteen years.

**Federal Reserve float.**   This arises when the Federal Reserve gives credit to a member bank on a check being processed before the Federal Reserve has collected on the check. This increases bank reserves.

**Federal Reserve notes.**   Paper money issued by the twelve Federal Reserve Banks, which are the bulk of U.S. money in circulation.

**Federal Reserve pricing for services.**   After the Monetary Control Act of 1980, the Federal Reserve was required to price its services, which previously had been free for member banks.

**Federal Reserve System.**   The American central bank consists of a Board of Governors, the Federal Open Market Committee, the Federal Advisory Council, and twelve Federal Reserve Banks. See *Central bank.*

**Federal Reserve System members.**   All national banks, after 1913, and eligible state banks are members of the Federal Reserve System.

**Federal Savings and Loan Insurance Corporation (FSLIC).**   The government agency that insures deposits in savings and loan associations up to $100,000 each.

**Financial innovations.**   Changes in financial institutions or in the assets they offer their customers. Financial markets also undergo such change.

**Financial institutions.**   These buy and sell financial assets, or borrow and lend money. See *Financial intermediaries.*

**Financial intermediaries.**   Financial institutions who receive funds from savers and make loans to borrowers.

**Financial sector.**   All borrowing and lending of money for whatever purpose and for whatever period of time.

**Financial transfers.**   Capital flows in and out of a country.

**Financing schedule.**   As much of the Treasury's debt management operations as possible are on a regular time period (i.e., once a week, once a month, and once a quarter).

**Fiscal policy.**   The conscious and deliberate use of government expenditures and tax rates to affect total aggregate demand.

**Fisher effect.**   The inclusion of a premium in the long-term market rate of interest to offset for lenders the expected rate of inflation. See *Inflation premium.*

**Flexible prices.**   Prices which change readily with little friction, if demand and/or supply changes.

**Floating prime rate.**   The key bank rate, which is charged the banks' best business customers, was changed each week for a period in the 1970s as certain money market rates changed.

**Flow of funds accounts.**   The national accounting system that measures where all of the money comes from to finance the purchase of all goods and securities in a given year, and where it goes.

**Forecasting interest rates.** Considers current and prospective rates of inflation, stage of the business cycle, and monetary policy.

**Forced saving.** Increased retained business profits in a period of inflation are saved.

**Foreign exchange markets.** Financial markets that buy and sell all foreign currencies used in foreign trade.

**Forward market.** Foreign exchange currency transactions for future delivery.

**Free banking.** The era in state banking after 1838 when bank charters became easy to get.

**Free reserves.** Excess bank reserves minus bank borrowing at the Federal Reserve Banks.

**Full employment.** This condition exists when most workers who want jobs have them, although there may still be a 5 to 6 percent unemployment rate.

**General arrangements to borrow.** An additional amount of funds furnished the IMF by ten major industrial countries available for borrowing by any one of these ten countries.

**General obligation bonds.** State and local bonds backed by the full credit and taxing power of the governmental unit.

**Gold bullion standard.** The international monetary standard of the U.S. after 1933, which permitted convertibility of dollars held by foreign central banks into gold.

**Gold outflow.** When a country's gold stock is falling, it is having a gold outflow to other countries.

**Gold standard.** All money is here ultimately backed by, and therefore convertible into, gold. Gold coins are used and are considered legal tender.

**Gold tranche.** The amount (or slice) of gold furnished the IMF by member countries. This is 25 percent of the borrowing quota of a member.

**Government securities.** Treasury bills, notes, or bonds sold by the federal government to finance budget deficits and to pay off maturing debt.

**Government sponsored credit agencies.** Privately owned financial institutions, which are backed indirectly by the Treasury (e.g., FNMA).

**Great depression.** In the 1930s until World War II in the 1940's, the major capitalist countries, including the U.S., were in a depressed economic condition with high rates of unemployment.

**Greenbacks.** Irredeemable paper currency issued during the Civil War.

**Gresham's law.** The principle that bad money, or overvalued money, drives out good money, or undervalued money.

**Gross national product (GNP).** The market value of all goods and services produced in the U.S. in a year or in a given quarter of a year.

**High employment budget surplus.** The surplus, or deficit, in the federal budget, which would exist if the economy were at high employment.

**Highly developed countries.** The major industrial countries of the world with a high standard of living.

**Hoarding.**  A speculative or asset demand for money that reduces the velocity of money.

**Housing starts.**  The number of new residential houses started in a month or a year.

**Humped interest rate curve.**  A graph of a term structure of interest rates that shows both short-term and long-term interest rates lower than intermediate rates.

**Hyperinflation.**  A period of inflation when prices are rapidly rising day by day. The classic example was in Germany in 1923.

**Implicit rates of interest.**  Calculated rates on retained business earnings, which should be equal to equivalent market rates of interest.

**Inappropriate borrowing.**  Borrowing at the discount window by a depository institution for profit rather than for need.

**Inelastic money supply.**  A constant supply of currency even though the needs of trade and commerce have changed, as under the National Banking system from 1863–1913.

**Inflation.**  An increase in the general price level.

**Inflation benefits.**  Recipients of variable income, debtors, or those unemployed gain during an inflation, when prices and jobs rise.

**Inflation costs.**  A redistribution of real income from existing creditors to existing debtors and from those on relatively fixed income to those on variable incomes.

**Inflation premium.**  An amount added for expected inflation to the real rate of interest to equal the nominal, or market long-term rate of interest.

**Intended investment.**  The aggregate investment schedule showing how much investment will be made at different rates of expected profits and different levels of aggregate income.

**Intended saving.**  The amount of aggregate saving at different levels of aggregate income.

**Interest inelastic.**  When the amount of money demanded is unaffected by the rate of interest.

**Interest rate.**  The price of borrowed money in nominal or market terms. In real terms it is the productivity of added real capital.

**Interest rate structure.**  Different interest rates on different maturities (time) of debt.

**Interest rate theory.**  Traditional neoclassical theory, abstracted from real markets, focused on why interest can be paid, why must it be paid, and how much interest will be paid.

**International Monetary Fund (IMF).**  The international organization which makes short-term loans for balance of payments reasons to its 143 member countries.

**Interstate branching.**  A bank headquarters in one state would have branches not only in that state but in other states as well.

**Inventory accumulation.**  An increase in raw materials stocks, semi-finished stocks, or finished goods stocks in the hands of business firms in a given period of time, which may be intended or unintended.

**Investment.**  An increase in the stock of real capital goods is real investment, while an increase in financial assets in one's portfolio is financial investment.

**Investment income.** The return flow of income in a country's balance of payments resulting from past investments abroad.

**Involuntary unemployment.** This results from forces beyond the control of the worker, such as a decline in aggregate demand.

**IS schedule.** Relates different rates of interest and different levels of income, when investment and saving are everywhere in equilibrium.

**Lagged and contemporaneous reserve accounting.** Lagged reserve accounting bases required reserves for this week on average daily bank deposits two weeks earlier. Contemporaneous reserve accounting bases current required reserves on current deposits.

**Law of diminishing returns.** Whenever a variable real factor, such as capital, is increased while other real factors are kept constant, a point will be reached where less and less output is added.

**Legal tender.** Money that must be accepted in payment of public or private debts, such as the dollar.

**Lender of last resort.** The Federal Reserve system, and other central banks are regarded as such for the financial system since they guarantee the ultimate liquidity of the economic system.

**Leveraged buyouts.** Purchases of companies using large amounts of borrowing.

**Liabilities of financial intermediaries.** Financial assets for those who hold them.

**Liability management.** Purchase of deposits and reserves by financial institutions, rather than simply managing earning assets.

**Liquidity.** The ease and certainty with which an asset can be turned into money.

**Liquidity preference schedule.** Relates the demand for money to hold as an asset to the long-term rate of interest.

**Liquidity trap.** The flat part of the liquidity preference schedule of Keynes, where the demand for money becomes perfectly elastic with respect to the rate of interest.

**LM schedule.** Relates different rates of interest and different levels of national income where the demand and supply of money are in equilibrium.

**Loanable funds doctrine.** Focuses on the demand for and supply of bonds as determining the long-term rate of interest.

**Loan-deposit ratio.** Total bank loans divided by total bank deposits.

**Loan portfolio.** The total of a bank's loans.

**Loans to individuals.** Loans to persons by banks for various purposes.

**Long-run equilibrium.** Optimum relationships between economic variables over a substantial period of time.

**M1, M2, and M3.** See *Monetary aggregates.*

**Macroeconomics.** The study of the aggregate forces which determine the total output, employment, and the price level in the economy.

**Making a market.** This consists of those large government securities dealers who stand ready to buy and sell reasonable amounts of government securities on a bid-asked quoted basis.

**Manager for domestic operations.** The Senior Vice-President of the Federal Reserve Bank of New York who manages the Trading Desk for the FOMC.

**Margin requirements.** The percentage of cash that customers must pay when they buy stocks on the regulated stock exchange. In 1982, the margin requirement was 50 percent.

**Marginal efficiency of investment.** The expected rate of return on added new investment.

**Marginal propensity to consume.** Added consumption divided by added income.

**Market basket.** The list of representative consumer goods and services included in the Consumer Price Index.

**Market segmentation.** Different parts of the financial markets that may be partly insulated from influences operating in other parts of the market.

**Marketable securities.** Government securities sold by the Treasury in the government securities market.

**Matched sale-purchase agreements.** Sales by the Trading Desk of government securities with an agreement to buy them at a later date. These sales temporarily reduce bank reserves.

**McFadden Act of 1927.** Prohibited interstate banking and thereby created major barriers to entry in various local banking markets.

**Measuring inflation.** Measured in the U.S. by the Consumer Price Index (CPI), the Producer Price Index (PPI), and the GNP price deflators used to convert current GNP into constant dollars.

**Member bank borrowing.** Borrowing of Federal Reserve member banks at the discount window.

**Members of the Federal Reserve System.** See *Federal Reserve System members.*

**Minimal intervention approach.** A policy adopted by U.S. in April 1981 to intervene in foreign exchange markets only to offset conditions of disorder in those markets.

**Monday auction.** Each Monday, unless it is a holiday, the Treasury sells at discount at auction equal amounts of 91-day and 182-day Treasury bills. The auction is the preceding Friday, if Monday is a holiday.

**Monetarists.** Economists today who prefer a sophisticated version of the quantity theory.

**Monetary aggregates.** Various definitions of the money supply (i.e., M1, M2 and M3). M1 is a currency component, demand deposits of commercial banks, other checkable deposits, and nonbank travelers checks. M2 is M1 plus overnight repurchase agreements (federal funds), Eurodollars, money market mutual funds, and savings and time deposits. M3 is M2 plus large time deposits and term repurchase agreements.

**Monetary base.** Consists of all bank reserves and all currency held by the public.

**Monetary Control Act of 1980.** This permitted the Federal Reserve Board to establish reserve requirements for all transaction accounts of financial intermediaries. See *Reserve requirements.* See also *Depository Institutions Deregulation Act of 1980.*

**Monetary multiplier.** The simple monetary multiplier is the reciprocal of the average reserve ratio requirement on transaction accounts. The more complex monetary multiplier includes other factors affecting the creation of money such as the ratio of time deposits to demand deposits, the ratio of currency held by the public to demand deposits, and the ratio of excess bank reserves to demand deposits.

**Monetary policy lag.** When monetary policy changes to restraint, or to ease, there is a considerable time lag before the full economic impacts are felt.

**Monetary reserves.** Each country has a gold stock, holdings of hard foreign currencies, and, quite often, Special Drawing Rights in the International Monetary Fund.

**Monetary rules.** Monetarists recommend that fixed rules, rather than discretion, govern the growth of the money supply. Similar rules, they believe, should apply to taxes and government spending.

**Monetization of debt.** A condition when banks exchange their debt (demand deposits) for public or private debt.

**Money.** Anything that is generally acceptable in payment for goods, services, and debt.

**Money creating process.** When commercial banks and other financial intermediaries make loans or acquire investments, they create money (i.e., transaction accounts). See *Monetary aggregates.*

**Money-demand equations.** These predict the impact of changes in the demand for money when GNP and interest rates are changed.

**Money flow.** The average total stock of money times its turnover or velocity in a given time period.

**Money illusion.** A belief that a change in prices alone results in real benefits or real losses.

**Money market.** The New York City-centered market that deals in short-term, highly liquid debt.

**Money market banks.** No more than 134 commercial banks, especially in the large cities, that do most of the buying and selling of money market assets by banks.

**Money market certificates.** Three-month and six-month certificates issued by banks and savings and loan associations, which pay an interest rate based on the latest three-month and six-month Treasury bill rates.

**Money market instruments.** Marketable short-term, highly liquid debt.

**Money market mutual fund.** Such a fund invests in money market instruments and sells shares to small savers, who receive a high interest rate.

**Money substitutes.** Highly liquid debt other than money.

**Money value.** Measured by the amount of goods and services that a given monetary unit will buy.

**Multiplier.** The reciprocal of the marginal propensity to save (added saving as a fraction of added income).

**Municipal securities.** Securities issued by state and local municipalities. See *Tax-exempt.*

**Mutual savings banks.** Financial intermediaries similar to savings and loan associations, which invest primarily in mortgages and offer demand deposits and NOW accounts.

**Myopia.** Short sightedness, as when persons prefer present to future income.

**National banks.** After the National Banking Act of 1863, any commercial bank securing a charter from the comptroller of the currency.

**National income.** The aggregate earnings of labor and property each year.

**Natural rate of interest.** Determined by the productivity of capital.

**Natural rate of unemployment.** The rate of unemployment when the entire economy is in equilibrium.

**Negative time preference.** Such unusual persons may prefer future income to present income.

**Neoclassical analysis.** Focused on the determination of prices in particular markets and was the traditional economic approach before 1936.

**Neo-Keynesians.** Economists who use the concepts and policy approaches of John Maynard Keynes, as modified by experience.

**Neutral money.** When a change in the stock of money has no effect on real output.

**Noise.** The randomness in any money-supply series.

**Nonintermediation.** When savers put their savings directly into the money market rather in a financial intermediary.

**NOW accounts.** Transaction accounts on which an interest may be paid.

**Numéraire.** This French word means that something, say money, is simply being used as a unit of measurement.

**Oligopoly.** A few sellers in a given market.

**OPEC countries.** An oil cartel of many of the major oil producing countries called Oil Petroleum Exporting Countries (OPEC).

**Open market operations.** The buying and selling of government securities by the Federal Reserve system to determine the total of bank reserves and the money supply.

**Opportunity cost.** Whenever an asset, such as money, could be earning a higher rate of return in some other form, the asset has an opportunity cost.

**Paper money, or fiat money, standard.** When legal tender is paper currency, irredeemable in specie, that money is fiat.

**Par exchange rates.** Pre-determined exchange rates set jointly by each country with the International Monetary Fund from 1946–1971.

**Pari Passu.** Latin for step by step.

**Penalty surcharge.** Large depository institutions making frequent use of the discount window had to pay an extra penalty rate in 1981–1982 in addition to the basic discount rate.

**Phillips curve.** The aggregate trade-off between inflation and the unemployment rate.

**Potential output.** Output that would occur at full employment. See *Full employment.*

**Positive time preference.** This condition exists when people prefer present to future income at a zero rate of interest.

**Primary reserves.** Cash held by banks, whether in their vaults, in Federal Reserve Banks, or in correspondent banks.

**Prime rate.** The very best business borrowers at commercial banks receive this interest rate on their short-term borrowing. Other bank interest rates are scaled upwards.

**Problem banks.** Banks that regulatory authorities feel have asset problems resulting from mismanagement and/or insider abuses, poor earnings, inadequate capital, and insufficient liquidity.

**Procyclical.** Some activities of the federal government, such as least-cost debt management, accentuate the private business cycle instead of dampening it.

**Producer prices (PPI).** The average prices of raw materials and other goods puchased by producers. The current period of the producer price index is shown as a percentage of the base period, which is 100.

**Propensity to consume schedule.** This Keynesian schedule relates aggregate personal consumption and aggregate personal saving to various levels of aggregate personal income.

**Proportional consumption function.** The same percentage of consumption and saving is maintained out of national income over a long period of time.

**Proxy.** One thing that represents another thing (e.g., the bank credit proxy is total bank deposits, while the federal funds rate prior to October 6, 1979 served as a proxy for monetary policy).

**Pure theory of interest.** See *Interest rate theory.*

**Quantity theory of money.** Value of money declines as the quantity of money increases and vice versa.

**Quarterly forecasts.** Made by the staff of the Board of Governors for the use of the FOMC in setting quarterly monetary aggregate targets.

**Quasi-governments.** Securities issued by federal agencies rather than the federal government directly.

**Ratchet effect.** Easier to push something up than push it down, (e.g., prices).

**Real-balance effect.** The theory that a decline in the price level, alone in a period of economic decline increases the amount of real money balances and thereby increases consumer and business spending. This assumes nominal money supply is constant.

**Real bills doctrine.** This doctrine argued that commercial banks should largely restrict themselves to making short-term self-liquidating business loans, since their major liability traditionally was demand deposits.

**Real estate loans.** Loans made by banks and other financial institutions for long-term financing of construction.

**Real factors.** Factors in nonmonetary terms.

**Real GNP.** Gross National Product in constant dollars.

**Real sector.** Actual, or real, goods and services produced by the economy, whether consumer or investment goods.

**Recession.** A broad decline in economic activity. Usually this means that real output has declined for two or more quarters.

**Regulation A.** This regulation of the Federal Reserve Board governs borrowing at the Federal Reserve discount window by depository institutions.

**Regulation Q.**   Interest rate ceilings on time and savings deposits at member banks by the Federal Reserve Board from 1933 to 1986.

**Repurchase agreement (RP)**   The selling of a government security at one price and the agreement to buy it back at a lower price in a week, ten days, or two weeks.

**Reluctance to borrow.**   A tradition encouraged by the Federal Reserve to restrict borrowing of reserves by depository institutions at the discount window.

**Required reserves.**   The dollar amount of reserves needed by financial intermediaries, depending upon the amount of their transaction accounts and the reserve ratios set by the Federal Reserve Board.

**Reserve requirement on transactions accounts after 1980.**   Set initially by Congress and the Federal Reserve Board, at 3 percent on transaction accounts less than $25 million and 12 percent on transaction accounts more than $25 million.

**Reserve requirements.**   The Federal Reserve Board, within limits set by Congress, sets reserve ratios behind transaction accounts of financial intermediaries, like commercial banks. See *Required reserves.*

**Reserve week.**   The reserve week is Thursday to Wednesday. This is the period for which various Federal Reserve statistics are reported.

**Revenue bonds.**   Bonds sold by state and local municipalities based on the anticipated revenue to be generated by some project, such as a tollroad.

**Review of quotas.**   Every so many years the IMF has a review of quotas, which is an increase in the borrowing available to the member countries. Sometimes this also means an increase in the SDRs allocated to each country.

**Risk premium.**   The part of an interest rate that relates to the danger of default of a debt.

**Safety valve.**   Borrowing by depository institutions at the discount window as a means of getting some relief from Federal Reserve credit restraint.

**Saving.**   A diversion from the current payments stream, which may be used to finance physical investment or financial investment.

**Saving gap.**   The difference between consumption and income at full employment must be filled by investment and/or government expenditures, or full employment will not be reached or maintained.

**Savings and loan associations.**   Financial intermediaries popular in the Midwest and the Farwest, which specialize in making mortgages. They offer transaction accounts with interest (NOW accounts), as well as time and savings accounts.

**Savings ratio.**   Ratio of current aggregate personal saving to current aggregate personal income.

**Say's law.**   This law of markets states that supply creates its own demand.

**Seasonal borrowing privilege.**   A privilege given to small member banks in 1973 to borrow reserves at the discount window up to 90 days.

**Secondary reserve assets.**   Money market assets, such as Treasury bills, held by commercial banks.

**Secular inflation.**   Chronic inflation of the price level over a long period of time, such as twenty years.

**Silver standard.** All money outstanding is backed and ultimately convertible into silver.

**Snake-in-the-tunnel.** The agreed-upon exchange rate with a certain band of possible fluctuations among the nine members of the Common Market after August 1976.

**Special Drawing Rights (SDRs).** New liabilities, which are backed by the gold and convertible currencies held by the IMF. All member countries receive new SDRs in proportion to their quotas, which they could use as monetary reserves like gold and other currencies.

**Specie.** Hard money coins, such as gold and silver coins.

**Spot transactions.** Current daily transactions in the present price of foreign currencies.

**Square root rule.** Holds that the proportion of money held declines as real income rises.

**Stagflation.** The economic condition that existed in the 1970s in the U.S. when both the rate of unemployment and inflation was high or rising.

**State banks.** Newly organized banks that receive their charter from one of the fifty states and comprise about two-thirds of all commercial banks.

**Structure of interest rates.** See *Interest rate structure.*

**Supermultiplier.** This coefficient is the result of the interaction between the multiplier and the accelerator and is larger than the simple multiplier. See *Multiplier.* See also *Accelerator.*

**Supply-side economics.** Lowering tax rates was expected to increase the labor supply, the rate of saving, and the rate of investment. All of this was supposed to increase real output, employment, and revenues to the government.

**Surveillance.** Large continuous borrowing at the discount window by depository institutions leads the Federal Reserve to determine whether such borrowing is appropriate or inappropriate.

**Swap arrangements.** Reciprocal currency arrangements between the Federal Reserve Bank of New York and other central banks. The foreign currencies borrowed can be sold in foreign exchange markets to support the dollar.

**T-Accounts.** A simplified balance sheet approach to the creation of money by depository institutions or the creation of monetary reserves by the Federal Reserves.

**Tax-exempt securities.** Securities issued by state and local municipalities that are exempt from federal income taxation. See *Municipals.*

**Term loan.** Any business loan made by a commercial bank for a period of time longer than one year. These comprise one-half or more of all bank business loans.

**Terms of trade.** The price of imports in terms of exports for a given country. These improve for a country when the value of its currency rises, and vice versa.

**Thin markets.** Some markets, such as the long-term bond market, have such a small daily volume of trades that a large purchase or sale can cause a considerable change in price of the asset.

**Thrift institutions.** Financial intermediaries that specialize in accepting deposits from small savers and then make mortgages, make other loans, or buy government securities. After 1980, they could have transaction accounts with interest (NOW accounts) in all states.

**Thrift problem.** The mismatch between low-earning assets and high-cost deposits, which many thrift institutions had in the late 1970s and early 1980s.

**Time deposits.** Deposits in commercial banks that have a specific maturity before turning into cash. They receive a higher interest rate than available on transaction accounts.

**Time lags.** After changes in monetary, or other macro, policy, there are time lags before a new equilibrium is reached in the economy.

**Trading Desk of Federal Reserve.** The Securities Department of the Federal Reserve Bank of New York is the operational arm of the FOMC. It does the actual buying and selling of government securities.

**Transaction accounts.** Accounts with financial intermediaries on which checks can be written. See *Demand deposits*.

**Transactions demand for money.** The most traditional view of the demand for money as a function of the level of income or transactions. This view emphasizes the medium of exchange function of money.

**Treasury bill.** The shortest maturity of government security available for periods of 91 days, 182 days and 52 weeks, plus cash management bills of less than one month in maturity.

**Treasury notes.** Marketable government securities issued originally in maturities of one to ten years.

**Two-sector model.** Dividing the economy into a real sector and a financial sector.

**Unanticipated inflation.** Inflation that has not been correctly anticipated by any economic groups and therefore may cause much harm to them (e.g., retired workers).

**Under consumption.** A doctrine first enunciated by Thomas Malthus that consumer spending might not be high enough to absorb all of the consumer goods and services that can be produced at present market prices.

**Underdeveloped countries.** Agricultural countries with a lower standard of living than the industrial countries. Also called less-developed countries.

**Underwriters.** Investment bankers who underwrite new bond issues by buying them from the issuer at one price, while planning to sell them at a higher price in the market. Banks and government security dealers provide similar underwriting functions for the Treasury.

**Unemployment.** The difference between total employed workers and the labor force (persons sixteen years or older looking for work). This number as a ratio of the labor force is the unemployment rate.

**Unified budget.** Government expenditure programs of the federal government and its agencies and expected tax revenues. It is similar to the former consolidated cash budget.

**Unique equilibrium set.** The intersection of the *LM* and *IS* schedules provides a unique equilibrium set of an interest rate and a equilibrium level of income.

**Unit banking.**   Banks that have only one office and no branches.

**Unitary elasticity.**   When any given percentage change in the price of goods is offset by the same percentage change in the amount demanded.

**Upward bias.**   Price indexes, such as the CPI, have an upward bias insofar as improvements in the quality of goods and services included in the index may not be adjusted for adequately.

**Unsatisfied demand.**   Because goods and services are in short supply relative to demand in wartime, unsatisfied demand results, which leads to inflation, then and after the war, as buyers bid up the price of goods.

**Velocity of money.**   The turnover of money per month, per quarter, or per year. Sometimes called the turnover of demand deposits or the income velocity of money.

**Vicious cycle.**   A country suffering serious inflation will have worse inflation if it devalues its currency since imports are now more expensive.

**Virtuous cycle.**   Countries with low inflation rates find that a higher currency value in foreign exchange markets lowers the price of their imports, which lowers their inflation rate further.

**Weights of index components.**   Each component of the CPI, such as housing costs, must be given a relative weight of importance to the consumer before calculating the average number of all consumer prices.

**Wildcat banks.**   Banks started in frontier states before the Civil War with little or no specie backing for their bank notes.

**World Bank group.**   International financial institutions that raise funds in credit markets and make low-cost loans to developing countries.

# INDEX